Tenth Edition

MANY PEOPLES, MANY FAITHS

WOMEN AND MEN IN THE WORLD RELIGIONS

Robert S. Ellwood

University of Southern California

Barbara A. McGraw

Saint Mary's College of California

Routledge
Taylor & Francis Group

LONDON AND NEW YORK

First published 2014, 2009, 2005 by Pearson Education, Inc.

Published 2016 by Routledge
2 Park Square, Milton Park, Abingdon, Oxon OX14 4RN
711 Third Avenue, New York, NY 10017, USA

Routledge is an imprint of the Taylor & Francis Group, an informa business

Cover Printer: Webcom/Toronto. Printed in Canada

ISBN-13: 9780205797110 (pbk)

Library of Congress Cataloging-in-Publication Data
Ellwood, Robert S.,
  Many peoples, many faiths: women and men in the world religions/Robert S. Ellwood, Barbara A. McGraw. — 10th ed.
    p. cm.
  ISBN-13: 978-0-205-79711-0 (alk. paper)
  1. Religions. 2. Religion. I. McGraw, Barbara A. II. Title.
  BL80.3.E44 2013
  200—dc23

                                                                                      2012033344

Cover Images:
  Top row, left: © Stuart Black / Robert Harding Images
  Top row, right: Karen Trist/Rough Guides/Dorling Kindersley, Ltd.
  Second row: © Patrick Foto / Shutterstock
  Third row, left: ©Getty Images / Santiago Urquijo
  Third row, right: Chuongy/Fotolia
  Bottom row: © Idris Ahmed / Alamy Stock Photo

A very good book, best on the market.

—Helena Gourko, Merrimack College

There is no competition for this book. It is a nearly perfect introductory textbook in my considered estimation.

—Dell deChant, University of South Florida

For Richard Scott Lancelot Ellwood

May your faith be always adventurous.

For Erin Eklund Roddy and Echo Anne McCollum,

Daughters not of my body, but of my heart,
May the world greet you with a door wide open
to the fulfillment of all your potential.

CONTENTS

Chapter 4 WISDOM EMBARKED FOR THE FARTHER SHORE
The Journey of Buddhism   113

PREFACE

For more than three and a half decades, this introduction to the world's religions, has combined factual information with empathic writing that seeks to instill in readers a sense of the richness of the religious lives of the peoples of the world. While striving for accuracy and depth, *Many Peoples, Many Faiths* is neither an encyclopedic compilation of data nor a survey of alternative philosophies. Instead, the goal is to present a sense and feeling of the total human experience of religious life from past to present, made up as it is in an inseparable mingling of concepts, worship and other practices, and social factors. Also, the hope is that readers will become curious about the areas of scholarship that lie behind this introductory presentation of the world's religions and will be inspired to explore these areas more deeply.

NEW MATERIAL AND SPECIAL FEATURES OF THIS EDITION

The tenth edition has been fully updated throughout with material reflecting new scholarship and general interest and, where appropriate, addressing rapidly developing and shifting areas, taking account of the dynamic, changing quality of religion. The authors call the readers' attention to special features of this book and a few examples of new material that are especially significant:

- This book places the world's religions in historical context, illustrating the complex dynamic of each religion over time, while also presenting current beliefs, practices, and group formations.

- The chapters include substantial sections on women in religion; religion governance and political life; and religion in America, which have been revised and updated and many of these sections include new narrative accounts.

- MyReligionLab, an online resource produced by Pearson Education, is available with this book and includes "Suggested Websites" and other helpful electronic tools for this book.

- Chapter Two on indigenous peoples has been fully revised, including a revised map and additional accounts of indigenous religions to enhance readers' understanding of these foundational faiths and their importance for understanding other religions.

- In Chapter Three, the discussion of the religions of India has been substantially revised to reflect new scholarship on the development of Hinduism from prehistory to the present, and the chapter now has more developed sections on "the Practice of Hinduism Today," "Sikhism," and "Jainism."

- Chapter Eight includes a new section on "Independent Christianities", including a new section on the "Church of Jesus Christ of Latter Day Saints (the Mormons)," and the sections on "Missionaries and the Modern Expansion of Christianity" and on "Christian Mysticism and Devotion" have been substantially revised.

- Chapter Nine reflects new developments in Islam and includes a new section on Islam in Europe.

- Throughout the book, some descriptive writing has been replaced by profiles of individuals who exemplify the same point in personal terms, and additional narratives of the authors' experiences have been included.

- Many new photographs and other art have been added to increase the attractiveness and accessibility of the book.

- The Glossary is a helpful tool for students, as are the bibliographies at the end of each chapter, which have been updated to reflect new scholarship, and the maps, timelines, and summary information tables.

- The Appendix gives practical suggestions on how to write papers for courses using this text and makes suggestions about how to do research in the library and on the Internet.

As always, true understanding of the many faiths of the many peoples of Earth requires a mixture of knowledge and empathy. While reading this book, keep the necessary facts in mind, but read it also with compassion, which alone can furnish an understanding of what those facts mean to human beings for whom they are gateways to ultimate meaning.

The Authors

Robert S. Ellwood is emeritus of the Religious Studies Department, University of Southern California. Generous in sharing with other scholars, whether young or old, his clear understanding of the deeper goals of education and scholarship, his breadth of knowledge and insight have resulted in numerous impressive works. Dr. Ellwood has a legacy with a long trajectory—*Many Peoples, Many Faiths* being one of his many significant contributions over the past more than four decades.

Barbara A. McGraw, Professor and Director of the Center for Engaged Religious Pluralism, Saint Mary's College of California, has been coauthor of *Many Peoples, Many Faiths* for half of all editions of this book, having joined Dr. Ellwood from the sixth edition forward in the rewriting, editing, updating, and additions to all sections of the book. Among other things, she contributed most of the material on women in the world religions, on religion, governance, and political life, and on the religions in America.

ACKNOWLEDGMENTS

The authors are indebted to many people who have helped to make this tenth edition possible. First, we would like to thank everyone at Prentice Hall who has worked on this book. Unfortunately, we cannot name them all here, but we would like to thank Sarah Touborg, the Editor in chief for Religion; Nicole Conforti, the Editorial Project Manager, whose perseverance and steady hand during a complicated production process was greatly appreciated; and Anandakrishnan Natarajan, Project Manager, whose swift and clear communications and attention to detail were invaluable to the success and timeliness of this edition.

We also wish to acknowledge the reviewers who offered suggestions for the improvement of this tenth edition. Our thanks and appreciation to: James Findlay, *California State University Northridge;* Theresa Gilbertson, *University of South Florida Sarasota-Manatee;* Tim Harrison, *McKendree University;* Cristobal Serran-Pagan, *Valdosta State University;* Curtis Smith, *Penn State University;* and Brandy Stark, *St. Petersburg College.*

1

Understanding the World's Religious Heritage

CHAPTER OBJECTIVES

After studying this chapter, you should be able to

- Talk about what you mean by religion, and what a religion includes.
- Discuss religion in terms of the human experience of a split-level universe—as conditioned and unconditioned reality.
- Cite and interpret Joachim Wach's Three Forms of Religious Expression, plus expression in ethics, religious experience, and art.
- Discuss other methods for approaching the study of religion: descriptive, critical, and historical.
- Begin the study of religion, governance, and political life and the role of religion in the lives of women.

A NEW DAY OF RELIGIOUS ENCOUNTER

The world's many religious pathways are no longer far away.

Think of your friends, neighbors, classmates, or workmates. The chances are many of them are of a different religious background than yourself. Think of the products you buy in today's global economy: electronics from Malaysia, household items from China, chocolate from Africa. The chances are the hands that prepared them for your use belonged to persons of diverse religions, or no religion at all.

The religions of the world—the words themselves may evoke a panorama of colorful images, perhaps drawn from a host of stories, movies, TV documentaries, the Internet, travel, or family background. Incense and temple gongs, yogis in contorted postures, ancient and mysterious chants, joyous shouts of praise, the slowness of ancient rituals—all these and more sweep past our inner eyes and ears. Sometimes, what most fascinates us is that which is far away or long ago. But the study of the religions of the world is no longer a matter of reading about what may seem strange or is faraway. In today's world of **pluralism*** and rapid travel, almost any faith anywhere is a presence and an option throughout the world. The temples of Hindu Americans and the mosques of Muslim Americans embellish larger American cities. American Zen centers, quiet with the great peace of

---

*Terms in bold throughout this text are defined in the Glossary.

the Buddha, teach Eastern meditation. Christianity and Judaism in all their manifold forms have long existed here side by side, just as Christianity has been carried by American and other missionaries to the homelands of Hinduism and Buddhism.

All of this makes "now" an exciting time to study religion. We who come to the study of religion today bring with us expectations shaped by these times. The presence of many options, and the ferment within most of them, is something we sense inside ourselves as well as in the outside world.

A glance at virtually any morning paper or evening TV news reminds us that now is also an important time to study religion for grimmer reasons. In the post–Cold War world, religion, often linked to passionate nationalism, appears as a major factor in many of the planet's tragic conflicts. Reports from India, the Middle East, the Balkans and, after September 11, 2001, New York and Washington, remind us of this terrible reality over and over. While the religions invoked in these often-bloody disputes cannot usually be solely blamed for them, no full comprehension of the Earth's current crises is possible without an in-depth understanding of the faiths involved. In assessing our own attitudes toward religious belief, we are forced to deal with the fact that religion is not always a good thing by ordinary human values.

Our increasingly global world and economy mean that the adult careers of many American students will bring them in close contact with, perhaps even residence in, societies like those in India, China, Japan, or the Middle East, while many of Americans' counterparts in those countries will come to the United States. Whether one's primary interests are in law, business, diplomacy, or academic study, the greatest success in these endeavors will be achieved by those with a deep understanding of how a society works, including sensitivity to its religious heritage. In this book we will see, for example, how a sense of enduring Confucian values helps one to grasp how both Japanese corporations and the Chinese People's Republic really function.

These examples indicate how complex religion is. It is now time to sort out this complexity by introducing some categories through which religion can be understood. Our task will now be to answer these questions:

- What do we *look for* when we look at the religion of another culture and try to understand what it means in that culture and to the people for whom it is important?

- What are different ways in which religion *expresses* itself? (For example, as beliefs, as ways of worship, as social institutions like churches and temples, through ethical values, in art and literature.)

- What kind of terms do we use when we are just trying to *describe* a religion?

- How do we look at religion *critically*, that is, when it may not be a good thing, in ways that are fair, that try to accept cultures different from our own, yet in ways that are also true to what we consider to be the highest human values?

- What have been the *basic stages* of religious history on planet Earth?

- Can religion be *defined*? or is it always just a fairly elusive word used to cover a variety of things?

VISITING A STRANGE LAND

What is religion, then?

Suppose you are taking a trip to a country whose culture is completely foreign to you, and you want to determine the religion of that culture. Suppose, further, that because you cannot speak the language of the country well enough to ask anyone about it, you have to look for clues in what you see around you and in what people do. What would you look for?

Most of what you see has obvious explanations—basic human needs for shelter, food, drink, security, and pleasure in this world. Most buildings up and down the streets are houses where people live or shops where craftspeople work or merchants sell goods to meet everyday needs. Most of the people scurrying about are out on business or seeking recreation.

Once in a while, though, you may see something that has no such "ordinary" interpretation. A structure may be neither a home nor a shop, yet it is obviously set apart and perhaps elaborately ornamented. A human activity may be neither work nor play; it may not produce food, exercise the body, or challenge one's skill in any ordinary way. Yet it is clearly of great importance. It may be marked by a solemn or festive air. Both the building and the activity may be associated with symbols and gestures that make no sense to an outsider; yet they seem to be of deep significance to people.

You suspect these are places and practices connected to the religion of the land. You know you could be wrong. The special building might be a court instead of a temple; the activity, a game or dance instead of a rite. The rites of state and of religion are often intermingled. Often games and dances combine pleasure with celebrating a religious festival or occasion: think Carnival in Rio or Thanksgiving football games in America.

Even ordinary activities like planting or harvest may come with religious "extras" to relate them to the people's beliefs, like the American harvest-time Thanksgiving festival. These "extras," like the mysterious buildings and practices, go beyond what it takes to meet everyday needs or ordinary fun and games. They may therefore point to the society's awareness of more-than-ordinary reality. The rhetoric of preaching and the quiet of meditation, the ornate garb and stylized motions of elaborate ritual, and the gladsome tones of gospel music—all say reality has more to it than the everyday. These "signs" also say that this extraordinary reality, this "something more," touches human life and can be felt, channeled, and made manifest by special means. Rites and symbols, preaching and meditation, are ways of connecting to that "something more."

CONDITIONED AND UNCONDITIONED REALITY

What is that "something more"? One thing many religions tell us is that we live in a split-level universe. Or, to use the expression of the historian of religion Mircea Eliade, that reality is "nonhomogeneous." In homogenized milk, the milk and the cream are thoroughly mixed together. When it is not homogenized, the cream is at the top and the milk at the bottom, making two layers. However, some religions, like Hinduism and many indigenous religions, tell us that reality is actually one homogeneous whole and that we just need to be enlightened to this truth.

Most religious people see two kinds of reality. As we have seen, there is ordinary, everyday reality, and there is also the special reality of the temple, the festival, the "extras" pointing quietly to "something more" mixed in with everyday life. Certain visible places, people, and events are more in touch with that "something more" than others. They are *sacred* places, persons, and activities.

We may think of the layers of this split-level, "nonhomogeneous" universe—the ordinary and the "something more"—as conditioned and unconditioned reality. (These relatively neutral terms are borrowed from Buddhist thought.)

Let's start by talking about **conditioned reality**, because that's what most of us are living in most of the time. To say something is conditioned simply means it is limited or restricted. We are all conditioned in time and space. If we are living in the twenty-first century, we are not also in the ninth century with Charlemagne or in the twenty-third century with *Star Trek*. If we are living in Ohio or Oklahoma, we are not also in Hong Kong or on the planet Neptune.

Furthermore, we are conditioned by the limitations and habits of our minds. We can think about only one thing at a time, and we forget far more than we remember. Even the greatest genius can know only the tiniest fragment of what there is to know or to think more than the minutest fraction of what there is to think. Moreover, we continually put limits around ourselves when we say, "I'm a person who does this but not that," "I believe this but not that," or "I like this but not that."

Consider now what **unconditioned reality**, the opposite of all the above, would be like. It would be equally present to all times and all places. Its knowledge, wisdom, and mental power would be unlimited, and would include all that could possibly be known or thought. If it (or he or she) had preferences as to doing, believing, or liking, they would be based on omniscient (all-knowing) wisdom, not the bundle of ill-informed fears and prejudices by which we too often act—and react.

Unconditioned reality would, in fact, be no different from the Divine, or Ultimate, Reality of religion and philosophy. It goes by different names and has varying degrees of personality, but in most religions, it is believed that some unconditioned pole of reality stands over our very-much-conditioned everyday lives. (Even the legions of secondary entities that inhabit the religious world—the many gods, buddhas, bodhisattvas, angels, spirits—have their significance because of ultimate unconditioned reality. They are in a special relationship to it and send out its light or energy in some special way.)

We can illustrate conditioned and unconditioned reality and its names in various religions like this:

Unconditioned Reality

Brahman (philosophical Hinduism)

Nirvana (Buddhism)

The Dao (Daoism)

Heaven (Confucianism)

God (Judaism, Christianity, Islam [called Allah in Islam])

Awareness of Presence of Spirits (Shamanism)

Conditioned Reality*

Maya (philosophical Hinduism)

Samsara (Buddhism)

Under Heaven (Daoism, Confucianism)

Choice of Death (Judaism)

The "World" (Christianity)

Realm of War (Islam)

Evil Spirits (Shamanism)

---

*These are only examples of the many terms that are used in different religions. It should be made clear that these "conditioned" categories are not necessarily evil; they are just arenas of ignorance and separateness where evil or sin is possible.

DOORS AND WINDOWS TO THE ULTIMATE

One point remains—a very important one. When religion is seen as split between conditioned and unconditioned reality, the wall between them nevertheless is not hard and solid. It is not as though the two realms are hermetically sealed off from each other. Instead, the main idea behind any religion is that the wall is full of doors and windows.

Gods and people can look through from one side to the other. Revelations, gods, angels, saviors, and spirits can walk through the doors from the other side to visit us; our prayers and good thoughts can go through from this side to the other; and a few favored people—and perhaps the souls of many of us after death—may pass through those doors to join that other level of reality.

This porous borderline, where the action is, is the sphere of religion. All religions believe that certain teachings, practices (such as prayer or meditation, rites, and services), and modes of ethical behavior best express or fit in with the nature of ultimate reality. Those things are therefore like doors and windows. Through prayer, mystical experience, or worship, we can open them and pass through them in spirit. Certain persons or institutions are also in especially close touch with unconditioned reality and are also like those portals. So also are works of religious art, music, and literature. By all these means, religious people may enable themselves to move through the windows or doors.

Some will object that not all of what is ordinarily called religious, or that has to do with gods and the like, is really concerned with unconditioned reality. They might point out that people go to church or temple or conduct rituals for social reasons or merely because they like the music. Yet understanding religion should not always be limited by the conscious intention of the religionist, often hard to judge in any event.

Even if a person goes to church only to meet someone, or if a particular hunting chant is a tradition that bonds the tribe, something more is implied. In the church or temple, God will be spoken of and things done that make no sense if there is no God. The hunting chant tells us that there is more to the hunt than just human beings hunting. Both chant and church open up in back, so to speak, to that invisible realm beyond ordinary existence. In the end, they imply doors and windows to ultimate reality.

FORMS OF RELIGIOUS EXPRESSION

What then is this religion with its doors and windows all about? What is it made up of? To start with, it is made up of what people say, do, and form organizations around. The essence of religion may be unconditioned reality, and teaching about that may vary. But the outer forms of these doors and windows have much in common throughout the world. When we look carefully at religion all over the world, we find that certain basic patterns, like old friends, keep reappearing despite all the variety.

The sociologist of religion Joachim Wach (1898–1955) gave us one useful set of pegs for those patterns.[1] While the essence of religion may be beyond words, he tells us, religion expresses itself in human life in three ways. He called these three ways the *theoretical* (meaning what is said: for example, beliefs and stories); the *practical* (meaning what is done: for example, worship, prayer, meditation, pilgrimage); and the *sociological* (meaning the kinds of groups: for example, social institutions and other groups; leadership; and a group's relationship to society). These will be referred to from time to time. Let's now consider more specifically what is meant by each.

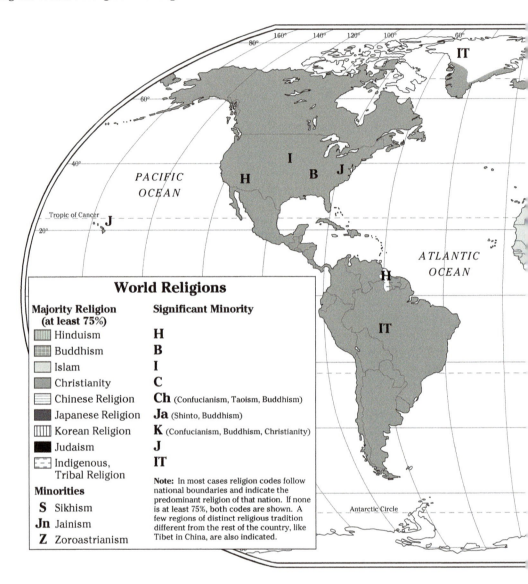

Theoretical Expression: What Is Said in Religion

Here we consider the query, "What do they say?"

People *say* things in religion. They talk about God, angels, salvation, answered prayers, and much more. They tell stories about what God or Gods did in times past and about great religious saints or heroes, and they say what their doctrines or beliefs are. Religions say things about certain basic, ultimate issues—how the spiritual universe is set up, what unconditioned reality is, where the world came from and where it is going, and where humans came from and where we are going. Religions talk about how we know ultimate truth and how we are helped to get from here to the ultimate. This is what Joachim Wach refers to as the **theoretical form of religious expression**.

The theoretical is expressed in two fundamental ways: **myth**, or narrative story, and **doctrine**. In the history of religion, the term *myth* is used in a special way to mean stories that express in narrative form the central values of the society and

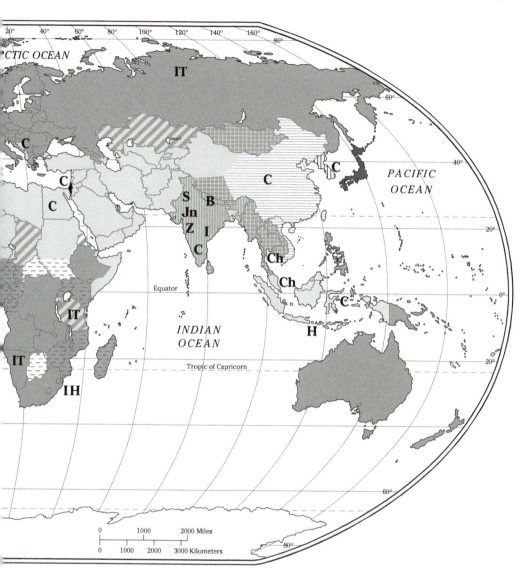

the way it views what the world means. This is different from the popular meaning of the word: a fable or story that is not true, as when we say, "That's just a myth." In the history of religion, the use of this word is only a statement of its function, and its use does not imply passing judgment on whether or not the narrative story is true.

What about myth?

A storyteller of the Australian aboriginal Arrernte tribes, an elder man or woman recognized as a lore keeper among these people who for some forty thousand years have inhabited the vast desertlike central areas of the island continent, is speaking to a group of young boys or girls, perhaps preparing them for tribal initiation. He is telling a story of how, according to wisdom now passed on to the latest generation, this immense and seemingly barren world came into being. For those whose lives have been so intimately a part of that rough terrain for so long, the immense emptiness is far from barren; rather, it is full of secrets and hidden wellsprings of life, and the storyteller knows how to crack its code. He recites in a reverent, chanting voice appropriate to ancient mysteries.

The Three Forms of Religious Expression

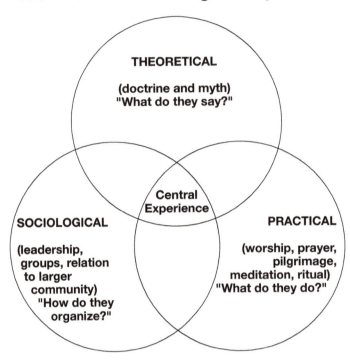

At first, he tells the young, all was a dark empty plain, containing neither life nor death. Then something stirred beneath the earth, as primal beings sleeping there moved from sleep without dreams to dreaming, then arose into what is called the Dreamtime. In this state they wandered the earth, calling to life plants, animals, and birds; as they wandered and worked, they sang. Their pathways are now called "songlines," and even now, by singing their songs, dwellers on Earth can follow their trails and renew their labors. In time, the Eternal Ones of the Dreamtime found deposits of plant and animal material for the making of human beings, usually near water holes or lakes; these they carved into final form. Labors done, the Eternal Ones then went back to sleep, but they left as marks of their presence sacred rocks and trees, often enhanced by rock paintings to show their presence. Today Arrernte can leave their harsh world to reenter the Dreamtime anew through dance and initiation and by following the songlines.[2]

Here we see, up close and in action, the theoretical form of religious expression as myth, or narratives that express the fundamental worldview and values of a society. Of these, none is more important than the story of creation, or how our world came into being, for we humans tend to assume that if we know where something came from, we know important things about its meaning and purpose.

What do you think is the basic message about our life as human beings in the Australian myth? Here creation is not an act of divine fiat or sacrifice; rather, it is more like acting out a dream, and the power of those primal times, the Dreamtime, can be accessed through dance and song, and storytelling.

Take another example, the Judeo-Christian creation account. The beginning of the Bible tells us that God created the universe from chaos and that God stood outside it as its maker and master, pronouncing it originally very good. This creation account tells us that God is not to be identified with the creation or with ourselves but that he is above it as its Lord and is One with whom we can have a deep relationship of faith and love, though not one of absolute identity.

A Hindu myth, in contrast, implies a very different kind of relationship between the Divine and the world. That myth tells us that God made the world out of himself by dividing up his body in a primal sacrifice. Thus, the world is, so to speak, God in disguise; in our innermost nature we are one with that same God.

What about doctrine?

Consider an assembly of bishops, teachers, or leading monks in one of the historical religions, like Judaism, Christianity, Buddhism, or Islam. They are reflecting on what general statements about religious truth can be deduced from the stories that have long been told about divine beings and their activities. It as though they are saying, "If the stories tell us that God, or Gods, at different times did this, and this, and this, what can we say about them that is true all the time?"

So they may say that stories and teachings like those of the Bible, the Qur'an, the Hindu Vedas and other sacred texts tell us that God is omnipotent or all-powerful, omniscient or all-knowing, or loving, and that he treasures those who believe and trust in him. They may say that the world was created at one definite point and will end at a later point in time with divine judgment. Or they may say that the universe is cyclical and eternal. Such statements give people something clear and definite to believe in that is relevant to all times and places and to all situations in which they find themselves.

Religions can present still other answers to "What do they say?": sermons, testimonials, lives of saints and heroes, folklore, poetry, novels. The list goes on and on.

Practical Expression: What Is Done in Religion

This form of religious expression answers the question, "What do they do?"

"Practical" here does not mean practical in the sense of something that works; it means "practices," what is *done*. It covers such aspects of religion as worship, rites, ways of prayer and meditation, pilgrimages—everything actually done for the sake of the religion from the most public to the most private. This is what Joachim Wach refers to as the **practical form of religious expression**.

All real religion has some kind of practice. If people were involved only in the realm of theoretical ideas, they would be involved in philosophy and not religion. But religious practices vary immensely, from an ornate ancient ritual to a simple Protestant-type service, from speaking in tongues to Zen meditation, from devotion to Gods in a Hindu temple to prayers in a Muslim mosque without images.

Many years ago, I* had an opportunity to see one of the noro, or priestesses, of Okinawa, a now-Japanese island in the Ryukyu chain, south of the main islands. The religion of these islands, though related to the Japanese religion known as Shinto, is often considered the only traditional religion in the world definitely under the full leadership of women, who are its clergy and spokespersons. The woman I saw, pointed out to me as a noro, was tall, dressed entirely in long white garments, and impressively dignified.

Four times a year, in one of their many rituals, a small group of noro gather at a shrine to the local kami, or local god, in the central square of the village. They light incense, pour sake (rice wine) from a cup over three sacred stones; then each takes a sip of the sake as a sort of communion, first offering it toward the altar and praying in a low voice.

---

*Robert Ellwood

They then proceed to the outer steps of the shrine, where they bedeck themselves in a five-piece white robe and a crown decorated with leaves and straw. This means the women are now, in effect, kami, or local gods, themselves. A male attendant hands each woman a small cup of sake anew; each woman lifts it and prays. The women then join the other villagers by taking assigned seats in the square and receive more offerings, and the occasion gradually becomes one of general festivity.[3]

Or, by way of contrast, consider the great variety of forms of worship within the Christian tradition. At one pole, there is the traditional Quaker meeting, in which persons sit in rows, or more often today, a circle, waiting in silence for the guidance of the Inner Light. From time to time individuals may feel moved to rise and say a few words or a prayer. At the end of the meeting, usually an hour, everyone stands to shake hands. A traditional Protestant service emphasizes the singing of hymns by the congregation, the reading of scripture, and the offering of prayers by the minister or other leaders, and it centers most of all on the sermon delivered by the minister, giving admonishment, advice, and support to those present who are endeavoring to lead a Christian life in this difficult world.

At another pole, the traditional liturgies of the Roman Catholic or Eastern Orthodox churches, while different, have in common a feeling of richness and timelessness. There are colorful vestments, offerings of incense, soaring music, and choreographed movements as the priests and others celebrate the offering and distribution of bread and wine by Christ at the Last Supper, now a festive banquet which is the central rite of a large part of Christianity.

What do these and all other "practical" forms of religious expression have in common? First, however different, one knows that these words and actions are "something extra" which cannot be explained solely in terms of ordinary everyday life, but have a special meaning outside it or pointing to something outside it. They construct a special "sacred time" in which, ideally, life is lived on another plane from the ordinary. Very often, this "sacred time" makes the place of worship different, too—a "sacred space"—perhaps a place in which one instinctively acts differently than one does on the street or in the shop. At the same time, worship is supposed to have meaning connected to everyday life, as "doors and windows" transmitting pardon and power for life's living.

The important thing for understanding is to look behind the form of the practice and see what the "message behind the message" is. How do the "doors and windows" of religious practices help people best get in touch with God or unconditioned reality? If it is an ancient rite, then it says we best get in touch with ultimate reality by getting out of the one-dimensionality of the present and entering something that has deep roots in the past, perhaps getting us in touch with family and ethnic heritage. The rite probably has a strong aesthetic component—the sight of gorgeous altars and vestments, the smell of incense, the sound of wonderful music—to make us feel lifted up into another realm. If, on the other hand, the rite is a simple service with emphasis on hearing scripture and sermon, then it says we best get in touch with ultimate reality through hearing and the feelings that hearing truth can evoke. If the rite is inner prayer or meditation, then it says we best get in touch by releasing our inner self, or by letting the Spirit speak freely within us.

Of course, remember that all worship has some kind of set form and in some way comes to us out of the past in a form that is traditional in a particular religion. This aspect of a rite, together with the sacred words used, is what makes it clear it is religious and not just entertainment or a lecture.

Sociological Expression: Groups and Leadership in Religion

This form of religious expression, dealing with the social organization of the religion, must encompass three questions instead of just one like the other two forms: What kind of groups do they form? What kind of leadership does the religion have? What is the religion's relation to the rest of society?

The main idea is that religion, as it appears in actual history and society, is generally social: followed by families, communities, and voluntary groups together. This means that, like any society, it has structure, that is, ways in which decisions are made and tasks assigned, as well as leadership and ways the group defines the boundaries between it and the outside.

From here on one finds countless variations. A moment's reflection should remind one of religious groups that are very democratic and of others that are very authoritarian in structure. Leaders may find their place in "institutional" ways, going through the established schools and ordination procedures of their group or denomination, or a religious group may be "charismatic," claiming a special inward call that manifests itself through the particular power of their preaching and perhaps miracles. Or a religious group may be a combination of each. So also there is considerable variation in the relation of religion to the outside. All of this is what Joachim Wach refers to as the **sociological form of religious expression**.

Religious groups are of many different kinds. Some religions are so dominant in a particular society as to be almost identified with it, as is, at least nominally, Roman Catholicism in Spain or **Lutheranism** in Sweden or Hinduism in much of India. Sometimes the predominant religion is divided into different, often competing groups or **denominations** with their own subsets of beliefs and practices, like Christianity in the United States or Buddhism in Japan. Some religious groups may be small and at odds with the larger society; these may be called **sects** or **cults**, though those words should be used with caution since they have become pejorative and stereotyping.

Like the practical expression, each kind of religious group has its own "message behind the message" about the "doors and windows" that help people to get in touch with ultimate reality. If it is a broad-based religion, having national churches or larger denominations, it will have an important role in that country's history and heritage; its leaders will be recognized as major spiritual figures, and it will doubtless have imposing churches or temples. At the same time, whatever its theoretical stance, because it includes so many people at all levels of spiritual development, in practice it will have to be fairly accommodating and tolerant. For those who sincerely adhere to this kind of religion, the message behind the message is, "It is better to go with a large religious group, even if there are imperfect people in it, than to set oneself apart; one can find everything one needs in that religion and help others in it, and in so doing one is identifying with a rich heritage."

On the other hand, those who join a small, probably more devoted, group are saying, "Large religions are inevitably corrupt and lukewarm; I have to be with a close-knit, intense group of people who are as serious as I am, who practice without compromise and who will give me the kind of support I need in my faith." Or those who join a small group may be saying, "I listen to a different drummer; what resonates with me seems to be a religion of a different kind from that of the majority; I have to seek it out and follow it whether it's popular or not." Without denying the validity of anyone's religious experience, one can probably imagine the kind of childhood and personality type that might go with each of the responses.

Take as an example the Prophet Muhammad and the beginnings of Islam with one man. It became the religion of a whole region, and eventually a major world religion.

As we will see in more detail later on, Muhammad started as a purely charismatic leader, first receiving the revelations that became the Qur'an, the sacred book of Islam, from an archangel while alone in a mountain cave. Soon enough, though, his religion was not purely private. The first convert was his wife Khadijah, who believed in his message. Today Islam is the second largest religion in the world with many sects, each with their own particular theoretical, practical, and sociological expressions of the revelation originally received by Muhammad.

Ethics, Religious Experience, and Art

Three more forms of religious expression, not mentioned by Joachim Wach as separate, ought to be cited: *ethics, religious experience,* and *art.* Although these forms could be included in either the theoretical or practical forms of religious expression—or both—each is so important that it ought to be discussed separately. We will look at ethics first.

ETHICS One has to deal with ethical issues all the time. Suppose someone shows you a way—or you figure out a way yourself—that you could cheat on an exam or plagiarize a paper in school, with very low risk of getting caught. How do you respond?

Or when you get home or get together with friends, you get into a hot and heavy argument about sexual morality. Is abortion ever justified? Is sex before—or outside of—marriage ever right? What about homosexuality?

Suppose a homeless person approaches you on the street wanting money. Should you give it to him or her or try to help in some other way, or should you say that just giving money doesn't really help?

Questions like these confront us almost every day. They are closely related to religion, because many people say that their religious teachings, or values, help them decide or actually provide the answers.

RELIGIOUS EXPERIENCE Another important vehicle is religious experience, sometimes called mystical experience. (Some authorities would define mystical experience as a sense of *oneness* with God or infinite reality, while saying a nonmystical religious experience simply offers a sense of divine presence, of deep prayer, or of being profoundly moved by a religious service or music.)[4]

For many people, the most important thing about religion is the experiences it provides: of closeness to or oneness with God, of conversion and inner purification, of prayers answered, of love for all beings. These feelings may be imaged and described in the language of various religions. But they are found in nearly all faiths, and appear to have some points in common everywhere. The recipient reports being inwardly moved, perhaps to sense a new start in life, and to know spiritual truth directly.

At the same time, characteristics of religious experience can vary, too. Shamans and others feel contact with, or possession by, individual deities rather than universal oneness, though these can be very powerful experiences. Sometimes the experience may be of what Rudolf Otto called the *numinous*—the sacred as fearsome as well as compelling.[5] More common today, though, are religious experiences described as warm and joyous.

Religious experience is not always intensely related to a particular religion. Roger Bannister, the first man to run the four-minute mile, tells of his first experiences running on the beach. After taking in the wonder of the nature all around him (though he says that he "could not absorb so much beauty"), he then started running virtually out of sheer joy: "No longer conscious of my movement I discovered a new unity with nature. I had found a new source of power and beauty, a source I never dreamt existed." Bannister added that it was from moments like this that his love of running grew.[6] Bannister's experience is what others might have termed a union with God.

ART   Let us use the term "art" broadly to include painting, sculpture, architecture, music, and literature—anything made by human craftsmanship for the sake of its beauty or truth-bearing capacity. Clearly, all these can serve as "doors and windows" to the Divine. The best analogy is a stained glass window in which the white light of the sun is colored and shaped to take on the form of haloed saints and conventional symbols of faith.

Art has always been important to religion. Indeed, it may well be that the earliest known art, the Paleolithic cave paintings, had religious meaning. The art of the earliest civilizations, in Egypt, Mesopotamia, and ancient India, was heavily religious—obviously because religion deals in beings that are ordinarily invisible— Gods, angels—or in beings from out of the past—saviors, saints, buddhas, prophets, sages. They must be portrayed to make them real. So also must basic religious symbols, or foci for meditation like the mandalas of the East, be made real.

Art can also tell us quite a bit about a religion's view of human nature and human society in the way it represents persons through art in all sorts of ways: as devout, as sinners, as wise and foolish, as turning to God or showing the nature of a life without religion. This last is especially the province of great novelists who have dealt with religious themes, such as Fyodor Dostoevsky or Graham Greene.

The Interrelationship of the Forms of Expression

In any religion, the forms of expression—three or six—work together to form a unified experience. It is usually a mistake to think that one comes first and the others follow after. Children learn about religion more or less through all forms of expression at once: they hear the stories and feel the special atmosphere of a church, a temple, or a religious rite when they are taken there by their parents, and they pick up the tone of its social life as they play with friends and relatives who share the same faith.

Even an adult convert will probably be drawn by all forms and will participate in all simultaneously. So the forms of religious expression unite to become a single unified experience, which points to the ultimate nature of the sacred and becomes a part of the inner life of each person touched by it.

DESCRIPTIVE AND CRITICAL APPROACHES

You may ask, is it enough just to talk, in a neutral way, about the shape of a religion's "doors and windows" as they open toward unconditioned reality?

It is not the purpose of a study such as this to decide about the truth or falsity of any religion. We are simply trying to know and understand religion better, using a descriptive and empathic approach—attempting to see each religion, in a sense, from the inside out. Even so, does one look on everything in the religious world— from human sacrifice to the healing work of a Mother Teresa—with exactly the same understanding gaze? Is there no place for a critical look that says one kind of religious practice is simply better than another?

In the twenty-first century, religion seems to have a newly important role in world affairs. The clash of religious beliefs and the cultures they foster have been painfully brought to the fore, making it all too clear that religion can have a dark side. In this environment, too much empathy certainly can get in the way of even seeing where the problems are, and world religion scholars realize that they need to be a part of the discussion about such matters.

Important questions have been raised around the world about religion and the oppression of women, about religion's role in maintaining exploitative economic systems, about ways in which religion can hinder (through allegedly outmoded religious beliefs) solutions to current problems, like overpopulation—solutions that are deemed more reasonable by those who propose them. The religious rhetoric and energies behind international conflict and terrorism, as well as scandals in major religious institutions, have alienated some people from religion, or at least some forms of it. On the other hand, some of those involved in such conflicts are moved to embrace a more profound commitment to their faith. And in the United States, divisive issues such as the conflict over the appropriate role of religion in politics and the conflict between science and religion (as in battles over teaching evolution or medical research using human stem cells) abound. Such issues have found some religious people on one side and some on the other. In any case, the power of religion to divide as well as to unite, to oppress as well as to uplift, and to seem dark as well as to enlighten is apparent. Yet in the thick of these conflicts, one thing is clear: beneficial change will not occur unless questions are asked and criticisms made.

Nevertheless, faith and effective change require the most accurate information and authentic insight possible. For this reason, there remains a vital place for religious studies that just attempts to present a clear and unvarnished account of the way things are. And that is why it is especially important to maintain an empathetic perspective when studying or observing a religion that is from a cultural context quite different from the one of the student or the observer.

If an attack is made, for example, on a certain religion's endorsement of war, one needs to be sure that one understands how this matter is understood *by believers*, not just how it looks from the outside. One also needs to know exactly who endorses the policy on behalf of the religion: the great majority of members, authoritative leadership, or only certain extremists that take it on themselves to interpret the religion's teaching. It is also important to analyze to what extent this policy differs from the teaching and practice (not always the same thing!) of one's own and other religions. One would also need to be clear about the values to which one is appealing in advancing the criticism and why she or he believes those values should be considered superior to those of the religion itself. Only then would one properly be able to make a critical yet responsible statement challenging the religion to reassess its position on war.

Our main goal in this book is to be descriptive. This is primarily a work that provides information and attempts empathetic insight. But it does not preclude criticism, and the authors hope that what is presented here will help readers to view religion both empathetically and critically.[7] Criticism made honestly on the basis of knowledge and insight is ultimately necessary if we are to come to our own conclusions about the validity or rightness of a religious expression that is foreign to us in our own cultural context. Criticism is essential in any open and honest inter religious discourse; we must be prepared to deal not only with our criticism of the religions of others, but also with their criticism of ours.

RELIGION THROUGH TIME

Think of pictures you may have seen of paintings on the walls of caves by our early ancestors, some going back as far as 35,000 years or more. They suggest that "something more" was added by human hand, mind, and spirit to nature. We do not know exactly why the lavish cave paintings were made. In part, they may have been a kind of magic to enhance the availability of animals the people hunted. The depth of the cave may have been considered an otherworldly kind of place, where access to a realm of divine beings or departed spirits was possible and through which animal and even human life entered our realm. There is evidence that the caves were not only art galleries but places of religious rite or initiation. In one cave recently studied, the archeologists found that the sandy floor was trampled by many tiny human feet some thirty millennia ago: children dancing in some ritual, perhaps their initiation?

These remains are from the Paleolithic era, or Old Stone Age: the time when hunters and gatherers predominated, before the discovery of agriculture. Religion is oriented, in part, toward what is perceived to be the source of our life, in this case the animal, and also what is perceived to be that other world that is the source of dreams, of the visions of shamans, of life itself and its invisible powers. The cave religion of Paleolithic peoples may be perpetuated in the barrows or underground artificial burial caves or tunnels of ancient Ireland and Britain, or even the pyramids of Egypt, which are like artificial mountains with their internal caves for burial and access to the world of the dead and the Gods.[8]

With the discovery of agriculture, the plant and its cycle of seedtime and harvest, of "death" and then "rebirth" were sacralized. Sometimes this mystery was viewed as a model of human life, and even of the life of the Gods, as well. In ancient Babylonian religion, Ishtar was the most loved and worshiped of all the Goddesses. Her brother and spouse was Tammuz, a vegetation God, and a dying-rising deity. Tammuz was said to die and go to the underworld in the fall. Ishtar then wept for him, descended into the realm of shades, and triumphantly brought him back in the spring with vibrant rejoicing. This myth had great worship expression among the common people. Women wailed with Ishtar for her charming yet dying child, and farmers danced when his return meant the return of fertility and new crops in a new year. This pattern was commemorated by the great temples of Babylon and by Babylon's kings as well.

That worship hints at something else too: agriculture meant people stayed in the same place, meaning villages, then towns, then great cities and empires like those of Egypt or Babylon or China. Such great civilizations meant bountiful trade, together with surplus wealth that could support priests and philosophers. That brought a momentous development, one even more important than cities, empires, trade, and priests, though it was related to them: the invention of writing. Writing first originated perhaps in the records kept by men of commerce. But soon it meant chronicles of kings and the sacred books of the priests. Oral traditions that had been passed down from generation to generation took on new significance as they were reified in the written word.

A quick glance at chronicles going back over years and centuries told readers that things change and do not change back. Empires rise and fall, peoples move about, plagues come and go. Take the Chronicles of the Hebrew Scriptures. They told ancient readers, as they tell us, that the people of Israel went through many vicissitudes: slavery in Egypt, entry under Moses into the Promised Land, innumerable wars, and exile. Each age brought new challenges, and none were quite the same as those of yesteryear.

This discovery of a sense of history called for a larger religious perspective than that of cave or tribe. In the new civilizations, lives were more specialized and individual than in the old tribes. In religion, too, there was more emphasis on individual responsibility, on one's own sin and guilt, on one's merit and salvation, and on how one's own life fit in the larger society.

Moses standing on the top of Mount Nebo.

All this was reflected in new religious visions, which were provided by a just a handful of persons—Moses, Zoroaster, the Buddha, Confucius, Laozi, Jesus, Muhammad—who were the founders of major religions, several of which came to dominate the spiritual landscape of vast expanses of the globe. Although their traditional lives have no doubt been mythologized, it is significant that the founders were, or were taken to be, historical personages who lived at a definite time in human history, not mythological beings. For the most part these founders lived over a relatively brief period within the whole scope of human history, from about 500 B.C.E. to 500 C.E. This period, or its first century, has sometimes been called the Axial Age, because on it so much turned.[9] Not least of this was the use and institution of sophisticated writing, which enhanced the awareness of historical time (mentioned above) and centered religion on set texts rather than oral tradition, which could evolve in its telling over time.

Although the major religions to come out of this period carried over much from before, cumulatively they marked a tremendously important new start in Earth's spiritual history. Believing that a definite word was delivered by a divine voice within the midst of human history, which was memorialized in sacred texts, like the Bible, the Sutras, or the Qur'an, they could sometimes be stricter and more intolerant than what went before. Yet they also showed that the onward march of human history can have sacred meaning: God or the Gods are working in it. In India, at approximately the same time as the emergence of the founder religions, the traditions that were to become Hinduism produced written texts of such teachings as the Upanishads and the Bhagavad-Gita. In them the central theme is the oneness of the true self with the Divine, transcending history through making absolute the state of consciousness or angle of philosophical vision in which timelessness shows is above time.

The founder religions that were successful, such as Buddhism, Christianity, Islam, Confucianism, and parallel developments in Hinduism, became associated with major empires, like Christianity and the late Roman Empire under Constantine, Buddhism with the Ashoka in India, Islam with the Caliphate, and Confucianism in the Han dynasty of China, which gave them a foothold from which they spread, sometimes over continents and many diverse cultures. Parallels among them can be seen in how they developed devotional patterns, had an era of reformation like that of Europe in the sixteenth century, and produced philosophies and literatures, ancient and modern.[10]

Golden Buddha, Lama Temple in Beijing, China.

Blue Mosque, Istanbul, Turkey.

Looking Forward

It is clear, then, that religion is always in a state of flux and transition. Each generation has always been melting into the next. There are always constant themes in religion, but their ways of expression continually shape themselves anew. The process is a complex interaction of tradition and new ideas, working through expression in word, act, and group formation, expressed through symbols or concepts that may be as old as cave art or inspired and imaginatively created only yesterday. And it should be remembered that virtually nothing of significance that appears in the long history of a religion is ever really lost.

RELIGION, GOVERNANCE, AND POLITICAL LIFE

In 1953, Elizabeth II was crowned Queen of England and the United Kingdom in a solemn and highly religious ceremony in Westminster Abbey. The actual coronation took place in the heart of the Eucharist, or Holy Communion, the central rite of much of traditional Christianity, celebrated according to the usage of the Church of England.

Later, in 1990, Akihito was made Emperor of Japan in ceremonies which included a very ancient Shinto rite called the **Daijosai**. Virtually alone, the ruler prayerfully took sips of rice wine twice in the dead of night in thatch-roofed structures, apparently communing with Shinto deities and his divine ancestors in this quiet and mysterious ceremony.

In the twentieth century, these impressive rituals had resonances of something from another era, when a state church or some other form of union of religion and government had real authority. For that matter, neither the British nor the Japanese sovereign possesses real political authority, but each is considered the embodiment of the whole people—a check on ordinary state power but whose function is actually symbolic. For traditionalists, the symbolic religious enthronement of symbolic rulers evokes warm nostalgia, from others, criticism for the apparent presumption that all citizens share one religion or that government has any business so endorsing a religion.

In the West, we tend to think of religion as a phenomenon more or less different from the public life of politics and government. Thus i may surprise many a Western reader to discover that in most cultures around the world, throughout time, there was not even a word to identify religion as something different from the society and culture as a whole.[11]

Even today, nearly all of what we now refer to as "religion" aims toward an ideal not only for individuals, family, and the religions' own institutions but also for all of society. So to study a religion without addressing its vision of society, including governance and political life, would be taking it out of context.

What we find is that the world religions' aspirations for government and society have much in common, in that they address common fundamental questions: How can society achieve stability, safety, justice, prosperity, and fairness for its people? What kinds of characteristics and character do we want our governors to exemplify? What role should religion play in politics or government, if any at all? What is a good society? Differences arise, of course, in the various ways in which the world religions have attempted to answer such questions. And the reader will want to keep these questions in mind as we explore religion, governance, and political life in the sections on that topic throughout this text.

WOMEN IN THE WORLD RELIGIONS

One might ask: Why have the authors included special sections on women in the chapters that follow and not a complementary one on men? The reason is that too often what we study about religion is a generalization of human experience using men's experience as the norm. This is called being **androcentric**. The study of women in religion is an effort to undo this androcentric perspective to provide a more holistic understanding of religion.

We have already looked at one example of women in religion, the Okinawan noro or priestesses. But a more typical situation would be that in medieval Europe, where women had no hope of a leadership position in the official hierarchy, from village priest to pope, but who might participate in what is sometimes referred to as the **"little tradition"** of folk myths and practices that were intermingled with officially sanctioned doctrines or through unofficial but sometimes significant influence from the sidelines as saint and advocate.

Take St. Catherine of Siena (1347–1380). This medieval Italian woman claimed to have had an ecstatic vision of Jesus when she was only five or six years old, and at sixteen she was asked by her family to marry the widower of her recently deceased sister, Bonaventura. Utterly unwilling to enter into this union, Catherine adopted a tactic she had learned from Bonaventura. The latter, callously treated by her spouse, had refused to eat until he changed his ways; he finally did so. Now Catherine, aware of the power as well as of the status fasting could give women in a society controlled by men, declined to eat until her father relented and let her remain unmarried.

Catherine later became a Dominican sister, and in a famous mystical experience, she believed she was inwardly wedded to Jesus. She now reportedly ate very little but the Holy Communion, and as a now-celebrated ascetic, she sent letters and traveled about, promoting church reform and, particularly, striving to end the papal schism, in which rival popes reigned in Rome and in Avignon in France. Gregory XI in Avignon was apparently sufficiently impressed by the spiritual power of this impassioned woman, evidenced by her fasts, that he returned his administration to Rome.

The role of women in religion will be a major concern of this book all the way through. Occasionally, as with the Okinawan noro and, more recently, in some religious communities in which reforms have equalized the genders, women have had positions of institutional leadership. But most of the traditional major faiths that, since the Axial Age, have dominated the spiritual landscape have been governed by males, regardless of what their founders may have intended. That is, a patriarchal social pattern, or

Woman praying at a temple in Thailand.

Fundamental Features of Religions

Theoretical

Basic Worldview	How the universe is set up, especially in its spiritual aspect—the map of the invisible world.
God or Ultimate Reality	What the ultimate source and ground of all things is.
Origin of the World	Where it all came from.
Destiny of the World	Where it is going.
Origin of Humans	Where we came from.
Destiny of Humans	Where we are going.
Revelation or Mediation between the Ultimate and the Human	How we know this and how we are helped to get from here to our ultimate destiny.

Practical

What Is Expected of Humans: Worship, Practices, Behavior	What we ourselves must do.

Sociological

Major Social Institutions	How the religion is set up to preserve and implement its teaching and practice; what kind of leadership and groups it has; how it interacts with the larger society.

"patriarchy" developed where the patriarch or the father is the authority. Because of this, women were subject to male religious leaders, fathers, husbands, and even sons on the basis of religious tenets that did not permit individual status and authority for women.

Still, the positions of women have been varied. As wives and mothers they have, of course, had a role in the shaping spiritual life and wisdom on the domestic level. Sometimes, perhaps like the noro, perpetuating shamaness and priestess roles going back long before the Axial Age, they have been folk religion visionaries and ritualists. Sometimes, as nuns and abbesses, they have carved out a niche with definite, though limited, authority within the system. Certain women, like Catherine of Siena, have exercised no small influence through their own inner spiritual charisma, whether as ascetics, saints, writers, counselors, or even founders of new religious movements, from Christian Science in the United States to Tenrikyo in Japan.

More often, though, women have found that their gender has caused them to face implacable barriers in life, whether in exercising institutional or intellectual spiritual leadership or in marriage, where the prevailing religion has often taught wifely submission to the husband and has made divorce or even remarriage after widowhood very difficult. Some women have invented ways around these situations; some have known deep inner happiness, nonetheless; some have found life very hard. All these matters will be reflected in the upcoming sections on women in the various world religions, as they ask the "woman question" what are the proper roles and status of women in religion and society?

FUNDAMENTAL FEATURES OF RELIGIONS

That each of the world's religions has a history and encompasses each of the forms of religious expression means that they all have common patterns. They usually ask and answer certain questions. All have a basic worldview, ideas about the Divine or Ultimate Reality, ideas about the origin and destiny of the world and of individual humans, a revelation or authority or mediation between the Divine and humankind, standards about what is expected of humans (that is, patterns of worship, spiritual practices, and ethics or behavior), and an institutional or sociological expression.

In order to provide a convenient guide to these fundamental features, a chart that presents the three forms of expression from Joachim Wach (the theoretical, practical, and sociological) has been prepared for each religion discussed in this text. An introductory outline for the charts is presented on page 19 so that the reader can see what will be covered in each of the categories used.

It should be remembered that these charts are able to present only the dominant or traditional interpretation of the religion; variations often exist but cannot be taken into account in the charts, although they may be in the text.

It is now time to turn to the religions themselves.

Summary

This chapter has tried to present some basic perspectives for understanding the religions of the world comparatively. We discussed religion as the "doors and windows" between conditioned and unconditioned reality. We presented the forms of religious expression: theoretical (narrative and doctrine), practical (styles of worship), sociological (forms of group life), ethics, religious experience, and art. We reflected on ways in which both descriptive and critical approaches to religion are valid and important. We discussed religion's aspirations for the political dimensions of society. We talked about the problems and possibilities inherent in discussing religion in terms of its history and summarized the major historical periods of human religion. We also discussed the "woman question" in the world religions and how the answer to that question impacts women's lives and shapes the societies in which they live. Finally, we indicated that each actual, living religion contains tensions and seemingly conflicting motifs that it tries to resolve into a pattern.

This may all make religion appear very complex and difficult, but if you will look within yourself, you will see that your own life is ordered in much the same way. By increasing your understanding of yourself as a human being, you will grow in your ability to understand the complexity of human religion.

Questions for Review

1. Discuss whether or not you agree with the contention that today is a particularly exciting time to study world religions.

2. Describe some of the problems in today's world that seem to be involved with religion and some ways religion can help intergroup and international understanding.

3. Explain the difference between conditioned and unconditioned reality and religion's role regarding them.

4. Name and explain Joachim Wach's three forms of religious expression, together with ethics, religious experience, and art.

5. Describe how religious doctrine develops from myths and narratives.

6. Discuss what sort of messages might be transmitted nonverbally by the practical (style of worship) and sociological expressions of a religion.

7. Explain how the forms of religious expression interact.

8. Present the values of both descriptive and critical approaches to the world religions. Give examples of both based on your own observation.

9. Discuss the advantages and possible pitfalls of an historical approach to understanding a religion.

10. Summarize the main periods in the history of human religion with an understanding of the importance of the Axial Age.

11. Indicate the main ways in which religion has responded to the experience of the "discovery of history."

12. Describe some common characteristics of founder religions, especially Buddhism, Christianity, and Islam.

13. Explain some of the major characteristics of the modern experience and how religion has responded to them.

14. Discuss some of the issues raised by postmodern consciousness and how religion has responded to them.

15. Summarize the main issues involved in the study of religion, governance, and political life.

16. Discuss the "woman question" in the world religions and how an androcentric point of view might provide only a limited perspective of religion.

17. Discuss how religions both contain and try to resolve the tensions common to human existence.

Suggested Readings on the Study of World Religions

Almond, Gabriel A., R. Scott Appleby, and Emmanuel Siran, *Strong Religion: The Rise of Fundamentalism Around the World*. Chicago: University of Chicago Press, 2003.

Armstrong, Karen. *The Great Transformation: The Beginning of Our Religious Traditions*. New York: Knopf, 2006.

Bowie, Fiona, *The Anthropology of Religion*, 2nd ed. Malden, MA and Oxford: Blackwell, 2006.

Bowker, John, ed., *The Cambridge Illustrated History of Religion*. Cambridge and New York: Cambridge University Press, 2002.

Browning, Don S., M. Christian Green, and John Witte, Jr., *Sex, Marriage, and Family in the World Religions*. New York: Columbia University Press, 2006.

Carmody, Denise Lardner, *Women and World Religions*. Englewood Cliffs, NJ: Prentice Hall, 1989.

——, and John Tully Carmody, *How to Live Well: Ethics in the World Religions*. Belmont, CA: Wadsworth, 1988.

Christ, Carol P., and Judith Plaskow, eds., *Weaving the Visions: New Patterns in Feminist Spirituality*. San Francisco: HarperSanFrancisco, 1989.

——, *Womanspirit Rising: A Feminist Reader in Religion*. San Francisco: HarperSanFrancisco, 1979, 1992.

Eliade, Mircea, *Cosmos and History*. New York: Harper Torchbooks, 1959.

——, *Patterns in Comparative Religion*. Cleveland: Meridian Books, 1963.

——, *The Sacred and the Profane*. New York: Harper Torchbooks, 1961.

Ellwood, Robert S., *Myth: Key Concepts in Religion*. London and New York: Continuum, 2008.

——, *Cycles of Faith*. Walnut Creek, CA: AltaMira, 2003.

——, *The Politics of Myth: A Study of C. G. Jung, Mircea Eliade, and Joseph Campbell*. Albany: SUNY Press, 1999.

——, *Introducing Religion*, 3rd ed. Englewood Cliffs, NJ: Prentice Hall, 1993.

Gross, Rita M., *Feminism and Religion: An Introduction*. Boston: Beacon Press, 1996.

Haddad, Yvonne Yazback, and Ellison Banks Findly, eds., *Women, Religion and Social Change*. Albany: State University of New York Press, 1985.

Hitchcock, Susan Tyler, with John Esposito, *The Geography of Religion*. Washington, DC: National Geographic Society, 2004.

Idinopulos, Thomas Athanasius, Brian C. Wilson, and James Constantine Hanges, eds., *Comparing Religions: Possibilities and Perils?* Leiden: Brill, 2006.

James, William, *The Varieties of Religious Experience*. New York: Longman, Green, 1902 (many later editions).

Jaspers, Karl, *The Origin and Goal of History*, Michael Bullock, trans. London: Routledge & Kegan Paul, 1953.

Lerner, Gerda, *The Creation of Patriarchy*. New York: Oxford University Press, 1986.

Lincoln, Bruce, *Holy Terrors: Thinking About Religion after Sept. 11*. Chicago: University of Chicago Press, 2003.

MacDonald, Margaret Read, *The Folklore of World Holidays*. Detroit, MI: Gale Research, 1992.

Matthews, Clifford N., Mary Evelyn Tucker, and Philip Hefner, eds., *When Worlds Converge: What Science and Religion Tell Us about the Story of the Universe and Our Place in It*. Chicago: Open Court, 2001.

Morgan, Peggy, and Clive Lawton, eds., *Ethical Issues in Six Religious Traditions*. Edinburgh, UK: Edinburgh University Press, 1996.

Neusner, Jacob, *World Religions in America: An Introduction*, rev. ed. Louisville, KY: Westminster John Knox Press, 2000.

Otto, Rudolf, *The Idea of the Holy*. London and New York: Oxford University Press, 1958.

Pals, Daniel L., *Seven Theories of Religion*. New York: Oxford University Press, 1996.

Sharma, Arvind, ed., *Today's Woman in World Religions*. Albany: State University of New York Press, 1994.

————, and Katherine K. Young, eds., *Feminism and World Religions*. Albany: State University of New York Press, 1999.

————, *Her Voice, Her Faith*. Boulder, CO and Oxford, UK: Westview Press, 2003.

Smith, Huston, *The World Religions: Our Great Wisdom Traditions*. San Francisco: HarperSanFrancisco, 1999.

Smith, Jonathon Z., *Imagining Religion*. Chicago: University of Chicago Press, 1982.

Smith, Wilfred C., *The Meaning and End of Religion*. New York: Harper & Row, 1962, 1978.

Swidler, Arlene, ed., *Homosexuality and World Religions*. Valley Forge, PA: Trinity Press International, 1993.

Thrower, James, *Religion: The Classical Theories*. Washington, DC: Georgetown University Press, 1999.

van der Leeuw, Gerardus, *Religion in Essence and Manifestation*, 2 vols. New York: Harper & Row, 1963.

Wach, Joachim, *Sociology of Religion*. Chicago: University of Chicago Press, 1944.

————, *The Comparative Study of Religion*. New York: Columbia University Press, 1958.

Waardenburg, Jacques, ed., *Classical Approaches to the Study of Religion*. New York and Berlin: de Gruyter, 1999.

Weber, Max, *The Sociology of Religion*. Boston: Beacon Press, 1963.

Winzeler, Robert S., *Anthropology of Religion*. Lanham, MD: AltaMira Press, 2008.

The student is also referred to good encyclopedic treatments of particular topics, such as those in the *Encyclopedia Britannica*; Keith Crim, ed., *Perennial Dictionary of Living Religions*. HarperSanFrancisco, reprint, 1990; Lindsey Jones, ed., *The Encyclopedia of Religion*, 2nd ed., 15 vols. Detroit: Macmillan Reference, 2005; Robert Wuthnow, ed. in chief, *Encyclopedia of Politics and Religion*, 2 vols. Washington, DC: CQ Press, 2007.

CHAPTER

2

The Sacred in Nature

Indigenous Peoples and Religion

CHAPTER OBJECTIVES

After studying this chapter, you should be able to

- Discuss common features of indigenous peoples' religions, especially how the sacred is found in nature.
- Explain the importance of initiations in indigenous peoples' religious practice.
- Explain the role of the shaman in indigenous peoples' religions.
- Discuss how remnants of archaic indigenous peoples' religions can still be found in cultural traditions in the West and elsewhere.
- Interpret how differences in procuring food influence religious orientations and symbolism.
- Talk about how social changes that arose in response to agriculture affected women and led to great cultural changes.
- Discuss the importance of understanding early religion for human life today, including ways in which its themes are found in religions around the world today.

ENCOUNTERING INDIGENOUS PEOPLES' RELIGION

In 2009, the Council for a Parliament of the World's Religions held its international conference in Melbourne, Australia. The conference opened with a welcome from an indigenous,* **Aboriginal** elder and the sounding of the *didgeridoo*, the aboriginal ancient horn, which when blown makes deep resonating, undulating tones that are haunting and comforting all at once. After all, a focus of the conference was **indigenous peoples** and their religions, and indigenous peoples had come from all over the world—from Asia to North America, from Europe to Africa, from South America to

---

* The authors acknowledge that the term "indigenous" is a contested term and is inadequate to express the variety of peoples and cultures, past and present, we discuss in this chapter. The term "indigenous" has been used to mean "native" in other senses than our usage here. Nevertheless, increasingly the identifier "indigenous" is being used to designate certain peoples who are, or believe themselves to be, descended from the original inhabitants and culture-makers in specific locations around the world. The designation specifically distinguishes such peoples from those who participated in the processes of colonization or otherwise came much later to a location.

the Pacific Islands and Australia. Any stereotypes that would characterize them as primitive, or any thought that their religions were all in the past, fell away as they shared the wisdom and practices of their ancient faiths with other representatives of the world's religions. Any stereotypes of what might be considered "typical" appearance or clothing became unthinkable as well. These indigenous peoples were of every skin color from the whitest white of the Sami People of the northern reaches of Scandinavia to the darkest Australian Aborigine. And they were attired in native costumes of every color and style imaginable and unimaginable.

In all of this, it was abundantly clear that the substance of these indigenous peoples' religions past and present is tremendously varied, for the roster of indigenous cultures, each with its own deities and rites, is almost endless, and undoubtedly very many from ancient times have been forgotten forever.

Because of the immense variety of indigenous peoples (estimated to consist of as many as 5000 communities worldwide, more than 5% of the world's population),[1] this chapter cannot hope to cover the subject in a systematic or culture-by-culture way. Our discussion is impressionistic and largely nonhistorical, drawing from cross-cultural observations to illustrate certain great themes and motifs. Not all of these are shared by all such cultures, of course, but they provide insight into a worldview that shares much across the religions of indigenous peoples. As you read this chapter, also keep in mind that today indigenous peoples' religion has frequently been challenged by disruptive modernizing and missionary influences from outside. In some places, though traditional feeling about sacred places, shamanic vision, and life-cycle celebrations remain, their expression may be mixed in with features of modern life, such as urbanization, and with nominal or integrated acceptance of another religion religions, such as Christianity or Buddhism.

THE FIRST FAITHS

Behind the panorama of the religions of the axial age with their founders and scriptures, behind even the world of the ancient empires with their writing systems and sprawling political-economic entities out of which the founder religions mostly emerged, is the religious world that went before all of them. That was a religious world without written texts but rich in art, myth, and dance. It was the religious world of the ancestors of all living human beings for hundreds of thousands, perhaps millions, of years between the emergence of a distinctly human way of life on Earth and the development of writing and large political units. Accordingly, such religious practices may be called "prehistoric religion," for written history had to await the development of writing.

We are speaking of ancient societies characterized by three features:

- They were nonliterate—that is, they did not have reading and writing, except in some cases through pictograms or markings, such as runic inscriptions;
- They were organized in very small political units, such as tribes or clans; and
- They subsisted by hunting and gathering only or practiced an ancient form of agriculture or lived as nomadic pastoralists.

As late as the nineteenth century, vast stretches of the Earth, from Siberia to Africa, from Australia to the Americas, still supported such indigenous societies, though under steadily increasing pressure. Their traditional forms of religion also flourished, though traditional ways of spirit, livelihood, and social organization were increasingly undermined with the incursions of "civilized" traders, settlers, colonial rulers, and missionaries, who all too often combined religious conversion (whether intentional or not) with an insatiable appetite for land acquisition and resources, sometimes using violent means. Today remnants of this prehistoric society and religion survive in what were once remote and largely isolated areas. Others, have found ways to practice their religion and continue their culture in the midst of the religion and culture of their conquerors.

To extrapolate from present-day indigenous peoples' religion back to worldwide prehistoric religion is risky, especially because evolving change is inherent in many indigenous peoples' religions, rather than maintaining consistency with an ideal of a golden past found in a book. Nonetheless, it seems safe to assume that at least the major themes of today's indigenous peoples' religions can be traced to roots in pre-historic religion. And if we're right, today's indigenous religions are the oldest living religions in the world.

Here is an example. The Sioux believe in four souls, three of which die with the individual's physical death.* When death comes to a person of the community, you would see his fourth **soul** kept present in the midst of his people in a kind of bundle, containing his hair wrapped in animal skins, and placed on a tripod in a teepee. Offerings of the Sioux's most sacred foods, buffalo meat and wild cherry juice, would be presented before this shrine to Wakan Tanka, the ultimate force behind the universe, on behalf of all creatures, "two-legged, four-legged, and flying." You would see those foodstuffs then actually consumed by four young girls, so that when it later comes time for them to conceive, through them something of that departing soul's power could be transmitted to a new generation.

Then, after a suitable space of time, you would see the soul released. The bundle would be carried outdoors, and its spirit-dweller told now to continue its great journey on beyond the circles of this world, but as she or he progresses onward, to "always look back upon your people that they may walk the sacred path with firm steps."[2]

While the Sioux are only one among an almost endless number of indigenous peoples around the world, certain basic ideas are found among a very great number of them, and that is so here. Several features of the worldview expressed in the above account may impress themselves upon you.

First, our planet is shared by many kinds of spirits, some as humans, animals, or forces of nature, some like those of ancestors or Great Gods disembodied at present, or dwelling in shrines or sacred hills or trees, yet also able to affect our lives.

Second, that life is like a journey with stages of transition, whether initiations, or birth and death themselves. Each of these may involve pain and sacrifice, yet confer new status.

Third, in this religion food, as the source of life, has very important significance: note the role of the buffalo and wild cherry juice in the funeral rite; for farmers, the plant and its symbolism have no less important roles.

Fourth, all classes of people, young and old, male and female, have their sacred parts and obligations, related to their biological nature but going beyond it; note the role of the four girls in the rite above.

Now let's explore general themes and motifs of indigenous peoples' religions, as they are found today, but also no doubt echo the long past from which they derive.

THE NATURAL WORLD IS THE REALM OF THE SACRED

Indigenous peoples' religions find and express the sacred in all aspects of nature and human life. The celestial sky, the earth, the seasons, sacred rocks and trees, life passages from birth to death, the community or tribe—all are alive with spirit and

---

* This belief in multiple souls, common in indigenous peoples' religion, is not as unusual as it may seem to others. Consider how many different natures or personalities—souls—most of us have, depending on who we're with, at work or at play, in church or temple or at a party; one of them may seem like a deeper and more abiding, even immortal, part of us than the others.

meaning. Here, there is no linkage to historical personalities or written documents as in founder religions. The sacred is immediate, here and now, not located in the past or in a book. With this idea of the sacred, one needs little focus on linear time or an idea of the progress of history. Mircea Eliade called this worldview **cosmic religion**.[3]

Indigenous nomadic peoples, or hunters and gatherers, celebrate the hunt and stories of Gods and spirits who lead the people to bountiful forests or meadows with abundant food and shelter. For religions of indigenous agricultural peoples, there also are festivals focused on seedtime and harvest. And there is always the veneration of nature—the sacred trees and mountains, the human spirit, and communing with the Divine, immanent in all that is.

In this way of being, ordinary daily life and the extraordinary experience of the natural world are inseparably integrated, full of divine beings and goblins, elves and spirits, the returning dead. The rites of hunting, gathering, and archaic agriculture make no sharp division between this world and an "other" world. Moreover, **shamans** are believed able to travel in trance to heaven or the underworld to recover strayed or stolen souls or to intercede with the Gods. Ritual then invokes the fundamental sacredness of nature and human beings' part in it.

Although these religions have rational worldviews expressed through rite and symbol and society, they do not have the formal written ideological statements that in other religions are all-too-tempting pegs for interpretation. For that reason, we have to see what the unified experience and the particulars alike are saying themselves.

So, it is the images—symbols, gestures, sacred art, and the mighty figures of sacred stories—that stand out in the world of indigenous peoples' religion. It is from the accounts of heroes in story, from masks, from spiritual leaders in the midst of a hunting rite, from carvings of ancestors, and from paintings on rocks and caves that these religions are learned. All of these go together to make up a world in which spirit and matter are thoroughly interwoven, and everything is more than it seems as myth, rite, and art make the invisible visible. In this universe, human life is only complete in its total relationships—with family, community, ancestors, the wind and the rain, the bounty of the Earth, the warmth of the sun—and all is spirit.

GODS, SPIRITS, AND THE WORLD

Indigenous religions have their demarcations between conditioned and unconditioned reality. Yet, as Clifford Geertz has pointed out, they generally seem complex, only semiordered, and deeply intermingled with all of life. The images they imprint on the mind, however, borne by the powerful languages of myth and ritual, are unforgettable.[4]

Most prominent of these images carried by myth and ritual may be stories about creation, the beginning, where the world and human beings came from. At the same time, humans are aware that the world is far from perfect and that if the creation was meant to be good, something must have gone wrong. Often an original or ultimate God will be portrayed as having made the world but then seeming to have little concern for humankind except perhaps to enforce the moral law. A deity like this is spoken of by those who study religion as a **deus otiosus**, a "resting god."

Sometimes a myth, comparable to the Garden of Eden narrative, accounts for the separation of humankind from primordial closeness to the creator. With the separation, death enters the world. The indigenous people of Poso, Sulawesi (Celebes) Island, Indonesia, said that originally the sky where the creator dwelt was very near the Earth and that he would lower gifts down on a rope to his children. Once he let down a stone, but the first men and women were indignant at such a useless gift and refused it. So the creator pulled it back up and lowered instead a banana. This the men and women took. But the creator called to them, "Because you have chosen the banana, your life shall be like its life. Had you taken the stone, you would have been like it, changeless and immortal."[5]

Or the creation itself may have been accomplished by lower deities. A traditional story from the Wahungwe Makoni of Zimbabwe, Africa, tells us that their **high God**, Maori, made the first man, Mwuetsi, and put him in the bottom of a lake. Mwuetsi wanted to go out on the land; the high God told him he would regret his wish, but he insisted on it. Indeed, Mwuetsi found the Earth cold and empty, with no plants or animals. Maori told Mwuetsi that he had warned him, but Maori did consent to give Mwuetsi one of his kind as a companion, a maiden called Massassi. After Mwuetsi took Massassi as his wife, they procreated the plant world: grasses, bushes, trees. But after two years, Massassi said her time was up, and Maori put her back in the lake. Mwuetsi complained loudly to Maori, so the high God gave him another consort, Morongo, and by her animals and children were procreated. Then Maori told Mwuetsi that his procreating was to cease, for the time of his death was coming. But Mwuetsi and Morongo defied this edict from the high God by continuing to procreate, concealed in a hut with a closed door.

Now, however, their progeny appeared as dangerous creatures: lions, leopards, snakes, and scorpions. Nonetheless, as their human children grew up, Mwuetsi became a great "Mambo," or king, reigning in his "Zimbabwe" ("royal court"). But when he desired to lie with Morongo again, he was bitten by a snake hidden under her bed and became sick. The children performed a divination ritual and found his time was over. They strangled him and sent him, along with Morongo, back to the lake and made another man king.

Mwuetsi became the moon, with its cycles of dying and returning to life, and Massassi and Morongo became the evening and the morning star. From that time on, life and death stayed eternally in balance.[6]

Though an indigenous peoples' creator high God (if there is one) may be far removed from ordinary human affairs, many more spiritual entities inhabit the world. Lesser deities, perhaps offspring of the creator, like Mwuetsi and his wives, may be closer presences in sacred mountains or in the forests that the hunter enters. **Ancestral spirits** are likely to be especially loved and feared, for they stay near their families to impart the strength that goes with the lineage, but they also punish individuals whose faults dishonor it.

Indeed, it is characteristic of many peoples to believe that the supreme God who created the Earth is remote from our affairs and that it is really the finite, but far more involved, ancestral or nature spirits with whom we mostly have to deal. The Luguru of east Africa, for example, say that the Earth was made by the high God Mulungu but that he is not normally concerned with human affairs. He is given no prayers or sacrifices; they are made rather to the *mitsimu*, or ancestral spirits. One Luguru authority said:

> Mitsimu are the spirits of our grandfathers who died, of our grandmothers. Some say these are mitsimu. They bring sickness to a person for his faults. Also, as I say, when your maternal uncle...departs and bequeaths you his name there must be a supernatural event, then they say the name is seeking a person, his maternal uncle's name, then they say that's *mitsimu*. Or suppose you want to go to Dar es Salaam, and you ask permission from your maternal uncle and he says "You can't go!" and you say "I'm going!" and then he says, "All right, you'll see for yourself!" Then where you are going there is sure to turn out some danger. From the *mitsimu*.[7]

In this matrilineal society, the chief authority figure is the maternal uncle, who is superior even to one's father or mother. Thus, the authority of the ancestral spirits is chiefly aligned with the maternal uncle. But they are more than just glorified uncles. The *mitsimu* are personages with the numinous enchantment of the Divine haloing them; they are part of the invisible world. The appearance of omens, such as a solitary unusual animal, is said to be a warning from these ancestral spirits. Places of awe and dread, like a burial ground, a deep lake, an underground river, or a striking hilltop, are thought to owe something of their uncanny feel to the presence of these haunts. The *mitsimu* are not mediators between the passive high God and men, but independent powers working according to the lights of their own path in the cosmos. The Luguru universe is pluralistic, although Mulungu may have created all souls in the remote beginning. Thus, there is an ultimate principle of unity that the powers now work all on their own. Yet they are not merely chaotic, for the ancestors work in support of the familiar and traditional values.

Indeed, the concept of the soul as a separable, undying part of oneself is extremely widespread, but ideas as to what happens to it after death are mixed. In fact, a notion of several souls to accommodate the different prospects is common. By far the oldest recovered evidence of human religious themes are those indicating burial rites, such as painting bones ochre, the color of blood and life, or leaving artifacts with the remains as "grave goods." These practices suggest the idea of a soul surviving the body and may go back many thousands of years.

One idea is that the departed spirit remains close to hearth and home, becoming an ancestral soul that must be propitiated at a nearby grave or shrine. Sometimes these spirits are personified by dancers in ceremonies, often wearing masks. Another idea is that they go to a distant land of the dead, perhaps a known but remote island or mountain, perhaps a more mythical place like the Australian Aborigines' "Dreamtime" world. But usually this place is less a fanciful paradise than a mirror image of this world, where life goes on much the same as here though perhaps more pleasantly, with days always mild and food always abundant. Finally, it is also sometimes thought that the dead reincarnate in the same community or family, perhaps after a stay in the alternative world. Sometimes one finds a concept of several souls evoked to deal with these varied destinies, as with the Sioux previously mentioned, one to become an ancestral spirit and others to go to another world.

INITIATION RITES OF MEN AND WOMEN

Indigenous peoples' religion is ritualized as much as it is thought. Among its best-known and most significant rituals are **initiations**. They may include rites of symbolic death and rebirth for the initiate.

Consider the experience of a young person of the Crow Sioux people of southern Montana undertaking the Vision Quest, an aspect of initiation into manhood, and also undertaken when renewed spiritual energy and improvement in one's fortunes as hunter and warrior are required.*

The initiate would begin the adventure by entering a sweat lodge with some companions. There he would pour water over hot stones to create vapors and

---

* In some Native American nations, the Vision Quest has been available to both men and women when the need or desire for visionary experience has been felt. George Sioui, indigenous of the Canadian Wendat nation, has noted that the Vision Quest was not offered to women partly out of fear they might be possessed by spirits, partly because they had spiritual "allies" "that help them to recognize their personal vision in a more natural way and to remain attuned to the forces of Creation." George E. Sioui, *Huron-Wendat: The Heritage of the Circle.* Trans. from French by Jane Brierley. (Vancouver: University of British Columbia Press, 1999), 214, Note 100.

intense heat. Then, that afternoon, he and his companions would climb a mountain, carrying a newly tanned buffalo hide. On the way, he would stop at a spring to wash and clean himself thoroughly, down to the fingernails, and then build a fire, dropping pine needles into it to purify himself with their incense. Finally, reaching the summit at evening after a long hard climb, he and his friends would each select his own spot, there making a stone bed and covering it with the buffalo robe. Fasting from both food and drink, they would fall asleep. In some cases, the initiate might have given himself still more suffering, knowing that only through pain and privation does true vision come: he might have cut off the joint of a finger or with the help of a mentor, put a wooden skewer through the flesh of his chest or back and swung from it or dragged something from it like a heavy buffalo skull.

That night he would receive no vision; nevertheless, he would continue fasting and praying throughout the next day. The following night, he would have a preliminary dream; perhaps a strange man would appear to his inner sight, telling him that later he would receive his message. So he would continue fasting and praying three more days. Then, as day fell dark and rain began to fall, a remarkable sight could appear, such as a face in the sky, clouds before it and birds flying around it. A wide red stripe on the visitant's forehead would tell him that seeing this sight is auspicious. A voice would tell him that he will be helped and perhaps tell him that he will become a great warrior and chief. Then, he would be given a song of power to aid him in making this wonderful dream come true.[8]

For most indigenous cultures, life is a series of initiations, and it is through them that the cultures' most meaningful signs of status are bestowed, as well as the deepest mysteries of the ultimate meaning of human existence revealed. Birth and death are themselves initiatory experiences and so are a part of the series; the great ceremonial initiations enhance, ratify, recapitulate, and prepare one for what is imparted by these two deepest of all sacred mysteries—birth and death.

For males, at least, initiation is a painful trial, like birth and death. Among the Papuans about Finsch Harbor (Finschhafen) in New Guinea (Papua), the traditional initiation ceremony for all male youths would be held every ten to eighteen years, and the boys who would undergo it would rang in age from four to twenty. The central feature, as in many such rites around the world, is circumcision or, more exactly, a ritual death and redemption of which circumcision is a lasting token.

At the appointed time, the young candidates would be taken by the men of the community into the forest. The bull roarers—flat, elliptical pieces of wood, which when twirled make an unearthly roaring sound—would be booming. The women of the community would look on from a distance, anxious and weeping, for they would have been told that the boys were to be eaten by a *balum* or ghostly monster, who would release them only on condition of receiving a sufficient number of pigs. (Significantly, the word "balum" means both bull roarer and ghost.) The women therefore would have been fattening pigs since the ceremony was announced in the hope that the pigs would be adequate to redeem their sons and lovers—or at least they would pretend to believe all this. One pig would be needed for each initiate.

Deep in the forest, the boys would be taken to a secret lodge designed to represent the belly of the monster. A pair of eyes would be painted on the entrance, and roots and branches would betoken the horror's hair and backbone. As they would approach, the monster would "growl"—in the voices of more hidden bull roarers.

The pigs would be sacrificed and eaten by the men and the boys, for the monster demands only their "souls." The boys would then enter the lodge and undergo the circumcision operation. They would remain in seclusion for three or four months, living in that long hut inside the "monster." During this time, they would weave baskets and play two sacred flutes that are said to be male and female and to be married to each other. No women would be allowed to see these flutes, which would be employed only during such sacred seasons as this.

At the end of the seclusion period, the boys would return to the village, but they would return in a special manner that bespeaks festival and rebirth. They would first be taken to bathe in the sea and would then be elaborately decorated with paint and mud. As they would go back to the village, they would have to keep their eyes tightly shut. An old man would touch each on the forehead and chin with a bull roarer. They would next be told to open their eyes and then would be allowed to feast and to talk to the women.[9]

In the Vanuatu island of Malekula, where a similar Melanesian culture prevails, the men spend their lives undergoing a series of higher and higher initiations, as they are able to obtain the requisite pigs (raised by the women) for sacrifice and feast. These achievements would be memorialized in the imperishable tusks of the boars and by wooden markers like **totem** poles in the courtyard of the men's lodges; these then would become ancestral spirits. By the spiritual power of the pigs, a man would be enabled to pass the lair of Lehevhev, the terrible spider woman who guards the road to the spirit world. In the highest of these degree rites, the initiates would be garbed in masks and in ghostly white webbing, as though they were already sacred ancestors with the dread power of one who has passed from death into unearthly life.

Part of a totem pole.

Besides these rites, there are special individual initiations. For some indigenous peoples, in fact, the initiation of all young men is more individualized than in New Guinea, like the story of the Native American Sioux at the beginning of this section. Similarly, a Native American Pawnee young man would be expected to remain alone in the bush until he personally receives a dream or vision of his guardian spirit.

By no means are initiation rites solely the province of men in indigenous peoples' religions. Aboriginal women of Australia, for example, have a role in male initiatory rites, albeit in ways differing from that of the men. Women may participate in dramatic separation enactments that precede the circumcision rite of a young man and may perform sacred dances during the circumcision itself at a place adjacent to, but removed from, that of the men.

Further, Aboriginal women have their own rites marking important passages in their lives. A young woman's first menstruation, probably her most important passage other than birth and death, marks her coming of age, and the ritual at this time is parallel in many ways to that for young males. (In fact, it is probably the case that the male initiation rite, with its birthing imagery and the shedding of blood through circumcision, mirrors women's life processes.) The women of the community would take the girl to a sacred, secluded location, separate from the men. Her menstrual blood, **taboo** for the men, is sacred to her as a source of great magic and power, and secret rites would be performed by the women in recognition of this. The return to the community is a celebration that acknowledges her new status as a mature and fertile woman who provides for the community.

> She is brought triumphantly into the main camp in formal procession, followed by an old woman who jokes and dances, clowning, stamping her feet, throwing her arms about, in contrast to the solemnity of the others: the girl's mother especially, is crying and wailing.... The girl steps ritually over a row of food ... then sits down while more food is heaped beside her. Afterward she distributes this.[10]

Such rites reflect the interplay of spiritual forces in the affairs of human life. They emphasize that the spirits of nature work through the natural processes of the human body (particularly in the case of women, whose bodily processes are, therefore, mimicked in the men's rites), and they emphasize that the rites celebrate that which sustains the community as being coextensive with the ultimate divine, imminent reality.

SHAMANS

There are persons singled out by the Divine to receive special ecstatic powers for dealing with spiritual things. These are the men or the women referred to variously as shamans, medicine men and women, or witch doctors. The word "shaman" is Siberian, and it is in that land of endless birch and evergreen forests, broad rivers, wide skies, and dark subzero winters that the classic form of **shamanism** is found, although shamanism or closely related phenomena appear in most parts of the Earth. Indeed, it has been argued that shamanism is the prototype of much of the religious world. (For that reason, although the term itself is contested in some places, we will use it as the name for those who take the special role described here.)

The **shaman** above all is one who on subtle planes of perception or soul travel, moves freely among the spirits. The shaman knows the geography and dynamics of the invisible spirit world that overlays and is present in this world. Thus, the shaman can serve as guide of the souls of the dead, as healer and intercessor, and as counselor to the community—for all matters are matters of the spirit.

Let us look at a few shamanistic practices and try to understand the common features of this phenomenon.

The Altaic shaman in Siberia would wear brown leather and elaborate decorations of metal disks, bird feathers, and colored streamers. He would entrance himself by sitting astride a horsehide-covered bench or a straw goose and beating a drum rhythmically for hours, the beat being the pounding of the hooves or of the wings of these spirit steeds as they bore him to the realm of the spirits. Finally, the shaman would dismount and, flushed with **ecstasy**, climb nine steps notched in a tree trunk. At each stage in the ascent, he would relate the difficulties of his journey, address the deities and spirits of that level, and report what they were telling him about coming events. Some of the episodes would be comic, such as a burlesque hare hunt on the sixth level. The shaman's scenario would generally be enacted with a rich dramatic sense for the right combination of spectacle, mystery, suspense, comic relief, and exalted sentiments. When the Altaic shaman had gone as high as his power permitted, he would conclude with a reverent prayer of devotion to Bai Ulgan, the high God, and collapse, exhausted.[11]

In his *Book of the Eskimos,* Peter Freuchen describes a shaman's séance, which he attended.[12] He emphasizes that the shaman, named Sorqaq, prepared seriously for the exercise by fasting and meditation on the cliffs. Sorqaq was to contact a deity who dwelt beneath the Earth to find out why the community had been suffering a series of accidents. Nonetheless, he opened the session by telling those who attended that they were a bunch of fools for coming, that nothing he did would have any truth in it. The audience responded with cries of belief and encouragement. The shaman then sat naked upon a sealskin on a ledge in the igloo, and his assistant bound him tightly with sealskin thongs. His drum was placed beside him. The lights, except for one small flame, were put out.

Then Sorqaq began to sing, and his voice grew louder and louder. Soon it was accompanied by the beat of the drum and the rustle of the sealskin, which seemed to be flying about the room. The awful din rose to a crescendo, with everyone joining in the singing. Sorqaq's own voice then became fainter and seemed to be coming from farther and farther away.

Shaman dancer at the City God Festival in Taipei, Taiwan.

The assistant suddenly put on the lights. Freuchen noticed that the audience was ecstatic—eyes gleaming, bodies twisting to the music of the shaman's song. Even more remarkable, the shaman himself was gone, his place on the ledge empty save for the drum and sealskin! Among the crowd, the spiritual intensity grew, with people experiencing seizures and speaking in strange words, including a special séance language in which persons and objects were referred to by alternative terms.

Then the assistant announced that the shaman was returning. People went back to their seats, and the lights were put out. The assistant told of the difficulty Sorqaq was having when he was swimming through the rocks beneath. Sorqaq's voice was heard growing in volume; once again the drum sounded louder and louder, and the sealskin crackled in the air. The room quieted after Sorqaq returned, and he was seen again seated on the ledge, his body tightly bound in straps. He told the audience what he had learned: "To avoid more tragedies, our women must refrain from eating of the female walrus until the winter darkness returns!" Afterward, Sorqaq said to Freuchen, "Just lies and tricks. The wisdom of our ancestors is not in me. Do not believe in any of it!" (It should be noted, however, that shamans have been known to make such disclaimers to researchers and other observers to avoid further intrusion into their secrets.)

These accounts should make evident that the shaman is distinguished from other types of religious specialists, such as the priest or the sorcerer, in part by the dramatic quality of his or her performance, with its semispontaneous appearance and the fact that the shaman seems to, and often does, undergo the psychic and physical changes attendant upon altered states of consciousness. Anthropological work has brought to light that taking hallucinogenic plants, such as the fly agaric mushroom in central Asia and plants of the datura family in the Western Hemisphere, is a part of shamanism in some cultures.[13] The altered state of consciousness and the visions of the shaman, while valid spiritually in the context of the culture, are often facilitated by the well-known effects of these drugs.

Native American performing ceremonial dance in traditional attire.

African tribal woman in traditional attire.

That is not the case with all shamanism, however. Trance-induced altered states of consciousness in which radically nonordinary perception and audition are obtained are quite possible without the aid of drugs. Trances of this sort are often accompanied by violent trembling, swelling, discoloration, and berserk behavior, as well as divine utterance. Sometimes seemingly superhuman strength is attained. Tibetan shamans have been reliably reported to be able to twist strong steel swords into knots while in this state. Afterward the shaman will be so exhausted as to sleep for days, and such shamans are said, in fact, to be generally short lived.

The shaman is also distinguished by a related factor, the nature of her or his "call." Other religious functionaries may have entered into their role by heredity, choice, or apprenticeship. But in the case of the shaman, although these factors may play a part, the important point will generally be that he or she has passed through a powerful spiritual ordeal of selection, testing, and "remaking" by divine beings themselves. Above all, he or she will probably receive an assisting spirit, who gives the shaman supernormal powers and control over other spirits.

Here is a vivid account of the manner in which an Eskimo shaman received his power:

> The angakok consists of a mysterious light which the shaman suddenly feels in his body, inside his head, within the brain, an inexplicable searchlight, a luminous fire, which enables him to see in the dark, both literally and metaphorically speaking, for he can now, even with closed eyes, see through darkness and perceive things and coming events, which are hidden from others: thus they look into the future and into the secrets of others.
>
> The candidate obtains this mystical light after long hours of waiting, sitting on a bench in his hut and invoking the spirits. When he experiences it for the first time "it is as if the house in which he is suddenly rises; he sees far ahead of him, through mountains, exactly as if the earth were one great plain, and his eyes could reach to the end of the earth. Nothing is hidden from him any longer; not only can he see things far, far away, but he can also discover souls, stolen souls, which are either kept concealed in far, strange lands, or have been taken up or down to the Land of the Dead."[14]

The future shaman's career begins typically with a "call" from a God or a spirit, perhaps the primordial master shaman, in the form of "voices" or strange impulses or seizures. For a time, unable to escape from a supernatural world for which the future shaman is not prepared, he or she may be tormented by cruel spirits in the head and the body. Extremes of anxiety and rapture may be suffered. The future shaman may wander about the village in a dissociated manner, have fits, be unable to eat or drink, even become criminal. The future shaman is, in a word, what those in western culture might call insane.

In terms of the future shaman's own culture, however, she or he is one marked by the Gods as a possible candidate for a mighty vocation. However much the future shaman may want to be merely "normal," that can never be; the Gods will not let the one they have designated as a shaman to scorn them. The shaman must either serve the Gods or face the unspeakable terrors of their punishment in mind and body.

Navajo Native American medicine man performs a ritual.

Even so, success is not inevitable. A great test lies ahead. The future shaman is already in the spiritual world. Now power must be acquired to master it. There is no choice; the spiritual world must be mastered, or it will destroy the tormented one. This power can be acquired only with the help of one who has it. An initiator must be found, either a great shaman in this world or a supernatural ally in the parallel spirit world, who will impart to him or her the techniques of control. In our terms, the future shaman, now a novice, must conquer this "sickness" and make it work for him. It must continue to produce knowledge-giving visions of the spiritual world, or the subjective world if one prefers, but only when requested by the novice to do so. This "sickness" must become an insanity that can be turned on and off at will, so one can learn the things only this state can teach, yet not be enslaved by it.[15]

To arrive at this kind of control, the novice must pass through a catharsis that is virtually a death and a rebirth. Alone in the wilderness, in sickness, as aide to a senior shaman, the novice meets this crisis. Among the Eskimos, it is said that the future shaman must take out all his bones and count them; among the Australians that the soft viscera must be replaced by organs of quartz.

But however exclusive the call, shamanism also expresses the social dimension of religion. The future shaman's spiritual attack, private as it is, is also a phenomenon expected in the society and has a conventional interpretation and resolution. Moreover, the shaman who has passed through the initiation has a role that is traditional in the society, a role that frequently has great prestige.

However genuine the call, the role—partly because of the conventional expectations—is not without an element of showmanship or even trickery, as the Eskimo shaman Sorqaq intimated. Perhaps his point of view was the same as that of Quesalid, a shaman of the indigenous people of British Columbia, the First Nation Kwakiutl, who told the anthropologist Franz Boas the story of his life.[16] Quesalid said that he started out as a skeptic and associated with shamans to learn their tricks and expose them. Invited to join with them, he learned plenty: sacred songs, how to induce trances and fits, how to produce seemingly magical feats by sleight of hand, and much else. In the meantime, knowledge of his training spread, and he was invited by a family to heal a sickness.

Despite Quesalid's disbelief, he felt constrained to accept the offer, and the healing was a success. As more triumphs followed, word spread that he was a great shaman. Knowing such things as that the "sickness" he pretended to suck out of the ill person's body was actually made of down he had previously concealed in his mouth, Quesalid was at a loss how to interpret to himself what he was doing. Finally, he came to feel that the healings worked because the sick person "believed strongly in his dream about me," and he apparently felt that the deceptions were justifiable insofar as they helped people believe. Nonetheless, he proved the superiority of his method in competition with shaman colleagues and was contemptuous of most other shamans as charlatans, saying he had known only one he thought was a "real shaman," who employed no trickery he could detect and who would not accept pay.

There are variations in shamanism. One major variation is the "traveling" shaman, such as shamans of the Altaic and Eskimo, already presented, who goes to the spirit world or underworld in his trance. The other is the "possession" shaman who draws the Gods to her rather than going to them and who is possessed like a medium by deities and spirits and lets them speak through her.

A good example of the latter are the *miko*, or shamanesses, of Japan. Now disappearing, they played a substantial part in the popular religion of Japan in the past. They are found today mostly in the far northern part of the island of Honshu. Every summer they gather there for a sort of convention on Mount Osore at the upper tip of that island. The Japanese shamans of this type are all female and, what is more, are all blind or nearly so. All are initiated into the vocation of shamanizing as young girls. While the vocation of shamanizing precludes marriage (unlikely for a blind girl in any case in traditional society), it does provide a respected place in the village for girls who would otherwise have had slim prospects.

Blind girls become apprentices of older shamanesses at six or eight years of age. After a strict training involving fasts, cold-water ablutions, observing of taboos, and the learning of shamaness songs and techniques of trance and divination, they are initiated.

For this rite, the novice wears a white robe called the "death dress." She sits facing her mistress and other shamanesses; these elders sing and chant formulae and names of deities. Suddenly the mistress cries, "What deity possessed you?" When the candidate gives the name of a Shinto deity or Buddha or bodhisattva (who will thereafter be her main supernatural patron), the mistress throws a rice cake at her, causing her to fall onto the floor in a faint. The elders then dash water onto her head as many as 3,333 times. Then they lie beside her and revive her with body heat. When she comes to, she is said to be reborn; she exchanges the death dress for wedding apparel, and a traditional Japanese wedding—with the traditional exchanges of cups of sake nine times—is performed. The new shamaness is the bride; her deity, the groom. Next a great feast of celebration follows, shared by relatives and friends of the new medium; she demonstrates her proficiency at communicating with spirits of the dead. For a week following, as a sort of divine honeymoon, she may live alone in a shrine of her deity.[17]

While doing fieldwork in Japan many years ago, I* visited a shamaness who consented to give me a "reading." One wall of the main room of her small house was taken up with altars—Shinto and Buddhist alike—reflecting the syncretistic nature of popular religion around the world. She sat on the floor facing the altars and sang in a sleepy, mystical tone as she swayed back and forth, going into a light trance. Then she called on the help of the sovereign deities, giving out a list of popular Shinto and Buddhist figures and calling on the patrons of the local mountains and districts. Next she received her modest payment and worked the 500-yen note in her hands slowly and placed it on an altar.

After this, she called down the guardian deity of my family, whom she said was Fudo, a **bodhisattva** prominent in popular Buddhism. Fudo gave me warnings, for example, that I was in danger of having a cold in the next ten days, that my wife would become ill in the middle of the year, and that a doctor from the South would help her to recover. This directional emphasis was doubtless due to the influence of Daoist geomancy, or the plotting of auspicious and unlucky directions, on folk belief in both China and Japan.

Next, at my request, the spirit of my grandmother was summoned. The *miko* had some diffidence about this request, since she had never before summoned a non-Japanese spirit. But she proceeded, and the shade of my American grandmother spoke in Japanese and as though she were an Asian ancestral spirit.

She started by saying, "Except when it is difficult, offer me water. In this matter I am not happy. The good faith my grandson would show in offering me water as a parting gift would make me happy." She continued, however, to say that although a good doctor was not called when she died, she had had a long enough life and had no regrets; that she was now happy in heaven but that she wanted to be remembered more by offerings of water, presumably at the small shrines of Buddhas and ancestral spirits found in a corner of a traditional Japanese home. She inquired about relatives, gave advice such as to watch out for pickpockets on buses and trains, made a few minor prophecies, and promised to be with her grandson.

---

* Robert Ellwood

The shamaness said nothing of much evidential value, but the session did provide a vivid insight into the shaman's role: to serve as a meeting ground between the living and the dead and as a reinforcer of popular spiritual lore. The altars and references in her home to many faiths indicated that she was not tied to the systematic beliefs of any one faith but rather was alive to the presence and powers of deities and spirits of any sort. She knew, so to speak, the secret shortcut paths to the parallel spirit world and seemed to link them. One got a feeling that the real value of what she did was in the presentation, with its atmosphere of mystery and of belief in the survival of the deceased, rather than in the things the departed were purported to have said. In all this, she belonged to the great tradition of shamanism.

TRACING SURVIVALS OF ARCHAIC INDIGENOUS PEOPLES' RELIGIONS

At first glance, the world of indigenous peoples and their religions seem very remote to adherents of the **Abrahamic religions** (Judaism, Christianity, and Islam). Yet many of the religious motifs of indigenous peoples come across as hauntingly beautiful or nightmarishly powerful. They hit one unexpectedly with all the impact of a half-remembered but very important scene from a dream or from early childhood. Or perhaps they *are* recollections of an ancient past, before an indigenous ancient religion was overtaken by those newer faiths in the Middle East and Europe—when the turn of the seasons, the hunt, the harvest, and the veneration of earth and sky prevailed. We know something of the religions of the ancient peoples of those lands from the writings of those who conquered them. What's more, there are countless survivals from those ancient religions that continue to flourish as much as ever—from Christmas trees to the Muslim pilgrimage to Mecca—albeit with changed or added meanings. It could be argued that most **popular religion** of ordinary people, whether in Buddhist, Christian, or Muslim lands, is only a partially altered version of an underlying religion akin to today's indigenous peoples' religion under another name—many holidays incorporating bits and pieces of earlier faiths.

Christmas, for example, is a festival of Christianity, which derives from the era of the discovery of history and which commemorates a historical event around which Christians believe all history turns. But consider the Christmas symbolism. It is a celebration of light at the darkest time of the year—the Winter Solstice—the inauguration of a new year, an ornamented tree symbolizing the mystical center of the Earth and a way of access to the divine world. Remnants of a pre-Christian past are found in the evergreen tree, which may in times past have represented ongoing life through the dark time of winter, just as the tree remains green throughout the winter season. Still today it is suggestive of celebration amid the dark time of winter. The evergreen tree is not only pre-Christian in origin; it also expresses the kind of emphasis that one finds among indigenous peoples: the spiritual experience produced by the turn of the seasons; the sacred meaning of landmarks of nature like trees and mountains; the sheer immediate evocative power of symbols like light and glitter; the perennial importance to spiritual life of family; and the sacred, set-apart time of festivals.

Then there is the orange-and-black feast, with its atmosphere of jack-o'-lanterns and tales of witches amid frost and falling leaves. Perhaps the oldest holiday that is a part of general American culture is Halloween. It is almost a pure memento of an archaic religion (although coming from Europe, rather than America). Halloween customs incorporate no small number of themes akin to those of indigenous peoples today—themes that invoke the beginning of this darkest time of the year, when the spirit world and the world of the living are believed to be closest. On this night, children masked and costumed as ghosts, skeletons, witches, and devils, or as

Venus of Willendorf, a statuette found in what is now Austria, is estimated to have been made as early as 24,000 B.C.E.

pirates, cowboys, or monsters, visit homes to receive candy with threats of "tricks or treats."[18] Pranks ranging from soaping windows to putting a farmer's wagon on top of his barn have also sometimes been part of Halloween. There are costume parties with spooky decorations and traditional games like bobbing for apples.

Perpetuated into Christian times as the eve of All Hallows or of All Saints' Day, Halloween was originally the autumn festival of the ancient Britons and their Druid priests, called Samhain. It was, many believe, the Celtic New Year. Like festivals of harvest and the new year everywhere, Samhain had motifs of settling accounts, the harvest moon, the celebration of the last harvest before winter, the return of the dead to visit the living, and the kindling of a new fire to light the way and warm the spirit as the darkest, coldest time of the year loomed near. It suggested a temporary return to the chaos before the world was created and thereby the release of the dark and uncanny denizens of chaos. Behind children's masks of monsters and witches, behind "tricks or treats" and bobbing for apples, lies the ancient religious orientation toward the turn of the seasons, rather than a historical event, as the time when reality is revealed.

An important motif is a feeling that the turn of the year is like a clock running down and coming virtually to a stop just before it is wound up again on New Year's Day. New Year's Day is like a recurrent Day of Creation, so the preceding eve is like replunging into that precreation flux when there were no controls. This is illustrated by dark, grisly entities coming out on Halloween, by the ancient New Year's Eve, and by our tradition of getting drunk on the modern New Year's Eve. In ancient Rome, the end-of-the-year festival was the Saturnalia, when masters and slaves exchanged roles in a gesture of turning upside down the ordinary structures of society.

May Day, another holiday, continues the pre-Christian spring festival of ancient Britain known as Beltane. As Halloween in the fall bears a mood of night, moon, the dead, and unwholesome visitants, so May Day is a celebration of day, sun, flowers, and all that is bright, warm, and fresh, although also supernatural. Dancing around the Maypole was an ancient practice to encourage fertility; May baskets were gifts of the bounty of the enchanting White Lady who rode through the land awakening the miracle of spring. A center of this belief was the town of Banbury in central England; until modern times the visit of the White Lady was enacted on May Day in a pageant culminating at the ancient market cross in the town square. As the old rhyme has it

> *Ride a cock-horse to Banbury Cross,*
> *To see a fine lady upon a white horse,*
> *With rings on her fingers and bells on her toes,*
> *She shall have music wherever she goes.*

Long after Christianity came, in fact, May Day celebrations were held in Banbury in which youths would gather boughs and make garlands; a Maypole would be set up: and a girl would be chosen as May Queen (in ancient times representing the goddess of fertility), who would ride to the festivities on a white horse. Today, May Day, or Beltane, celebrations have been revived in Banbury, other locations in Britain, and elsewhere.

But survivals such as Halloween and May Day contain only a few of the themes of early religion in its fullness. They suggest a typical (at least in temperate climates) seasonal emphasis, but the pantheon of Gods and Goddesses and the full relation of the religion to society in these holidays are less evident as those relations recede from memory and into the realm of fantasy. Yet there are those, many of whom call themselves "Pagans," who do want to remember and are reviving these "Old Religions." We will turn to them in Chapter 10 in our discussion of new religious movements.

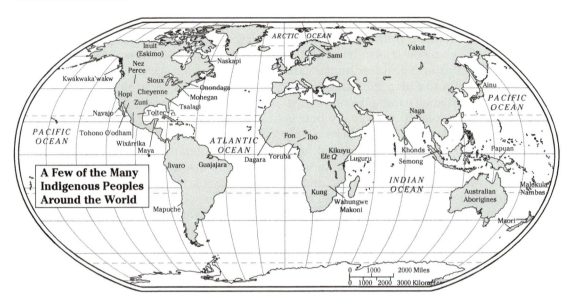

A Few of the Many Indigenous Peoples Around the World

INDIGENOUS HUNTER-GATHERS AND AGRICULTURALISTS

Indigenous Hunters

Religion past and present concerns itself not only with crossing the bar to contact ancestors and spirits but also with ordinary human needs. People have always viewed the object that is the source of their lives materially and subjectively to be the very presence, or at least a symbol, of the Divine: the animal for hunters, the plant for agriculturalists, the king as giver of order for the ancient city and empire, and for people today, the psychological sense of oneself in relation to community and the Earth.

Thus, the relation of the indigenous hunter to the game makes hunting more than mere killing. It is an important part of religious life. Going into the field, tracking, and taking the animal is an act of interplay with spiritual forces and in this respect is comparable to going to church or temple. Even though some of the hunters' tactics may seem cruel and can be as exploitative as those of any other people, the relation to the animal is that of one power or soul with another. To take the animal requires in some sense the consent of the animal or that of its divine masters, due propitiation for the wrong done to it, and proper magic to make anything happen at all.

It is necessary to prepare spiritually for a great hunt. Ceremonies set the hunters apart. Rites, such as drawing a picture of the animal sought and charming it, strive to attract the game, even as apologies to the animal are offered. As the hunters leave for the field, a sacred silence is sometimes observed. While out, they may observe taboos of diet, remain continent, and speak in a special vocabulary. They stir up the animal's attention with a ritualized dance to draw it into an ambush, or they may wait for it by a watering hole with a meditative quietude. When the animal is taken and devoured, the remaining bones are treated with respect, for the animal's soul may return to see how its remains were treated, or the bones may be mystically animated to make them magical instruments of great potency. Killing, in other words, entails all sorts of responsibilities. This is a very different world of human-animal relations from that of the modern slaughterhouse or of many a modern sportsman with his high-powered rifle, telescopic sight, and desire for a "trophy."

Indigenous hunters frequently believe in a divine "master (or mistress) of animals" who has control over the forest or a major species and who is able to "open" or "close" the forest, making game available or impossible to find. Among the indigenous Naskapi people of Labrador, for example, the Caribou Man is said to live in a world of caribou hair as white as snow and as deep as mountains. These mountains comprise the immense house of the Caribou Man, who is white but dresses in black. He is surrounded by thousands of caribou two or three times normal size—both living caribou and caribou ghosts. Along paths lined several feet deep with hair, the animals pass in and out of the Caribou Man's caribou paradise and shed caribou horns, as the Caribou Man releases them into our ordinary world for the proper use of humankind.

No human is allowed within 150 miles of the Caribou Man's house. Yet it is said that a hunter who really comes to know the ways of the caribou—virtually thinking like one and sharing its life, observing all the proprieties in his hunting, not taking too much game and respectfully using every part of an animal he does kill—becomes almost one with the Caribou Man and is always given what he needs.

When the Naskapi shamans address the animals, they say, "You and I wear the same covering and have the same mind and spiritual strength." This attitude governs their understanding of the animals that is so crucial to their survival in a harsh climate. Souls of animals circulate; the ghosts dwelling with the Caribou Man are waiting to be sent back into the world in fleshly bodies to be killed once again. It is therefore important that humanity live in reverent harmony with the biological and spiritual ecology of nature. Animals treated rightly will cooperate and return to offer themselves as game to hunters again; those who are not will be enemies, now and hereafter.[19]

A comparable view of life was reflected in the bear sacrifice of the Ainu, formerly a hunting people who live on Hokkaido, the northernmost island of Japan.[20] They believe that a spirit world reflects this world virtually as a mirror image; life circulates between there and here. When it is night here, it is day there, and so forth. In one traditional ritual, the Ainu took a small bear cub, which they had raised in their village and had treated with great affection, like a spoiled child. When it had nearly reached adulthood, it was killed and sent back to the spirit world in a long and elaborate rite, which was the greatest event in Ainu religious life. Before being sacrificed, the young bear was solemnly addressed. It was told that it had been sent into the world to be hunted and to remember how much care and love were showered upon it. They begged it not to be angry but to realize what an honor was being conferred upon it. They said that it was being sent back to its parents in the spirit world, and they asked it to speak well of the Ainu before them. Finally, they begged the bear to come back into the world to be sacrificed again.[21]

Indigenous Gatherers

Hunting is not the only spiritually charged economic activity of indigenous peoples. The relation of the gatherer to the land also reveals an especially rich center of spiritual life. Here, too, there is an interplay of ordinary activities for the well-being of the community with spiritual forces. Archeological and anthropological evidence indicates that from prehistoric times, the main diet of indigenous gatherers has consisted not of large game (an occasional and special food) but of plant foods and small animals gathered, for the most part, by women. The gatherers, then, have special knowledge of the Earth spirit (or spirits) who provide these "gifts" out of her (or sometimes his) bounty.

The important role of women as gatherers is reflected in the high status accorded them in gatherer/hunter societies where there appears to be an egalitarian bent exhibited by a great degree of complementarity in the roles of men and women. Although not universal, this remains so in many extant gatherer/hunter societies, such as the !Kung of the Kalahari Desert in Southern Africa.[22]

Indigenous Farmers

Where did agriculture come from, in the eyes of its first practitioners? Indigenous farmers are often aware that their craft came later than the activities of earlier humans. Yet hunters and gatherers no doubt continue, sometimes even in the same general region, as have the !Kung of the Kalahari Desert, who have said "Why bother to grow crops when there are so many mongongo nuts in the world?"[23] Indigenous farmers have sometimes thought that farming may have involved some kind of crime, something that produced goods of great value but that destroyed a primal innocence of the first children of Mother Earth, as her body was cut open by the plow. We find an echo of this in the words of a nineteenth-century Native American who, when urged by the United States government to take up farming on a reservation, refused in these words:

> You ask me to plow the ground! Shall I take a knife and tear my mother's bosom? Then when I die she will not take me to her bosom to rest. You ask me to dig for stone! Shall I dig under her skin for her bones? Then when I die, I cannot enter her body to be born again. You ask me to cut grass and make hay and sell it, and be rich like white man! But how dare I cut off my mother's hair?[24]

Yet agriculture also means a new importance for the Earth Goddess and in some ways women, Earth's kin by gender.

The *Kojiki*, the ancient Japanese mythology, tells of the moon god, Tsukiyomi, who came down to Earth and after going to the home of the food goddess, requested something to eat. She gave him a meal, but he considered it all repulsive food. In his anger he slew the food goddess and found in her body all sorts of food plants of a new sort—rice, beans, and so forth. These Tsukiyomi took back to heaven, and the high Goddess Amaterasu said they would be for planting in the broad and narrow fields of heaven and earth.

A myth from Ceram, in Indonesia, relates the same experience to the *dema*, divine creators and helpers who lived with human beings in mythical times. It tells us that a hunter long ago found a coconut on the tusk of a boar he slew. That night he was commanded in a dream to plant it. Immediately it grew into a great tree, and shortly after, a girl child was born out of the tree after the hunter had spilled blood on it accidentally. He named her Hainuwele. In three days, she was of marriageable age. Hainuwele then attended a great dance. For nine days, she stood in the midst of the dancing area and passed out gifts to the dancers. Nonetheless, on the ninth day, the dancers dug a grave, put Hainuwele in it, filled it in, and continued dancing on it.

When Hainuwele did not come home the next morning, the hunter sensed that she had been murdered. He found the body, cut it into pieces, and buried the pieces in different places. The interred pieces gave birth to previously unknown food plants. The hunter carried Hainuwele's arms to a leading *dema*, Satane, who took them into the dancing ground, drew a nine-spiral figure with them on the ground, and went to the middle of it. She said, "Since you have killed, I will no longer live here. I shall leave this very day. Now you will have to come to me through this door." Satane vanished through the mystic spiral into another mode of existence, and since then humans have been able to meet her only after death. After the agriculture-giving murder, the *dema* have no longer lived in companionship with humankind.[25]

Through stories such as this, a grim basic principle came to affect the agricultural worldview even more than the hunter's: the principle of death for life. Agriculture seems to have brought out a new and darker sense of the interconnection of death and life. This interconnection is not unknown to the hunter; the Naskapi believe that by a reverent treatment of the bones of a slain beast, the soul of the

Hani Akha women sift rice at a festival in Yuanyang, China.

animal can be influenced to return and offer itself again. The Ainu believe that by sacrificing the precious bear cub, they can persuade it and its relatives in the spirit world to return and replenish the supply of game.

But in agricultural society, all of this becomes more accentuated. The relation of life and death, and of gender, to agriculture is evident in the case of the head-hunting Jivaro of the upper Amazon. A Jivaro male who had taken and shrunk a head would perform a dance with it and two female relatives, usually his sister and his wife. He would hold the head in his outstretched hand, and they would hold on to him as they danced; this would empower these women to gain greater productivity from the crops and animals it is their province to tend. The dance seemed to make power flow from the head through the husband and then through his sister and his wife into the crops. After this rite, the head would no longer be powerful and could be discarded.[26]

Yet in most places the agricultural harvest is both a joyous and a ceremonial time, in which dancing is appropriate but everything must be done right.

Say, for example, you are visiting the Venda, an agricultural people in what is now South Africa. They plant mainly maize, sweet potatoes, beans, pumpkins, and melons, among other kitchen plants. Before planting, each farmer sends a small amount of mixed seeds out of those he will use to his chief, who cooks them all together to make a sacred meal, which is then presented to the ancestors. As with many African peoples, ancestral spirits like those of the Luguru of East Africa (discussed above) are especially potent in practical, everyday matters. The wood to cook this offering is gathered by young girls, who hit with a stick anyone they meet as they undertake this task; perhaps that quasi-ritual gesture is intended to heighten general fertility. As this hopeful gift, so auspiciously prepared, is presented, an abundant harvest is asked of those ancestral powers.

Then, when the harvest is ready, the chief announces that the time has come. No one may commence his harvest before this announcement. The chief then, after a private rite, leads a public ritual in his own fields. A sacred bull and cow are led through the field, sprinkled with beer that must have been prepared by the women. The young people follow, dancing, and a prayer is offered by a woman who is the sister of a former chief. As first fruits are presented to the ancestors, she says, "I give you the first grains of the yearly harvest; eat and be well; but what is still in the fields, leave to us." She then lists the names of all the ancestors she can remember and adds that the prayer is also directed at those whose names have been forgotten. Ancestral tombs and places where the dead dwell are then visited with offerings, and food is also left for those wild animals, such as leopards and serpents, into which some of the dead are believed to have been transformed.

Thus the harvest is a time for linking with family and spirits both living and departed, as is still the case in Halloween and Thanksgiving in the West. Moreover, harvest, like seed time, makes the year into a circle and binds one close to place, to family fields, and to family shrines.

THE SOCIAL IMPACT OF AGRICULTURE, THE ROLE OF WOMEN, AND THE PATRIARCHAL REVOLUTION

The beginning of agriculture, perhaps at several places, some 12,000 years ago, and the subsequent spread of the practice of planting and harvesting produced probably the most far-reaching religious changes of any transition in the history of religion. Significantly, the sedentary character of agriculture in itself effected extensive changes in religion and culture as time progressed. Because cultivation could sustain far more people than hunting and gathering on the same acreage, the advent of agriculture led to a marked increase in population in fertile regions. Of course, farming and population increase also brought new problems: poor health due to overdependence on a few crops, rather than the variety available to hunter-gatherers, and famines and epidemics sweeping through crowded, sedentary settlements.

Nonetheless, an expanding population and established communities grew into towns and cities, elaborate trade relationships, and extensive division of labor. A flourishing agricultural economy could support not only the farmers but also various traders, artisans, rulers, priests, and even a few scholars and philosophers. Finally, the susceptibility of the agricultural routine to commerce, taxation, and control, and its need in many lands for large-scale public works such as market roads and irrigation systems, led to the development of writing and the ancient empires in which civilization as is now known emerged. The religious products of this new economy were far reaching. Elaborate polytheism mirrored in the heavens the new extensive division of labor, and the coming together of many tribes and sacred scriptures were a first result of writing. Even more far reaching were the fruits of the leisure of priests, scholars, and philosophers—and the impact on the role of women in society.

Recall again the ritual roles of girls and women among the Sioux, the Venda, and the Jivaro. It may be that in such societies (and their **Paleolithic** and early **Neolithic** forbears), men and women are roughly equal religiously in the sense that both have indispensable sacred functions and an honored place. But in agricultural society, which became more complex, it often meant women (like many men) were caught in a social order that was becoming more and more hierarchical—that is, with a set place and set jobs for everyone, from kings and queens to the peasant man and woman. While many of the Great Goddesses of later antiquity—Isis, Demeter, Ishtar, Kali, Amaterasu—clearly stem from the powerful agricultural mother of ancient farming culture, the societies that held them sacred moved toward social conventions that proved more limiting for women than had been the case for the earlier women. As wife, mother, and homemaker in such an order, women's lives became more and more restricted to a narrow sphere subordinate to men.

In this regard, the continued development of agriculture was marked by significant and long-ranging reactions on the part of the men. Some of the men's initiations that are kept most secret from the women and that most obviously imitate women's mysteries, such as those from New Guinea, emerged from archaic planting societies. Sometimes these movements took extreme shape in their reassertion of the remaining masculine virtues of group loyalty, strength, prowess in waging war, and spiritual skill, such as head-hunting of the Leopard Society of West Africa. One men's society in Melanesian New Britain, the Dukduk, traveled from place to place with the function of enforcing the law in a rough-and-ready way wherever they landed.

An important development along these lines in ancient times was **megalithism**, or the erection of giant stone monuments such as those at Stonehenge in Britain. A period of making bigger and bigger constructions of this type as temples, observatories, or tombs occurred in many parts of the globe just before ancient civilization marked by cities arose. Megaliths are found in England, Malta, China, and Japan, and they are followed by even greater edifices, such as the pyramids of Egypt, the ziggurats of Mesopotamia, and the various monuments of Mesoamerica. It is as though the megalith were an extension of the custom in many men's lodges of erecting great totemlike figures as memorials of initiatory feasts and of ancestors.

The last stage has been called the "Patriarchal Revolution." At the onset of the ancient civilizations—whether in Egypt, Mesopotamia, India, or China—we see a vigorous assertion of male primacy in powerful sovereigns and a corresponding suppression of female religious figures, whether queens, goddesses, or shamanesses. In China and Japan, early edicts may be found forbidding or limiting the work of various sorts of priestesses. In addition, the celibate **asceticism** of early Hindu yogis and Buddhist monks asserts male primacy by implying that men do not need women for spiritual fulfillment. The ascendancy of the pharaoh, who made the Great Goddess Isis his throne but who identified himself with the male Ra and Osiris, signifies the same thing. We may ask ourselves whether now, after several thousand years of patriarchy, the pendulum is swinging again toward egalitarian values in religion and culture.

Stonehenge, Wiltshire, England, a megalith stone monument that some archeologists estimate was constructed as early as the 2400 B.C.E.

PROGRESS AND RETURN

In many ways, we are still living in the age set in motion by the development of agriculture. The modern city is an extension of the village of the first sedentary planters. At least until the twentieth century, the average person almost anywhere in the world lived close to the soil and the seasons—whose life and values were more like those of Neolithic indigenous agriculturalists than those of contemporary technological society. It may be that today, as developed societies finally move away from the world shaped culturally by the farmer's way of life into a truly urban world of computers and space travel, religious changes as marked as those that separate the farmer from the hunter-gatherers will happen. Or perhaps there is wisdom in the religion of the remaining indigenous peoples of the world, who still live close to the Earth and hold it sacred. If so, that wisdom might be instructive for peoples of the modern world, who continue to reach outward when it may be that a return to respect and gratitude for nature and its cycles is what is called for in our time.

Fundamental Features of Indigenous Peoples' Religions

Theoretical

Basic Worldview	The universe is a place animated by many spirits, some friendly and some not. Humans have a real place in the order of all things, the cosmos, which works by rules and cycles that can be known.
God or Ultimate Reality	Many deities and spirits; but perhaps a high God or unifying force over them.
Origin of the World	Either no point of origin or created by the Gods or a high God who may subsequently have withdrawn from activity.
Destiny of the World	Usually not clear.
Origin of Humans	Often children of Gods, Gods, or semidivine primal parents.
Destiny of Humans	Frequently we go after death to another world, not unlike this world, sometimes also to be reborn here in this world.
Revelation or Mediation between the Ultimate and the Human	Myth, often told and enacted at festivals and by shamans; benign deities and ancestral spirits as helpers.

Practical

What Is Expected of Humans	Worship, practice, behavior to undergo initiation; to honor and sacrifice to the Gods and ancestors; to observe communal norms of behavior and taboos.

Sociological

Major Social Institutions	One's immediate ethnic community as a spiritual unit; shamanism.

Summary

Indigenous peoples' religions, the precursor of all later religions, are a vast and complex phenomenon. But the phenomenon possesses certain basic themes that, in modified forms, appear centrally in later religion as well. It is, first of all, concerned with showing the relation of humankind to nature, and it celebrates the turn of the seasons and the places of special sacred power. It has myths telling of the creation of the world by divine powers but often also adds a mythic account of a "fall" that explains why humanity is no longer as close to the creative powers as at the time of creation.

Second, indigenous peoples' religions are concerned with soul or spirit. Endeavoring to explain the diverse feelings people have within them, indigenous people sometimes speak of two or more souls. Confronting the eternal human dread of death, their religion describes the destiny of the soul in the afterlife: sometimes different souls have different destinies; sometimes one at least goes to an alternative world; sometimes another aspect of the self remains around its familiar haunts as a ghost; sometimes one is reincarnated in this world. The spirits of ancestors or unappeased ghosts are usually feared and propitiated.

Initiations are very important for many indigenous peoples. They serve the end of social cohesion by inducting adults into the community after proper training and a potent shared experience, and they often serve the end of individual fulfillment as well by giving status and perhaps secrets of value in the soul's journey after death. Initiations involve a process of separation, marginality when one is separated from the social structure but is close to divine powers, and reincorporation of the individual into the social order. Such initiations also emphasize that the spirits of nature work through the natural processes of the human body (particularly the female body, the processes of which are mimicked in men's initiations rites) and celebrate what sustains the community as coextensive with ultimate cosmic reality.

The shaman is usually a person with a very special and personal, often lonely, initiation. She or he is believed to have powers of controlling spirits, healing, and confronting the Gods, expressed through dramatic scenarios of trance and dance.

The religion of hunter-gatherer peoples expresses the hunter's sense of dependence on the animal, as well as the gatherer's dependence on the natural world to provide the staples of the diet of the community. The hunter knows that the hunted animal, and often a "master or mistress of animals" deity in charge of a species, must be kept in good spirit if game is to be taken; the gatherer knows that the secrets of nature must be unlocked in order to receive the gifts of the Earth spirit's bounty.

Agriculture gave a tremendous impetus to human culture but often seems to have been perceived as a sort of fall from a purer state. The religion of agriculturalists tends to involve more blood and sacrifice and more antagonism between the sexes than that of hunters and gatherers. Agriculture tore the Earth deeply but also allowed the rise of sedentary societies, great increases in population, and the ancient empires, giving rise to the "Patriarchal Revolution."

Our world is in many ways still shaped by the patterns set in motion by the advent of agriculture. Perhaps there is wisdom in the religion of indigenous peoples that would be instructive for modern society today.

Questions for Review

1. Explain how some features of indigenous religion are more related to individual needs and other features to community needs, some features more to humanity's relation to the natural world, and other features to the destiny of the individual soul. Notice that some features more than others combine an interest in two or more of these motifs, as indicated by their placement on the chart.
2. Discuss what human problems and experiences lie behind common myths of Gods and spirits.

3. Talk about what indigenous peoples' religious myths may be trying to say through their accounts of the soul, their often multiple characters, and their destiny in the afterlife.
4. Explain the scenarios of initiation and their meaning in terms of indigenous peoples' interpretation of human life.
5. Understand shamanism, and describe how a shaman characteristically acquires special powers and what he or she is believed able to do.

6. Present the main features of hunter-gatherer religions, the worldview that lies behind them, and how that worldview is reflected in the relations between men and women.
7. Explain what impact agriculture had on ancient societies, transforming them and leading to what some people call the Patriarchal Revolution.
8. Following the chart, explain some fundamental features of indigenous peoples' religions.

Suggested Readings on Indigenous Peoples' Religions

American Museum of Natural History, "*The First Humans: Human Origins and History to 10,000 B.C.*," in Goran Burenhult, ed., *The Illustrated History of Humankind* series. San Francisco: HarperSanFrancisco, 1993.

Blakely, Thomas D., Walter E. A. van Beek, and Dennis L. Thomson, eds., *Religion in Africa: Experience and Expression*. London: James Currey and Portsmouth, NH: Heinemann, 1994.

Bowei, Fiona, *The Anthropology of Religion: An Introduction*. 2nd ed. Oxford UK, & Malden, MA: Blackwell Publishing, 2005.

Cauvin, Jacques, *The Birth of the Gods and the Origins of Agriculture*. trans. Trevor Watkins. Cambridge UK & New York: Cambridge University Press, 2000.

Douglas, Mary, *Purity and Danger*. Baltimore, MD: Penguin Books, 1966.

Ehrenberg, Margaret, *Women in Prehistory*. London: British Museum Publications, 1989.

Eliade, Mircea, *A History of Religious Ideas*, vol. I. *From the Stone Age to the Eleusinian Mysteries*. Chicago: University of Chicago Press, 1978.

——, *Shamanism: Archaic Techniques of Ecstasy*. New York: Pantheon Books, 1964.

Evans-Pritchard, Edward E., *Nuer Religion*. Oxford, UK: Clarendon Press, 1956.

Gill, Sam D., *Beyond 'The Primitive': The Religions of Nonliterate Peoples*. Englewood Cliffs, NJ: Prentice Hall, 1982.

——, *Native American Religions: An Introduction*. Belmont, CA: Wadsworth, 1982.

Gimbutas, Marija, *The Civilization of the Goddess: The World of Old Europe*. San Francisco: HarperSanFrancisco, 1991.

Glazier, Stephen, *Anthropology of Religion: A Handbook*. New ed. Westport, CT: Praeger, 1999.

Graham, Harvey, *Shamanism: A Reader*. London & New York: Routledge, 2003.

Gross, Rita M., "Tribal Religions: Aboriginal Australia," in Arvind, Sharma ed., *Women in World Religions*. Albany: State University of New York Press, 1987.

Humphrey, Caroline, with Urgunge Onon, *Shamans and Elders*. Oxford and New York: Oxford University Press, 1996.

Jenkins, Philip, *Dream Catchers: How Mainstream America Discovered Native Spirituality*. Oxford and New York: Oxford University Press, 2004.

Lewis, I. M., *Ecstatic Religion: A Study of Shamanism and Spirit Possession*. 3rd ed. London & New York: Routledge, 2003.

Miller, Christine, and Patricia Chuckryk, eds., *Women of the First Nations: Power, Wisdom, and Strength*. Winnipeg: University of Manitoba Press, 1996.

Marcos, Sylvia, ed., *Women and Indigenous Religions*. Santa Barbara, CA: Praeger, 2010.

Peters, Virginia Bergman, *Women of the Earth Lodges: Tribal Life on the Plains*. North Haven, CT: Archon Books, 1995.

Olupona, Jacob, ed., *Beyond Primitivism: Indigenous Religious Traditions and Modernity*. New York and London: Routledge, 2004.

Ray, Benjamin, *African Religions: Symbol, Ritual, and Community*. Englewood Cliffs, NJ: Prentice Hall, 1976.

Thomas, Douglas, *African Traditional Religion in the Modern World*. Jefferson, NC and London: McFarland, 2005.

Walter, Mariko Namba, and Eva Jane Newmann, eds., *Shamanism: An Encyclopedia of World Beliefs, Practices, and Culture*. Santa Barbara CA: ABC-CLIO, 2004.

Welch, Robert J., Virginia Lee Webb, and Sebastian Haraha, *Coaxing the Spirits to Dance: Art and Society in the Papuan Gulf of New Guinea*. Hanover, NH: Hood Museum of Dartmouth College, 2006.

3

Life Against Time
The Spiritual Paths of India

CHAPTER OBJECTIVES

After studying this chapter, you should be able to

- Discuss the major features of Hinduism, including basic terms and common concepts.
- Present the central message of the Hindu classics, such as the Upanishads and the Bhagavad-Gita.
- Be able to recognize the chief Hindu Gods and Goddesses and the religious narratives associated with them.
- Discuss the importance of Hinduism and other religions of India in the contemporary world.
- Understand Hinduism's ancient and contemporary views of governance and political life.
- Understand the impact of Hindu worldview on attitudes toward and practices with respect to women in India.
- Discuss Hinduism's impact on the American religious landscape.
- Discuss the major features of Jainism and Sikhism.

THE FACE OF INDIA

I* first entered India many years ago by plane from Kabul, Afghanistan, and followed, at jet speed, the track over the famous Khyber Pass of countless migrants, invaders, and pilgrims from the hard but exhilarating highlands of central Asia. With them, I dipped down into the heat-thick air of the Ganges River basin. Long before, at the dawn of history, cattle herders had perhaps taken the same trail, and after them Alexander and his Greeks, then Huns, Turks, and the cavalry of the opulent Moghal emperors. Others had come over the passes for reasons other than physical spoils, for India has never failed to draw seekers of all sorts: Chinese monks seeking authentic scriptures of the Buddha, son of India, who became the Enlightened One, and God-intoxicated mystics of Islam who were partly to conquer India in turn.

After I had landed and entered the city, I was lost amid labyrinthine crooked streets, open-air shops, houses of earth and corrugated metal, and rain-browned official buildings. The narrow ways

---

*Robert Ellwood

Statue of Ganesha.

were thronged with oxcarts, countless bicycles, ancient buses and trucks, and once in a while a chauffeured auto. On the most important streets as well as the byways, traffic was backed up as a inviolable cow ambled along or stood still, staring at the bustle of the human world with placid, indifferent eyes.

Today this past remains—adjacent to and in stark contrast with the new India of glittering steel and glass buildings in vibrant, bustling cities that are becoming centers of global commerce. The many department stores and office buildings rise amid city streets of tight, continuous traffic of fast-moving luxury cars, motorized and bicycle rickshaws—every kind of vehicle imaginable, old and new—while shining, beautiful, and elaborate new universities and temples and ancient walls, forts, and religious shrines stand proud. Yet a turn off main thoroughfares leads to inner cities of stark poverty, teeming with people in cramped stone or wooden buildings or in makeshift hovels and tents of tin, canvas, and broken ancient stone. And in many places rural India remains much as it has been for hundreds of years.

India is everything. As if in a high dream, India opens a crack in a door to let one glimpse something of an alternative world where the extreme potentials of human life in all directions—ecstasy, beauty, deprivation—are starkly revealed. And through it all, India's ancient and deep spirituality thrives—in the reverence of its people; in the myriad temples in city centers and in every nook and cranny; in the chanting that wafts through the early morning air; in the sunset prayers sung to Ganga, the Ganges River Goddess, and the God Shiva through whom she flows; in the ubiquitous images and statues of Gods and Goddesses and venerated spiritual leaders, teachers, and ancestors; and in the sweet "Namaste" greeting that acknowledges the Divine in everyone, high and low. India's religious traditions endure, for they lie at the heart of this spirited and complex society and suggest to the world that religion cannot be contained in one doctrine or institution or set of practices, but is and always has been dynamic.

UNDERSTANDING HINDUISM

The religion of approximately 80 percent of the people of India is Hinduism. This religion with a very distinctive flavor, sometimes referred to as Sanatana Dharma—"the eternal truth"—is now found all over the world. The first real Hindu temple I* visited was not in India but on the island of Fiji, where many people from India have settled. The air was humid and heavy; the place of worship was located by the side of a road and was largely open air. The first thing I saw was a large *Lingam*, the phallic pillar, which is the expression of **Shiva**, set in an oval base called the *Yoni* (a name for the female organ), which is the expression of **Shakti**. Shiva is the absolute cosmic Being, the sheer life force, and Shakti is the absolute power of the phenomenal universe, both creative and destructive—the whole of the cosmic their progeny. In the presence of the *Lingam* and *Yoni*, one has the feeling that the Indian worldview is deeply biological, tending always in the end to see the cosmos as a great living organism.

Betty Heimann has suggested that it is the biological flavor of Hinduism to which one must turn for understanding.[1] Her suggestion is a deep insight because Hinduism presses biology beyond the point where other religions set humankind and nature, or mind and body, against each other. But as is represented in the *Lingam* and *Yoni* of Shiva and Shakti, respectively, in Hinduism the biological and the Divine are one.

---

*Robert Ellwood

The dynamic of Shiva and Shakti further represents how Hinduism tends to see thought and life in terms of unity hidden within an apparent duality: of two things that seem to be set against each other but that are ultimately one. There is **Brahman**, Absolute God, Unconditioned Reality, and **Maya**, the World of Illusions, which mistakenly sees things as separate and other than God. Or one can think of **moksha**, the state of liberation into Unconditioned Reality, and **dharma**, the world of form, the social order, and the universe in its ideal sense, as harmony in which all things work together as they should and which is expressed in the basic polarity throughout Hindu thought and life—between **dharma** and **moksha**.

The word *dharma* is one of those terms so broad that it requires more of an intuition than a precise definition. But basically it can be understood as the social order of human civilization when it is righteous—that is, when it is in accord with the cosmic order, which is called **rita**. The rites of the priests sustain both the social order and the cosmic order. But *dharma* also implies the righteousness and the duty of the people themselves—in the sense that it means moral behavior that upholds the social order. Dharma includes the duty to pay the "Five Debts," with which everyone is born: to the Gods, to the sages and saints, to one's parents, to other human beings in society, and to all other living beings. Finally, *dharma* includes rituals that uphold the great cosmic-social order by demarcating one's place in society and by sustaining the work of creation by "fueling" the divine forces that move it.

Actually, seeing the world as *dharma* means regarding life as ritual. It means that one suppresses one's individualistic predilections in order to harmonize with the swing of the total pattern so that the world becomes like a great dance. There are rituals dealing with virtually every aspect of life: for rising, for brushing one's teeth, for bathing, for eating, for love, for study, for worship. One's personal *dharma*, **svadharma**, his or her particular steps in the great dance, are determined by individual birth and **karma**.

Humans and even the Gods of nature can live in accordance with or rebel against *dharma*, but they cannot escape the consequences that *dharma* imposes through *karma*. Karma, related to the English word "car," means basically action or activity, as in **Karma-yoga**, which we shall see means the way of union with God through right actions. But action always implies cause and effect, for nothing in this world acts or moves without an impelling cause. Therefore, *karma* also refers to that chain of cause and effect set in motion by one's deeds in the world. Sooner or later, through inexorable laws of justice built into *dharma*, one's deeds rebound to affect one's own future as retribution or reward. As one sows, so one reaps. One could just as well attempt to defy nature by jumping off a cliff and trying to fly, but he or she would be met by the consequences. Retribution or reward will include (but is not limited to) the state in which one is reborn—as a monarch or a slave, as a God or a dog.

Dharma is the realm of endless and ultimately self-correcting change driven by striving and by cause and effect in which we dwell. This realm is an interesting level but in the end wearisome. However, it is not necessary for us to remain forever running with its tides and tossed hither and yon by the self-made waves of *karma*. There is always the possibility of our leaping aboard a raft and skimming to a different level altogether—to a state as opposite to it as land is to water. This "skimming to a different level" is **moksha**, "leaping out" and finding liberation. It is the final quest, after all other quests have run out. The quest for *moksha* is undertaken under the guidance of a **guru**, a spiritual guide who initiates the seeker into the path he is qualified to impart and who directs the initiate along. Later we will examine some of these paths.

According to the Laws of Manu (c. 100 C.E.), there are four basic goals that motivate humanity, also known as the "Four Ends of Human Life": pleasure (*kama*), gain (*artha*), righteousness (*dharma*), and liberation (*moksha*). Each goal has its own place and, indeed, its own rituals, such as those for *kama* in the well-known **Kama-sutra**. Yet all the Laws of Manu, except *moksha* finally exhaust themselves in our craving for something beyond our level.

We may imagine a young man (since the pattern was designed with the male in mind) starting out in life motivated mainly by *kama;* he becomes a playboy, a hedonist. But after a whirl at this way of life, he finds that pleasure alone, without direction or purpose beyond today, gives him a sense of disintegration. He feels that if he keeps up that way of life, he will just keep wanting more and more to provide the same satisfaction, and he will finally end up enslaved, more anxious to avoid losing pleasures and their symbols than enjoying them.

So next he decides to attempt some real goals: getting ahead, making money, getting a big house and car (or, in ancient India, a chariot). This is the second stage, *artha*, and over time, he meets this goal increasingly well.

But still he senses an inner disquiet. He has neither self-respect nor a desire for the respect of others. He wants not only to be successful but also to be substantial—to be a solid, respectable citizen or a community leader. He wants to exemplify and uphold *dharma* in this world. So he becomes active in organizations that address social issues and perhaps even gets into politics—highly motivated, of course. (Or in ancient India, he is active in the *panchayat*, the local governing body of his village, or he is a faithful ritualist or even a gracious and just king.)

Yet when a busy day is done and he goes to bed, he may later wake in the middle of the night with empty despair, as though he were all straw, with gnawing rats inside. What he is doing, exemplifying and upholding *dharma* in this world, is good, yet somehow it ultimately means nothing, or it would mean nothing if it is all that people do, age after age, generation after generation, and getting nowhere because it all has to be done time and time again, for all eternity. The big questions are now unavoidable: Why does nothing fully meet my unquenchable yearning? What will become of me in the end? What is the real purpose of life, and why is it so hard to discover? Who am I, anyway? He is now ready to tackle the last goal—*moksha*.

In India, these developments would ideally occur in tandem with the four **ashramas**, also known as the "Four Stages of Life": student, householder, hermit or forest dweller, and renunciant. *Dharma* has priority in all stages except the last, when the renunciant lives outside of the social order. Gain and pleasure—*artha* and *kama*—would coincide with the householder stage, since before that the student was expected to practice continence as well as application to his work and was under obedience to his father and teacher. Then, after he had seen his first grandchild or his hair had begun to turn gray, he could retire to a hermitage to begin the quest for *moksha* and to culminate it by becoming a **sannyasin**, or renunciant, a wandering monk free from all ties. His wife could accompany him if he desired and if they maintained celibacy. Of course, no more than a small percentage of the people of India have followed this regimen, and frequently the "retirement" of the last two stages actually occurs in a private room within the family's house. But the tradition is still alive and answers to something universal. One feels many Westerners would be happier by accepting that, in the last half of life, pleasure and gain should be put aside in favor of another quest, which can be repressed but which deep inside them becomes more and more insistent.

The traditional goal of Hinduism may be given many labels—God realization, identification with the absolute, supreme bliss, cosmic consciousness—but it is perhaps best spoken of by more negative terms such as release, liberation, or freedom. For the goal is really beyond all concepts and labels. It is simply freedom—not freedom in any political or individualistic sense but inner freedom from everything that circumscribes or conditions the sense of infinity one has within, that is, freedom from all relation to the cause and effect of *karma* within or without. One is to rise above and master the goal, to become as lithe and free as sunlight and clouds in the sky. Then one knows the answer to the secret of who one really is.

The prevailing Hindu answer is that, in the great quiet of meditation, in hearing the sonorous words of scripture, in the joy of devotion, the realization comes through that there is only One—**Brahman**, Universal Being, God beyond all personalities—and that "Thou art that."

There are many paths to *moksha*, bespoken by the many Gods and Goddesses, temples, and teachers of Hinduism—many of which we will be encountering in the pages to follow. But before we begin that exploration, it is important to recognize that Hinduism is not so much *a* "religion" as it is a general term covering all those religions and spiritual paths that have a common base in the Vedas—Hinduism's ancient scriptures. In fact, the culture and religion of India are neither monolithic nor divided into watertight compartments. Like America, but more so, they are a mix of many colors. Individual components can be distinguished, but, in a sense, the mixture has always been slowly stirring, blending, and receiving new inputs throughout history. As we now turn to that history, we will also be identifying distinct religious trends that, through the centuries, have been stirred into the mixture known as Hinduism. Let us begin with the ancient Aryans and their Vedic scriptures.

ANCIENT INDUS VALLEY RELIGION

The Indus Valley, in what is now Pakistan, was the scene of a remarkable ancient civilization (around 3200 B.C.E., although its origins have been traced by some to as early as 6500 B.C.E.) in the vicinity of a now-extinct river, which has been identified as the famed Sarasvati River extolled in the Vedas (discussed later). Several cities, including Harappa and Mohenjo-Daro, together with numerous smaller towns and villages, constituted it, covering an area of 800,000 square miles. In all, archeologists have located more than 1,200 sites. Each city was laid out on a grid plan, and the houses, although often identical and extremely functional, were technologically advanced; the plumbing has been equaled only by that of the ancient Romans and the modern world. The writing of this culture has not been deciphered, and many mysteries about it remain, not least its religion. However, archeologists have found what they believe to be fire altars, domestic shrines, and figurines showing yogic postures and usages of the red dot (the *tilaka*) in the center of the forehead, all of which suggest some confluence with Hindu practices today, as we shall see in the pages that follow. The cities contained no obvious temples, though on high ground in Mohenjo-Daro, there was a cloisterlike complex, with a pool perhaps used for ritual bathing and which may have been the stronghold of a powerful priestly order. Enigmatic religious motifs appear on many of the seals and small art objects that have been found. These suggest a Mother Goddess, sacred bulls, phallic Gods, and a Deity in perhaps a yogic meditation posture. Some scholars have theorized that the sides of Hinduism that center on the Shiva-Shakti dynamic, bulls, the Mother Goddess, water ablutions, and yoga come out of the indigenous cultures of the Indus Valley and that some of the practices associated with ancient Vedic scriptures began there.[2]

Around 1500 B.C.E., the cities of the Indus Valley declined into ruins. The reason why is not clear. An older theory, propounded mainly by Western scholars,

HISTORY OF RELIGION IN INDIA

GENERAL HISTORICAL CONTEXT

End of Indus Valley civilization
Spread of Indo-Aryan Culture

Kashi (Benares) prominent
Urban civilization beginning in
Ganges basin
Invasion by Alexander 326
Mauryan Empire 321–185
Gupta Empire in N. 320–540
Classic Hindu period

PERSONALITIES AND MOVEMENTS

The Buddha 563–483

Mahavira c. 540–468

First Buddhist Council c. 480

Buddhism prestigious

Ashoka r. 273–232

SACRED LITERATURE

Rig Veda

Brahmanans

Early Upanishads

Buddhist Tripitaka
Later Upanishads
Heart Sutra and other
early Mahayana
writings

Yoga Sutras

| 1500 B.C.E. | 1000 B.C.E. | 500 B.C.E. | 1 B.C.E./C.E. |

Small states, largely Hindu

Delhi sultanate (Muslim) 1211–1398

Small states, many Muslim ruled

Moghul Empire 1526–1765

British rule in India
18th century–1947

Independent India,
Pakistan 1947

Bangladesh 1971

Nagarjuna c. 150
  Decline of Buddhism in India
  Rise of Bhakti
    Growth of Hindu Tantrism

Kabir 1440–1518
  Nanak 1470–1540 fdr.
  of Sikhs
    Akbar r. 1556–1605
      Ramakrishna 1836–1886

Shankara c. 8th century
and Advaita Vedanta

Ramanuja d. 1137   Gandhi 1869–1948

Laws of Manu

  Bhagavad-Gita

    Lotus Sutra and other later Mahayana sutras

      Puranas

        Tantras

          Guru Granth Sahib

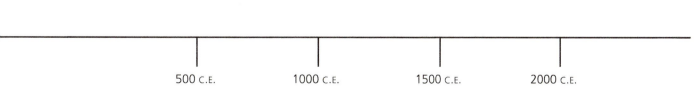

500 C.E.   1000 C.E.   1500 C.E.   2000 C.E.

postulated an invasion, or at least a migration, of outsiders called Aryans who spoke an Indo-European tongue which was the original form of Sanskrit, the language of the ancient Vedic scriptures.[3] More recent scholarship has proposed that there is no real evidence of such an "invasion" and that Indo-Europeans may have entered the Indian subcontinent much earlier than the originally proposed date of 1500 B.C.E. and become part of the Indus Valley culture.[4] The decline of that ancient civilization may be attributed to the drying up of the Sarasvati River and other natural or human causes, but these are only speculations.

THE VEDAS

The Indo-European speakers in India are chiefly known as the people of the **Vedas**, the most ancient and fundamental official scriptures of Hinduism, which may be the oldest scriptures that have a continuous tradition to our times. They are considered to be divinely revealed and are revered in the Hindu religious tradition today.

On their earliest level, they are dominated by the hymns and rituals of their priests. Their poetic style splendidly reflects freshness of vision, heroic virtues, and ritual precision. The oldest and most important of the Vedic scriptures is the Rig Veda, hymns to the Gods sung while sacrifices were being presented. Parallel to it are sets of songs and chants for auxiliary groups of priests and of charms called the Sama, Yajur, and Atharva Vedas, respectively. These in turn have sets of commentaries called the Brahmanas, Aranyakas ("Books of the Forest Schools"), and **Upanishads**. They not only offer ritual instructions, but also, over the centuries, present more and more esoteric content and philosophical reflections on the meanings of the rites. The Vedas were transmitted orally and not committed to writing until recent centuries.

The original Gods of the Vedas were vital, flashing, brilliant beings of sky and storm. They dwelled in the three levels of the known cosmos—sky, atmosphere, earth—and those of the middle atmospheric level acted most vigorously.

The most popular deity was Indra, the prototype of the Indo-European warrior and comparable to Thor (after whom Thursday is named) in European mythology. He wielded a thunderbolt and dwelled in the atmosphere, where the action is. He was accompanied by the Maruts, a boisterous band of warrior companions who rode in chariots like the armies of ancient India. Every dawn was a victory for Indra. Abetted by the morning sacrifices of the priests, he and his Maruts would arise and defeat the demonic powers of darkness. Indra consumed countless cattle and, in preparation for heroic exploits, vast lakefuls of the sacred drink, Soma. Indeed, it was Indra who had originally brought Soma down from high in the mountains. Indra slew the monster Vritra, representing drought, in mythical times. But finally, as his age gave place to another, he was superseded by other Gods closer to the heart of wisdom.

The Vedas speak of Dyaus—whose name is obviously cognate to the Latin *Deus* and the Greek *Zeus*—as sky father, but he is shadowy and remote, virtually a **deus otiosus**. Equally mysterious is the vague but profound-seeming figure of Aditi, light (or mind) beyond shadow or stain, and Mother of the Gods. Then there are two sky Gods of somewhat more concrete personality, Varuna and Mitra, kingly figures whose main task is the upholding of *rita*, the cosmic laws. There are few female figures, and the ones that are referred to, like Aditi and Ushas (the Dawn), seem passive and indistinctly conceived, although they are the subject of lovely hymns. It is as though the Vedic people thought naturally in the ways of the masculine world (in contrast to the Indus Valley with its Mother Goddess), so the feminine appears as beautiful but rare.

In a sense, however, all the bright Gods and Goddesses of the Vedas are elusive; all are described interchangeably as shining and benevolent, and each is addressed in turn as though he or she were the only deity, until finally we come to wonder if there is just one God who bears a series of names and parts. A mantra in the Rig veda reads: "The sages describe one and the same Divine Being in various ways and call it Agni, Yama and Matarisvan."[5] Still, a tremendous vitality and sense of divine force is at work in the Vedas. Nowhere is this more apparent than in the two deities Agni and Soma.

These are the deities of the rituals. They are only barely personified but extremely important. Agni, whose name is cognate to the Latin *ignis* and the English "ignite," is fire. Fire is the crucial mystery in the cycle of conception and consumption that keeps life in process; all its transitions—from sex through eating to death (in which we are eaten in turn, whether by microbe, worm, or tiger)—are various gradations of oxidation, that is, of fire. This lively magician of life and death is Agni, and he is the central actor in the drama of the sacrifice. On Earth, it is said, he is fire; in the atmosphere, lightning; in the sky, the sun. Existing in principle in all strata, he is also the quick messenger of the Gods: he bears prayer and sacrifice to them.

Soma is the deity representing the sacred drink of power and immortality that the Gods consumed, especially Indra, and that was manufactured, offered, and consumed in the sacrifices. The drink has an exhilarating, empowering effect: Indra fortified himself with Soma for his battle with Vritra and on one occasion he felt frenzied, exalted, as though he had passed beyond the Earth and the sky, and he asked himself rhetorically if he had been drinking Soma.

To understand Vedic thought, we must glance at what actually went on in the Brahmin rites. The group of words related to the word "Brahmin" appears to come from a root meaning a "magical force" or "spell."[6] From the earliest times, shamans and wizards have employed words of power that encapsulate the essence of a God or a line of force in the cosmos, so such words can be used to control that power or force. The Brahmins used them in connection with their sacrificial rites. Just as through words of power and sacrifice the Gods made the world, Brahmins said, so by words and sacrifice the Gods could themselves be controlled. Thus, the sacrifices controlled the Gods, and the Brahmin priests controlled the sacrifices, becoming like higher Gods themselves.

It would be a great misconception to imagine these rites as gorgeous ceremonies along the lines of a high Mass or the processions and offerings of later devotional Hinduism. For while the Brahmin rites required much preparation and many priests, outwardly they were quite plain. They were performed outdoors but often under a temporary shelter, in a quiet place with only the priests and the lay patron who was paying for them present. Three fire pits of different shapes—representing Earth, atmosphere, and sky—and a grass-covered pit for preserving offerings and utensils were dug. Offerings of butter, vegetables, or flesh were placed into the pits, now alight with fire; the plainest offering was slowly pouring melted and strained butter (*ghee*) from two spoons into the fires. While the offerings were being presented, other priests would chant the proper hymns; sometimes still another would stand in the center, meditating on the whole procedure, unifying it in his thought. Yet these relatively undramatic acts had to be done precisely right. The fuel was gathered and arranged, and the fires were built with immense care as to detail, and if a single syllable of the hymn was mispronounced or a single gesture was wrong, the rite might be stopped and started all over again from the beginning, or it might be recommenced only after atonements for the ritual lapses had been performed. The whole rite was so crisp, sharp, and exact that it had the atmosphere of a modern laboratory experiment.

Indeed, the Vedic rites were a sort of science; the old Brahmins saw themselves less as enthusiastic lovers of their Gods and more as technicians making precise adjustments in the cosmic order to correct an imbalance or to produce some desired result. For the sacrifice was nothing less than "making the world" and calling into life the Gods who rule over it. Its purpose then was to meditate on what the cosmos is like and to make adjustments in it in such a way as to keep it on course or direct its power in desired directions: prosperity, the inauguration of a king's reign, a son, long life, immortality in heaven.

It was as though a reducing lens had been held up to the cosmos. The sacrificial spread was a miniaturization of the universe as a whole, made much smaller, and its processes correspondingly speeded up. The fire was the destruction and transmutation of material—food—through heat that keeps the universe going. The words of the chants, the **mantras**, or "thought-forms," were sounds whose "vibrations" were in tune with those of the Gods and with those of the subtle currents of reality itself. On this "laboratory" world the priests performed their delicate technical operations. The rites to keep the universe on course and to help humans were like making tiny adjustments in a tremendously huge and intricate machine—perhaps only by turning a single screw a quarter of a turn. But a trained technician, who knows exactly what he is doing, can by such minute modifications make the difference between whether the machine works as desired or not. Or so the Brahmin priests understood their ritual activities.

But as time went on, as the Brahmin sages pondered over and over the meaning of the rites, new questions arose. They thought of the web of vibrations, which the mantras and the miniaturization process seem to suggest, as orchestrating the universe. The whole was like a magic web that held the universe of humans, Gods, and substance together, "the thread stretched out on which these creatures are strung together" (Atharva Veda 10:8:37). Within even this thread was "the thread of the thread," the fundamental unity, subtle beyond all sight yet inextricably there, beneath the world's multiplicity—Brahman, originally the power of the mantras or sacred words that held the world in course. Upon this secret, the Brahmin priest, who supervised and by his thought unified the sacrifice, was to meditate.

Other questions concerned Agni, the sacred fire. Fire is at the center of the world and therefore the center of the sacrifices—but is it only the fire that burns visibly? What of the fire that burns within a person's own body—the fire of joy, of concentration, even of fever? Does this make the person also an altar, and a world?

In Brahminical thinking, the sacrifices of their rites were, in effect, "interiorized." *Tapas*—interior heat—was generated by the real sacrifice, which was within a person. And this interiorization of the sacrifice, in time, paved the way for philosophy and yoga.[7] Through the **asceticism** of fasting and concentration, one built up *tapas*, and this power could be used by the **adept** to bless or to curse or to gain cosmic vision. For the person was now the cosmos; one replaced the cosmic sacrifice with oneself; all without was also within, the greater in the smaller and the smaller in the greater. This is the secret of the Upanishads, the last and most philosophical commentary of the Vedas.

THE UPANISHADS

The portion of the Vedic literature called the Upanishads is a collection of texts that attempt through words to point its adherents to the inner or final meaning of things. These words would be imparted by a father or a master to his most advanced pupils as the culminating stage of their learning. They are not for beginners, for until one has had enough experience of life or has matured enough to ask the right questions, the highest wisdom would be only empty sounds. Far from preaching it to everyone, the wise jealously preserved Upanishadic wisdom for those ready for it. The dozen or so ancient Upanishads, composed as early as 800 B.C.E., were transmitted orally as a part of larger Vedic scriptures in an unbroken chain of select teachers and students.

Thus, the Chandogya Upanishad tells of a Brahmin father who sent his son to study in a "Forest School." When the son returned, full of pride in his Vedic scholarship, the father deflated his son's ego and increased his wisdom by telling him of a further knowledge, "that knowledge by which we hear the unhearable, by which we perceive the unperceivable, by which we know the unknowable."

This arcane knowledge was that, as different things made of clay or gold go by different names yet are still clay or gold, so all things are One Existence under many names. At the beginning, this One Existence thought to itself, "Let me grow forth." "Thus out of [itself] it projected the universe; and having projected out of itself the universe, [it] entered into every being. All that is has [itself] in it alone. Of all things [it] is the subtle essence."

And the father adds the crucial words about the One to his son: That Art Thou.

Other analogies are used in this passage: Nectar gathered by bees from many flowers becomes one honey; all rivers flow into one sea. The One Existent is the invisible essence of all things, like the "nothingness" at the heart of a seed of a giant tree. And after each example of the essence, the father repeats: That Art Thou.

This essence is Brahman. The great inner knowledge to which the wise ones of the Upanishads came is "Atman is Brahman." **Atman** is the innermost self, the "soul"; Brahman is the universal One Existent. "He is pure, he is the light of lights." All persons and all things are really Brahman, taking many shapes, like fire taking the shape of every object it consumes or air taking the shape of every vessel it enters.

As the Svetasvatara Upanishad, quoting the ancient mantras of the Yajur Veda, puts it beautifully,

O Brahman Supreme!

Formless art thou, and yet

(Though the reason none knows)

Thou bringest forth many forms;

Thou bringest them forth, and then

Withdrawest them to thyself.

Fill us with thoughts of thee!

Thou art the fire,

Thou art the sun,

Thou art the air,

Thou art the moon,

Thou art the starry firmament,

Thou art Brahman Supreme:

Thou art the waters—thou,

The creator of all!

Thou art woman, thou art man,

Thou art the youth, thou art the maiden,

Thou art the old man tottering with his staff;

Thou facest everywhere.

Thou art the dark butterfly,

Thou art the green parrot with red eyes,

Thou art the thundercloud, the seasons, the seas.

Without beginning art thou,

Beyond time, beyond space.

Thou art he from whom sprang

The three worlds.[8]

The movement from Veda to Upanishad is well expressed in the Katha Upanishad. It begins with the account of a young man named Nachiketa. Nachiketa's crusty old Brahmin father presented a sacrifice of the Vedic sort in which he was supposed to offer all his possessions but was careful to present only old and scroungy cattle. The boy, shocked by this, told his father he also was one of his possessions and asked him to whom he would give his son. The irritated parent responded that he would give him to Yama, the ancient King of the Dead.

Nachiketa, taking this very seriously, proceeded to the home of this king, Death. Death was not at home, forcing Nachiketa to wait. When he returned, Death, in compensation, offered the sincere young Brahmin three wishes, which Death agreed to fulfill.

The first two wishes were clearly rooted in the traditional Vedic world. Nachiketa asked that his father's anger be appeased; this wish concerned the worldly social obligations of patriarchal society. Second, he asked to know the fire sacrifice that led to heaven, for as we have seen, the power of the sacrifice extends from this world to the next. But the son's second wish was only a worldly matter, too, for life in the Vedic heavens extended only as long as the warping of cosmic energy by the rite lasted. Depending on one's skill and power, knowing the fire sacrifice that leads to heaven might ensure bliss for a very long time, but being just a matter of technical craft, it would ultimately wear down, for within the cosmos there is no such thing as perpetual motion or energy.

But the third question was a shift to another level of discourse. Nachiketa said, "When a man dies, there is this doubt: Some say, he is; others say, he is not. Taught by thee, I would know the truth. This is my third wish."

Understanding the thrust of the question, that Nachiketa is probing the fringes of an entire new spiritual world different from that of the Vedic rites and that he might well be ready to enter it, Death parried with him. He went through the time-honored conventions of the master seeming to frustrate and discourage the novice in order to test him. He informed Nachiketa that the Gods themselves find the answer hard to understand and urged him to select some other favor. He urged him to select sons, cattle, elephants, gold, a mighty kingdom, or celestial maidens so beautiful as not to be meant for mortals.

But Nachiketa stood fast, pointing out that these things are only grasped for a fleeting day, then vanish like smoke; in the process, they wear away the senses. How can one desire them, he asked Death, who has once seen Death's face? There is a secret of imperishability and immortality that is beyond them, he insisted, and he would not yield till Death had imparted it.

Inwardly well pleased, Death confirmed that there is another secret, one that cannot really be taught at all but that can be caught from a true teacher by the student who is truly prepared—that the Self within is the imperishable, changeless Brahman, the One beyond and, at the same time, in all these forms and changes. The mantra, or sound, that expresses Brahman himself and whose recitation can give rise to his consciousness is "OM." The King of Death continues:

Om, a symbol of Hinduism.

> The Self, whose symbol is OM, is the omniscient Lord. He is not born. He does not die. He is neither cause nor effect. This Ancient One is unborn, imperishable, eternal: though the body be destroyed, he is not killed.
>
> If the slayer think that he slays, if the slain think that he is slain, neither of them knows the truth. The Self slays not, nor is he slain.
>
> Smaller than the smallest, greater than the greatest, this Self forever dwells within the hearts of all. When a man is free from desire, his mind and senses purified, he beholds the glory of the Self and is without sorrow.
>
> Though seated, he travels far; though at rest, he moves all things. Who but the purest of the pure can realize this Effulgent Being, who is joy and who is beyond joy.
>
> Formless is he, though inhabiting form. In the midst of the fleeting he abides forever. All-pervading and supreme is the Self. The wise man, knowing him in his true nature, transcends all grief.
>
> The Self is not known through study of the scriptures, nor through subtlety of the intellect, nor through much learning; but by him who longs for him is he known. Verily unto him does the Self reveal his true being.
>
> By learning, a man cannot know him, if he desist not from evil, if he control not his senses, if he quiet not his mind, and practice not meditation.[9]

The Self—Atman, who is really Brahman—is the only Being, the Sole Existent, the One Mind. He is everywhere yet indivisible. Brahman alone exists; all else floats insubstantial on the face of the shoreless ocean of his being, his wisdom, and his bliss, like reflections in an unstained mirror. Yet the ordinary consciousness grasps only the things and not Brahman, for the simple reason that Brahman is consciousness. In the same way, the eye cannot see itself or a pair of pliers grab itself. Brahman plays hide-and-seek with itself in the world, dwelling in myriad things while elusive to human thought and dream. Why? None of us groping about in the world of the many can fully know, just as those inside a house can know only incompletely the whole plan and shape of the structure. They would have to step through the door and look at it from outside as well.

The sages of India tell us there are doors that the wise and the intrepid can find. As the end of the preceding passage tells us, it is through meditation, that is, quieting the senses and the mind, that the door to the infinite dimension can be unlatched. For it is the play of the senses and the mind that turn one away from one's true nature—Brahman—to the phantasmagoria of many things to which feeling and thought attach themselves like leeches.

It is as though a play has been going on for a very long time—not weeks and weeks but countless years. It has been going on for so long that the actors have forgotten they are merely playing parts and have come to identify themselves with the parts. They think that when one actor murders another, the victim is really dead and that the red gore on the floor is not ketchup but real blood. They think that when two members of the cast fall in love or break up with tears and angry words, these are absolute and final realities of life, not just events woven into the web of a greater drama with higher purposes beyond their ken. So the show becomes so mad, with the actors' involvement and anxiety rising out of control, that the prompter behind the stage must send out messengers to remind them that the show is only a play, to remind them who they really are.

This is like the Upanishadic view of the world. The messengers are like the great sages who remind us of how things really are; the *rishis*, or seers, who composed the Vedas, are the God-realized teachers who bring students into Brahman consciousness in all ages. But the difference is that in the Upanishadic vision, there are not many actors but one actor—the One Mind—who is playing all the parts and is also the prompter. He who is playing the part of the one you love and also the one you hate and the stranger to whom you are indifferent is none other than the Self, of whom our outward-directed thoughts have been forgetful.

One other message from the Upanishads: The Mandukya Upanishad tells us that the Self, as consciousness, has three aspects—and beyond them, a fourth.

The first is the "ordinary waking consciousness." It is you or I walking down the street, perceiving other objects and people as outside of oneself, and thinking of oneself as separate from them, while enjoying the pleasures of the senses.

The second aspect is the mental nature turned upon itself, enjoying a mental world created within the head. It is the "dreaming state of consciousness" and, by extension, the worlds of imagination, fantasy, and the deep archetypes of the unconscious. The images that dance behind the curtains of the mind in this state derive from things remembered by the senses and so come from outside, and except in advanced yogic states, they are more or less out of control: we cannot usually tell ourselves what to dream. Yet although the second aspect is not a divine state of consciousness but an inward turning of the first, it does have some similarity to Brahmanic consciousness; it is one mind growing a whole world of bright and transient forms, which do not exist elsewhere, out of itself.

The third aspect is the self in the state of "deep sleep without dreams." When all forms, external and internal, vanish into formlessness and when mind and sense are still, like a windless lake in the midst of night, one enters the third state. Significantly, it is called the **prajna** state. *Prajna* means wisdom, not in the sense of factual knowledge about all sorts of things, which obviously would not apply, but that sharp, intuitive insight that simply knows, without the confusion of words or ideas from the world of the many. And what is known in this way, all that is known in this way, is Brahman.

In an important sense, then, the "deep-sleep-without-dreams" state is the closest of these three aspects to Brahman consciousness. A fundamental principle of Hindu (and Buddhist) philosophy is that all outward, particularized perceptions and concepts, such as those one has in the waking state, are really limitations. If you are thinking about one thing or a thousand, there are still millions of things you are not thinking about; and the very things you are thinking about cut you off from the others and so limit you. Only when this part of thought is quieted does the mind become like Brahman's—thinking of nothing in particular, and thus horizonless, infinite, in tune with the All. In deep sleep, one is functioning just on the biological plane and so becomes an integrated part of the dance of the atoms and galaxies, without being cut off by any individualizing thoughts from this infinite play of Brahman.

This is really the fulfillment attained in the fourth state of consciousness, for the Mandukya Upanishad tells us that the true Self, OM or AUM, is the unification of all three other states. It is the state of a person who walks through the world bearing the gifts of all three. That person has the fearlessness and sense of oneness of one at ease in our universe-home, or of one dead, or of Brahman. He has under control all the delights and occult powers of the inner dream world yet lives and works with acute capability in the outer world, for he knows things as they really are, down to their roots. In the vision of the Upanishads, such a person alone is a complete human being.

SPIRITUAL FERMENT AND THE RISE OF BUDDHISM

The Upanishadic vision is the epitomizing expression of the classic lore of the most prestigious scholarly class, the Brahmins. It enjoys a unique status and is accepted as authoritative, along with the rest of the Vedic literature, by all who consider themselves orthodox. But to think that the Upanishadic vision is the tool by which Hindu culture is to be interpreted or that it plays a role in Hinduism exactly parallel to the Qu'ran in Islam or the Bible in Christianity would be to oversimplify.

Although reference to the Upanishads greatly illuminates the mentality that underlies India's Gods, art, and institutions, one who tries to understand what is happening in an average Hindu village temple or pilgrimage center solely on the basis of the Upanishads would be quickly at sea. It must be borne in mind that through the centuries, the majority of the people of India, illiterate and provincial, have doubtless never heard much of the teaching of the Vedas directly. Bits of their light must have reached the peasants through the lips of wandering holy men or veiled in stories or song, but the people would know them as treatises no more than they knew the Sanskrit language to which the Vedas were traditionally confined.

The spiritual movement in India, which produced the "interiorization of sacrifice" of the Upanishads, also produced other equally important results. At the time the Upanishadic vision was crystallizing, much else was also happening across the dusty face of India. Although the Indus Valley cities declined, much of their culture persisted, with its religious emphasis on fertility, the Mother, purity, and (presumably) the mystic states of consciousness attained by techniques of the yogic sort. Doubtless this heritage did much to influence the direction that the Upanishadic culmination of Vedism took. Not only did the thinkers in India move toward mystical **monism** rather than **monotheism**, as in Iran, but the doctrine of **reincarnation**, central to later Hinduism and Buddhism, appears first in the Upanishads. In the earlier Vedas, it is found only in a very rudimentary form.

It was a time when the Vedic culture was pressing across northern India and had established itself virtually to the Ganges Delta. No great unified empire had yet arisen, although the sub-Himalayan plain was a patchwork of kingdoms large and small. Material civilization was still scanty, but spiritual and philosophical cultures were vigorous and moving ahead rapidly.

Spiritual teachers strolled from village to village in the company of bands of disciples, even like **sadhus**, or "holy men," in India today. Typically, they would walk in the morning and would arrive at their destination by noon, when they would beg for food. In the afternoon, they would rest and meditate; in the evening, the townsfolk would gather around them. The visitors—intriguing and the subject of much local talk because they came from "outside"—would pay for the hospitality they had been afforded with spiritual instruction and doubtless also by reporting news from the outside world. The next day, unless a local magnate persuaded them to stay on as his guest, they would leave, possibly taking with them a local lad or two who had been impelled by both an itch for adventure and a hunger for higher things to leave home in the company of a peripatetic master.

The masters' teachings were wide ranging and circumscribed by few dogmatic presuppositions, for these teachers were not Brahmins defending the Vedic tradition, performing the sacrifices, and interpreting them along Upanishadic lines. The Brahmins were mostly priests retained by the courts or living in their own communities. But new teachers—Brahmins and non-Brahmins—began looking for truth everywhere. One teacher might say that the world was created, another that it is eternal; one might say that all is mind, another that there is nothing but matter.

One assumption that the new teachers shared in common, however, was that philosophical teaching was not to be merely abstract but also was to aid in attaining a state of inner liberation. Each school should include a spiritual path that could be tested empirically. Most advocated methods involving extremely rigorous self-denial and self-control.

Many wanderers are now forgotten, but two are not: Vardhamana, called Mahavira ("Great Hero"), c. 540–468 B.C.E., who was the founder of the Jain religion (which we shall look at in more detail later in this chapter), and Siddhartha Gautama, of the Sakya clan and a contemporary of Mahavira, called the **Buddha** ("Enlightened One"), 563–483 B.C.E. (who will be discussed in more detail here and in the next chapter). Both founded faiths that have persisted through twenty-five centuries; both have symbolized for many the highest conceivable human state; both have structured the lives and blessed the deaths of innumerable spiritual children through the ages. Moreover, both were of similar background: each was the son of a minor ruler afforded more or less honorary warrior-caste status; each was considered by his followers to be the last of a great chain of mighty teachers. Indeed, similar legends are told about the nativity and life of both, so much so that scholars once wrongly concluded they were the same person going by different names in two different religions. They did, however, roam the Eastern Ganges River Valley contemporaneously.

Beyond these characteristics, however, their destinies differ, and by far more, so do the destinies of the two faiths. **Jainism**, profoundly Indian, has remained remarkably unchanged in teaching and practice through the ages, but at the price of remaining small and of being restricted primarily to India. Buddhism has reached hundreds of times more adherents than Jainism. It has spread over vast continental areas, has exfoliated into incredible diversities of sect and practice—and, again in contrast to Jainism, it essentially died out in its homeland (although it has had something of a modern revival there), while spreading from Siberia to Sri Lanka and from the Caspian Sea to China and Japan, not to mention its influence in the West.

While Mahavira taught a way of stern denial and control, the Buddha called his path the "Middle Way," for it was a spiritual tack of dwelling in the calm spot of equilibrium between all polarities, such as asceticism and indulgence, love of life and desire for death, even being and nonbeing. The Buddha, we are told, had been brought up in luxury and had tried the extremes of fasting and asceticism, but he came to see both sides as forms of egotism. It should not be supposed, however, that Buddhism is any sort of easygoing, moderation-in-all-things philosophy. To hit the exact spot of equilibrium where one is in precise balance with the universe and so has all power is no easy act of spiritual archery. It involves neutralizing all the outward and subtle desires that keep us shooting impulsively this way and that, scarcely seeing the target, much less hitting the bull's-eye.

Although the Buddha and Buddhism are discussed in detail in the next chapter, it is important here to place the inception of Buddhism in its historical time and place. Initially, Buddhism prospered in India, doubtless because of its close relation to the indigenous tradition and the moderation and attractiveness of its monks. They found favor in the homes of the mighty. In particular, the Buddhists won the support of the Emperor Ashoka (r.c. 273–232 B.C.E.), one of the noblest rulers of all time, whose patronage sustained and advanced Buddhism throughout northern India.

Buddhism, being inherently tolerant of Hindu and other Gods, is glad to acknowledge them as long as they are seen as pupils of the Buddha, "teacher of Gods and men." In this sense, Buddhism did not self-consciously assert itself as *the* religion in society. Yet Hinduism and Buddhism were also consciously or unconsciously competitive in India. Even in the high tide of the Buddhist period, the Hindu tradition was providing responses and alternatives to the Buddha's way that would eventually help it supersede Buddhism in India itself, at the same time tremendously enriching and broadening the appeal of Hinduism in order to answer the questions raised by the Buddhist experience. But in so doing, Hinduism capitalized on the older religion's strong points as a total religious expression: Hindu concern was not only with liberation but also with the organization of society, the pluralism of spiritual paths and stages implicit in its many representations of the Divine.[10]

THE LAWS OF MANU

The Laws of Manu, which some scholars hold were given in their current form around 100 C.E., are a systematization of the Hindu view of society and contain the teaching about the "Four Ends of Human Life" and about the "Four Stages of Life," described earlier. The Laws of Manu also rationalize the caste system of India, which places one in the great social order believed to be prescribed by *dharma*. The Laws of Manu, therefore, speak of the four great divisions of society, called **varnas** (literally "colors"): *Brahmins* or priest-scholars; *kshatriyas* or rulers and warriors; *vaishyas* or merchants, shopkeepers, and farm owners; and *shudras* or domestic help and ordinary manual and farm laborers. It is said that these divisions come from different parts of the body of the primal man: *Brahmins* from the head, *kshatriyas* from the arms, *vaishyas* from the thighs, and *shudras* from the feet.

In addition to securing the place of the priests at the pinnacle of society, the caste system was probably intended to provide stability by distributing societal power among the top three *varnas* (sacerdotal, military, and economic) and to pass the duties and preserve the occupational skills of each *varna* from one generation to another. However, the caste system became rigid, leading to social disjunction, the development of a hierarchy of classes, and a static society. The lower castes suffered disabilities in education and occupational choices. Furthermore, although the requirements were not sanctioned by the Vedas or the Laws of Manu, eventually a large segment of society deemed to be "outcastes," and known as "untouchables," were required to live outside village and town boundaries.

Still, in all of this, the Laws of Manu were clearly trying to deal in a unified way with the two great but hard-to-reconcile poles of Hindu experience: *dharma* and *moksha* (or one's duty in society and liberation). So *dharma* and *moksha* are seen as appropriate concerns for different stages of life, and through the caste system, the social many are made manifestly compatible with oneness through the image of the great social organism, with each cell and organ playing its part, but some with much better roles than others.

YOGA SUTRAS

What would one do during the course of seeking liberation? One important answer was given by yoga, which had ancient roots, having been founded, it is said, by the ancient sage Hiranyagarbha. But it was Patanjali who synthesized the yoga system in his Yoga Sutras (c. 300 C.E.). Buddhism had emphasized introspective meditation, with analysis of sensation and consciousness; the Yoga Sutras returned to India's deeply biological, psychosomatic understanding of human nature as the background for liberation through methods of meditation, breath, and physical discipline. Thus, **hatha-yoga**, the physical yoga of postures and breathing exercises, plays a major role in the spiritual quest. Rightly understood, breath and body are indispensable tools. Brought under control of spirit as precision instruments, they can facilitate states of consciousness that evoke the goals of spirit.

The goal of the *yogi*, the practitioner of yoga, is control of the modulations of the mind—in other words, *kaivalya*, "isolation," independence of the anxiety and

limitations imposed by interaction with the changing world of sight and feeling and fantasy. This goal is accomplished when the *yogi* gets the mind and the body strictly under control and then uses this control to withdraw attention from the outer world so that the inner light shines unimpeded.

According to the Yoga Sutras, the process is composed of eight steps, called "limbs." The first two steps, *yama* and *niyama*, are positive and negative moral rules aimed at a life of quietness, gentleness, and purity, for one's manner of life must be prepared and purified before yoga can hope to succeed. Releasing yoga's potent spiritual forces into an unworthy vessel can, in fact, be most dangerous to both the individual and society. Then come the two steps of *asana* (posture) and *pranayama* (breath control), in which the psychosomatic powers are lined up to move in the one direction of liberation.

After the *yogi* gains control of his or her own bodily and emotional house in this way, *pratyahara*, the stage of the disengagement of the senses and of the attention from outer things, becomes possible. This makes for acute inner, subtle ways of awareness. Just as a blind person develops especially sharp touch and hearing, so yoga tells us that when all the gross senses are withdrawn, other undreamed-of capabilities latent in the human being begin to stir. When they come to be mastered, the *yogi* has awareness of things near and far and the ability to use occult forces, beside which the ordinary senses and capacities are as an oxcart to a rocket ship. The Yoga Sutras tell us how to read minds, walk on water, fly through the air, make oneself as tiny as an atom, and be impervious to hunger and thirst.

But these powers, called *siddhis*, doubtless tempting to many, are to be given up for an even greater goal—true liberation of the true self. This is the work of the last three steps, which are interior: *dharana*, concentration; *dhyana*, meditation; and *samadhi*, the absolutely equalized consciousness of perfect freedom.

THE BHAGAVAD-GITA

The wisdom of the Upanishads, the way of society described in the Laws of Manu, and the methods and goals of the *yogi* synthesized by Patanjali are found together in what many hold to be the greatest Hindu statement, the **Bhagavad-Gita**, or simply the "Gita." The Gita probably was originally an oral account. The date of the written text as we know it is disputed, suggested dates ranging from 500 B.C.E. to 100 C.E. It is really a section of the Mahabharata, which is one of the two most famous Hindu epics, the other being the Ramayana (to be discussed later). The Mahabharata describes a great war between cousins over the succession to the throne of an Aryan state, but it is also a deep philosophical and spiritual work. But the Bhagavad-Gita, or "Song of the Lord," is especially revered and stands by itself once its setting is understood.

The Bhagavad-Gita tells the story of Prince Arjuna, whose charioteer is the heroic God **Krishna** in human form. Arjuna is setting out to lead his army into bloody battle against the foe. Appalled at what he is about to do, Arjuna pauses in deep moral distress. The book is a series of answers that Krishna gives the prince to resolve his irresolution. It discourses on why Arjuna can and must fight, but its implications go much further than this. The pacifist Mahatma Gandhi (to be discussed later) greatly treasured this book, taking it as an allegory of nonviolent struggle against injustice and for spiritual purity.

Krishna gives three basic answers, reflecting three kinds of spiritual paths: **Jñaña-yoga**, the way of knowledge, which emphasizes the Upanishadic-type realization of the oneness of all things, attained by meditation; **Karma-yoga**, the way of activity, a liberation reached by selfless action; and **Bhakti-yoga**, the way of love for God in personal form.

So it is that Krishna's first answer is along the lines of Upanishadic thought. He emphasizes that there is no reality behind the talk of life and death, behind killing and being killed:

Some say this Atman	*Unborn, undying,*
Is slain, and others	*Never ceasing,*
Call It the slayer:	*Never beginning*
They know nothing.	*Deathless, birthless,*
How can It slay…	*Unchanging forever.*
Or who shall slay It?	*How can It die*
Know this Atman…	*The death of the body?*[11]

But if it does not make any difference, the question could be asked: Why kill instead of not killing? This question Krishna answers, in effect, "Because you are a *kshatriya*, a warrior, by birth and caste, and therefore fighting is your role in the drama of the universe; there is no honorable way you can shirk it, and right is on your side since the enemy has gone against *dharma*."

Further questions arise. Does this mean, then, that one born as a warrior has no hope for salvation comparable to that of the Brahmin whose hands are unstained with blood and who enacts the mystic sacrifices? Does it mean that he whose place in society makes it almost mandatory that he stay in the world cannot compete with one who is able to become an ascetic or a *yogi*?

No, replies Krishna. It is all a matter of how one lives in the world. The object is to become one with the Absolute, so that nothing in one's thoughts or deeds causes separation. But if Brahman is truly All, the world of the activist is just as divine as that of the recluse. Brahman is expressed through *dharma* as much as *moksha* if it is truly All—in the caste laws and in all of life's stages together. One can realize God in acting as much as in meditation, if one's actions are as selfless as meditation and as passionless. Thus, Krishna gives his second answer and teaches Arjuna the secret of *karma-yoga*, yoga in the midst of doing. The point is to be in the world impersonally, objectively—doing so not out of personal desire for the fruits of one's actions but fearlessly and dispassionately, as it were by proxy for God, motivated solely by the duty and righteousness of the act. Then, with one's feelings not getting in the way, one's actions are a part of the great dance of the cosmos, of the life of the whole social and natural organism, and they are as quiet and far reaching as meditation.

> You have the right to work, but for the work's sake only. You have no right to the fruits of work. Desire for the fruits of work must never be your motive in working. Never give way to laziness either.
>
> Perform every action with your heart fixed on the Supreme Lord. Renounce attachment to the fruits.
>
> Be even tempered in success and failure; for it is this evenness of temper which is meant by yoga.
>
> Work done with anxiety about results is far inferior to work done without such anxiety, in the calm of self-surrender. Seek refuge in the knowledge of Brahman. They who work selfishly for results are miserable.[12]

Traditionally, *karma-yoga* was interpreted in a highly conservative way to mean that one must accept the role given by caste. Some modern Hindus, however, see it instead as a view that liberates one for bold and selfless acts of service to humankind, however risky, unpopular, or likely to fail—if one is acting out of impersonal righteousness rather than for the gratification of pocket or ego, which do not matter.

A philosophy like this does not satisfy all the spiritual needs of most people. However noble it may be, by itself it has a quality of dry resignation that does not answer one's thirst to know the Real. Yet something like *karma-yoga* can be an invaluable preparation for what seems to be its opposite, a religion of deeply felt awe and love in the presence of God. Only the person whose ego self is unobtrusive can truly know God in any case.

This philosophy reflects the spiritual progression of the Bhagavad-Gita. After the Upanishadic and *karma-yoga* stages, the dialogue moves more and more into a sense of a mystical presence.

Now I shall tell you
That innermost secret:
Which is nearer than knowing,
Open vision
Direct and instant.
Understand this
And be free for ever
From birth and dying
With all their evil.[13]
Who burns with the bliss
And suffers the sorrow
Of every creature
Within his own heart,
Making his own
Each bliss and each sorrow:
Him I hold highest
Of all the yogis.[14]

Something else begins to arise in the tradition, a sense that the relationship of the individual and this mystical presence can be one of love and that love is greater than success or failure in keeping the formal obligations of law and rite.

Great is that yogi who seeks to be with Brahman,
Greater than those who mortify the body,
Greater than the learned,
Greater than the doers of good works:
Therefore, Arjuna, become a yogi.
He gives me all his heart,
He worships me in faith and love:
That yogi, above every other,
I call my very own.[15]

The verses quoted above contain the very essence of **bhakti**, the spiritual path of devotionalism or love for God in personal form.

The greatest spiritual explosion, however, is yet to come. Nearness and love, in place of philosophy and duty, lead to a radically different relationship between humankind and God and one far more analogous to the relationship between people than between persons and natural law. Moving into this spiritual sphere, Arjuna culminates the discourse by asking to see Krishna in his full splendor and glory. Krishna obliges:

> Then...Sri Krishna, Master of all yogis, revealed to Arjuna his transcendent, divine form, speaking from innumerable mouths, seeing with a myriad eyes, of many marvelous aspects, adorned with countless divine ornaments, brandishing all kinds of heavenly weapons, wearing celestial garlands and the raiment of paradise, anointed with perfumes of heavenly fragrance, full of revelations, resplendent, boundless, of ubiquitous regard.
>
> Suppose a thousand suns should rise together into the sky: such is the glory of the Shape of Infinite God.
>
> Then the son of Pandu [Arjuna] beheld the entire universe, in all its multitudinous diversity, lodged as one being within the body of the God of gods.
>
> Then was Arjuna, that lord of mighty riches, overcome with wonder. His hair stood erect. He bowed low before God in adoration, and clasped his hands, and spoke.

Arjuna:

Ah, my God, I see all gods within your body;
Each in his degree, the multitude of creatures;
See Lord Brahma throned upon the lotus;
See all the sages, and the holy serpents.
Universal Form, I see you without limit,
Infinite of arms, eyes, mouths, and bellies—
See, and find no end, midst, or beginning.
Crowned with diadems, you wield the mace and discus,
Shining every way—the eyes shrink from your splendour
Brilliant like the sun; like fire, blazing, boundless.
You are all we know, supreme, beyond man's measure,
This world's sure-set plinth and refuge never shaken,
Guardian of eternal law, life's Soul undying,
Birthless, deathless; yours the strength titanic,
Million-armed, the sun and moon your eyeballs,
Fiery-faced, you blast the world to ashes.[16]

Here Arjuna sees Krishna as **Vishnu** (to be discussed later), brighter than a thousand suns, expressed through endless multiplicity, the same infinity that can also be expressed as the One, as Brahman, as God. God is here represented by the myriad things, and among them, he is as an enthroned sovereign. But God as infinite series or infinite multiplicity also brings out the dark side of God: infinite series expressed through time as well as space, and in time, all things perish. So God appears as destroyer: "By me these men are slain already," Krishna says a little later of Arjuna's foes. Hence, this vision, too, is a justification of Arjuna's fighting, and of much more as well. Yet God as a personal being with whom one can have a relationship of knowledge and love and who, moreover, comes among people as a friend and a brother, like Krishna, engenders a new spiritual sensitivity, too.

ADVAITA VEDANTA

The tradition of Hindu philosophy that has generally been most prestigious in India for the last 1,000 years and is best known outside India today is **Vedanta**. The word literally means "the end (i.e., the culmination) of the Vedas." The school centers itself essentially on the teaching of the Upanishads, the last and most philosophic of the Vedas, about Brahman as one with Atman and as the Sole Existent. Other texts, such as the earlier Vedas and the Bhagavad-Gita, are interpreted in this light.

The most influential school of Vedanta has been **Advaita Vedanta**, which may be rendered as "nondualism in the Vedic tradition." Its leading exponent was Shankara (?700–?750 C.E.), who argued forcefully and uncompromisingly for radical oneness in a universe of apparent "manyness." Commenting on the Upanishads, Shankara brought home in metaphysical language its intuition that there is only one reality—Brahman. Only Brahman exists; all else—every idea, form, and experience—is "superimposed" on Brahman owing to our *avidya*, our ignorance of the true nature of reality. What we ordinarily see is **maya**, often translated "illusion," but illusion that has to be understood in the right sense, for *maya* is an appearance of Brahman and so is not unreal. The world is really there; it is not on a level with the pink elephants of the proverbial drunk. But it is *maya* when the world is not seen for what it is. Shankara liked to use the simile of a man who saw something lying on the ground and jumped, thinking it was a snake; he looked again and saw it was only a piece of rope. In the same way, we really see something when we see the world, but we misapprehend what it is we see; we think it is really many separate things, when actually it is but one "thing"—Brahman.

Shankara's influence on the practical side of Hinduism was comparable to his philosophical influence. He reformed and promoted **monasticism**, establishing four great monastic centers of learning in the quarters of India. He tried to modify the harshness of caste distinction and encouraged devotion to the Hindu Gods as aspects of the One., Through his reforms and achievements, although he would not admit they were a goal, he was establishing Hindu parallels to the intellectual monasticism, the subtle nondualist philosophy, and the devotion to the Buddhas and bodhisattvas of Buddhism.[17]

TANTRISM

Another movement starting in these centuries cut across both Hinduism and Buddhism and deeply affected the course of both. It is the complex and mysterious set of spiritual attitudes and practices called **Tantrism**—a road to enlightenment through powerful initiations, "shock therapy" techniques, the negation of conventional morals and manners, magical-seeming acts and chants, and, for a small number, the use of sexual imagery and ritual. Tantrism seeks through radical means to induce powerful consciousness-transforming experience, while preserving something of the technical aura of the old Vedic rites.

One reason why Tantrism's origins and teachings are so hard to trace is that it has often attracted persons in reaction against the current religious establishment of Brahmins, of princely rulers, and of Buddhist monks. Tantrism presented itself to people who were marginalized in society as a secret, underground path far more potent than the official teaching, if one were bold enough to reject conventionality by accepting it. If the adept, it says, does not shrink back or go mad at its "steep path," then, in a single lifetime, Tantrism can bring one to a state of realization and power that would take countless lifetimes by ordinary means.

Roughly, the procedures of Tantra are as follows: The novice is initiated into the practice of a particular Tantric path by a *guru* (spiritual teacher); this impartation of power is said often to be physically felt and is extremely important. Being empowered, the aspirant then seeks identity with a deity like Shiva or Kali (a manifestation of Shakti) through magical evocations of the God's visible presence, through visual fixation on diagrams (**mandala** and **yantra**) of his or her powers, and through the recitation of a **mantra** that encapsulates his or her nature. By becoming one with the Divinity, the aspirant hopes to share the Divinity's cosmic realization and omnipotence.

In this process, the Tantrist seeks to experience the totality, the unity beyond all opposites. To do this, one may liberate oneself from "partiality" by getting outside of structure—living independent of caste and morality. In some Tantric traditions, "forbidden" things—such as meat, alcohol, and sex outside of the social conventions of marriage and caste—are partaken, either symbolically or actually, in specific rites. In this latter case, the male Tantrist identifies himself with a male deity like Shiva, the absolute, and his female partner with Shakti, who is the phenomenal universe; as the Tantric couple unites, they mystically unite the absolute and the universe in a flash of ecstasy. Sexuality is important to Tantrism, not only because it offers the "shock therapy" effect of sexual rites but also because it is a tremendous evoker of energy (which the skilled practitioner can then sublimate to the spiritual quest) and is a symbol and sacrament of the Tantrist view of reality.

But the rite cannot do this sacramentally, nor can moral reversal be spiritually efficacious, nor the sexual energies transmuted to spiritual realization until the novice is well advanced in a Tantric *sadhana*, or path. Unless one has truly negated self and identified with the God, sex is merely lust and not participation in divine mysteries.

Tantrism had an influence far beyond the schools that taught it in its strictest form. All Hindu worship on a serious level is now likely to show some influence of Tantra, if only in the use of *yantra* and the repetition of the name of a deity and a mantra over and over. It has also had a substantial impact on Indian art.

The important concepts of **kundalini** and the **chakras** come out of the Tantric tradition, although they are represented today in most systems of yoga. They are an interiorization of the Shiva-Shakti dynamic. The *kundalini*, or "serpent power," is a feminine energy believed to dwell, coiled three and a half times, below the base of the spine. Through *yogic* techniques of posture, breathing, and concentration, the *kundalini* is awakened and aroused to be drawn up the spinal column. In the process, it "opens" seven *chakras*, "circles," or lotus centers of dormant psychic energy located along the spinal column at the base of the spine, the lower abdomen, the solar plexus, the heart, the throat, and the forehead (the "third eye"), culminating in the *sahasrara* or the thousand-petaled lotus at the top of the head.

This process, together with the withdrawal of senses from the outer world incumbent upon yogic practice, is said to produce remarkable states of awareness. The final objective, however, is only achieved when the *kundalini* reaches the inside of the skull, where, with a psychic explosion at the crown *chakra*, it awakens a thousand-petaled lotus that grants cosmic consciousness and God realization. The awakening brings into the light an entire world within the head, replete with its own miniature mountain, lake, sun, and moon, and in its midst Shiva is enthroned.[18]

DEVOTIONAL HINDUISM

The early Middle Ages were times of realization of both the social and devotional promise of the Hindu reactions to Buddhism. In the process, Hinduism became a system integrating all the population of India into a loosely knit organism, providing for a multitude of spiritual drives and social needs. New tribes and peoples throughout the land were brought into the system by being recognized as branches of major castes; thus thousands of subcastes, or *jati*, were created. The folk gods of all these people were recognized as representations, or aspects, of one of the great Gods of Hinduism—which by now owed as much or even more to the indigenous traditions as to the Vedas. To these Gods, *bhakti* or devotion, the service of a loving heart, weighed more than legal righteousness, caste, or ritual.

Accounts of these Gods, their religious narratives and words and methods of worship, are presented in books called **Puranas**, which were written over hundreds of years, some as late as the fifteenth century C.E. The devotional Gods, some many-armed or animal-headed, rejoice in colorful images and pictures; they enjoy lavish temples and dramatic processions. It is this Hinduism that most moves the average Indian and that is most conspicuous to the visitor today.

In Hinduism, **devotionalism** is the spiritual path of *bhakti*—the way to liberation or *moksha* through losing one's egocentricity in love for the chosen God. Love is, for most people, the human drive in which one most readily forgets (if only now and then) self-centeredness. In these moments, one's feelings go outside of one's self to share in the subjective life of another human being through caring and empathy. Why not, then, *bhaktas* ask, utilize this drive to propel the ultimate quest, for loss of self in the Divine? Through the love of God in any of various forms, whom one can visualize and adore but who are themselves not separate from the absolute, one shares their nonseparateness, for one becomes what one loves.

Nondevotional Hinduism may take very austere forms in the case of renunciants who "interiorize" it all and worship without priest or temple. But it has never entertained much the Puritan idea that there is something virtuous about making ordinary worship drab. Rather, India (outside Buddhism) tends to feel that genuineness is found at extremes; whatever path a person takes, it should be taken all the way, with the abandon of the mystic. **Ascetics** may starve their eyes and ears as they starve their bellies, striving to find God in the all by negating God in any particular form. The *bhakta*, the devotionalist, goes the other way and characteristically follows that path without restraint, using particular Gods as stepping-stones to love of the All. This is the Hinduism of the temple, where nothing is spared of lights, music, flowers, jewels, pomp, incense, and offerings to create an atmosphere of royalty (the Gods and Goddesses as kings and queens), love, and heavenly delight, which takes the worshipper out of the ordinary and into the transforming circle of the sacred. Images of God may be sheathed in gems worth a royal ransom; during festivals the bejeweled deities may be taken through the streets on festooned elephants or giant chariots. A vast scriptural corpus, the Agamas, detail the ritual ceremonies, theologies, and spiritual practices that are to be followed and that are specific to the various devotional Gods and Goddesses.

The greatest theologian of *bhakti* was Ramanuja (born 1017 C.E.). Although trained in Shankara's nondualist Vedanta, Ramanuja was of strong religious bent and a devotee of Vishnu. He criticized Shankara's system as being both inconsistent and spiritually unsatisfying. If everything is Brahman, he argued, but this is not known because of *avidya*, ignorance, then this would mean that the ignorance lies in Brahman himself. It would be better, he argued, to postulate a different model for the relation of the universe and God—an organic model in which God is like the indwelling soul and the cosmos the body, the two inseparable and interacting but having distinct modes of life. In this theistic system, God is personal and loving. Souls, in lifetime after lifetime, can respond to his love and grace, and by purifying themselves through *bhaktic* worship, they can draw near to God until they gain blissful eternity with God in a paradisal heaven. Through highly sophisticated philosophical argument, Ramanuja defended the religion of the love of a personal God, which was and is the faith of the great majority of his countrymen.

The devotional Gods are best thought of as belonging to two families—the Vishnu family and the Shiva family. The difference can be thought of in this way: Vishnu and his religious system are somewhat like the Western concept of God, in that the masculine figures are heroic and dominant and the feminine figures rather demure; Vishnu as God represents not so much the cosmic totality as the forces on behalf of order or righteousness. He descends incarnate from highest heaven whenever righteousness declines and works to restore good in the world. Krishna of the Bhagavad-Gita is one such descent of Vishnu.

In the Shiva system, God is, above all, simply the Absolute, and therefore the union of all opposites—creation and destruction, male and female. Shiva and Shakti thus have equal prominence, and she is far from unassertive. But although they may appear in visions, they are not usually claimed to be born incarnate among humans. Shiva is like the Brahman of the Upanishads personified.

The Vishnu Family of Devotional Gods

Statue of Brahma, Hinduism's creator God.

Vishnu, it is said, slept in the cosmic ocean on a great serpent made up of the remains of the last universe before this one was formed; time is immense cycles of divine sleep and waking. When it came time for the cosmos to be made again, a lotus grew out of Vishnu's navel, and on the lotus appeared Brahma, the creator God (not to be confused with Brahman). Brahma defeated the imps of chaos and fabricated the world with his second wife, Gayatri, at his side (because the ceremony required to create the world could not be performed without a wife). Then Vishnu rose, seated in high heaven on a lotus throne with his consort Goddesses Lakshmi (Fortune) and Bhu-Devi (the Earth). The serpent arched his hoods over the divine sovereign to make a canopy; the lesser gods attended him.

But as time progresses, the set moral order of the world—*dharma*—declines, and the power of demons grows. To counteract the latter, Vishnu periodically enters the world in various bodily forms; these are called his **avatars** (descents or **incarnations**). The most popular list gives ten incarnations: as a fish, a tortoise, a boar, a man-lion, a dwarf, Parasurama (a *Brahmin* hero), Rama, Krishna, Buddha, and Kalkin, who is the incarnation yet to come.

The most important avatars are Rama and Krishna. Rama is the hero of the Ramayana, the great epic very popular among all classes in India and Southeast Asia. It relates that Rama was a prince of the ancient city Ayodhya but, owing to intrigue, was wrongly exiled from court. His brother, Lakshman, and his faithful wife, Sita, accompanied him as he went to live a simple life of a renunciant deep in the forest. But Sita was abducted by the demon Ravana and carried off to his palace in Lanka (Sri Lanka). Assisted by a monkey army, especially the mighty monkey hero Hanuman, Rama waged war against Ravana and prevailed. After rescuing his wife, his exile ended and the three returned to Ayodhya. There he presided over a long reign of peace and paradisal prosperity. In one telling of the story, Rama's reign of peace did not occur until Rama was forced to send Sita away, because many people thought she may have been unfaithful to him while with Ravana. In that version, Sita finally called on the Earth Goddess to take her if she were pure. This the Earth Goddess did, appearing on a golden throne, embracing Sita, and disappearing with her. (In an alternative, popular version of the story known as the Ramcharitmanas, however, this sad ending to the story does not occur.)

While Rama does not seem to have been considered divine at first, devotion to him as an avatar of Vishnu increased and his devotion was firmly established by the sixteenth century. He remains, however, essentially God as supreme human ideal: gentle, brave, devoted. Sita, regarded as an incarnation of Lakshmi (Vishnu's consort), is the supreme model of the traditional Hindu wife, utterly pure and loyal. Hanuman's loyalty is also extolled, and he has come to be seen as the incarnation of supreme devotion, being one of the most worshipped deities in all of India, especially in the northern and central regions where shrines dedicated to him are quite common. In some cases, he is shown with his breast torn open to reveal Rama and Sita reigning in his heart.

Krishna's languid poses, his impudent charm, and his effortless omnipotence fascinate India because they are like the beguiling paradoxes of God. Indeed, he is God himself, and when he came to Earth long ago to counter the decline of righteousness, he brought with him the whole sensuous and rapturous ambience of his highest heaven—slow rivers; gemlike flowers cascading everywhere; the frolics of the *gopis*, or milkmaids, who eternally love him—all under a moon as big as one remembered from a childhood summer evening.

His name means "The Dark One" or "The All Attractive One." His commonest title is Govinda, popularly regarded as meaning "Cowherd" or "Cow Finder." Because of attempts of the king, Kansa, to kill him, Krishna was brought up by a plain cowherd family. The homely tales of his youth are full of milk, butter, and the warm smells of cattle barns. In this simple and relatively innocent world, Krishna is delightfully naughty and much beloved.

Krishna appears in three basic modes: the marvelous infant, the divine lover, and the great hero of the Bhagavad-Gita.

As an adorable but mischievous infant, Krishna was given to transcendent pranks. He once ate some dirt, and when his irritated mother opened his mouth to check on it, she saw there the entire universe. He then stole some butter, but when his exasperated mother sought to tie him up in punishment, no matter how much rope she used, it was never quite enough.

Legs flexed and eyes half-closed, Krishna, as divine lover, would sound his flute deep in the woods, and the *gopis* (milkmaids) burning with intermingled human and divine love, would leave their legitimate husbands and dash into the forest of delights to revel with the young God—for the devotees of Krishna agreed with the troubadours of the Age of Chivalry in the West that extramarital love is a closer simile for the love of the worshipper for God than the nuptial tie. The former is a passion freely given for the beloved's sake and with no heed for the cost in shame and suffering, while the latter was (in old India and medieval Europe) probably a legal bond arranged in childhood by the families without regard for the individual's feelings.

Krishna, playing his flute, with Radha, his favorite gopi.

Deep in the forest, Krishna would dance with the *gopis*, miraculously multiplying himself so that each would think she alone was his partner. Or he would hide himself and make the *gopis* seek him—pining—so that the celebration might be all the greater when he was found. Or he would steal the devotees' clothes while they were bathing in the river, to have them show their pure trust by emerging naked. In all that he did, Krishna was as capricious and infatuating as a coy lover, for God also seems capable of playing cruel tricks on humans; yet we, like the *gopis*, continue to run after God, accept his changing moods, and feel something lifeless in us till we have once danced in abandon with him.

The Srimad Bhagavatam, the classic text of the life of Krishna that beautifully combines luminous simplicity with hints of the divine profundity beneath its surface, tells us:

Sri Krishna is the embodiment of love. Love is divine, and is expressed in many forms. To Yasoda his foster-mother, the God of Love was her own baby Krishna; to the shepherd boys, Krishna was their beloved friend and playmate; and to the shepherd girls, Krishna was their beloved friend, lover, and companion.

When Sri Krishna played on his flute, the shepherd girls forgot everything; unconscious even of their own bodies, they ran to him, drawn by his great love. Once Krishna, to test their devotion to him, said to them, "O ye pure ones, your duties must be first to your husbands and children. Go back to your homes and live in their service. You need not come to me. For if you only meditate on me, you will gain salvation." But the shepherd girls replied, "O thou cruel lover, we desire to serve only thee! Thou knowest the scriptural truths, and thou dost advise us to serve our husbands and children. So let it be; we shall abide by thy teaching. Since thou art in all, and art all, by serving thee we shall serve them also."

Krishna, who gives delight to all and who is blissful in his own being, divided himself into as many Krishnas as there were shepherd girls, and danced and played with them. Each girl felt the divine presence and divine love of Sri Krishna. Each felt herself the most blessed. Each one's love for Sri Krishna was so absorbing that she felt herself one with Krishna—nay, knew herself to be Krishna.

Truly has it been said that those who meditate on the divine love of Sri Krishna, and upon the sweet relationship between him and the shepherd girls, become free from lust and from sensuality.[19]

The preceding excerpt shows the very heart of Krishna bhakti devotion—this loss of self in the Divine through the rapture of passionate love until oneself, others, and the whole world become Krishna. His favorite among the milkmaids was the lovely Radha, whose image often stands beside his.

However, he could not continue forever on Earth—although he did continue in his heavenly world—in these pastimes of a divine youth. The time came for him to take up arms, to slay the wicked king Kansa, to take over Kansa's kingdom and later another, and to work against the forces of evil. He slew demons all over India, took part (as we have seen) in the great battle of the Mahabharata, during which he delivered the Bhagavad-Gita. He was a worthy and magnificent ruler. Rukmini, a princess of Berar, became his chief queen among 16,018 wives, and he had ten sons with each wife.

This happy estate, however, was not to last. In a scenario reminiscent of European mythology but oddly unique in India, Krishna's chief men fell into a drunken brawl and soon had the whole capital city in a tumult. Krishna's chief son and best friends were all slain in the rioting. Unable to stop this disintegration into chaos, Krishna left the city to wander dejectedly alone in the woods. There a hunter accidentally killed him as he sat meditating. As with Achilles, his heel was his only vulnerable spot, and there an arrow struck. He then returned to his eternal spiritual world.

Krishna's story, then, begins with a divine infancy, a flight, and a murder of innocents, all reminiscent of Christianity, and ends on a note more suggestive of Greek tragedy or some bleak Nordic myth than a tale from mystic India. But, in between, the aura of divine mystery about the pranks of infancy and the dalliance of love evokes the warm maternalism and poetic passions of India.

Above all, in the worship of Krishna, devotees lose themselves in graceful dance and chanting to exciting music. Women place images of the infant Krishna in tiny cribs, and while calling themselves "mothers of the God," they rock him back and forth as an expression of love. In devotional services, images of Krishna and Radha are often put together on the swing the bride and groom share in Hindu weddings and are rocked back and forth. Always, the motive is put in terms of casting aside self-restraint and just asking, "What more can I do to show my love? What more can I do to please the beloved God, to make myself his indulgent mother, lover, or companion?"[20]

Devotion to Vishnu, Rama, and Krishna takes equally expressive forms. *Vaisnavas*, devotees of Vishnu or one of his forms, tend to be vegetarian, and flesh offerings are not used in their worship, only plant and dairy products. Some mark themselves with a V-shaped symbol on the forehead and perhaps on the upper arm.

The Shiva-Shakti Family of Devotional Gods

The Shiva-Shakti family has a different feel about it. Instead of sunny Vishnu, heroic Rama, and playful Krishna, here is a fierce ascetic crowned with the mysterious moon, or a wild dancer whose hair is serpents, or one whose presence is simply the heavy stone pillar of the *Lingam*. Rama is allied with an army of monkeys, but Shiva is companioned by a retinue of ghosts, and instead of the decorous Lakshmi or the charming Radha, his consort is Shakti who may manifest herself as the grim Kali, with bulging eyes and tongue hanging out to lap the blood of her victims.

Yet the Shiva-Shakti family is also comprised of deities of immense power, mystic depth, and ultimate goodness. The difference is that while the Vishnu family, like the Western monotheistic God, represents all that is good, the Shiva-Shakti family represents simply the All, the totality, the union that lies beyond all dualities of matter and spirit, creation and destruction: their "goodness" lies in the wisdom that comes from initiation into this ultimate unity.[21]

Dancing Shiva or "Auspicious One" representing Absolute Being as "Lord of the Dance."

Shiva Nataraja, Tamil Nadu, India, 13th Century, Chola period (ca. 890-1279). Bronze, 34 1/4 × 27 1/2 × 13 inches

Shiva is descended from the deity of the Vedas named Rudra. A cross-grained God who lived by himself in the mountains and who sang and danced in his solitude, Rudra could capriciously bestow healing herbs or send an epidemic. Worshippers called him Shiva ("Auspicious One") more in fearful hope than in trusting love, for his lonely power was great. Shiva seems then to have assimilated much of the mystic and yogic divinity of the ancient indigenous cultures of the Indus Valley. In a late Upanishad, he is already called the All—and, indeed, to those who lack the eye of wisdom, the universe itself does seem to sing and dance like a mountain madman with more zest than moral precision.

Shiva, serpent-entwined, is a much more enigmatic figure than Vishnu; one is less sure how to read his subtle, ambivalent smile. His four most important representations are the Lord of the Dance, the Master Yogi, the Ultimate Teacher, and the *Lingam*. As Lord of the Dance, he dances with perfect equilibrium and pounds his drum down through all the changes of the world until the time comes for an age of the world to end; he then beats the drum louder and louder until its vibrations shatter the cosmos into its primal elements.

As the Master Yogi, he is enthroned high in the Himalayas, on skull-faced Mount Kailas, his body covered with the white ash that symbolizes the ascetic's burning away of passion. The deity sits on a tiger skin pallet; his symbol, the trident staff, is in place beside him; the holy Ganges River leaps off the topknot of his long matted hair. He is sunk deep in meditation, and his concentrated thought sustains the world; if he were to cease his meditation for even a moment, the world would begin to vanish like a dream and leave not a trace behind. The story is told, in fact, that once his wife, Parvati, came up behind him and playfully put her hands over his eyes—but removed them in a hurry when she saw the mountains and forests fade and the sun and stars start to blink out.

Or as the cosmic being, the sheer life force, and the sole reality that underlies all that is, Shiva can be simplified and abstracted still further, to the still, upright column of the *Lingam*—the pivot on which the wheel of the universe turns or the phallus of an unquenchable will to live or the infinite pillar of light or fire of Upanishad stories.

As Shiva represents absolute Being, Shakti (or Power) is the whole of the phenomenal world, in all its bounty, danger, and change, forever wedded to the Absolute. She is thus a being of fierce splendor and power, equal to Shiva just as, in an even deeper sense, the two are one. She is the fullness of the Eternal Divine Feminine, the Goddess, the Great Mother and Mistress in all her moods, and she goes by countless names.

As Parvati, she is the world at rosy dawn, nature at its gentlest and loveliest. As Annapurna, she is the bountiful mother, the Goddess of food and abundant harvest. But as Durga, the coloration shifts a bit. Durga is good and slew a mighty demon, but the Great Goddess in this form is more chancy: she proudly rides a lion and wields a great sword. It is in this latter form that she is said to be most accessible to her devotees today.

Finally, in the form of Kali, Shakti is also good and the object of the devotion of mild and wise saints. But she is good in a dark way that only the wise can understand—for on the face of it, she is time and death. She bears a sword and carries the severed head of a victim said to be a demon, killed out of mercy lest his bad *karma* become too weighty. Her tongue hangs out; around her waist are the arms of other victims, and their severed heads are garlanded around her neck. She is dark, often standing or dancing on the prostrate white body of Shiva, the passive Absolute whose being she draws upon. She is worshipped with offerings of male goats slain in her temples, and in the past, was presented human sacrifice.

Thus, Kali is the world of appearances, the world of time, change, and multiplicity. In it, all that comes into being is sooner or later destroyed. So it is said that Kali will give birth to a child, fondle it at her breast, and then wring its neck. The ways of Kali are not pleasant to contemplate, and one may wonder why such a Goddess would be worshipped. Although the deities of other traditions, including the Western, also have their dark sides, India is unrivaled in its exuberance of expression of both the light and dark colors of the sacred.

Statue of Kali.

But there are those who say that until Kali is fully understood and loved, one cannot truly find peace or know God, for peace and God are beyond the vicissitudes of creation and destruction, so one must confront them and pass through them first. They say Kali is standing there with her blood and her victims, and one cannot simply go around her; one day a person on the way to liberation must face her squarely, if not embrace her.

Devotees of Shiva are called *Shaivas*. Ascetics of this tradition live austere lives. They cover themselves with white ash to symbolize the ascetic's burning away of the passions, and they put three white horizontal bars across the forehead as a symbol of Shiva to whom they are devoted. Devotees of Shakti (as Kali), called *Shaktas*, focus on the worship of the Great Mother. Forgetting Shiva, *Shaktas* hold that in Kali alone is the power of the universe and the wellspring of bliss.[22] And, as we have seen, in Tantric practices, Shiva and Shakti are worshipped together in a unique way.

The Mixing of the Families of Gods and Goddesses, and the "Holy Trinity."

Although, generally, the Gods and Goddesses are known in these families, one studying Hinduism should not be attached to a too-neat categorization of the Hindu Gods and Goddesses. In practice, one will find the Shiva-Shakti family of Gods and Goddesses together with the Vishnu-Lakshmi family of Gods and Goddesses in the same shrine or temple, although nearly always one God, one Goddess, or one divine couple is prominent. In addition, many stories bring Gods and Goddesses from different families together, and some of the stories vary in their telling, if not in the message they convey. One is the story of Brahma's creation of the world. In one version of the story, his first wife, Savitri, is delayed, requiring Brahma to marry Gayatri so he can complete the required ceremony; in another version, it is Sarasvati, the Goddess of wisdom and the arts, who is the delayed first wife. One important example of the mixing of the families of the devotional Gods and their various aspects is what many Hindus refer to as the "Holy Trinity" of Hinduism (the *Trimurti*) and the particular way that the Gods are understood in it: Brahma, the Creator; Vishnu, the Preserver; and Shiva (here as Rudra), the Destroyer. Yet in devotional practice, Shiva is all of these aspects and more.

Devotionalism in the Meeting of Hinduism and Islam

Another style of devotionalism emerged at the very end of the Middle Ages—on the spiritual frontier between Hinduism and Islam. The faith of Muhammad was then coming into India in force, together with Muslim rulers. Eventually as many as a fifth of the people of India—the present populations of Pakistan and Bangladesh, as well as a scattered minority in what is now the Republic of India—became Muslim. Some were drawn by Islam's practical advantages, the greater simplicity of this faith without image or caste, and the attractiveness of many of its Sufi preachers and mystics.

Others, however, were converted by coercion, even violence, when many Hindu temples were demolished and public celebration of Hindu festivals was prohibited.

Nevertheless, the majority of Hindus, especially those of higher caste, remained Hindu and indeed became very conservative about it. The meeting of two cultures alien to each other, like Islam and Hinduism, produces two kinds of reaction. Some, generally the great majority, will respond with a conservative withdrawal into their own culture or faith—especially if they are also politically subjugated; indeed, they will say, "They can take everything else from me; they will not take my faith," and they will cling to their faith all the more tenaciously and inflexibly. The ultratraditionalism for which Hindu society was famous until recently—rigid adherence to caste, rite, and the authority of past models of life and relationships of the people—was not so much the heritage of the great creative periods of ancient India as it was a response, understandable in context, to the more recent centuries of Muslim and British rule, when Hinduism was the only possible vehicle for a Hindu sense of identity.

For others, the confrontation of faiths effects a different reaction. These are sensitive souls who say, "If one faith claims one truth and another a different truth, then is not everything we have taken for granted thrown into question? Perhaps reality is instead a truth beyond them both." There are some, from the great Moghal emperor Akbar (r. 1556–1605) to lowly weavers and washerwomen, who out of this situation were driven to adore God beyond all particular places and rigidities of orthodoxy. The wandering ecstatic of God in all persons and places, who is loved in a *bhaktic* way, became a new and attractive style of pilgrim. A good example is the poet Kabir (1440–1518), who was born into a Muslim family but was spiritually nurtured by a Hindu guru. Alluding to the Kaaba (**Ka'bah**) in Mecca, the center of Muslim devotion, and to Mount Kailas in Tibet, venerated as the abode of Shiva and a place of Hindu pilgrimage, he sings:

> *O servant, where dost thou seek Me?*
>
> *Lo! I am beside thee.*
>
> *I am neither in temple nor in mosque: I am neither in Kaaba nor in Kailash:*
>
> *Neither am I in rites and ceremonies, nor in Yoga and renunciation.*
>
> *If thou art a true seeker, thou shalt at once see Me; thou shalt meet Me in a moment of time.*
>
> *Kabir says, "O Sadhu! God is the breath of all breath."*
>
> *It is needless to ask of a saint the caste to which he belongs;*
>
> *For the priest, the warrior, the tradesman, and all the thirty-six castes, alike are seeking for God.*
>
> *It is but folly to ask what the caste of a saint may be;*
>
> *The barber has sought God, the washerwoman, and the carpenter...*
>
> *Hindus and Moslems alike have achieved that End, where remains no mark of distinction.*
>
> *If God be within the mosque, then to whom does this world belong?*
>
> *If Ram be within the image which you find upon your pilgrimage, then who is there to know what happens without?*
>
> *Hari is in the East: Allah is in the West. Look within your heart, there you will find both Karim and Ram;*
>
> *All the men and women of the world are His living forms.*
>
> *Kabir is the child of Allah and of Ram: He is my Guru, He is my Pir.*[23]

A comparable mystic poet was Nanak, founder of the Sikh religion and a follower of the teachings of Kabir. We will turn to **Sikhism** later.

Devotionalism in the Meeting of East and West

Hinduism has undergone slow changes in modern times, as it has all through its long history. Just as the meeting of Hinduism and Islam produced challenges, so the basic problem of thinking Hindus from the nineteenth century to the twenty-first century has been the meeting of Hindu and Western values. How can the ancient faith respond to Western science, education, democracy, and the economic and social dislocations they bring? How does Hinduism fit in among the religions of the world? Dealing with questions like these while living in two worlds at once has led Hindu intellectuals to produce a fascinating array of new philosophical and spiritual options, some of which have had considerable influence in the West.

One great influence was Ramakrishna (1836–1886). Not an intellectual himself, this Bengali was in many ways a traditional Indian saint and mystic, deeply devoted to Kali, the Great Mother, and able to go into deep, ecstatic trance, all the while profoundly aware of God in all things. Yet he was also aware of modern religious pluralism. He intentionally tried and experienced from within several religious traditions, including Islam and Christianity, finding to his own satisfaction that all religions are of the same essence and are paths to God realization. Disciples of his, particularly Swami Vivekananda (1862–1902), brought his message to the West. In his writings and in the work of the Ramakrishna Order, Vivekananda did much to make Vedantic Hinduism and the mysticism of Ramakrishna an intellectually vigorous and compassionate faith relevant to the modern world both in India and the West.

THE PRACTICE OF HINDUISM TODAY

When I* was in Jaipur, India, I woke early and made my way to the Govind Dev Ji Temple for morning *darshan* (vision of the Divine). The curtains were drawn across the enclave in the altar where the priests were preparing Krishna and Radha in a sanctifying ritual of flowers, milk, oil, spices, and adornment of the deities in fine, colorful, sparkling robes and headdresses—all out of the view of the devotees congregating in the great hall. The gathering devotees joined in beautiful chanting to the rhythm of deep drumming while facing the altar's curtains, which concealed the deities, and while holding flowers in anticipation of seeing their God. As anticipation grew, the chanting swelled and hundreds of celebrants joined with more and more voices and clapping hands in the joyful song for the Divine.

Then, suddenly, as if by surprise, the curtains opened to reveal Krishna and Radha arrayed in their splendor, while the celebrants gasped or cried out with joy to see with their own eyes this beautiful manifestation of Divinity and to be seen by Krishna and Radha, too. The chanting and clapping continued even more strongly as the community of devotees offered their flowers to the priests to adorn the deities. What a beautiful way to begin the day!

Such rituals have been practiced for millennia, as the long past we have looked at in this text so far is still present in India. Much has been poured into the melting pot of Indian culture over the millennia, but little has been lost. The earliest continues alongside the latest, as jet planes bring seekers of the sacred from all over the world. Let us look at some of these phenomena.

---

*Barbara McGraw

Temples

Temples are ubiquitous in India. One can hardly turn a corner and not find a shrine or a small or great temple with elaborate carvings and depictions of deities.

The temple, through the medium of art and architecture rather than that of a human life, bespeaks the Divine. Even as one approaches it, one senses the nearness of another kind of realm. Here are lively people in a festive mood, and here are special shops selling flowers for offerings. The temple may be alive with monkeys and birds, with sacred cows grazing on the lawn, but it is also a throne room, and a brilliant image of deities or a *Lingam* and a *Yoni* stands toward the back. The arrangement and the schedule of the temple are those of a king in his court, and the sanctuary containing the main divine image is called the *garbha* or the "womb." The deity is awakened in the early morning with conch trumpets, is given his or her meals with regal ceremony, and is presented entertainments of music and dance. There is even a siesta at midday when the curtains about his or her throne are closed. At regular hours, the deity holds court; then his or her subjects come for *puja* (worshipful ritual offerings) with their gifts, most commonly wreaths of flowers, which are handed to a priest who is customarily bare-chested, except for the Brahmin's sacred thread, and who takes the flowers to drape them over the deity. The priest receives a token payment and often bestows a blessing on the worshipper by placing a touch of color, known as a *tilaka*, on the forehead.

The interior of many temples is splendid and colorful, suggesting the heavenly delights of the pure realms of the deities, who in turn shatter like prisms the clear light of the Absolute into these gay hues. The deities, too, suggest that beyond mere purity is the playful delight of the Divine, rolling out world after world. This warm and vivid atmosphere, of a piece with India's rain and sun, remains deeply impressed on a visitor long afterward.

The typical Western church, in comparison, is more lifeless but for cut flowers, and it is tightly sealed against all nonhuman life. But through feast, sacrifice, or offering, the throbbing and dying life of the universe flows in and out of the Hindu temple like a vast tide of monkeys, cows, birds, flowers, and fruit. Indeed, the temples themselves with their knobby, often intricately carved shapes seem almost more botanical than architectural. Like Hindu society itself, they grow out of the soil of India like prodigious plants, reaching away from nature yet still linked to its maternal arteries.

Home Rites

In a devout Indian household, the day begins early. It is understandable that dawn should seem the most apt time for worship in India. Not only is it natural that one should turn to God at the beginning of a day's activities, but the Indian dawn also has a special quality. Except in winter, the day soon enough becomes wearisomely hot, muggy, or dusty. But for a short time, just before and during sunrise, it is as though an enchantment has fallen over the ancient land. The air is limpid, fresh, and inviting; dew gems the grass; all is as still and hopeful as the deep meditation of Shiva just before a new world streams forth from his thoughts. At this hour, the head of the household arises, splashes himself with water, and going out on his porch or rooftop, says his morning prayers, such as the Gayatri mantra, a hymn to the sun. He may place on his body sacred marks, indicating the deity of which he is a devotee, who represents his "chosen ideal."

He then proceeds to the household shrine of the chosen deity, maintained by his wife. There he performs morning *puja* with his wife, who assists her husband especially in preparing the offerings to be presented. (When her husband is not present, she may conduct all of the home rites, and in many homes, she may present the food and conduct some of the rites, even when her husband is present.) Then there are ritual chanting of praise and mantra of the deity, presentation of cups of water, the washing of the image, and offerings of food. There may also be study and meditation. In a deeper sense, through the ritual, the wife honors the Divine through her husband, as the family priest and the family deity become identified; and the husband honors his wife as the Divine Shakti—the power that animates the family.

The household, in fact, is the real center of Hinduism, although, of course, its religious life is rarely seen by the foreign visitor, unlike that of the spectacular temples. But many devout Hindus never go to public temples. They express their faith through home customs and rites. To follow the home rites of one's caste and lineage is expected for social standing, at least in such matters as coming-of-age and marriage; worship at the temple is much more a matter of personal preference.

In the upper castes, there are **samskaras**, or sacraments, that mark the stages of life for boys and that are marked by appropriate family ceremonies with a Brahmin officiating: the child's birth, his first eating of solid food, his first haircut, and his attainment of manhood, when he is invested with the sacred cord. In some households today, similar rituals of passage are conducted for girls as well.

Weddings

No occasion is greater in Hindu family life than a wedding. Neither man nor woman is considered complete until married. But for a woman, the marriage ceremony is the decisive event in her life.

A Hindu marriage involves a long and elaborate ceremony, often at the bride's home, which can last several days. The groom may arrive, arrayed in red and gold robes, wearing a colorful turban and with a canopy of corresponding colors overhead. If the family can afford it, during the last part of the groom's journey, he will be accompanied by a band and will be seated on a decorated horse at the end of a long procession of numerous, bright, electrically lit candelabra (generator in tow) lighting up the streets and with drums (and sometimes fireworks) booming. Upon the groom's arrival at the entrance of the place where the ceremony will occur, the men of both families join in celebratory dancing, while tossing money in the air to invoke the blessings of prosperity for the bride and groom.

Later, there are offerings and formal meetings of the two families and the bride and the groom (who if they are from very traditional families, would not have seen each other before the wedding day). The bride, too, is usually dressed in red and gold, which are especially auspicious colors, in an elaborately decorated *sari* of swaths of sweeping material and detailed embroidery, with a matching veil and a gold-colored crown or headband. As lavish a feast as can be made is provided for the numerous guests, because weddings, whether for rich or poor, bind the new couple with a whole community of extended family and friends.

There are vivid rites, depending on the community and region of the couple. These rites might include the bride and groom sitting together on a swing and later binding their hands to each other, and the bride and groom's reciting of the *Saptha Padhi* (the Seven Steps). While taking each of the seven steps together around *agni* (the sacred fire), the bride and groom make these corresponding promises: to share healthy, abundant food; to be strong in body, mind, and spirit; to be prosperous while following *dharma*; to be happy and harmonious; to be blessed with good children; to exercise self-control; to live a long, comfortable, and peaceful life together; and to be friends through life.

Hindu wedding with guests throwing rice grains over the couple to symbolize abundance and good fortune.

Funerals

Funerals are not generally performed by Brahmins, at least not by those of high status. Although a member of a class of funeral priests may officiate, the chief functionary at a funeral of a man is the deceased's eldest son, who lights his father's funeral pyre and who, in some traditions, when the skull becomes red hot, cracks it with a stick. The ashes are then thrown into a sacred river. The most famous cremation site lies in Varanasi (Benares), where the fires have burned continuously since time immemorial. Even if it is not possible to bring a body to Varanasi, the ashes may later be brought to that site, and thousands of Hindus travel to Varanasi when they are mortally ill, in the hope that they will die and be cremated there.

The funeral fire reminds us of the Vedic sacrificial fire and tells us that death is but another stage in the cycle of conception and consumption through which the sacred fire dances. The sacramental structure of life and the role of the eldest son suggest the organic, biological view of life of which we have also spoken.

Caste

Another usage that suggests the biological view of life is the caste system. Caste presents its own paradox: on the one hand, it suggests the organic unity of life, while on the other, it suggests a desire for symbols of separateness, with each group in its own place and not eating or marrying outside a small unit. Although the ancient classification of society had only four great orders, the practical division of modern society resulted in thousands of sub-castes, known as *jati*, literally "births," each with their own caste rules. They range from various types of Brahmins through bankers, silversmiths, and farmers, and down to the "untouchables," to whose lot falls such tasks as sweeping, washing, and tanning hides.

The real principle of division is not occupation, as many think, but commensality—who can cook food for whom, who can eat with whom, and by extension, who can marry whom, or, for that matter, who can even come near to whom without pollution. It is a question of relative purity and impurity. One is made impure by contact with a member of a lower caste—sharing water or food, being touched by the lower one's spittle. These contacts would require ritual purification. A basic principle is that products of the body pollute; thus barbers and washermen, handling hair and grime from human bodies, are low on the caste scale.

Discrimination on the basis of caste has been abolished legally in modern India, though attitudes based on it remain in many places, and it is still entrenched in family relations, especially in marriage.

Water

Water has great symbolic and spiritual power in India, as a purifier and as a transformative medium. The main places of pilgrimage, like Varanasi and Haridwar, lie near rivers, lakes, or the sea.

The Ganges is the most sacred water of all. That great river is the Divine herself, the Goddess Ganga, who flows through Shiva to bless the millions who have turned to her for sustenance and spiritual renewal for millennia. Hindus in the millions throng to bathe in the Ganges River, and each evening at sunset, the people gather at the river to sing beautiful chants in *aarti* (prayers) with fire and smoke, bright-colored lights, and the ringing of bells.

As mentioned above, the dead are cremated at the river's shores. The ashes of the dead are scattered into that sacred river, returning them to the eternal flow where the cycle of birth and death become one with the river.

Sangams (confluences) of sacred rivers also have special significance throughout India. At the Sangam at Prayag (Allahabad) of the Ganges and Yamuna rivers and the now ancient, lost Sarasvati River (located by tradition here), a small boat

Aarti at the Ganges River, Haridwar, India.

Devout Hindus bathing in the sacred Ganges River.

rowed by a local villager takes one on a peaceful, almost silent journey to meet the rivers at their exact confluence with its unmistakable cross-waves. There one will find a string of boats all across the river where priests are available to those who seek the blessings of the rivers. The Kumbh Mela, a major month-long festival held at Prayag (and at three other holy places in India, each on its own twelve year cycle), sometimes draws millions of people for the celebrations, especially at Prayag. During the festival that occurred there in 2001, an estimated 20–25 million people attended on the day of the new moon with as many as 70 million people (by some estimates) attending sometime during the month, and estimates are even higher for that festival in 2013.

Sadhus

Since caste itself is founded on a sense of the pure versus the impure, we get a glimmer of that basic thinking in terms of dualisms or polarities that carry up to the distinction of *dharma* and *moksha*. But some things are simply pure and purifying in themselves; they stand as symbols of transition, on the borderline between the realm of *dharma* and that of *moksha*.

Visible reminders of the *moksha* side of things are the numerous *sadhus*, the holy renunciants or wandering ascetics of India. Virtually every Hindu village and homestead may from time to time have strange, yet familiar, visitors. They may be sons from the house or the village, or they may have come from far away. But they will no longer be bound by family ties or have any claim other than charity upon the support of anyone.

The *sadhu* has, in principle, cut himself loose from society to be free for the greatest of quests. For what he represents—even if personally unworthy—he is welcomed and fed, his blessing sought and his curse feared. *Sadhus* have no centralized discipline like that of Western monastics, although most do acknowledge the absolute authority of their own *guru* or in a few cases, the absolute authority of an order. A *sadhu* may in turn establish his own "family," for disciples may join him, and devout lay people may seek him out and become his spiritual pupils. To these, the *sadhu* becomes formally a *guru*; he initiates them into his method, be it Vedantic, Tantric, or devotional. He takes on the burden of the disciples' karma and becomes their means of grace; followers worship the "lotus feet" of their *guru*. As the means to God for them, he becomes their personification and presence of God.

The way of life among *sadhus* varies greatly. Some wander as of old from village to village, teaching and begging. Some frequent temples and pilgrimage sites, where they seek alms and instruct others in the appropriate devotions. Many are childlike, jovial spirits, going in merry bands from festival to festival. Others are unspeaking recluses deep in the woods, known only to a few who supply their meager needs. Some are charlatans, some are crazed, some are wise and learned, and some are true saints. Some were born to the holy life and have really followed no other. Some were prominent in business or civic affairs and only made the renunciation late in life. Some are devotees of Vishnu, wearing the V-shaped marks; others wear the three horizontal bars of Shiva and cover themselves with white ash. Traditionally, the ochre robe is the token of asceticism; some wear it, while others wear rags or nothing at all. Some shave their heads; others wear hair and beard as long and matted as old vines. But all are part of the pageant of Hinduism and are venerated by traditional Hindus. Insofar as they are God-realized, they are God, for they have become transparent to the God within, who is as much God as God anywhere. God is believed to be nowhere more present and visible than in Great Souls: to venerate them is to venerate God. Their diversity and the strangeness of some of them only bespeak the mystery and infinity of the Divine Sea, whose waves crest in its lovers.

Festivals

Hinduism is an especially festive religion. In fact, there are so many holy festivals throughout India that one can lose count. Hindu festivals commemorate the heroes and heroines of myth and history, the changing of the seasons, Gods and Goddesses, gurus, sacred places, and more.

The most widely celebrated holy day is Diwali, the festival of lights, which begins on the day before a new moon in the fall. Numerous stories are taken up in Diwali, involving Rama, Krishna, Lakshmi, Yama, and others. But mainly the holiday celebrates family and community harmony and the triumph of good over evil. Many colored lanterns are lit in homes and communities, and sumptuous feasts of special sweets and savory treats are served. Customarily, Diwali sweets and blessings are sent to family and friends.

The playful Holi festival of colors, which marks the new moon near the beginning of spring, invokes the colors of nature's bounty. The night before, bonfires are lit in neighborhoods throughout India's cities, towns, and villages to signify leaving behind all that impedes one as one embarks on spring's renewal. It is a kind of spiritual spring cleaning. Then, on Holi (which in some parts of India lasts several days), the multitude of colors takes over with smiles in abundance. "Children" of all ages take to the streets, splashing each other—friends, neighbors, even strangers—with brightly colored water, sometimes squirted with water pistols, and colored powders are thrown in the air. To be out in the street, especially wearing white, is an invitation to play! Stories of Krishna and Radha are especially enjoyed at Holi, reminding everyone of Divine love and that the Divine is found in fun, laughter, friendship, community bonds, song, dance, and all of the joys of life.

Many festivals celebrate and invoke special blessings of specific deities. The Krishna Jayanthi, Navaratri, Mahasivarati, and Rama Navami are a few examples. Navaratri festivals involve the celebration and reverence of the Goddess Shakti, as the Divine Mother of All. Starting on a new moon in September or October, the Fall Navaratri continues for nine days and nine nights, during which Shakti is venerated in several forms: as Durga, Lakshmi, or Sarasvati, depending on local custom. Offerings are made of sweets and nuts; artistic skills are displayed; and blessings are sought for courage, prosperity, fertility, wisdom, and inspiration, as well as for the consecration of the tools of one's livelihood. Women's friendships are especially honored at this time. As in much of Hindu practice, there is joyful music, dance, and chanting. In many places, on the tenth day, Durga's victory over a famous demon is celebrated—a story that evokes the overcoming of ignorance and selfishness.

Cows

An unforgettable sight confronting every traveler to India is that of innumerable white, humpbacked cows wandering freely about streets, marketplaces, and all but the busiest sections of cities. The sensitive observer may see in the cows' warm and much-beloved frames, which appear in the most unlikely places, a different concept of the relation of human and animal from that of the West, one of living together rather than the superiority of human over beast. Mohandas Gandhi, with his keen, non-Western perception, once remarked that the cow is really the most universal Hindu symbol, and cow protection its most expressive principle. Hindus, he said, may agree on nothing else, but they unite on the veneration and protection of the cow, a token of maternity, simplicity, nonmaterialism, and nonviolence. The products of the cow—its milk, its urine, and even its dung—are purifying and are therefore used in purificatory rites.

Vegetarianism

Not only do Hindus eschew the slaughter and eating of cows, many Hindus are vegetarians. Many Hindus hold that killing animals violates *ahimsa*, the nonviolence and nonharming principle in Hinduism, and they believe that the killing and eating of animals and fish leads to negative *karma* and impedes the clear consciousness needed for spiritual advancement. There is support in the Mahabharata for a vegetarian diet in its injunctions against violence and eating flesh (Mahabharata 115:40).

Ashrams and Swamis

Hinduism in India, and in fact throughout the world, is known for its ashrams—places of meditation and sanctuary where the seeker of the sacred may stay for a day or a lifetime. Sometimes

One of India's ubiquitous wandering cows.

the ashram houses only those who have taken monastic vows. But often they are yoga retreat centers for meditation and yogic exercises, as well as for learning one or more of the many spiritual traditions of Hinduism. Often the ashram is the abode of a swami or a revered saint whose work is dedicated there.

Swamis are men or women who have taken ascetic, monastic vows to dedicate themselves to a particular Hindu tradition—usually through a guru, although they may espouse a new spiritual revelation, which forms a new or breakaway tradition. A swami may remain alone at his or her monastic home or allow visits by spiritual seekers there, or may travel throughout the world to share his or her wisdom.

The Parmarth Niketan Ashram is the abode of H. H. Pujya Swami Chidanand Sarawatiji and his dedicated followers in Rishikesh, India. Here visitors meditate and find peace amid gardens filled with statuary scenes of the activities of the Gods and Goddesses, share vegetarian meals in silence,

Shiva statue on the banks of the Ganges River near the Parmarth Ashram in Rishikesh, India.

take yoga posture classes, and receive the wisdom of the teachings. And every evening at sunset, they join in chanting and *aarti* (prayers) at the bank of the Ganges River, which flows only a minute's walk from the ashram's gate. Through an archway depicting a scene from the Bhagavad-Gita of Krishna and Arjuna in a chariot drawn by charging horses, visitors descend to a point where there are steps on which they can sit, chanting prayers and passing the plates of fire and incense from one to another. And just across the river they see the beautiful white statue of Shiva in meditative repose with Goddess Ganges on his head and the river itself below—his youth, strength and vigor bringing confidence that the world will be sustained regardless of the particular vicissitudes of the moment.

HINDUISM, GOVERNANCE, AND POLITICAL LIFE

Classical Concepts: Dharma and the Holy Kingship

Hinduism, as we have seen, did not arise out of the mission of a particular founder, as did, for example, Buddhism, Christianity, and Islam. Instead, it emerged from the cultural traditions of the ancient inhabitants of the land now called India, which had been informed by the Vedas, the Upanishads, and other subsequent texts, such as the Bhagavad-Gita and the Puranas. In them, religion, governance, and political life were not understood as separate phenomena but as aspects of the sociocultural whole. When aligned with *dharma* (the social order that reflects the cosmic order), that sociocultural whole would exist in harmony and righteousness and would avoid descent into chaos. In its classic expression, the foundation of government is a moral vision, inseparable from religion, where everyone participates in ways appropriate to their station—or caste—to uphold the *dharma*. Classic Hindu literature reflects the central role of a holy kingship. The king, properly of the *kshatriya* (warrior/ruler) caste, has specific obligations and prerogatives consistent with his status in the grand hierarchical order of caste. And government conforming to the *dharma* would be *Ram Rajya* (the rule of God).

So now imagine the dramatic procession of a traditional Indian king—rajah or maharajah— as he presented himself to his subjects. In western India, in particular, you would hear thundering footsteps and see the long line of elephants with their bright caparisons and many-colored banners, the most splendid of all bearing the noble ruler waving to the awestruck crowds. After touring the capital, as was his occasional wont, he would return to his many-towered palace, with its legendary storerooms of treasures and women's quarters.

Yet for all its opulence, the king's pomp and magnificence was not for himself alone. In principle, he was just as much a servant of *dharma*, the right eternal order of things, as the Brahmin or the shudra peasant. His pageantry bespoke his place in the universe as surely as the Brahmin's ritual did his, and like Arjuna in the Bhagavad-Gita, he had to fulfill his duty whether it was to his taste or not. Indeed, it was the Brahmins' obligation to see that he did, for the temporal was subject to the spiritual, and the priests were his monitors. The king's duty—*rajadharma*—was not to innovate, for righteous law had been set from the beginning and had been laid out in the sacred texts. His obligation was to maintain order and protect his people, as well as to see that law was followed and justice administered in accordance with *Ram Rajya*. Furthermore, the king was himself to be an exemplar of virtue, showing self-restraint in temperament and personal morality. Insofar as he does so, he is like God on Earth, in the image of Rama, the ideal warrior king of the Ramayana.

Such kings continued even during the more than two centuries of British rule, for a number of them were maintained as colorful but subordinate rulers by the British administration. But by independence in 1947, history had largely passed them by, although the succession of maharajas and maharanis (kings and queens) of various principalities remains today. The leaders at the forefront of the independence movement were mostly motivated by other ideologies: democracy in the Western sense, socialism, Marxism—and a wholly revisioned style of Hinduism. It was Gandhi, among others, who created and maintained the ideal of independence.

The Hindu Nationalist Movement

Hindu nationalist sentiments played no small part in the efforts to achieve independence from British rule, efforts that had begun gradually during the mid-eighteenth century. Over their long tenure, the British studied India, its culture, and its religion, and in so doing, they categorized and rationalized a Western conception of Indian religion for the West, which was then reconveyed to India. After nearly two centuries of rule by the British empire and of rule by Muslim potentates of much of India for centuries before that, Indian religious identity was unclear. The Neo-Vedanta philosophy that arose among upper caste Bengali intellectuals reflected and responded to this Western conceptualization of Hinduism.

Vinayak D. Savarkar, in *Hindutva: Who Is a Hindu?* (1923), wrote persuasively to associate Hindus with place (the territory known as India) and with the philosophy and cultural expressions derived from the Vedas. His arguments were significant for the continued development of Indian national self-identification, which was needed to mobilize Hindus for the struggle for independence. Many nationalist proponents found in Hinduism resources for harmonizing Hindu identity with modernity, espousing religious pluralism and tolerance as inherent in Hinduism and its many manifestations, as well as promoting reform of caste and family law. Traditionally subjugated castes, as well as women, were mobilized to assert rights as the nationalist movement took hold. Yet at the same time, there was also a strong movement for the **secularization** of society, while non-Hindu populations, especially the

Muslims, fearing a Hindu hegemonic revival that might relegate them to a lower status, threatened reprisal. These were the tensions that existed when Mohandas K. Gandhi came to prominence.

Mohandas K. Gandhi and Indian Independence

Undoubtedly the most significant of all modern Hindus is Mohandas K. Gandhi (1869–1948), who led the movement for Indian independence through "truth force." Popularly referred to as Mahatma ("Great Soul") Gandhi, he drew the theory behind his nonviolent resistance—by noncooperation, demonstrations, and fasting—from yoga and Jainism's **ahimsa** (non harming) and from the Bhagavad-Gita's *karma-yoga*.

In the life of Gandhi, we see the Indian religious tradition working once again to weave together in a new pattern two realms of the Divine—the social order and the infinite within the self.

Gandhi was the son of a prime minister of a small princely state in western India and a deeply religious mother. Though Hindu, he was raised in a part of India where Jainism was influential, and he studied law in England, where he also came in touch with the Christian "Sermon on the Mount" and the Bhagavad-Gita of his own religion. Upon his return to India, he met with little success in his practice of law until 1893, when he undertook to represent a Muslim

Followers support Mahatma Gandhi as he arrives at Simla for a political conference.

firm in South Africa. He stayed there until 1915, increasingly involved in struggles against racial prejudice and discrimination in that country. Upon his return to India, he took up the cause of India's independence from Britain.

Gandhi became convinced that this cause was a spiritual as well as a political struggle. He opposed abuses within Hinduism, such as caste discrimination and particularly the ill treatment of women and the "untouchables," or *harijan*—"children of God" as he called them—as much as he opposed foreign rule. Ancient Indian values, he asserted, were superior to European values, but they needed to be affirmed through spiritual self-purification. This he called *satyagraha*, "holding to Truth." It was the basis of his well-known methods of "fighting"—by fasting, by nonviolent demonstrations, and by selected acts of deliberate disobedience of laws believed to be unjustly imposed or enforced. On other levels, by his simple, ascetic living, including strict vegetarianism, by adherence to non-violence at all costs, by the self-reliance shown by his famous spinning wheel, and by wearing only homemade cloth (an affront to British manufacturing), Gandhi set an example of inner, spiritual freedom alongside political and economic emancipation. Moreover, he showed they were related; India could be truly free only if it lived simply and self-reliantly enough to eschew outside entanglements. And its people could fight effectively in Gandhi's way only if they were inwardly purified by such ascetic means, together with meditation and the practice of compassion to all beings.

By 1947, Gandhi and his followers not only achieved their political goal—independence from Britain—they also successfully demonstrated a new method of political activism. The Hindu politician-saint profoundly influenced Martin Luther King Jr. in the United States; land reformers in India like Gandhi's disciple Vinoba Bhave; and many others. At the same time, he showed the continuing vitality and adaptability of the ancient Hindu religion.

Tragically and ironically, however, independence initially brought great suffering to India. The country was partitioned into two states, the predominantly Hindu India and the Islamic state of Pakistan. The resulting bitterness between the two faiths produced terrible riots and many deaths, especially as people on the wrong side of the new borders tried to make their way to the other side or were driven out. Gandhi, who had opposed partition and who had always tried to care for Muslims as well as Hindus and enlist their support, was deeply saddened. He fasted for the sake of peace with some success. Then, early in 1948, he was assassinated by a Hindu extremist who thought he had gone too far in making concessions to the Muslims.

India Today: Tension, Change, and Promise

India's constitution largely employed the **secular** language of rights, liberties, and equality rather than offering religious justifications for the new government. Nonetheless, despite some inroads from **secularization**, religion has flourished.

India is the world's largest democracy. However, its political identity is still in flux with many competing visions. Some view India's secularizing trends as necessary for modernization, while others are concerned that the abandonment of Hindu traditions will lead to moral chaos, especially as Western-style consumer capitalism takes hold. Some, including Hindu nationalist political parties such as the BJP (Bharatiya Janata Party), draw on India's ancient traditions in reasserting Hindu identity as the foundation for a tolerant Indian society, while they also view the rise of other religious groups' political power and cultural influence, especially Islam, as a potential threat to that vision. At the same time, the legacy of the caste system, although discrimination based on caste is technically abolished, continues to create barriers to a unifying vision of Hinduism for politics. Low-caste political movements continue to challenge the existing social order, and tensions remain between the more orthodox and vocal Hindu traditionalists who interpret Hinduism in doctrinally rigid ways and most other Hindus who embrace Hinduism's inherent heterogeneity and tolerance.

Tensions between Hindus and Muslims have resulted in flare-ups, sometimes with disastrous results. Hindus point to incidents in Kashmir, the only region with a significant Muslim majority, which resulted in essentially forcing, through violence and harassment, the Hindu minority, numbering more than 200,000 people, to leave. Then, later that same year, a dispute over a mosque in the city of Ayodhya, reportedly the capital of Lord Rama, God and king of the Ramayana, led to dire consequences. Hindus held that the mosque was built on the site of a previous temple marking Rama's birthplace. The seven-century-long Muslim rule in much of India, which led to the destruction of numerous Hindu shrines and sometimes their replacement with mosques, is deeply embedded in many Hindus' consciousness. Determined to recover the temple site, Hindus rioted and destroyed the offending edifice, exacerbating religious animosity nationwide. This episode was followed a decade later with arson that resulted in the deaths of fifty-eight Hindus on a train at Godha, a town with a majority Muslim population. Although they were never confirmed, some reports recounted confrontations between Muslims and Hindus at the Godha railway station in previous weeks, when Hindu activists took the train to Uttar Pradesh to lobby the government to build a Ram a temple at the ruined mosque's Ayodhya site. On the day of mourning and funerals, riots broke out in the state of Gujarat's largest city, where revenge was taken against Muslims.[24] After decades of litigation, the Hindus' claim to the temple site in Ayodhya was validated in a landmark court judgment in September 2010, although no further development has been permitted at the site since the Supreme Court stayed the ruling. Tensions remain.

Yet, as India increasingly becomes a global economic force, with economic growth rates surpassed only by China's, there are signs of a change in mentality, especially in the younger generation. Writer Anand Giridharadas, in *India Calling: An Intimate Portrait of a Nation's Remaking*, describes a subtle but significant change: the sense of caste-bound hierarchy that had once defined Indian life is fading; software engineers are the new Brahmins; and the Indian people conceive of possibilities their grandparents never imagined existed.[25] Former "untouchables" ("Scheduled Castes," "Harijan," or "Dalits) have greatly improved their lot. Some have become very successful in the business world and in government.

Along with India's growth in world political and economic importance, some Hindu spokespersons have shown increasing energy and confidence in promoting the ancient religion's values at home and abroad. In the midst of the rapid changes wrought by India's growing economic power in the global marketplace and rising religious tensions around the world, many Hindus are promoting what they see as Hinduism's inherent valuing of holistic self-realization and religious pluralism, which together, they believe, could serve as a beacon for global peace. Hence, the personal will not be the self-centeredness that they hold is the hallmark of the economic West's preoccupation with the individual; rather, the personal will be the self with a deep sense of connection to all and, therefore, to global welfare—because ultimately the self is all, is Brahman. These Hindus have been reaching across the globe to join forces with like-minded religionists of all faiths in their efforts to make a better world.

WOMEN IN HINDUISM

When visiting Udaipur, I* attended a reverent, celebratory Shiva *puja* at the 2000-year-old Eklingji temple, not far from the city. I was struck by how the temple and the ritual bespoke of the difficulty of any attempt to locate Hinduism's attitudes toward women in Western cultural categories. The community of worshippers, men and women with no particular advantage of one over the other, respectfully waited in a long line to approach the temple priests to receive a blessing and the red *tilaka* (the dot at the center of the forehead, the third eye) and to give an offering of flowers and a donation. Mothers came with their children of all ages, guiding them on how to participate in the ritual customs. Aged women with bent backs, assisted by younger women or

Hindu women paying homage to deities at the altar of sacred trees and symbols before they enter the main temple.

---

*Barbara McGraw

male family or community members, and women of all ages in between, including me, made their way as well.

After receiving a blessing, the women were seated on the floor in a place of honor in front of the congregation, while the men took their place on the floor in the back of the temple. As the chanting and clapping rose, the women exchanged happy smiles of acknowledgment—curious little girls and aged, ancient women with wise eyes, as well as young women and proud mothers.

Still, the *garbha,* the sanctuary "womb" in the far wall of the temple where the deity was being adorned with flowers and which the seated congregants faced, was clearly the province of male priests and their *puja* ritual. Yet somehow I didn't feel an unbalanced exclusion in that sanctuary. Male and female were represented everywhere. Even though this was Shiva's temple, there were paintings and carvings acknowledging Shakti, too. And the main temple was surrounded by 107 smaller temples (108 being Shiva's sacred number) for the veneration of numerous male and female deities—the botanical architecture creating the impression of a limitless, paradisal temple forest. Male and female, nature and spirit, the phenomenal universe and the absolute—all swirled together with the incense and the song, the smiles and the drums, the youth and the elderly, the rhythm of the cycles of life and death. It all seemed to say that women are in everything—as demur and wild, wise and playful, controlled and uncontrollable.

Yet Hinduism's history was not kind to women. As we see in other world religions, while there always have been extraordinary women who have overcome religion's norms and traditions that justify the circumvention of women's lives and potential, overall, for too long, patriarchal patterns prevail. Yet, as we will see, today Hindu women are on the rise.

Sources of Classical Hindu Ideals of Womanhood

The earliest Vedic scripture, the Rig Veda, establishes the family as the central component of the socioreligious structure of Hinduism. Consequently, although the society was patriarchal and patrilineal, women held important positions in the social structure as wives and mothers. Because home was the center of religious worship and the Gods were understood to bless the family as a collective, women's presence was considered necessary in rituals. High-caste women experienced relative freedom in comparison with their counterparts in later periods with respect to marriage, divorce, remarriage, and education.[26] In addition, there is evidence in ancient texts that women participated in Vedic rituals.[27]

Later, however, although some Vedic texts cite women as authorities on Vedic rituals and the texts suggest that there is no difference between man and woman in performing Vedic rites,[28] overall the Brahmana texts reveal a shift in the religious orientation of the Vedic peoples, which was eventually to have a profound effect on the status of women in the society. Religious rites became complicated, and the knowledge required to conduct them gave rise to specialists. As a consequence, religious education became a growing necessity.

Women's participation in religious rites declined, and certain social trends occurred that were to become problematic for women as such trends became exaggerated in later periods. Hindu tradition advised that women should marry soon after the onset of puberty, which resulted in early childbearing. Thus, education became the province of men, while women remained focused on the home. The result was a visible disparity in the education of women and men and a greater separation in their social roles. Significantly, the status of Brahmin men was tied to education and related abilities. Because women were denied this education, their status was lowered, and as a result, they were denigrated in writings by men. Such attitudes were no doubt internalized by the women themselves. At the same time, however, women were permitted a derivative status attained by producing sons who would be educated and, therefore, qualified to perform rites for the family.

The ascetic ideal developed with the writing of the Aranyakas and the Upanishads, with its ultimate focus on Hindu life as the realization of the One—Brahman. Asceticism, an option effectively foreclosed to women, brought a further attitudinal shift toward them. Women were perceived by male ascetics as an impediment on the road to liberation. "Many misogynist passages in the texts can be traced to the perspective of an ascetic-in-the-making who stereotyped women as temptresses before he had conquered his passions so that he was truly indifferent to the world."[29] Even the order of Shankara, the great nondualist master of Advaita Vedanta, was open only to men, and it represented the feminine principle only as *maya*, which is the realm of ignorance or unreality, the only reality being Brahman in Advaita Vedanta.[30]

Attitudes toward women shifted with social change, and so did the doctrinal authority of the religion. Although women poets had been authors of some of the hymns in the Vedas, women now became equated with the *shudra* and were not permitted to study or recite the Vedas.[31] While one may find favorable passages regarding women in the Hindu texts, they generally express a negative stance, proclaiming that women are pervaded with countless vices and faults.[32] In addition, authoritative works memorialized the subordination of women. You may recall the four stages of the ideal Hindu life set forth in the Laws of Manu: student, householder, forest dweller or hermit, and renunciant. It is interesting to note that this ideal was the province of men and that only one of the stages—householder—relates men's lives to women's. On the other hand, women's lives were centered completely on and subordinated to men's. Most important, except in the very rare case of a woman ascetic, women's lives were oriented toward marriage. As a consequence, their stages of life revolved around maidenhood (being eligible for marriage); wifehood (living the married life), and widowhood (having been married).[33] Moreover, the Laws of Manu dictated standards that were to govern many Hindu women:

> In childhood a female must be subject to her father, in youth to her husband, when her lord is dead to her sons: a woman must never be independent....
>
> Though destitute of virtue, or seeking pleasure (elsewhere), or devoid of good qualities, (yet) a husband must be constantly worshipped as a god by a faithful wife....[34]
>
> Day and night, women must be kept in dependency by the males (of) their (families), and if they attach themselves to sensual enjoyments, they must be kept under one's control....
>
> Through their passion for men, through their mutable temper, through their natural heartlessness, they become disloyal towards their husbands, however carefully they are guarded in this (world).
>
> Knowing their disposition, which the Lord of creatures laid in them at the creation, to be such, (every) man should most strenuously exert himself to guard them.[35]

It is clear, then, that such texts reflected a perceived need to control women. Many have speculated as to how this may have developed. One theory is that any perceived threat to ethnic purity results in the subjugation of women to male control. This may result from warfare or occupation by an outside authority or merely from the desire of the patriarchal head of the household to ensure that the children of the marriage are his own. Nevertheless, practices that involved subjugation and control of women were justified by selective readings of Hindu scriptures where the feminine ideal of purity, chastity, and unflinching loyalty were emphasized.

All these various influences in some combination gave rise to the classical Hindu ideal of womanhood: She is married with at least one son and preferably more. She is chaste, humble, and devoted to the point of self-sacrifice to the welfare of the family, in particular to her husband, as was exemplified in the story of Sita who followed her husband, Rama, into exile and steadfastly defended her chastity. The classical, ideal Hindu wife bathes, sleeps, and even eats only after her husband has done so. She is uneducated (this fact having become a status symbol among those of the higher castes), and she is to contribute to at least three of the four goals of life of her husband, but sometimes she is to join him as, in effect, his servant in the fourth stage. She is to provide pleasure (*kama*) by providing sexual enjoyment and contributing aesthetic richness by maximizing personal desirability in appearance and manner, as well as beauty in the home. The husband's gain (*artha*) is advanced by providing him with sons who add to the auspiciousness of the home by their achievements and who are also able to perform the funerary rites that ensure safe passage for their father into the next life.

The classical Hindu wife also contributes to righteousness (*dharma*) by generally fulfilling her duties in her role as wife, including fasting, making vows and sacrifices to the Gods for the well-being of the family, and exhibiting all of the characteristics of the ideal Hindu wife. In this way, she participates in upholding the social and cosmic order.[36] Because the classical ideal woman was oriented to the worldly aspects of her husband's life, her own highest goal was to fulfill her role as wife in order to be considered a good woman—that is, a woman who gained good *karma* by attending to her husband as a God so that she would attain a more auspicious reincarnation in the next life.

The Subordination of the Ideal Hindu Wife

Classical attitudes toward women dictated the shape of women's lives, particularly the lives of upper-caste women, and resulted in a series of religio-cultural practices that came under severe attack in the nineteenth century both inside and outside India. One such practice was child marriage. Initially, the age of marriage was linked to puberty, perhaps to ensure virginity in marriage. But eventually it became the practice to marry girls as children, sometimes no more than five years old.[37] Presumably this was to limit a girl's social context extremely in order to guarantee her sole devotion to her husband, even if she did not leave her natal home to join her husband until later. In rare cases, however, physical injury from sexual relations at too early an age resulted in deformities in adult life.[38] Even if child marriage and its consequences did not occur, it was common for a woman married as a teenager to have many children, which restricted and shortened her life.

Other practices came into vogue that severely limited women's lives and led to abuses. One such practice in northern India, where there had been considerable Muslim influence, was **purdah**. This is the practice in which the wife is confined to the home and when movement outside of the home is necessary, she must be veiled. The effect then is to isolate her from society.

Dowry is another custom that became ubiquitous, not only among Hindus but among other religious groups in India (and elsewhere, for example, in Pakistan and Bangladesh). The traditional Hindu practice of presenting family gifts to the bride upon her marriage devolved (during British rule of India, some Hindus contend[39]) into the dowry custom of the bride's family giving money and other valuables to the family of the groom. Dowry is a considerable financial burden on a girl's family, while at the same time it provides a means for attaining wealth for the family of the groom. This practice has, for obvious reasons, contributed to the Hindu preference for sons.

Other practices evolved out of the ideals of purity and chastity. Women were not permitted to divorce, and if a woman's husband died before her, she was not permitted to remarry, although divorced and widowed men could remarry.

Most criticized of all, however, have been the attitudes and practices associated with widowhood itself. Because a woman's focus is the well-being of her husband, if he dies before her, his death is, in effect, her fault. Her in-laws, others in the family, and society consider such an unfortunate event the result of the widow's own bad *karma*. When one considers that women were to be self-sacrificial and otherwise live a severely restricted and controlled life, including many childbirths, one can discern that her early demise, in advance of her husband's, was evidence that she had been properly performing her duties as a wife. The practice of childhood marriage, however, sometimes to men well advanced in age, made widowhood more likely than it might have been otherwise. As a result, there were numerous young widows, many of whom were under ten years old.[40] Even so, although one can find authority in some Hindu scriptures for remarriage and evidence of widow remarriage in ancient India, the custom of prohibiting Hindu widows to remarry prevailed.[41] The widow was (and remains today in many parts of India) the most scorned figure in Hindu society.

There was, however, another, more "auspicious" way out of the predicament of widowhood. In some parts of India and among some of the higher castes, women could choose to become a **sati** (or **suttee**) in the ritual by the same name in which she was burned alive on the funeral pyre of her dead husband. This was the noble choice, which permitted the wife certain status as the "good wife," who was deserving of the good *karma* and therefore needed to join her husband in the next life or to be reincarnated as a man eligible for *moksha*. Muslim traders and European travelers recount witnessing a *sati* that was not forced or induced.[42] Yet one wonders what kind of choice *sati* was, considering the enormous social burden of the alternative.

At the same time, however, there may have been women so devoted to their husbands that this supreme sacrifice was actually experienced by them as recognition of, or transformation into, the exalted ideal, the self-sacrificing and devoted wife that the practice of *sati* was intended to exemplify. In other cases, the shame and burden of having a widow in the family provided incentive for the family to impose *sati* when it was not actually chosen. A case reported in 1776 recounts a widow being thrown into the pyre by her own son.[43] Katherine K. Young has noted that "[i]t is significant that *sati* became common in regions where a wife could inherit her husband's property."[44]

Places of Power and Participation

It is important to remember, however, that we must not assume that the authoritative texts written by men for women and the accounts of women in historical writings accurately portray the full extent of women's lives. Although it is extremely difficult to trace evidence of women's lived experience, it is possible to make some assumptions on the basis of the little evidence there is and by looking at the contemporary experiences of Indian women to discover places of divergence from orthodoxy and custom.

First, it must be remembered that what we have been describing so far is the classical Brahminical ideal. Yet most of India consists of the lower castes. Scholars have noted that there is more equality between men and women as one descends on the caste hierarchy.[45] On the other hand, since the practices we have been discussing were associated with status, those who sought to elevate themselves would be drawn to them.

Hindu women at the holy waters of the Galta Temple near Jaipur, India.

Second, the popular practice of a religion often differs in large degree from the orthodox canon and traditions. Undoubtedly, there have always been rituals associated with women's lives, such as those for childbirth, and women's rites and festivals in contemporary India's popular religion are evidence that women's religious lives may have been richer in the past than authoritative texts indicate.[46] There is also evidence that authoritative religious texts were unknown in many parts of India and that therefore they were not used where the "little tradition" of local custom prevailed.[47] In addition, because the home has always been the center of Hindu religious practices, rather than the temple, it is likely that women have been more involved in family ritual than one might think from reading only the texts.

More significant, however, there were religious movements within Hinduism that provided opportunity for the participation of women. As previously discussed, *bhakti*, the path of devotion, was indifferent to caste. Not noted earlier, however, is that *bhakti* also was largely indifferent to role restrictions for women. In *bhakti*, women found a path to liberation that was denied by the Brahminical ideal. Since women had already been prepared for a devotional life at home, it was an easy transition to complete devotion to a chosen deity. So it is no surprise that women have been acknowledged as *bhakti* saints. Examples of famous *bhakti* saints are Andal of South India (eighth century C.E.) and Mirabai (sixteenth century C.E.), both Krishna devotees. Upon the death of her husband, Mirabai refused widowhood and *sati* and declared herself the wife of Krishna himself.[48] Another famous woman saint is Akka Mahadevi, a twelfth-century poet who is believed to have reached union with Shiva.[49]

Many *bhakti* devotional Gods are male. Hence, the model worshipper is female, which is exemplified, for example, in the stories of Krishna and the devoted *gopis* who chase after and dance with him in the forest. As a consequence, even male devotees are considered "spiritually female" and may "suspend their masculinity" by taking on feminine devotional behavior and even dressing like women, as did Ramakrishna, the great saint and teacher discussed earlier, in order to identify as the devoted lover of the beloved God.[50]

On the other hand, Hindu popular religion, which incorporates *bhakti* devotionalism, often focuses on female representations of the Divine, such as Shakti (phenomenal power), *prakriti* (primordial nature), Kali (creatrix and destroyer), or the Great Goddess as Divine Mother. In some areas, such as Bengal, *bhakti* devotion to the Goddess is dominant.[51] Although such devotionalism often did not translate into improved status for human women, no doubt the *bhakti* Goddesses were exemplars that may have influenced attitudes toward women as well as provided sources of self-esteem and models for the empowerment for women.

The religious narratives of the Gods and Goddesses also elevate femaleness. One traditional story tells of Parvati domesticating the wild, itinerant Shiva through marriage. This narrative runs counter to those that show male control of female

Worship of Durga in Calcutta.

Adinath Jain Temple in Ranakpur, India.

energy, for example the traditional narrative of Shiva taming the turbulent, seething Ganga, the Ganges River Goddess, so that her flow nurtures and sustains rather than endangers the inhabitants of the world. Such narratives support the view that it is together that the Gods and Goddesses make order out of chaos, just as it is together that men and women can be civilizing influences on each other. Another traditional narrative recounts Parvati admonishing Shiva for neglect of his duties as a husband and father and Shiva admitting his failings and correcting them. These narratives suggest that when a husband does not perform his duties adequately or otherwise unduly disrupts his wife's life, it is appropriate for her, as the Shakti of the household, to complain and that the husband should right the situation.[52]

There are also historical accounts of queens and other influential women who were instrumental in the establishment or support of temples and educational institutions and who were even revered as warrior queens. One example is Queen Ahalyabi Holkai (1725–1795), who inherited the kingdom of Indore in central India after all of the male heirs had died. Ruling for thirty years, she was a great benefactor of temples and pilgrim sites, even many outside of her own kingdom. Legendary as an example of an ideal Hindu sovereign, she ruled with skill and compassion, fostering increased prosperity among her people.[53] Then there is also the heroine Queen Lakshmibai (1835–1858), martyr of Jhansi, in northern India. She refused to submit to British rule and led an army (which accounts say included many women as well as men) in the first war for Indian independence. In 1858, under threat of British armed forces, she led her army into the battlefield mounted on a horse, with her young son strapped to her back. After a victory in a subsequent fierce battle, she suffered a mortal wound and died on the battlefield. An icon of the Indian people's fight for freedom, she remains an inspiration to Indian women and men as a brave Hindu warrior queen and is memorialized in poetry, paintings, and statues portraying her with sword held high, riding a charging horse, her son bound closely behind her.[54]

Another example of places of power and participation can be found in Tantrism (beginning about the sixth century C.E.). Its practice of societal reversals offered leadership opportunities to women, who became *gurus* to men. On the other hand, Tantrism may also have resulted in the sexual use of women only for the purposes of the man's enlightenment or in legitimizing prostitution at the expense of women. Yet Tantrism's exaltation of the female Divine must have provided a source of power and esteem, at least for some women practitioners. Its cosmology does not elevate God over Goddess as the supreme expression of the Divine. Instead, Tantrism adheres to an ideology and practice that is intended to promote balance between male and female principles of the universe (which can be found in most forms of Saivism (Shiva bhakti), as well).

In some forms of Tantrism, identification with and immersion in the Goddess is the supreme goal of its practice, whether by male or female adepts. Immersion in the Goddess is apparently to reverse the unbalancing effects of mainstream religion and culture, which emphasize maleness. Some Tantric texts and practices also sought to reverse the prevailing social order by teaching men to recognize that the Goddess exists in every woman and that therefore women should be venerated, not subjugated. In Bengal, for example, women have been recognized as Tantric teachers.[55]

William Dalrymple's *Nine Lives* gives an account of a woman in Bengal named Manisha, a Tantric priestess of the Great Goddess Tara (the Tantric manifestation of Kali). Tara is fearsome and very powerful, with her tongue lolling out and her hands holding her bloodstained cleaver as she stands over a dead body. Manisha lives here, with several ash-covered *sadhus*, and according to Dalrymple, she is not afraid of the gruesome representation of the Divine. "'Tara [Ma] is my mother,' she said. 'How can your own mother evoke fear?'"

> When I first came here in a distressed condition, Ma protected me. I had been beaten by my husband, rejected by my mother-in-law, and had lost my home and my three daughters. It was she who brought me to Tapan Sadhu [a benefactor] to protect me and give me love. In this place of death, I have found new life. Now I don't want to go anywhere. To me, Ma is all. My life depends on her.[56]

Nor, according to Dalrymple, was Manisha a fearsome person. Though her gray hair was matted and her saffron robes ragged, she was a large, warm woman in her sixties, soft-spoken and with gentle eyes, a woman who after much turmoil had clearly found her place. Now, as an organizer of Tara's worship—including the careful seasoning and preparation of skulls—she had responsibilities, respect, and a sphere of influence, even if in a form of religion that reaches to the Divine through blood and death. Her Tantric faith shows that through flouting convention, violating taboos, and forcing one to confront grisly signs of our mortality, we can break out of the social cocoons that all too often only shield us from the ultimate things.

Women and Reform in India

Western history has generally credited the British, who controlled vast areas of India and ruled India for over two centuries until 1947, with reforms for Indian women. However, although some of the British pushed for reforms, foreign rule in India actually exacerbated the problem for Hindu women, resulting in a more insistent cry for reform from some within Indian society itself.[57] Not wanting to interfere with the status quo of long-held custom and religious practice, the British enforced Hindu laws regarding women in their courts. As a consequence, many practices adverse to women were not addressed by the British. *Sati* was not made illegal until 1829, when an educated Indian man, Raja Ram Mohun Roy, was successful in convincing the British that *sati* was not sanctioned by the Rig Veda as the Brahmin priests had contended.[58] Furthermore, intending to provide uniform laws, the British imposed strict Brahminical standards and practices regarding the family on the Indian population as a whole. For example, the British embraced the Laws of Manu in lieu of other texts, such as Narada Smriti, which held less restrictive views regarding women.[59]

The severe restrictions of the Brahminical ideal for Hindu women, which primarily had been confined to the higher castes, were now imposed on Indian women regardless of caste. For example, where women had once been permitted divorce or remarriage, these practices were abolished. However, as the greater Indian female population was subjected to the severe restrictions of the Brahminical ideal, a backlash resulted against the British. The British, who had claimed that one of the primary justifications for their occupation of India was to improve the lowly status of Hindu women, appeared hypocritical to reform-minded Indians, and the nineteenth-century Hindu reform movement was born, which included women such as Pandita Ramabai (1858–1922). As a result of the movement, the British reversed course and passed several reforms, such as prohibiting marriage for girls under the age of twelve and permitting women to remarry.

In the early 1900s, the Indians, including the Women's Indian Association (founded in 1917), pushed for reforms beyond those the British had envisioned. In many parts of India, for example, Indian women won the right to vote before British women were allowed to do so. As a consequence, the Indians were able to argue that their own attitude toward reform ran against the British contention that India's women needed British imperialism; therefore, they argued, Indian independence from British rule was in order.

Reforms for Hindu women, then, were inextricably bound with the Indian independence movement. Gandhi, although he held to traditional roles for women, made a call to Indian women to join him in the struggle for independence. Having fully integrated the idea of self-sacrifice for the benefit of others, many Hindu women turned their attention from the home and directed their efforts toward the broader context of the Indian homeland. Sometimes their peaceful protests found them, with babes in arms, standing up to British authority. Many made the supreme sacrifice by giving their lives when fired upon by the British.[60]

After independence was won in 1947, women's rights were enshrined in the new constitution, in which women such as Kitty Shiva Rao had considerable input. In addition, legislation was passed that, for example, provided equal pay for equal work; that outlawed polygamy; that raised the age of marriage to eighteen and twenty-one for women and men, respectively; that permitted divorce; that provided maternity benefits; and that prohibited sexual harassment, among other things. As a consequence, the legal context for women was radically altered. The new secular state took hold, and in 1954, Jawaharlal Nehru, India's first prime minister, called on women to become full partners with men in the development of a new India.[61]

Implementation of reform in the actual villages of the vast Indian countryside proved to be a daunting task, however, leaving many Indian women unaware of their rights—a problem that continues to this day. What is granted by law is easily taken back by custom and tradition that have a firm hold on the minds of the people.

Traditional attitudes have been difficult to change in many parts of India. The notion of the ideal Hindu wife is well embedded in Hindu culture, and the practices and attitudes associated with widows continue to be a source of subjugation of women in today's India, having, despite reforms, never been eradicated completely from Indian society.

On the other hand, the ideals of *lokasangraha* ("acting for the welfare of the world") and *satyagraha* ("grasping or insisting on the truth," or as Gandhi put it, "soul force") have helped women to move forward in their work to improve the status of women in India.[62]

Today's Hindu Women

What we see is that, despite the traditional low status of Hindu women and despite the preeminence of authoritative religious texts asserting the importance of women's subordination, there are resources in scripture and history on which women can draw today in their struggle for liberation.

Many reform-minded Hindu women and men are quick to assert that it is not Hinduism that is inherently patriarchal but those things that have been superimposed onto it over the millennia. They proudly point out that unlike all of the other major world religions, Hindus do not have to "tie themselves in knots" to locate sources of the veneration of femaleness as Divine. They note that Hinduism is the only major world religion (having nearly one billion adherents) that recognizes the Divine in female form, including powerful Goddesses who defy conventional stereotypes. Durga and Kali come to mind as aspects of the Divine power that manifests the phenomenal universe: Shakti.

In an article published in 2011, an American Hindu activist described Shakti as power that is "quiet yet strong, graceful yet fierce, subtle yet capable of unmatched rage," the sort of power on which Hindu women have drawn from the time of the Vedas to the present. Although the softer side of Shakti power has often been emphasized in Hindu culture, the article notes, at times women draw on their Shakti power when the time comes to manifest change. The article recounts the example of twenty women Hindu activists who were not about to stand for women's exclusion from the sanctum of male province in Hindu worship. In April 2011, they stormed the Mahalakshmi temple in Maharashtra, taking over the *garbha*, the heart of the temple where only male priests preside. In contradiction of the male-dominant tradition there and while fending off the priests and police who tried to stop them, they performed the *puja* themselves, adorning the deity with new raiment.[63]

Significantly, Hindu reformists have been scouring Hindu scriptures and history for evidence of strong, influential, empowered women, locating many sources that contradict the conventional view that Hinduism is essentially responsible for the suppression of women. Reformist Hindus and others have found historical and scriptural references to Hindu women as learned scholars and teachers of the Vedas and of Sanskrit grammar, as experts in Vedanta philosophy, as founders of temples, as saints, and (as mentioned earlier) as powerful Hindu sovereign queens.[64]

Hence, it is not only Indian secularists who have contributed to the advancement of women in India but religious Hindus as well. Exceptional Hindu women and men have opened the doors to education for women, and women have taken prominent positions in the professions, business, and government. Indira Gandhi (1917–1984), who was prime minister of independent India from 1966 through 1977 and from 1980 through 1984, serves as a reminder that even the highest offices of government are available to women.

Significantly, as attitudes toward women have changed, women's roles in religious societies have changed as well. During the nineteenth century, Ramakrishna (1836–1886), who was discussed earlier in this chapter, authorized his wife, Sarada Devi, to administer *mantras* during his lifetime. Today, she is considered by Ramakrishna followers as a saint. Furthermore, many monasteries in India now welcome women ascetics into their folds, and many women have become spiritual teachers in their own right. Mate Mahadevi ("The Great Mother Goddess") (1946–) is a prominent example. "She is perhaps the first woman in history who has ascended [in 1980] to the pontifical seat of Jagadguru ('world teacher'…) so far reserved for men[.]"[65] Moreover, the worship of the Divine Mother or Great Goddess is a growing phenomenon. Many Hindus believe the Divine Mother is present to them in Hindu's women saints. For example, Anandamayi Ma (1896–1982) is thought to have been an incarnation of the Goddess Kali, and Mata Amritanandamayi ("Mother of Bliss") (1953–), also known by her followers as Ammachi ("Beloved Mother") and dubbed by the media as the "hugging saint," is revered today as the Divine Mother by her numerous followers around the world.

Furthermore, many respected Hindu masters have worked for gender parity, and several have handpicked women successors for their movements, such as Gurumayi Chidvilasandanda, successor to Swami Muktananda, and Mathru Sri Sarada, successor to Swami Lakshamana.[66] Moreover, women are finding new avenues of religious devotional expression in other places as well. For example, women are *bhakti* poets, composers, singers, choreographers, and dancers—all roles traditionally denied to all but the most exceptional women in history, such as Andal, mentioned previously.[67] And there are now institutions that teach the Vedas and the performances of Vedic rites to women—Kanya Kumari Sthan in Sakori and Udyan Mangal Karyalaya in Pune, where women are being taught to become priests.

All of these developments have led many to believe that Hindu women will be an even greater political and religious force in the years to come, not only in India but all around the world.

JAINISM

As we have already noted, Jainism was established in its historic form by Vardhamana, called Mahavira, an approximate contemporary of the Buddha, in the fifth century B.C.E. Mahavira is believed by his followers to have been the last in a series of

Tirthankaras ("Crossing-Makers") who attained full liberation and taught the way to it. These men are honored as the greatest of *jinas* ("victors" or "conquerors"), from which the word "Jain" is derived. The ideal of conquering through great struggle is pervasive in Jain literature. But it is not a triumph over a human enemy that is lauded, for the foe is oneself and one's own material nature, which can be defeated by perseverance in asceticism or self-denial. This kind of triumph is often reflected in Jain art, which may portray the *Tirthankaras* as heroically rigid, immobile figures over which vines have extended their tendrils, in contrast to dancing or flute-playing Hindu deities.

Jainism teaches that sentient, feeling life dwells in all that exists—God, humans, animals, plants, and even in stones, dust, and air. These *jivas*, souls or particles of life, are entrapped in the material shells of these substances as a result of *karma*. The Jain view of *karma* is somewhat different from the Hindu or Buddhist views; for Jains it is more like a material coating that covers souls as a consequence of action based on desire and that thereby condemns them to the suffering incumbent upon material existence.

One can look at it this way: *Karma*, or action, is inevitably directed toward some particular object and so "grows" the material form it needs to attain that object. If you want a piece of candy, you need an arm to reach out and grab it, and you need a mouth with which to eat it. *Karmic* law says that in such matters you get what you want—but then you have

Women praying in a Jain temple.

to live with it. You now have a body so that you can enjoy candy, but you are also trapped inside that body, with all its limitations and its capacity for pain—and you will have a very hard time getting out of it. According to Jainism, since it was action that got us into the material predicament, it must be its opposite—quietness and abstention—that begins to reverse our predicament, as well as suffering induced by asceticism that wears down the *karmic* shell until the soul can break free, floating up to the top of the universe to enjoy an eternity of bliss and omniscience.

Inflicting suffering on another soul, whether through cruelty or indifference or even apparent necessity, adds to one's burden of *karma*. For this reason, Jains go to great lengths to counter the callousness of the world toward life. Virtually all Jains are strict vegetarians and go so far as to put screens around lamps to keep insects from flying into them. Many Jain temples maintain homes for unwanted animals and hospitals for injured birds.

Practice differs, however, between laity, on the one hand, and monks and nuns, on the other. The former live essentially in order to add no more to the burden of *karma*, in the hope of becoming a monk or nun in some future life and ultimately attaining *kaivalya*, or liberation.

Monks and nuns, however, are determined to make real headway toward that goal in this lifetime. They not only practice the great Jain virtue of *ahimsa*, harmlessness, but also undertake great asceticism—fasting, meditating in the hot sun, enduring discomfort—to wear down the *karmic* shell. Jain monks are divided into two orders: the *Digambaras*, who are "sky-clad" or naked in many settings, and the *Svetambaras*, who wear a thin white unstitched robe. Nuns, too, wear a thin white unstitched robe and sometimes a white cap. Monks and nuns also pluck out their hair as another austerity. Many also hold or tie a white cloth in front of their mouths so that when they speak, their outgoing breath does no harm to others. Sometimes their asceticism may even lead to *sallekhana* or self-starvation. They often take extra precautions to ensure that even as they walk, they do not inadvertently harm a living being. Take, for example, Prasannamati Mataji, described by William Dalrymple in *Nine Lives*.

When Dalrymple first laid eyes on Mataji in a Jain temple, he was struck by the fact that, despite her bald head, Mataji was in fact a surprisingly young and striking woman. She had large, wide-apart eyes, olive skin, and an air of self-contained confidence that expressed itself in vigor and ease in the way she held her body. But there was also something sad and wistful about her expression as she went about her devotions; and this, combined with her unexpected youth and beauty, left one wanting to know more.

The "more" was that Mataji, unlike some others who may have wanted to escape a difficult life elsewhere, came from a loving, prosperous Jain family, having by her own account enjoyed a very happy childhood, treated like a little doll. With her beauty and a good dowry, she could undoubtedly have had virtually any marriage she wanted, or perhaps she could have gone into one of the modern secular careers, from flight attendant to politician, which are increasingly available to Indian women. Yet, after hearing a Jain monk at the age of thirteen, she had no desire but to follow the life of his austere religion. She reduced her eating to monastic levels, and a year or two later, she visited a Jain monastic community for a short retreat. But she simply refused to leave the community until her angered father had to come to get her forcibly. Once back home, however, she refused to eat, or drink even a drop of water, till her family gave in and let her return. Back in the community, she swept the road in front of her to make sure it was clear of living beings, and she ate very little, aspiring to the *sallekhana* ideal (referred to above). Though her family continued to stay in touch with her, she was on her own and seemed to have had no doubts as to the rightness of her path.[68]

Jain *ahimsa* symbol.

The high value placed on asceticism, however, has not inhibited a respect for learning and beauty among the Jains. Monks and nuns go among Jain communities as teachers and preachers; a great number of the laity is well educated in the faith. Historically, Jain monks have played a very creative role in the letters and philosophy of India. As we have seen, Mohandas K. Gandhi and through him such Americans as Martin Luther King Jr. were deeply influenced by Jain teachings about harmlessness and nonviolence.

The Jains, typically merchants and bankers, are a prosperous and gifted class in India today, influential beyond what their numbers of only about 4.5 million would suggest. Their well-maintained temples are among the most exquisitely beautiful in India.[69]

SIKHISM

The Sikh religion arose early in the sixteenth century on the spiritual boundary between Hinduism and Islam. It answered the needs of those who, perturbed by the coexistence of two mighty but conflicting faiths, sought a higher truth beyond them both. It taught the simple monotheistic worship of a God who can be called by many names as long as one does not limit him to any of them. Yet Sikhism, over time, became a movement with its own distinctive outlook and its own role in the complex and tumultuous history of India.

According to tradition, Guru Nanak (1470–1540), the first revealer of Sikhism, received his divine call at the age of thirty, when God came to him and charged him to teach humankind the worship of the true name of God through simple prayer, charity, cleanliness, and service. Nanak was lost in the rapture of this experience for three days, and when he reappeared, he said to his companions, "There is no Hindu; there is no Muslim."

Nanak had strong ties to both the Muslim and the Hindu traditions. He had an ordinary upbringing and marriage, but after his call at thirty, he left his family to take up the renunciant life. Then, when he was about fifty, a decisive special vision was granted him. God above and beyond human places and faiths came to him, Nanak said, and pledged him to worship and teach faith in his Divine Name.

The God of this revelation was neither the God of Islam or Hinduism's Gods and Goddesses, but the one all-powerful, loving God who is above them both, who makes no unfavorable distinctions among humanity as to creed or caste but looks into the heart. He may be called by any name—Brahma, Rama, Hari, or Allah—as long as the worshipper recognizes that he is not limited to any of them. Sikhs love, above all, just to call the Lord *Sat Nam*, the True or Absolute Name. The repetition of his name is itself true devotion and equal to any pilgrimage to Mecca or Benares (Varanasi). In submission to his name lies freedom.

Nanak spent a number of years, surrounded by disciples, as an itinerant poet and minstrel of this God. Here is one of his most expressive poems:

The Golden Temple (Sri Harimandir Sahib Amritsar), the holiest Sikh temple.

> *Those who believe in power,*
> *Sing of His power;*
> *Others chant of His gifts*
> *As His messages and emblems;*
> *Some sing of His greatness,*
> *And His gracious acts;*
> *Some sing of His wisdom*
> *Hard to understand;*
> *Some sing of Him as the fashioner of the body,*
> *Destroying what He has fashioned;*
> *Others praise Him for taking away life*
> *And restoring it anew.*
> *Some proclaim His Existence*
> *To be far, desperately far, from us;*
> *Others sing of Him*
> *As here and there a Presence*
> *Meeting us face to face.*

To sing truly of the transcendent Lord
Would exhaust all vocabularies, all human powers of expression,
Myriads have sung of Him in innumerable strains.
His gifts to us flow in such plenitude
That man wearies of receiving what God bestows;
Age on unending age, man lives on His bounty;
Carefree, O Nanak, the Glorious Lord smiles.[70]

Nanak believed he had been called to serve as the guru, or teacher, of this faith in the true God. After him, a succession of nine more gurus bore his authority. Following the tenth and last, the Holy Granth (the Sikh scriptures composed of poems of Nanak, Kabir, referenced earlier, and others) took the place of a living teacher. The story of how **Sikhism** inevitably became another religion, instead of a faith beyond all religion, is a colorful and fascinating one.

Nanak inculcated in his growing band of followers an inclusive religion focused on the name of one universal, all-powerful, and all-loving God, who makes no distinction among men and women on the basis of caste or creed but who looks into their hearts. The simple worship of God is sufficient; pilgrimage, ritual, or ascetic practices add nothing to it.

As the Sikh ("disciple") movement grew, the idea of the *guru* and of the Sikhs as a distinct community also became more and more important. Some of the succession of nine *gurus*, each appointed by his predecessor, following Nanak left a distinctive stamp on the character of the faith. The Sikh fellowship, too, came to be clearly defined.

Khanda, symbol of Sikhism.

The fifth *guru*, Arjun (1563–1606), did much to make the religion institutional. He compiled the Sikh scriptures, the Granth, from the writings of Nanak, Kabir, and other poets and *gurus*. He enshrined the Granth in the famous Golden Temple in Amritsar, which is Sikhism's most venerated site. A strong administrator, he organized local Sikh communities efficiently and pushed for a high measure of self-government for the movement as a whole. Arjun was imprisoned and then martyred after he offended the successor of the great Moghal emperor Akbar by supporting a rebellion. The martyrdom served virtually to absolutize Arjun's reforms and to teach the Sikhs they would need to look out for themselves in increasingly dangerous surroundings.

That lesson was not lost on Gobind Rai (1666–1708), descendant of Arjun and the tenth and last *guru*. The Moghal Empire in north India, with its many peoples and faiths, was deteriorating under the rule of the fanatically Muslim Aurangzib. Rai advocated the right of the Sikhs to defend themselves and did much to enhance the military tradition for which Sikhism was to become noted.

In 1699, Gobind Rai inaugurated the *Khalsa*, the Sikh military fraternity. Standing before the great assembly of believers, Gobind Rai asked if there were any here, now, today, who were willing to give their lives for the faith. The crowd was astounded by this awesome request. But eventually five brave men came forward. Gobind Rai took each into his tent, a thud was heard, and when he came out, his sword was dripping with blood. Finally he led the five out before the terrified assembly. They were unharmed—the blood had been that of a goat—but the men were now accounted heroes and the first members of the *Khalsa*. Though of different caste backgrounds, they drank *amrit*, sacred nectar, together and were required to wear five tokens, called *kakaars*: uncut hair covered by a turban (*kesh*), a comb (*kanga*), a steel bracelet (*kara*), a special pair of undershorts (*kachehra*), and a *kirpan*, or two-edged dagger. They took the surname Singh, "lion." Others rushed to join the *Khalsa*, pledging never to turn their backs on an enemy. Rai, now Guru Gobind Singh, took to the field with some success, but he died of wounds inflicted in battle in 1708. Before he died, he said that he would be the last *guru* in human form and that after him, the Granth itself would become the *guru*, and so it has been. In time, Sikh rulers governed most of Punjab until the largest of their kingdoms was subjugated by the British in the Sikh wars of the nineteenth century. However, the remaining smaller kingdoms were allowed to continue under British sovereignty.

The Sikhs have no formal priesthood. Their worship, similar in some ways to that of Protestant Christianity, may be conducted by any qualified Sikh. It consists of hymns, prayer, scripture reading, sermons, and the sharing of food together, both in a sort of communion rite at the end of worship and in communal dinners afterwards. Sikh gurdwaras (temples) are alive with the beautiful and moving chanting of the Granth, and the hospitality of Sikhs there is well-known, especially in the offering of food. Private worship in the home morning and evening is also emphasized. In its mainstream form, Sikhism gives little place to asceticism or celibacy, though it teaches simplicity of life.

The twenty-three million Sikhs in the world today—nineteen million of them in India—form a highly distinctive community. Among various groups following Sikh teachings, those associated with the Khalsa are the most numerous. Devout males among them are recognizable by the turban and the other *kakaars* of the Khalsa, known as the "Five Ks." Emphasizing the primacy of the householder life, Sikhs are known for their strong family values, their work ethic, their egalitarian view of men and women, and their renowned generosity and hospitality. The Sikh military tradition lives on, and a number have served honorably in the Indian army. These values have generally served well those Sikhs who have immigrated overseas. Most have become well established in business or the professions. The first Asian American and member of a non-Western faith to serve in the U.S. Congress was a Sikh, Dalip Singh Saund, who represented a California district from 1957 through 1963.

Sikhism, then, can be characterized as a monotheistic religion with a strong sense of community, a devotion to family life, a tradition of ethical and military virtues, and a belief in a universal God beyond sectarian divisions.

Sikhism has spawned several additional religious movements, typically based on the belief that the lineage of authentic *gurus* is still living. Among them are Radhasoami and Eckankar, which have spread to the West.

INDIA IN AMERICA

Hinduism Comes to America

The World Parliament of Religions at the Chicago World's Fair in 1893 marked the introduction of Hinduism to America. Before 1893, the number of Hindus in America was insignificant, though Hindu philosophy had had a profound effect on Emerson, Thoreau, and other Transcendentalists; it greatly influenced their writings and thus made an impact on the American religious landscape. The charismatic Swami Vivekananda took the World Parliament by storm with the introduction of Advaita Vedanta, based on the teachings of the Indian saint Ramakrishna (1836–1886). Hinduism was at once an exotically foreign religion for late nineteenth-century Americans, yet at the same time welcome because of its openness toward all religious views. Swami Vivekananda soon established Ramakrishna, or Vedanta, Societies in the United States, the first in New York in 1896. By the time of his untimely death in 1902, Vedanta had solid footing in the United States and elsewhere. Vedanta's blend of devotion, service, meditation, acceptance of all forms of piety, and a harmonious view toward the religious life, along with a style of worship that brings together Protestant-style services imparting Vedanta philosophy with Hindu *puja* worship, has attracted many followers in America of both Indian and Western descent. Vedanta in America thus paved the way for other varieties of Hinduism to follow, including the Self-Realization Fellowship and the International Society for Krishna Consciousness (also known as the Hare Krishnas).

Early twentieth-century America displayed an interest in Eastern philosophy and religion, including Hinduism, but at the same time, it showed an ambivalent attitude toward Indian immigrants themselves, who found the immigration door alternatively opened, then closed, then opened again in 1965.

Hindus of Indian descent in America have had to strike an uneasy balance between their religion and cultural identity, on the one hand, and American pressures to Westernize, on the other hand. The establishment of a significant number of Hindu temples constructed in America in the architectural styles of northern or southern India and dedicated by Hindu priests from India have become centers of Hindu worship and culture for Hindus of various Indian backgrounds. The temples, in effect, create oases of purity for the orthodox in the midst of the various pollutions of modern America, where eating meat, class and racial intermarriage, considerable mobility in society, and rapidly transforming family structures are commonplace.[71]

Today, Hindu temples generally welcome the serious seeker of non-Indian descent as well as the merely curious, creating a congenial atmosphere for all visitors that speaks well for Hindu hospitality. At the same time, second and third generation Hindus are forging a "Hindu-American" identity, bridging their Hindu spiritual traditions with American culture and finding common ground in religious freedom and diversity.[72]

Other Indian Influences in America

Hinduism has had a wide influence on American religion and culture since it was first introduced. As previously mentioned, even before Vivekananda set foot on American soil, it was a presence in the influential writings of Emerson and Thoreau. Hindu ideas have almost imperceptibly become woven into American culture at places where there is concordance. For example, Vedanta's tolerant universal view of religion has found a kindred spirit in certain forms of liberal Christianity and Judaism, no doubt enriching each. And "New Age" religious movements and the Theosophical Society have also benefited from the wisdom of India. Even certain words, such as *mantra*, *yoga*, and *chakra*, have been incorporated into the American lexicon as quasi-religious practices permeating American society. Yoga practices have become so widespread in America today that it is even probable that new generations will perceive them as entirely "American."[73] Hindus are now prominent scholars of religion in American universities, as well. The first non-Judeo-Christian President of the American Academy of Religions was a Hindu woman, Vasudha Narayanan, in 2002.

Jain, Sikh, and Parsee (Zoroastrian) temples also are found in major centers of population, adding their distinctive notes to the American spiritual symphony. The first Sikh *gurdwara*, the Sikh place of worship, was established in Stockton, California, as early as 1912. In the 1960s and afterward, many Euro-Americans became Sikhs through the influence of Yogi Bhajan (1929–2004; b. Harbhajan Singh Puri) and his organization, now called Sikh Dharma. Large-scale Jain immigration and the establishment of Jain centers in the United States began after 1965. The same is largely true of Parsees.

We see, then, that India's religions have been substantial contributors to the American religious melting pot, as well as to America's rich diversity.

Fundamental Features of Hinduism

Theoretical

Basic Worldview	The universe is profoundly one. Even though it goes through surface changes and cycles, its ultimate nature as expression of the Divine does not change.
God or Ultimate Reality	Brahman, the one Mind or Life, is the one reality. Its essence is beyond knowing, but it expresses itself in all that is like a flame taking many shapes.
Origin of the World/ Destiny of the World	The world goes through endless cycles of creation and destruction but has no real beginning or end.
Origin of Humans	Like the world, the individual has no known beginning. He or she goes through countless lifetimes, the nature of which is determined by karma.
Destiny of Humans	The series of lifetimes continues and may include episodes in heavens and hells. Finally, one transcends karma through God realization.
Revelation or Mediation between the Ultimate and the Human	The Vedic scriptures; the Bhagavad-Gita; the Brahmin priesthood; the Gods and God-realized saints as expressions of the One; following one's guru as spiritual guide.

Practical

What Is Expected of Humans; Worship, Practices, Behavior	To follow *dharma* through rituals, behavior, and righteous deeds. If one seeks *moksha*, or liberation, one would practice *yoga*, meditation, or devotion under the guidance of a guru.

Sociological

Major Social Institutions	The family; temples as places of the worship of the Gods and the Goddesses; holy men; the Brahmin priesthood; the caste system.

Summary

India has been the cradle of several religions: Buddhism, Jainism, Sikhism. But the great majority of its people follow Hinduism, which can be taken to mean simply "the religion of India." As such, it embraces a vast diversity of Gods and Goddesses, practices, and spiritual paths. It includes the worship of the Divine through images and concepts and through taking those images and concepts away. It strives to reconcile the following of *dharma*, the cosmic law, and the way of righteousness in this world and the quest for *moksha* or liberation from all that is limiting in the attainment of God realization.[74]

Beginning with Brahmin sacrificial religion and its cosmic Gods, such as Indra, Varuna, and

Agni, the Vedas end with the "interiorization of sacrifice" in the Upanishads, with their message that Brahman, the universal Absolute, is one with Atman, the True Self of each individual. Brahman, taking many shapes, is all that is, and only in knowing him is there joy.

During the period of the Upanishads, other spiritual teachings were arising as well. The Buddha and Mahavira of the Jains taught inward paths to liberation not dependent on the Vedas. Patanjali and others taught the essence of yoga: self-control attained through virtuous life, postures, and ordered breathing, then withdrawal from the outer senses to reach mastery and freedom within.

The Bhagavad-Gita, the great Hindu classic, showed the direction religion was taking by beginning with teachings like those of the Upanishads and culminating in a great revelation of Vishnu that established the foundations of *bhakti*. In the process, it also presented the *karma-yoga* teaching (which much later greatly influenced Mohandas K. Gandhi) that one can know liberation through work in the world if that work is done selflessly. A little later, Advaita Vedanta, the philosophical teaching that speaks of the sole existence of Brahman, and Tantrism, the path to liberation through radical initiations and paradoxical sexual and other practices, added their flavors to Hinduism. In the sixteenth century, the Sikh faith sought to worship the God above Hinduism and Islam.

Hindu deities are numerous, but the major ones fall into two great families: the Vishnu family and the Shiva family. Vishnu represents the forces working for good in the cosmos; from time to time he comes to Earth in the form of *avatars*, such as Rama and Krishna, to restore righteousness. Shiva, though also ultimately good, represents the life force or the totality, and Shakti, the Great Goddess who goes by many names, such as Kali, Durga, and Parvati, is the power and manifestation of the phenomenal universe. She is a powerful religious force in her own right.

Home and family are all-important centers of Hindu religious life. In a devout home, the head of the family offers daily devotions. In traditional India, one's caste was an important determinant of spiritual life; however, the power of caste is weakening, and discrimination based on it is illegal, although adherence to caste remains in attitudes toward it and in marriage alliances. Many Hindus worship in colorful temples as well as at home,

presenting garlands of flowers or other offerings to the Divine, perhaps with the help of a priest; temples are especially associated with pilgrimage and festival. Some Hindus, especially toward the end of life, become *sadhus*, renouncing the things of this world for the sake of the spiritual quest. They, like others serious about spirituality, may become disciples of a guru or spiritual teacher, or *sadhus* may become gurus themselves.

Modern Hinduism has made vigorous efforts to relate its ancient tradition to the modern world. Ramakrishna and his followers in the nineteenth century endeavored to show that the philosophical basis of the religion has universal value.

The great majority of Hindus practice some form of *bhakti*, or devotion, toward the Gods and the Goddesses. *Bhakti* devotees believe that love for one's chosen deity is the easiest yet most supremely effective road to liberation. *Bhakti* somewhat minimizes the importance of caste and the restrictive roles for women in Hindu society and so has permitted participation by those in the lower castes, as well as by women—many of whom have become recognized saints.

Classical Hindu literature reflects the central role of a holy king who is to rule in ways consistent with the *dharma*. The king's rule is monitored, therefore, by the *Brahmins*, who are of the highest caste and whose duty it is to maintain the *dharma*. The *dharma* inextricably links the political order and the social order, of which the obligations and structures of caste and family are essential constituents. Moreover, the king is to be the exemplar of virtue. The ideal is Rama, the archetypal warrior king hero.

In the twentieth century, Mohandas K. Gandhi drew from Hinduism to pioneer nonviolent methods of political and social change. Today, the political situation in India, the world's largest democracy, remains in flux, with many competing visions for the future of India and tensions between Hindus and those in other religions in India, such as Muslims and Sikhs. In the meantime, India has risen to become a global economic and political force, and its society is changing, with many Indians fostering a Hindu worldview of holistic self-realization and religious pluralism at home and abroad.

The development of the ideal of the Hindu wife in the Brahminical period led to religio-cultural practices, such as child marriage, *purdah*, dowry, and *sati*, together with attitudes such as those toward widows that greatly restricted women's lives and led to abuses. These became the subject of reform in the nineteenth century. Today Hindu women have leadership roles in government, business, and religious institutions.

Hinduism has had a profound influence on the American religious landscape. American Hindu temples are centers of worship for Indian immigrants, who strive for balance between Hindu culture and Western values. Hindu practices and ideas have been almost imperceptibly woven into aspects of American life. There are numerous Hindu-based religious movements in America,

including the Vedanta Society, the Self-Realization Fellowship, and the International Society for Krishna Consciousness. New generations of Hindus are forging an identity as "Hindu-Americans," finding much in American culture that is compatible with Hinduism's emphasis on holistic self-realization and religious pluralism.

Jainism is an ancient Indian religion emphasizing life in everything and the liberation of the *jiva*, or soul, from bondage to *karma* or to matter through self-denial.

Sikhism, emerging on the border of Hinduism and Islam, presented a simple monotheism taught by a lineage of true gurus.

Questions for Review

1. Explain how Hinduism has reconciled the "affirmative way" in religion—the way of moving toward unconditioned reality through devotion to Divine images and ideas—and the "negative way"—the way to God by taking away all that is not God, all lesser images and ideas. See what persons, concepts, and practices are on each side and where they meet.
2. Explain how Hinduism reconciles the following of *dharma*, the divine social order, in accordance with *rita*, the divine cosmic order, and the way of righteousness in the world, with the pursuit of *moksha*, liberation into divine infinity.
3. Interpret the view of human life indicated by Hinduism's four goals and four stages of life.
4. Present the main features of Vedic religion: its worldview, its Gods and Goddesses, the inner meaning of its sacrifices, and how it set the stage for the development of later Hindu philosophy and religion.
5. Talk about the central message of the Upanishads.
6. Explain what is meant by Brahman.
7. Discuss the Buddha in the context of his times and how Buddhism may have influenced Hinduism.
8. Understand the theory and practice of *yoga*.
9. Show how the thought of the Bhagavad-Gita moves from the insights of the Upanishads to those of *bhakti*, or Hindu devotionalism.
10. Explain the philosophy of Advaita Vedanta.
11. Describe some features of the thought and practice of Tantrism as a path to liberation.
12. Describe the two main families of Hindu Gods and Goddesses, as well as the religious narratives

and worship of two or three deities in detail, and Hinduism's "Holy Trinity."
13. Explain how home and family are the main centers of Hindu worship for a large number of Hindus.
14. Interpret the fundamental meaning of the Hindu caste system.
15. Discuss the meaning and role of *sadhus*, or holy men.
16. Briefly describe the practice of Hinduism today—its main features.
17. Discuss the development of the model of the ideal Hindu wife from the early Vedas to the Upanishads and how it had an impact on women's lives.
18. Discuss the holy king model based on the dharma and its potential influence today.
19. Discuss the reform movement of the nineteenth and twentieth centuries in India and its relationship to the Indian independence movement and nationalism, as well as the role of women in it.
20. Explain how Ramakrishna and Gandhi, each in his own way, related Hinduism to the modern world.
21. Talk about the insight of Hinduism that you found of most value for yourself.
22. Using the chart on page 107, summarize the fundamental features of Hinduism. How does it answer the great questions about God and the meaning of human life?
23. Give the fundamental features of Jainism.
24. Give the fundamental features of Sikhism.
25. Describe Hinduism and other religions of India in America, including the Hinduism of Indian immigrants and India's influence on the American religious landscape.

Suggested Readings on the Religions of India

General—Ancient

Basham, A. L., *The Wonder That Was India*. New York: Grove Press, 1959.

Benton, Catherine, *God of Desire: Tales of Kamadeva in Sanskrit Story Literature*. Albany: State University of New York Press, 2006.

Clothey, Fred W., *Religion in India: A Historical Introduction*. London and New York: Routledge, 2006.

Deutsch, Eliot, *Advaita Vedanta: A Philosophical Reconstruction*. Honolulu: East-West Center Press, 1969.

Doniger, Wendy, *The Hindus: An Alternative History*. New York: Penguin, 2009.

Eck, Diana L., *Banaras: City of Light*. New York: Knopf, 1982.

Eliade, Mircea, *Yoga: Immortality and Freedom*. New York: Pantheon Books, 1958.

Fuller, J. Christopher, *The Camphor Flame: Popular Hinduism and Society in India*. Princeton, NJ: Princeton University Press, 1992.

Heehs, Peter, ed., *Indian Religions: A Historical Reader of Spiritual Expression and Experience*. New York: New York University Press, 2012.

King, Ann S., ed., *Indian Religion: Renaissance and Renewal*. London and Oakville, CT: Equinox, 2006.

Klostermeier, Klaus, *A Survey of Hinduism*, 3rd ed. Albany: State University of New York Press, 2007.

Lopez, Donald S., ed., *Religions of India in Practice*. Princeton, NJ: Princeton University Press, 1995.

Madan, Triloki N., *India's Religions: Perspectives from Sociology and History*. New Delhi: Oxford University Press, 2004.

Michaels, Axel, *Hinduism: Past and Present*. Princeton, NJ: Princeton University Press, 2004.

Mittal, Sushil, and Gene Thursby, *Studying Hinduism: Key Concepts and Methods*. London and New York: Routledge, 2008.

Miller, Barbara Stoller, *Yoga: Discipline of Freedom: The Yoga Sutra Attributed to Patanjali*. Berkeley: University of California Press, 1996.

O'Flaherty, Wendy P., ed., *Karma and Rebirth in Classical Indian Traditions*. Berkeley: University of California Press, 1980.

———, *The Rig Veda: An Anthology*. Harmondsworth, UK: Penguin Books, 1982.

Prabhavananda, Swami, and Christopher Isherwood, *How to Know God: The Yoga Aphorisms of Patanjali*. New York: Mentor Books, 1969.

———, *The Song of God: Bhagavad-Gita*. New York: Mentor Books, 1951.

Prabhavananda, Swami, and Frederick Manchester, *The Upanishads: Breath of the Eternal*. New York: Mentor Books, 1948.

Rinehart, Robin, ed., *Contemporary Hinduism: Ritual, Culture, and Practice*. Santa Barbara, CA: ABC/CLIO, 2004.

Rosen, Steven J., *Essential Hinduism*. Westport, CT: Praeger, 2006.

Sullivan, Bruce M., *Historical Dictionary of Hinduism*. Lanham, MD: Scarecrow Press, 1997.

Zimmer, Heinrich, *Myths and Symbols in Indian Art and Civilization*. New York: Harper Torchbooks, 1962.

———, *Philosophies of India*. New York: Meridian Books, 1956.

Hindu Gods and Goddesses

Carman, John B., *The Theology of Ramanuja*. New Haven, CT: Yale University Press, 1974.

Chandra, Suresh, *Encyclopedia of Hindu Gods and Goddesses*. New Delhi: Sarup & Sons, 1998.

Coomaraswamy, Ananda, and Sister Nivedita, *Myths of the Hindus and Buddhists*. New York: Dover, 1972.

Hawley, John Stratton, ed., *The Divine Consort*. Berkeley: University of California Press, 1982.

———, and Donna Marie Wilffieds, eds., *Devi: Goddesses of India*. Berkeley: University of California Press, 1996.

Kinsley, David R., *Hindu Goddesses*. Berkeley: University of California Press, 1986.

———, *The Sword and the Flute*. Berkeley: University of California Press, 1975.

O'Flaherty, Wendy P., *Asceticism and Eroticism in the Mythology of Siva*. London and New York: Oxford University Press, 1973.

———, *Hindu Myths: A Sourcebook*. Harmondsworth, UK and Baltimore, MD: Penguin Books, 1975.

———, *The Origins of Evil in Hindu Mythology*. Berkeley, CA: University of California Press, 1980.

Pintchman, Tracy, ed., *Seeking Mahadevi: Constructing the Identities of the Hindu Great Goddess*. Albany: State University of New York Press, 2001.

Singer, Milton, ed., *Krishna: Myths, Rites, and Attitudes*. Chicago: University of Chicago Press, 1968.

Singh, R. Raj, *Bhakti and Philosophy*. Lanham, MD: Lexington Books, 2006.

Tantrism

Kinsley, David, *Tantric Visions of the Divine Feminine*. Berkeley: University of California Press, 1997.

McDaniel, June, *The Madness of the Saints*. Chicago: University of Chicago Press, 1989.

Silburn, Lilian, *Kundalini: Energy of the Depths*, Jacques Contier, trans. Albany: State University of New York Press, 1988.

Urban, Keth, *Tantra: Sex, Secrecy, Politics, and Power in the Study of Religion*. Berkeley: University of California Press, 2003.

White, David Gordon, *Kiss of the Yogini: "Tantric Sex" in its South Asian Contexts*. Chicago: University of Chicago Press, 2003.

———, *Tantrism in Practice*. Princeton, NJ: Princeton University Press, 2000.

Modern India

Blank, Jonah, *Arrow of the Blue-Skinned God*. Boston: Houghton-Mifflin, 1992.

Bonner, Arthur, *Averting the Apocalypse: Social Movements in India Today*. Durham, NC: Duke University Press, 1990.

Dalrymple William, *Nine Lives: In Search of the Sacred in Modern India*. New York: Knopf, 2010.

Giridharadas, Anand, *India Calling: An Intimate Portrait of a Nation's Remaking*. New York: Times Books/Henry Holt & Co, 2011.

Isherwood, Christopher, *Ramakrishna and His Disciples*. New York: Simon & Schuster, 1965.

Juergensmeyer, Mark, *Radhasoami Reality: The Logic of a Modern Faith*. Princeton, NJ: Princeton University Press, 1991.

Luce, Edward, *In Spite of the Gods: The Rise of Modern India*. New York: Anchor Books, 2008.

Religion, Governance, and Political Life

Iyer, Raghavan, *The Moral and Political Thought of Mahatma Gandhi*. London: Oxford University Press, 1973.

Sahu, Sunil K., "Religion and Politics in India: The Emergence of Hindu Nationalism and the Bharatiya Party (BJP)," in *Religion and Politics in Comparative Perspective: The One, the Few, and the Many*, Ted Gerard Jelen and Clyde Wilcox, eds. New York: Cambridge University Press, 2002.

Smith, Brian K., "Hinduism," in *God's Rule: The Politics of the World's Religions*, Jacob Neusner, ed. Washington, DC: Georgetown University Press, 2003.

Zavos, John, *The Emergence of Hindu Nationalism in India*. New York: Oxford University Press, 2000.

Women and Hinduism

Dietrich, Gabrielle, *Reflections of the Women's Movement in India*. New Delhi: Horizon India Books, 1992.

Falk, Nancy Auer, *Women and Religion in India: An Annotated Bibliography of Sources in English, 1975–1992*. Kalamazoo, MI: New Issues Press, 1994.

Harlan, Lindsey, and Paul B. Courtright, eds., *From the Margins of Hindu Marriage: Essays on Gender, Religion and Culture*. New York: Oxford University Press, 1995.

Jacobson, Doranne, and Susan S. Wadley, *Women in India: Two Perspectives*, 3rd ed. Columbia, MO: South Asia Publications, 1995.

Kinsley, David R., *Tantric Visions of the Divine Feminine: The Ten Mahavidyas*. Berkeley: University of California Press, 1997.

Mitter, Sara S., *Dharma's Daughters: Contemporary Indian Women and Hindu Culture*. New Brunswick, NJ: Rutgers University Press, 1991.

Mukherjee, Prabhati, *Hindu Women: Normative Models*, rev. ed. Calcutta: Orient Longman, 1994.

Narayanan, Vasudha, "Brimming with *Bhakti*, Embodiments of Shakti: Devotees, Deities, Performers, Reformers, and Other Women of Power in Hindu Tradition," in *Feminism and World Religions*, Arvind Sharma and Katherine K. Young, eds. Albany: State University of New York Press, 1999.

———, "Hinduism," in *Her Voice, Her Faith*, Arvind Sharma and Katherine K. Young, eds. Boulder, CO and Oxford, UK: Westview Press, 2003.

Pintchman, Tracy, ed., *Women's Lives, Women's Rituals in the Hindu Tradition*. Oxford and New York: Oxford University Press, 2007.

Ramabai Sarasvati, Pundita, *The High Caste Hindu Woman*. New Delhi: M. C. Mittal Inter-India Publications, 1888, reprinted in 1984.

Robinson, Catherine A., *Tradition and Liberation: The Hindu Tradition in the Indian Women's Movement*. New York: St. Martin's Press, 1999.

Young, Katherine K., "Hinduism," in *Women in World Religions*, Arvind Sharma, ed. Albany: State University of New York Press, 1987, pp. 60–72.

———, "Women in Hinduism," in *Today's Woman in World Religions*, Arvind Sharma, ed. Albany: State University of New York Press, 1994, pp. 77–135.

The Jains

Dundas, Paul, *The Jains*, 2nd ed. New York: Routledge, 1992.

Jaini, P. S., *The Jaina Path of Purification*. Berkeley: University of California Press, 1979.

Long, Jeffrey D., *Jainism: An Introduction*. London and New York: I. B. Tauris, 2009.

Shah, Natubui, *Jainism*, 2 vols. Brighton, UK and Portland, OR: Sussex Academic Press, 1998.

Tobias, Michael, *Life Force: The World of Jainism*. Fremont, CA: Jain Publishing, 1991.

The Sikhs

Cole, W. Owen, and Piara Singh Sambhi, *The Sikhs: Their Religious Beliefs and Practices*. London and Boston: Routledge & Kegan Paul, 1978.

Dogra, Ramesh Chander, and Urmila Dogra, *The Sikh World: An Encyclopedic Survey of Sikh Religion and Culture*. New Delhi: UBS Publishers, 2003.

McLeod, W. H., *Guru Nanak and the Sikh Religion*. Oxford: Oxford University Press, 1968.

————, *Sikhs and Sikhism*. New York: Oxford University Press, 1999.

————, *The Sikhs: History, Religion and Society*. New York: Columbia University Press, 1989.

Singh, Pashavra, *The Guru Granth Sahib: Canon, Meaning, and Authority*. New Delhi: Oxford University Press, 2000.

Singh, Trilochar, et al., *Adi Granth: Selections from the Sacred Writings of the Sikhs*. London: George Allen & Unwin, 1960.

Hinduism in America

Coward, Harold, John R. Hinnells, and Raymond Brady Williams, eds., *The South Asian Religious Diaspora in Britain, Canada, and the United States*. Albany: State University of New York Press, 2000.

Crawford, S. Cromwell, *Dilemmas of Life and Death: Hindu Ethics in North American Context*. Albany: State University of New York Press, 1995.

Ellwood, Robert S., *Eastern Spirituality in America*. New York: Paulist Press, 1987, Chapter II.

————, and Harry B. Partin, *Religious and Spiritual Groups in Modern America*, 2nd ed. Englewood Cliffs, NJ: Prentice Hall, 1988, Chapter 7.

Forsthoefel, Thomas A., and Cynthia Ann Humes, *Gurus in America*. Albany: State University of New York Press, 2005.

Jackson, Carl T., *Vedanta for the West: The Ramakrishna Movement in the United States*. Bloomington: Indiana University Press, 1994.

Kurien, Prema A., *A Place at the Multicultural Table: The Development of an American Hinduism*. New Brunswick, NJ: Rutgers University Press, 2007.

de Michelis, Elizabeth, *A History of Modern Yoga*. London and New York: Continuum, 2004.

Syman, Stefanie, *The Subtle Body: The Story of Yoga in America*. New York: Farrar, Straus and Giroux, 2010.

4

Wisdom Embarked for the Farther Shore
The Journey of Buddhism

CHAPTER OBJECTIVES

After studying this chapter, you should be able to

- Outline the traditional life and essential teaching of the Buddha.
- Discuss the major schools of Buddhism and how they spread to various parts of Asia.
- Present the importance of practice, especially meditation, in Buddhism.
- Talk about why Buddhism can be thought of as a particularly "psychological" religion.
- Understand ancient and contemporary views of Buddhism, governance, and political life.
- Discuss the role of and attitudes toward women in the major schools of Buddhism.

A RELIGION OF TRANSFORMATION OF CONSCIOUSNESS

Buddhism is many things. On the flat Ganges plains east of Benares (now Varanasi), it is an ancient enshrined tree said to be a descendant of the very tree under which he who is called the Buddha, on the night of a full moon, ascended through the four stages of trance and attained full, perfect, and complete enlightenment. In Southeast Asia, Buddhism is steep-roofed temples, rich in gold and red, that house conventionalized images of the same Buddha, perhaps standing to teach, perhaps seated in the meditation posture of enlightenment, perhaps reclining as he makes his final entry into **Nirvana**. The images will probably be gilded, gleaming with transcendent golden light, and the figure's eyes will be half-closed and enigmatic. Around his head may be a many-pointed crown or a simple burst of flame. Outside the temple, saffron-robed monks of the Blessed One (as the Buddha is called) walk with begging bowls, seeking alms.

    In the snowy Himalayas, Buddhism is a prayer wheel, a cylinder on an axle inscribed with a mantra such as "Hail the Jewel in the Lotus" and set up on a roadway or around a temple to be spun by passing pilgrims. In Japan, Buddhism is an old Zen monk making tea or contemplating the rocks in his monastery garden, as well as vigorous, dynamic young people organizing rallies that combine Buddhist chanting with marching bands and rock concerts.

The Lotus Flower, an important symbol in Buddhism.

What is it that ties this tradition together? Buddhism is not rooted in a single culture or area, as is Hinduism, but is an international religion, a movement introduced in historical time into every society where it is now at home. It has deeply pervaded these cultures and deeply identified with them. But the perceptive observer never quite loses awareness that, on the one hand, this religion is not identical with all of the spiritual life of the culture and that, on the other hand, it is a movement wider than the culture and has brought in gifts from outside.

All of this gives Buddhism a somewhat different atmosphere from the Hindu context out of which it emerged. Buddhism always combines something of the Indian spiritual tradition with very different cultures. However, instead of the rich, heavy "biological" flavor of Hinduism, of which we have spoken in the preceding chapter, Buddhism has a more psychological thrust.

What is distinctive about Buddhist altars is that, instead of portraying the archetypal hero, mother, or cosmic pillar, as do Hindu altars, the image communicates a unified psychological state—profound meditation, warm compassion, or even unambiguous fury against illusion. Buddhist practices, too, are focused on strong and clear states of unified consciousness. Either they produce clear states, or they draw power from beings who have achieved unfettered clarity.

Given this fundamental psychological thrust, let us briefly look at Buddhism in terms of the three forms of religious expression. We shall examine them in reverse order.

The basic sociological fact in Buddhism is the **samgha**, the order of monks. The monastic order is not a unified organization throughout the Buddhist world, and its structure and role vary. In modern Japan, it is often no longer celibate, but almost always, where there is Buddhism, there are men and women who have given up "natural" life and its goals to take formal vows that orient life in another direction, the realization of a different state of consciousness from the ordinary. They are the teachers and bearers of Buddhist tradition, and by their distinctive garb, by their monasteries and temples, and by their way of life, they make the Buddhist presence unavoidably visible in the midst of society.

Buddhist practice is immensely varied, but it centers on three foci: the ideal of the Buddha, the transformation of consciousness, and *karma*, or doing works that gain merit and that thereby bring good things in this life and the next rebirth. As for the first focus, the Buddha is revered and presented to the world as the fully realized being who teaches and epitomizes the true nature of all other beings. He has attained realization through profound psychological self-analysis and self-control. Second, the Buddhist practice for transformation of consciousness works in the same way and so is most fully expressed in meditation, but it also includes chanting and ritual. Third, good *karma* is gained through good works—both ritual works, like gilding a statue of the Buddha or building a temple, and works of compassion, like kindness to a needy person or a mistreated animal. Conversely, evil deeds of irreverence or cruelty to man or beast bring bad *karma*, and with it bad luck and a worse rebirth than this one.

Buddhist theoretical expression is then concerned with the meaning of the Buddha, how consciousness is transformed, and *karma*. Above all, it is psychological in emphasis. Concerned with the analysis of human perception and experience, it studies how people see the world and how they think. It looks at how our perceptions and our thoughts really center on our own egos.

Buddhist philosophy is not a vague, diffuse mysticism but a sharp, precise tool that delights in hard logic and numerical lists of categories. It holds that ordinary life is unsatisfactory, for it is based on ignorance and desire, and is unable to realize that there is no real "self." All entities within the universe, including human beings, are impermanent compounds that come together and come apart. The answer is a different kind of mind, a "wisdom mind," which finds the "middle way" between all attachments and unites all opposites—being, like the Buddha, free of partiality toward any segment of the cosmos—and which is therefore, in its unclouded clarity, open to omniscience, skill, and compassion.

We shall now look at the life of the Buddha to see how these themes are expressed in the traditional account of his quest and achievement.

THE LIFE OF THE BUDDHA

At the beginning of the tradition, of which all these forms and much else are branches, lies the life of one man, Siddhartha Gautama of the Sakya clan, called the Buddha, dated by modern scholars to have lived between approximately 563 and 483 B.C.E. While the following story of the Buddha's life is legendary and not historical, it is important because it reveals how traditional Buddhists have thought of him over some twenty-five centuries.

The Buddha was born, according to tradition, at Lumbini, about where the border between India and Nepal now lies, north of Varanasi, also known as Benares. His father was ruler of a tiny state in the foothills of the Himalayas.

Tradition has it that a wise old Brahmin came to the court and, having observed certain remarkable signs on the infant's body, predicted that the wonderful child would become either a world emperor or a Buddha, that is, an Enlightened One and a World Savior. The father, being more political than spiritual in orientation, preferred that his son follow the path of a "world emperor." Realizing that if the gifted boy saw the suffering of the world, he would be so moved by compassion that he would prefer to save humankind from pain rather than rule from a throne, the king determined to shield the prince from any sight of ill. He built Siddhartha Gautama glorious pleasure palaces, equipped with everything from chariots to dancing girls to delight the heart of a young prince. All were surrounded by high walls.

There, the future Buddha matured, married, and had a son. But even unbroken amusement palls eventually, and the prince persuaded his charioteer to take him down the road toward the nearby city. He took four trips in all and, despite his father's previous efforts to shield his eyes, saw four thought-provoking sights: an aged man, a man suffering in agony from a hideous disease, a corpse, and finally an old wandering monk who appeared content. After this, Siddhartha viewed even his dancing girls in a different light, and large disturbing issues clouded his mind.

What is the meaning of life, he asked himself, if its initial promise of joy ends long before its dreams can possibly all be fulfilled—in the old age in which one totters backward into infantilism again, or in sickness and pain that can reduce a man or woman full of zest and hope to the state of a howling animal, or, finally, in the apparently blank extinction of death? How can one be delivered from these ghastly conditions of birth, fantasy, and agony?

Siddhartha did not know the answers to these questions, but he knew that until they were answered, he could no longer live for anything else than finding the answers. The last sight, the itinerant monk with his staff and begging bowl, inspired him with the idea of a life wholly dedicated to finding the answers he sought. Not long after, in the middle of the night, the prince kissed his wife and son farewell without waking them and slipped off with his faithful charioteer to the banks of a river. There he exchanged his fine raiment for the coarse garb of a renunciant. He then proceeded alone on the great quest.

In his search, he sampled the web of paths to realization that crisscrossed the spiritual map of India. He talked with Brahmins. He worked with teachers of trance meditation and went the route of extreme asceticism, getting to the point of eating only one grain of rice a day and becoming so emaciated that his ribs and spinal column stood out as if he were a walking skeleton. But he found that neither philosophy nor fasting and self-control alone brought what he desired. He gave them up and went back to a moderate diet.

Then, late one afternoon, as he wandered not far from the banks of a river, he felt that the time had come. After purchasing a pallet of straw from a farmer, he seated himself on it under a huge fig tree. He placed his hand firmly on the ground and swore by the good earth itself that he would not stir from that spot until he attained complete and final enlightenment. All night he remained there, sunk in deeper and deeper meditation. Mara, an old Vedic nature god or demon, buffeted him with furious storms and sweet temptations, but a wave of the Blessed One's hand was enough to dispel them. His consciousness refined itself by moving through four stages of trance, beginning with the calmness of the passions that concentration brings and ending with the transcendence of all opposites. He also passed through several stages of awareness. First, he saw all of his previous existences. Then, he saw the previous lives, the interlocking deaths and rebirths, of all beings, and he grasped at the *karmic* forces at work; the universe became like a mirror to him. Finally, he saw with full understanding what principles underlie this web of paths and how extrication from it is possible. He saw the mutual interdependence of all things and how egocentric ignorance leads sentient beings inevitably through desire to suffering, death, and unhappy rebirth. The **Four Noble Truths** (to be discussed later) appeared in his mind: all life is suffering; suffering is caused by desire; there can be an end to desire; the way is in the **Eightfold Path**.

Siddhartha Gautama was now a Buddha, an "Enlightened One" or "One who is awake." He was also called the **Tathagata**, an expression difficult to translate but meaning something like, "He who has come thus and gone thus," in the sense of, "He who passed beyond all bounds; one cannot say where he came from or where he is but can only point in the direction he went," referring to his overcoming of all conditioned reality in his enlightenment to become "universalized." He was one with the universe itself and not any particular part of it in principle. And after death and entry into Nirvana, he no longer continued to have a physical body. (Another title for the Buddha commonly used in Asia is *Sakyamuni*, *Shaka* or *Shakamuni* in Japanese, meaning "Sage of the Sakya Clan.")

After remaining in meditation many days, he arose and went toward Benares. On its outskirts, in Sarnath, the "Deer Park," he met five ascetics with whom he had been associated before and who at first mocked him for giving up the austere life. He preached to them about the **Middle Way** and the Four Noble Truths. They were converted and became his first disciples.

As he wandered about teaching, other disciples came to join him, until there was a band of some sixty accompanying the Enlightened One. Upon entering the Buddha's order, each accepted the **Three Refuges**, or the **Three Jewels**. These refer to three fundamental points of orientation in Buddhism, three things that a Buddhist affirms. They are expressed in the form of these assertions: I take refuge in the Buddha; I take refuge in the *dharma*; I take refuge in the *samgha*. The *dharma* here means the Buddha's teaching; the *samgha* is the order of monks.

Thus, the Three Jewels affirm that the Buddha is the supreme embodiment of the potential of human life; his teaching tells how he can be emulated and what his wisdom is; the order of monks is the custodian of the Buddha and the *dharma* for future generations and is the social context in which the potential can best be reached. We see here Buddhism taking the three forms of religious expression: an intellectual teaching; an emerging object of worship, together with the practices prescribed by the Eightfold Path, meditation being a central practice; and a sociological expression, the *samgha*, which today is probably the oldest continuing nonfamilial social institution in the world.

The life of monks was strictly governed by rules, of which the basic ten are prohibitions against (1) taking life; (2) taking what is not given; (3) sexual misconduct; (4) lying; (5) taking intoxicants; (6) eating after noon; (7) watching or participating in dancing, singing, and shows; (8) adorning oneself with garlands, perfumes, and ointments; (9) sleeping in a soft bed (taken to represent living luxuriously); and (10) handling money. (These rules are still followed by Buddhist monks, although they are sometimes interpreted in an allegorical sense in northern traditions. Devout lay people often undertake the first five.)

The Buddha's ministry, which lasted forty-five years after his enlightenment, was generally successful. Of those to whom he preached, many were said to have become **arhants**—fully liberated beings who will suffer no more rebirths. Since being a Buddha is unique, the *arhant* state is the spiritual goal of the Buddha's disciples. When the band of disciples reached sixty, he sent them out as missionaries. Thousands came to the Buddha or to his disciples, seeking lay or monastic initiation, many from the highest ranks of society. Sometimes whole tribes or ascetic orders were converted at once. In time, an order of nuns was established (to be discussed later). Valuable pieces of land were given to the order.

Bronze Statue of Buddha in the Asakusa district, Tokyo, Japan.

There was, of course, opposition. Certain Brahmins murmured against the Buddha's doctrine. One disciple, Devadatta, egged on by a hostile king, became a traitor and tried to kill the Buddha, but his plots were foiled by the sage's perception. The Buddha's end finally came from eating tainted food; he died meditating in great peace and surrounded by his disciples, passing again through the stages of trance, imparting final wisdom to the *samgha*, such as "Be ye lamps unto yourselves," "All compounds are transitory," and last, "Work out your own salvation with diligence." Breathing his last, he then transcended all particularized existence and attained Nirvanic consciousness.

This is the story traditionally told of the Buddha. Much of it is legendary or a reading back of later Buddhist developments, but it is nonetheless important, for it presents the image of the Buddha that has shaped the 2,500 years of Buddhist history.[1]

BASIC BUDDHIST TEACHING

The Middle Way

When the Buddha returned to preach to the five ascetics in the Deer Park after his enlightenment, he preached to them the Middle Way. When they first saw him and recognized him as one who had been with them but had left, they mocked him as a pleasure lover who had gone back to soft living. But when he opened his mouth to speak, they could not resist a wisdom that went beyond their mere pride in denying the flesh.

Of the Middle Way he said:

> Those foolish people who torment themselves, as well as those who have become attached to the domains of the senses, both these should be viewed as faulty in their method, because they are not on the way to deathlessness. These so-called austerities but confuse the mind which is overpowered by the body's exhaustion. In the resulting stupor one can no longer understand the ordinary things of life, how much less the way to the Truth which lies beyond the senses. The minds of those, on the other hand, who are attached to the worthless sense-objects, are overwhelmed by passion and darkening delusion. They lose even the ability to understand the doctrinal treatises, still less can they understand the method which by suppressing the passions leads to dispassion. So I have given up both these extremes, and have found another path, a middle way. It leads to the appeasing of all ill, and yet it is free from happiness and joy.[2]

The Middle Way is, on its deepest levels, an attitude that seeks to find the delicate, infinitely subtle point of absolute equilibrium between all extremes and polarities—from the obvious balancing off of asceticism and self-indulgence to the deep metaphysical reaches of eschewing attachment either to life or death to the desire for being or nonbeing. Everything comes in pairs of opposites, the Buddha taught, in our world of partialities, multiplicity, and conditioned reality: day and night, pleasant and unpleasant, life and death, being and nonbeing. The senses, the desires, and the unexamined life get hung up on one side or the other in these pairs of opposites, thinking one side or the other is better. The way of wisdom is for one to find a balance in the totality that includes them both—and so have the permanence and invincibility of the totality. The person of wisdom is stable, like the sky—not like clouds now blown this way, now that, and finally dissipated.

The Four Noble Truths and "No Self"

The Four Noble Truths go deep into the psychological analysis behind the Middle Way and into the process to attain perfect equilibrium and totality. In his Deer Park sermon, the Buddha went on to say:

> What then is the Holy Truth of Ill [Suffering]? Birth is ill, decay is ill, sickness is ill, death is ill. To be conjoined with what one dislikes means suffering. To be disjoined from what one likes means suffering. Not to get what one wants, also that means suffering. In short, all grasping at any of the five Skandhas involves suffering.
>
> What then is the Holy Truth of the Origination of Ill? It is that craving which leads to rebirth, accompanied by delight and greed, seeking its delight now here, now there, i.e., craving for sensuous experience, craving to perpetuate oneself, craving for extinction.
>
> What then is the Holy Truth of the Stopping of Ill? It is the complete stopping of that craving, the withdrawal from it, the renouncing of it, throwing it back, liberation from it, nonattachment to it.
>
> What then is the Holy Truth of the steps which lead to the stopping of Ill? It is this holy Eightfold Path, which consists of right views, right intentions, right speech, right conduct, right livelihood, right effort, right mindfulness, right concentration.[3]

These Truths can be summarized as consisting of two pairs. The first is

All life is suffering (or ill, or pain, or anxiety, or bitter frustration). Suffering is caused by desire (or craving, or attachment).

This pair is the analysis of the ordinary human condition: a mad circle dance, fueled by ignorance, of suffering and desire chasing each other. The more we suffer, the more we want things to assuage or distract the suffering. The more we get, the more we suffer anxiety that we shall lose it and so experience frustration at the transience of all things. And so around and around.

Thus, we find the good news in the second pair:

There can be an end to desire. The way out is the Eightfold Path.

Buddhism is sometimes thought of as a pessimistic religion, but that interpretation is true only in its assessment of the ordinary life governed by the suffering and desire of the first two Noble Truths. In fact, Buddhism is one of the most optimistic of religions in its vision of the ultimate potential of humankind once that vicious circle is broken, for the third of the Noble Truths says suffering can be ended by stopping the craving. At this point, the vicious circle can be halted. One can throw sand in its gears and pull the plug on its turbulence.

Desire, then, is the vulnerable point at which the circle can be broken. It is vulnerable because there is something we can do about it. Craving, or desire, the Buddha says, is like a fire, and any fire requires fuel. If fuel is taken away, the fire must die down. The fuel of the fire of desire consists of the many things to which the senses are attached. How does one pull back the senses from these attachments? One does so by concentration or meditation, the last and culminating point of the Eightfold Path, which focuses one's awareness on something other than objects of desire and so lets the senses quiet down from burning for things they can never really have.

One of the fundamental points of Buddhist psychology, and a key to understanding the whole system on a deep level, is **Anatman**—"No Self." This Buddhist teaching can be compared to the Upanishadic doctrine that the Atman, the innermost self or soul, is really identical with Brahman. The Buddhist negative expression Anatman, or "No Self," is a difference of emphasis rather than a contradiction, for if the "Self" is simply the one universal Brahman, it is also "No Self" in any individualistic sense. But the difference points to the Buddhist tendency to psychological analysis rather than an **ontological** statement (i.e., a statement about reality).

Reflection on the idea of No Self provides a line of insight into the meaning of the Four Noble Truths, the Middle Way, and the Buddhist experience. This insight happens because the fundamental craving, or desire, that keeps us in the suffering–desire syndrome is ultimately the desire to be a separate individual self.

The first Noble Truth—that all life is suffering—tells us that there is something unsatisfactory, something anxious, frustrating, and incomplete about all life as it is ordinarily lived. It does not mean that all life is excruciating pain or that there are no pleasant moments. The Buddha, who supposedly lived his first twenty-nine years in a round of extravagant pleasure, could hardly have said that. But what he does say is that there is something frustrating and unsatisfactory in life, and it can get worse and worse.

The second Noble Truth tells us that the reason for this sense of inadequacy in ordinary life is that we are always trying to cling to things—objects, persons, ideas, experiences—that are partial and not permanent and so keep us in anxiety lest we lose them, as sooner or later we shall. Yet, nonetheless, we want to keep grasping.

The only conclusion that can be drawn is that somewhere we have acquired a distorted idea about the whole nature and possibilities of human life, that we are basing life on a false premise. And just as when we try to do a complex mathematical problem with the wrong formula, sooner or later everything will begin to come out wrong. So it is with human life. According to Buddhism, the false premise that underlies all other delusion, suffering, and grasping is that one is a separate, independent, individual self—rather than a transitory compound of several elements that is *completely interdependent with the whole universe.*

Buddhism teaches that instead of being a "Self," in the sense of a separate enduring "soul" stuck in a body, we are all compounds made up of several different constituents. The five parts that make up a human being are called **skandhas**; the word *skandha* means "bundle" and reminds us that these constituents themselves are collocations of *dharmas*, the pointlike primary particles that flash out of the void. The human *skandhas* are the form (the physical shape), the feelings, the perceptions (the "picture" the mind forms out of data transmitted by the sense organs), the inherent impulses (*karmic* dispositions), and the background consciousness. Note that both physical and psychological entities are brought together.

The problem is that when these five entities get together, they interact in such a way as to make the "person" think of himself or herself as a separate individual "Self." Although understandable, this way of thinking, according to Buddhism, arises from a misreading of the data.

Consider what happens when you, as a collection of the five *skandhas*, walk down the street and meet another such collection. You interpret everything in terms of reinforcing the illusion that you are a "Self," yet a moment's analysis would show how false this premise is.

As you walk, you could think, "I must be a separate individual self, for my physical body gives me the impression of being a detached unit, self-propelled and separate from other objects as I walk past them." (Such thinking is not really true, for even the physical body is in continual and necessary interaction with the environment in the course of breathing and eating. It is only a certain perspective that makes me include the stomach when I say "myself" but not the field that grows the food it digests or the sun that makes that food grow.)

As you see the other person, you could say to yourself, "I must be a separate individual self, or else why would I perceive that unit out there as other than myself?" (But it is not really "I" who sees the other; it is just a phenomenon of light waves hitting sensitive nerves.) The *skandha* of the senses then stimulates the *skandha* of perception to form a mental picture on the basis of this data.

You may react emotionally to the person you see—with joy and desire if the person is a someone you love, with anger if the person is someone you dislike. You may say, "I must be a separate individual self, for if I were not, who would be feeling these emotions of joy or anger?" (But these feelings are not a "Self"; they are just something that comes and goes like billowing waves in response to data fed to you by the senses, interpreted by the perception, and probably conditioned by the *karma* of patterns of behavior toward that person, or similar persons, carried over from the past, along with much else.)

Finally, you may say, "I must be a separate individual self because I am aware of all this." (But the human capacity for self-consciousness is not itself a "Self." It is just the *skandha* of consciousness that accompanies physical form, feeling, perceptions, and impulses; for it can neither generate nor erase the latter four; it is only a mirror in which they reflect as they act and react.)

Through such analysis as this, Buddhism concludes that we are not separate, individual selves but collections of elements temporarily brought together and bound to break apart. A life that disregards this fact is basing itself on a false premise and can experience only the syndrome of anxiety and craving as it faces old age, sickness, and death.

Nonetheless, this collection perversely wants to be a separate, individual self. From birth on, a human being asserts selfhood as the real reason for most of what he or she does. The newborn baby cries as if to say, "I must be a separate individual self, or else who would be crying and who would be hungry?"

Through life, one wants to learn, to achieve, to be loved, to accumulate goods, to acquire fame, to become a saint, to win life in heaven—all for oneself, all as though to say, "I must be a separate individual self, for if I were not, who would be learned, famous, beloved, immortal?" Nevertheless, all these dreams bring their own syndromes of anxiety and craving, and the body and, perhaps, the mind fall apart before they can more than begin to be fulfilled.

The Buddhist would put the question another way: *Who* is rich, famous, wise, holy, immortal? A name? A process? A set of memories? None of these is a "Self." Is there any one who can be abstracted from the round of rising and falling feelings and forms of a human life, who is independent of the continual flux of the universe? If there is no one, then we cannot properly think of anyone as being the recipient of wealth, fame, and wisdom or as experiencing perception, anger, joy, and so forth; there is only wealth, fame, wisdom, perception, anger, and joy, and so forth. But these are not things to be grasped, and there is no one to grasp them. For the Buddha's final words are reported to have been, "All aggregates are transitory." Every compound, including the human, is unstable and will come apart.

The reason is *karma*, the force of universal action and reaction that keeps everything moving and changing. Your activities, mental images, and thoughts, even your desire to perpetuate yourself as a separate individual self, set up "waves" in the cosmos around you as you try to gain this object or fulfill that dream. No energy is lost, and sooner or later the waves based on the false premise will come back to afflict and finally shatter the compound.

If there is no separate individual self, one might ask how Buddhism can talk as it does of reincarnation. What is there to reincarnate?

In one sense, of course, the answer is nothing. But *karma* also means that you get what you want—or rather, you continue to be what you think you are. Every cause, including the illusion of being a separate individual "Self," has an exactly corresponding effect. The illusion then becomes self-perpetuating, life after life.

It might be called a kinetic view of reincarnation. There is nothing solid taken out of one body and put in another. Rather, a deceased person's *skandhas* are dispersed into the universe. But the *karmic* waves that one has generated continue to operate until the precise kind of energy they bear has been appropriately transferred, just as ripples may continue to spread on the face of a pond even after a dropped stone has hit the bottom. The *karmic* waves will move until they have put together another set of five *skandhas* having shape, circumstance, and dispositions that are what they are because of the *karmic* energies left by the previous person. In terms of energy, then, if not actual substance, this person can be spoken of as the "reincarnation" of the other person.

Nirvana

What is the goal of meditation? Ultimately, it is Nirvana, the state absolutely transcending all pairs of opposites, and so all conditioned reality, by the blowing out of all flames of attachment. In Nirvana, all conditioning and, therefore, attachment, including the notion of being a separate individual self, are gone utterly beyond.

It must not be supposed that Nirvana is simply a state hardly distinguishable from annihilation. It is rather the opposite—universalization, the falling away of all barriers so that the mind becomes undifferentiated from horizonless infinity. The full, attractive, positive nature of Nirvana must be stressed. The word "Nirvana" is said to mean "extinguish" or "blow out," in the sense of blowing out a flame. Yet it does not mean disappearance in a negative sense; rather, it is the blowing out of all the fires of desire that constrict us. It does not mean extinction of consciousness but extinction of desires that cage and enslave consciousness. Our present consciousnesses are usually bound up with relishing sensory input and the accompanying mind-fogging cravings and self-delusions. It is virtually impossible for us now to know what genuine Nirvanic consciousness, free of such cravings and self-delusions, would be like. Nirvana is truly the opposite of life as we know it. In Buddhist literature, it is portrayed as the Otherness that is utterly desirable, a sparkling and golden light, a calm beyond all imagining.

Nor is the quest for Nirvana escapist. Far from being less alive, less active, or less useful, the person who passes into it (if one can so speak), or who is brought near to it, is far more—infinitely more—alive, active, and useful, as well as blissful to an unlimited degree. Freed from the shackles of self, one can live purely on the level of universal compassion and oneness with the joy of all beings. But one cannot express, in mere words, the full meaning of such statements. All language comes out of making distinctions and so is bound up with the pairs of opposites that rack the conditioned world. Nirvana is beyond all opposites; it is what is left, so to speak, when the last of them are surpassed. Therefore, although we know, from the unsatisfactory nature of life within attachments, contraries, and conditions, that Nirvanic transcendence would be supremely desirable and glorious, mere words cannot tell what it is, only what it is not, and those who have been there can only smile.

According to Buddhist belief, when the Buddha died—or attained Nirvana absolutely—an effect occurred that can only be called an implosion on the spiritual level. An implosion is the opposite of an explosion; it is what happens when a vacuum is suddenly created and all surrounding molecules of matter rush in to fill the void. The Buddha made no *karmic* waves, as we do when we try to grasp at things to fulfill desires. But his passing was like an implosion in the *karmic* field—suddenly there was nothing there—and a stream of *karmic* force (good *karma*) is still rushing in, striving to enter the gateless gate through which he had passed.

The best way to go in the direction he went, of course, is to meditate, emulating the means he used to get there. Next best, if one must act, is to act in ways that harmonize one with the onrushing waves of this stream flowing into the implosion void and let them bear one along. This is the meaning of being a Buddhist who accepts the Three Refuges. It is the meaning of the ordinary acts of kindness that follow the four "unlimited" virtues—unlimited friendliness, unlimited compassion, unlimited sympathetic joy, and unlimited even-mindedness. It is the inner meaning of the merit-making acts of lay people toward the meditative monks, such as giving them food, clothing, and donations. It is the meaning of acts of pure devotion that win good merit, like having **sutras** read, gilding images of the Buddha, burning incense, and offering flowers at shrines.

THERAVADA BUDDHISM

The Buddhist world is now divided into two great traditions.

Theravada ("Path of the Elders") Buddhism[4] is found in the nations of Sri Lanka (formerly Ceylon), Myanmar (formerly Burma), Thailand, Cambodia, and Laos. **Mahayana** ("Great Vessel") Buddhism has spread throughout China, Korea, Japan,

Buddhists praying at the Shwedagon Pagoda (Golden Pagoda) in Yangon, Myanmar at dusk.

Tibet, Mongolia, Nepal, Bhutan, Vietnam, and corners of India and Russia.[5] Let us look first at Theravada Buddhism.

Theravada Buddhism is based on what is known as the **Tripitaka**, or "Three Baskets." The Tripitaka, written in the Pali language (a variation of Sanskrit) several centuries after the time of the Buddha but based on oral tradition, presents the Buddha's life and teaching in three parts: the rules of monastic conduct, the Buddha's discourses, and the Buddha's doctrinal principles.

Theravadists (the "Elders") hold that Theravada Buddhism is the original form of Buddhism, which emphasizes individual enlightenment and the monastic community. Significantly, Theravada Buddhism claims an unbroken lineage of monks that extends back to the *samgha* established by Buddha himself. Theravadists believe themselves to be following the Buddha's teachings more literally than other Buddhist traditions and place greater emphasis on the historical Buddha.

If you were to visit one of the Theravada nations, it would not be long before the practical and sociological expressions of Buddhism became evident to you, and, through them, you would perceive the wide and deep influence of Buddhism in these lands. You would be struck by the great number of temples dotting the cities and lush tropical hills of the countryside. The temples are ornate and elaborate. Curved eaves mount up to pitched roofs. Soaring spires, in the case of large and lovely edifices such as the Shwe Dagon Temple in Yangon (Rangoon), seem to catch the very soul of the East. Guarding the temple gates are fierce-looking mythological beings; these, like the sculpture and murals one may see of epic heroes, such as Rama and Hanuman, are Gods borrowed from Hinduism. Shrines to indigenous spirits of nature and weather, *nats* in Burma and *phis* in Thailand, lurk in the temple shadows. Like the borrowed Hindu Gods, they are pupils of the Buddha on another plane than the human.

Within the cool temple, however, it is the Buddha who is supreme; his image gleams richly amid lamps and delicate offerings of incense, flowers, fruit, and water. He may be seated, standing, or reclining; these three postures represent, respectively, the Buddha's enlightenment, his teaching, and his entry into Nirvana. Worshippers come and go, performing worshipful acts of merit, which will benefit them in this life and in coming lives and will prepare them for ultimate release into Nirvana.

On the streets walk monks in their saffron-yellow robes, their heads shaved and their arms bare in the warm humid air. If it is early morning (Theravada monks do not eat after noon), each may be holding an offering bowl. At the door of a house, a monk will stand silent, head lowered and hands upraised, accepting whatever the indulgent householder places in his dish.

Most of the monks are young, for in all the Theravada countries except Sri Lanka, it is a custom (not always observed today) for every young man, from prince to peasant, to spend a year of his life as a monk. This experience serves to stabilize his religious life and is an initiation into manhood. A youth will not marry until after he has served as a monk, and his closest lifelong friends are likely to be those with whom he shared this experience. The great majority of men, of course, do not remain in the cloister. However, among the morning mendicants will be a few gentle old veterans of the monastic path, and they are afforded great respect.

If you followed one of the monks, you would return after him to a neighborhood temple with its attached monastery. Here the monks gather after begging to consume the simple meals they have garnered. During the afternoon, they will rest, study, and meditate.

The temple may be just a village or town **vihara**, rustic and no tourist attraction, but a center of community life. Here, traditionally, children go to school, festivals public and private are celebrated, and the dead are remembered. For the plain people of the town, monks are counselors, healers, exorcists, and friends.[6]

Or the temple might be one of the popular places of pilgrimage, where the faithful hope to win merit by gilding the Buddha's image or burning incense before the Buddha's giant footprint—a significant and popular shrine that suggests the Enlightened One was here and is no longer, but we can follow in the direction he went.

Or the monk you followed might be one of the many who throng the great national temples of the Theravada lands—the Temple of the Emerald Buddha in Bangkok, the Shwe Dagon Temple in Yangon, the Temple of the Tooth in Kandy, Sri Lanka. The skyward-curved towers of these splendid buildings, their pitched roofs and carved beams, their brilliant gold and color, their inner atmosphere of incense and contemplation, all murmur something of the sense of wonder and glory at the heart of Buddhism—and remind us that it is far more than just a philosophy.

In theory, the main task of the monk in the monastery is meditation, for he is to emulate the Buddha himself, and it was through meditation that the Awakened One went thence. That the young novice is emulating the Buddha is shown by the procedure through which he enters the monastery, if only for a few months. He goes to the monastery dressed as a prince, accompanied by a friend who plays the role of the Buddha's charioteer. At the monastery, he will have his head shaved, don his coarse monkish robe, and, kneeling before the abbot, take refuge in the Three Jewels.

Having taken refuge, the monk knows he is to emulate the silent image of the Buddha in the temple, with its serene and inward gaze. He is to explore and know, through meditation, the inward realm. Finally, he is to break through it into the Unconditioned—Nirvana. He is ultimately, though perhaps not for many lifetimes, to become an *arhant*, a perfected and enlightened one who has attained Nirvanic consciousness. What does he need to know to reach this end?

First, the monk must recognize that there are many worlds besides this one. Except for the animal world, the others are generally invisible, but they are accessible to inner organs of vision and are places of possible reincarnation. Like the shaman of old, the monk plunges into them through meditatively altered states of consciousness.

Hinduism and Buddhism speak of six *lokas*, possible "locales" or places where one can be reborn. These are, starting with the lowest,

> *The Hells (realm of extreme self-imposed punishment for those who have violated the most basic laws of life and have the worst karma)*
>
> *The Realm of Hungry Ghosts (place of creatures said to have large bellies and tiny mouths, so always hungry; destiny of slaves of the appetites)*
>
> *The Animal World (lives of impulse and suffering without knowing why; fate of those who do not live by understanding or reason)*
>
> *The World of the Asuras or Ogres (realm of warrior-like beings continually enraged and fighting; place of those governed by anger and violence)*
>
> *The Human Realm (world of good and bad, and ability to understand; only from here is liberation usually possible)*
>
> *The Heavens of the Gods (worlds of perpetual delight, but where one is so absorbed in pleasure that true liberation is difficult)*[7]

The upper reaches of the heavens, although still part of conditioned reality and so not Nirvana, correspond to very rarefied states of consciousness. Attaining them is considered excellent spiritual exercise. Theravada Buddhism, then, has two basic kinds of meditation: **samadhi** meditation (which explores the *jhanas*, or higher states above matter and form) and **vipassana** meditation (which breaks through directly to Nirvana).

Samadhi meditation must begin with the practice of *sila*, ordinary morality and simplicity of life. It then moves to the technique of "one-pointed" meditation, focusing on one thing to concentrate the mind. There are forty traditional topics for this concentration, ranging from discs of various colors to Buddhist virtues to grisly objects such as the repulsiveness of digested food and gnawed corpses—these last considered salutary for those overattached to the lusts of the body. After learning to focus entirely on the object, one can then leave it behind to enter the calm of formless realms of thought.[8]

Nirvana itself requires a more direct thrust. The way is through *vipassana*, the meditation of insight. Instead of forty, it employs only three hard-hitting topics: that all things are impermanent, that all is "ill" or unsatisfactory in conditioned reality, and that one

Theravada Buddhist monks in Thailand.

is not a real ego or self. *Vipassana* gets back to the fundamental Buddhist outlook of the Four Noble Truths and *Anatman*. *Vipassana* meditators analyze themselves until they realize the truth of these three points. Then, as it were, in the gaps left by the breakdown of the ordinary ego-centered way of handling experience, flashes of Nirvanic consciousness break through. The meditator is now "entering the stream" and continues in it until he becomes an *arhant*, one who has full, continuous Nirvanic realization and will not be reborn.[9]

Nirvana, the other shore or the transformation of consciousness, is the goal of Buddhism. Yet it must not be forgotten that Nirvana, for most, is far away and that the life of the religion is something quite other than a direct quest for Nirvana or *samadhi*. Even among the monks, the great majority are perhaps more interested in passing exams, in community affairs, and in the daily monastic round than in assiduous meditation.

Theravada laity do not generally expect to make formal meditations in the manner of monks. Rather, for them the tableau of the Buddhist map of the invisible world—its temples, pilgrimage places, and cosmic lore—becomes ways they can align themselves with streams of good karmic force set in motion by the implosion of the Buddha's Great Departure. Buddhism, for them, is a noble instrument for making merit, which will transform destiny to bring good things in this and future lives.

It must not be supposed, however, that the layperson's Buddhist orientation toward merit making means a diminished Buddhist vision. It may well be morally richer than that of many monks. The splendors of the temples that the layperson loves offer a hint of Nirvana itself, which illumines the mind on deep levels. The observant visitor is often made aware that popular attitudes toward time, human relations, and good or bad fortune in Theravada cultures reflect such basic teachings as "No Self," *karma*, and the Four Noble Truths. But the layperson relates to the Buddhist vision differently: through what he or she does rather than what is experienced in meditation.

The layperson tries to follow, as well as possible, the five precepts: not to take life, not to steal, not to engage in sexual misconduct, not to lie, not to take intoxicants. He or she tries also to exemplify the four unlimited virtues: unlimited friendliness, unlimited compassion, unlimited sympathetic joy, and unlimited even-mindedness. Through practicing the four unlimited virtues, one can be reborn in a divine heaven.

Merit can also be made by donations of robes and food to the monks, building **pagodas** and making monastery improvements, undertaking pilgrimages, sponsoring a candidate entering a monastery or sponsoring a formal scripture-reading, working for community good, or giving food to the poor and to animals. The relation of monk and layperson is mutually profitable in terms of merit: The laity win merit by donations to the monks; the monks win merit, by preaching and teaching to the laity and by giving them the opportunity to win merit through gifts. The relation between monks and laity exemplifies one of the deepest Buddhist doctrines, the interdependence of all things.

In Theravada countries, there are services in local temples four times a lunar month, at the four phases of the moon. The chief annual festival is Wesak in the spring, commemorating the Buddha's birth, his enlightenment, and his entry into Nirvana. In various places on this day, trees are watered, candles and incense wave in processions, and rockets blaze through the sky—all aimed in part at producing the rain that will be so critical in the coming growing season.

A month later, the rainy period (May through July) begins in Southeast Asia. During this time, following the example of the Buddha himself, the monks remain in retreat in the monasteries. Many of the laity, in this Lentlike season, make a special effort to keep the precepts—or even to enter the monastery temporarily, for just being a monk gives them merit and benefit.

The monks and the monastic life are like a reservoir of merit. The Buddha, the teaching, the order, and the laity are like concentric circles going around the absolute center, Nirvanic consciousness. Every circle profits through interaction with its neighbors, especially the one next closest to the center.[10]

MAHAYANA BUDDHISM

The northern tier of Buddhist nations, including the great and distinctive Buddhist cultures of Tibet, China, Japan, Korea, and Vietnam, are in the Mahayana tradition. This style of being Buddhist, and of exploring the meaning of the historical Buddha's experience, is different from that of the Theravada Buddhism we have just discussed. It is a tradition almost as old as Theravada, although not as conservative.

The first appearance of what was to become Mahayana was the school called the Mahasamghika ("Great Monastic Order"), which arose within the Buddhist order about a century after the Buddha's death. The points of difference with the Theravadists lie in the Mahasamghika's insistence that monastic meetings be open to all practitioners, that popular religious practices be reconciled with Buddhism, and that the Buddha was really a supramundane and perfect being who came into our midst as a teacher. These are theoretical points that led directly to Mahayana's universalism, accommodation, and transcendence. (By the time it became the popular Buddhism of several countries, Theravada had made its own adjustments in the same directions.)

So it was through the early centuries of Buddhism, a consistently liberal and innovative group was pushing for more flexible forms of the tradition. By the first century C.E., this group appeared as a distinctive tradition marked off by the fact that they accepted not only the Tripitaka but also a growing body of Sanskrit scriptures called **sutras**. Acceptance of the body of *sutra* literature, rather than any particular **doctrine**, is the formal test of a Mahayanist.

A broad consensus of attitude and doctrine runs through the Mahayana *sutras*, although they were written over several centuries and add up to a hundred times the bulk of the Christian Bible. (In theory, the *sutras* are put into the mouth of the historical Buddha and are ascribed by commentators to various stages of his life; many are said to have been "hidden" for hundreds of years to await times when they would be most needed.)

These scriptures start from a universal rather than a historical perspective, holding that there is a universal true reality everywhere—known variously as the Void, Nirvana, Buddha-nature, **dharmakaya**—that is, capable of being realized by anyone. Gautama Buddha realized it at the moment of his enlightenment, and so he manifests it and comes from it—but there are an infinite number of other Buddhas, too, and in a deeper sense everyone is actually an unrealized Buddha. Any means of attaining this realization is acceptable insofar as it works; the gradated practice of Theravada may be dispensed with, and techniques of devotion, chanting, even quasi-magic, brought in from *bhakti*, Tantrism, and folk religion, can be employed.

In all of this, the key figure is the **bodhisattva**, who becomes for Mahayana the ideal in place of the Theravadin *arhant*. The *bodhisattva* is on the way to Buddhahood but holds back at its very threshold out of compassion for the countless beings still in ignorance and suffering. This figure dwells both in Nirvana and in the phenomenal world, having the power and reality of both. As a borderline figure, he or she also imparts grace and receives devotion.

Mahayana Hall, Chengde, Hebei Province, China

All of Buddhism is built on the Buddha's experience of infinite consciousness at the moment of his enlightenment. Mahayana says that any method of getting at the way he saw the universe at that moment, which is the way it really is, is true Buddhism.

In Theravada, this means "entering the stream" left by the historical Buddha. In Mahayana, there is more emphasis that the world perceived by the Buddha at enlightenment is the true reality everywhere present at all times and so it can be apprehended directly by a number of different means. The historical Buddha, although respected, is relatively deemphasized in Mahayana. In the final analysis, all reality is full of Buddhas and is one's teacher of Buddhahood. Everywhere one can see sages, gods, and Buddhas who are essentially aspects of one's enlightened mind, and the Buddha-nature is in every blade of grass and every grain of sand.

Visiting a Mahayana country, one is immediately struck by a difference in Buddhist tone from Theravada countries. There is still the great splendor and peace of the Buddhist temple. But now, instead of a single, solitary Buddha image on the altar, attended by mere gods and men, one will see radiant Buddha after Buddha, *bodhisattva* after *bodhisattva*, all transcendentally aware, but all in different moods and poses, from serene meditation to explosive wrath and from deep withdrawal to many-armed compassionate activity.

This reflects that Mahayana is, in effect, a "multimedia" way to Buddhahood. The "turning of the head" needful to see one's true Buddha-nature is not something that must be done only one way. Because it relates to the ungraspable, it cannot be put into a box. Thus, Mahayana has many methods, some very complex and some so simple as to seem insulting until one realizes that simplicity is the point. Mahayana disdains none of the senses and no "level" of religion—from peasant folk faith to the most advanced metaphysical system.

Thus, Mahayana is **Zen** monks in Japan in long and immensely calm rows, "sitting quietly, doing nothing." It is followers of **Pure Land** Buddhism chanting "Hail, Amitabha Buddha" and hoping to be brought into the "Pure Land" or Paradise of the Buddha of Infinite Light and Life from where attainment of Nirvana is sure—or perhaps just experiencing the "beingness" of doing the chant. It is Tibetan Tantric Buddhists blowing on trumpets of human thighbones and evoking, through chanting

Buddhist monks at the royal temple in Bangkok, Thailand, beneath the figure of a giant mythological guardian.

The Great Buddha of Kamakura, Japan (Daibutsu). The bronze statue represents Amida, the Buddha of the Pure Land.

and intense visualization, the form of one's patronal spiritual ideal. Mahayana is finally the great peace of massive temples, the brazen images of supernal figures glowing dimly in incensed air.

The ultimate experience of Mahayana is ineffable, and so can be "turned on" by many different means: meditation; the numinous wonder of a temple that causes one to forget oneself for a moment; the quasi-hypnotic rhythm of chanting; the magical concentration of evocation.

The **Lotus Sutra**, one of the most important of all Mahayana texts, tells us that a simple offering of flowers or of a tiny clay *pagoda*, presented by a child to a Buddha, is of far more worth than all the proud efforts of an aspiring *arhant*—for any distance we can advance toward Buddhahood by our own self-centered efforts would be only as an inch to a thousand miles. But if one just forgets oneself in a childlike sense of wonder and giving, one is already there, for in that moment, one's high walls of ego have vanished away. True, the temples and gilded images of Buddhist temples are meaningless from an ultimate point of view, but it is they that can bring us across, for they invoke that childlike wonder with the natural effectiveness of bright baubles.

The Lotus Sutra also tells the parable of a father who, returning home to the house in which his children were waiting, was appalled to see it on fire and the children apparently unaware of the danger. Thinking quickly, he realized that if he shouted a warning, they might panic and be in a worse state. So instead he cried out that he had new toy carts outside for them. Laughing and skipping eagerly, they ran from the house and were saved. Images, rites, and devotion are like toys that draw us from the flames of desire and begin the process of self-transcendence.

The Buddha acts in a manner consistent with this view. The Lotus Sutra pictures him as like a rain cloud over all the Earth that waters vegetation of all sizes and shapes equally. He is universal, ineffable reality, who appears on different levels of reality in different forms, in countless worlds over and over again—as godlike heavenly Buddhas and *bodhisattvas* and in the human worlds, as teachers like Gautama. He is, in the climax of this astounding document, portrayed as descending in a tremendous, bejeweled temple to turn the wheel of his teaching in this universe.[11]

Nagarjuna's Two Basic Principles

The greatest philosophical force in the emergence of Mahayana was the teaching of Nagarjuna (c. 150–250 c.e.). His two basic principles are that **samsara** (the phenomenal world) and Nirvana are not different and that the most adequate expression for this totality is "Void."[12]

That *samsara* is Nirvana and that Nirvana is *samsara* means that one does not "go" anywhere to "enter" Nirvana. It is here and now; we are all in it all the time, so we are all Buddhas. Experiencing as Nirvana getting up, walking down the street, or washing dishes, rather than experiencing those things as *samsara* is simply a matter of how they are seen. The way to see them as Nirvana is with complete nonattachment and nonegotism, which means making nothing within the web of our experience more important or more prior than anything else. Neither self, nor any god, nor Buddha, nor the *skandhas*, nor any concept or idea or principle, is to be made into a basis upon which reality is constructed. None of these exists or persists of its own power. All are "hollow"—impermanent and part of the flux of entities and ideas out of which the cosmos is constructed. All exist not of their "own being" but only in their interrelationships.

The Nirvanic vision, then, is to see all things, including (and this is perhaps the most difficult angle to get) oneself, the observer, equally and as an endless series of interdependencies and interrelationships. This universe neither starts nor stops anywhere. In it all things are continually rising and falling and moving in and out of each other, and nothing is stable except the totality itself, the "framework" in which this frameless and endless moving picture is situated.

Because the cosmos has no pivot or foundation or point of reference within itself (i.e., no starting or ending line), Nagarjuna believed that the only adequate word for it is "Emptiness" or "Void." To say the cosmos is "Void" is not to say that nothing exists. The term "Void" is only a metaphor. But "Emptiness" and "Void" are the only appropriate words for Nagarjuna's cosmos, because any other word would imply some standard or "reality" to be grasped in order to understand it, and he taught that there is none. Void or Emptiness communicates the ungraspable quality of unconditioned reality. Like the inside of a dewdrop or a soap bubble, Mahayana reality is, so to speak, done with mirrors: it is full of light and color, but everything is just a reflection of everything else, and there is nothing to seize. One who tries will be like a person who attempts to lasso a rainbow or bring home a sunset in a bucket.

The secret is the insight-wisdom called *prajna*. It is able to see things as they are without being attached at the same time to any structure of thought or theoretical concept. Theories try to make it possible to see things by interpreting them, but the use of such tools also twists them out of shape.

Bronze statue of the bodhisattva Kuan Yin at Kek Lok Si Temple, Penang, Malaysia

The importance of *prajna* came about in this manner: Mahayana began, in part, as a discussion of the six *paramitas*, or areas in which one could attain Buddhist perfection: donation (giving of gifts), morality, patience, zeal, meditation, and *prajna*, or wisdom.

The supreme *paramita* is **prajnaparamita**: it must be built on the foundation of perfection in the other *paramitas*. But it is *prajna* that gives the lightning flash of final insight uniting one firmly and invincibly through every corner of one's subjectivity with the marvelous Void itself and so makes one as secure as it. This is *prajnaparamita*, the "wisdom that has gone beyond" or the "perfection of wisdom." The earliest distinctive Mahayana literature deals with it. Indeed, in devotional Mahayana, *prajnaparamita* (like wisdom in the biblical Book of Proverbs) came to be personified as an initiating maiden greatly to be desired.[13]

The Bodhisattva

The key figure in Mahayana thought is the *bodhisattva* ("enlightenment being"). *Bodhisattvas*, almost endless in name and number, dwell rank on rank in Mahayana heavens and flame out from countless Mahayana altars; there are also many of them, known and unknown, at work in this world. Virtually everything that is distinctive and of general interest in Mahayana is related to the *bodhisattva* and the *bodhisattva's* path. To understand this category of being, his or her meaning and methods, is to have the surest key to understanding Mahayana teaching, symbols, and practices.[14]

First, the *bodhisattva* epitomizes the ideal of *samsara* and Nirvana being the same, for the *bodhisattva* lives in both simultaneously. The *bodhisattva* is in the world, but without attachments, and therefore is able to see everything as it really is and to work with all its power. Thus, the *bodhisattva* lives on the level of Void consciousness.

Mahayana lore tells us that the *bodhisattva* is one who has taken a great vow to attain supreme and final enlightenment, however long it takes and at whatever cost, but at the same time a vow to practice unlimited compassion toward all sentient beings while remaining active in this world without passing into absolute Buddhahood until all other beings are brought to enlightenment. Its fulfillment requires great sacrifice and suffering on his or her part. The Lotus Sutra portrays the *bodhisattvas* as superior to the Theravada *arhants* and "private Buddhas," who allegedly attain enlightenment only for themselves, falling short of the ideal of universal compassion.

In the *bodhisattva's* work in the world for liberation of other beings, the *bodhisattva* is activated by two principles, skill-in-means and compassion. Both of these derive from unconditioned awareness of the total interrelatedness of all things, and this interdependency shows up the error of centering life on private goals. Compassion is the ethical consequence of this knowledge; it is merely stating the fundamental Buddhist realization of "dependent co-origination" in ethical terms. If one truly realizes that everything in the cosmos is dependent on everything else and that nothing and no one can exist apart from the rest of the cosmos, the only logical consequence for behavior is love, which negates all egocentricity. The *bodhisattva*— like the historical Buddha in a previous life—would think nothing of giving his or her physical body to feed starving tiger cubs, for the *bodhisattva* knows that body and time are all transitory and mean nothing, whereas compassion is affirming the basic truth of existence, and any holding back would be basing life on a false premise.

The *bodhisattva's* compassion is not merely a vague, diffuse force, well intentioned but capable of doing almost as much harm as good because of a lack of knowledge of all factors in a situation—as is the "compassion" of some. The *bodhisattva's* compassion is instead a sharp, precise instrument, for it is combined with the accurate insight that the *bodhisattva's* freedom from "thought-coverings" allows. This is what is conveyed in the attribute "skill-in-means." He or she is able to see all the *karmic* factors in a life situation and thus to know just what changes can be wrought to set a person's steps in the right direction.

Moreover, the same deep awareness, undistorted by any egocentricity, gives the *bodhisattva* control of appearances in the world, control that seems magical but actually is based on a deeper awareness of subtle forces than the ordinary person has. The *bodhisattva* is able to take any apparition-body he or she wants, or, rather, compassionate knowledge provides the insight as to what would be most beneficial in a particular situation. *Bodhisattvas* have worked in the world, according to Mahayana scriptures and stories, as monks, abbots, orphans, beggars, prostitutes, rich philanthropists, and gods.

In his or her work in the world, the *bodhisattva* is able to make those small but precise adjustments in a situation that will achieve maximum effect. He or she works with subtlety and skill to help the objects of compassion rise above a discouraging life to one of joy and enlightenment.

Above all, the subtly skilled and compassionate *bodhisattvas* impart a sense of sublime serenity, except in some of the wrathful manifestations of the **Vajrayana** tradition (which we will be discussing later). Whether the transcendentally tranquil princes of the Ajanta caves of India, crowned and holding flowers, or the many-armed and enigmatic-eyed Kannon of Japan, the *bodhisattvas* impart a feeling of attainment so perfect as to be effortless and exude mercy like the perfume of a lotus. The concept of the *bodhisattva*, whose beauty has moved hundreds of millions, is the supreme achievement of Mahayana Buddhism. It superbly exemplifies the ultimate meaning of the Middle Way by dwelling at once in *samsara* and Nirvana.

"Mind Only" (Yogacara)

After Nagarjuna, further developments in Mahayana thought and practice were in store. Some Mahayana thinkers, probably influenced in part by the developing nondualist Vedanta tradition in Hinduism, came to feel that merely to call the fabric of reality a "Void" was inadequate. A new tradition, found in the Avatamsaka and Lankavatara Sutras and the thinkers Asanga and Vasubandhu (c. fourth century C.E.), said that what Nagarjuna had called Emptiness or Void is more like mind, like pure consciousness in which particular forms or thoughts rise and fall. This position, called *Yogacara* or *Vijnanavada* and best labeled in English as "Mind Only" or "Consciousness Only," was immensely influential.[15] Most important, subsequent schools of Mahayana, including Zen and Vajrayana (both discussed below), are exponents of the Mind Only philosophy and are intellectually grounded on it as well as on Nagarjuna's Middle Way.

Buddhist Mind Only is comparable to idealistic philosophies of the West, such as that of George Berkeley. Mind Only holds that fundamentally only one clear mind or field of consciousness exists, the Buddha-nature or Nirvana. It is the basis of each person's own existence, and we are therefore all Buddhas. But we do not realize this because we each "project" an apparent world of many different things, which we think we see outside of us but which is actually in our heads. It is really like an illusion made by the preconceptions and the habitual but false modes of perception in which our individual *karmas* have bound us up and blinded us.

One can understand this by thinking of a movie projector. The screen is the one mind, the clear universal consciousness. The light source in the projector is the one mind within, which is our own true nature. The reel of film, cassette, or DVD is the "movie" put into the head by *karmic* forces reaching out of the past through preconception and habit to make us see and experience the kind of world they have made for us. We think we see forms—mountains and trees, cities and people, pleasure and suffering, joy and sadness—marching across the screen and invading our lives. But actually they are pictures cast by the movie running through our heads.

One might ask why, if each of us projects an individual "movie," we all seem to see the same world. Actually, this is not strictly the case; the world appears different to a child and to an adult, to people of different language and culture, and, in subtle ways, even to brothers and sisters. Yet admittedly there is general consensus about the "lay of the land." Mind Only philosophy says that this is because we carry over shared past impressions from collective as well as individual experience. This is called "store consciousness." The way we "see" the world is formed basically by human and community input, such as the common experiences of birth and having parents, language, education, and culture. What is added by individual *karma* is only like frosting—although it may seem very important for individual destiny.

Mind Only, like most Eastern philosophies, is not just a theory. It is also a practice, as it is a path to transformation of consciousness. It describes the projections and store consciousness as a prelude to teaching how to get beneath them and live without coverings on the unstained mirror of the One Mind. One method, developed by **Chan**, or Zen, is found simply through still meditation—"sitting quietly, doing nothing"—settling down until one lives beneath the coverings and projections.

Another method, developed by Vajrayana Buddhism, is a kind of experiential shock therapy where one experiments with different "movies" by putting in one after another. This is the role of the psychic experiments and the visualizations of

Buddhas and *bodhisattvas*, characteristic of the Tantric-influenced "esoteric" tradition in Mahayana. Through sacred and powerful words, gestures, and hard meditation, one creates before oneself alternative realities in which unlikely things are as real as rain. One may create a world in which one is a tree, or in which magic works, or in which armies of gods battle in the sky, or—and this would be the goal—in which Buddhas and *bodhisattvas* appear visibly on one's altar. Then one would "merge" with an evoked Buddha or *bodhisattva* and so share his or her bliss and enlightenment.

To do this, of course, one needs to have a good idea of what the universe of innumerable Buddhas and *bodhisattvas* envisioned by Mahayana—in countless worlds, in aspects of one's mind, in great lineages—is like: what they look like, how they are organized, how one goes about contacting each one. This is laid out in the diagrams called ***mandalas***. Furthermore, in Mahayana, each Buddha and *bodhisattva* may have his or her own heaven, a sort of aura around the *bodhisattva* from which entry into Nirvana through his or her aid is possible; these are different from the *karmic* heavens, the highest of the six *lokas*, also accepted by Mahayana. By devotion to a particular figure, one might enter the *bodhisattva*'s Buddha-heaven.[16]

Tibetan Sand Mandala

The Three Forms of Buddhic Expression (The Three "Buddha Bodies")

We see that the Buddha-reality (reality as seen by the enlightened eye) is encountered in so many different "styles"—in the Void, in the One Mind, in Nirvana, in the many transcendent Buddhas and *bodhisattvas*, which seem more like gods in heaven than people of this earth, and finally in this world, where the historic Buddha and the *bodhisattvas* did their works of teaching and mercy. Accounting for these many "styles" led to yet another development in Mahayana, one that seems to have emerged in Mind Only circles. It is the **trikaya** concept, the idea of three "Buddha bodies."

The three "Buddha bodies," or forms of Buddhic Expression, are the three ways or levels in which the Buddha essence is expressed. First there is the **dharmakaya**, the "truth body," what the universe ultimately is, the one mind through which the atoms and galaxies dance. It is the way the universe looks to a Buddha at the moment of enlightenment and entry into Nirvana, when all distinctions disappear and the universe and the Buddha's mind are absolutely one. This absolute nonduality is the Buddha-nature, the unstained mirror of the One Mind, the Void, Nirvana.

The second form of expression is the **sambhogakaya**, the "bliss body." It is the *dharmakaya* expressed in paradisal heavens ruled by radiant Buddhas, and it is represented in art and altar as golden Buddhas surrounded by gilded lotuses. But it must be remembered we are not talking about Buddhas or heavens literally "out there" but of the floating world of Buddhist reality, which is both (and

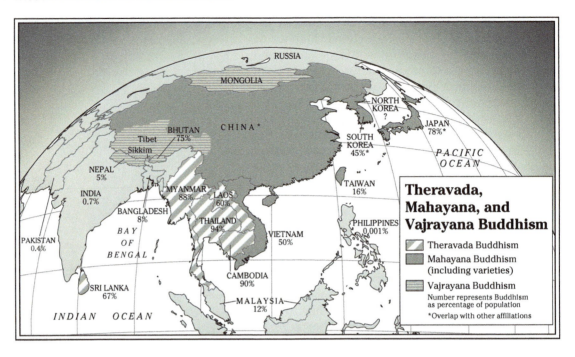

neither) subjective and objective. In a profound sense, the *sambhogakaya* is the absolute Buddha-nature insofar as it can be put into form—so it is now represented by the most luminous "otherness" kinds of forms possible, those that come out of the realms of dream, vision, and artistic creativity.

The *samboghakaya* centers on the radiant cosmic or meditation Buddhas, which are important in esoteric meditation. They are not Buddhas who were at one time historical human beings like Gautama, although sometimes legends about human lives in the remote past were given to them. Essentially, they are subjective–objective aspects of reality, which come into being in meditation and visualization as embodiments of aspects of the mind and the universe in their highest ratios. Above all, they are forms that give shape to the wonder of the Buddha-nature, and by bringing them into being in meditation, one provides bridges to it.

The **nirmanakaya**, the "marvelous transformation body," is the Buddha-nature expressed in this world of ordinary, "waking" reality. Because it is a world of seeing people and objects as separate, here the Buddha-nature comes to us as other persons—as Gautama the Buddha and all the other Buddha-figures. This is only a development of the mighty concept of the Lotus Sutra that the Buddha-nature is really a universal reality without beginning or end, which comes into the world from time to time in apparent, apparition bodies.

VAJRAYANA (TANTRIC) BUDDHISM

The form of Mahayana that most developed these kinds of things is Vajrayana—the "Thunderbolt Vessel" or "Diamond Vessel." Today this is the Buddhism of Tibet, Nepal, Bhutan, and Mongolia, and it has much affected some schools in China and Japan. But like so much else, it originated in old India. It stems from a confluence of Mind Only Buddhism with the same forces that went into Hindu Tantrism, and it can be thought of as Buddhist Tantrism. In the end, Vajrayana produced colorful art, potent devotional techniques, and philosophy no less deep than that of any other Buddhism.

As we have seen, Tantrism had its roots in the adaptation of obscure indigenous rites by questing persons who hoped, in their secret conclaves, to attain greater power than the Brahmin and Buddhist "establishments." These practices centered on magic spells, mighty initiations, and usages that sought to generate the power of a kind of shock therapy by deliberately defying ordinary caste, ritual, sexual, and dietary conventions.

Buddhist Tantrists took very seriously the dictum that *samsara* is Nirvana. To them, this meant that nothing in the *samsaric* world is intrinsically evil and that everything can be used as a means to liberation. Above all, this is true of the passions, and the most potent among them is clearly the sexual. Rather than seeking to circumvent the passions, which only leaves them lurking behind in one's psyche as potential depth charges, adherents of Vajrayana hold that one should wrestle with them, master them, and then deliberately arouse and direct their energy as dynamos of force for the breakthrough to the ultimate goal.

The Tantric scriptures warn that this is a dangerous tack and that what the adept does would cost the ordinary bumbler eons in the hells. But Tantrists were nothing if not bold, and they prided themselves on their skill at dangerous occultism. Indeed, if *samsara* is Nirvana, it is necessary to bring all polarities together in the perfected human. The defiance of cultural prohibitions is a way of expressing this.

The dangers meant that secrecy was necessary, and much Tantric literature is veiled in a code called "twilight language." It also meant that only the qualified, or those who were supposed to be, were admitted and that the student of these techniques had to work under the close supervision of a master, or guru. The one absolute in the Tantrist's world of inverted values was strict obedience to the master,[17] even if the master commanded, as some deliberately did, the most puzzling or perhaps shocking things—presumably to teach lessons about the emptiness of the universe.

By the early Middle Ages, Buddhist Tantra, as Vajrayana, had attained a literature and scholastic exponent. It became the prevailing form of Buddhism in some areas. Inevitably the rough edges were smoothed off; practices that violated conventional Buddhist morality were (because mind is all) translated into subjective meditations, restricted to marriage, or otherwise legitimatized, save in fringe groups. But it never quite lost its wildness either. Tantric adepts have always tended to be fierce, vivid, shamanlike characters, given to heroic spiritual strife deep in mountains or jungles, shunning the more staid academic and religious circles and leaving behind beguiling tales of wizardry.

In Vajrayana thought, the *dharmakaya* is made equivalent to *prajna* (wisdom) and is regarded as feminine, the supreme mistress, the cosmic womb. Often Tantric practice is described in the texts and by teachers from the male point of view. When so described, the adept, from novice to Buddha, is masculine and personifies skill-in-means, seeking to penetrate and unite with *prajna*. But there are also descriptions of the sexual union as occurring between male and female adepts, where each envisions the other as a Buddha—male or female, respectively. Thus, in Tibetan art, the cosmic Buddhas and *bodhisattvas* are often shown locked in sexual embrace, as a "father–mother deity" with their respective personifications of *prajna*—joining dualistic otherness in eternal ecstatic unity. This represents the supreme enlightenment achievement. The great Vajrayana *mantram* of Avalokiteshvara, *Om Mani Padme Hum*, "The Jewel in the Lotus," expresses all this, the union of Nirvana and *samsara*, of the male and female principles. In Vajrayana lands, it is chanted continually by priest and peasant alike, and it is the message of a million prayer wheels and prayer flags.

A novice being brought into the Vajrayana path will be given by his or her guru a particular deity or *yidam* (a male or female Buddha or *bodhisattva*, such as Green Tara, who is active compassion) as patron, from out of the vast Vajrayana ranks that crowd the *mandalas*. The novice will then seek to evoke the patron's presence through concentrated means and will study the deity's conventional picture until it appears in the mind even when the novice is not looking at it. The novice will seek to unify with the deity's lines of spiritual force by repeating an assigned *mantra* and making *mudra* (ritualized hand gestures). Stemming from the Mind Only presuppositions, the practice strives to create for the adept a new universe revolving around the adept's "god." Finally, it is hoped that the deity will appear visibly on the altar to accept the adept's worship. The student will then pull closer and closer to the deity until the ultimate goal is attained, and the student becomes one with the assigned deity, sharing the deity's intimate, divine embrace and Buddha-enlightenment.

In the process, there is no lack of powers of sorcery the Tantrist can wield, generated as byproducts of the *mantras* and supernormal friendship that is possessed. But the true goal is enlightenment—realizing that all is mind—all gods, *bodhisattvas*, and Buddhas, and all souls and phenomena, arise out of mind and sink back into it. In this respect, far from being credulous, Vajrayana is psychologically both sophisticated and boldly experimental. It knows that the numerous celestial beings and forces it calls into service exist only in mind. They are projected out of it and then, once isolated and confronted, called back into it to reign over a liberated mind equal to their power. This is the Vajrayana expression of Mind Only philosophy. It is as if one were taking out one DVD and putting in another, until forced to recognize that one can in fact create any universe one wants, and so one knows that no DVD is more "real" than any other, and only the One Mind is "truly real." To learn this is to attain the true liberation.

Vajrayana Buddhism in Tibet

Tibet, "Land of Snow" and "Roof of the World," has long had a very particular place in the imagination of the other peoples who dwell in lower, more prosaic places. For India, the realm behind the white ramparts of the highest mountains on Earth, out of which the sacred Ganges flowed, was the abode of mystic Shiva and of mighty *siddhas*, wizard-adepts. For China, it was the paradise where the Queen-Mother of the West presided over a happy nation of Daoist immortals. For many in Europe and America, Tibet has been no less a land of magic and mystery, a cloudland of abominable snowmen and lost monasteries where occult lore is the specialty and weird psychic phenomena are everyday occurrences. Today, traditional Tibet has been severely disrupted, indeed nearly destroyed, by Chinese Communist rule, which began in 1951. The tradition is maintained by Tibetan exiles, like the country's monk-ruler, the Dalai Lama, in India and elsewhere.

Although many stories about religious Tibet may be romanticized, there is no doubt that it would seem a very strange place to those of contemporary Euro-American Western culture. But it also is significant, for the real Tibet represents a unique and often profound interpretation of Buddhism and of the human experience.

In Tibet, as much as a quarter of the male population wore the reddish robes of monks, and the great thick-walled monasteries were centers of trade, finance, and government; there were even monk-soldiers who battled with each other. Other monks concerned themselves with complex meditations calling up the visible presence of strange, colorful deities of fierce or benign countenance or perhaps with the casting of spells or the writing of histories.

The religion of the common people was equally colorful. Houses, as well as the squat, domed temples, were decked with bright prayer flags—pennants with brief *mantras* inscribed on them, flapping in the mountain wind. Prayer wheels—large drums around the outside of a temple, small ones held in the hand, each containing strips of paper inscribed with *mantras*—turned everywhere, sending out auspicious vibrations into the thin, crisp air. On holy days, particularly New Year's Day, brilliant dance pageants were enacted by the local priests and villagers wearing masks of grotesque demons and radiant heroes. Life in old Tibet was hard, and doubtless the ordinary people were, from a Western point of view, backward and exploited by their nobility and monk-rulers. But they were sturdy, immensely proud of their country and its religion, and, according to travelers, a cheerful folk.

The unique Tibetan spiritual culture was essentially a combination of indigenous shamanism with Tantric Vajrayana Buddhism imported from India and allowed, by the unusual degree of isolation Tibet's geography afforded, to develop in its own way. From shamanism came the desire of the adept of power to undergo initiation, to demonstrate courage and vision, to explore the infinite new worlds of the psychic plane, and to manifest accomplishments through preternatural talents. From Buddhism came a sophisticated philosophical framework by which to explain these things. One has acquired unlimited full power because one has become one with the universal, invincible void; one travels to strange realms because one is realizing that one creates all one sees out of the *karma*-twisted mills of one's own mind.

This combination, and something of the profound Tibetan point of view, is made evident in the well-known *Bardo Thodol*, or **Tibetan Book of the Dead**, which is Tibet's most famous contribution to the world's religious thought.[18] The Tibetan Book of the Dead is essentially an account of the experience of a deceased person between death and, if destined by *karma* to be born again, the next entry into a womb. In it all levels of the Mahayana Buddhist cosmos are touched. The deep Vajrayana teaching that we create our lives, and our own heavens and hells, out of "Mind Only" is expressed.

Tibetan monk painting a mandala that is used for meditation.

The newly deceased entity starts with the "highest" level to encounter the "Clear Light of the Void," the *dharmakaya* or absolute essence of the universe. It is of "terrifying brightness," and out of it comes a roaring louder than a thousand thunderclaps at once, the light and vibrancy of an entire cosmos. If the pilgrim recognizes the *dharmakaya* as one's own true nature, however, the pilgrim can merge with it and attain the ultimate liberation immediately. Most, though, will be insufficiently prepared, shrink back, and lose the priceless moment of opportunity.

Still, other opportunities present themselves. The pilgrim next faces, one at a time and then all together, a *mandala* of five great cosmic Buddhas in their "peaceful" aspects. They are like heavenly forms of Universal Reality—the cosmic meditation Buddhas of the *samboghakaya*. Each of these corresponds, among other things, to one of the five *skandhas*. It is as though form, feeling, perception, *karmic* dispositions, and consciousness are not merely inside human beings but also reflect attributes or potentials that come into a lower level of manifestation in humans and into a higher one in this realm. If the traveler in this **Bardo** realm recognizes them as "Mind Only" projections, that individual will merge into one of them and be liberated. But if that test is failed, the pilgrim will be frightened and pass quickly by. The next encounter is with the same deities in their horrible, terrifying aspect, full of wrath but with the same opportunity for recognition. If it is missed, the process of rebirth now firmly takes hold. The pilgrim is propelled by winds of *karma* reaching hurricane force, and the entity experiences flash visions of judgment and of his or her future parents in copulation, and finally swoons, forgetting all on a conscious level, all that has transpired between the worlds, to awaken in the womb of whatever animal or human that is fated to give birth to him or her in the upcoming life. But even in these last stages the process can, with tremendous spiritual effort, be cut short and redirected. The most effective way is to meditate on the "father–mother" guru, the union of Buddha and Wisdom as male and female locked in erotic/ecstatic embrace, which is a popular subject of Tibetan sacred art. For the greatest power comes from the union of all opposites. And, psychologically, the deepest polarity that needs to be rejoined is our partiality toward the male and the female.

This account of the experience after death really expresses what Buddhism is about, for in the end all of its language, symbols, and practices are expressions of the union of opposites, the reconciliation of all polarities. From the Buddha's proclamation of a Middle Way, which finds infinite bliss in keeping a breathtakingly delicate balance between indulgence and asceticism, life and death, being and nonbeing, to the Tibetan vision of coupled father–mother gods in the *Bardo* sky, we have met with pointers to an experience of oneness. That experience makes one aware that it is a self-made shell of ego encrustations that keeps one from full consciousness; out of this egg one has to break with a shout of awakening.

CHAN OR ZEN BUDDHISM

Chan is a form of Buddhism that developed in China, but the tradition is known better under its Japanese name, Zen. Chan means the school of *dhyana*, Sanskrit for "meditation."[19] For Chan and Zen, enlightenment arises unexpectedly, often suddenly, in the course of "sitting quietly, doing nothing" in meditation, or perhaps in response to an unconventional teaching gesture by a master. This is the Chan or Zen expression of Mind Only philosophy where one's goal is to embrace the Void that is the Really Real underlying all projections.

Chan teaching and practice are "therapeutic" means of bringing people to inward realization of the basic ideas of Mahayana, especially the Void teaching of Nagarjuna and the Mind Only insight of Yogacara. What is distinctive about Chan is the fierce and direct means used to shake aspirants into inward realization of basic Mahayana truth. That was the truth of nondualism—that getting entangled in making distinctions keeps us from realizing that we and all else are the indivisible Buddha-nature now and forever. Chan masters claimed that their tradition was one of getting at the truth by "direct pointing" and that it was transmitted "outside the scriptures," in that it did not depend on words and letters but on immediate experience passed from master to disciple.

The experience, tradition said, began long ago when the Buddha silently handed a flower to a disciple named Kashyapa and smiled. The disciple smiled back and knew—the flower and smile conveyed a universe of wisdom indefinable by any words or books.

After Kashyapa, the secret of the smile was passed down through a lineage of "patriarchs" in India, until the twenty-eighth, a sage from India called **Bodhidharma** brought the tradition to China, where it became Chan about 520 C.E. To exemplify it, Bodhidharma spent years meditating in front of a brick wall and did not hesitate to tell an emperor to his face that all the temples he had built, all the scriptures he had ordered copied, and all the monks and nuns he had supported, had won him no merit whatsoever.

In several ways, this account is fictitious and misleading. The line of patriarchs in India is undoubtedly an invention, and Chan was well on the way to formation in China even before

Effigy of Bodhidharma, at the Shaolin Temple, Dengfeng, Henan Province, China.

the time of Bodhidharma. The claim of Chan to be "outside the scriptures" requires qualification, for the Heart Sutra and others are chanted and expounded in its monasteries, and Chan is nothing more than a means toward realization of the central Mahayana concepts that these *sutras* proclaim. But Bodhidharma does dramatize that Chan is interested not in learning for its own sake but in hard, sharp, direct realization—and that colorful stories and exaggerated making-of-points are among its armory of techniques.

So it is that the ideas of Emptiness or Void and of the Buddha being found only in one's own consciousness (for all sentient beings are Buddhas and need only to be awakened to realize it) are shown in Chan's disparagement of conventional Buddhist piety. In some places, Buddha-images were chopped up periodically. In the early days of Chan, monks worked in the fields like peasants. A disciple once went up to his master, who was apparently weighing out a harvest of flax, and asked him, "What is the Buddha?" The master, continuing with his work, answered, "Three pounds of flax."

Another master had a habit of remaining silent and merely pointing up his thumb when asked a question like this. A disciple, seeing this gesture and thinking cleverly to himself that there was some occult significance to it, began to imitate his mentor by holding up his thumb in the same way. One day the master saw the boy do this, and, quick as a flash, he whipped out a knife and cut the thumb off. After the disciple recovered, he approached the master once more and brought himself to ask again the question, "What is the Buddha?" As though nothing had happened, the master held up his thumb. At that moment, the disciple attained enlightenment.

Perhaps this anecdote is related to the Chan saying, "When a finger is pointing at the moon, do not look at the finger." Scriptures, practices, and a good master may indeed point to the moon (a Buddhist symbol of Nirvana), but the idea is not to look at them but at where they are pointing. For the reality to which Chan points

Statue of Zen master Sawaki Kodo Roshi, Sengaku-ji Temple, Tokyo, Japan.

comes before words and cannot be reduced to them. A Chan master was once asked what the "First Principle" is. He replied, "If I told you, it would become the Second Principle!"

Once again, the truth before words, which Chan and Zen radiate, is that one is the Buddha and in Nirvana now, in the "unborn mind" before thought, and that this realization is attained not by effort but by "doing nothing" and seeing who one is when one is not oriented toward doing anything. That "empty-handed" truth is well presented in a legend of Huineng (638–713), called the Sixth Patriarch of Chan in China, author of the Platform Scripture, and the man most responsible for the development of the Chan tradition.

Huineng came as a youth to the monastery of the Fifth Patriarch, Hongren. Only a poor obscure novice from the far south, then considered on the fringes of civilization, Huineng was set to such menial tasks as pounding rice. One day the Fifth Patriarch called the monks together and announced that he would make the Sixth Patriarch whoever of them could write a poem portraying deep understanding and true enlightenment. One promising monk, Shenxiu (who later became patriarch of the now extinct "Northern School" of Chan), wrote:

Our body is the tree of Perfect Wisdom
And our mind is a bright mirror.
At all times diligently wipe them,
So that they will be free from dust.

The Fifth Patriarch said that these lines showed understanding, but he perceived that this rather pedestrian and moralistic approach did not come near the great breakthrough possible in Chan. The next night, an anonymous verse was posted for all to see. It read

The tree of Perfect Wisdom is originally no tree.
Nor has the bright mirror any frame.
Buddha-nature is forever clear and pure.
Where is there any dust?

Here was the insight Hongren had been looking for. True enlightenment cannot consist of obsessively trying to wipe away symbolic dust particles; rather, it is the marvelous freedom of realizing that one's mind, one's self, and the dust are all equally "empty," and so unbounded. The Fifth Patriarch grasped that Huineng had written this poem, secretly called him in from the rice-pounding room, and made him his successor as Sixth Patriarch.

How is the realization of one's true nature to be attained? By not striving to attain it. How does one reach a state of nonstriving? Chan masters used several means. The most important is meditation: just sitting, doing nothing, striving for nothing, attaining nothing. However, Chan sitting does mean a definite posture and long hours. It produces a situation of nonstriving in which something can happen.

Many masters found that other techniques could hurry along the process of reaching nonstriving in their pupils. Some would fiercely scold, strike, and beat the disciples when they showed signs of trying too hard while missing the point, like the pupil who got his thumb sliced off. All this was intended as shock therapy to knock the novice out of the rut of his thinking and into a different perspective.

Many masters used the enigmatic Chan anecdotes, riddles, and sayings (known in the West by the Japanese name **koan**), such as "What is the sound of one hand clapping?" or "Where was your face before you were born?" While these puzzles can be answered in terms of the Void and Mind Only philosophies, the real point is that such conundrums bring the ordinary, rational "monkey mind" to a stop. They stop its perpetual chatter by feeding it something it cannot handle in its usual way. Perhaps, Chan says, if the relentless mental process can be quashed for just a moment, the mind will have a chance to see what it is when it is not chattering and chewing.

But liberating what is genuinely free and spontaneous within is not easy. Unlike some shallow romantics, Chan does not confuse true spontaneity with mere self-indulgence. Liberation is not doing what you want to do, for the tradition is well aware that what the ordinary, unenlightened person thinks he or she wants to do is merely the compulsions of those attachment-rooted desires that, fulfilled or not, can only enslave one in the bitter syndrome of craving, anxiety, and despair. The life of a well-ordered Chan or Zen monastery is very much the reverse of a hedonistic life; through the deprivation techniques of celibacy, scanty food and sleep, hard work, long meditation in freezing halls, and on top of that, sometimes physical and verbal abuse, it is hoped that the monk will find out who he is, apart from the desire-wrought illusion of being a separate person.

When success comes, the seeker is then truly free—for he lives on the level of spontaneous enlightenment and Buddhahood everywhere, even in the most trivial aspects of life. One master, Huihai, when asked if he did anything special to live in the *Dao* (the Way of the Universe), replied, "Yes; when hungry I eat, when tired, I sleep." When asked how this way differed from what ordinary people did, he replied, in effect, that ordinary people do not just eat when they eat, but they use eating as an occasion to let the desire-stimulated imagination run wild, thinking of what food one would like or having conceits of how the food one is eating symbolizes one's prosperity, lifestyle, and the like; similarly, ordinary people do not just sleep when they sleep; they also lie on their beds awash with waves of restless worries, fancies, and lusts. The goal of Chan, however, is just to eat when you are hungry and sleep when you are tired—nothing more.

In the same vein, another master, Qingyuan, said that before he had studied Chan for thirty years, he saw mountains as mountains and waters as waters. When he had made some progress, he no longer saw mountains as mountains and waters as waters. But when he got to the very heart of Chan, he again saw mountains as mountains and waters as waters.

PURE LAND BUDDHISM

The other important East Asian style of Mahayana Buddhism is Pure Land. While the scriptures that describe the Pure Land derive from India, it was only in China, Korea, Japan, and Vietnam that Pure Land became an important and distinct form of Buddhism. Like Chan, Pure Land evokes the freedom of nonstriving and nondependence on one's ego-self. A highly seminal early Chinese Buddhist philosopher, Daosheng (d. 434), spoke for both Chan and Pure Land when he argued that enlightenment has to be a sudden leap. Because it is a leap into the indivisible, he said, one can no more go through gradual stages of partial enlightenment than one can jump across a chasm in several jumps.

But in Pure Land, the structure is different; one has freedom from gradualism, striving, and self by dependence on the marvelous help of another, **Amitabha Buddha**, who can instantaneously and effortlessly give, out of his endless store of merit and grace, assurance to all who call upon his name that they will be reborn in his Pure Land where full enlightenment is easily available.

Chinese Bronze statue of Buddha Amitabha, savior in Pure Land Buddhism.

Photograph © 2012 Museum of Fine Arts, Boston.

Amitabha, called Emiduo in Chinese and **Amida** in Japanese, is the Buddha in the West of the esoteric *mandala* and of the Tibetan Book of the Dead, and his Pure Land is also called the Western Paradise. It was said that countless ages ago he was an aspirant who, in setting foot on the path, vowed (the "Original Vow") that if he attained full and perfect enlightenment, out of compassion he would bring all who called upon his name into his Buddha-paradise (an enlightenment world that surrounds a Buddha like an aura, in which his devotees can dwell; not to be confused with the desire-heavens among the six *lokas*). Amitabha's paradise is described in marvelous terms. There are jeweled trees linked by gold threads, fields of lapis lazuli, and perfumed rivers that give off music.

In China and Japan, Amitabha became, for vast numbers of worshippers, virtually the only Buddha, assisted by the usually female **Kuan-Yin**, also known as Guanyin, and as Kannon in Japan, who as the mercy-working *bodhisattva* has generally been closely linked to Pure Land Buddhism. Amitabha came to be, in effect, the universal Buddha-nature, and placing trust in him is an act of release that negates the individual ego in favor of harmonizing it with Nirvana or the universal. The Pure Land experience, then, ideally is not really different in character from the enlightenment experiences described in quite different words by other Buddhists.

BUDDHISM, GOVERNANCE, AND POLITICAL LIFE

Bodhidharma (fl. c. 480–520), who according to historical legend brought the Chan or Zen tradition of Buddhism from India to China, once came before the Emperor Wu of Liang. That monarch, who considered himself a devout Buddhist, recounted to the monk all he had done to promote the faith and asked what merit he had thereby received, undoubtedly expecting to be highly complimented for his good works and told that he had gained much karmic reward. The visitor, with more courage than most would have felt in the face of such a potentate, replied, "None whatsoever."

Wu, shaken in his concept of Buddhism, then asked what the first principle of the faith's sacred doctrine was. "It's just empty, nothing sacred," was the unexpected answer.

The sovereign, clearly becoming irritated by this impertinence, shouted: "Who then are you to stand before us?"

"I don't know," responded the other, and he left to meditate, it is said, for nine years in a cave.

Here we see confronting each other two roles of Buddhism in relation to the state: the ruler who sees himself as a practitioner and promoter of the faith, a dharma-king, an honorable office in much Buddhist lore, and the monk, or the *samgha*, in this case from an extreme wing of the religion, standing independent of the state, free to criticize or support it, or go his own way.

The Tradition of the Dharma King

As we have seen, Buddhism began with Buddha's rejection of the political and his disengagement from ordinary society when he left the kingdom of his father to pursue enlightenment. With the *samgha* that soon developed, adherents were largely removed from worldly concerns to live in community. Still, as we have seen, an understanding of the reciprocal interrelationship of laity and the *samgha* developed and was based in part on the doctrine of dependent co-origination. It was not long before this reciprocal arrangement led to the involvement of Buddhism in society and the engagement of politics with Buddhism.

Borrowing from, but extending and liberalizing, the idea of the holy kingship we found in Hinduism, Buddhism developed its own *dharma* king ideal, informed by the moral implications of Buddhism's basic teachings. Dependent co-origination was reflected in the interdependency of the Buddhist king and the *samgha*. The ideal was the king as the foremost patron of the *samgha* and the recipient of merit for the whole kingdom, which in turn legitimized the king's rule. The king was to rule in accord with the *dharma*, which requires of him (or, in rare cases, her) the virtues of compassion, honesty, selflessness, justice, kindness, and righteousness.[20]

All of this was especially epitomized in the paradigmatic rule of the Emperor Ashoka (r. c. 273–232 B.C.E.), a historic and legendary figure who exemplifies in Buddhist tradition the ideal ruler committed to *dharmic* rule. Making the *dharma* central to political and social stability and the general welfare, Ashoka articulated key principles of Buddhist morality for society, including the idea of equal justice across social categories, especially caste; he issued edicts advancing Buddhist moral prescriptions and promulgating policies instituting Buddhist moral norms throughout his realm.

> Dharma is good. But what does Dharma consist of? It consists of few sins and many good deeds, of kindness, liberality, truthfulness and purity. (Pillar Edict I)[21]
>
> My officials of all ranks—high, low, and intermediate—act in accordance with the precepts of my instruction. . . . For these are the rules: to govern according to Dharma, to administer according to Dharma, to advance the people's happiness according to Dharma, and to protect them according to Dharma.[22]

Thus, Ashoka joined the sacred and the temporal through what later came to be known as the "two wheels of the *dharma*"—the *samgha* and the civil rule of the king.

The effects of Ashoka's patronage of Buddhism during his reign were substantial for the future of Buddhism. During Ashoka's era, the *samgha* flourished, the first

Buddhist monasteries were built, and the oral teachings of the Buddha began to be collected and systematized. Ashoka unified northern India and then, under Buddhist influence, ceased to make war, proclaimed tolerance for all beliefs, and promulgated noninjury to life. While Ashoka supported and approved worthy teachers of whatever persuasion, the Buddhists were closest to his heart.

His patronage, extended by various later kings who were inspired by his example, gave Buddhism a prestige that it was to enjoy in India for centuries—and far beyond to Afghanistan and China and elsewhere. He reportedly sent the first Buddhist missionaries outside India to the island now called Sri Lanka, to Southeast Asia, and to Greece.

As Todd Lewis has written, "The tradition's memory of Ashoka, then, established that charity, justice, concern with the common good, and generosity toward the *samgha* became the norms by which 'a good Buddhist ruler' was to be measured."[23] Following in the model of Ashoka, later rulers who were held to be especially good *dharma* kings were venerated as if they were saints; some were even thought to be incarnations of the Buddha.

Generally, however, Buddhism's engagement with politics was more of a general moral influence than a confluence of Buddhist directives and state power, since its doctrines were compatible with existing social and cultural traditions, including other religious orientations, and with varying social arrangements. The exceptions were Mongolia and Tibet, where a theocratic political arrangement developed gradually. In the seventeenth century, the Dalai Lama became the monk ruler of Tibet, and by the nineteenth century, the authority of the Dalai Lama in succession was consolidated. Rule by the Dalai Lama continued until the 1950s, when China asserted sovereignty over Tibet.

For the most part, Buddhism was not directly involved in social and political reform. Monks and nuns were admonished to follow the laws and customary practices of the realm and generally suffered punishment within the *samgha* commensurate with the corresponding civil punishment, even risking expulsion from their monastic community if they failed to comply. Furthermore, the power of the state was often invoked to enforce the internal rules of the *samgha*.[24] However, there also has been a tradition of independence and resistance.

Colonial Rule and Recent Developments

Although other factors led to the decline of the kingship, in the nineteenth century, monarch patronage was disrupted under colonial rule in Theravada Buddhist South and Southeast Asia, primarily by the British, and in the twentieth century by Communism in China and North Korea, where Mahayana Buddhism is practiced. This disruption undermined existing institutions and threatened the viability of the *samgha*. Colonial rule and other influences resulted in the usurpation of key functions of the *samgha*, for example education, as well as the centralization of state control of the *samgha* in most places, and the "purification" of Buddhism of folk customs and practices.[25]

All of this, together with the imposition by colonial powers of nation-state boundaries and institutions in South and Southeast Asia, led to the reassertion of religion as central to national identity. Eventual independence after such disruptions has had varying results in different nations.

Theravada Buddhism has been caught up in the crises of nationalism, modernization, and ideological conflict that have tormented much of its corner of the world. In Sri Lanka and Myanmar (formerly Burma), some monks played a vigorous role in the movement for independence from Great Britain. Postindependence leaders, especially U Nu in Myanmar, made much of Buddhism, in part as a symbol of the national non-Western culture. In Myanmar both the military junta and the opposition look to Buddhism for legitimacy; tensions there led to marches, riots, and violent suppression of Buddhist monk activists. However, recently, the political situation in Myanmar has been much alleviated. In Thailand, which was not colonized but was greatly influenced by events elsewhere, developments included a strong national identity merged with Buddhism (co-opted to promote state goals), the rise of a militant Buddhist movement, and the eventual emerging of various parties holding different views of the significance of Buddhism for politics. The Thai government has made the rural monasteries centers for official programs in health and agriculture.

In Cambodia, Vietnam, and Laos, Buddhist life has been disrupted by war and political instability. In the 1970s, the abusive Communist regime of the Khmer Rouge nearly wiped out the *samgha* in Cambodia, which was especially targeted. There was some recovery under the Vietnamese occupation that followed. Since the end of the Vietnamese occupation in 1989, signs of Buddhist revival in Cambodia have appeared; however, it has been difficult there because so many of the elders were assassinated or fled during the Communist takeover. In Laos, the transition to Communism did not result in the extreme suppression that was experienced in Cambodia. Rather, the Buddhist monks were enlisted in support of the Communist regime, and the *samgha* exists under strict state control. Today, Buddhists in Laos are expected to participate productively in their communities, and the government oversees Buddhist doctrine and practice, purging it of subversive elements.

Yet, despite the incursion of modern problems, visitors to the Theravada Buddhist countries will still find cultures deeply shaped by centuries of Buddhism. The temples still gleam, and yellow-robed monks still walk the streets.

In China, Mahayana Buddhism was suppressed for a time under Communist rule, but now, under more liberalized policies, most Buddhists enjoy freedom of worship, though religious institutions are regulated and some dissident sects are banned. There is little religious freedom in Communist North Korea, though official Buddhist institutions exist. In Japan and South Korea, Buddhism has flourished under secular government—Japan seeing the rise of a Buddhist Soka Gakkai political party.

Implications of Buddhism for Politics Today

Traditional Buddhist literature provides little direct wisdom for contemporary political challenges. On the one hand, some have even called into question the relevance of Buddhism to politics today when its teachings do not address modern developments that have gone well beyond the relative simplicity of the kingly rule of the world of Buddhism's origins.[26] On the other hand, Buddhist social activists find resources in Buddhist tradition for challenging governments, structures, and policies that do not foster the Buddhist values of compassion and reciprocity, among others, which many activists hold are universal. Such "Engaged Buddhism" is now a transnational, global movement promoting compassion for the poor, social justice, and environmental responsibility.[27]

Nevertheless, in many ways and in many places, Buddhism is divorced from politics—where it deals with personal liberation and not much with religion's role of legitimizing social institutions. In many countries where Buddhism is prominent, these legitimizing roles are often taken care of by other traditions, for example in China by Confucianism, and later, by Communism, or in Japan, by Shinto. (Confucianism and Shinto will be discussed in the next chapter). And in countries where Buddhism is in the minority, for example the United States, it is primarily the *samgha*, the order of Buddhist monks dwelling within the society but in a sense standing outside it, that provides guidance, and is quietly available, for those ready for Buddha's teachings.

WOMEN IN BUDDHISM

The Dharma: Opening the Door to Women's Enlightenment

After observing Buddhist statuary in a museum, a modern American woman reflects:

> If you have looked at Buddhist art, you've noticed that many representations of the Buddha or other embodiments have decidedly feminine characteristics: breasts, delicate facial features, softly draped clothing. Buddhists believe that as beings achieve more refined levels of enlightenment, the distinctions of sex and gender fall away, leaving a transgendered or genderless figure. Nevertheless, the Buddhas or other figures with breasts and sweet girlish smiles are always referred to as "he." Similarly, male Buddhist teachers who have studied with or venerated female teachers of forebears may express feminine qualities in their teachings, but they retain their conventionally masculine assumptions and sense of entitlement.[28]

For this woman, the inherent privileging of masculine language and gender roles in traditional Buddhism was all too apparent on the religion's surface, yet the gender equality deeply implied in the Buddhist worldview was there peeking out, waiting to be realized.

Arguably, from early in its development, Buddhist philosophy supported a more egalitarian role for women than previously had been known in Hinduism. The concepts of "no-self," "codependent origination," and the illusory nature of distinctions and polarities provide a fundamental basis upon which to argue that "maleness" and "femaleness" are illusory categories. To contend otherwise is to be ego-attached—valuing one category over the other. Still, the practical and sociological manifestations of Buddhism over the centuries have perpetuated gender stereotypes to greater and lesser degrees, making true equality as yet unachieved.

But Buddhism must be taken in its historical context. For its time, it provided a tremendous shift in attitudes toward women. Most significantly, it acknowledged that women, too, can attain Nirvana. Interestingly, this gave rise to the "woman question." No longer was women's place deemed a settled matter by the religiously orthodox. Instead, Buddhism opened the door for consideration of such questions as, What are the proper role and status of women? What capacities and qualities are attributable to women? What goals are appropriate for women?

The "woman question" has been a much-debated topic in Buddhism from the very beginning of its history and remains so today. Consequently, when contemporary feminists raise it in the Buddhist tradition, it is not an innovation. Rather, feminists enter a long-standing debate for which many resources are found in Buddhist teachings.[29]

Women in Early Indian Buddhism and Theravada Buddhism

As we have seen, Buddhism arose out of the social and religious context of old India. Hinduism was a religio-cultural vision of an entire social–cosmic structure. Buddhism, on the other hand, did not provide an alternative vision for society. Instead, it offered an alternative life—the life of the *samgha* and the *dharma*—to those willing to leave behind the conventions of traditional society. This was a life focused on the goal of overcoming the suffering attachments of ordinary conditioned existence and realizing the bliss of Nirvana.

Thus, Buddhism moved the locus of religion outside the sphere of the home. Instead, the *samgha* became the center of religious life. Consequently, Buddhism provided an opportunity, an option, not available to women before. Women could become or continue in their roles as wives and attempt to exemplify the Hindu ideal; or women could reject convention, live outside the constraints of society, and follow the Buddha's *dharma*.

It is important to recall that early Buddhism developed in India at a time when Indian women led lives that were severely restricted by the dictates of Hindu religious law and custom. Women were focused on (and in many cases bound to) the home and generally were uneducated. Consequently, when the Buddha decided to include women in the *samgha*, it was nothing less than radical. The Buddha's *dharma* supported an egalitarian view toward women and men; nevertheless, these ideas were in conflict with an existing cultural bias in favor of female subjugation to male authority. The tension between the *dharma* and sociocultural attitudes toward women was, therefore, present from the beginning.

The story of the founding of the order of nuns (*bhiksuni-samgha*) and the debates surrounding the story's authenticity illustrate the uneasy compromise between the egalitarian *dharma* of the Buddha and the sociocultural views toward women at that time. The story, as told in the *Vinaya* (The Book of Discipline), is that, approximately five years after the Buddha's enlightenment and the founding of the order of monks (*bhiku-samgha*), women who had been following the *dharma* sought recognition in the new religion. **Mahaprajapati**, the Buddha's aunt and foster mother, approached the Buddha, asking that she and five hundred women followers be permitted to join the Buddha in the life of the renunciant. The Buddha rejected Mahaprajapati's request, but she was not easily dissuaded. Twice more she approached the Buddha with her request, and twice more she was denied.

At the third rejection of Mahaprajapati's request, however, Ananda, the Buddha's attendant, successfully argued the case of the women to the Buddha. He asked: Did not the Buddha hold that women could attain enlightenment? Accordingly, they, like men, would benefit from living the life of the renunciant, Ananda reasoned. The Buddha agreed and thereby assented to the founding of the order of nuns on the condition that the nuns were to accept being subjected to eight special rules (*garudharma*),[30] which clearly subordinated nuns to monks:

Buddhist Nuns at Grand Palace, Bangkok, Thailand.

(1) Any nun, no matter how long she had been in the order, must treat any monk, even the rudest novice, as if he were her senior; (2) Nuns should not take up residence during the annual rainy-season retreat in any place where monks were not available to supervise them; (3) Monks would set the dates for the biweekly assemblies; (4) During the ceremony at the end of the rainy-season retreat, when monks and nuns invited criticisms from their own communities, the nuns must also invite criticism from the monks; (5) Monks must share in setting and supervising penances for the nuns; (6) Monks must share

in the ordination of nuns; (7) Nuns must never revile or abuse monks; and (8) Nuns must not reprimand monks directly (although they could and did report one monk's offensive behavior to another, who then might take the appropriate actions to correct it).[31]

As Nancy Falk has written, however, women were likely to have found their situation to be greatly liberating as compared with their previous positions in traditional society. More important, the eight rules did not interfere with their main purpose for participating in the *samgha*—the pursuit of those practices that would lead them to enlightenment. In addition, it has been noted that the rules may have been enacted, at least in part, for the protection of the nuns from violence by the monks and from being treated like servants by the monks who might wrongly think it appropriate for nuns to clean and prepare food for them. Or, possibly, the Buddha may have wanted to preserve the order of nuns against the condemnation of Hindu householders. Keeping the nuns in check under male authority may have mitigated the arguments of those who viewed the inclusion of nuns in the *samgha* as leading to societal decay in that women were not upholding the Hindu social order by remaining at home.[32]

Despite some negative views of women attributed to the Buddha,[33] the Buddha is said to have acknowledged that women could be, and were in his time, exemplary adepts. The **Therigatha** (*Songs of the Female Elders*), which has been preserved and which complements the **Theragatha** (*Songs of the Male Elders*), contains beautiful accounts of the enlightenment of over seventy women who are believed to have been among the first nuns. It is interesting to note that the Therigatha "may be the only canonical text written by women in the world religious literature."[34]

On the other hand, the lower status of nuns as compared with monks limited the development of the order of nuns and probably adversely affected their ability to obtain sufficient charitable support for their activities.[35] As Nancy Schuster Barnes has said, "Women were there, are there, but most often seem to remain on the shadowy fringes of the religious life, not at the creative, influential center of religious activity."[36] This is thought to have been a major contributing factor in the decline and eventual demise of the order of nuns in those countries in which it first developed (i.e., India, Sri Lanka, and Burma) and a possible explanation for the fact that the order of nuns never developed fully in other Buddhist countries, such as Thailand, Cambodia, Laos, or Tibet. Today the only unbroken existing lineages of nuns are in China, Korea, Japan, and the northern part of Vietnam. In those Mahayana Buddhism lands, nuns have been more visible and influential as teachers of laity and as spiritual guides to emperors and their families.[37]

The tension between Buddhist teachings, on the one hand, and Buddhist institutions and practices, on the other, is further illustrated in writings that contain misogynistic passages, particularly from the later period of early Buddhism. One passage in the Pali canon states: "Even when…stricken or dying, a woman will stop to ensnare the heart of a man."[38] As in Hinduism, such passages may be attributed to the biases of unenlightened male renunciants who viewed women as obstacles to attaining Nirvana. The Buddha himself is reported to have cited men's lust as the problem.[39] Nevertheless, misogynistic attitudes reflected in important texts most likely contributed to the tendency to relegate the nuns to a lower place in the *samgha*, despite the obvious egalitarian doctrine of the *dharma*, and as Theravada Buddhism developed, to the tendency to exclude women from the *samgha* entirely.

In addition to the *samgha*, the Buddha established an order of laywomen (*upasika*) and laymen (*upasaka*). The lay disciples did not leave behind their conventional lives but practiced a Buddhism that accommodated their worldly vocations. The records reflect a measure of ambiguity regarding early Buddhist laywomen. On the one hand, these women, even more than the nuns, presented a temptation to the monks who would meet them while the monks obtained daily offerings of food.[40] On the other hand, laywomen constituted some of Buddhism's most ardent benefactors. The many passages praising the exemplary qualities of certain laywomen can be attributed, in part, to their substantial economic support of the *samgha*.[41]

In general, laywomen fared reasonably well under Buddhism. They were given the same instruction that the laymen received. And both men and women were encouraged to contribute to the well-being of their communities by upholding the traditional social order more in the sense of a partnership than was so in Hinduism. Significantly, the status of wives seems to have improved considerably under Buddhism, probably because of Buddhist recognition of women as being able to reach the highest spiritual achievements and, therefore, being given the option of the renunciant life, making marriage somewhat of a choice and not merely a social and religious obligation.[42]

Nevertheless, rebirth as a woman was considered unfortunate. The misfortunes of womanhood include the "five woes": "that she must leave her family at marriage; that she must suffer the pain of menstruation, pregnancy, and childbirth; and that she must always work hard taking care of her husband."[43] In addition, a woman must always observe the "three subserviences," which are "in youth, [to] her father, in maturity, [to] her husband, and in old age, [to] her son." Consequently, she was never independent and always subject to a man.[44]

When the Theravada and Mahayana schools split, one central issue was the proper role and status of women. Theravada tended toward a more negative view of women and their capabilities. Mahayana, on the other hand, tended to develop a more positive and egalitarian view toward women.

Women in Mahayana Buddhism

It is important to recall at this point that Mahayana Buddhism is the "Great Vessel," a vehicle for an all-inclusive notion of the *samgha*. In this view, all have the universal Buddha nature and are capable of realizing Nirvana now. As a consequence of this altered view of the *samgha* and the belief that enlightenment is not only for renunciants, there is not the sharp division between the renunciants and the laity that is seen in Theravada Buddhism. Householders, both men and women, are recognized as advanced and capable of attaining Buddhahood. This shift in doctrine made Mahayana Buddhism more accessible to all, which resulted in a tendency toward an egalitarian approach to women not only in theory but also in practice.

Nevertheless, the Mahayana order of nuns remained subject to the eight special rules as in Theravada Buddhism, and some Mahayana Buddhist texts reveal a continued ambivalence toward women. This ambivalence is revealed in writings that question whether one can reach Buddhahood while remaining in female form. Many texts claim that the "highest levels of wisdom and insight" can be attained by women who are able to espouse the "highest truths and most complex philosophical arguments of Mahayana thought."[45] Other texts argue, however, that it is only after one ceases to be reborn in female form that Buddhahood can be attained. Some Mahayana texts claim that the Buddha himself ceased female rebirths even before he ceased rebirths as animals.[46]

There are many stories of exemplary women adepts being challenged by men on this point. Often such stories recount that, when challenged, the woman transforms herself into a man, revealing that she has attained Buddhahood. One such story is the Lotus Sutra account of the miraculous feats of the Naga Princess. She was challenged by Sariputra (who symbolizes conservative Buddhism) because, he claimed, the female body is unsuited to the five ranks of existence that one must pass through on the way to Buddhahood. Upon being so challenged, the Naga Princess's "female organ disappeared and the male organ became visible" and she became a *bodhisattva* and then, immediately thereafter, a Buddha.[47] In another story, when asked why she did not change her female sex, the woman transformed her challenger into her own form and herself into his and then asked: "Why don't you change your female sex?" The story concludes with the man realizing that "[t]he female form and innate characteristics neither exist nor do not exist."[48]

There is some dispute regarding the significance of these stories for women. Some, such as Diane Paul, argue that the accounts of a woman's transformation into male form, in effect, derogate the female body, implying that it is inadequate for the enlightened state of complete wisdom and compassion.[49] However, Rita Gross's interpretation is probably more to the point. She concludes that the sexual transformation stories do not show the superiority of the male body but show that the woman already had the power of enlightenment and was unattached to any particular form. Thus, she exemplifies the wisdom that "gender, like every other phenomenon, has no fixed essence and so does not limit those who bear its illusory outward signs."[50] This view is supported in other texts by stories of women who teach the *dharma*, who are recognized as having achieved enlightenment, and who are not challenged regarding their female form. The story in the Sutra of Queen Srimala Who Had the Lion's Roar (i.e., was enlightened) is a notable example. As Nancy Schuster Barnes puts it: "The Mahayana sutras demonstrate dramatically that the man who clings to his maleness is not an enlightened being, and the women who does not worry about changing her sex is genuinely enlightened. This is a dramatic demonstration of the meaning of emptiness."[51]

The *bodhisattva* ideal of wisdom and compassion also supports the view that Mahayana Buddhism, in general, promotes an egalitarian approach regarding women. While a few texts claim that one cannot become a *bodhisattva* in female form, in general, there are numerous references to female *bodhisattvas* in Mahayana Buddhism. Kuanyin or Guanyin (Kannon in Japan), the *bodhisattva* of mercy, is one of many. Although she originated in India as Avalokitesvara, who was male, in China and Japan she became the Goddess of Compassion. She is a central figure and is nearly always given a prominent place on the altars of Mahayana temples and homes. In addition, *Prajnaparamita* (the Perfection of Wisdom) is the primordial female principle—the universal expression of absolute wisdom and the mother of all Buddhas and *bodhisattvas*. The Perfection of Wisdom in 8,000 Lines, an early example of Mahayana literature, beautifully expresses the centrality of the feminine principle:

Heiwa (Peace) Kannon (Bodhisattva of Compassion) carved after WWII in the famous Oya stone, Tochigi Prefecture, Japan to promote peace.

The Buddhas in the world-systems in the ten directions
Bring to mind this perfection of wisdom as their mother.
The saviours of the world who were in the past, and
also are now in the ten directions
Have issued from her, and so will the future ones be.
She is the one who shows this world (for what it is),
she is the genetrix, the mother of the Buddhas.[52]

We can see then that while Mahayana Buddhism continued to exhibit some ambivalence toward women, its texts presented a significant move toward an egalitarian Buddhism. And Buddhism has enriched many women's lives.

Consider the moving story of a young woman who became a Mahayana Buddhist nun in contemporary Taiwan. Wang Jinyun, like most girls of her generation, completed only middle school. (She dropped out to help her family because of her mother's illness.) Then, when she was twenty, her father, whom she had clearly admired greatly, suddenly died. Devastated, she put family affairs in order as best she could, then began seven years of wandering. She performed solitary meditation and experienced crucial encounters with wise women: several Buddhist nuns, devout laywomen, and three Catholic nuns. She also sought out a distinguished priest, Venerable Xiudao, head of a nearby temple. Then one day she saw two nuns affiliated with that temple working in a rice field and joined them in their work.

By her account, the plants seemed to float in the wind like a song; suddenly she gained an understanding, like an awakening. At that moment, she said, she felt really happy as if all the secrets of the heavens were revealed to her heart. She knew she was to become a nun herself, and did. She took tonsure, received the nuns' precepts, studied, and in time became a well-known teacher with disciples of her own; she was especially famous for public lectures on the Lotus Sutra.

Women in Vajrayana (Tantric) Buddhism

At the core of Vajrayana, or Tantric, Buddhism is recognition of the apparent duality of the universe in male and female forms, which is seen as the most profound fact of existence. Thus, ultimate realization requires the merging of both into an all-encompassing unity—one devoid of such distinctions as male and female. *Prajna* (discussed earlier) is the feminine principle, which represents primordial infinite space—that emptiness that is also ultimate wisdom out of which the phenomenal world manifests. The masculine principle, **karuna**, represents "form, activity, compassion"—that which is manifested. Yet ultimately space and form are not separate for, as is said in the Heart Sutra: "Form is emptiness but emptiness is also form."[53]

The central symbol of this unity is the sexual embrace of male and female *yidams* or Buddhas, as we have said. Accordingly, unlike many other religions (including other forms of Buddhism) where the human body is eschewed as an obstacle to spiritual perfection, Vajrayana Buddhism celebrates the body as the vehicle through which one may realize Nirvana in this lifetime. As a result, there is much praise for the female body. Tantric texts are replete with passages describing in detail the wonders of the sacred lotus (symbol of the female sex organ—*bhasa* or *yoni*) through which ultimate wisdom may be sought and received. And female symbolism is pervasive—as the masculine must always appear with its counterpart in what Rita Gross calls a "dyadic unity."[54] This appreciation of the female body, together with abundant female symbolism, makes Vajrayana especially hospitable to women, who in some texts of Vajrayana Buddhism are venerated as goddesses.

As we have already seen, Vajrayana Buddhism has an elaborate pantheon of Buddhas and deities, which include many in beautiful, powerful, and wrathful female forms. A central and formidable female cosmic Buddha is Vajrayogini—the liberator. In Tantric art, she appears as a blood-red goddess with flowing black hair, dancing with passionate abandon on the corpses under her feet and offering a skull cap full of ambrosia to the Tantric seeker. Another central female cosmic Buddha is Tara—the giver of wisdom. Tara appears as a beautiful, emerald green, nurturing goddess, sitting on her lotus flower, inviting the seeker with joy and peace into the calm assurance of her maternal embrace. There are also many *dakinis*. These are enlightened beings who represent the female principle and can appear in human or nonhuman form. They surround the *yidam* or *yidam* couple, providing insight and enhancing passionate energy that is evoked to bring about spiritual ecstasy, which leads to enlightenment.[55]

Tantric Buddhism in some of its forms, like Tantric Hinduism, attempts to work against social conventions, which are considered to be obstacles to attaining ultimate wisdom. It is not surprising, therefore, to find the traditional subjugation of women to be reversed. Consequently, one can find many passages requiring men not only to overcome their prejudices against women (which is evidence of their own ignorance) but also to worship women because the veneration of women is the surest path to enlightenment.

An especially beautiful passage from the Candamaharosana-tantra instructs a man how to worship his Tantric partner:

> *The man [sees] the woman as a goddess,*
> *The woman [sees] the man as a god.*
> *By joining the diamond scepter and lotus,*
> *They should make offerings to each other.*
> *There is no worship apart from this…*
> *Then the yogi lovingly*
> *Makes a mandala in front [of himself],*
> *And the woman enters that.*
> *As the embodiment of Perfection of Wisdom,*
> *He continuously worships [her] with flowers,*
> *Incense, butter lamps, and other articles.*
> *After uniting the five mandalas,*
> *He should prostrate to her,*
> *Circumambulate [her] clockwise, and*
> *Worship the ardently passionate yogini.*
> *The man worships the woman in that way,*
> *With a mind full of reverence.*[56]

One might expect that a religion so imbued with female imagery—whose very essence requires the presence of the feminine—would be devoid of patriarchal characteristics. Unfortunately, here too in the institutions of Tantric Buddhism, we find a tendency toward male control of authority, less education and support of female adepts, and a suspicion of such women for stepping outside the norms of conventional society.[57] And there is evidence that women have been sexually exploited by men who have used them as objects in the attainment of their own spiritual goals.

Still, women have many options in Tantric Buddhism. They may be nuns and laywomen, as in other forms of Buddhism. Unique to Tantric Buddhism are the *yoginis* or *tantrikas* who live their lives neither as monastics nor as laywomen but as full-time practitioners who wander the countryside alone or in groups, teaching the Tantric methods to both men and women. Tantric texts include stories of extraordinary *yoginis* who were gurus of renown, such as the story of Yeshe Tsogel, the famous and revered eighth-century *tantrika*, who, together with her Tantric partner, Padmasambhava (Guru Rinpoche), is believed to have established Buddhism in Tibet.[58]

Yet women do not participate equally in the religious practices of traditional Tibetan Buddhism, where male authority is nearly absolute. Tibetan sexual Tantric practices tend to be "right-handed" (i.e., symbolic). Thus, the male adept can perform the rites in meditative trance, visualizing the unity of the male *yidam* and *prajna* without the aid of actual physical contact. Apparently, the irony of the incongruence of the unabashed acceptance, even reverence, of women in the Tantric texts and the sociocultural attitudes that severely limit women's actual involvement is not recognized by Tibetan Buddhists. This discrepancy is inherent in the very word for "woman" in the Tibetan language. It means "born low."

> This word carries a conscious social status that Tibetans everywhere recognize as low. Yes, they say, a woman is not as capable as a man; she cannot enter into new areas of development; her place is in the house; she lacks a man's intellectual capacity; she is unable to initiate new things; and finally, she cannot become a Bodhisattva until she is reborn as a man.[59]

Even the women themselves accept with resignation the misfortune of their female births and validate the belief that women's subjugation is a matter of the natural state of their existence rather than something that can be overcome through the sharing of power by and with men.

Nevertheless, there are roles for women in Tibetan Buddhist religious practice. There is, for example, an order of nuns. Because there is no ordination lineage, however, the nuns remain novices with all of the implications of a reduced status that one would expect from such a situation, leaving all institutional power in the hands of the monks or lamas. A woman can choose to become a *yogini*. Clearly, however, there is much to overcome when a woman decides to walk the path of the *tantrika*.[60]

Women in Chan (Zen) and Pure Land Buddhism

It is important to recall here that Chan or Zen Buddhism and Pure Land Buddhism are specific developments within the Mahayana tradition. Consequently, what has been said already with respect to women and Mahayana Buddhism applies here—for example, with respect to the continuing ordination lineage for nuns in China. It is important to note specifically, however, a couple of additional things with respect to Chan (Zen) and Pure Land Buddhism.

The ideas and practices of Chan (Zen) Buddhism are grounded in *Prajnaparamita*, which, as we have already seen, is the expression of the ultimate primordial source as the Female Divine. Not surprisingly, then, many issues surrounding femaleness that are found in other forms of Buddhism, including other forms of Mahayana Buddhism, are not present here. Femaleness does not present a bar to enlightenment or Buddhahood in Chan. Significantly, women in Chan Buddhism have been permitted to teach both men and women, and there is historical evidence that there were great women teachers at court with considerable influence. However, this certainly was contrary to the prevailing customs of the host cultures of China and Japan. As a result, the institutions of Buddhism in Japan and China remained male-dominated.

In Pure Land Buddhism, on the other hand, femaleness is treated as problematic because it is deemed to be an unfortunate birth. Traditionally, Buddhism was not concerned with changing the social order. Therefore, in its Pure Land form, it merely acknowledged a fact of society—women's lot was indeed unfortunate. The good news is that there are no unfortunate rebirths in the Pure Land. Accordingly, it is believed that all who reach the Pure Land are reborn there as males!

Women in Contemporary Buddhism East and West

The "woman question" in Buddhism continues to be debated to this day, and contemporary women in the East and West are considering the degree to which Buddhism, in its many forms, is in need of reconstruction in order to give effect to what is perceived by them as its egalitarian core. In most of Asia, there is now a Buddhist women's movement that is actively seeking reform.[61] And American feminist Buddhist scholars, such as Rita Gross in *Buddhism after Patriarchy: A Feminist History, Analysis, and Reconstruction of Buddhism*, have made convincing arguments that negative stereotypical attitudes toward women are due to sociocultural encrustations from Buddhism's various host countries.[62] Such scholars point to the problem of the record keepers nearly always being men, which results in the effective erasure of the history of women's participation and in an androcentric point of view that minimizes women's experience within the traditions of Buddhism. As a result, important information about women's own processes and practices in the quest for enlightenment and their contributions to the tradition has generally been lost.

Significantly, Buddhist women scholars have uncovered many nearly forgotten texts that do recount the lives and practices of exemplary Buddhist women. And such scholars have found evidence that the failure to tell women's stories has obscured what may have been a more prominent role for women than the majority of texts seem to indicate. For example, in relatively recent times, a male Tibetan university student, Namkhai Norbu, who had studied with the yogini Ayu Khandro (d. 1953), wrote a biography of his teacher. As feminist scholar Rita Gross surmises, "Without this almost accidental preservation of her biography, we would probably have no idea that such a woman had lived so recently. She may not have been as rare as the impression given us by the records that were preserved."[63]

Furthermore, Buddhist feminists find that there is a "quasi-feminist" strain in classical Buddhism on which they can draw to support arguments for reform. For example, it has been pointed out that the "five woes," referenced above, illustrate that male dominance of women has long been recognized as a "woe" rather than a benefit for women as many other religions have contended.[64] Another example is found in Vajrayana Buddhism where the denigration of women is held to be a "root downfall."[65]

A significant issue for contemporary Buddhist women is the ordination of nuns. This is an especially difficult issue in Theravada Buddhism where, as noted earlier, no ordination lineage for nuns is extant. Southeast Asian Theravada monks are especially resistant, some say even hostile, to the reinstitution of a nuns' ordination lineage. They argue that because there has been no nun's ordination tradition for centuries in some areas and because no such tradition has ever existed in others, to have one at all at this point is not in accord with the Theravada tradition. Interestingly, some nuns oppose it as well, arguing that ordination makes them subject to the eight rules and, therefore, subjects them to control by the monks.

There is, however, an unbroken ordination lineage for nuns in the Mahayana tradition. Contemporary Buddhist women have argued that Theravada nuns' ordination could be reestablished through that lineage. Even though the monastic tradition is virtually the same for both Theravada and Mahayana, Theravadists argue against conflating their tradition with that of the Mahayanists and conclude that Mahayana ordination is not valid for Theravada. However, some Theravada monks with more exposure to the West support the reinstitution of the nuns' ordination. Attempts to restore an ordination lineage for nuns have been made in Sri Lanka since the mid-1990s; however, the validity of the lineage remains in question.

Nuns' ordination has support on other fronts. Significantly, the Dalai Lama has ordained nuns and thus supports nuns' ordination in the Tibetan tradition, which since the Chinese invasion of Tibet in 1959 continues in India and in the West. But as Nancy Barnes has noted, the overwhelming majority of monks worldwide in traditions without a nuns' ordination do not support women's struggle for institutional recognition and support.

Still, Buddhist women have made tremendous strides in the twentieth century. In modern times, there have been many women teachers of renown. Among them are Ayu Khandro (Tibet), Sister Sudharma (Sri Lanka), Achan Naeb (Thailand), Daw Panna (Burma), Venerable Bhiksuna Tae-heng se Nim (Korea), and Venerable Bhiksuni Hiu Wan (Taiwan). Jiyu Kennett Roshi (1924–1996), who was the head of a Zen monastery in Northern California, was especially esteemed by the several women who have become prominent Buddhist leaders in the West.

The main issue for Buddhist women is that, even though most schools of Buddhism today espouse an egalitarian doctrine, there is continued reluctance on the part of Buddhist institutional establishments to provide opportunities for women's full participation and leadership and that, therefore, Buddhism remains androcentric and patriarchal. Part of the problem is that Buddhism has generally tended to be focused on spiritual advancement and not on the social problems of this world, including the relative status of women. Hence, women arguing for "equal rights" can be criticized as being "attached." The result is that their efforts to better their lot in life can be maligned as evidence of ignorance of the Ultimate Reality, which knows no such distinctions.

Turning that argument around, however, and demonstrating that "gender identity" and "gender fixation" are manifestations of ego that are at odds with Buddhism's No Self doctrine of egolessness, Rita Gross has argued that "gender hierarchy" and "gender privilege" constitute a "samsaric trap,"[66] and she has pointed out, therefore, that

> If gender equality is normative, then actively working to undercut gender hierarchy and privilege is a required ethical norm for all Buddhists, not merely a marginal position for a few feminists.[67]

In other words, feminism can be a resource for Buddhism itself, not only helping Buddhism to reveal its "non-sexist core" by lifting the "patriarchal overlay" of its practices and institutions but also helping Buddhism to apply more consistently its fundamental teachings.[68]

So we see that Western influences have resulted in rethinking Buddhist values and that Buddhist influences have resulted in rethinking Western values, particularly with respect to the role of women. Western feminist scholarship has brought attention to the discrepancy between Buddhism's egalitarian doctrine and its institutional practices, while Buddhism's vision of a nondualistic universe has contributed to an examination of the West's tendencies to see polarities as oppositional rather than complementary. Anne Klein, Rita Gross, and Nancy Barnes see this interplay as a potentially positive development in the modern world, particularly in efforts toward women's equality. One can certainly argue that, in many places, it is leading not only to a more egalitarian Buddhism but has contributed to a more egalitarian perspective in the West as well.[69]

BUDDHISM IN AMERICA

Buddhists in substantial numbers first came to the United States as laborers. Chinese workers were brought to California just after the Gold Rush of 1849. By 1880 more than 100,000 Chinese were to be found in the country, largely on the West Coast. To this day there are Chinese temples in San Francisco and other northern California cities, which, in a characteristically popular Chinese way, combine Buddhist and Daoist (to be discussed in Chapter 5) deities and which are important historical mementos of that era. Japanese Buddhists came to work in the sugar fields of Hawaii even before the islands' annexation to the United States in 1898. The first strictly

Buddhist temple in what is now the United States was built in Hilo, Hawaii, in 1889. It is in the Japanese Jodo Shinshu (Pure Land) tradition, and this form of Buddhism has been most active among Japanese Americans. A little later, however, temples of other schools of Buddhism—Nichiren, Shingon, and Zen particularly—appeared in the Japanese-American community.

At the same time, interest in Buddhism was growing among American intellectuals. The way had been prepared by the oriental concerns of New England Transcendentalism. Sir Edwin Arnold's poetic story of the Buddha, *The Light of Asia* (1879), had a considerable impact. In addition, the 1893 World's Parliament of Religions was a catalyst for the development of Western Buddhism, just as it was for Western Hinduism. One of the Asian speakers at the parliament, the Japanese Zen monk Soyen Shaku, returned to the United States in 1905 with several followers to establish the beginnings of Western Zen. A student of his, the layman D. T. Suzuki, wrote and spoke extensively on Zen in English up through the 1950s. By 1930, the first continuing Zen center for Westerners had been founded in New York.

Zen Buddhism was something of a vogue in the 1950s, influencing the art and letters of "Beat" writers like Jack Kerouac and Gary Snyder. At the end of that decade and in the 1960s, a number of Western Zen centers were organized in the United States. Another form of Japanese Buddhism, the Nichiren Shoshu school, then promoted by Soka Gakkai, also became widely popular among non-Asian Americans in the 1960s and afterward.

Other styles of Buddhism also reached American shores in midcentury and continued to arrive thereafter. The devastation of Tibet by the Chinese Communists since 1951 has sent many Tibetans, including learned *lamas*, into exile. Some have taught in American universities; some have established centers where Tibetan Buddhism has been presented to the general public. Helped by the immense prestige of Tibet's spiritual leader, the Dalai Lama, Vajrayana or Tibetan Buddhism, seen as a difficult but rewarding spiritual path by many Westerners, became popular in the second half of the twentieth century.

Those years also saw substantial immigration from other traditionally Buddhist countries: Korea, Vietnam after the fall of Saigon in 1975, and the Theravada nations of Southeast Asia. These peoples brought their religion and monks to teach Buddhism with them. The presence of Theravada in addition to Mahayana Buddhism in the New World is now shown by the graceful and colorful architecture of Thai, Burmese, Cambodian, and Sri Lankan temples in several U.S. cities.

Some Americans of non-Asian descent have taken up the study of Theravada spiritual practice, especially the quiet but deeply penetrating *vipassana* form of meditation. There are Western-oriented centers and teachers of it, as well as Asian. It may be mentioned that Chinese Buddhism has also flourished in America. The supreme symbol of this prosperity is undoubtedly the vast and spectacular Hsi Lai Temple outside Los Angeles.

Buddhism, though very much a minority religion in America, has taken root there in two forms: temples ministering largely to Americans of traditionally Buddhist ethnic background and Buddhist centers geared chiefly to the requirements of persons of non-Asian culture who are interested in Buddhism as part of their personal spiritual quest. These two wings of the Buddhist movement are slowly coming together as a distinctive Buddhism gradually emerges in America, just as it has in every other country to which the *dharma* has spread. That may be a task of centuries, and Buddhist centers catering to national, cultural, and religious interests will understandably also remain important for some time to come. Buddhism is now, however, a significant part of the United States' highly pluralistic spiritual community.

Fundamental Features of Buddhism

Theoretical

Basic Worldview	Reality is an indescribable unity. Humans find themselves in a realm of suffering governed by karma.
God or Ultimate Reality	Unconditioned reality beyond all opposites: Nirvana, the Void.
Origin of the World/Destiny of the World	While the cosmos may go through cycles, it has no known beginning or end.
Origin of Humans	An individual is a process of cause and effect rather than a self; to this there is no beginning.
Destiny of Humans	Unending lifetimes in this and other worlds, good or bad according to karma and merit. One then breaks through to attain the Nirvana state.
Revelation or Mediation between the Ultimate and the Human	Through the Buddha, who attained full enlightenment, and the scriptures attributed to him.

Practical

What Is Expected of Humans; Worship, Practices, Behavior	To do good. Religious and moral works that gain good rebirth. To seek Nirvana by meditation or related practices.

Sociological

Major Social Institutions	Temples; the *samgha*, or order of monks.

Summary

Buddhism can be thought of as a religion with a psychological emphasis. It teaches the transformation of consciousness from attachment to ego, suffering, and objects of craving to the unattached bliss of Nirvana. Its fundamental teaching is that the Buddha, through his enlightenment, showed the way out of the wheel of rebirth or conditioned reality created by ignorance and attachment. Its fundamental practice is meditation and comparable methods of transcending attachment. Its fundamental sociological expression is the *samgha*, or order of monks in the succession of the Buddha's disciples.

According to Buddhist tradition, the Buddha, among the first of the great religious founders, attained a state of perfect enlightenment after a spiritual quest. He then taught that liberation comes by following a Middle Way between all attachments. He taught the Four Noble Truths: suffering, attachment, and freedom from suffering in Nirvana through the Eightfold Path, which culminates in Right Meditation. He taught that the ego is the supreme delusive object of attachment, for we are really not egos but impermanent collections of parts called *skandhas*.

Theravada Buddhism, the "Way of the Elders," predominant in the Buddhist parts of South and Southeast Asia, adheres closely to these teachings and views itself as standing in the tradition of the historical Buddha. For monks, who claim a lineage that extends back to the Buddha's original *samgha*, it emphasizes meditations leading to spiritual agility and nirvanic consciousness. For the laity, it emphasizes acts and attitudes that will lead to merit and good rebirths.

The Mahayana Buddhism of North and East Asia stresses the presence of the "Buddha-nature," the essence of the universe as the Buddha saw it in his enlightenment, in all beings. Thus, the universe is spoken of as Void and as one with Nirvana, for there is nothing within it to be grasped. The *bodhisattva*, an "enlightenment being" who realizes this and is at once in the world and Nirvana, is a key Mahayana figure. Because liberation is a matter of realizing one's own Buddha-nature, Mahayana teaches the accessibility of salvation to all and offers many diverse paths to the final goal. An important later Mahayana school is "Mind Only" or Yogacara, which holds that one creates reality out of one's mind. It led in turn to teaching about the three "bodies" or forms of expression of the Buddha-nature, in the cosmos (*dharmakaya*), in the heavens (*sambhogakaya*), and on Earth (*nirmanakaya*). Yogacara led to Vajrayana, the Tantric school of Buddhism which presents rigorous initiation and training, leading one to evoke or visualize helping Buddhas and *bodhisattvas*, among other techniques.

Vajrayana, Chan (Zen), and Pure Land are particular developments in the Mahayana tradition. Vajrayana is the Buddhism of Tibet, a land that traditionally had a unique Buddhist culture. The Tibetan text best known in the West is the Bardo Thodol, or The Tibetan Book of the Dead, which describes after-death experiences and emphasizes that all that one meets after death is a manifestation of one's own true nature. Chan began in China and later became an important Buddhist sect in Japan. It is the Buddhism of meditation—"sitting quietly, doing nothing." Pure Land is the Buddhism of Amitabha, also known as Emiduo in Chinese and Amida in Japan, who vowed that he would bring all who called upon his name to his Buddha-paradise—the Western Paradise of jeweled trees and perfumed rivers where there are no unfortunate rebirths and everyone can easily attain enlightenment. It is an important Buddhist sect in China, Japan, and Korea.

The *samgha* ideal that developed in Buddhism primarily involved the separation of its adherents from worldly concerns to live in community with their companion seekers. However, the reciprocal relationship of laity and *samgha* was eventually reflected in the relationship of the *dharma* king to the *samgha* as patron and receiver of merit for the whole community and in the relationship of the *samgha* to the king as teachers and advisers—the *samgha* and the king's civil rule being the "two wheels of the *dharma*." Emperor Ashoka, who made the *dharma* central to political and social stability and justice and who promoted Buddhism throughout his empire, is venerated as the ideal. Colonial rule disrupted this pattern where it existed. Since then Theravada Buddhism has been caught up in the crises of nationalism, modernization, and ideological conflict, which have tormented much of its corner of the world. Mahayana Buddhism in China and in North Korea has been suppressed under Communist rule, although in China it is now permitted, albeit regulated, while it has been practiced freely in Japan, South Korea, and Taiwan.

Early Buddhism offered new opportunities for women. For the first time, women were able to adopt the life of the renunciant. Significantly, Buddhism offered a more egalitarian worldview than did Hinduism at that time. Still, prevailing societal attitudes toward women have held sway throughout Buddhism's history. As a consequence, the women's *samgha* has generally been under the authority of the monks. Theravada Buddhism developed a more socially conservative doctrine toward women, resulting in a limitation of their role in that form of Buddhism, where the ordination lineage for nuns has died out. On the other hand, the many forms of Mahayana Buddhism tended toward a more egalitarian view of women and men that Western and Eastern feminist scholars see as the core of the Buddhist teachings of "No Self" and nonattachment. The debate as to whether the female body can be a vessel for enlightenment is still continuing and is dealt with variously by the many Mahayana sects, and Mahayana Buddhist institutions remain patriarchal in many respects.

Buddhism has come to the United States in both traditional ethnic forms and in forms designed to appeal to Western seekers. There are now a number of beautiful Buddhist temples and centers in America.

Questions for Review

1. Interpret Buddhism in terms of the three forms of religious expression.
2. Show how a religion ultimately focused on individual liberation also functions as a religion for society. Point to the significant contrasts between Theravada and Mahayana Buddhism in both respects.
3. Talk about the meaning of the Buddha's quest and enlightenment, as presented in traditional accounts of his life.
4. Explain basic Buddhist teaching: the Middle Way, the Four Noble Truths, the Eightfold Path, No Self, and Nirvana.
5. Explain why meditation is important in Buddhism.
6. Understand and be able to put into simple words the fundamental teachings of Nagarjuna that underlie Mahayana Buddhism: *Samsara* is Nirvana, and Void or Emptiness is the best metaphor for what we call reality.
7. Discuss the distinctive features of Mahayana: the Buddha-nature in all things, the *bodhisattva* concept, the "multimedia" approach to salvation, and the Sutras.
8. Mention some features of Mind Only (Yogacara or Vijnanavada) Buddhist philosophy and discuss its influence, especially its impact on spiritual practice as well as on theory.
9. Explain the three "bodies" (*trikaya*) or forms or expressions of the Buddha-nature as presented in developed Mahayana thought: the universal essence, the heavenly essence, and the earthly (or transformative) essence.
10. Discuss some features of Vajrayana, the Tantric Buddhism of Tibet, Mongolia, and elsewhere, especially its use of initiation and evocation and its foundation in the Mind Only philosophy.
11. Discuss the scenario and the deeper meaning of The Tibetan Book of the Dead (Bardo Thodol).
12. Explain the "two wheels of the *dharma*" in the classical expression of Buddhism, governance, and political life and how that concept is disrupted or has evolved in Buddhism today.
13. Explain how the advent of Buddhism in India affected women's lives.
14. Discuss the issues surrounding the advent and development of the nuns' *samgha*.
15. Discuss the role of women in Buddhism, especially the issues surrounding the appropriateness of the female body for Buddhahood.
16. Using the chart provided in the chapter explain the fundamental features of Buddhism. How does it deal with the great questions of the nature of ultimate reality and the goal of human life?
17. Talk about the aspects of Buddhism that seem most meaningful to you.

Suggested Readings on Buddhism

General

Bechert, Heinz, and Richard Gombrich, eds., *The World of Buddhism: Buddhist Monks and Nuns in Society and Culture*. New York: Facts on File, 1984.

Becker, Carl B., *Breaking the Circle: Death and the Afterlife in Buddhist Thought*. Carbondale: Southern Illinois University Press, 1994.

Byrom, Thomas, *Dhammapada: The Sayings of the Buddha*. Boston: Shambhala, 1993.

Ch'en, Kenneth, *Buddhism: The Light of Asia*. Woodbury, NY: Barron's Educational Series, 1968.

Conze, Edward, *Buddhism: Its Essence and Development*. New York: Harper Torchbooks, 1959.

———, *Buddhist Thought in India*. New York: Harper Torchbooks, 1962.

———, *Buddhist Wisdom Books*. London: George Allen & Unwin, 1958.

De Bary, William Theodore, ed., *The Buddhist Tradition in India, China, and Japan*. New York: Modern Library, 1969.

Harvey, Peter, *An Introduction to Buddhist Ethics*. New York: Cambridge University Press, 2000.

Jiang, Tao, *Context and Dialogue: Yogacara Buddhism and Modern Psychology on the Subliminal Mind*. Honolulu: University of Hawai'i Press, 2006.

Kasa, Stephanie, ed., *Hooked: Buddhist Writings on Greed, Desire, and the Urge to Consume*. Boston: Shambhala, 2005.

Kinnard, Jacob N., *The Emergence of Buddhism*. Westport, CT: Greenwood, 2006.

Mitchell, Donald W., *Buddhism: Introducing the Buddhist Experience*. New York: Oxford University Press, 2008.

Olson, Carl, *The Different Paths of Buddhism*. New Brunswick, NJ: Rutgers University Press, 2005.

Robinson, Richard H., and Willard L. Johnson, *The Buddhist Religion*. Belmont, CA: Wadsworth, 1982.

Snelling, John, *The Buddhist Handbook: A Complete Guide to Buddhist Schools, Teaching, Practice and History*. Rochester, VT: Inner Traditions, 1991.

Strong, John S., *The Experience of Buddhism: Sources and Interpretations*. Belmont, CA: Wadsworth, 1995.

Tsomo, Karma Lekshe, *Into the Jaws of Yama, Lord of Death: Buddhism, Bioethics, and Death*. Albany: State University of New York Press, 2006.

Williams, Paul, *Mahayana Buddhism: The Doctrinal Foundations*. New York: Routledge, 1989.

The Buddha

Griffiths, Paul. J., *On Being Buddha: The Classical Doctrine of Buddhahood*. Albany: State University of New York Press, 1994.

Karetzky, Patricia Eichenbaum, *The Life of the Buddha: Ancient Scriptural and Pictorial Traditions*. Lanham, MD: University Press of America, 1992.

Percheron, Maurice, *The Marvelous Life of the Buddha*. New York: St. Martin's Press, 1960.

Rahula, Walpola, *What the Buddha Taught*. New York: Evergreen Press, 1962.

Buddhism in Southeast Asia

King, Winston L., *A Thousand Lives Away*. Cambridge, MA: Harvard University Press, 1964.

Langer, Rita, *Buddhist Rituals of Death and Rebirth: Contemporary Sri Lankan Practice and Its Origins*. London and New York: Routledge, 2007.

Lester, Robert C., *Theravada Buddhism in Southeast Asia*. Ann Arbor: University of Michigan Press, 1973.

Swearer, Donalk K., *The Buddhist World of Southeast Asia*. Albany: State University of New York Press, 2010.

Wickermeratne, Swarna, *Buddha in Sri Lanka: Remembered Yesterdays*. Albany: State University of New York Press, 2006.

Tibetan Religion

Bernbaum, Edwin, *The Way to Shambhala: A Search for the Mythical Kingdom Beyond the Himalayas*. Garden City, NY: Doubleday Anchor, 1980.

Blofeld, John, *The Way of Power*. London: George Allen & Unwin, 1970.

Dalai Lama, The, *The Buddhism of Tibet*. Ithaca, NY: Snow Lion, 1987.

Powers, John, *Introduction to Tibetan Buddhism*. Ithaca, NY: Snow Lion Publications, 2007.

Thurman, Robert A., Jr., *The Tibetan Book of the Dead: The Great Book of Natural Liberation through Understanding in the Between*. New York: Bantam, 1994.

Chan/Zen and Pure Land Buddhism

Addison, Stephen, ed., *Zen Sourcebook: Traditional Documents from China, Korea, and Japan*. Indianapolis: Hackett, 2008.

Amstutz, Galen Dean, *Interpreting Amida: History and Orientalism in the Study of Pure Land Buddhism*. Albany: State University of New York Press, 1997.

Bodhidharma, *The Bodhidharma Anthology: The Earliest Records of Zen*, Jeffrey L. Broughton, trans. Berkeley: University of California Press, 1999.

Dumoulin, Heinrich, *Zen Buddhism: A History*, James W. Heisting and Paul Knitter, trans. New York: Prentice Hall Macmillan, 1994.

———, *Zen Buddhism in the Twentieth Century*. New York: Weatherhill, 1992.

Hershock, Peter D. *Chan Buddhism*. Honolulu: University of Hawai'i Press, 2005.

Hoover, Thomas, *The Zen Experience*. New York: New American Library, 1980.

Kapleau, Philip, *The Three Pillars of Zen*. Boston: Beacon Press, 1967.

Suzuki, Daisetz T., *Zen Buddhism*. Garden City, NY: Doubleday, 1956.

Buddhism, Governance, and Political Life

Friedlander, Peter G., "Buddhism and Politics," in *The Politics of Religion: A Survey*, Jeffrey Haynes, ed. London; New York: Routledge, 2006, pp. 3–12.

Hershock, Peter D. *Buddhism in the Public Sphere*. London, New York: Routledge, 2006.

Jerryson, Michael K., and Mark Juergensmeyer, *Buddhist Warfare*. New York: Oxford University Press, 2010.

Lewis, Todd, "Buddhism: The Politics of Compassion," in *God's Rule: The Politics of the World's Religions*, Jacob Neusner, ed. Washington, DC: Georgetown University Press, 2003, pp. 233–56.

Queen, Christopher S., *Engaged Buddhism in the West*. Boston: Wisdom Publications, 2000.

———, and Sallie B. King, eds., *Engaged Buddhism: Buddhist Liberation Movements in Asia*. Albany: State University of New York Press, 1996.

Women in Buddhism

Arai, Paula Kane Robinson, *Women Living Zen: Japanese Soto Buddhist Nuns*. New York: Oxford University Press, 1999.

Barnes, Nancy Schuster, "Buddhism," in *Women in World Religions*, Arvind Sharma, ed. Albany: State University of New York Press, 1987, pp. 105–33.

———, [Schuster] "Striking a Balance: Women and Images of Women in Early Chinese Buddhism," in *Women, Religion and Social Change*, Yvonne Yazback Haddad and Ellison Banks Findly, eds. Albany: State University of New York Press, 1985, pp. 87–112.

———, [Barnes] "Women in Buddhism," in *Today's Woman in World Religions*, Arvind Sharma, ed. Albany: State University of New York Press, 1994, pp. 137–69.

Blackstone, Karthryn R., *Women in the Footsteps of the Buddha: Struggle for Liberation in the Therigatha.* Richmond, UK: Curzon, 1998.

Boucher, Sandy, *Discovering Kwan Yin, Buddhist Goddess of Compassion.* Boston: Beacon Press, 1999.

———, *Opening the Lotus: A Woman's Guide to Buddhism.* Boston: Beacon Press, 1997.

———, *Turning the Wheel: American Women Creating the New Buddhism*, 2nd ed. Boston: Beacon, 1993.

Campbell, June, *Traveler in Space: In Search of Female Identity in Tibetan Buddhism.* New York: George Braziller, 1996.

Cheng, Wei-Yi, *Buddhist Nuns in Taiwan and Sri Lanka: A Critique of the Feminist Perspective.* London, New York: Routledge, 2007.

Dresser, Marianne, ed., *Buddhist Women on the Edge: Contemporary Perspectives for the Western Frontier.* Berkeley, CA: North Atlantic Books, 1996.

Gregory, Peter N., and Susanne Mrozik, *Women Practicing Buddhism: American Experiences.* Boston: Wisdom Publications, 2008.

Gross, Rita M., *Buddhism after Patriarchy: A Feminist History, Analysis, and Reconstruction of Buddhism.* Albany: State University of New York Press, 1993.

Schireson, Grace, *Zen Women.* Boston: Wisdom Publications, 2009.

Shaw, Miranda, *Passionate Enlightenment: Women in Tantric Buddhism.* Princeton, NJ: Princeton University Press, 1994.

Tisdale, Sallie, *Women of the Way: Discovering 2,500 Years of Buddhist Wisdom.* San Francisco: HarperSanFrancisco, 2006.

Tsomo, Karma Lekshe, ed., *Buddhist Women Across Cultures: Realizations.* Albany: State University of New York Press, 1999.

———, ed., *Buddhist Women and Social Justice.* Albany: State University of New York Press, 2004.

Tsomo, Karmas Kekshe, *Buddhism Through American Women's Eyes.* Ithaca, NY: Sno Lion, 2010.

———, *Innovative Buddhist Women: Swimming Against the Stream.* Richmond, UK: Curzon, 2000.

Willis, Janice D., "Nuns and Benefactresses: The Role of Women in the Development of Buddhism," in *Women, Religion and Social Change*, Yvonne Yazback Haddad and Ellison Banks Findly, eds. Albany: State University of New York Press, 1985, pp. 59–86.

Buddhism in America

Coleman, James Wilson, *The New Buddhism: The Western Transformation of an Ancient Tradition.* New York: Oxford University Press, 2001.

Fields, Rick, *How the Swans Came to the Lake.* Boulder, CO: Shambhala, 1986.

Friedman, Lenore, *Meetings with Remarkable Women*, rev. ed. Boston: Shambhala, 2000.

Learman, Linda, ed., *Buddhist Missionaries in the Age of Globalization.* Honolulu: University of Hawai'i Press, 2005.

Morreale, Don, ed., *The Complete Guide to Buddhist America.* Boston: Shambhala, 1998.

Paine, Jeffrey, *Re-Enchantment: Tibetan Buddhism Comes to the West.* New York: W.W. Norton, 2004.

Prebish, Charles S., *Luminous Passage: The Practice and Study of Buddhism in America.* Berkeley: University of California Press, 1999.

———, and Kenneth K. Tanaka, eds., *The Faces of Buddhism in America.* Berkeley: University of California Press, 1998.

Seager, Richard Hughes, *Buddhism in America.* New York: Columbia University Press, 1999.

Storhoff, Gary, *The Emergence of Buddhist American Literature.* Albany: State University of New York Press, 2009.

Sutin, Lawrence, *All Is Change: The Two Thousand Year Journey of Buddhism to the West.* New York: Little, Brown, 2006.

5

Dragon and Sun
Religions of East Asia

CHAPTER OBJECTIVES

After studying this chapter, you should be able to

- Cite the major religious traditions of China and Japan.
- Explain the different roles of Confucianism, Daoism, and Buddhism in China and Japan.
- Explain the role of Shinto in Japan.
- Interpret the relation of these spiritual traditions to East Asian societies today.
- Understand the Confucian vision for governance and political life, as well as the historical and current trends for religion and politics in China and Japan.
- Discuss the role of women in traditional Chinese and Japanese societies and the effect of East Asia's religious traditions on women's lives.
- Present the religious traditions of Korea, Vietnam, and Mongolia.

THE EAST ASIAN SPIRITUAL WORLD

Some years ago, I* encountered a non-Western religion in its homeland for the first time. That religion was **Shinto**, and the country was Japan. I saw Japanese Buddhist temples on the same visit, of course, but it was Shinto shrines I saw first and which for some reason buried themselves most deeply in my memory.

I could not forget the **torii**, the gently curved archway that led into the precincts of a shrine, separating the noisy bustle of the street from the quiet shrine with its ancient architecture. The *torii* was like a mystic portal between one age and another, and even one dimension and another. In the midst of a modern industrial city, these plain but graceful sanctuaries of the **kami**, Shinto deities, are set amidst sacred groves of gnarled old trees, and they communicate just a touch of the past, the natural, and the wondrous. In the countryside, where shrines grace mountaintops, clear rushing streams, or inlets of the sea, they lend an aura of the Divine to vistas already beautiful.

I felt strangely stirred by these wooden shrines, simple and rustic in construction, with their pitched roofs and heavy doors. The porticos presented such understated but effective symbols of

---

*Robert Ellwood

deity as zigzag strips of paper, immense rope lintels, and gleaming eyelike mirrors. I liked the way the shrines seemed never to clash with nature but only to embellish it. If a *kami* presence dwelt within the shrine, one felt that the divine presence was a deity who knew and respected the old trees in the parish down to their deepest roots and felt the insides of the ageless stones, as well as the grandmothers, young people, and babies who lived in the streets around this shrine home. While musing on dreams of the mythic past, the *kami* watched with spirit eyes the frenetic life of a modern nation.

Nor were these *kami* presences easily forgotten. Once the official religion of Japan, since World War II Shinto has no longer been under state control. Now shorn of ultranationalistic overtones, it retains its shrines under local democratic administration. It has not withered away as some thought it would but has prospered as a popular religion. To be sure, few of those frequenting the shrines would call themselves exclusively Shinto. Most are also Buddhist, at least nominally, or members of one of the "new religions" of Japan (to be discussed later). And many would hardly think of themselves as religious at all. Yet they may pause for a moment as they pass a shrine.

At a shrine of any importance, the visitor will not wait long before seeing an individual or family pass through the *torii*, wash hands and mouth in a basin, approach the shrine, clap twice, bow, murmur a prayer, and leave a small offering in a grill.

The fortunate observer may have the opportunity to attend a Shinto festival, or **matsuri**. Then, he or she will notice a dramatic change in the atmosphere of the shrine. Instead of a quiet, shy deity in a leafy refuge, the *kami* now becomes a dynamic presence in the midst of the people, calling explosive festivity into being.

First, pure offerings of rice wine (*sake*), vegetables, and seafood are very slowly presented to the *kami* by white-robed priests, together with green boughs of the sacred *sakaki* tree brought forward by leading laypeople.

Then, suddenly and startlingly, this mood of classical dignity breaks. Sacred dance in vivid and fantastic costume is performed. A carnival may be held on the grounds of the shrine, with everything from cotton candy to sumo wrestling. The *kami* presence is carried through the streets in a palanquin (a *mikoshi*) by running, sweating young men, who shout "*Washo! Washo!*" as they zigzag down the ways and byways of the *kami*'s parish.

Shinto has a highly distinctive personality of its own, yet it also illustrates several characteristics of the religion of East Asia in general. In Shinto shrines, and also in Chinese and Japanese Buddhist and other temples, one senses a close harmony of the human and natural orders. The deities and guides of humankind dwell in virtual symbiosis with woods, streams, and mountains, suggesting that in a larger sense, society is a part of nature, and that *kami*, immortals, Buddhas, and humans are all parts of a greater cosmic unity.

Very often, then, the Divine is finite and tied to particular places. There may indeed be an indefinable universal divine principle that underlies all particular manifestations of the sacred and is infinite. But the individual deities one can know are limited, although impressive, as if no more than glorified human beings. Indeed, in China for the last two thousand years, nearly all deities except Heaven and Earth themselves were conceived of as having once been humans who acceded to divine status by exemplary merit. Their ranks and titles were confirmed by the emperor as though such beings were simply another class among his subjects—and the emperor alone was permitted to worship Heaven and Earth directly. In Japan, although only occasionally designating a deity, the government did assign the sacred status of the various shrines.

East Asian religion has tended to see a world in which divine beings and humans both have places and interact with each other more by agreement and respect than on the model of master and servant. To be sure, Chinese and Japanese worship is capable of mystery, awe, and wonder. Buddhism, particularly through the Mahayana philosophies and techniques described in the previous chapter, has made spiritual culture aware of mystical and metaphysical profundities oriented toward the infinite. Yet in East Asia, it all finally comes down to a human-centered view of mystery and metaphysics—the Chinese and Japanese are rarely forgetful that these things are important to humans insofar as they enrich human life and help validate its central institutions, the family and the state. Religious style is likely to be more restrained and pragmatic than the ecstatic abandon of the Hindu *bhakta* or the certainty of the Christian believer. Religion is not that kind of commitment; rather, it is part of a ring of reciprocal commitments whose real center is inflexible norms or propriety for human and divine relations: these are the true obligation. The value center, in other words, is one's proper place in society and therefore one's means of integration into family and community.

The sociological expression is extremely important in understanding religion in East Asia, particularly, "natural" sociological units—family and community, which for most East Asians are one's link with the infinite. It is through worship of one's particular ancestors that one expresses filial relation to the primordial infinite ancestors, Heaven and Earth. It is through one's particular *kami* or patronal deity that one integrates oneself into the hierarchy of the Divine. It is through reverence to particular Buddhas and *bodhisattvas* that one acknowledges tacitly the unbounded wisdom a Buddha represents.

All these features come together when one thinks of East Asian faith as centered in a "one world" concept. There is no God or Heaven outside the world system of which we are a part here and now. Gods, heavens, hells, society, nature, family, and individual are all parts of a single unity of which humankind is (at least for humans) the pivot. This means the individual has to be a part of the whole; if there is only one unified system, it is absurd to try to opt out of it. On the other hand, it means that one is under no obligation to emphasize one part of the system more than another—heaven more than this world, a deity more than family. All are parts of the same thing, so one's approach is made according to one's circumstances or bent. Most would probably agree that a balanced outlook is wisest.

Some commentators have so stressed this supposedly "humanistic" and "this-worldly" East Asian attitude to suggest that religion, life after death, heavens, and supernatural entities are unimportant to the Chinese and Japanese. At least in regard to traditional society, such an assessment is very wide of the mark. Whatever some rationalist philosophers may have held, the popular culture of East Asia has certainly not been behind any other in energy and expense devoted to worship of deities, propitiation of spirits, and the assurance of a good fate on the other side of death. It has also been possible to enlist religion in support of revolutionary and nationalistic causes.

But it is fair to say that the visible and invisible realms are parts of one unity, like the obverse and reverse sides of a coin and that what is really important to humanity is the continuation and well-being of individual, family, and social life on both sides of the line between this world and the next. Except for the most mystical of Daoists (to be discussed later) and Buddhists, the unending perpetuation of the good life for humans, together with the maintaining of family obligations, is the supreme good. The apparatus of religion is appreciated by the many who accept it for the contributions it can make to the good life here and hereafter. It is an invisible world that interlocks with this world.

In East Asia, as we can readily see, religion is not divided neatly into distinct categories, such as "Buddhism" or "Shinto"—each as a "religion" unto itself. Rather, religion is integrated into the cultural landscape of each East Asian region. Accordingly, we will be looking at religion in East Asia by country: first China, then Japan, then Korea, Vietnam, and Mongolia.

Religion in China

ANCIENT CHINA

To get a perspective on the specifics of East Asian religion, let us start with China— and at the beginning. One of the most distinctive features of the Chinese mentality is its feeling that the Chinese people and the soil on which they live are inseparable and have been so as far back as tradition goes. In most other major societies, a tradition of having come from some other place and conquering the land in which the people now dwell is a feature of incalculable weight in the national image. Consider the significance of the Exodus and the taking of the Promised Land to the Israelites, the journey of Aeneas from Troy to Italy for the Roman mystique, the importance of Indo-European arrivals in both ancient India and Northern Europe, the myth of the conquest of Japan by the first emperor Jimmu for Japanese nationalism, or the immigration and pioneer motifs in America's national consciousness.

In China, there is none of this. Instead, the Chinese have felt a quieter but even more secure assurance that they have always been in China, were created there, and belong there as surely as the rivers and mountains and rice fields. Consequently, a sense of place, of the cycles of nature, and of lineage were fundamental to the religious outlook of the earliest known Chinese, as they have been ever since.

The cultural line that led to Chinese civilization began around 4000 B.C.E. in tiny villages in the Yellow River basin where millet, vegetables, and pigs were raised. One of the oldest motifs of Chinese religion is the Earth God. The central sacred feature was often a stone or mound, like a concentration of the forces of the soil into a central focus. These mounds are the ancestors of the city-god temples of today, as well as the great **Altar of Heaven** in Beijing, built like an artificial mountain where the emperor offered worship at the Winter Solstice.[1] Worship was also offered very early to the spirits of rivers and of rain, the latter immemorially represented as the dragon, for the rivers and rain bless the fertile Earth with moisture.

In burial and **ancestrism**, continuity of the three identity-giving factors of family, ancestors, and place was emphasized. Burial, the return of the tiller of the Earth to its bosom, has always been very important in China. As the peasant works his fields, he may see on the side of an overlooking hill the site he has selected for his tomb. He knows that from there he will in spirit watch his progeny generation after generation work the same fields. At the tomb, at the family shrine with tablets bearing the names of ancestors, and in the home shrine, his descendants will remember him with offerings of food and drink and with information concerning family events. This reverence may be tinged with awe and dread, for even the humblest family head grows mightily in power when he returns to union with the Earth, and he can reach out from the grave to bless those who keep bright the family honor or to afflict its enemies. From another perspective, perhaps the continuity of life and death made death less feared than it may have been in other cultures. Here, the afterlife was understood to be a continuation of family and community, and to be remembered by one's family through the ages must have been some comfort in itself.

Gate to the Round Altar, Temple of Heaven, Beijing, China.

The concern with burial goes as far back as Chinese culture. **Neolithic** farmers buried children in urns under the house and adults in reserved fields. In the first period of real civilization, the Shang era, great pits were dug in earth for the burial of a king. In what must have been a scene of incredible barbaric horror and splendor, the deceased monarch was interred brilliantly ornamented with jade, together with the richly caparisoned horses who had borne his hearse, hundreds of sacrificed human retainers and prisoners, and a fortune in precious objects.[2]

The Shang **Dynasty** and its successor, the Zhou Dynasty,[3] lasted from about 1750 to 221 B.C.E. The basic motifs of religion in these eras represent, in developing form, the fundamental ideas of Chinese religion and philosophy.

The thinkers of those days talked of a supreme ruler or moderator of the universe, Di or **Tian**, usually translated as "Heaven," who gave rain, victory, fortune or misfortune, and regulated the moral order. All things ultimately derived from Tian, but it was more a personification of natural law than a real personality and was not directly worshipped; Heaven was like the high God of many archaic and indigenous peoples—sovereign but remote.

Other deities, lesser but more accessible to worship, were those of sun, moon, stars, rivers, mountains, the four directions, and localities. These were given offerings, some seasonally, some morning and evening. Above all were the ancestral spirits, treated to meals and remembrance and expected to intercede on behalf of the living with Tian.

The dead, in other words, were made a part of life. They could communicate with the living through the lips of shamanesses and oracles, and unpropitiated ghosts of the dead were much feared. There were also myths of culture heroes who combated floods, built irrigation systems, and taught the people agriculture. If not directly worshipped, such figures as Yu and Hou Ji had marvelous births, precarious and miracle-fraught childhoods, and lives of self-sacrifice and superhuman works comparable to those of divine heroes and saviors elsewhere.

The Shang era is most famous for divination with the "oracle bones." The procedure was that kings would ask their ancestors questions and the answers would be determined by cracks made in a tortoiseshell when it was heated over a fire. Thousands of these shells, with the questions and sometimes the answers inscribed on them in an archaic form of writing, have been preserved.

Archaic Chinese religion is also noteworthy for the importance it gave to ceremonial elements. Highly stylized and exact rites were performed for each season, for deities and ancestors, and for the major occasions of life. These were done at court and apparently had their parallels among the common people as well. Court ceremonies were elaborate affairs; as we have seen, they sometimes involved grisly but solemn animal and human sacrifices.

Divination, the seasonal cycle, and ceremonialism all suggest one basic principle that has run through Chinese thought from the beginning—that the universe is a unity in which all things fit together. If humanity aligns itself with it, all will fit together for us as it does for nature. On this assumption, traditional Chinese lived with the turning of the seasons, and in their ceremonies, they strove to make life into an image of their harmony. Divination is based on the same worldview, for it presumes that if the world is a unity, each fragment of it—like a tortoiseshell—must contain clues to what is happening or what will happen in other parts.

THE DAO: FOUNDATIONAL TO CONFUCIANISM AND DAOISM

The unity in which all things fit together harmoniously is called the **Dao (Tao)**. The word is most often translated "way," and it originally meant a road but can also mean "speak." Among philosophers it came to mean the inexpressibly broad track down which all things roll; in philosophical writing, it has been translated by such terms as "way," "nature," "existence," and "God."

Dao—how to know it, live it, and construct a society that exemplifies it—is the great theme of Chinese thought and the religious expressions closely related to it. Never was this more the case than in the last two centuries of the Zhou Dynasty, 403–221 B.C.E. Called the "Warring States" period, this was an era when because the emperor had been reduced to a powerless figurehead, rulers of feudal states battled unceasingly with each other. Although it was a time of cultural and material advance, people felt that all sense of restraint and morality had been lost. Even the rough warrior codes no longer held, and society was caught up in a madness of rapacity, intrigue, and violence punctuated by a depraved brutality in which prisoners were routinely killed by slow and horrible means. The peasants, exploited in the best of times, suffered most.

Yet this was a time of creativity for the human spirit. New concepts that could be the foundation of high civilization emerged, if only because thoughtful people were forced to ask themselves such questions as, Where did we go wrong? How can we get society back on the right track and find the Dao? How can a sensitive individual find meaning in the midst of so much crassness?

In asking how to get back on the track of Dao, the Chinese believed there were three realms where Dao could be experienced: nature, human society, and one's own inner being. The question was, How are these to be lined up, with what priorities, and with what techniques for ascertaining the "message" of the Dao?

The answers fell into two categories: Confucian and Daoist. (There were other schools that have not survived or did not develop significant religious expression.) The basic difference was that Confucianists thought the Dao, or Tian (the will of

Heaven), as they often called it, was best found by humans within human tradition and society and so was explored through human relationships and rituals and by the use of human reason. The Daoists thought that reason and society perverted the Dao—that it was best found alone in the rapture of merging with infinite nature and the mystical and the marvelous.

The difference is comparable to that between rationalists and romantics in the West. Needless to say, Confucianism in China has been mainly associated with moralism and the ruling "establishment" elite together with their education system. Daoism, on the other hand, is linked with sensitivity of feelings, with artists and poets, and with all sorts of colorful, bizarre, "nonestablishment" things—from fairy tales to unusual sexual techniques, from exorcising devils to revolutionary secret societies and esoteric temple rites.

But it is important to recall that relatively few Chinese would think of themselves as exclusively Confucian or Daoist or Buddhist. In the lives of most people, features from all sides would have a place. Confucian attitudes would undergird family and work ethics; Buddhism would help to answer questions about what happens after death; a dash of Daoist color would meet aesthetic and spiritual needs in family and personal life. (It has been said that Chinese officials were Confucian at work and Daoist in retirement.)

Statue of Confucius at the main entrance of the Confucius Temple, Beijing, China.

CONFUCIANISM

Confucius (Kong Fuzi) and the Confucian Classics

The Confucian tradition is named after the philosopher **Confucius** (551–479 B.C.E.). We must distinguish Confucius as the man of his time from the almost-deified, incredibly wise, and remote figure of the Confucian educational tradition and state cult. But at the same time, we must remember why this particular man was selected as the symbolic embodiment of that tradition.

First, we must take into account the winsome, wise, persuasive, and utterly sincere personality of Confucius himself. Born in the feudal state of Lu (modern Shandong Province) as the son of a minor official or military officer, Kong Fuzi—to give Master Kong his Chinese rather than Latinized name and title—received an education and sought employment by a prince. He was a member of a class called **ru**, who were specialists in the "six arts"—ceremonial, music, archery, charioteering, history, numbers—and so custodians of what passed in those days for a classical and cultivated tradition. But Confucius had great difficulty in finding a position, apparently because he was too outspoken about proper conduct on the part of rulers and seemed hopelessly to have "his head in the clouds." He had to settle for a role that to him seemed second best but in the long run proved far more epochal than that of government minister.

He became a teacher. Among his students were young men who were successful in attaining practical influence and who over the years—and through subsequent generations of students over the centuries—reshaped the values and structures of Chinese statecraft, education, and social organization. It was they who understandably added honor upon honor to Confucius's memory until temples redolent of incense and sacrifice enshrined his name.

Confucius was not revered just for himself but because he was associated with the classical literature that was the real bedrock of the traditional culture. Five books, which existed in early form by the time of Confucius and which were the basic texts of the *ru*, are now often called the Confucian Classics. These are the Book of History, the Book of Poems, the Book of Change (the famous Yi Jing or I Ching), the historical Spring and Autumn Annals, and the Book of Rites. Tradition said, with greater or less exaggeration, that Confucius had written parts of them and edited them all; in any case, he became the symbol of their authority.

Four other books from shortly after the time of Confucius are also canonical and bear the putative seal of the master's authority: the Analects (containing the remembered words of Confucius himself), the Great Learning, the Mean, and the Book of Mencius.[4] (Mencius is the next best known philosopher in the Confucian tradition.)

These books are important because they reflect basic Chinese values and ways of thinking. Their tradition went back before Confucius and continued after him. Confucius is not a peerless sage because he created this tradition. On the contrary, he is unequalled because the tradition "created" him, and he reflected it faithfully.[5]

Fundamentals of the Confucian Tradition

It was not unfair to Confucius to honor him as the embodiment of the tradition, for the burden of his teaching was above all to maintain this heritage and apply it fully and properly. He was a creative and deeply principled conservative. He believed that the way to get society on the right track again was to go back to the example of ancient sage-emperors. The basic structures of society, he felt, were adequate. The needful thing was to convince people they must act in accordance with the roles society has given them. The father must act like a father; the son, like a son; the ruler must be a real ruler like those of old, wise and benevolent; the ministers of state must be true civil servants, loyal and fearless and self-giving.

This change to becoming what one "is" (called **rectification of names**) must first of all take place within. One must be motivated by virtue or by **ren**, a typically vague but eloquent term suggestive of humanity, love, high principle, and living together in harmony. It is the way of the **junzi**, the superior man, who, as the Confucian ideal suggests, is a man at once a scholar, a selfless servant of society, and a gentleman steeped in courtesy and tradition; as an official and family head, he continually puts philosophy into practice.

Confucius conceded that this noble ideal is enforced by no outside sanctions except the opinion of good men, for it was based on no belief in divine rewards or punishment after death. Its sincere practice in this life might, as often as not, result in exile and hunger rather than honor from princes. Yet in the end it draws men by the sheer attractiveness of the good and by the fact that it embodies Dao, so to follow *ren* is to align oneself with the way things are.

A fundamental satisfaction follows from acting in accordance with the real nature of things that the virtueless devotee of passion and gain can never know and that finally makes such a person's life hollow. For Confucianism has generally

MAJOR ERAS: CHINA

End of Shang (c. 1750–c.1050)

Zhou (1123–221)

Qin (221–206)

Han (206 B.C.E–220 C.E.)

PERSONALITIES AND EVENTS: CHINA

Court rituals
Laozi (?)
Confucius (551–479)
Zuangzi (c. 300)
Mencius (372–289)
Tung Zhungshu
(179–104) and
Han Confucianism

MAJOR ERAS: JAPAN

Prehistoric   Protohistoric

PERSONALITIES AND EVENTS: JAPAN

Shamanism very
influential

Clan period

1500 B.C.E.   1000 B.C.E.   500 B.C.E.   1 B.C.E./C.E.

Three Kingdoms (220–265)
Jin (265–420)

Yuan (1280–1368)

Ming (1368–1644)

Six Dynasties (420–589)
Sui (589–618)
Tang (618–907)

Qing (1644–1911)

Republic (1912–)

People's Republic on mainland (1949–)

Song (960–1280)

Han synthesis

High point of Buddhism

Ge Hong (283–343)

Zhu Xi (1130–1200)

Beginning of Chan and
Pure Land Buddhism

Neo-Confucianism dominant

Huineng (638–713)

Wang Yangming (1472–1529)

Taika (645–710)

Kamakura (1185–1333)

Nara (710–784)

Muromachi (1333–1568)
Monoyama (1568–1600)

Heian (794–1185)

Tokugawa (1600–1867)

Modern (1868–1945)

Postwar (1945)

Introduction of Buddhism
(early 6th century)

Honen (1133–1212)

Hakuin (1685–1768)

Kojiki (712)

Zen dominant Dogen
(1200–1253)

Confucianism
dominant culturally

Eisai (1141–1215)

Kobo Daishi
(773–835)

Shinran (1173–1262)

Nationalism

Esoteric Buddhism

Nichiren (1222–1282)

New Religions

500 C.E.   1000 C.E.   1500 C.E.   2000 C.E.

believed that the basic nature of mankind is good. It is only perverted by bad external example or bad social environment, and people will turn naturally to the good when good examples and social conditions are present. To make them present is the weighty responsibility of the ruler, advised by Confucian sages.

External influences, then, can aid in the inner development of *ren*. This leads to another very important Confucian term—**li**. It indicates rites, proper conduct, ceremonies, courtesy, doing things the right way. Despite a professed lack of concern about ghosts and gods, for Confucius the performance of rituals was extremely important.

It may seem to us excessive that a man, at the height of his career, upon the death of his father would go into retirement for three years, wearing sackcloth, wailing through day and night, eating only tasteless food. It might seem that the government of a nation ought to have better things to do than spend endless hours and money in the preparation and execution of seasonal ceremonies, one after the other. But *li* needs to be understood as Confucius understood it, not as cold or mere "formalism" but as a supremely humanizing act. Animals act out of the lust or violent emotion of the moment, but humankind can rise above this in the societies it creates, and *li* exemplifies this potential. *Li* expresses a society that becomes a great dance and thus acts in harmony. In ritual, everyone acts out proper relationships and has a structured place. Ritual generates order in place of chaos and nurtures "rectification of names." It can be hoped that if a person acts out, if only ritually, the proper conduct of his or her station in life often enough, in time she or he will interiorize the action, and the inner and outer will become one: the ritual father a true father, the ritual prince a true prince. *Li*, then, is meant to stimulate *ren*, even as melodious music induces calmness and heroic poetry valor.

It is within society that humanity comes to its best, for here the mutual stimuli of *ren* and *li* can be operative. Here is the key point of difference with the Daoists, who contended that society, or at least its regulations and rituals and mandatory relations, obscure the Dao. For Confucius, it was precisely in these social expressions that the Dao became visible and "spoke" to mankind.

Society for Confucius was founded on the **five relationships**: (1) ruler and subject, (2) father and son, (3) husband and wife, (4) elder and younger brother, (5) friend and friend. In all of these, proper behavior, *li*, was required to give what is simply biological or spontaneous the structure that makes it into human society—calm and enduring for the benefit of all.

The cornerstone relationship is the second—father and son. A son was expected to negate his own feelings and individuality in deference to the wishes and pleasure of his father in **filial piety**.[6] It was in this relationship, which is (at least according to Freudian psychoanalysis) the most feeling-laden and difficult of all, that fundamental attitudes of *ren* and *li* and societal orientation were to be learned. It was as though to say, if love and virtue are to be learned truly, they must be learned at home and by making this difficult, but all-important, relationship the pivot. Father–son becomes the primal model of an interpersonal relationship, and in Confucianism it is in interpersonal relationships that man is humanized and Dao is manifested. If this relationship can be rectified, then all other relationships will also fall into place.

One might ask, Why is the relation between father and son, rather than that between mother and child, the key? Perhaps it can be looked at in this way: The mother–child relationship is essentially a given—biological, fraught with deep feelings and instincts that humankind shares with most of the higher animals. The father–son relationship, on the other hand, is more social in nature. This is not to say, of course, that the father does not have a biological role and some instinctual equipment to go with it. But in many archaic societies, the father's biological role does not in itself establish social responsibility for a child. Rather, the crucial factor is the father's taking responsibility for the child in his social role as head of the household. The role is defined by his picking up the child, giving him a name, and recognizing him as his ward and heir. In other words, the father–son relationship is the most basic *social* relationship. It is inextricably intertwined with the social as well as the biological components of human culture, such as language (giving a name), moral responsibility, family as a legal entity, and the combination of privilege and repression that makes learned behavior—all that flows into *li* and *ren*—possible. It is therefore significant that in Confucianism, with its emphasis on human society as the key bearer of the Dao for human beings, the father–son relationship—the primal social, structured relationship—should be central. (In contrast, Laozi, whose Daoism, as we shall soon see, emphasized the natural and biological and spontaneous as better than the social for manifesting Dao, several times uses the mother–child relationship as a metaphor for the relation of a person with Dao.)

Needless to say, this perspective has meant that Confucianism, like many other traditional religions and social orders, has presumed and established an essentially male-centered worldview and society. Women, while given a place in the pattern of relationship, have found that place to be distinctly subordinate—something we will be addressing in more detail later. (We have not hesitated to use the terms "man" and "mankind" in the discussion of Confucianism, for this usage certainly conforms to the Confucian outlook.)

Subsequent Confucian philosophers talked about human nature and how society can be organized best to manifest the Dao within it. **Mencius** (372–289 B.C.E.), for example, held that human nature is basically good and is only impeded by an evil social environment, while **Xunzi** (fl. 298–238 B.C.E.) said that man is basically evil in the sense of being self-centered and, therefore, needs education and social control to become good.

We must give more attention, however, to the ways in which Confucianism clearly understood the three forms of religious expression, presenting a unified structure of teaching, rites, and sociological forms. In Confucianism, these three forms appeared simply in the "natural" units of family and traditional community. Because Confucius wanted to enhance and sanctify these units, he did not want to establish a center of sacred value elsewhere. His teaching was about the family and community, for which his rituals were performed, and through which they made their own sacred community. The secular was the sacred.

But as Confucianism became a quasi-state religion in the Han Dynasty (206 B.C.E.–220 C.E.) and afterward, it found it needed a quasi-theology, a quasi-divinity, and a quasi-priesthood with its own rites. Quasi-divinity it found in Confucius himself, and quasi-priesthood in the powerful class of Confucian scholar/bureaucrat elites—the *ru* or **mandarins**—who staffed the bureaucracy of the empire. Confucius, as the peerless infallible sage, was seen as a sort of mystic king, with a true right to rule the inward kingdom of ideas and values upon which the outer realm, administered and educated by the mandarins, was based.

The Han Synthesis and Yin–Yang

This kind of thinking, which may be called the **Han Synthesis** because it generously incorporated Daoist and other traditional motifs into Confucianism, was the work of **Dong Zhongshu** (c. 179–104 B.C.E.) more than of any other individual. His thought is like that of cosmic religion in that it is interested in the total interrelationship of all things rather than the ethical and political questioning of early Confucianism. Dong presented a doctrine of correspondences, in which humanity and nature are parts

Yin-Yang Symbol of the Dao.

of an interwoven web. A portent in heaven may be related to a forthcoming event on earth, and the moral decisions of a ruler may affect the prevalence of rain in his nation's fields.

Unlike many moderns, traditional Chinese did not see people and nature as separate, going by different laws. Instead they assumed that humanity, human history, and government cooperate with nature and are controlled by the same laws. It is as though we were to say that perpetual motion is as impossible in the history of a nation as it is in mechanics, if inertia is a true law. To further the comparison, it would be as though we then said that the nation must have a public ritual once a year to counteract its slowing down and to wind the energy up again.

For Dong, the key to the whole web of correspondences of which life is woven is the **Yin–Yang** concept. This theory had very early origins in occult speculation connected with astrology, alchemy, and *Yi Jing* divination, but it did not emerge fully into the mainstream of Chinese philosophy until the Han Synthesis.

In this view, the Dao—that is, all the ten thousand things—is divisible into two great classifications: *Yang* things and forces, and *Yin* things and forces. Fundamentally, *Yang* is associated with the masculine and *Yin* with the feminine, but their respective meanings go far beyond gender. *Yang* is what is male, but also day, sky, spring, and all that is bright, clear, hard, assertive, growing, moving out. Its symbol is the dragon. *Yin* is female and also night, earth, moisture, autumn and harvest, spirits of the dead, and all that is dark, underneath, recessive, pulling in, connected with the moon, mysterious. Its symbol is the tiger, which may be thought of as Blake's "Tyger, tyger burning bright/In the forests of the night"—emblematic of the arcane, the inward, the unfathomable, yet the inescapable in human life.

It must be emphasized that philosophically *Yang* and *Yin* are by no means either "good" or "bad." Neither is "better" than the other. They are both neutral, like gravitation. To keep going, the universe needs both, and they need to interact in a balanced way. Too much of either brings disaster, just as rain and sun are both necessary in their places but too much of either brings flood or drought. (In popular religion, however, *Yang* is often preferred because of its fertility associations and no doubt also because of the male predominance in the culture.)

The task of humanity is to keep these two eternal antagonists and partners, the dragon and the tiger, in proper balance, for our place is between them, and we are finally to interiorize them both. An elaborate art called **feng-shui** arose to determine, according to *Yin–Yang* "bearings," the most auspicious locations for houses, businesses, tombs, and temples, between, say, a rock considered *Yang* and a pond determined as *Yin*. (Much more is involved in the full system of *feng-shui* and of correspondences, too: the values of the five "elements" or modes of natural activity—fire, water, earth, metal, and wood—each of which corresponds with seasons, colors, tones, and so forth.) Finally, particularly in esoteric Daoism, one sought through alchemical potions and *yogic* practices to bring to equilibrium the two forces within oneself and thus achieve immortality. It is *Yin–Yang* imbalance that results in decay and death; one who has them in as perfect harmony as the great Dao itself will be as deathless as the great Dao. Confucianism has always emphasized finding a balance and keeping away from too much or too little of anything.

The ritual year, both at the imperial palace and in the humblest village, strove to "work" Yang and Yin. The object was to support what the Dao was doing at that time. The first half of the year, the time of growing and the outgoing of nature as it awoke from the sleep of winter, was the time of the dynamic, rain-giving dragon. The Chinese New Year is marked by a parade through the streets of a gigantic, weaving dragon borne by many men. In midsummer, to consummate *Yang*, dragon boat or horse races are held. Then to inaugurate the *Yin* months of ingathering and the

Chinese New Year Celebration.

darkening of days, lion or tiger dances are held. The traditional harvest festival when the dead return (as at Halloween) is full of *Yin* symbolism: it is held at night, and cakes in the shape of the moon, decorated with moon castles where immortals live, are placed in the courtyards.

Mandarins (Ru)

Han Synthesis thinking fit the needs of the *ru*, or *mandarin*, class who studied the lore, enacted the rites, and made Confucius the symbol of learning and authority. His **cultus** grew apace. In 56 C.E., sacrifices to Confucius were ordered in all schools. By the end of the empire in 1912, he had (in 1908) been declared coequal with Heaven and Earth themselves, as though to say the best of human culture was no less a great thing than cosmic nature.

The importance of the *mandarin* scholar class in Chinese tradition can hardly be overemphasized. Three things set them apart: (1) They were bearers of the ongoing tradition as dynasties rose and fell; (2) they were unique as a class in ability to read and write well; and (3) in theory they were not a hereditary aristocracy but an elite of brains who attained their positions in academic competition. As both teachers and administrators, they were indispensable to generations of rulers who found that sooner or later they had to conform to the values and usages of this class because they could not rule without its support.

The role of these Confucian scholar/bureaucrats meant that the real focus of power was not the sword but the pen and that the vessel of cultural continuity in this society was a class of refined elites, who scarcely hid their disdain of the rough soldier, but who made the written language and the ability to wield it elegantly the supreme symbol of superiority over the toiling masses. This situation involved no small flourishing of class privilege, yet it also enabled a rudimentary democracy, for the means of entry into the privileged class came through education and civil service examinations—ostensibly through merit. In nearly all periods, there were young men of humble background who managed to succeed in that grueling ordeal to become a *mandarin*.

Dynasties periodically rose and fell, and with the transfer of the Mandate of Heaven, a peasant or outlander might well come to the throne. There was no official nobility, and all families experienced years of bad fortune as well as good. China, then, did not know the domination of intermarrying noble lines like the Bourbons and Hapsburgs of Europe century after century; what lasted instead was the gray-gowned meritocracy of the learned.

The *mandarin* class naturally developed its own internal traditions and style. Its members grew fingernails inches long to prove that they did not do manual labor. Anything in writing, however trivial, was treated by them with respect and would be reverently burned rather than thrown out. They would typically be skeptical of beliefs concerning ghosts, spirits, gods, and an afterlife but would treat such beliefs among the common people (or even the womenfolk in their own households) with a disdainful tolerance. It was better that the masses believe in such things than that their discontent with their lot in this life get out of hand. In this spirit, the *mandarin* scholar who was appointed governor of a city would conduct the rites of the city-god, even to whipping the image of the deity when that divine protector failed to protect his people from misfortune. He would, however, know that beliefs like this were unworthy of a philosopher.

Rituals of the Mandarins (Ru)

On a more serious level, the *ru* would manage the execution of the state ceremonies, culminating in the emperor's worship in the middle of the night at the Winter Solstice and the worship of Earth at the Summer Solstice. The drama of the Midwinter worship of Heaven has been described by many observers before its last enactment in 1911. In icy darkness broken only by flaring torches, the sovereign and his ministers, clad in the heaviest furs, would arrange elaborate presentations of food, wine, and cloth on the huge, tiered mountain of masonry in Peking (now Beijing) called the Altar of Heaven, and the emperor would read an elegant prayer. In principle, only the emperor, as mediator, could worship Heaven and Earth, the greatest ultimates; others had to be content with ancestral and divine intermediaries. For the Confucianist, these rites were of grave importance as expressions of *li*; they contributed to making society into a vast harmony or dance rather than a mere collection of thinking animals.

Another set of rituals was of special meaning to the Confucian elite. These were the major sacrifices to Confucius himself, held at the Vernal and Autumnal Equinoxes, significantly midway between the two great rites of Heaven and Earth. These would be conducted at the temples of Confucius located in the more important cities. Although formerly they contained images of Confucius, since the Middle Ages they gave tribute to the superior worth of writing in the eyes of devotees of the philosopher by presenting only an upright tablet with the inscription "Confucius the Wise and Holy Sage," flanked by similar tablets to the master's disciples. At these rites,

Confucian followers burn incense at the tomb of deceased great scholars.

the local scholar-rulers would gather; *kowtow* (kneel deeply so that the forehead touched the floor) before the altar; present offerings of a whole slaughtered bull, pig, and sheep, together with wine and vegetables; offer a tribute; present music and dance supposed to be from the time of Confucius; and finally feast on the offerings.

Understanding this ritual, as enacted by presumably skeptical scholars, for whom no one was considered exactly a god, creates difficulty for the Westerner accustomed to quite different styles of thought. Clearly, it was an act of reverence and sacrifice that was less than divine worship yet more than Western civil ceremonies. It was somewhere between what might be done at Arlington National Cemetery on Memorial Day and a cathedral service, with the difference that animal victims were sacrificed in a way that Westerners consider barbaric (despite the butchering of thousands daily with less ceremony in our slaughterhouses).

Apart from their value simply as *li*, the Confucian rites can be thought of best in connection with the ancestral system. The Confucian scholars greatly valued their own family shrines and lineages, yet they were also, as a special called-out class, members of another "family," a spiritual clan of all of their vocation. Of this family of literati, the supreme scholar Confucius was the ancestor.

Neo-Confucianism

A word should be said about **Neo-Confucianism**, which began as a movement in the eleventh and twelfth centuries during the **Song Dynasty** (960–1280 C.E.) and became the authoritative interpretation of the Confucian intellectual tradition. Partly in response to the issues raised by Daoist and particularly Buddhist thought, Neo-Confucian philosophers greatly enhanced their tradition's metaphysical foundation. It became a comprehensive worldview concerned with the nature of mind and the ultimate origin of things and with simple methods of meditation, as well as a social philosophy, although it never lost the ideal that the philosopher finds joy in the midst of family and social life, not in permanent withdrawal from them. Two leading Neo-Confucianists were **Zhu Xi** (also written as Chu Hsi, 1130–1200) and **Wang Yangming** (or Wang Shouren, 1472–1529). Zhu Xi taught that one great ultimate is manifested in the principles of the myriad separate things, as the light of the moon is broken onto many rivers and lakes. Through reflection on particulars, especially human morality, one can know the ultimate. The more idealistic Wang Yangming

Fundamental Features of Confucianism

Theoretical

Basic Worldview	The universe a unity under heaven, of which humans are an integral part. For humans, family and society are the most important links to the universe.
God or Ultimate Reality	"Heaven" or *Tian*, regulating the world and moral order.
Origin of the World/ Destiny of the World	Vague, but world originates from heaven and proceeds through interaction of Yin and Yang and the five "principles" or elements.
Origin of Humans	Vague; ultimately from heaven and earth.
Destiny of Humans	No stress on afterlife except in terms of ancestrism. Ideal is to live a good life in this world through family and society.
Revelation or Mediation between the Ultimate and the Human	The teaching of Confucius and the classics; mediated by the educational system.

Practical

What Is Expected of Humans:	To observe official and ancestral rites; to honor parents and meet other ethical Worship, Practices, Behavior obligations. One works for a good society by exercising benevolence and practicing mutuality with others, especially through the "five relationships."

Sociological

Major Social Institutions	Great importance of family and of elite class; aligned to state under empire.

taught that the principles are actually within the mind itself, so the supreme requisite is sincerity of mind. Through reflections such as these, the spiritual and intellectual side of Confucianism was given a transcendence that made the practice of Confucian rites and virtues more deeply religious, even developing a sort of mysticism in the midst of a life of service.

Confucian Moral and Social Values

The most important impact of Confucianism on China lay in the area of moral and social values. Although ancestrism, the family system, and the ideal of selfless work for the common good have pre-Confucian roots, Confucianism gave these values ultimate prestige through the civilized centuries. It was of a piece with Confucianism that all important families had ancestral shrines in which the names of parents, grandparents, and great-grandparents were lined up on higher and higher shelves for each generation and that worship was offered to them, as it was at the tombs, so it was in the home. Inseparable from ancestrism was the Confucian-based family system in which loyalty and filial obedience were obligations that gave precedence to no others. Confucianism also underlay the Chinese "work ethic," the high regard for diligence and productivity, bringing honor and prosperity to one's family name. Without the mental image of the wise and sober sage from the state of Lu, and the words from his followers' pens, China would be very different from what we have known it to be for more than twenty centuries.

DAOISM (TAOISM)

Fundamentals of Daoism

Confucianism, even in its most expansive forms, does not exhaust the spiritual heritage of China. Few people can be wholly devoted to sober virtues all the time, and the Chinese are no exception. There is another side that demands its due. This is the side of human personality that is attracted to what expresses the private fears, fancies, and aspirations of the individual. It is the side that feels for communion with nature and aspirations toward/for mystic rapture, imaginative works of art and letters, rebellion against social conformity, inward fear of evil, and love for gods. This side affirms the needs of personal life against the demands of structured society, and it affirms the place of the feeling, symbol-making, nonrational side against the cool, word-oriented rational side. In China, all this side has danced about under the broad umbrella of the Daoist tradition.

As one would expect from this, Daoism has been many things to many different people and has taken an immense variety of forms over the centuries. It has included hermit poets, temples with lavishly robed priests burning clouds of incense before resplendent gods, and "underground" secret political societies. It has ranged from "nature mysticism" to occult quests for immortality to the rites of spiritualists who call up the dead.

Some commentators have talked about a "pure" philosophical Daoism and a "degenerate," "superstitious" religious Daoism, but such presuppositions get in the way of real understanding. It is more instructive to comprehend how all of Daoism forms a unity of experience around a single pole, focusing on the feeling-oriented, nonrational side of life. Here it is simple to move rapidly from mysticism to occultism to revolution and back, and from "nature" to the most elaborate religious robes and rites, as long as they express something imaginative and personal. Daoism in China is really a tapestry of countless strands of folk religion, ancient arcana going back to prehistoric shamanism and private vision.

Daoist Priest.

Laozi and the Dao De Jing

Daoism's supposed founder is the sage **Laozi (Lao-tzu)**. Appropriately for such a romantic tradition, he is more legend than fact, and his very name suggests anonymity, for Laozi means only "The Old Man." Stories say that the bearer of this epithet was an older contemporary of Confucius and indeed that Confucius once met him, found him hard to confront, and said, "Of birds I know that they have wings to fly with, of fish that they have fins to swim with, of wild beasts that they have feet to run with. For feet there are traps, for fins nets, for wings arrows. But who knows how dragons surmount wind and cloud into heaven? This day I have seen Laozi and he is a dragon."

Lao-Tzu riding an ox.

Laozi was, according to tradition, a "dropout." It is said he was an archive keeper at the Zhou Dynasty court and a popular fellow who kept a good table. But he became disgusted with the grasping and hypocrisy of the world, and at the age of 80, he left his job, mounted a water buffalo, and wandered off to the West. At the Western portals of the empire, the gatekeeper is reported to have detained him as his guest, refusing to let him pass until he had recorded his wisdom. So the Old Man wrote down the book called the **Dao De Jing (Tao Te Ching)** and then departed in the direction of Tibet, becoming mysteriously lost to the world.

Other ways may be found to interpret the emergence of the Daoism in the Dao De Jing. Some have pointed out that at the time of Confucius, there were apparently a number of fairly well-educated people around, more than there were government or literary jobs available; Confucius's own difficulty in finding a position may testify to this. Such persons, unable to work at the level of their abilities and too proud to return to the fields, formed a floating intellectual class for whose way of life early Daoism could provide at best an inspiration and at least a rationalization.[7]

Others have noted that, on the other hand, the Dao De Jing does contain a political philosophy aimed at rulers as well as reflections for the solitary individual; it must not have been intended only for people without place. Still others have seen in it the veiled, but rather technical, manual of a *yogic* school.[8] In sum, the origin of the Dao De Jing is as mysterious as its meaning; each reader must get from it what he or she can.

Let us now look at the message of the Dao De Jing. It is a book about the Dao, that universal way or track down which all the ten thousand things roll and which is their substratum and the only lasting thing there is; the name "Dao De Jing" means something like "The Book of the Dao and How to Apply Its Strength."

Although a book about the Dao, it begins with the curious affirmation that nothing can be said about its subject matter:

> The Tao that can be trodden is not the enduring and unchanging Tao. The name that can be named is not the enduring and unchanging name. (Conceived of as) having no name, it is the Originator of heaven and earth; (conceived of as) having a name, it is the Mother of all things.[9]

This means there is no word that adequately expresses the Dao. That is obvious when we consider that all human words come out of finite human experience. They do convey something of what really is but only as human beings with their limited sensory equipment and limited field of experience have known it. When someone says to you the word "tree," certain images pop up into your mind, but these images derive only from your own limited experience with trees.

The image you have may be of a tree in your backyard as a child or one that you saw in a picture book when you learned the word; you let this tree represent for you all the trees theoretically covered by the word. The word says little about all the trees you have not seen or about how trees are experienced by other people or animals, much less about how a tree experiences itself! The word "tree" is really only a very pale thing, calling up few hints of what "treeness" means to a human being who is alien to a tree's life. It scarcely touches the vast untapped richness contained in the reality of trees "out there"—how they were in ages past before humankind arose, what they may be like on other planets, what they seem like to squirrels and birds who live in them, how they "feel" deep down in their own lives.

If this is true of something that is still only a part of creation, how much more must the limitations of language apply to the infinite whole? Add to the limitations of our experience that language by definition cannot really apply a meaningful label to the whole because the purpose of words is to categorize the particular. We use words to distinguish one thing from another. To call something "rice" implies there are other things that are not rice from which it needs to be distinguished.

Even to use a word ostensibly for the whole, such as Dao or existence, does not avoid this limitation. All these words can do is point in a certain direction of comprehension, but they cannot make clear that there is really nothing comparable to Dao or existence from which it could be distinguished.

Philosophical discussion like this may begin to open up the kind of realizations that seized the writer of the Dao De Jing. But for him, the book was no mere metaphysical nitpicking—nothing would have won his contempt more. Rather, these reflections opened up a different, ecstatic mode of being in the world.

Once you realize that the Dao, which flows in and through everyone and everything, cannot be labeled and put in a box, you can respond to it in a different way, with simple wonder, turning to it as an infant turns to its mother. The first chapter ends, "Where the Mystery is the deepest is the gate of all that is subtle and wonderful." Elsewhere we read, "When one gives undivided attention to the (vital) breath, and brings it to the utmost degree of pliancy, he can become as a (tender) babe.... In the opening and shutting of his gates of heaven, cannot he do so as a female bird?" And again, the writer, seeing himself as a misfit in artificial society, although marvelously near the Dao that others miss, says, "The multitude of men look satisfied and pleased; as if enjoying a full banquet, as if mounted on a tower in spring. I alone seem listless and still, my desires having as yet given no indication of their presence. I am like an infant which has not yet smiled." In contrast to the Confucian cornerstone—the father–son relationship—the Dao De Jing, which emphasizes the natural, biological, and spontaneous as being better than the social manifestation of the Dao, makes becoming feminine or becoming a child in a mother's arms a basic image for the relationship of the individual with the great Dao.

In the seemingly weak stance of the female or the child is tremendous strength—the strength of water that wears down the hardest rock or of wind and rain that can come and go as they wish. In yielding, bending with the wind like a supple tree and then springing back renewed, is a vital strength that will weave its way subtly through all the permutations of the Dao. But that which is stiff like a man standing on tiptoe will break and fall. We are told that the best ruler is he who guides his people unobtrusively, so that they say, "We did this ourselves."

Making comparisons are inimical to this way of life, for they induce partial views and keep one from seeing life and the Dao whole:

> All in the world know the beauty of the beautiful, and in doing this they have (the idea of) what ugliness is; they all know the skill of the skilful, and in doing this they have (the idea of) what the want of skill is . . .

> Therefore the sage manages affairs without doing anything, and conveys his instructions without the use of speech.

All things spring up, and there is not one which declines to show itself; they grow, and there is no claim made for their ownership; they go through their processes, and there is no expectation (of a reward for the results). The work is accomplished, and there is no resting in it (as an achievement).

The work is done, but how no one can see; 'Tis this that makes the power not cease to be.[10]

This outlook has political implications, and they are quite contrary to the elitism of "getting the best man for the job" of the Confucianists. There is also an attack on the philosophy of advertising: nothing would be more contrary to Daoist political and economic ideas than our system of choosing leaders through elective competition and creating prosperity by encouraging consumption.

Not to value and employ men of superior ability is the way to

keep the people from rivalry among themselves; not to prize articles

which are difficult to procure is the way to keep them from becoming

thieves; not to show them what is likely to excite their desires is

the way to keep their minds from disorder.[11]

Elsewhere, we are told in the Dao De Jing that the ideal community would be a village of simple, hardworking, prosperous farmers, so unsophisticated that they did not even use writing but kept records with knotted cords and so content that even though they could hear the dogs barking and the cocks crowing in the next village, they never visited it.

Needless to say, this approach was quite at odds with the Confucianists' earnest talk of cultivating virtue and their moral norms such as filial obedience. Laozi instead refers back to a primordial paradise where people lived simply in harmony with the Dao spontaneously. Only when deterioration sets in, he thought, did rules and norms appear, and they were both cause and effect of the deterioration.

When the Great Tao (Way or Method) ceased to be observed, benevolence and righteousness came into vogue. (Then) appeared wisdom and shrewdness, and there ensued great hypocrisy.

When harmony no longer prevailed throughout the six kinships, filial sons found their manifestation; when the states and clans fell into disorder, loyal ministers appeared.[12]

In other words, what for the Confucianists was the very essence of true civilization, for the Daoists was the token of decay and hypocrisy. To them, true virtue, like that of nature or of a child with eyes full of wonder, could never be forced by bookish ethics. If we got rid of formalized learning and duty, Laozi said, people would be a hundredfold happier and would do naturally what they now resist just because they are told to do it.

Here we can see clearly the Daoist reaction against ordinary conventions of thought and behavior. It is but a step from this generalized sense of wonder and of the limitations of ordinary words and attitudes to the affirmation of the most extraordinary seeming ideas: the possibility of deathlessness, the reality of fabulous secrets, powers, and worlds. In fact, even the Dao De Jing appears to affirm that one who is in inseparable harmony with the Dao is as immortal as the Dao is and that through the way of yielding one can find mysterious powers so great as to seem miraculous. But it remained to subsequent Daoist writers to make this potential of Laozi's vision more explicit.

The Development of Philosophical Daoism

The first and greatest of the Daoist writers to expand on Laozi's vision more explicitly is **Zhuangzi** (Chuang-tzu, died c. 300 B.C.E.).[13] Little is known of Zhuangzi apart from his book, *The Zhuangzi*, but it is enough. Written in a vivid, fanciful, and humorous style, it immediately brings the reader into a world of expanding horizons. One is first told of strange marvels, as though from tales of Sinbad—of an immense fish thousands of miles long that changes into a bird just as large and flies to a celestial lake in the South. The writer then juxtaposes these examples of the fabulously large with mention of the tiny motes in the air that make the sky blue and tells us that to a mustard seed a teacup is an ocean. As the reader's imagination is swung violently from the microscopically small to the immensely huge, from fairy tales to the homey, the reader gets a sense of mental vertigo. One feels that one is spinning and things are coming unfastened.

That is just what Zhuangzi wanted one to feel, for he wanted to shake the reader loose from the ordinary way of seeing things. Zhuangzi wanted a person to be free—above all, free from oneself, one's own prejudices, partial views, categories, and from judging everything in terms of oneself. To this Daoist, man is not the measure of all things. The way the universe happens to appear to a biped six feet tall is no more the way it is than the way it appears to a fish, a mote, an eagle, or a star. Only the Dao itself is the measure.

In the same way, ordinary rational waking consciousness is no more the measure of all things than the world of dreams and fancy and of the improbable. Zhuangzi tells us that he once dreamed he was a butterfly and that when he awoke, he did not know whether he was Zhuangzi who had dreamed he was a butterfly or a butterfly who had dreamed he was Zhuangzi. The dream world, in other words, is just as real as any other.

Unlike the sober Confucianist, Zhuangzi delights in the world of fantasy: of rocs and leviathans, wizards who can fly over the clouds, and islands of immortals. The world of the unconscious and the imagination, he is saying, is just as much a manifestation of the Dao as the rational—and may indeed better lead us to comprehending the Dao. At least it opens us to that sense of wonder and infinity beyond all limits that is necessary to comprehend the Dao—for the Dao is precisely the unbounded.

This was the direction in which Daoism went. A later Daoist thinker, Ge Hong (283–c. 343 C.E.), put it even more clearly, both in his life and in his writing. He lived during the three and a half centuries (221–589 C.E.) when division and political confusion reigned in China after the fall of the **Han Dynasty** in 221 C.E.—a time that nonetheless was culturally quite creative. Buddhism spread extensively, Daoism revived, and brilliant new forms in art and literature emerged to express the visions of these new, and newly personal, spiritual visions.

Confucianism was still accepted as normative, but the collapse of the social order rooted in its "Han Synthesis" version discredited it for many. In any case, the Confucian view of life oriented toward social usages and interpersonal obligations simply could not "work" well in a time of social confusion. Many were driven to look for more personal paths that promised inner meaning in spite of what was going on around them.

To this effect it is interesting that Ge Hong's book, the *Baopuzi*, contains what are called "Outer" and "Inner" parts. The "Outer" presents conventional Confucian teaching; the "Inner" offers Daoist material centering on the achievement of personal immortality through alchemy and *yogic* techniques. It is as though to say that while Confucianism may still be adequate for social ideology, a new self-consciousness and sense of social failure have made Confucianism hollow without something for the individual as well.

This quest for personal immortality was a basic theme of the new Daoism, and with it came interest in the worlds of miracles and of immortal supernatural beings that the quest implied and almost predicted. It had, as we have noted, philosophical roots in Laozi's implication that harmony with the Dao is immortality and in Zhuangzi's that truth is found in unfettered openness to all levels of consciousness and all possibilities, however fantastic.

The consequent distinction between Confucian and Daoist styles of thinking is very clear in a fictional debate that Ge Hong composed between a Confucianist and a Daoist on the possibility of immortality. The Confucianist argues that every living thing that anyone has ever heard of dies and that belief in immortality is therefore untenable nonsense. Baopuzi, the Daoist, responds that there are exceptions to every rule and that just because things of which we know die, we cannot say that everything in this universe, of which we really know so little, must die. In effect, the Confucianist says, "You can't prove immortality," and the Daoist says, "You can't prove there isn't immortality." Perhaps little is proved in this particular argument except that, for Confucianists, the instinctive response to a query is the safe, rational, common-sense answer and for Daoists, the romantic, speculative approach open to nonrational, mystical possibilities. The cleavage is temperamental and comparable to the gulf between Enlightenment rationalism and the Romanticism that followed it in the West.

Other Daoists of this period of uncertainty followed lifestyles that seemed almost to repudiate the importance of personal immortality (as did earlier Zhuangzi), so much did they emphasize spontaneity. To them, living with the Dao meant a **feng liu** ("wind and stream") life, acting according to the movement of what was happening day by day. Many were artists and poets, or at least aesthetes; the unplanned life, which savored the beauty of each event and the richness of each impulse, well suited the temperament of their callings. Philosophical works that went with this Daoist stance made much of Dao as **wu-wei**, nonbeing or not doing, in the rather technical sense that the Dao is not a "thing" or a "cause" and does not produce by plan or through work. Instead, all things just flow out of it freely or spontaneously in an endless stream of flux and change; the person who is attuned to Dao lives life in this way.[14]

Religious Daoism

It was religious Daoism with its popular gods and quest for immortality that took lasting institutional form. Its roots are complex, reach far back into the murky past, and are far from adequately traced.[15] We have noted that magical techniques to attain deathlessness, and *yogic* practices to control breath and induce joy, may be reflected in the Dao De Jing and are very ancient. We have also mentioned that in the Han Period, popular religious movements emphasizing healing and revolution were attached to the Dao De Jing tradition. For example, Zhang Ling in the second century C.E. started a revivalistic healing movement that established itself as a state within a state in mountainous areas. Zhang Ling said that Laozi had appeared to him from the realm of spirits and had given him a sword and other apparatus by

Fundamental Features of Daoism

Theoretical

Basic Worldview	The universe is one, yet always moving and changing.
God or Ultimate Reality	The Dao, the great Way down which the universe moves.
Origin of the World/ Destiny of the World	An expression of the Dao, without a known beginning or end.
Origin of Humans/ Destiny of Humans	An expression of the Dao, to share in its never-ending evolution. One may become immortal by mastering the Dao and its power.
Revelation or Mediation between the Ultimate and the Human	The teachings of Laozi and other sages. Benign immortals or gods can be honored and serve as helpers.

Practical

What is Expected of Humans: Worship, Practices, Behavior	To live spontaneously and close to nature; in more formal systems, to mediate and perform rites that draw one close to gods and immortals.

Sociological

Major Social Institutions	Temples, monasteries, the Daoist priesthood.

which he was able to exercise control over the spiritual world. Zhang was called Heavenly Teacher, and his direct descendants (sometimes misleadingly called the **"Daoist Popes"**) have continued the title to the present, the present holder of the title now living in Taiwan. Formerly, they dwelt on Dragon and Tiger Mountain in central China, exercised a tenuous spiritual authority over Daoist priests in the South, and sold mysterious charms that were distributed far and wide.

The popular Daoist religious system, which embraces the "Daoist Pope" and his charms and priests, presents a rich and colorful face. Perhaps no religion in the world has had a vaster pantheon of gods—many said to have once been human beings who became immortal and finally reached divine status. Some deities are ancient, although many were "appointed" to divinity by the **Tang Dynasty** (618–907 C.E.) and especially by the **Ming dynasty** (1368–1644) emperors.

This recalls the extensive interaction between Confucian and Daoist systems in China. Not only did the emperor, in designating approved worship, act out the role of mediator between Heaven and Earth assigned by Confucian thought but the pantheon itself also exemplified a heavenly reflection of the earthly bureaucracy manned by Confucian officials. Many of the deities, like Kuan Di, a strong military god who is considered a protector against evil forces, were originally earthly officials immortalized in the heavenly court.

The supreme deity in religious Daoism was the Jade Emperor, a personal high god for the masses that were ineligible to worship Heaven directly; he was enthroned in the Pole Star. Around him was his court: the Three Pure Ones—Laozi, the Yellow Emperor (the mythical first sovereign of China), and Bangu (the primal man); the Eight Immortals, very popular in art and folk tales; and gods of literature, medicine, war, weather, and so forth. The gods and immortals lived in numerous heavenly grottos, in Islands of the Blessed to the East, and the Shangri-La of the Mother Goddess to the West, deep in the mountains.

The priests of this faith were a varied lot, affiliated with several different **sectarian** strands with differing specialties. Some were celibate and monastic; others were married. Some were contemplative, concerned above all else with perfecting in themselves the seeds of immortality. Some were custodians of lavish temples with huge and ornate images of the Jade Emperor and other worthies; to these temples believers would come to receive divination, have memorial services performed on behalf of their departed, and worship at important festivals, which were also occasions for carnival and feasting. Other Daoist clergy were mediums, male and female, who would deliver messages from the Other Side; some were sellers of charms, perhaps issued by the Daoist Pope; some were exorcists who performed dramatic rites of driving demons out of possessed persons and places.

Behind all of this lay the affirmation of immortality and of immortal entities. The panorama of religious Daoism made visible the invisible but deathless realm of gods and sages who had won the priceless secret. Those who would reveal the secret were not lacking, however. Religious Daoism pointed to three main highways to immortality: (1) alchemy, (2) yoga, and (3) merit.

Alchemy referred to the preparation of elixirs supposed, in combination with spiritual preparation, to circumvent death through the manipulation of Yin and Yang and the "five elements." Most were based on cinnabar or mercury ore (HgS). Some seven Chinese emperors are said to have died of mercury poisoning as a result of taking this medicine of immortality! Yet, as scholars such as C. G. Jung and Mircea Eliade have pointed out, both Chinese and Western alchemy contain important spiritual and protoscientific insights that cannot be neglected by the serious historian of ideas.[16]

Daoist yoga is equally complex. Its central motif seems to have been the holding of the breath to circulate it throughout the body inwardly, awakening the gods of various physical centers. Finally the breath is to unite with semen to produce an immortal "spiritual embryo," which emerges as new life within the self. As it flourishes, the old mortal shell can fall away like the chrysalis of a butterfly. Diet and sometimes sexual practices of the Tantric sort were important supports of this process.

The hope of attaining immortality for the masses who were not adepts lay in merit. The idea was approached with typical Chinese concreteness. Some popular temples even had a large abacus or calculating machine in full view to recall to the faithful the reckoning of good and bad deeds that would be required. Various texts cite the number and kinds of good deeds—building roads, acts of charity, compassion to living things—that would win immortality at diverse grades; even one demerit, however, would require the aspirant to start at the beginning of his labors again.

Daoism is usually presented as but one of the spiritual traditions of China, and not the most prestigious in the eyes of traditional scholars. But the attitudes of religious Daoism came closest to the spiritual world of the vast majority of ordinary people. Even Buddhism and Confucianism became "Daoicized" in cultus though not in doctrine and morals. Whatever their origin, most plain people thought of the Buddhas, bodhisattvas, and even Confucius himself as immortalized humans having now become spirits and able to send down blessings from above. Daoist and Buddhist priests served interchangeably in many localities, but their major functions, such as funerals and exorcisms and village festivals, were Daoist (that is to say, popular Chinese) in style. To be sure, popular Daoism borrowed the use of images and its quasi-monastic clerical organization from Buddhism and the bureaucratic model of its pantheon from Confucianism—but those are historical matters, not at all readily apparent to the person on the street.

Daoism, as the pervasive tone setter of the nonestablishment side of Chinese life, has contributed to those undying elements of cheerful fancy, fairy tales, colorful festivals, bright pictures, and striking spiritual practices that are as much a part of Chinese life as Confucian common sense.

BUDDHISM IN CHINA

Buddhism first entered China during the Han Dynasty (206 B.C.E.–220 C.E.), spread widely during the three and a half centuries of disruption that followed the fall of that dynasty, and reached its peak of maturity and creativity during the Tang Dynasty (618–907 C.E.).[17] It was chiefly brought in the caravans of traders, not directly from India but from central Asia. The new faith first took root in the major cities and among the aristocrats. In the late Han and post-Han times, as we have seen, many of this class were searching among occult, mystical, and aesthetic possibilities for a richer inner life than could be offered by a decaying social order and its tired Confucian rationale. The wilder side of Daoism naturally appealed to some of them, but the profound mysteries of Buddhism, brought by exotic foreigners and bearing a whiff of the mystic perfume of India, as well as a more substantial philosophical and ethical base, were to many even more appealing. It speaks of both the power of Buddhism and the dissatisfaction of those times that until the modern Western influence and the subsequent Marxist triumph, no outside cultural force other than Buddhism has ever succeeded in making a major impact on China.

In the period when Buddhism was taking root in China, it was quite fashionable among the upper echelons of society. Aristocrats entertained visiting Buddhist priests, commissioned the translation of scriptures, and built temples in the mountains to which they would retire for genteel retreats. They also built hospitals and orphanages in the cities in accordance with the dictates of Buddhist compassion.

Buddhism opened up a new world of artistic possibilities with its demand for massive sculpture, mystic painting, and temple architecture. Buddhism also broadened ethical horizons more than many were prepared to accept with its very new (and very controversial) notions of universal compassion, monasticism, and the relative independence of religion from the state cultus. These emphases, although suggested in Daoism, went strongly against the Confucian grain, with its feeling that the arts are more frivolous than civil service and that obligation to family and sovereign is primary. In particular, the ideal of the celibate Buddhist monk stood contrary to Confucianism, which put family life and the subordination of self to society at the center of value.

But Buddhism also made its adjustments to China. Indeed, for a long time the Indian religion was considered a variant of Daoism—an illusion promoted by some Daoists who even claimed that Laozi, after disappearing into the West, had gone to India and become the Buddha. In the translation of Buddhist texts from Sanskrit to Chinese, Daoist and Confucian terms were used, with inevitable shifts in connotation. Thus, *dharma* became Dao, *arhant* became immortal, and Buddhist morality was couched in the terms of submission and obedience hallowed by Confucian usage.[18]

Even the monastic system was modified in the direction of supporting rather than challenging the Chinese family unit. Young monks acquired a filial relation to their teachers, in imitation of obedience to father, and moreover were expected to assist their natural families dutifully by devoting much attention to prayer on behalf of relatives living and dead. Sometimes boys were dedicated to the monastery by their families for this reason or in fulfillment of a vow made in prayer, because it was

Miluo, the laughing Buddha.

considered beneficial for a family to number a monk among its members. Finally, monasteries were brought under the control of the throne, which licensed them and regulated the number of ordinations they could perform.

On the level of popular religion, Buddhism accommodated itself to China even more thoroughly. As already mentioned, popular Buddhas and *bodhisattvas* came to be regarded as blessing-giving deities little different from indigenous gods, except perhaps more broadly compassionate. The bodhisattva Avalokiteshvara in India became Kuan-Yin or Guanyin in China (Kannon in Japan), the Goddess of Mercy who answered prayers for healing, women in childbirth, and wanderers. **Maitreya**, the Buddha of the future who would bring to pass a new paradisal era, was transformed from the lean, elegant, poised contemplative of Indian art to the immensely fat, laughing **Miluo** of China, who suggests a heartier, earthier vision of the joys of the new age. He has also been associated with revolutionary religio-political movements. In fact, even the Indian origin of Miluo, as of other Buddhist figures, came to be forgotten. Folklore identified him with a popular wandering wise-fool monk of the tenth century.

Probably the most important contribution of Buddhism to popular religion in China was in concepts of life after death. Previously, the Chinese had known belief in survival as ancestral spirits, as ghosts, or as Daoist immortals in blissful hermitages. To this Buddhism added the novel ideas of reincarnation and of elaborately gradated heavens and hells. Both these notions, however inconsistent with each other and with indigenous belief, were widely received, even by many who understood little else of Buddhism.

Reincarnation appears as a popular theme in literature. The hells were described in religious tracts, temple paintings, and sculpture displays (such as the well-known Tiger Balm Garden in Hong Kong), with a blood-splattered realism that even the dullest countryman could not ignore. The officials of hell, presided over by Yanluo (originally the Indic Yama, whom we previously encountered in the Katha Upanishad), were Confucian bureaucrats. As a reward for years of conscientious service, they were allowed to continue in the same line of work on the other side, where they saw to it that demons administered horrendous (but not eternal) punishments for infractions of both Confucian and Buddhist moralities.[19]

On the intellectual level, a number of different traditions of Buddhist thought and practice were introduced into China. Only the broad, tolerant, and variegated Mahayana had any success, however. But within it, the Void school, Yogacara or Mind Only, and esoteric Buddhism or Vajrayana all had early followings at various monastic centers. On Mount Tiantai, the syncretistic Tiantai school endeavored to reconcile all styles of Buddhist thought into a system that made the Lotus Sutra the summit of many planes of accommodation in the Buddha's teaching.

When the dust settled, however, two strands of Buddhism emerged as the most important in China: Chan and Pure Land. The concept of clearly defined denominations, like those of Christianity or even of Japanese Buddhism, is alien to China except for minority sectarian movements. But it has ended up that most monasteries in

China proper largely followed Chan teaching and practice, and Pure Land Buddhism was most popular among lay followers.

Historically, the prevalence of Chan and Pure Land is in large part the result of a suppression of Buddhist monks, nuns, and monasteries in 845, under the instigation of Confucian and Daoist rivals who persuaded the court that the persons and institutions of the imported Buddhist tradition were unproductive parasites on society. Chan, because its monasteries were less wealthy and more scattered throughout rural areas than the others, and Pure Land, because it was largely a popular lay faith, best survived the despoliation.

Significantly, both (while having ultimate Indian roots) are highly **Sinicized** styles of Buddhism, owing much to different sorts of Daoist belief. Chan enlightenment is really like following the Daoist concept of *wu-wei*, not-doing, and so letting events happen spontaneously. The assumption is that what is truly spontaneous is the Dao at work—or in this case, one's true Buddha-nature—while what is planned is of human egoistic contrivance, artificial and inauthentic. Pure Land could also easily be related to Daoist ideas—in this case, not only effortless and spontaneous release, but also popular belief in paradisal realms to the West where immortals dwelt amid fairy-tale loveliness. But both Chan and Pure Land embraced the realization, emergent early in Chinese Buddhism's independent development, that true enlightenment is a sudden, spontaneous happening rather than a laborious process.

These two doctrinal traditions, usually working closely together and not seen as inconsistent, formed the basis of Chinese Buddhism in recent centuries. The nation boasted scores of large monasteries. They followed a Chan regimen for the most part, modified by concessions to Pure Land, esoteric practices, and the economic necessity that Buddhist monks perform funeral and memorial rites; for many these rites were quite time-consuming, but they kept monks in touch with the lay public.

The monasteries were headed by an elected abbot, and they were flourishing economic units busy with administering lands and dealing with pilgrims. The monks would often devote themselves to meditation and work on half-year shifts. Monastic novices were ordained by a rite that included burning incense in several spots on the candidate's shaved head, a painful practice leaving scars intended to exemplify the bodhisattva vow to work and suffer at whatever cost for the salvation of all beings. Many monks traveled frequently from one monastery to another in a manner akin to the wandering students of medieval Europe. Others might become hermits.

Four monasteries on mountains in the four directions were especially important as pilgrimage centers. The roads to them were lined with colorful shrines and hermitages. Travel to these places for the sake of a vacation, enjoyment of natural beauty, and spiritual renewal all together was very popular.

The majority of those who were students in a major monastery, however, received training like a seminarian and would sooner or later become priests in village temples. There the priest would live a fairly easy life, unless he were given to much study or spiritual practice. He would keep his temple in order as a place for prayer and performing funerals, memorial rites, and other services as his parishioners required and could pay for them. Although the priest probably had Chan training, the temple would doubtless give principal encouragement to the Pure Land and Kuan-Yin devotions as being more suitable for the laity. However, among more sophisticated urban lay Buddhists, especially of more recent times, many took one or another of the monastic vows, such as celibacy or vegetarianism, as a lay associate of a major temple and received advanced training in meditation or other practices from a distinguished master.

RELIGION IN TRADITIONAL CHINA: A SYNCRETISTIC PRACTICE

We began by observing that East Asian religion is generally religion of the particular place and social unit, deeply rooted in soil and family. We have, however, devoted much attention to exploring historical tracks made by the Confucian, Daoist, and Buddhist traditions. This has necessitated portraying them as three major traditions extending through time as though they were great independent causes. It is not possible to understand religious China fully without this historical and philosophical background. But in popular religion, the major traditions unite to form a single spiritual world. It is now time to refocus on the particular to see how they are combined in practice.

Consider a single family in old China, the Changs. They lived in a home in the countryside. The setting and ornamentation of the house itself reflected some ideas we have discussed, for when it was built its location was carefully determined so it would be at the meeting point of *Yin* and *Yang* forces in the environment and would be spiritually protected. Open places and straight lines dissipate the benevolent breath of nature and encourage invisible evil forces, so the house was situated between a sunken pond and a bamboo grove, and the road up to it was curved.

The Changs took the veneration of their ancestors very seriously. They were memorialized in three places: in the home at a small shrine with tablets bearing their names; in the chapel of the Chang clan or extended family where large tablets were set up, rank on rank, rising on higher and higher tiers, the further back in time the generations went; and at the cemetery. A bit of water, incense, and food would be presented daily at the household shrine. Several times a year, the clan shrine and cemetery would be visited, cleaned, and given larger offerings and a report on family events. Ancestrism, combining very old spiritist beliefs with Confucian filial piety toward departed parents and grandparents, was most important.

The biggest annual holiday was the New Year. At the end of the year, debts would be settled and the house cleaned. On New Year's Eve, the picture of the protective kitchen-god, which had been hanging in the house all year, would have its mouth smeared with honey, to put it in a good mood, and would then be burned—for it was believed that this deity would then ascend to the court of the Jade Emperor to give his report on the merits and demerits of the family for the past year. On New Year's Day itself, members of the Chang family would be gathered from far and wide and extensive offerings of food and drink—together with a plate of soup set out for lonely spirits without family to care for them—would be placed with bows and prayers before the family shrine, full of ancestors and protective gods. Then the family would join in a feast. Outside, they would hear firecrackers and doubtless see a *Yang* dragon parading down the road, animated by the feet of many men.

The Harvest Festival in the autumn would have a different, *Yin* sort of atmosphere, oriented toward the moon, the night, and the returning spirits. Round cakes would be made, and tables would be set up in the courtyard of the house, both showing the fabulous palaces of the moon where Daoist immortals dwelt.

In the Chang household, sober Confucianism would have its due, as well as Daoist fancy. The sons would bow to their father, and if educated, they would study first and foremost the Confucian classics. When the elder Chang died, the sons would mourn for him according to Confucian ritual—although somewhat modified and shortened—kneeling before the father's portrait or tablet, wearing gowns of rough sackcloth, and eating coarse and tasteless food.

For the funeral and subsequent memorial rites, Buddhist or Daoist priests would be called in. They would chant *sutras* or prayers and burn elaborate paper houses and imitation money offerings to be used by the deceased on the Other

Side. They would pray to the protecting city-god to serve as his advocate before the dread court of Yanluo. The family might discuss the possibilities for the deceased amid the many hells, heavens, and paths back to reincarnation in this world. They might well consult a medium, of Daoist ties, who would contact the departed spirit to find out what the disposition of his case had been, how he had fared, and what the living could do to help him. There were even shamanistic Daoist priests who cut themselves with knives in order to take on themselves the after-death suffering of their clients.

For answers to problems in this life, the Changs might consult a diviner who would use the ancient *Yi Jing*. He would throw coins or sticks to determine which of the sixty-four "hexagrams" or sets of six lines (some unbroken *Yang* lines; some broken *Yin* lines) that unfolded the meaning of the situation in question. The text in the *Yi Jing* for that hexagram would suggest, in fairly cryptic language, whether favorable or unfavorable lines of force were in operation, whether it was a time for action or waiting, and the like. This book, now popular in the West, is perhaps the oldest extant Chinese book in its most ancient parts; it is one of the Confucian classics, yet it also expresses a Daoist philosophy. In its own way it epitomizes a Chinese worldview that underlies both traditions based on a profound sense of the continual, rhythmic interaction of visible and invisible forces within a unified world process to which humankind must gently and wisely accommodate itself.[20]

From time to time a representative of the Chang family would go to one of the temples in the locality. The temples vary from tiny edifices with images the size of a doll to huge structures with giant, superhuman gods of awesome countenance. Some would be Daoist, some Buddhist, some mixed. But it should be realized that they were homes of the gods, not generally places of congregational worship. When Mr. Chang or another of the family visited the temple, it was generally to ask a favor or pay respects, as one would to a powerful neighbor. Most frequently the purpose of the visit would be to ask advice of the deity, performed by throwing two woodblocks, by drawing a printed oracle, or perhaps by consulting a medium retained by the temple. Sometimes the family representative would make an offering of incense or of paper temple money in thanksgiving for a favor or in response to a vow. This worship would be done especially at earth-god shrines—humble but ubiquitous temples to deities of the soil older and closer to the people than any of the major faiths—in the spring for the crops and in the fall in thanksgiving for the harvest. Food might be presented to the deity, but it would be brought back home for a feast.

At irregular intervals, depending on local custom, the temple would hold a great festival. Brilliant red candles would be burned around the divine image, priests would perform elaborate rituals, and villagers and visitors alike would throng the temple with offerings and divinations. The temple courtyard would be set up like a fair, with booths and amusements and colorful pageantry. There would be ranks of offerings, particularly pigs, presented by families and businesses. Here the Chang family might be represented, and the family members (except women in traditional middle- or upper-class families) would delightedly attend.

If Mr. Chang were of the *mandarin* class, he would also go to the nearest Confucian temple at the two equinoxes to join with his peers in the old dances and offerings presented to the Wise and Holy Sage by his latter-day disciples. He would probably also take part in the rites of the city-god, the protector of the town, honoring him with thanks for good times and perhaps punishing him when misfortune struck, for the city-god's *cultus* was part of the official religion.

Then again, one day Mr. Chang or someone else in the family might become pious, or at least acquire a wanderlust, and go on a pilgrimage to some Buddhist or Daoist monastery situated on a cloud-wrapped mountaintop or an isolated island.

There he would break his routine by living with the monks for a spell, sharing their meals and conversation, and renewing his spirit in a setting of exalted beauty.

The Chang family, then, would be touched by the attitudes and institutional life of all three of the great traditions and by ancestrism and the earth-gods, as well. This combined experience is nowhere better expressed than in the first part of the old Chinese fantasy novel *Monkey*.[21] In it, the Buddha and the Jade Emperor visit and consult with one another. Dragon-kings, bodhisattvas, and sages with the secret of immortality move in and out of the narrative—yet the monkey-hero, like the sturdy peasant farmers of China, employs both wiles and wonders to combat authority, even the hosts of heaven itself, to preserve the autonomy of himself and his household.

RELIGION IN CHINA, GOVERNANCE, AND POLITICAL LIFE

Confucianism as a Holistic Sociopolitical Vision

As we have seen, classical Confucianism was expressed as a holistic vision of the good society, extending from individual self-cultivation to the cultivation of proper familial roles and relationships to the relation between the individual and family to government—all well-balanced with Heaven and Earth, all ritualized in a harmonious "dance" for the good of all. For that reason, it is not possible to separate religion or politics from the overall sociocultural vision of the Confucian worldview, nor is it possible to conceive of the individual as inhabiting a private realm disconnected from or unconcerned with the state. Rather, the Confucian sociopolitical vision interrelated all parts as interdependent constituents of each other. Heaven and Earth, government and family, and the individual becoming fully human, as he strives to be a *junzi* within the context of the culture and the totality of the social relationships of Confucian society (which impart to him what that means) were all understood as being of a piece within the cosmic whole. Hence, the reader will notice that the political dimensions of Confucianism are interwoven into the discussion of Confucianism generally throughout this chapter.

Yet it is important to understand that the practical effect of the Confucian ideal was realized incompletely. The vastness of the empire and variety of local officials, customs, and even deities meant that the actual power to exercise authority, even though it was autocratic, was decentralized. Consequently, the varieties of religio-cultural expressions we have been exploring, for example as illustrated by the Chang family, were tolerated so long as they did not become disruptive elements in society. If they did, the heavy hand of the state would resort to suppression. In this way, an official orthodoxy prevailed, thwarting challenges from the margins or subsuming them into its overarching cosmic vision. Still, commoners generally were permitted to venerate local deities, which often were given official status by the state, and to participate in new religious developments, such as Buddhism, as long as such practices did not pose a threat to the state's orthodoxy.

Let's explore that orthodoxy further to have a sense of its centralizing influence, even if such orthodoxy was not thoroughly imposed.

The Sage King and the Mandate of Heaven

At the outset, it must be noted that although the mandarin class had significant influence as advisors to emperors, they generally did not wield the power of the state directly. Rather, the Confucian worldview contemplated sole imperial authority. Confucius, himself, sought to re-establish what he understood to be the sociopolitical ideal that had been realized under the height of the Zhou Dynasty.[22] This ideal required the ruler's cultivation of the Confucian virtues discussed earlier to establish

The Torii or ceremonial gate of the Miyajima Shinto shrine in Japan, located offshore.

Carved stone statue of Confucius at the Temple of Confucius in Nanjing, Jiangsu Province, China.

the legitimacy of his authority, and also to ensure that the ruler would serve as a model of virtue for the populace. He was to serve as the full expression of the *junzi* as a "sage ruler."

Furthermore, as was mentioned earlier, the ruler's authority was subject to the **Mandate of Heaven**: signs that Heaven, the fundamental order of the universe, approved his rulership. A good social order under the guidance of a true monarch was understood to be no less than human society rightly integrated into the universe as a whole: into the turn of the seasons, the cycles of nature, the stars in their courses. Under a true sovereign not only would society be harmonious but weather would be benign, crops would flourish, and all would be prosperous.

If the state displayed these auspicious signs, it could be taken for granted that it enjoyed the Mandate of Heaven; if disaster followed disaster, that meant that the Mandate of Heaven had passed from it, no doubt first of all because of moral corruption at the top, for it cannot be expected that the people will be any better than the example set for them by their rulers. If the ruler did not appear to have such mandate either at the start or at any time during his rule, his authority was no longer deemed sanctioned by Heaven and therefore others could legitimately challenge or even replace him—or circumstances might be such that a virtuous person would be elevated, presumably by Heaven, to take his place. Mencius argued pointedly that corrupt kings are not legitimate rulers but usurpers and may rightly be deposed. In effect then, if not explicitly identified, there was a dialectical interplay between the self-cultivation of the ruler based on a sage king model and the divining of Heaven's mandate—the ruler as individual fulfilling his role as sage king within the hierarchy of relationships in society, all within the cosmic whole.

Narratives of ancient sage kings in classic Confucian texts, specifically in the *Book of History*, served as models for the ruler and for those in hereditary succession who were educated in such teachings. At the same time, a tradition of discerning Heaven's mandate was also at play. This came to involve the divining of omens but also consideration of the relative welfare of the populace as a whole, as well as whether the people expressed satisfaction or dissatisfaction with the conditions of their lives.

As a result, eventually the people themselves were understood as an expression of Heaven to the imperial authority: "*Tian* [Heaven] sees through what my people see, *tian* listens through what my people hear."[23] Those to whom the people gave their trust and loyalty were understood to have the Mandate of Heaven; consequently, hereditary succession could be thwarted under circumstances where the people's allegiance was drawn elsewhere. In addition, it was incumbent upon Confucian scholars to raise their voices in protest when administrators showed laxity that might lead to the passing of the Mandate. That role might often be dangerous, since Chinese rulers welcomed criticism no more than most and had sufficient absolute power to silence critics, often in very unpleasant ways. But as Mencius nobly said, "[A] gentlemen never abandons rightness in adversity, nor does he depart from the Way in success."[24] Students were considered especially suitable for the duty of expressing principled dissent, since they were presumably idealistic, close to the wellsprings of wisdom, and had less to lose than established mandarins.

In the Han Period, *Yin-Yang* ideology also became political as a part of the Han Synthesis. The emperor was *Yang*, the people *Yin*, and the ruler was to serve as activator of proper response by the ruled. Moreover, the sovereign was mediator between Heaven and Earth, the midpoint in a triad of Heaven, Earth, and human society. In his lawgiving, he was representative of Heaven, the great origin, to the people; as chief priest in his worship, he represented humankind before Heaven. In all of this, it was his responsibility to promote the proper working of *Yang* and *Yin*.

Such notions, derived from classical Confucianism and integrated into the social fabric of the imperial realm, remained authoritative in Chinese culture even when imperial rule was abolished. They were even invoked much later when political upheavals led to a rejection (in name) of the traditional Chinese cosmic vision. That vision remained in the background culture, as the events of history took their toll on China, and China forged a new course.

Religion and Politics after the Fall of the Empire

Today the tradition illustrated earlier by the Chang family and the idea of virtuous rule under the Mandate of Heaven has been disrupted completely. To understand how such an immense cultural and religious change could come about, it is necessary to know something of the history of China and the impact of that history on Chinese religion.

During the long, wrenching, and often dreadful hundred years from the middle of the nineteenth to the middle of the twentieth century, China underwent tremendous shock and change, not the least to its traditional ideological and religious systems. The fundamental factor that made the shocks of this era even more climactic and catastrophic than those that accompanied earlier changes of dynasty was the incursion of the Western powers—demanding trade, missionary rights, and often inordinate influence on Chinese affairs.

The impact of these humiliations and of the countless subsequent little humiliations inflicted upon a proud people by the presence of privileged and often insensitive and exploitative foreigners went far beyond the immediate terms of the treaties forced on China by these foreign powers. It resulted in the discrediting of Chinese authority itself; in the eyes of many thoughtful persons, the whole system upon which Chinese authority was based, down to its ideological and religious roots, seemed anachronistic and discredited as well. It was clear by 1911, after numerous such humiliations, that the ancient empire had lost its mandate and a new governmental vehicle would be needed to bring the nation into modern times. A host of alternatives, ranging from reactionary to radical, arose to try to fill the void.

In 1912, after other traumatic vicissitudes, such as the **Boxer Rebellion** of 1900 (with its roots in magical Daoism), the lingering death of Imperial China was finally consummated with the establishment of a republic. Drawing on the Mencian "right of revolution" as their justification, the founders of the republic called upon Confucian relationship ethics and ideals of social harmony to rationalize adherence to often-corrupt officials and often-changing policies as they tried to deal with China's overwhelming problems. Consequently, although inspired by Western democratic idealism, the history of the republic was, in reality, rocky and sometimes ignoble. The principle of the separation of religion and the state was adopted formally. Moreover, the central government was rarely able to control either large-scale corruption or the power of avaricious local warlords. Just after it seemed, in the late 1920s, that headway against China's immense problems was being made, the Chinese republic was dealt further staggering blows by Japanese military incursions and then World War II.

During the period of the republic, Confucianism declined in influence with the disestablishment of the state cultus; Buddhism experienced a modest revival; there was considerable Christian missionary activity; and the Communist Party of China, full of high dedication and radical solutions, flourished more and more. Then, upon the triumph of Communism in 1949 and the establishment of the People's Republic of China, numerous Christian missionaries and Buddhist monks, together with the Daoist Pope, fled to Hong Kong and Taiwan, but the bulk of their followers remained behind to contend as best they could with the new regime. That government, the

People's Republic of China, did not profess any sympathy for religion, for in accordance with general Marxist theory, Chinese Communism saw religion as essentially the product of feudal conditions and was bound to fade away as the circumstances of alienation and exploitation between classes disappeared. However, in many ways the Communist regime seemed to embody the best of the old Confucian virtues combined with the prestige of a modern Western ideology (Marxism), a level of dedication beyond corruption, and a commitment to the sort of industrial and military strength that would restore greatness. Like Confucianism, though without the name, Communism offered a worldview that related human society to the way history and the universe work, and like Confucianism, Communism emphasized a good social order as the supreme human good. The new order viewed mutuality—negating oneself for the good of all—as the noblest virtue, and "Serve the People" was a ubiquitous slogan. At the same time, the regime was very much like the Confucian state, authoritarian but now with a Communist Party Chairman **Mao Zedong** (1893–1976), who had led the Communist revolution, in the imperial role, supported by Communist Party "cadres" serving in place of the mandarins of old.

Differences obtained, of course. Perhaps most significantly, the Communists objected to the primacy of the family in Confucianism, seeing it as a major obstacle to their goals for society, which were stated to be based on gender and age equality, collectivization, and the total mobilization of the workforce for whatever tasks needed doing. Loyalty, they said, should be to "the people"—in effect the Communist Party and the state rather than to one's parents and family. Time would show that the demands of this loyalty could be very stringent indeed. At the same time, much was accomplished which, at least for a people imbued with the Mandate of Heaven idea and used to authoritarian rule, seemed to demonstrate the legitimacy of the People's Republic.

The Communist approach toward religion generally in China passed through several clearly defined stages. The first (1950–1952) was a period of consolidation of the new regime. All foreign elements were forced out of China. This meant a mass exodus of missionaries together with many Christian Chinese clergy and believers. Religious bodies remaining on the mainland were pressured into forming themselves into "patriotic" organizations with corresponding nationalistic allegiances. While Confucianism was only criticized and Daoism received little consideration, some Buddhist institutions were permitted to survive in the People's Republic, chiefly as showplaces to enhance the new China's image in the rest of the Buddhist world.

The period of 1952 to 1960 was a time of relative cooperation between the new society and reorganized religious bodies. There was an increasing tendency to align religious thought with Marxism. This was particularly true among "patriotic" Buddhists, who did not hesitate to compare the Marxist utopia with Nirvana—because desire is eliminated in both—and the revolutionary struggle to the tortuous quest for enlightenment. But the 1950s were also a time when persecution of uncooperative religionists was harsh. Innumerable churches and temples were confiscated for "more productive" use as

Bronze statue of Mao Zedong, Zhongshan Square, Shenyang, China.

schools or warehouses, and the great majority of monks were defrocked to join the workers in factory and field. In particular, the great Buddhist religious and cultural tradition of Tibet was brutally extirpated.

Nonetheless, in the early 1960s reports came of a resurgence of religion, particularly Buddhism. Accounts of foreign visitors interested in religion between 1960 and 1965 indicated that, at the least, religion of all sorts was ostensibly being practiced routinely and without hindrance; churches and temples, while far diminished in number from before the revolution, were in full swing—but it was the proverbial calm before the storm.

The **Great Cultural Revolution** of 1966 to 1969, with the young Red Guards in its vanguard, swept through China, leaving virtually no locale or institution untouched. They were fired by a drive to suppress all that was old and a desire, perhaps contrived by the aging **Mao Zedong**, to renew revolutionary fervor at the expense of social stability. As a consequence, they disrupted education, harried enemies, defaced monuments of the past, and left nearly all religious places ransacked and closed. Such religious life as survived went deep underground.

Much was made in this period by outside observers of the religious character of "Maoism" itself. Certainly the phenomena suggested such an interpretation. Chinese Communism had a "sacred history" repeated over and over in dramas and monuments. Its great programmatic rallies had a quality little short of sacred ritual, reminiscent of Confucianism, while rejecting it at the same time. The famous "little red book" containing the sayings of Chairman Mao was read like scripture, carried constantly about, and eagerly held up by the faithful; it doubled as a holy talisman. Above all, Mao himself was hymned and praised in language that made him hardly less than deity or perhaps replacing Confucius as the revered authority. During these years, however, the official attitude of the state to Confucius was one of disdain. Mao, for his part, clearly identified the ancient sage with the China he disliked and wanted to remake into something entirely new.

Yet if Maoism was a religion, it turned out to be one of the world's most ephemeral. After the Great Cultural Revolution had run its course by around 1970 and the need for a return to normality was apparent to almost everyone, fervent Maoism was definitely in recession, and more traditional religious practice recovered its foothold. Following the death of Mao in 1976 and the subsequent purging of the "Gang of Four," who allegedly wanted to return to the policies of the Cultural Revolution, little more was heard of it.

Religion and Politics in China Today

After the Cultural Revolution, due in large part to the efforts of Deng Xiaoping (1904–1997), a very influential Communist Party leader from 1977 to his death, government policy became more open to the world, especially economically. The Communist Party has become pragmatic in its outlook at home regarding political, economic, and social life—decentralizing control of economic ventures and decision making, although retaining an authoritarian character. In this atmosphere, religion has generally been allowed to flourish openly, though under tight control. At the same time, the situation in Tibet remains tense, and new religious movements outside of official control, such as the neo-Daoist Falun Gong, which received much publicity in 2000 and afterward, have been regarded as subversive and are harshly repressed.

A perspective on Confucianism in the new China can be seen in the Tiananmen Square crisis of 1989 (in China, called the June Fourth Movement), when some 100,000 dissident students and workers demonstrated peacefully in Beijing, demanding democratic reforms. Refusing to disperse, after a month the uprising was crushed by troops with tanks, at a cost of an estimated 5,000 dead, and many injuries and arrests. This tragic event may be seen as an illustration of conflict between the Confucian principle of hierarchical control from above and the Confucian principle of the obligation, especially of students and scholars, to protest what they see as unjust policies on the part of the government. Though it cost lives, it may be that this action prepared the way for further liberalization in years to come. As far back as 169 C.E., during the Han Dynasty, over a thousand students from the Confucian university protested the corruption of a prominent official and were tortured and killed for their pains. But that official, Hou Lan, has been dishonored in Confucian history ever since.

Recent research indicates that traditional religious practice, such as those of the Chang family, have reemerged in the liberalizing atmosphere of China after around 1980, though sometimes in curtailed form.[25] Indications are that the number of those willing to call themselves religious is rising, and includes members of the Communist Party. A sampling survey conducted on behalf of the Ministry of Education of the People's Republic of China in 2004 reported that 31.4 percent describe themselves as religious adherents; of these 66 percent were followers of traditional Chinese religions, 15 percent were Muslims, and 12 percent were Christians.[26] The astute scholar of global Christianity, Philip Jenkins, has estimated the number of Christians in China at about 5 percent (65–70 million).[27] It is of course unclear how reliable these findings are, but undoubtedly it is true that religion has flourished in the more open atmosphere of recent decades under the liberalized policies of the Communist leader Deng Xiaoping and those who have followed, as compared with previous periods.

In the meantime, traditional Chinese religion survives in Taiwan, Hawaii, Singapore, and other Chinese outposts outside the People's Republic of China.

Taoism has flourished in a significant revival under the greater tolerance of recent years. Recently Yin Xinhui, a 47-year-old Taoist abbess, consecrated a newly rebuilt temple to the Jade Emperor, which, as we have seen, is one of the religion's most important deities. This edifice had been trashed by the Red Guards during the Cultural Revolution, but it was now reconstructed under the aegis of Communist officials, with one eye to tourism and the other to the religious yearnings of many ordinary people.[28] Other Taoist and Buddhist temples, like the famous Shaolin temple, the legendary home of Kung Fu, have prospered from the worldwide popularity of Chinese martial arts.[29] Reports have also related that such folk religion cults as that of the Goddess Mazu, a maiden who became a sea deity protecting sailors and fishermen on the south coast of China, once condemned as superstition by the Communist Party, are now encouraged. Officials recognize, if not the religious reality, at least the economic and social value of popular temples and festivals of figures like Mazu.[30]

Confucianism is currently enjoying another kind of revival in mainland China. Economic, social, and political institutions and their constituents have begun to look to traditional Confucian values, including the conception of individuals and families as constituent parts of the whole in service of the collective good, as the grounding for a unique Chinese approach to politics, business, and society—at home and globally. This approach is contrasted with what the Chinese see as a stark individualistic materialism proffered by the West, which some of them claim undermines community, as well as virtue itself. As China's United Nations Ambassador Wang Guangya has said, Confucian principles offer the world hope for a new era of "harmony between man and nature and among mankind."[31] As China rises in our increasingly globalized world, will China's newfound power and influence foster such an ideal or will they lead to an increasingly authoritarian outlook for the globe as well? Only time will tell.

Certainly bedrock Confucian values regarding work and education, whether explicitly religious in the Western sense of the word or not, are making a difference not only in China but in the world as a whole. A 2011 article by the respected journalist and *New York Times* columnist Nicholas D. Kristof opens with these words: "An international study published last month looked at how students in 65 countries performed in math, science and reading. The winner was: Confucianism!"[32] At the top in all three categories, by a wide margin, was the Chinese city of Shanghai. Three of the next four top performers were other societies with a strong Confucian tradition of reverence for education—Hong Kong, Singapore, and South Korea. (The other nation in the top five was Finland. The United States, by comparison, was fifteenth.) Education, together with strong values, is of course the foundation of all lasting success. In this respect Confucianism, though secularized, seems highly competitive in the globalized twenty-first century.

WOMEN IN CHINESE RELIGION

As we already have said, Chinese religion is an amalgamation of many different ideas, myths, practices, and institutions. Obviously, this amalgamation is characteristic of women's experience of religion as well. Women play important roles in the syncretistic Chinese popular religion's "little tradition" as shamans, diviners, mediums, and the like. Still, for discussion purposes, rather than attempt to tackle the subject as a whole, it is easier to ferret out those themes, myths, practices, and institutions by considering the component parts themselves. This is important, too, because some women's lives have been influenced or directed more by one component than another. With this in mind, let us now turn to what is one of the most defining aspects of Chinese culture and, therefore, the most defining of attitudes toward women and their lives.

Women in Classical Confucianism

Confucianism, as we have seen, provided an entire social vision grounded in relationships. In the Confucian worldview, each person is to perform his or her role in accordance with the Confucian idealization of that role. It was believed that this resulted in a well-organized, well-functioning society—as if everyone in society were performing a great dance. While the cosmic implications of this were not emphasized by Confucius himself, Confucianism nevertheless related its social vision to the cosmic order. As we shall see, this resulted in the religio-cultural institution of the subordination of women to men, greatly limiting women's participation in and influence on the "dance," while at the same time acknowledging the role of women in Confucian society as a respected and necessary one.

In Confucianism, women's lives were centered on the family. Women were the "inside" members of the family, while the men were the "outside" members. This reflected the ideal of women as homebound and the ideal of men as participants in society at large. In particular, the father was the representative head of the family to the world outside the home. In upper-class families, this arrangement was reflected in the very structure of the house, which included inside compartments for the women and outside compartments for the men.

As in Hinduism, Confucian women were to remain under the dominion of the men in the home in accordance with the "three obediences" of the Book of Rites:

> The woman follows (and obeys) the man: in her youth, she follows her father and elder brother; when married, she follows her husband; when her husband is dead, she follows her son.[33]

Moreover, a young girl was not considered a part of her natal family and, therefore, was not a part of any ancestral line. It was not until marriage that she attained a recognized place in a family and that her name was included on the ancestral tablets on the family altar. It is not surprising then that the marriage ceremony was the most significant and life-transforming event in a Chinese woman's life. She then had a recognized and respected role in the Confucian social order as wife.

Because a female child was not deemed a part of her natal family, the birth of a female child often was not greeted with joy, giving rise to such proverbs as "Raising a daughter is like weeding another man's field" and "The best daughter is not worth a splay-footed son."[34] Not surprisingly, with such attitudes prevalent, female infanticide was a continuing practice throughout the centuries, although discouraged by Confucian authorities.[35]

At birth, the baby girl's anticipated place in society was acknowledged. As the *Instructions for Women* by Pan Chao (?–116 C.E.) states:

> On the third day after the birth of a girl, the ancients observed three customs: first to place the baby below the bed; second to give her a potsherd with which to play; and third, to announce her birth to her ancestors by an offering.[36]

Theresa Kelleher's interpretation of the passage is, "The first action indicated that as female she should be lowly and submissive, humbling herself before others, the second that she should be hardworking and diligent in the domestic sphere, and the third that she should enter fully into the wife's responsibilities to the ancestors of her husband's family."[37] Thus, at birth, the girl's destiny was fixed, and accordingly her education was devoted entirely to learning the "wifely way" (*fu-tao*)—sewing, meal preparation, how to serve the parents-in-law, the development of a proper demeanor, and the like.[38]

The marriage relationship itself, in accordance with the Confucian ideal, involved very defined roles and much formality between the couple. Generally, the couple was segregated in the household except for sleeping. A wife was to exemplify *Yin* (passive, pliant) in order to provide the harmonious complement to the husband's *Yang* (active, firm). Thus, instead of a harmonious complement of power and status between husband and wife, the goal of harmony was to be achieved by the wife's submission to her husband. Again, we can return to the analogy of the dance. It is the husband who leads and the wife who follows with movements that complement, that is, harmonize with his. This was perceived to reflect the cosmic order, where Heaven (identified with the husband), which is creative, is superior to Earth (identified with the wife), which is receptive.

Divorce was very limited in Confucian society. Husbands could divorce wives only under seven specific circumstances: incurable sickness, no male heir, talking too much, stealing, disobedience, promiscuity, and jealousy. However, he was not permitted to divorce her if she had performed funerary rites for one of his parents, if he had become rich during the marriage, if her parents were no longer living, or if she otherwise had no home to which to return. On the other hand, a woman was never permitted to divorce her husband. Her filial piety obligations to his (and now her) family would not accommodate that. Furthermore, she was not to remarry after the death of her husband because this would disrupt the family ancestral line of which she was a part.

In Confucian society, as we have seen, parents and ancestors were honored by all. Accordingly, the wife was to join her husband in making the happiness and comfort of his parents their prime focus. But the parent who most shaped the life of the young wife was her mother-in-law whose every wish was to be served by her.

Upon marriage, a young woman in effect became the servant of her new mother-in-law and was to be her "shadow and echo" in all things. Moreover, the new wife was the lowliest person in the family hierarchy and was thus expected to be submissive to everyone else in the household as well. In her *Classic of Filial Piety for Women*, which was an authoritative text for Confucian women through the centuries, Ch'eng wrote (ca. 700 C.E.):

> A virtuous wife never dares demean the younger concubines, how much more is her solicitation for her sisters-in-law. Therefore they are all happy and get along with each other, and are able to serve their parents-in-law. In managing the household, she never dares mistreat the chickens or dogs, how much more is her care for the servants. Therefore those of all ranks are content with their lot and are able to serve their master well.... In these ways, the nine degrees of relatives are kept in peace and harmony, calamities do not arise, nor disorders occur.[39]

A woman was expected to be completely devoted to her husband—her highest goal being to win his love. "To obtain the love of one man is the crown of a woman's life, to lose the love of one man is to miss the aim in woman's life."[40] Moreover, she was to win her husband's love by exhibiting correct behavior. She was to be obsequious, quiet, demure, and industrious in her work in the home, as well as pure, clean, and chaste (although her husband would be permitted concubines, to whom the wife was to be courteous)—such behavior being called the "womanly virtues."

The Confucian ideal for women was set out in several very influential texts, for example, *Instructions for Women* and the *Classic of Filial Piety for Women*, both already mentioned, as well as the *Analects for Women* by Sung Jo-chao (ca. 800 C.E.). Another important text regarding women is the *Biographies of Exemplary Women*, collected by Lui Hsian (77–6 B.C.E.), which chronicles the lives of exemplary women and their contributions to their husbands. Most involve extreme self-sacrifice for virtue, chastity, and honor. Some recount the woman's choice to commit suicide rather than violate the dictates of filial piety. And the work of Margery Wolf indicates that suicide was indeed the choice made by many young wives who found themselves unable to exemplify the ideal in family situations that they could not endure.[41]

With marriage as the central focus of women's lives, it is easy to see that women who did not marry were not accorded many options in traditional Confucian society. Prostitution or domestic labor were their only viable options—with their concomitant shame. Women for whom there was an insufficient dowry or who for other reasons were unmarriageable were often sold.

Yet unlike some other patriarchal social systems in history and in various parts of the world that seem to hold a view that the world would be a better place without women, Confucianism never took so harsh a view, for Chinese ideologies have always had at their core a profound respect for the cycles of life. Accordingly, the greatest joy (and thus duty) of a couple is to bring new life into the world. Hence, the woman's role as wife and mother is not deemed extraneous to something else perceived as central to life (e.g., meditation) but is integral to the family—the center of life. Therefore, regardless of her subservient status, the wife is nonetheless a necessary part of the life cycle. This unfortunately did not undercut the repetition of some of the taboos we see in other cultures, such as those requiring men to avoid the "impurity" of menstruation and childbirth. Still, the arrival of children, particularly sons, greatly increased the status of the wife in the household. All recognized upon the birth of a son that the new mother, herself, will eventually attain to the status of mother-in-law with all its concomitant privileges. And as mother, she can develop what Margery Wolf has called the "uterine family"—a network of family affiliations surrounding the mother of married children, which contributes to the enrichment of her own life and those around her.[42]

Women in Confucian society were not without their means of exerting power to influence their situations. One way in which women could exert power was to work through other societal relationships. In Chinese society, decorum, proper behavior, and harmony might mean that a wife could not complain directly about improper treatment by her husband. However, if the husband were to drink too much alcohol, shirk his responsibilities, or become abusive, his wife could report it to other women who would then urge their own husbands to take action. The threat of shame—"losing face"—was probably a powerful deterrent to wayward husbands.[43] In addition, the considerable power of the mother-in-law must not be underestimated. On the other hand, because this power was exercised, for the most part, over daughters-in-law, on balance the societal arrangement seems to represent more a control of women in general than an expression of women's power in society as a whole.

Women in Daoism (Taoism)

Filial piety and the role of wife place considerable demands on women in China but also offer status and respect in the Confucian worldview. But Confucianism is not the only religious influence to have shaped Chinese women's lives. There is another side of life to which women could appeal as a spiritual source—that provided by Daoism.

Daoism, as we have seen, has taken an immense variety of forms over the centuries, which include philosophical and religious forms, the latter incorporating mysticism, shamanism, sexual practices, and magic in a syncretistic blend that is virtually indistinguishable in many cases from Chinese popular religion. We can find Chinese women in most all of Daoism's manifestations, perhaps because of Daoism's emphasis on nature and the feminine, which opened the pathway for women's participation.

As we already have seen, the Dao De Jing makes ready use of feminine symbolism to describe the Dao. The Dao is the creative source, which is potential itself and out of which flows existence—an existence sustained by the Dao "stream," just as a mother gives birth out of her womb to a child, who is then nourished at her breast. As said in the Dao De Jing:

> The valley spirit dies not, aye the same;
> The female mystery thus do we name.
> Its gate, from which at first they issued forth,
> Is called the root from which grew heaven and earth.
> Long and unbroken does its power remain,
> Used gently, and without the touch of pain.[44]

Because feminine symbolism is so pervasive in Daoism, some scholars, such as Ellen Marie Chen, have

Woman praying with incense at a temple in China.

concluded that Daoism has ties to an ancient Mother Goddess and the Dao itself is the Great Mother.[45]

Daoism seeks a balance of *Yin* and *Yang* just as Confucianism does, but for Daoism that balance is struck by grounding it in the *Yin*. Thus, the way of the Dao is *wu-wei*—"going with the flow," which is associated with the "natural" passivity and flexibility of women. Thus, women were deemed to be naturally good Daoists. But Daoism does not appear to have moved women beyond patriarchal norms.[46] Instead, perhaps because Daoism was a reaction to the rigidity of Confucianism and perceived Confucianism as "too *Yang*" in its striving to construct a structured society, Daoism used the patriarchal stereotype of *Yin* as an antidote. Significantly, whatever influence Daoism had, it never had much of an impact on the social order prescribed by Confucian norms and thus did not generally move women out of their subordinated roles. Still, Daoism's emphasis on the inner self, feelings, and imagination must have provided a spiritual outlet for women—the "inside" members of the family.

Religious Daoism drew from shamanism (which had been central to Chinese popular religion) the belief that women especially are receptive to divine inspiration. This, together with the perceived need for a complementary balance of *Yin* and *Yang* in all aspects of life, paved the way for an openness toward the participation of women in nearly all levels of religious Daoism, despite the patriarchal norms of mainstream Chinese society.[47]

Yet early on, Daoism developed patriarchal leadership with Celestial Masters, who, being men, were the highest administrators. However, even then women held prominent leadership positions equally with men as libationers (who provided the ritual and moral leadership of Daoism) and as officials over the districts. Women were ordained equally with men in all ranks, except the highest rank—that of Divine Lord.[48] Women also founded Daoist sects and were revered adepts, masters, alchemists, and scholars. And convents were founded so that women could be free of ordinary social ties in order to pursue spiritual lives.

Significantly, there are women among the Daoist Immortals, and the Daoist spirit world is filled with many female entities—jade maidens, fairies, spirit-generals, and beautiful, as well as gruesome, female spirits.[49] There are also many female deities, for example, Toumu, a powerful deity who is the Mother of the Pole Star, and other celestial goddesses. And there are goddesses of the household who appear with male deities, such as the kitchen god and his wife, who keep track of the good deeds and indiscretions of members of the household.[50]

As in Tantric Hinduism and some forms of Tantric Buddhism, the participation of women was essential in those forms of Daoism that include sexual practices in the attainment of the spiritual goal. Here, the sexual union represents the balance of *Yin* and *Yang*, and the goal is to prolong life—even to achieve immortality by forming an incorruptible embryo as a culmination of the practice. Still, in Daoism, as in many other religions, the texts are often written from a male perspective, making it difficult to ascertain the participation and techniques for women in the sexual practices and indicating that sexual practices may, in some instances, have led to the exploitation of women.[51]

On the other hand, there is an interesting contrast here between Daoism and Buddhism. The highest spiritual levels were deemed by Daoists, for the most part, to be achievable only in female form, as opposed to male form as we saw in Buddhism. (See Chapter 4.) As Barbara E. Reed's research has shown: "Pregnancy is a basic [D]aoist model for attaining immortality. A [D]aoist, male or female, creates and nurtures an immortal embryo within the corruptible physical body. According to this model, males must become females, at least metaphorically, to achieve their goal of deathlessness."[52]

Daoism provided an alternative view that venerated women and thus opposed the subjugating tendencies of patriarchal society. Moreover, it offered significant leadership opportunities for women and provided an option for women outside the strictures of mainstream, patriarchal Confucian society as Daoist priestesses, nuns, and shamanesses. But in all this we must take note that Daoism as a religious institution was marginal at best in Chinese society, relegated to the lowest levels. Consequently, the participation of women, even at the highest levels, did little to raise the social status of the women involved.[53]

The "Golden Lotuses"—Footbinding in China

Partly religio-cultural, partly fashion, partly eroticism, the one-thousand-year practice of binding the feet of young girls remains an enigma. No one knows with certainty how the practice became tradition, but one fairly credible account has it that it began in the royal palaces in Southern China in the mid-tenth century as an outgrowth of a kind of ballet toe dancing, in which the dancer wore silk socks wound with strips of silk.[54] As the practice developed, however, it involved molding girl's feet into perfect "golden lotuses"—three inches long and shaped like the bud of a lotus flower. The resulting tiny feet and their accompanying tiny, embroidered silk shoes were a source of great pride and perceived beauty. Although the practice began with royalty, nobility, and the very rich, it eventually worked its way into the entire range of Chinese social strata—even the peasant classes—and became a central feature in the Chinese family, at least for the women, as the practice became linked to marriage and tradition.

A perfectly formed bound foot would appear to extend "naturally" from the leg, rather than veer off at a 90-degree angle as do unbound feet. This was accomplished by binding the feet tightly with cloth to break the arch of the foot and all the toes except the big toe, which was left to protrude forward to create the lotus flower point, while the other toes were curled under and molded into the sole of the foot. This extremely painful procedure usually took two years, generally when girls were five to seven years old, but sometimes it took longer in order to achieve the desired result. Thereafter, bindings would be worn throughout the woman's life.

We have already seen the central place marriage and its traditions played in the lives of Chinese women under the influence of the Confucian ideal. Tiny lotus feet and the accompanying "lotus gait" that the women acquired, because of her slight steps, were highly desired in a wife. Significantly, the tiny feet provided evidence that the girl was obedient, submissive, and able to endure great pain; moreover, her sexuality was controlled because she could not easily "run around."[55] There is also literature showing that bound feet even became an erotic fetish for men. All of this made the young woman with bound feet an excellent selection for a wife.

It was not only Confucian ideals that contributed to the religious overtones of footbinding. Much family ceremony and tradition were associated with it. Generally, all the women in the extended family would come together for the first binding of the young girl's feet. The mother would choose an auspicious day for the event by consulting astrologers, fortunetellers, or diviners. She would also have made the first shoes to be worn by her newly bound daughter and would have placed them the night before the event on an altar to Kuan-Yin, the Goddess of Mercy, or "Little Footed Miss," an obscure goddess associated with footbinding. The hope was that the deities would ensure the success of the binding and a perfect result, so that the daughter would make an excellent match in marriage. Moreover, it was thought that even if those prospects were not realized in this lifetime, the girl would attain to a higher status in the afterlife if her feet were bound.

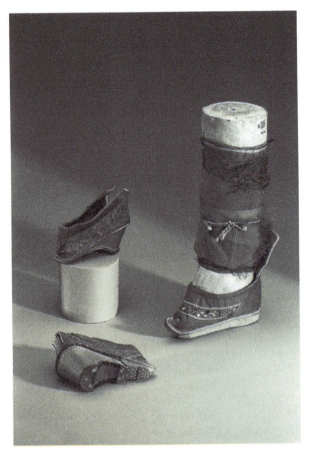

Shoes for women with bound feet. Each "lotus slipper" would be meticulously crafted and embroidered by the women who wore them.

In the nineteenth century, as China had more contact with Westerners who viewed footbinding as barbaric, the antifootbinding movement began. The Manchus, who were in power through 1911 and who had never bound their feet, banned the practice, but without much success. Long-held traditions die slowly, but the antifootbinding movement, which was inextricably linked (for obvious reasons) to women's liberation in China, eventually held sway, especially as more and more people began to feel shame in the face of condemnation of the practice from the rest of the world.[56] The practice was abolished in 1949 when Mao Zedong came to power. There are still women alive as of this writing whose feet were bound when they were girls before an end was finally put to the practice.[57]

Chinese Women in Buddhism

We have already discussed Chinese women in Buddhism in the context of Mahayana Buddhism in Chapter 4. Also, it is important to emphasize here, however, that Chinese Buddhism brought with it a pervasive female symbolism for the Divine, including *Prajnaparamita* (the Divine source, which is analogous to the Dao) and Kuan-Yin, the Goddess of Mercy. Chinese Buddhism provided a rich mythology and history filled with female deities, adepts, and laywomen to be woven together with other religious influences into the popular religion practiced by many women.

Buddhism also offered an alternative life for Chinese women as nuns, but because the Buddhist convents operated outside the conventional social order, women's participation in them was viewed by those adhering to traditional Chinese standards as subversive to the social order. Nevertheless, the convent provided women with a viable alternative to the role of wife and mother in traditional Chinese society and a place wherein women could exercise considerable leadership as respected teachers.

Women in the People's Republic of China

As we have already seen, the Communist revolution brought with it a suspicion, even disdain, of religion. As a consequence, Buddhist convents were destroyed, and nuns were moved into the workforce. Daoism and popular religion were suppressed. Hence, the doors were closed to the options these religions offered to women.

In their efforts to purge Chinese society of religion, however, the Communist reformers opened new doors to women. They sought to eradicate the oppressions they saw as pervading Confucianism, and these included the oppression of women. Mao Zedong saw in women a great resource for his cause as revolutionaries and as workers in the new Communist economic system. Accordingly, he was a great supporter of the reform of women's role in Chinese society, declaring that "women hold up half the sky." Although the trend had begun in the Republican period, under Communism women were encouraged to find roles "outside" in the economy and in politics, as well as "inside" as participants in family life.

No doubt some hypocrisy obtains in these claims. To be made a part of a regimented and overworked labor force along with men is not necessarily liberation. And few women attained top leadership roles. The hidden history of Communist China includes terrible but long-concealed famines, the result of misguided government policies, in which women and children suffered most of all. Nonetheless, the Communist Party sought to end dowry and expensive wedding ceremonies, made divorce more readily available, and promoted education for women. These social changes radically altered women's lives.

But women's lives have been altered in other ways as well in Communist China. In an effort to curb the population explosion in China, the Communist Party has imposed a one-child rule on families, which has had a profound impact on women's lives. The preference for sons has created an atmosphere conducive to the revival of female infanticide and places women who bear daughters in danger of abuse. A woman may be forced to endure an abortion if she becomes pregnant after bearing a first child. Moreover, the limitation to one child has undermined the traditional role of women, which was a source of pride and status for some. A woman can no longer look forward to developing a "uterine family."

Still, in many respects women's lives are often better today than in traditional Chinese society. Women are now full citizens, having gained to a large degree equal status with men under the law, if not in practice. Women now work outside of the home in factories, sales, other business roles, politics, educational institutions—in all aspects of Chinese society, albeit still not to the same degree or level as men. Infanticide has been curbed, but not eliminated as noted above; footbinding has been abolished; and the sale of women is no longer permitted. And in recent years, the Communist Party's hard line toward religion has softened, providing renewed opportunities for women in the religions of China.[58] Yet there continue to be reports of the repression of women, especially those involved in religiously motivated dissident activity, including Tibetan Buddhists, Roman Catholics, Protestants, and those in banned religious groups.

Today, China remains in transition and, therefore, what this all means now for women under Chinese Communism—a blend of an authoritarian political structure and an evolving capitalist economy—remains to be seen.

THE INFLUENCE OF DAOISM AND CONFUCIANISM IN AMERICA

Daoism in the New World has had two kinds of vehicles: the practice of religious Daoism by Chinese Americans, and the general cultural influence of Daoist themes. Appropriately, for a spirituality that sees its path as like that of water, which though seeming soft and weak in the end wears down the hardest rock, the Daoist impact has been unostentatious but surprisingly pervasive.

I* once observed the characteristic religious Daoist interaction of mystery and community in Hawaii. I was visiting the annual festival of a large interrelated group that had immigrated in the nineteenth century from a single village in south China. The deity on the brightly decked altar in the community hall was Kuan Di, a stern military god who is considered a strong protector against evil forces. He was a famous general back in the third century C.E., who was so exemplary that after his death an emperor declared him a god. He became known and worshipped all over China.

As members of the community entered the hall, they lit sticks of incense and set them upright before the deity. Spread before Kuan Di were food offerings including a roast pig, paper boxes and houses, and firecrackers. Also on the altar were esoteric symbols of the Daoist craft: scissors, a measuring stick, and the symbol of Dao, the mystic universal unity.

Then an old Daoist priest vested in a red and green robe put on a peculiar black cap. He stood before the altar, waved incense, and opened a worn liturgical book. The *jiao* or Daoist service offered by the priest had nothing to do directly with the community. It was essentially a priestly rite, although he performed it in the community's presence. Through chanting occult formulae, the officiant called up a series of high spirits—the spirits of the eighteen stars of the Big and Little Dipper and the Three Pure Ones—hierarchical rank upon rank, a celestial court like the old imperial bureaucracy. Each level contained fewer but more powerful entities than the one below it. Meditatively, then, the adept brought the cosmos into greater and greater unity until *Yin* and *Yang*, the two ultimate polarities into which all other multiplicity is resolved, remained alone. Then the priest merged them and stood before the ritually presented great Dao itself, the endless, incomprehensible stream down which all things visible and invisible flow. He did not become Dao, but he stood before it in awe.

In a real Daoist temple, such as examples still found on Taiwan, this *jiao* ritual might be performed in a great ceremony involving several priests and lasting for days at an important festival—and the ritual would be secret, the temple closed to all but the priests participating. In Hawaii, however, the members of the community were mostly seated in a big half-circle around the priest and altar, many talking and laughing quietly—not out of disrespect but just because priest, rite, spirits, community, Kuan Di, the Dao itself, were all part of one big family in which one felt at home. The incoming spirits wanted the community to be happy and prosperous, to enjoy the good things of life, good food and good companionship—they were in fact inducing the ripples of merriment and kindly gossip to roll around the room as waves in the tide of Dao.

Suddenly the tempo changed. The esoteric part of the mystery was over. The spirits were dispatched by burning the paper offerings outside in a big fire; firecrackers were set off. The roasted pig was quickly cut up and served. Everyone received a heaping plate of food and turned to enjoying a lavish banquet; a leading community official discreetly handed the priest of Dao the traditional bright red envelope containing payment for his services.

This is one side of Daoism in America. The other side is martial arts studies, surfers wearing emblems with the *Yin-Yang* symbol of the Dao, macrobiotic diets, exercises like *tai chi chuan*, Chinese medicine practices like acupuncture and the taking of traditional Chinese herbs, the practices of *feng shui*, and even important concepts that have influenced the ecological movement. Not all of this is Daoist in the strictest sense of the word, but all are based on cultural imports from China or the Chinese cultural sphere and stem from broadly Daoist concepts: the importance of balancing energies; of humans living in harmony with nature, working with nature rather than against it; and of isolating and releasing the inner biological/spiritual energy called **chi**.

A few centers and movements teaching philosophical and spiritual Daoism, sometimes including Daoist yoga and meditation, have appeared in America. Much more widespread have been martial arts studios. While not exactly religious, the martial arts centers often help students prepare for training through meditation and "centering" of consciousness and above all, emphasize the importance of releasing the *chi* and the intuitive direct insight that goes with it—all fundamentally Daoist, whatever the nationality or formal affiliation of the center. Somewhat the same can be said of clinics practicing Chinese medicine. Its premises are that health is recovered through opening clogged channels through which the *chi* should pass, using such techniques as acupuncture, and through restoring a proper harmony of *Yin* and *Yang* and the five elements in the body.

---

*Robert Ellwood

Even more widespread is the influence of a basically Daoist mentality through such instruments of popular culture as *Star Wars*. The combination of myth, fantasy, otherworldliness, and the idea of the mystical Force (analogous to *chi*) in those films is profoundly Daoist in spirit—and their immense popularity indicates just how broad an impact the ancient Chinese religion has had in the West. The enigma is typical of Daoism, the watercourse way of weakness and near-invisibility that is really strength. It may be that Daoism actually has had more cultural influence in America than other Eastern religions, whose temples and centers are far more visible.

Confucianism is also found in America, not directly in temples or institutions, but in the continuing attitudes toward family, work, and obligation of many Americans whose families originated in Confucian societies, such as China, Japan, Korea, and Vietnam.

Religion in Japan

SHINTO

Four Affirmations

The word "Shinto" actually means "The Way of the Gods." Shinto is a broad path offering a pattern of rites, attitudes, and subtle experiences that harmonize humankind with the many faces of its spiritual environment in the context of an ancient culture.

Like the Chinese city-god and ancestral chapel, the Shinto shrine expresses Japanese religion's rootedness in place and family. But typically the Shinto shrine will have a light, lean construction, contrasting with the heavy and ornate quality of Chinese temples. Shinto shrines, and the Shinto religious complex, have distinctive attitudes and practices to go with the unique architecture. If we were to remain around a Shinto shrine and observe its activity, we would see things happen that would bring out four basic affirmations that are inherent in Shinto: (1) of tradition, (2) of life in this world, (3) of purity, and (4) of festival.

Virtually every Shinto shrine has its unique set of traditions: the festivals that are celebrated and the rituals that are performed. Some are ancient and some less so, but all strongly link the present with the past. They appear in the midst of modern Japan like time capsules from earlier centuries. The traditions of some shrines present brilliant spectacles drawing vast throngs of tourists; others are of only local interest. But in any case, the observer will note that while Shintoists may have little idea exactly why a rite is performed in a certain manner or what it means theologically or philosophically, the action will be performed in a precisely prescribed way.

The fire to cook the offerings may be started with a traditional fire drill, a ring of evergreen may be set up in the same way each year for people to walk through to remove pollution. What is really being affirmed is not so much the importance of this or that particular custom as the importance of having tradition itself and of living in the presence of visible carryovers from ages gone by, with all their color and evocative power. For millions of modern Japanese living in a rapidly changing technological world, this role of embodying a traditional past they do not want entirely to lose is the most important function of Shinto and one very precious to them.

The affirmation of tradition is clearly related to the motif of affirmation of life in this world. Shinto, the religion of clans and their communal spirit of joyous festivals and bountiful harvests affirms the good things of this world and natural relationships. Its land of the dead is shadowy, and its mystical and intellectual life relatively undeveloped. But in the exuberant festivals of harvest or the stately splendor of ancient dance and ritual, Shinto comes into its own.

This is related to another important Shinto affirmation: the distinction between purity and pollution. Shinto shrines, demarcated by their *torii*, represent pure spaces in the midst of a polluted world. Upon entering the shrine precincts, one washes, and rituals begin with the symbolic sweeping away of impurity with a green branch. What is fresh, lively, and bright is pure; what is stagnant, decaying, sick, or dying is impure. Blood, disease, and death are the most impure things. A dead body would not be brought into a shrine; on the rare occasion of a Shinto funeral, the rite is held at another place. Through its avoidance of impurity, Shinto affirms the persistence and superiority of life and joy.

The fourth affirmation is festival. As we have seen, the quiet, inactive shrine in its wood or beside its stream may have an air of still purity, but it is not until the *kami* (the deity of the shrine) is stirred to vigorous life by the drums of a *matsuri* (a Shinto festival), that the full color and dynamism of the divine side of reality is manifested. For one who has been at a *matsuri*, the sylvan quietude of the shrine on ordinary days, when only individual worshippers approach it to clap twice and pray, has a feel of expectant waiting about it. The still drum, plainly visible on the open porch at the front of the shrine, and the dance pavilion remind one of another mood.

To fully understand Shinto worship and festival, it is necessary to have a mental picture of the structure of a shrine. After the visitor has entered under the cross-beams of the *torii* and passed the purificatory font, he or she approaches the porch with its drum, **gohei** (zigzag paper streamers), and other accoutrements; this is the **haiden**, or hall of worship, where the laity pray and sacred dance is offered. Behind it, but visible from the front, is a second segment with a curious eight-legged table for offerings; this is the *heiden*, or hall of offerings. Behind the table, the observer will note a set of extremely steep steps leading up to a massive, richly ornamented door. It leads to the *honden*, an enclosed room much higher than the rest of the shrine and the symbolic dwelling place of the *kami*. In this room will be a heavily wrapped object called the *shintai*, a representation of the god—an old sword, a mirror, an inscription, or something else, which from ancient times has been the sacred presence of divinity in this shrine, in a manner somewhat analogous to the reserved sacrament in a Roman Catholic church.

Formal Shinto worship occurs at varying intervals, depending on the importance of the shrine. Some small shrines without a resident priest will enjoy offerings only two or three times a year; others will have services monthly, or every ten days, or daily in a few major shrines. Special rites commissioned on behalf of families and groups are common at larger shrines, too. The spring and fall festivals will usually be the most important *matsuri*. However, many shrines also have very colorful and dramatic midsummer rites directed against evil influences. New Year is a time of considerable shrine activity too, especially for private visits.

Shinto Worship

All full Shinto worship follows a basic structure. It can be remembered by a series of four words, each beginning with the letter P: purification, presentation, prayer, and participation.

First, a priest, dressed in white or perhaps lightly colored garments and a high black hat (derived from ancient court costumes) may, according to local usage, wave a branch or stick with paper streamers on it (the *onusa*) or sprinkle salt or water over the heads of the people gathered in the courtyard as a rite of purification. Then the priest will enter the shrine and present the offerings, very neatly arranged, before the *kami*-presence on the eight-legged table—or on very important occasions he will open the great doors and lay the offerings on the floor of the *honden*. The presentation is accompanied by dramatically accelerating drumbeats and perhaps the eerie tones of reed flutes. The offerings, mostly fruit, vegetables, rice,

Priest and entourage accompanies a wedding group at the Meiji Shrine in Central Tokyo, Japan.

seafood, salt, water, and rice wine, are borne up and arranged with reverent care. Then, all in order on the altar, the priest reads a formal prayer, either silently or in a high chanting voice.

Next follows one of several possibilities, depending on the elaborateness of the occasion and the resources of the shrine. While the offerings are still on the altar, formal dance may be presented as part of the offering and as a representation of the divine presence to the worshippers. At the close of the service, individuals may present a small branch as an offering, as though to show their participation; and, as a kind of holy communion after offerings have been solemnly removed from the altar, they may partake of a tiny bit of the wine and perhaps other offerings.

As soon as the offerings are removed, it is understood that the solemn part is over. Then a dramatic change of pace takes place as the *kami*-spirit animates the people with a festival spirit. Particularly at the main annual *matsuri*, vivid local activities occur, affording everyone participation in the festivities. These will be as exuberant as the offering and prayer were solemn. The *kami* may be borne through the streets in a palanquin by young men zigzagging and shouting. All over the shrine grounds, booths are set up as for a carnival, with cotton candy stalls and sumo wrestling exhibitions, and crowds throng onto the carnival grounds with laughter and squealing children.

In some great shrines, splendid parades, historical pageants, folk dances, medieval horseracing or archery performances, fireworks, indeed, an almost endless variety of traditional activities, may be parts of the "participation" aspect of the *matsuri*. Some are rustic fairs little known outside the locality; some take months of professional preparation and draw spectators from around the world.

The Kami and Their Myths

So far we have described only Shinto shrines and worship, saying nothing about the particular deities who are the recipients of this worship. This is not inappropriate, for to most Japanese the name and story of a particular *kami* mean little; it is the shrine, the worship, and the festival itself that count. Partial exceptions are the familiar *Inari* shrines, distinguished by their red *torii* and stone foxes, to which people go to pray for prosperity. But Shintoists are far from having the kind of relation to their *kami* that Hindu *bhaktas* have with Shiva or Krishna. Japanese religion, like the Japanese temperament, is much more reserved and formal.

Nonetheless, the *kami* do have names and myths. Many Shinto *kami* are only local, but many of those of national importance are named in the two great collections of Shinto mythology—the **Kojiki** (712 c.e.) and the **Nihonshoki** (720 c.e.), two of the oldest books in Japanese[59] compiled by order of the imperial court of the time to present its divine descent and commission. They tell the story of creation and give an account of the Sun Goddess, Amaterasu, believed to be ancestress of the Japanese imperial house. She is worshipped at the grand Shrine of Ise, a sort of Shinto national cathedral.

The national myth in the *Kojiki* and *Nihonshoki* tells us that in the beginning the High *Kami* in heaven sent the primal parents, the male **Izanagi** and the female **Izanami**, down from the High Plain of Heaven. They indulged in a virtual orgy of procreation, giving birth to islands and gods, until Izanami was burned to death upon the birth of the fire-god. Izanagi tried to bring his wife out of the underworld, but he was unable to do so because she had already eaten of its food. Izanagi then exchanged boasts with Izanami about the greater power of life over death. He bathed in the ocean to cleanse himself of the pollution of the underworld. From his washings were born several great deities, above all Amaterasu. In heaven, Amaterasu once hid herself in a cave when her brother greatly offended her at the harvest festival. She was drawn out from the cave when a goddess did a ribald dance and another *kami* held up a mirror to the solar Goddess's curious emerging face. Later, Amaterasu gave the

Fundamental Features of Shinto

Theoretical

Basic Worldview	Universe is pluralistic, having many gods. It is growing and changing. Nature, humanity, and the Divine are not sharply separated.
God or Ultimate Reality	Many *kami*.
Origin of the World	Generated by the gods.
Destiny of the World	Unknown, but historical progress has meaning.
Origin of Humans	Descended from *kami*.
Destiny of Humans	Unclear; perhaps to become *kami* or merge with *kami*.
Revelation or Mediation between the Ultimate and the Human	Myths, traditions, and festivals of shrines where one approaches the *kami* presence.

Practical

What Is Expected of Humans: Worship, Practices, Behavior	To remember and celebrate the gods, remain pure and sincere, enjoy life. Support the societies of which *kami* are patrons.

Sociological

Major Social Institutions	Shrines, with the *ujiko* community of each. Family, work, and regional ties with particular shrines important.

Meoto Iwa (wedded rocks) representing the union of Izanami and Izanagi at Honshu, Japan.

same mirror (now said by tradition to be enshrined as a sacred object in the Grand Shrine of Ise) to her grandson, Prince Ninigi, who was sent down from heaven to establish the line of sovereigns on earth. This brings us to another aspect of Shinto, its relationship to the Japanese state, to be considered later.

BUDDHISM IN JAPAN

Nearly as common as Shinto shrines, and also of graceful wooden architecture but without the *torii*, are the Buddhist temples of Japan. However, the Buddhist edifices are likely to be larger than the shrines, with room for throngs of worshippers within. The temple is dominated by imposing Buddhist images, some large and of a deeply glowing gold. These images personify a spiritual force that is not as old in Japan as the *kami*, who go back to misty prehistory, but it is as old as history itself. For with the coming of Buddhism to Japan came writing, new models for art and governmental organization, many material boons of continental civilization, the keeping of records, and consciousness of history.

Buddhism arrived in Japan from Korea in the early sixth century. Early Japan long had closer ties with the Korean peninsula than with China proper, even to the extent of maintaining military and trading settlements there. In the sixth century, Buddhism had just come to Korea from Tang Dynasty China, and in China itself it had only been a strong influence for some three centuries. It still was a young and dynamic enthusiasm in that part of the world, and the *Ninonshoki* says a Korean king, anxious to cement an alliance, sent the Japanese emperor a Buddhist image and scriptures.[60]

But we must remember that as new as Buddhism seemed then, that faith already had behind it nearly a thousand years of development. Mahayana, Tantrism, temple architecture, *sutras*, images, *mandalas*, schools such as Chan and Pure Land—all these had reached mature forms before Buddhism touched the shamanistic and nearly unlettered people of old Japan. Buddhism came, therefore, as a powerfully more sophisticated culture, with splendors of art and subtleties of concept undreamed of before. It was far from well understood, but it was a force and a presence that could hardly be avoided.

As they have done repeatedly since, the Japanese responded initially with debate between the desire to keep their culture intact and the desire to be open to everything foreign that seemed advanced and advantageous. Then, as later, the Japanese swung between extremes on each hand. But from then on, Buddhism was an increasingly deeply rooted part of Japanese culture.

Tendai and Shingon

Japanese Buddhism has taken several forms. The first major denominations of Buddhism in Japan, which flourished in the Nara Period (710–784) and the Heian Period (794–1185), were elaborate and complex, with temples honoring many Mahayana Buddhas and *bodhisattvas* with colorful rituals. They often verged toward Vajrayana practices. The most important denominations of this type, which stem from the beginning of the Heian Period and still exist in large numbers today, are **Tendai** and **Shingon**.

Tendai, founded by Saicho or **Dengyo Daishi** (762–822), holds that the Lotus Sutra is the fullest expression of Buddhist truth but that under that "umbrella" it is tolerant of a great diversity of Buddhist devotions, holding that there are innumerable ways to enlightenment.

Shingon, founded by Kukai or **Kobo Daishi** (773–835), is more Vajrayana-like in style. It emphasized the Great Sun Buddha (Dainichi) who is the universal Buddha nature everywhere and taught esoteric practices—*mantras*, or chants, *mudras*, or hand gestures, meditations that visualize the Buddhas—by which one could express one's inner Buddhahood. Its temples and rituals often presented *mandalas* or *yantras*,

Main Hall of the Great Buddha Temple in Nara Japan.

sometimes three-dimensional, showing the interrelationships of the many Buddhas and *bodhisattvas*.

The Kamakura Reformation: Pure Land, Nichiren, and Zen

In the **Kamakura Period** (1185–1333) the religious picture changes. Politically, the Nara and Heian Periods had centered on the imperial court in the cities of Nara and then Heian (modern Kyoto). The courtiers had appreciated and patronized those many-faceted forms of Mahayana Buddhism. But in the Kamakura Period, a new force came to power, the warlords or **shoguns**, who established their capital in the city of Kamakura far to the north of Kyoto. With their rise to power came a religious change that has sometimes been compared to the Protestant Reformation in sixteenth-century Europe.

If Heian was dominated by the elegant refined courtier and the esoteric monk, Kamakura was characterized by the simple, direct warrior. Moreover, times were troubled, and pessimism was in the air. People talked of the Buddhist idea of the **mappo**, the last age, when doctrine and morality would deteriorate so much that one could be saved only by faith, if at all. To meet the new age, three new forms of Buddhism arose in Japan—Pure Land, Nichiren, and Zen.

Each in its own way represented a popularization of Buddhism as a path to liberation for the masses. Each also represented a radical Buddhist simplification. Kamakura Buddhism was a reaction against the deep metaphysics and ostentatious rituals of the Heian Period. The soldier and peasant, in a time of disorder and death, wanted assurance of salvation, but they were not attracted by monasticism or beautiful but impersonal rites or subtle philosophy. They insisted on some simple and sure key to salvation, as dependable in the field as in the monastic temple.

Hence, synthesis and mystery gave way to simple faith, popular preachers, and practical techniques. An age can be understood as well or better through the questions it asks as through the answers it gives. The Heian period (like medieval Europe) had asked, "How can all knowledge and spiritual experience be brought into a great inclusive system?" Kamakura Japan (like Reformation Europe) was asking instead, "How can I know that I am saved?" It was eager to shuck the mysteries of the cosmic **mandala** and the three Buddha-bodies for a sure answer to this desperate question that anyone could understand. Its new forms of Buddhism—Pure Land, Nichiren, and Zen—can be called products of the Kamakura Reformation.

Pure Land Buddhism was taught in Japan by **Honen** (1133–1212) and his disciple **Shinran** (1173–1262), who founded respectively the **Jodo-shu** (Pure Land) and **Jodo Shinshu** (True Pure Land) denominations.[61] The basic practice is expressing faith in the vow of Amida Buddha to save all who call upon his name through faith by the *Nembutsu*—the chant "*Namu Amida Butsu*" ("Glory to Amida Buddha"). It is a very simple but deep faith in which one loses ego not by meditation, as in some other forms of Buddhism, but by trust in the help of another far more powerful—Amida. Shinran taught an even more radical salvation by faith alone than Honen, and he implemented it thoroughly—allowing married clergy, requiring the removal of all figures in temples, except Amida and the bodhisattva Kannon, and promoting a new "secular" Buddhist way of life. If salvation is by faith and faith alone, he argued, all the rest of Buddhic rites and rules is unnecessary.

The militant Kamakura spirit in religion is supremely manifested in **Nichiren**.[62] The son of a poor fisherman, Nichiren (1222–1282), an intelligent and perceptive youth, was haunted by two questions. He wondered why, in the struggle between the old Heian regime and the rebellious warlords, the imperial armies had been defeated despite the countless incantations offered on their behalf by the Tendai and Shingon

Buddhist Priest praying in a temple in Tokyo, Japan.

clerics. And he asked, like so many others in his day, how one could experience the certainty of salvation. Both of these are serious themes, which were to become pillars of the faith he finally offered the world.

In 1242, Nichiren went to study at Mount Hiei, where he stayed until 1253. Under the influence of Tendai, he became convinced that the answer to his problems lay in the Lotus Sutra. Salvation was not only in its teachings, although they are the supreme expression of Buddhist truth, but also in the gesture of accepting the Lotus Sutra as the sole bearer of Buddhist faith and authority. This acceptance is expressed through the recitation of the chant, "Nam Myoho Renge Kyo," meaning "Hail the Marvelous Teaching of the Lotus Sutra." In 1253, he began a prophetic mission, urging the whole nation to return to the Lotus Sutra.

From the beginning, Nichiren Buddhism had a rigorous quality; his disciples did not shrink from using contentious and disruptive means to spread the faith. While for several centuries his faith settled down to become a fairly ordinary denomination, Nichiren's thought was not without its effect on Japanese nationalism and modernization. After World War II, a new Nichiren movement, the **Soka Gakkai** (actually a lay organization originally within Nichiren Shoshu, the largest of the Nichiren sects) was founded by persons who suffered persecution from the wartime nationalist regime. Soka Gakkai ("Value-creation Society"), which grew remarkably, places special emphasis on the power of chanting to achieve results in this life. Following the "this-worldly" promises of Nichiren faith to augur a new age of human fulfillment, this tightly organized order has shown the force of Nichiren as a prophet for the modern world. The movement declined in the late twentieth century.[63]

Because the basic principles of **Zen** have already been presented in connection with its sources in Chinese Chan in the chapter on Buddhism, it will be sufficient here to make just a few comments on its Japanese development. Chan was transmitted to Japan by two men, Eisai (1141–1215) and Dogen (1200–1253). Both were priests educated at Mount Hiei, and both, like many others, were looking for something more. Each went to China, and each came in contact with one of two major traditions of Chan, which in Japan became the Zen Buddhist **Rinzai** and **Soto** schools.

Besides being a denomination that administers temples, Zen in Japan is a distinctive esthetic and cultural influence. Zen cultural expression—in poetry, painting, the tea ceremony, the garden—suggests the Zen experience of the absolute in the ordinary and in the natural in that perfect simplicity that comes out of perfect control. For example, let us look at the Zen garden. A Zen monastery may possess a garden with raked gravel and moss and gnarled trees. The objects will not be spaced in the geometric patterns of a European formal garden, as at Versailles, but in a seemingly natural and irregular way that nonetheless enchants and satisfies. Like all the other Zen arts, it manifests the truly natural by pruning and control.

Early one mild spring morning, I* sat overlooking the world-famous stone garden of the Ryoanji Zen temple in Kyoto. This garden is simply a large rectangle of raked white gravel in which fifteen rough stones are set in five clusters, like "islands" of rock, with bits of moss around them. The stones are in a seemingly random pattern, yet one cannot quite leave them alone. For long periods I gazed at them, torn between the intellect's insatiable desire to make everything into meaningful relationships

Rock garden in Japanese Zen monastery.

and the inherent meaninglessness of this, which was yet a work of art. Over and over again, I felt that I had almost, but not quite, seen the meaning of the rock "island" relationships; I seemed to know it but could not quite say it. Finally, like a koan, the rocks and their relationships brought me up against the futility of the pattern-making mind in dealing with certain ultimates. In gazing at the garden, I now saw random bits of moss and stone, now a cluster of galaxies in the trackless void of space.

CONFUCIANISM IN JAPAN

Confucianism is an "invisible" but profoundly pervasive spiritual presence in Japan. With one or two exceptions, it presents no eye-catching shrines like Shinto or splendid temples like Buddhism. Yet its influence on the structures and values of Japanese society can hardly be overestimated. However diverse their metaphysical positions, the practical, this-worldly ethics of all accepted religions in Japan are essentially Confucian in character, stressing family, loyalty, harmony, and fulfilling obligations. More than anything else, Confucian values have made Japan the industrious, harmonious, hierarchical, sometimes repressive, web of intricate loyalties and mutual obligations that it is. And more than anything else, these values lie behind Japan's success as a world-class economic power, even given recent setbacks. It is vital, therefore, to understand something about the Japanese adaptation of Confucianism, which in certain ways is different from what it means in China.

Confucianism has been taught in Japan since the earliest arrival from the continent, although it rarely took explicitly religious expression in that land. A Confucian

*Robert Ellwood

university taught the Chinese classics during the Heian Period. Confucianism's Japanese heyday, however, was the Tokugawa Period (1600–1867), when it flourished as the state ideology and also as the main inspiration of several popular or deviant philosophical movements.

Influential popular movements during that time inculcated broadly Neo-Confucian values. Some embraced worship at both Shinto and Buddhist sites but made central the cultivation of the heart's original purity, holding that human nature is one with the natural moral order. Others taught respect for the social order and its laws, seeing in them human expression of that natural moral order—a characteristic Neo-Confucian perspective and one well calculated to produce a hard-working, law-abiding society.

Still, loyalty and obligation—the two values that have shaped Japanese social character more than any others—are deeply rooted in Confucianism. (Some say they go back even further than Confucianism, to the life of the archaic village and tribe, but certainly they have been articulated in historical times through Confucian language.) Loyalty in Japan goes beyond literal filial piety to apply to anyone who can be seen as being in the place of a parent. Thus, feudal lords and many others have made extensive use of adoption to continue their line when suitable natural heirs were not forthcoming. Moreover, the concept has been extended to include loyalty of students to teachers, workers to their employer or corporation, even gangsters to their underworld bosses, and subjects to state and sovereign. In Japan these obligations could, and often did, take precedence over family. Such obligations were prevalent because they were based on another key principle, the **on-giri** relationship, that of *on*, or benefaction, and *giri*, the resultant supreme obligation to repay by work and loyalty; this makes the benefactor a parent substitute.

Although outer forms continually change, these attitudes are virtually as alive today as ever. No understanding of contemporary Japanese politics or corporations is possible without a grasp of how Confucian values make such institutions complex networks of loyalties and obligations, or of how the other Confucian-based ideals of harmony and cooperation lead to decision-making as a sort of consensus-seeking process—one often quite mysterious to outsiders. The Japanese way tends to make superiors—including the emperor—figureheads and facilitators and to exalt the collective responsibility and consensus decision making of the whole family, group, or network involved.

After the disastrous Tohoku earthquake and potential nuclear disaster of 2011, observers were deeply impressed by the response of workers and ordinary Japanese people in the afflicted area. Virtually no looting was reported, and the dedication of relief and particularly atomic technicians, defying danger and fatigue as they worked together as a team, surely showed the Japanese spirit, often articulated in Confucian terms, at its best.

Japan, then, is a fundamentally Confucian society and a very effective one that in many ways displays the tradition's potential for making human life work smoothly in the twenty-first century as well as in the days of the Ancient Sage. But it is Confucianism with a difference, without the *mandarins* or the rituals—save as the former are now captains of industry, and the latter, the interpersonal courtesy for which Japan is famous.[64]

THE JAPANESE "NEW RELIGIONS"

One of the most fascinating of all contemporary religious phenomena is a set of groups in Japan called **shinko shukyo**, "newly arisen religions." Although most of them have earlier roots, they grew and flourished tremendously in the post–World

War II years of disillusionment with traditional life, including conventional Shinto and Buddhism. The golden age of these religions was the 1950s, when many were growing at fantastic rates and, in some, the original charismatic leader was still alive. At the beginning of the twenty-first century, the *shinko shukyo* are still very much a part of the Japanese scene.

The new religions have generally been based on revelations given through the lips of their founders, often women. Sometimes they have seemed to be in the tradition of ancient Japanese shamans and shamanesses. Generally, they have emphasized new teachings and practices suitable to the rapidly changing modern world. One example is **Tenrikyo** ("Religion of Heavenly Wisdom"), founded in 1838 by Miki Nakayama (1798–1887), who said that "God the Parent" is seeking to call the human children back to himself through telling them the forgotten story of creation. The main temple of the faith, in Tenri city near Nara, centers around a pillar said to mark the place where creation began and a new paradisal age in the future will be inaugurated. Rituals include beautiful sacred dances acting out the creation story. Other new religions with Buddhist roots, like the Soka Gakkai, already mentioned, or based on other modern messages from the divine are also found, such as the **Church of World Messianity**, in which adherents channel the "Divine Light of God" through cupped hands to a recipient. Another new religion is **Konkokyo**, in which adherents are given personal spiritual guidance channeled by the priest.

In the 1980s and 1990s, the "classic" new religions just mentioned, while still important, leveled off somewhat in terms of growth. Soka Gakkai was affected in 1993 by conflict and separation between the Nichiren-shu priests, who had authorized or conducted the movement's strictly religious rites, and the dynamic lay organization that had done so much to evangelize Nichirenism. However, some new movements, often called **shin-shin-shukyo** or "new new religions" have appeared, often with a healing, charismatic, and individualistic emphasis, similar to the "New Age Movement" in the West. Examples are Mahikari, a healing faith similar to World Messianity, and Agonshu, a faith of Buddhist background emphasizing ancestrism and the enactment of spectacular *goma* or fire rituals like those of Shingon.

Another is Aum Shinrikyo, founded by Asahara Shoko in 1984 as a yoga and meditation group, but which came to anticipate a final battle between good and evil around the end of the twentieth century, with Aum Shinrikyo at the head of the forces of good. That apocalyptic expectation led to violence on the part of the faith. The most notorious episode was its murderous release of nerve gas on the Tokyo subway in 1995, leading to arrests of Aum Shinrikyo leaders. The upshot was a decline in the prestige of religion in Japan, especially the new religions.

RELIGION IN JAPAN, GOVERNANCE, AND POLITICAL LIFE

The Japanese political structure, and its underlying rationale, has had four sources: Shinto, especially in the form of the myth of imperial descent from the Goddess Amaterasu; Buddhism, as an imported religion able to help unify the country; Confucianism, particularly in its values of community, relationships, hierarchy, and filial piety; and more recently, imported Western-style democracy. Let's look at each of these.

As we have seen, the ancient myths recorded in eighth-century *Kojiki* and *Nihonshoki* tell us that the first emperor was a grandson of the sun-Goddess Amaterasu, who sent him down from heaven to pacify and rule the land. Therefore, the sovereign was a kind of divinity, and he ruled by divine right. Though this doctrine has been differently emphasized at different times and the monarch has seldom exercised real power, the monarch's presence served, and still serves, as a kind of symbol to legitimate the state.

Buddhism came to Japan in the sixth century. Early in the next century, a powerful Buddhist figure, Prince Shotoku (573–621), became regent to the empress, who was his aunt. Shotoku realized that because Buddhism was imported, unlike the Shinto *kami* (mostly gods of particular clans), this faith did not belong to any one local chieftain, so it could be used to unify the country as a whole around the imperial house. He built major national temples, dedicated to *dharma*-teaching and protection for the entire nation.

Confucianism has had immense influence on moral values in Japan, and these imported but compatible teachings apply to political as well as family culture. The idea that the individual owes a debt of loyalty to the larger community, which is made up of mutually supportive relationships, and that those relationships are usually hierarchical with one side superior to the other, have all made for a polity that is, ideally, benign but authoritative. In addition, Japanese Confucianists (unlike the Chinese) often said that loyalty to the emperor was the highest obligation, taking precedence over family and all others.

After the "opening" of Japan to the West in the late nineteenth century, Japan went through the period Japanese call the "Dark Valley"—the trauma of extreme nationalism, militarism, and war in the first half of the twentieth century—when the state was aligned with Shintoism. But after the nation's defeat in 1945, especially during the American occupation, Shinto was separated from the state, and in principle government was freer of religious ideology than in any previous regime. Since then Japan has striven to adapt to Western-style democracy, with an elected parliament. While there have been problems, it would be fair to say that today Japan is politically a quite democratic nation by world standards and that the democratic values of equality, the right of all citizens to participate in government, and freedom of expression, religion, and way of life are very widely accepted, if sometimes in tension with Shinto, Buddhist, and Confucian values.

However, there has been some retrenchment because of what has been termed the "post-Aum effect." This is the name given in Japan to government reaction to the sarin gas attack in a Tokyo subway in 1995 by the religious group known as *Aum Shinrikyo*. Not only were laws regulating religions tightened in its aftermath but many observers detected an enhanced public mood of skepticism toward religion generally, which many believe has had the effect of accelerating Japan's drift toward becoming a highly secularized state.

WOMEN IN JAPANESE RELIGION

As in China, religion in Japan involves a confluence of many diverse elements. In addition to Shinto, which is indigenous to Japan, imported Buddhist, Daoist, and Confucianist themes were woven into the Japanese social fabric. Due in particular to Confucian influence, Japan has been notably patriarchal at least since the feudal era (twelfth to seventeenth centuries), during which the status of women was lower than in the proto-historic days of powerful shamanesses or the Heian era with its brilliant women poets and novelists. Not less important, Buddhist attitudes toward women as obstacles to male enlightenment and objects of negative karma were conflated with Confucian notions to bolster the view that women's subjugation was warranted.

Prior to the importation of these religious influences, women were significant religious figures in their own right as shamanesses, who were skilled in trance and able to contact the *kami* and the dead and proclaim their messages to others. The first centuries of the common era have been referred to as the "golden age" for

Japanese women.[65] It was Empress Gemmei (ruled 707–715) who ordered the completion of the *Kojiki* (referenced earlier). Also, shamanesses, such as Pimiko or Empress Jingu, were charismatic ruler queens. Such shaman queens were thought to be mediators of the Divine for the people. This prominent role of women as religious and political leaders contributed to the high status of women at the time. Family lineage was traced through the mother. And there is evidence that, unlike in other religions and later in Japanese religion, menstruating women and childbirth were not considered to be impure but were thought to be closer to the sacred and perhaps even to provide purification.[66] (As Karen A. Smyers has noted, "It is a curious fact that in the *Obaraekotoba*, the ritual prayer for the very solemn semiannual purification of the Japanese nation, the four kami who are invoked are all female."[67]) Further, because sexuality was sacred in early Shinto, virginity was not valorized as it later came to be. Rather, the body of the Japanese shamaness was believed to be a sacred vessel, which received the *kami* presence.

Miko, temple servant, offering sake at a ritual ceremony at the Shimogamo Shrine in Kyoto, Japan.

The elevated and prominent social role played by shamanesses was nearly eclipsed, however, by Chinese religio-cultural influences eagerly appropriated by the Japanese who regarded China as a more advanced civilization.[68] The matriarchal organization of Japanese society was undermined by Confucian and Buddhist influences from China, as hierarchical bureaucratic structures, organized by men, developed in political institutions and society. The patriarchal patterns we have seen in other religions took hold. Sexuality, menstruation, and childbirth came to be considered polluting taboos. Now unclean and subjugated to father, husband, and son, women's charismatic political authority was no more. However, some virgins were believed to retain the powers of the shamanesses, and their role was institutionalized at the Ise Shrine (referenced earlier).

Confucianism provided the foundation of Japanese family life where Confucian ideals regarding the formality of family hierarchical relationships prevailed. As a consequence, family and society became the province of male authority, and the woman's role reflected the Confucian ideal of wife and mother, including the importance of purity, chastity, submissiveness, and the bearing of sons. A woman's place was inside the home and her main objective was complete devotion to her husband. As in traditional China, women in Japan joined the families of their husbands and lived under the authority of their mothers-in-law.

Family loyalty developed a considerable role in Japanese life—a confluence of Confucian notions and ancient clan allegiances. This and Buddhist doctrines of selflessness (together with the influence of the Daoist *wu-wei*) merged to make acceptance of one's lot in life, and service to the familial group, the religious ideal. For women this meant accepting their subservient status without complaint. Attitudes that developed over the long period of these religio-cultural influences and the political and social structures based on them (much of it codified in the Meiji Civil Code of 1898), prevail to this day, despite Japanese women's suffrage in 1945 and constitutional and statutory reforms in 1947.

Against these religio-cultural attitudes, and the institutions they engendered, Shinto retained, in many respects, the distinctly Japanese folk wisdom and mythology of the prior age. A "little tradition" of traveling women diviners survived, and the shamaness tradition lives on in Shinto's rural folk religion manifestations. That tradition provides the impetus behind the acceptance of the charismatic women leaders of the "new religions," such as Miki of Tenrikyo (discussed earlier). Moreover, the creation myth, as we have seen, provides a prominent place for the female divine as one deity in the primal divine couple: Izanagi and Izanami. And their progeny, Amaterasu (the Sun Goddess), is the patroness and ancestor of the imperial family and the Japanese people. Significantly, as well, the many *kami* include both male and female deities.

However, even in Shinto where female symbolism abounds, we find a reiteration of the cosmic order as requiring the submission of women to men. For example, in the creation myth, when Izanagi, the male, is to join with the female, Izanami, the female speaks first. As a result, their first offspring is defective. Clearly, she was to have deferred to her male counterpart. Yet it is Shinto's emphasis on the beauty and divinity of nature (bolstered by analogous Daoist thinking and practice) that provides the aesthetic sensibilities so central to Japan. This added to women's vocation the development of elegance and grace in her person and her home. Thus, under Shinto influence, combined with Confucian ideal family life and Daoist reverence for "naturalness," especially as manifested in Zen Buddhism, women are to serve and beautify. Interestingly, some aesthetic aspects of Japan associated with Zen are performed by women—the tea ceremony and flower arranging come to mind.

The role of women in contemporary Japanese religion can only be described as mixed and in flux. Women retain some traditional religious roles from the past, as *miko* or shamanesses, as founders of new religious movements, and occasionally as Shinto priests or priests in temples of new religions. Even in religions where the hierarchy is officially male, in a characteristically Japanese way, active women—sometimes as wives or mothers of priests—are expected to exercise considerable influence.

At the same time, the secondary status of women in Buddhism is increasingly being challenged, no doubt under the influence of Japanese and worldwide feminist movements. For example, Buddhist nuns have agitated for equality in the *samgha*. The wives of Buddhist priests have long had an anomalous place. Although most Japanese priests are married, that they are theoretically supposed to be celibate has put many of these women in the position of persons whose role is not supposed to be openly recognized. They have formed organizations to try to rectify this situation in order to give them the dignity to which they are entitled.

A matter that has attracted much attention, and that affects women profoundly, are the *mizuko kuyo* rites, memorial services for aborted fetuses. Abortion is common in Japan, and these rites, offered by many Buddhist temples, have provided ways for women to deal with the feelings of loss and guilt evoked by the tragedy in ways consistent with Buddhist beliefs in the afterlife and reincarnation.[69]

Most significant for Japanese women generally, however, contemporary Japan is undergoing a crisis of its traditional Confucian family values. One often sees articles in the print media and presentations on television treating, in tones of either enthusiasm or despair, the reality that young people no longer seem to regard elders with the veneration of old and that women are increasingly expecting equal opportunity in business, professions, and politics. At the same time, change is often slow. Many Japanese, both women and men, remain influenced by the Confucian tradition of recognizing the importance of one's integration into larger social units—family, community, corporation—and therefore they are skeptical of the extreme individualism promoted by the West. As a result, efforts to "liberate" women from the patriarchal family model have run headlong into tradition, as we have seen elsewhere. This has been especially difficult in Japan, however, where patriarchal family tradition joins national pride in an "ideology of familialism." In that tradition, as first manifested in the Meiji period (1868–1912) but still influential today, the ideal woman is to be a "good wife and wise mother," not only for family, but also for the state.[70]

Meanwhile, feminism has had an uneasy road in Japan. The early decades of the twentieth-century saw suffrage and labor movements, and the desire of women to obtain control over their bodies, in particular reproductive control. These developments spawned the "New Women" debate in Japan and the influential *Seitosha*, a feminist literary association and publisher of *Seito*, a journal that inspired many women to resist patriarchal norms.[71] While, these rumblings eventually led to a nascent women's liberation movement in the 1970s, that movement's efforts and social and legal reforms have not led to women's equality. Yet Japan has not developed a feminist movement quite as strong as those in other modern, developed industrial nations. Perhaps the reason for this is that many Japanese women remain family-oriented, consistent with religious ideas, and wield considerable power in the home. Perhaps the reason is that Japanese women were not subjected to the extreme oppressions of women in other societies. Perhaps it is that the traditional Japanese Confucian worldview does not permit a notion of liberation. Everyone is part of the group—the clan—and is not an individual in one's own right. Whatever the reason, women are well-rooted in traditional Japanese society, and many accept their role without a perceived need to mount a strong resistance. Still, there are women whose voices are being raised in debates about the "woman question" in Japan, while tradition and modernity remain in tension.[72]

Religion in Korea

Korea has been called the "Bridge of Asia." This peninsula, reaching from the mainland toward Japan, has long been a melting pot of religious and cultural influences and a pathway by which they have been transmitted to Japan. As we have seen, Buddhism first entered Japan from Korea. At the same time, with a population of some sixty million (now divided between the Republic of Korea in the South and Communist-ruled North Korea), Korea is an important cultural sphere in its own right.

Korean religion may be looked at in terms of five constituents: indigenous shamanistic faith, Buddhism, Confucianism, modern new religions, and Christianity. These are the main ingredients in the contemporary Korean religious melting pot, together with a dash of Daoism from China that is, among other things, represented in the *Yin–Yang* symbol found on the Republic of Korea's flag, but that is less of a definable religious stratum in Korea than the preceding five.

The ancient indigenous religion of Korea is comparable to early Shinto, to which it is probably related. It presents a myth of the origin of the Korean people in the union of a god descended from heaven who made a she-bear into a human and mated with her. Their son, Tangun, was the founder of Korean society. He then worshiped the high god of heaven, Hananim. Shamanism was very important, persisting today in the role of *mudangs*, colorful shamanesses who may perform a rite called *kut* to drive away evil spirits and restore good fortune.

Buddhism came into Korea late in the fourth century C.E. and quickly took hold owing to patronage by rulers of several Korean kingdoms. Buddhist influence was all in the Mahayana tradition; monastic life has come to be predominantly *Son* (Zen), while lay Buddhism has focused on Pure Land faith and the worship of the *bodhisattva* Kwanseum (in Chinese, Kwan-Yin; in Japanese, Kannon), the heavenly bestower of mercy. The great Buddhist temple and monastic centers of Korea tend to be in isolated places, quiet retreats often stocked with invaluable Buddhist libraries and works of art.

The golden age of Korean Buddhism was the early Middle Ages. The Yi Dynasty (1392–1910) favored Confucianism and tended to restrict Buddhist activity. National temples performed Confucian rites, and Confucian (especially Neo-Confucian) values deeply affected Korean life. The patriarchal family, filial piety, and the honor of traditional learning among the elite were as absolute in old Korea as anywhere, and the impact of centuries steeped in Confucianism is far from gone today.

But in the nineteenth and twentieth centuries, the closed Confucian cultural world of the Korean "Hermit Kingdom" was harshly violated by Western and Japanese incursions, ranging from extensive Christian missionary activity to bitterly resented Japanese rule, and then to the Korean War and the shocks of modernization. These traumatic events have created an ardent sense of Korean cultural identity and messianism, reflected in several new religious movements. Tonghak ("Eastern Learning") was founded in the 1860s and renamed **Ch'ondogyo** ("Way of Heavenly Teaching") in 1905. It inculcated the worship of the God of Heaven but combined features of shamanism, Buddhism, and Confucianism. It also advocated social change against the anachronistic, ultraconservative Yi Dynasty, and it lay behind a great rebellion in 1894 that nearly toppled that regime and produced in turn the Sino-Japanese War of that year. Another group, which combines Christian, shamanistic, and messianic features, is that founded by the Rev. Sun Myung Moon (1920-2012), known in the West as the **Unification Church**.

Christianity, brought by Catholic and Protestant missionaries, has been more successful in Korea than in most other parts of East Asia except the Philippines, embracing nearly half the population of South Korea as the twenty-first century began.[73]

Religion in Vietnam

Situated on the southeast corner of the Asian mainland, Indochina is an area where Indian and Chinese cultural influences meet. Two of the Indochinese countries, Laos and Cambodia, are Theravada Buddhist and are traditionally oriented toward the Indian cultural direction. The third and largest, Vietnam, has sometimes experienced Chinese rule and has been more dominated culturally and religiously by its great neighbor to the north. In the early centuries c.e., however, the southern tip of Vietnam, then the kingdom of Funan, was a center of Indianization.

But China ruled major parts of Vietnam, mostly in the north, for more than a thousand years, from 111 b.c.e. to 939 c.e. Despite ardent Vietnamese resistance to their rule, the Chinese succeeded in Sinicizing Vietnamese culture to no small extent. This is reflected in the dominance of Mahayana Buddhism, largely in the form of Thien (Chan or Zen) Buddhism and in the traditional role of a Confucian *mandarin* elite imbued with the values of that tradition. However, these institutions have adapted to Vietnamese culture; in recent centuries, monk and *mandarin* alike have embodied Vietnam.

Like the other societies of Southeast Asia, Vietnam in the nineteenth and twentieth centuries suffered severe shocks that gave rise to new questions about the nature of its spiritual identity. The decades of French colonial rule, the missionary presence of Roman Catholicism, the demise of the traditional Confucian order in China itself, and some thirty-five years of war and confusion all left traumatic marks. Vietnamese felt caught between a Catholicism frequently benign but associated with alien rule, a moribund Buddhism, and a Confucianism linked to a social order clearly passing away. In this situation, it is not surprising that not only did Communism win support but highly nationalistic "new religions" also gained large followings. The two most important new movements, **Hoa Hao** and **Cao Dai**, both controlled whole provinces and fielded their own armies in the complicated struggles of Japanese, French, and various Vietnamese forces during the 1940s and 1950s. They continued

Cao Dai Holy See (Great Divine Temple) in Long Hoa near Tay Ninh, Vietnam.

as powerful factors in Vietnamese life until the unification of the country under the Communist Hanoi regime in 1975.

Hoa Hao was a Buddhist movement with Theravada leanings that sought to restore "pure" Buddhism. Cao Dai, on the other hand, was a highly syncretistic church based on spiritualistic communications, reminiscent of Daoist sectarianism. It embraced Confucian morality, such Buddhist doctrines as *karma* and reincarnation, and spiritist mediumship, while possessing an organizational structure under a "pope" clearly inspired by Roman Catholicism.

Since 1975, religious activity has generally been severely curtailed in Vietnam itself, but Buddhism, Catholicism, and Cao Dai continue to be practiced in Vietnamese refugee communities around the world.[74]

Religion in Mongolia

This vast country of horses, deserts and grasslands north of China, the homeland of Genghis Khan, was originally dominated religiously by shamanism, and practitioners of the shaman's art are still important in Mongolia and are on the rise. A recent bestseller, *The Horse Boy* by Rupert Isaacson, tells the true story of a father and mother's journey to Mongolia with their autistic son, and of the healing a famous Mongolian shaman was reportedly able to accomplish in him.[75] In the narration, much is also told about the worldview and craft of Mongolian shamanism. In addition to healings, this involves such things as ceremonies at the solstices, all of which are to bring everything into balance with the natural world.

Since the sixteenth century, however, Buddhism of the Tibetan or Vajrayana school has been the official religion, with the Dalai Lama its head. As in Tibet, monasteries were thronged, and the conspicuous piety of Vajrayana was visible everywhere until Soviet-allied Communism took control of the nation after the Russian revolution.

Buddhism was banned in 1937. At least 20,000 lamas were executed, and many other monks sent to Siberian labor camps. After the fall of the Communist regime in 1990, however, Buddhism resurfaced, and monasteries are again busy. Most Mongolians identify themselves as Buddhist, and the Dalai Lama has made several visits to the country since 1900.[76]

Christianity has also entered Mongolia since 1990, largely owing to the work of Korean evangelical missionaries, though Mormon and other American representatives of Christianity have also been active. Though Christians make up no more than a tiny percent of the overall population, churches can be found in Ulan Bator, the capital, frequented by young people in blue jeans who appreciate their casual worship and the Western pop-style Christian music. Here, in addition to its spiritual appeal, Christianity must seem like a suggestion of the outside world in a land long isolated and repressed.

Summary

The religion of East Asia has emphasized the unity of the cosmos and the integration of the individual with nature as well as with family and society. Ancestrism has been an important way of meeting both ends. It has, however, also been a religious tradition deeply influenced by outstanding individual teachers and leaders.

Confucianism, deriving from the teaching of Confucius and other philosophers, as well as from ancient Chinese attitudes, is perhaps the most pervasive spiritual force of all in East Asia. It has emphasized the importance of inward virtue, the obligations of the individual to family and society, and rites and forms through which these are expressed. Daoism, with its stress on mystical unity with all of nature and with such nonrational aspects of human life as love of beauty, fantasy, and personal immortality, has provided compensation for the rational and ethical character of Confucianism. Both sought to align human life with the Dao, the universal Way, or with the will of Heaven; for Confucianism it was supremely found in a good society; for Daoists, it is in nature, beauty, fantasy, and mystical experience outside the corrupting influence of society.

Hardly less influential in East Asia has been Buddhism. In China, it was considerably affected by Daoism. Its main forms were Chan (Zen, in Japan; Son, in Korea), emphasizing meditation and nature, and Pure Land Buddhism, emphasizing rebirth in paradise through faith in Amida. In the popular religion of traditional China, Confucianism, Daoism, and Buddhism combined with ancestrism, seasonal festivals, and local deities to make up a colorful complex.

China's Confucianism was expressed as a holistic vision of an ideal good society, in which the sage king or emperor, in consultation with the mandarin, ruled with virtue. However, the ruler's authority was subject to the Mandate of Heaven, which could be gleaned from omens, the conditions of the empire, or even the general opinion of the populace. Since 1911, China has experienced significant developments in a different direction. After a brief experiment with a republican form of government, a Communist takeover led to major cultural shifts imposed by the authorities for the People's Republic of China. Religion was originally suppressed under this Communist regime. It is experiencing a minor revival; yet it still remains severely circumscribed. China is generally a secular society, although there are recent reports of increased religious adherence.

In Japan, Confucian values have been and still are important, but formal religion has been mainly a matter of the indigenous Shinto faith and Buddhism, imported at the dawn of Japanese history. Shinto is the worship of the *kami* or polytheistic gods of clans and places. The *kami* are housed in simple but lovely shrines and worshiped either privately or in community *matsuri*, which stress tradition, purity, and the festive spirit.

Japanese Buddhism has centered more on major leaders and has changed character through the production of new denominations with major changes in historical eras. Its earlier forms, such as Shingon and Tendai, stressed comprehensiveness and often used esoteric forms. The newer denominations of the Medieval Kamakura Period—Pure Land, Nichiren, and Zen—moved in the direction of the simplification and popularization of Buddhist salvation.

The Japanese political structure, and its underlying rationale, has had four sources: Shinto (its myths of emperor descent from the Goddess Amaterasu), Buddhism (to unifying the country around the Imperial House), Confucianism (its relational values, in particular that of the people and the emperor), and more recently Western-style democracy. However, during the period called the "Dark Valley," the ideology of the Imperial House led to authoritarianism and military aggression, which ended in Japan's defeat in World War II, the U.S. occupation, and the adoption of Western-style democracy. This form of government has been retained to this day, permitting toleration and religious freedom, albeit with a skeptical eye in light of recent domestic terrorism from a militant religious sect.

Women in East Asia have held a centrally important role in the social order prescribed by religious norms regarding family and the social order. Although considered integral to the "good life," women's significance in that regard did not mitigate against patriarchal patterns that required subordination of women to men. A woman's accepted vocation involved only the realm of the home, where she was highly restricted. Buddhism and Daoism offered alternative avenues of religious and personal expression for women. As Buddhist nuns, women may become teachers and leaders, although, for the most part, they are subordinated to monks. In Daoism, East Asian women have found an accommodating theology, and, therefore, more opportunity for significant roles than found elsewhere in these cultures. Yet religious Daoism itself is marginal in its impact on the great society. Consequently, advancement there does not provide women with social status.

In modern Japan, a number of new religions have arisen in response to times of rapid change, and women have played important roles in them.

Two other important East Asian countries, Korea and Vietnam, also share a heritage of Confucianism and Buddhism in the Chinese Chan and Pure Land styles, and, in the context of a modern experience devastated by upheaval and war, they have generated major new religious movements. Religion in Mongolia is dominated by Shamanism and Vajrayana Buddhism.

Questions for Review

1. Discuss the main general features of East Asian religion: its stress on cosmic unity, its orientation toward family and society, and its practicality.
2. Interpret the meaning of the important theme of ancestrism.
3. Discuss the thematic chart for Chinese religion, showing how it brings out the aspects of Chinese religion oriented toward society and those oriented toward nature, and how it sorts out those aspects that stress a rational approach to ultimate meaning and those that give vent to the nonrational side of human nature.
4. Talk about the meaning of Dao.
5. Present the main features of Confucianism. Be sure to distinguish the features of philosophical Confucianism and the religious aspects of Confucian worship, but also show how the two fit together in traditional China through the values and role of the *mandarins*.
6. Discuss the Han Synthesis and its significance.
7. In the same way, explain the main features of Daoism (Taoism), distinguishing between the outlook of the Daoist philosophers and religious Daoism, but also indicating how they are related.
8. Discuss the main forms and features of Chinese Buddhism, explaining how Buddhism was modified through interaction with Chinese culture.
9. State the major points of popular religion in traditional China, such as ancestrism, the celebration of seasonal festivals, and the relationships involved in family and place.
10. Explain Confucianism's view of society as holistic and the roles of the ruler and mandarin in it.
11. Explain what the attitudes and policies of the People's Republic of China toward religion have been and what has happened to religion under its rule.
12. Discuss the principal features of Shinto.
13. Discuss Buddhism in Japan, stressing the role of the great leaders who have shaped it and how its character has changed with changing historical periods.
14. Interpret the general characteristics of the "new religions" of Japan.
15. Using the charts provided in the chapter, explain the fundamental features of Confucianism, Daoism,

and Shinto. How do they answer the great questions about the nature of ultimate reality and the meaning of human life?

16. Discuss the role of women in traditional Chinese and Japanese societies.

17. Explain how Buddhism and Daoism offered alternative roles for women in China.

18. Discuss women's aesthetic role in Japanese society.
19. Give an account of the four sources for Japan's political structure.
20. Describe the religious traditions of Korea.
21. Summarize the religious heritage of Vietnam.
22. Summarize the religious heritage of Mongolia.

Suggested Readings on East Asian Religion

Chinese Religion

Ahern, Emily M., *The Cult of the Dead in a Chinese Village*. Stanford, CA: Stanford University Press, 1973.

Bauer, Wolfgang, *China and the Search for Happiness*. New York: Seabury Press, 1976.

Blofeld, John, trans., *I Ching*. New York: Dutton, 1968.

Chau, Adam Yuet, *Miraculous Responses: Doing Popular Religion in Contemporary China*. Stanford, CA: Stanford University Press, 2006.

Clart, Philip, and Charles R. Jones, eds., *Religion in Modern Taiwan*. Honolulu: University of Hawai'i Press, 2003.

Eberhard, Wolfram, *Guilt and Sin in Traditional China*. Berkeley and Los Angeles: University of California Press, 1967.

Fowler, Jeaneane, and Merv Fowler, *Chinese Religions: Beliefs and Practices*. Brighton, UK and Portland, OR: Sussex Academic Press, 2008.

Fung Yu-Lan, *A Short History of Chinese Philosophy*. New York: Macmillan, 1960.

Lopez, Donald S., ed., *Religions of China in Practice*. Princeton, NJ: Princeton University Press, 1996.

Poceski, Mario, *Introducing Chinese Religions*. London and New York: Routledge, 2009.

Shahar, Meir, *The Shaolin Monastery: History, Religion, and the Chinese Martial Arts*. Honolulu: University of Hawai'i Press, 2008.

Sommer, Deborah, ed., *Chinese Religion: An Anthology of Sources*. New York: Oxford University Press, 1995.

Thompson, Laurence G., *Chinese Religion: An Introduction*. Belmont, CA: Wadsworth, 1969.

———, *The Chinese Way in Religion*. Encino, CA: Dickenson, 1973.

Van Glahn, Richard, *The Sinister Way: The Divine and the Demonic in Chinese Religious Culture*. Berkeley: University of California Press, 2004.

Yao, Xinzhong, and Paul Badgham, *Religious Experience in Contemporary China*. Cardiff: University of Wales Press, 2007.

Confucianism

Bahm, Archie J., *The Heart of Confucius*. New York: Harper & Row, 1971.

Littlejohn, Ronnie L., *Confucianism: An Introduction*. London and New York: I. B. Tauris, 2010.

McArthur, Meher, *Confucius: A Throneless King*. New York: Pegasus, 2011.

Oldstone-Moore, Jennifer, *Confucianism: Origins, Beliefs, Practices, Holy Texts, Sacred Places*. New York: Oxford University Press, 2002.

Yao, Hsin-chung, *An Introduction to Confucianism*. New York: Cambridge University Press, 2000.

Daoism

Blofeld, John, *The Secret and Sublime: Taoist Mysteries and Magic*. London: George Allen & Unwin, 1973.

Clark, John J., *The Tao of the West: Western Transformations of Taoist Thought*. London and New York: Routledge, 2000.

Cleary, Thomas, *Immortal Sisters: Secrets of Taoist Women*. Boston: Shambhala, 1989.

Kirkland, Russell, *Taoism: The Enduring Tradition*. London: Routledge, 2004.

Kohn, Livia, *Daoism and Chinese Culture*. Honolulu: University of Hawai'i Press, 2005.

———, *The Taoist Experience: An Anthology*. Albany: State University of New York Press, 1991.

Littlejohn, Ronnie J., *Daoism: An Introduction*. London and New York: I. B. Tauris, 2009.

Buddhism in China

Ch'en, Kenneth, *Buddhism in China: A Historical Survey*. Princeton, NJ: Princeton University Press, 1964.

Ferguson, Andrew, *Zen's Chinese Heritage: The Masters and their Teachings*, 2nd ed. Somerville, MA: Wisdom Publications, 2011.

Wright, Arthur F., *Buddhism in Chinese History*. Stanford, CA: Stanford University Press, 1959.

Religion in China, Governance, and Political Life

Ashiwa, Yoshiko, and Donald L. Wank, *Making Religion, Making the State: The Politics of Religion in Modern China*. Stanford, CA: Stanford University Press, 2009.

Csikszentmihalyi, Mark, "Confucianism," in *God's Rule: The Politics of the World's Religions*, Jacob Neusner, ed. Washington, DC: Georgetown University Press, 2003.

Yu, Anthony C., *State and Religion in China*. Chicago: Open Court, 2005.

Religion in Japan

Ama, Toshimaro, *Why Are the Japanese Non-Religious?* Lanham, MD: University Press of America, 2005.

Blacker, Carmen, *The Catalpa Bow: A Study of Shamanistic Practices in Japan*. London: George Allen & Unwin, 1975.

Bowring, Richard John, *The Religious Traditions of Japan, 500–1600*. Cambridge University Press, 2005.

Ellwood, Robert S., *Introducing Japanese Religion*. New York and London: Routledge, 2008.

Hori, Ichiro, *Folk Religion in Japan*. Chicago: University of Chicago Press, 1968.

Reader, Ian, *Religion in Contemporary Japan*. Honolulu: University of Hawai'i Press, 1991.

Swanson, Paul L., and Clark Chilson, *Nanzan Guide to Japanese Religions*. Honolulu: University of Hawai'i Press, 2006.

Tanabe, George, ed., *Religions of Japan in Practice*. Princeton, NJ: Princeton University Press, 1999.

Buddhism in Japan

Bloom, Alfred, *Shinran's Gospel of Pure Grace*. Tucson: University of Arizona Press, 1965.

Covell, Stephen Grove, *Japanese Temple Buddhism*. Honolulu: University of Hawai'i Press, 2005.

Hoover, Thomas, *Zen Culture*. New York: Random House, 1977.

King, Winston, *Zen and the Way of the Sword: Arming the Samurai Psyche*. New York: Oxford University Press, 1993.

Shinto

Breen, John, and Mark Teeuwen, *Shinto in History: Ways of the Kami*. Honolulu: University of Hawai'i Press, 2000.

Hay, Jeff, *Shinto*. Farmington Hills, MI: Greenhaven Press, 2006

Kasulis, Thomas, *Shinto: The Way Home*. Honolulu: University of Hawai'i Press, 2004.

Nelson, John K., *A Year in the Life of a Shinto Shrine*. Seattle: University of Washington Press, 1996.

New Religions of Japan

Hardacre, Helen, *Kurozumikyo and the New Religions of Japan*. Princeton, NJ: Princeton University Press, 1986.

———, *Lay Buddhism in Contemporary Japan: Reiyukai Kyodan*. Princeton, NJ: Princeton University Press, 1984.

Ooms, Emily Groszos, *Women and Millenarian Protest in Meiji Japan: Deguchi Nao and Omotokyo*. Ithaca, NY: Cornell University Press, 1993.

Stalker, Nancy K., *Prophet Motive: Deguchi Onisaburo, Oomoto, and the Rise of New Religions in Imperial Japan*. Honolulu: University of Hawai'i Press, 2008.

Religion in Japan, Governance, and Political Life

Hall, Robert King, and John Owen Gauntlett, *Kokutai no Hongi: Cardinal Principles of the National Entity of Japan*. Cambridge, MA: Harvard University Press, 1949.

Hardacre, Helen, *Shinto and the State, 1868–1988*. Princeton, NJ: Princeton University Press, 1989.

Toyoda, Maria A., and Aiji, Tanaka, "Religion and Politics in Japan," in *Religion and Politics in Comparative Perspective: The One, the Few, and the Many*, Ted Gerard Jelen and Clyde Wilcox, eds. New York: Cambridge University Press, 2002.

Religion in Korea

Baker, Don, *Korean Spirituality*. Honolulu: University of Hawai'i Press, 2008.

Buswell, Robert E., Jr., ed. *Religions of Korea in Practice*. Princeton, NJ: Princeton University Press, 2007.

Grayson, James H., *Korea: A Religious History*. London and New York: RoutledgeCurzon, 2002.

Kang, Jae-eun, *The Land of Scholars: Two Thousand Years of Korean Confucianism*. Paramus, NJ: Homa & Sekey, 2006.

Kendall, Laurel, *Shamans, Nostalgias, and the IMF: South Korean Popular Religion in Motion*. Honolulu: University of Hawai'i Press, 2009.

———, *The Life and Hard Times of a Korean Shaman*. Honolulu: University of Hawai'i Press, 1988.

———, *Shamans, Housewives, and Other Restless Spirits*. Honolulu: University of Hawai'i Press, 1985.

Kim, Chongho, *Korean Shamanism*. Aldershot, UK: Ashgate, 2003.

Religion in Vietnam

Blagov, Sergei, *Caodaism*. Huntington, NY: Nova Science, 2001.

Do, Thien, *Vietnamese Supernaturalism*. London and New York: RoutledgeCurzon, 2003.

Pham, Quynh Phuong, *Hero and Deity: Tran Hung Dao and the Resurgence of Popular Religion in Vietnam*. Chiang Mai, Thailand: Mekong Press, 2009.

Taylor, Philip, *Goddess on the Rise: Pilgrimage and Popular Religion in Vietnam*. Honolulu: University of Hawai'i Press, 2004.

Religion in Mongolia

Heissig, Walther, *The Religions of Mongolia*. Geoffrey Samuel, trans. Berkeley: University of California Press, 1980.

Lane, George, *Daily Life in the Mongol Empire*. Westport, CT: Greenwood Press, 2006; especially Chapter 9, "Religion and the Mongols."

Women in East Asian Religions

Arai, Paula Kane Robinson, *Women Living Zen: Japanese Soto Buddhist Nuns*. New York: Oxford University Press, 1998.

Baptandier, Brigette, *The Lady of Linshui: A Chinese Female Cult*. Kristen Ingrid Fryklund, trans. Stanford, CA: Stanford University Press, 2008.

Batchelor, Martine, and Son'gyong Sunim, *Women in Korean Zen: Lives and Practices*. Syracuse, NY: Syracuse University Press, 2006.

Cahill, Suzanne, *Divine Traces of the Taoist Sisterhood*. Honolulu: University of Hawai'i Press, 2006.

Cole, Alan, *Mothers and Sons in Chinese Buddhism*. Stanford, CA: Stanford University Press, 1998.

Despeux, Catherine, and Livia Kohn, *Women in Daoism*. Honolulu: University of Hawai'i Press, 2005.

Grant, Beata, *Eminent Nuns: Woman Chan Masters of Seventeenth-Century China*. Honolulu: University of Hawai'i Press, 2009.

Iwao, Sumiko, *The Japanese Woman: Traditional Image and Changing Reality*. New York: The Free Press, 1993.

Kelleher, Theresa, "Confucianism," in *Women in World Religions*, Arvind Sharma, ed. Albany: State University of New York Press, 1987, pp. 135–59.

Ko, Dorothy, JaHyun Kim Haboush, and Joan R. Piggott. *Women and Confucian Cultures in Premodern China, Korea, and Japan*. Berkeley: University of California Press, 2003.

Laughlin, Karen, and Eva Wong, "Feminism and/in Taoism," in *Feminism and World Religions*, Arvind Sharma and Katherine K. Young, eds. Albany: State University of New York Press, 1999.

Levering, Miriam, "Women, the State, and Religion Today in the People's Republic of China," in *Today's Woman in World Religions*, Arvind Sharma, ed. Albany: State University of New York Press, 1994, pp. 171–224.

Lowie, Dina, *The Japanese "New Woman": Images of Gender and Modernity*. New Brunswick, NJ and London: Rutgers University Press, 2007.

Mackie, Vera, *Feminism in Modern Japan: Citizenship, Embodiment and Sexuality*. Cambridge and New York: Cambridge University Press 2003.

Meeks, Lori Rachelle, *Hokkeji and the Resurgence of Female Monastic Orders in Premodern Japan*. Honolulu: University of Hawai'i Press, 2010.

Ruch, Barbara, ed., *Engendering Faith: Women and Buddhism in Premodern Japan*. Ann Arbor, MI: Center for Japanese Studies, University of Michigan, 2002.

Sered, Susan Starr, *Women of the Sacred Groves: Divine Priestesses of Okinawa*. New York: Oxford University Press, 1999.

Wong, Eva, "Taoism," in *Her Voice, Her Faith*, Arvind Sharma and Katherine K. Young, eds. Boulder, CO and Oxford, UK: Westview Press, 2003.

Woo, Terry, "Confucianism," in *Her Voice, Her Faith*, Arvind Sharma and Katherine K. Young, eds. Boulder, CO and Oxford, UK: Westview Press, 2003.

6

One God, Many Words and Wonders

The Family of the Three Great Monotheistic Religions and Zoroastrianism

CHAPTER OBJECTIVES

After studying this chapter, you should be able to

- Understand the unique features of monotheistic religions and their relation to the historical period in which monotheism as we know it emerged.
- Discuss the relation of the major Western monotheistic religions to each other.
- Discuss the common features of the history of the Abrahamic faiths.
- Understand Zoroastrianism and its influence on the three great monotheistic religions of the Middle East and the West.

THE NATURE OF MONOTHEISTIC RELIGION

Monotheistic religions are those professing belief in one all-powerful and personal God and in no other gods. The largest and most influential of these faiths today are Judaism, Christianity, and Islam, each of which will be discussed at length in the chapters that follow. Zoroastrianism, small today but of profound historical importance in the development of monotheism, will be presented later in this chapter. Here we are concerned with showing how Judaism, Christianity, and Islam are a family, for they all explicitly go back to one source: the experience of the one God of ancient Israel recorded in the Hebrew Scriptures. The God of Judaism, Christianity, and Islam is the God of Abraham, Moses, and the prophets; these fathers in faith are venerated by all three.

There are other monotheisms, too: Zoroastrianism, Sikhism, and in a sense bhaktic Hinduism and Amidist Buddhism. Overtones of monotheism appear in the primal high god and in nondualist Hinduism and Buddhism. But Judaism, Christianity, and Islam are uniquely bound together in origin and history, as discussed below.

Yet, for all their shared past, we find divergences both among and within the three faiths every bit as great as between one of them and, say, Hinduism or Shinto. Thus, the following discussion of the characteristics of the monotheistic traditions may appear full of qualifications, exceptions, and

Rooftop view of the old city of Jerusalem. On the left is Al-Aqsa Mosque; on the right is the Mount of Olives.

statements that this or that trait is or is not shared by other traditions, too. That is because religious life is simply that way. A distinctive belief, such as a belief in one personal God, does not necessarily make the religion different in practice all the way through—and different people may experience the same religion in different ways. There is certainly a distinctively monotheistic style of relation to God, a relation of interpersonal awe, love, and obedience unshared by polytheism or mystical monism. But not everyone in a monotheistic tradition is really concerned with that sort of relationship to God or feels one ought to be. Rather, for many the practical and socio-logical aspects of a monotheistic religion—worship, law, customs, society, mysticism, the institutional structure of leadership and clergy—are important.

Within the monotheistic family itself, the messages communicated by the practical and social forms, including art and architecture, could hardly be more contrasting. Compare the Muslim mosque in the Alhambra in Granada, Spain, with a Spanish Roman Catholic church. The mosque has clean lines, devoid of pictures or images, the worshippers who pray in it having been oriented only by a bare niche in the wall to the direction of Mecca. Yet far from giving an impression of barrenness, the cool, still arabesque interior of the mosque is, in an almost indescribable way, sym-bolic of fullness and light. It turns thoughts to God, for all that is not God is expunged; nonrepresentational designs of arabesque fantasy line the walls and dome, raising the mind beyond image to dimensions of meditation where God is pure spirit.

The traditional Spanish Roman Catholic church also evokes feelings of wonder and awe, but in a very different way. Here one is typically confronted with a richness and diversity of forms to rival a jewel box. The altar is a gleaming shape of gold and brocade, and behind it the reredos, or decorated screen, reaches to the ceiling as an ornate waterfall of gilt, lights, and statues of saints. Indeed, images are not exhausted at the altar but continue around the church, each in its own little chapel—sorrowful and bleeding Christs; the Blessed Virgin Mary, Queen of the Universe in imperial crown and robe; St. James of Compostela on his horse; and so on. Apostles, monks, nuns, bishops, and kings, each unique yet each part of a larger mosaic, suggest that in this church the power of the beam of monotheistic light is shown by the many different colors and forms into which it breaks as it interacts with the world. This faith appears close to polytheism, though it is not that. Yet neither is it the clear, austere monotheism of Islam, whose simplicity, oddly enough, is matched by the rustic grace of many shrines of that most polytheistic of religions, Shinto.

On the other hand, if one were to compare a New England village Protestant church with an Islamic mosque, one would feel, at least, in the same world. Orders of monks and nuns bring Roman Catholic and Eastern Orthodox Christianity closer to Buddhism, in this particular sociological respect, than to most of their Protestant, Jewish, and Muslim neighbors. So we can see that many different grids can be laid over the religious world to produce different configurations of similarity and difference.

Each monotheistic religion traces itself back to a historical founder, such as Moses, Jesus, Muhammad, or farther East, Zoroaster and Nanak. Monotheism is never a continuation of something growing out of a timeless past, as we saw, for example, in Hinduism. The idea of a special revelation through a known historical figure, who at a known point in time gave an authoritative word from the one personal God, which the monotheistic faith proclaims, seems to be inseparable from monotheistic expression.

Thus, monotheism generally has strong roots in the teaching of great individuals. It tends to stress intense individual commitment and emphasis on verbal expression. This means that the written word, scripture, is of great importance in monotheistic religion. While other religions have also constantly studied and chanted scriptures, in the monotheistic religions, scriptures (characteristically short and clear-cut compared with Vedas or Sutras) are especially decisive statements of law and belief, as well as mystical hymns, monastic rules, and philosophy. They are to be proclaimed universally and are given through the founder, or at least they are fruits of a process started by him, at the pivotal moment.

In keeping with its linkage to the discovery of history, monotheism is inevitably tied to what we have spoken of as a linear concept of time. While the idea has played different roles in different times and places, Zoroastrianism and the three great monotheisms now under discussion have taught that the world was created by God at the beginning of time and is moving toward a climax at an equally definite end: the coming of the **Messiah**, the final judgment, the making of a new heaven and earth. Monotheisms are, in other words, **eschatological**. As noted earlier in Chapter 2, in connection with Christmas, monotheistic religion may carry over many symbols from cosmic religion. But its fundamental view of the world and human life will place these symbols in linear time and history—in this case, the one-time event of Jesus's birth.

THE ABRAHAMIC FAITHS

Judaism, Christianity, and Islam, which together comprise about half the religious world, are a family having, like most families, a common ancestor. That common ancestor was the patriarch Abraham, who, as we will see, according to the Hebrew Bible was led by God out of the Valley of the Two Rivers (modern Iraq) into Promised Land (Israel and Palestine today), where he made a covenant with God; he and his descendants would keep this covenant, and they would be given this land, and through them all the peoples of the Earth would be blessed. Jews see Abraham as their forefather, and his covenant as the beginning of their special relationship with God. For Christians, he inaugurated a historical process that culminated in Jesus Christ and the New Covenant, or New Testament, of their faith. Muslims see the faith of Abraham (Ibrahim in Arabic) as the prototype of the original pure monotheism restored by Islam; he is also ancestor of the Arabian people and the builder of the Kaa'ba or holy shrine in Mecca, now the central place of pilgrimage.

HISTORY OF THE THREE MAIN WESTERN MONOTHEISTIC FAITHS

GENERAL INFLUENCES

Pyramid texts

Zoroaster

Sumerian decline
Egypt and
Mesopotamia
dominant in
Near East

Cyrus
Persian Empire

Trojan War

JUDAISM

Abraham

Early prophets:
Amos, Elijah

Moses

Exodus (c. 1290)
Judges
David (r.c. 1000–962)
Solomon (r. 961–922)

First Temple (c. 957)

Exile (586)
Jeremiah, Isaiah
Return from
captivity in
Babylon (538)
Most wisdom
literature
Apocalyptic
literature

CHRISTIANITY

ISLAM

| 2000 B.C.E. | 1500 B.C.E. | 1000 B.C.E. | 500 B.C.E. |

Alexander
  Hellenistic
    Culture
      Roman Empire
        Byzantine Empire
          Feudalism

Renaissance
  European
    preeminence

    French & American
      revolutions
        Marxism

Maccabees/temple rededication (164)
  John the Baptizer
    Temple destroyed (70)
      Talmud
          Jewish dispersion
            throughout Europe, Asia,
            and N. Africa

Maimonids (1135–1204)
  Zohar (1275)
    Kabbalah

Hasidism
  Reform
    Conservative

                Holocaust
                  State of Israel (1948)

Jesus (c. 30)
  Gospels (60–100)
  Paul (d. 62)
Constantine (r. 312–337)
Council of Nicaea (325)
Augustine (354–430)
Conversion of Europe

Rise of medieval papacy
  Monasticism
    Great Schism (1054)
      Crusades begin
    St. Francis (1181–1226)

    Aquinas (1225–1274)
    Medieval Catholicism

Luther (1483–1546)
Calvin (1509–1564)
Radical reformers
English Ref. (1534)

John Wesley
  (1703–1791)
    American
      Christianity

Muhammad (570–632)
  Muslim conquests
    Rise of Sufism
      Baghdad Caliphate
      (750–1258)
        Avicenna (980–1037)

Al-`Ghazali (d. 1111)
Al-Arabi (d. 1290)
Islam spreads to India,
  Malaysia, Indonesia

Rise of Ottoman Empire

Sufi orders and devotion
  prominent
    Growth of Islam in
      Africa
                Nationalism

| 1 B.C.E. | 500 C.E. | 1000 C.E. | 1500 C.E. | 2000 C.E. |

Even the quarrels in these religions have the special bitterness of family fights, and rarely have other religious hatreds and persecutions matched those among and within them. It is an unhappy fact that family quarrels can often be far more bitter than those with someone who just lives down the street, for it is our family members who we live with most intimately, whom we know best in all their faults and virtues, and in whom we may see ourselves for better or worse.

Nevertheless, these three monotheistic faiths have common features, both historically and practically. Significantly, the **Axial Age** of the founders of these three great monotheistic traditions was also the time that writing emerged in the Middle East. Human consciousness emerged from cosmic religion into a state in which it was apparent that things change and do not change back—that human history is a process in which the new and more complex is always unfolding. This increasing consciousness of history suggests a force, greater than seasonal natural forces, that governs this larger process. Awareness of history also makes possible monotheism's central pivot in history—the distinctive revelation, the prophet, and the scripture—which can give meaning to the new and more complicated historical world.

Common features (as the religion is understood by most ordinary believers) include the following:

- A belief in one personal God (ordinarily identified as masculine) who was Creator of the world, who establishes personal relationships with individuals and peoples, who is in charge of history, and who intervenes in history to work his will.

- A history, or time as we know it, that is linear, running from the creation to the Last Day. Within this time, the religion was established by a special divine revelation to or through individual figures—Abraham, Moses, Jesus, Muhammad—in the Axial Age.

- A succession of prophets who bespeak the message of God for their time, who denounce evil, and who establish the ethical orientation of the religion.

- A definite, relatively compact book of scripture—the Hebrew Scriptures, the New Testament, the Qur'an—believed to be the word of God.

- A belief in angels and in Satan (Iblis in Islam), believed to be the adversary of God.

- An eschatology affirming a future divine judgment and end of history as we know it.

- The origin of each among Semitic peoples in the ancient Middle East.

- The importance of Jerusalem: the holiest city in Judaism and Christianity and the third most important in Islam.

- An orientation toward the desert: Abraham and Moses meet God in the desert; Jesus and Paul retire to the desert before beginning their active ministries; Muhammad receives the Qur'an in a desert cave.

- The importance of the Sabbath, or seventh day, as the day of worship.

- In Judaism and Islam particularly, the importance of a ritual and ethical law, including special provisions about food.

Some of these features, of course, are echoed in other religions, but they are prominent in a particular, family-resemblance way in the three Abrahamic faiths.

Needless to say, there are significant differences among the three religions, as well as modernizing interpretations of them today. These will become evident as we proceed to examine each in more detail in the following chapters.

Finally, it can be noted that monotheisms arise or become socially important in periods of rapid cultural change, that is, in conjunction with the emergence of national cultures and political institutions—ancient Israel, the Arabs at the time of Muhammad, Christianity in the flux of the Roman world and subsequently providing a cultural focus for the dying Roman Empire and the new European nations. (Of course, other religions that emerged in this era, such as Buddhism and Confucianism, have followed the same pattern as the three monotheistic religions.) Monotheism, with its idea of a universal God who can legitimize one sovereign and one law below, helps greatly in a transition from tribalism to nationhood.

But monotheism, by its own intrinsic logic, is also universalist, for if there is but one God with one message, it must be available for all people everywhere. This universality is modified considerably in Judaism, with its idea of the "chosen people" with a special calling by the one God, but even in Judaism, the chosen people are to mediate a blessing to all the families of the Earth. In Islam and Christianity, monotheism and belief in one revelation have at various times served as an ideological undergirding for the creation of empires uniting many cultures and people—even though systematic polytheism can also serve this function. But an international, universal gospel serves especially well as a dynamic for the vigorous missionary expansion of culture. It is usually personal monotheism, then, or a psychologically similar form of Buddhism, such as that of Kamakura in Japan, that strongly missionizes and spreads cross-culturally.

Monotheism is like a river running through religious history. The obscure springs where it arose are located very far back indeed, doubtless with the primordial high God of archaic hunters. The river flows through the fertile lowlands of the inevitable polytheism of archaic agricultural religion, with its emphasis on the marriage of heaven and earth to produce the divine harvest-child, and of the ancient empires uniting the local gods of many tribes and towns into an organized composite. Even then, however, monotheism glimmered faintly in the usual concept of a controlling universal principle associated with an often vague but sovereign deity: Tian, Varuna, Amon, or Zeus. In the ancient Judaism of Abraham, Moses, and the prophets, the river first emerges as a distinct current. It is then fed by tributaries such as Zoroastrianism and Greek philosophy, and at the same time, it spreads out like a delta to form its three main branches—Judaism, Christianity, and Islam. Sometimes these branches flow torrentially. More often they become slow, amiable, domesticated streams and millponds, which coexist comfortably with diverse landscapes of cosmic religion, folk religion, and local culture. But the river never quite stops moving toward a destination.

We will now look at one important example of a monotheistic faith—Zoroastrianism.

ZOROASTRIANISM

Between Mesopotamia and India lies the vast expanse of the land called Persia, or Iran. It is a land of paradoxes: a land nearly empty, yet the homeland of an ancient and immensely creative civilization; a land forbidding, with its endless deserts and stony mountain ranges, yet a country incomparably important as the transmitter of goods and ideas between East and West. Persia had, and Iran still has, a distinctive and splendid culture of its own. It has given its own gift of the **magi** to the religious world in Zoroastrianism, a faith now much diminished in numbers but one which has had immense influence in both East and West. Even after Persia formally submitted to the Muslim crescent, its ancient faith made rich contributions to the art, literature, and thought of Islam.

Zoroaster.

Wherever Persian spiritual influence has been felt, Zoroastrianism has given or reinforced three basic motifs: a battle between light and darkness as respectively good and evil; **eschatology** (or emphasis on an end to history) as a divine judgment and the making of a new purified Earth; and the concept of paradise (derived from a Persian word) as an ideal heavenly realm with a divine court and an abode of the blessed. In turn, these ideas have impelled religion in Persia and elsewhere toward monotheism, ethics, and a sense of the religious meaning of history. These Iranian contributions have done much to move Western religion away from mystical identification with the forces of nature or states of consciousness and toward "ethical monotheism."

Indeed, while the ancient Hebrews believed in one God who judged and punished those with whom he was angry in this life, it was not until after they had had some contact with Persia that such ideas as **resurrection** of the dead at the end of the world, a final judgment, the making of a new Earth, and heaven and hell, became important in the Hebrew Scriptures. These ideas, all part and parcel of Zoroastrianism, entered the biblical tradition after the exile of the Judeans to Babylon, from which they were released by the great Persian king Cyrus; thereafter, contact between Jew and Zoroastrian was frequent. Today, ideas like final judgment and heaven and hell are important to traditional Judaism, Christianity, and Islam. The exact nature and extent of Iranian influence on Judeo-Christian eschatology is a matter of scholarly dispute, and other factors such as Greek and Egyptian influence and indigenous development played a part, too. But nowhere in the ancient world, before late Judaism, Christianity, and Islam, is there an eschatological scenario with the grandeur of the Persian; one cannot doubt its vision would strongly stimulate those who came to know it.

The prophet Zoroaster (or Zarathustra; perhaps 628–551 B.C.E.) was a great son of Persia about whom we have little reliable information, despite all the influence he had. The traditional religion of his people at the time, similar to that of their kin in Vedic India, centered on a sacred fire, the sacrifice of cattle, and a sacred drink, *haoma*, comparable to the *soma* of farther east. But though himself a priest, Zoroaster was profoundly dissatisfied with these rituals and set out wandering in search of greater truth. One day, it is said, a transcendent vision came to him by the side of a mountain stream. He saw **Ahura Mazda**, as he named the high God, in all his splendor and glory above and beyond the old gods. Ahura Mazda was accompanied by six Amesha Spentas, Holy Immortals or Good Spirits, angels or perhaps aspects of God himself. Zoroaster understood then that religion reflects an ongoing universal battle. Ahura Mazda and his forces of light are in combat against the legions of **Ahriman** or **Angra Mainyu**, the evil spirit, also called the Lie, and the *daevas* in his following. Boldly, Zoroaster gave the dark army the name *daeva*, meaning *deva*, or god in the old polytheistic sense. The great battle was a battle between the Truth and the Lie. Ahura is a god of goodness and morality; Ahriman is the Lie. Humans must choose, out of free will, which side they are going to be on.

The battle of good and evil was the most satisfactory way Zoroaster could explain the ill he saw around him. Ahura Mazda, he believed, is only good; therefore he could create only good things and could do only good deeds. Like all who wrestle with the problem of evil and find it very hard to explain its coexistence with an all-powerful good God, Zoroaster and his followers had difficulty explaining theologically the relation between Ahura Mazda and Ahriman—whether they are both eternal realities, meaning that Ahura's power is limited, or whether, as many thought, Ahriman is an offspring of Ahura who rebelled against him. But there is no question of the moral force of what Zoroaster was trying to say: We are combatants in a war of ultimate significance and cosmic dimension. No one can be just neutral; in every area of life, day by day, everyone must decide which lord he or she will side with, the Lord of Light or the Lord of the Lie.

Ahura Mazda, we are told, made this present world as a trap in order that his masterpiece, humankind, might ensnare the enemy. Humans are the bait. By drawing Ahriman, eager to tempt and win over humanity, into Ahura Mazda's world and by then freely choosing the good when tempted, humans weaken Ahriman's force and wear him down so that he can eventually be destroyed.[1] Each person, then, is under judgment. Here the eschatology of Zoroastrianism comes in. While Zoroaster himself undoubtedly had strong eschatological ideas, they have been preserved in a later form. That form centers on reward and punishment (although, in contrast to the Judeo-Christian tradition, punishment in hell is not eternal) and on the making of a new world.

Zoroastrians said that on the fourth day after death, a deceased person had to cross the bridge called Chinvat, which connects humanity with the unseen world. The righteous will find it broad as a highway, and they will take it to enter the House of Song, where they will await the Last Day. Yet to the wicked, the bridge will seem narrow as a razor, and they will fall off it into hell.

But on the Last Day, Ahura Mazda will defeat evil. He will purify the entire world and reign over it. All persons will be raised in a general resurrection. The souls of the wicked, having been purified along with the Earth, will be brought out of hell with their sentences terminated. All will enter together a new age in a new world free from all evil, ever young and rejoicing.

Just before the Last Day, it was said, Zoroaster would return in the form of a prophet conceived of a virgin by his own seed, stored in a mountain lake. A prophet would in fact appear in this way at one-thousand-year intervals during the three thousand years between Zoroaster and the renovation of the world.

The Zoroastrian priests, or *mobeds* (*magi*), were great practitioners of magic as well as profound philosophers. In the days of the Roman Empire (as the New Testament account of the visit of several of them to Bethlehem bears witness), they were a byword for astrologers and wizards. Zoroaster himself was accounted a great magician. However, many of those called *magi* around the ancient Mediterranean were probably only from Mesopotamia, where the occult arts flourished mightily. The Parthian Empire, Rome's great rival, ruled the Persian and Mesopotamian regions from 250 B.C.E to 224 C.E. It was a melting pot of polytheism, Zoroastrianism, Hellenism, Babylonian religion, and teachings from East and West, out of which mystical and esoteric movements bubbled continually.

How widespread or exclusive a religion Zoroastrianism was in this period is disputed. Its heyday as an official, organized religion in Persia was during the Sassanian Dynasty (224–651 C.E.). The **Zend Avesta**, the Zoroastrian scriptures, were then compiled. Although they contain the *Gathas*, hymns ascribed to Zoroaster himself,[2] there is much material of a later and more sacerdotal character.

After the fall of the Sassanian Empire, Persia was converted to Islam, and the minority of Persians who wished to remain faithful to the old religion were under pressure. Some—about 14,000—remain in Iran to this day. Others moved to the more tolerant atmosphere of India. Zoroastrians there, now called Parsees ("Persians") and living mostly around Mumbai (formerly Bombay), number perhaps 150,000.

The Zoroastrianism that survives today in India is life affirming. It says that the world, having been made good by Ahura Mazda, is to be accepted with thanks. One's basic duties are to confess the religion, to take a mate and procreate offspring, and

Fundamental Features of Zoroastrianism

Theoretical

Basic Worldview	The universe is a battleground between good and evil.
God or Ultimate Reality	The good high God, Ahura Mazda, whose adversary is the evil force.
Origin of the World	Made by Ahura Mazda to entrap the evil force.
Destiny of the World	At the end of the age, to be remade as a new, pristine paradise.
Origin of Humans	Judgment after death, sentence to paradise or hell; resurrection in the new world at the end of the age.
Revelation or Mediation between the Ultimate and the Human	Revelation through the prophet Zoroaster; mediation by priests.

Practical

What Is Expected of Humans: Worship, Practices, Behavior	To choose the good, do right, keep pure; to maintain the faith by supporting its rites and institutions.

Sociological

Major Social Institutions	Temples, priesthood, a close-knit community; now mostly Parsees in India.

to treat livestock justly. Asceticism and world negation are not approved. The main places of worship are the clean, attractive fire temples, where a perpetual flame is kept burning as a symbol of the purity of God and is fed five times a day with prayers. Here the scriptures are chanted, and other rituals are performed.[3]

The faith of cosmic battle and renewal given us by Zoroaster, once the religion of a powerful empire, has now greatly declined in numbers. But no decrease can erase its immense influence on the history of religions, an influence that reaches us today in the great monotheistic religions that arose out of the Middle East—Judaism, Christianity, and Islam.

Questions for Review

1. Discuss the nature of monotheism.
2. Explain why the present great monotheistic religions have their origin in the period of the "discovery of history."
3. Tell why those religions have given an important place to a single individual founder, to revelation in history, and to scripture.
4. Discuss the relationship of Judaism, Christianity, and Islam to one another.
5. Discuss Zoroastrianism and its influence on the great monotheistic religions of the Middle East and the West.

Suggested Readings on Monotheism and Zoroastrianism

Monotheism

Kirsch, Jonathon, *God Against the Gods: The History of the War Between Monotheism and Polytheism.* New York: Viking, 2004.

Niebuhr, H. Richard, *Radical Monotheism in Western Culture.* London: Faber & Faber, 1960.

Peters, R. E., *The Voice, the Word, the Books: The Sacred Scriptures of the Jews, Christians, and Muslims.* Princeton, NJ: Princeton University Press, 2007.

Zoroastrianism

Boyce, Mary, *Zoroastrians: Their Religious Beliefs and Practices.* London and Boston: Routledge, 2000.

———, ed. and trans. *Textual Sources for the Study of Zoroastrianism.* Chicago: University of Chicago Press, 1990.

Choksy, Jamsheed K., *Evil, Good, and Gender: Facets of the Feminine in Zoroastrian Religious History.* New York: Peter Lang, 2002.

Clark, Peter, *Zoroastrianism: An Introduction to an Ancient Faith.* Brighton, UK, and Portland, OR: Sussex Academic Press, 1998.

Duchesne-Guillemin, J., *Zoroastrianism: Symbols and Values.* New York: Harper Torchbooks, 1970.

———, *The Hymns of Zarathustra.* Boston: Beacon Press, 1963.

Kreyenbroek, Philip G., *Living Zoroastrianism: Urban Parsees Speak about their Religion.* Richmond, UK: Curzon, 2001.

Zaehner, Robert C., *The Teachings of the Magi.* New York: Oxford University Press, 1976.

_____, *The Dawn and Twilight of Zoroastrianism.* London: Weidenfelt and Nicolson, 1961.

CHAPTER

7

Keeping Covenant with God in History
The Unique Perspective of Judaism

CHAPTER OBJECTIVES

After studying this chapter, you should be able to

- Present the ancient and modern history of Judaism.
- Interpret the basics of Kabbalistic and Hasidic mysticism.
- Discuss the uniqueness of the Jewish religion.
- Explain the importance of practices and observances in Judaism as a way of life.
- Understand the history of the Jewish polity and contemporary views of Judaism, governance, and political life.
- Discuss attitudes toward and the role of women in traditional and contemporary Judaism.

JEWISH UNIQUENESS

Judaism is the first of the three great monotheistic religions; Christianity and Islam are really Judaism's offspring. The Jewish faith, then, has special importance in the history of religion, well out of proportion to its present numbers—for here it all began.

Every religion is unique in its own way, but none is perhaps as distinctive or has as remarkable a history as that of the Jews. Judaism seems always to be the exception to every rule of history, just as Jewish thought or even the mere presence of the Jewish community has so often pointed up the limitations of whatever "universal" truth and practice someone else has tried to lay out. Toward the ancient empires and polytheisms, toward Eastern mysticism and Christian salvationism, toward modern nationalism, dictatorship, Communism, mass culture, and disbelief, Judaism—or at least some segment of Judaism—has always said, "Yes, but...".

It has not opposed all of these things: Judaism has had mystical systems that compare with those of India, and it also has its share of skeptics, and it has been, and is today, expressed in nationhood. But it has always been wary of making an "ism" out of them and then saying that mysticism, or skepticism, or nationalism is the end of meaning and truth. Jews have always had a tendency, fired by centuries of living as a minority "different" from the majority culture of whatever nation they happen to be inhabiting and honed by centuries of hard study of the bristly legal texts of their law, to say, "Yes, but perhaps there's another side. If the majority worldview leaves us out, it's not the complete and final truth."

The questions have not always been put verbally. The mere presence of the Jewish community as an all-too-visible exception to a nation's spiritual and cultural homogeneity has stated them more eloquently than words. Needless to say, such questions, whether verbal or implicit, are not always welcome to those who prefer to leave the waters of a religious or cultural unity unruffled. Jewish "differentness" and the awkward queries it implies for others have given Jews much suffering. But they have persisted in making the question felt and have thereby also pressed human society not to settle for partial truths.

Jews have been exceptions from the beginning of the tradition among the Israelites of the Hebrew Scriptures (which Christians call the Old Testament). They were developing toward the monotheism of a personal God while polytheism became richer and richer among their neighbors.

Why this reliance on one God and the belief that he is the only God and sole king of the universe developed uniquely among the Israelites is hard to say. It may have arisen in part out of the climatic situation of pastoral peoples wandering over the face of the hard desert. That humans are like aliens in these lands, caring for flocks that would die were they not taken to pasture and kept well by shepherds, suggests that God, in the infinite desert sky above, guides his people as a shepherd guides his flock. That the shepherd, like Abraham, sets up an altar and worships the same God in many different places, wherever his wanderings take him, implies that his God is universal, not tied to place or nature like an agricultural deity. (Yet although the early monotheists were pastoralists, many pastoralists did not become monotheists.)

The traditional Jewish interpretation is that God himself, for reasons of his own, selected this people and made himself known to them. This did not mean that he meant to make their life smooth and easy; the call involved heavy responsibilities and frequent suffering. He established a covenant, or agreement, with them that they would worship him, follow his Law, and be faithful to him. On his part, God would preserve them throughout history, even to a consummation at the end of history when the meaning of this relationship would be made known. A core, at least, of Jews have maintained this trust. No people so dispersed as they have been for two thousand years, so much a minority and so persecuted, has ever kept a faith intact for so long.

This faith has not been centered on belief in an afterlife or an experience of salvation in personal or mystical terms or a philosophy or a technique of meditation or even a set of doctrines. It has been centered on awareness of this unique relationship with God, but it has taken different forms at different times.

THE ANCIENT STORY OF JUDAISM

The ancient religion of Syria and Palestine, and no doubt of the earliest Hebrews, was related to that of the major Semitic civilization, the Mesopotamian. These peoples were all Semitic (except the Sumerians of ancient Mesopotamia) and believed in common deities, like the Great Mother Ashtoret (Ishtar) and the dying–rising vegetation god Tammuz or Baal. The account in the Book of Genesis tells us that Abraham, father of the Hebrews, came out of Ur in the Valley of the Two Rivers. This origin affirms the common cultural background. It is reinforced, in turn, by many passages in the Hebrew Scriptures—from the obvious parallels between the flood story featuring Noah in Genesis and that of Utnapishtim in Babylon (though the monotheism of the former and the polytheism of the latter afford quite a difference in tone) to the reference in

Ezekiel to the practice in Israel of "wailing for Tammuz" (of which the **prophet** much disapproved). The difference was that the Hebrews were originally herder Semites, like the Arab Bedouins of today, in contrast to the more numerous and prosperous sedentary agriculturalist Semites of Mesopotamia and of the fertile regions of Syria and Palestine, who worshipped fertility-giving lords of the land such as Baal.

However, the Hebrews—wandering herders originally on the fringes of the great Semitic civilizations—had their own God. They were familiar with Baal, Ashtoret, and Marduk, for from time to time, they must have come into the cities to trade and could not help noticing the massive temples, the powerful priests, and the sacred prostitutes. But for themselves, at sacred stones and mountaintops deep in the desert, they worshipped their own God, Yahweh, who was not tied to one place but could be served wherever the tribe wandered.[1] Moreover, he was not pleased with the offerings from the cultivated field but preferred instead the odor of roasting flesh from the herds of his own poor but free people, as the story of Cain and Abel tells us (Gen. 4:3–5).

It was not until most of the Hebrews themselves became sedentary agriculturalists after settling in the land of Canaan (now, for the most part, Israel and Palestine) that the issue of Baal, Ashtoret, and the other gods of neighbors became acute. Should the tribes stay with a god of the desert after they had become people of the soil, or go to Baal and their kin, whose province seemed to be the agricultural way of life? Many understandably took the latter option.

But there were always those, led by the prophets, who contended that the Hebrews should continue to worship Yahweh even in the new way of life—because Yahweh was particularly connected with the basic rules of their nation, the Law of Moses, and with inspiration (originally more or less shamanistic in type) that seized the nonpriestly spiritual leaders called "prophets." Because the Law of Moses hearkened back to the nomadic period with its simpler ways, the parties favoring continuing loyalty to Yahweh had a rigid, conservative appearance, and the other side doubtless a suggestion of judicious flexibility.

Ironically, the faith in Yahweh had far more future to it and apparently far more potential for adjusting to various cultural levels—from planting to modern industrial life—than Baal. The desert god of the Hebrews lives today, while the Semitic agricultural religion, which seemed the height of sophistication in 800 B.C.E., did not outlive the cultural level it served.

A statement like this is, of course, only one side of the situation. A deity can keep the same name and become different or change names and remain the same. Although the name of Yahweh was kept among the agricultural Hebrews, his worship evolved to include farming feasts and offerings, and these in turn have been retained among Jews long after they became urban.

A fundamental feature of the Hebrew Scriptures is what we have spoken of as a historical or linear concept of time, in which God himself imparts new revelations in history. A picture steadily emerges of the relation between God and the Children of Abraham as a dialogue in which God's faithfulness is constant, but as his people are more or less loyal to their pledge, the situation takes different forms: reward for obedience and punishment for disobedience. It is a history in which God is himself acting and revealing more of himself. The Books of Deuteronomy and Chronicles in particular interpret the history of Israel in these terms, as do the prophets regarding the events of their day. One can think of it as a "graph," with the high peaks representing the moments when Israel was seen as close to God and the low points the periods of apostasy.

The story begins with a very high point, the creation of the world and the placing of Adam and Eve in the Garden of Eden. But suddenly the graph falls to near the bottom as the primal couple disobey God in the matter of eating the forbidden fruit and are expelled from the original paradise. From then on, the dealings of God with the people of Israel are really a part of his plan to bring humankind back to the original high level of the relationship.

The story of Noah, the ark, and the flood tells us that the process began as God exercised judgment toward the fallen world and also mercy, as he saved one righteous family and specimens of the animals, in the destruction of the wicked. But the plan did not really get underway until Abraham and his family were called to leave Ur of the Chaldees, in order to go to a new land that God promised to give Abraham, where he would make of him a mighty nation. This was not for Abraham's sake alone but was part of a plan for the good of the whole Earth, for God said, "[B]y you all the families of the earth will bless themselves" (Gen. 12:1–3). An ancient city of Ur has been excavated. People called Hapiru (which are thought by some to have meant Hebrews) seem to have resided in Ur, a Sumerian capital, before roughly 2000 B.C.E. That is about the time Abraham and his people left for the Promised Land by way of Haran, a city in northern Mesopotamia that was a center of the cult of Sin, the moon god.

This covenant of God with Abraham was ratified by Abraham's sacrificing to God, and it was confirmed by God's giving Abraham a son, Isaac, in his old age. The promise then passed to Isaac and to his son Jacob, also called Israel, the name by which the Hebrew people became known. Under Abraham, Isaac, and Jacob, the line on the graph clearly moved upward; for all their human failings, a new relationship was being established between God and humankind in the patriarchs. Indeed, the sharp difference between Hebrew religion and some others could scarcely be more evident than in the personalities of the father of faith, Abraham, and his son and grandson. They are not mystics or meditators, magicians or philosophers, but shrewd, barely literate, sometimes coarse, obscure wanderers on the edge of civilization, who fought and made love and drove hard bargains and (at least in the case

of the young Jacob) were not above trickery to get their ends. In the Bible, however, it is not the self-purification or spiritual achievements of a yogi or adept or Buddha that makes one available to God to advance his work. It is rather that the one God, with true omnipotence, is able to reach to the "bottom of the barrel" if he wishes and select whomever he wants, however unpromising.

Very hard times came in the latter days of Jacob, and he went down to Egypt (where Jacob's son Joseph had been taken earlier and had risen to power) to try to buy food. But in time the Children of Israel ended up in bondage there, and this was a low point on the graph, for the God of the patriarchs and his worship may have been nearly forgotten.

After four hundred years, we are told, this situation was reversed through the labors of Moses, the most outstanding figure in the Hebrew Scriptures. Moses appears as a member of the oppressed Hebrew class in Egypt who nonetheless advanced high in the service of the pharaoh. But he killed an Egyptian he saw beating a Hebrew and was forced to flee to the deserts of Midian (now northwestern Saudi Arabia), where he kept the flocks of distant kinsmen. There God spoke to him in the vision of a burning bush, and Moses returned to Egypt to lead the Hebrew people out of bondage. He succeeded, and the event was fraught with great drama. Moses and his brother Aaron pronounced ghastly plagues upon Egypt to force the pharaoh's hand, culminating in the death of the firstborn, save those of the Hebrews, who marked their homes with sacrificial blood so that this final plague would pass over them. That night, too, they ate a hurried meal in preparation for the flight from Egypt; this is commemorated in the **Passover** (to be discussed more later).

The **Exodus** has been dated to about 1300 B.C.E., although some put it a couple of centuries or so earlier, and many scholars regard the whole account more as significant legend than history. The narratives of the parting of the Red Sea, so that the escaping slaves could thwart their last pursuers, and of the forty years of wandering in the desert, are well known. At Mount Sinai, in the midst of this trek, the final definition of the covenant, or agreement, between God and Israel was made. Amid the thunder and lightning of a great storm, Moses on the mountain received the Ten Commandments and the rest of the Law recorded in the **Torah** (the first five books of the Bible containing the "Law of Moses"). At this point, the line on the graph moves sharply upward.

Moses himself died before he could lead Israel into the Promised Land. This difficult and warlike task was undertaken by his successor, Joshua. Gradually, a nation was put together from an assortment of restless herding and raiding tribes, who were at best a rough democracy under the leadership of the emergent charismatic prophets called "judges." As the Hebrews adapted to the agricultural way of life indigenous to the area, sedentary institutions like kingship came to seem more and more appealing. Finally, it was written that God had consented to the anointing of the first king, Saul, though Yahweh had expressed only reluctant approval through the prophet Samuel for this development, indicating the conservative nature of the Yahwist and prophetic faith.

Saul, however, proved unworthy of the kingship. He failed to liquidate completely the people and flocks of the Amalek folk, as Samuel said Israel was commanded to do by the Lord. David, who was designated by Yahweh to succeed Saul, began his reign c. 1000 B.C.E. He was succeeded by one of his sons, Solomon.

Under Solomon a great temple to Yahweh was built in which all the ritual prescriptions of the Law of Moses for temple worship could be carried out. From the time of Moses until then, Yahweh had been worshipped in a movable shrine called the **tabernacle**, which contained the written Torah. After Solomon, the kingdom was divided into Israel in the North and Judah, around Jerusalem, in the South, and the glory of the people began to decline.*

During these times the line on the graph, as read by devout later historians, wavered up and down like a fever chart. In the time of Joshua and the judges, it was presumed that whenever Israel won, the Lord was pleased with them; but when Israel lost, it did so because there had been sin. But then came the early prophets (such as Samuel, Elijah, Elisha, and Nathan) and after them, the writing prophets (Amos, Isaiah, Jeremiah, and the rest), who argued that this was not necessarily the case. The prophets were apparently originally members of a class of seers who entered into some sort of visionary, divinatory trance, not wholly unlike a shaman's, and there they gave out the direct word of God for a situation. As in the case of Samuel reproving Saul even as the king stood victorious over the Amalekites or of Nathan reproving David at the height of his glory for having taken Bathsheba, another man's wife, the word of the Lord that came through these envoys could well indicate that God was displeased even when his people seemed successful. It could still happen that they were forgetting the fullness of God's commandments. Even in prosperity, they might, as Amos said, be too much "at ease in Zion" and sell the needy for a pair of shoes.

From a wider religious perspective, it may be pointed out that the Hebrew Scriptures characteristically offer a "minority report" on the matter of whether

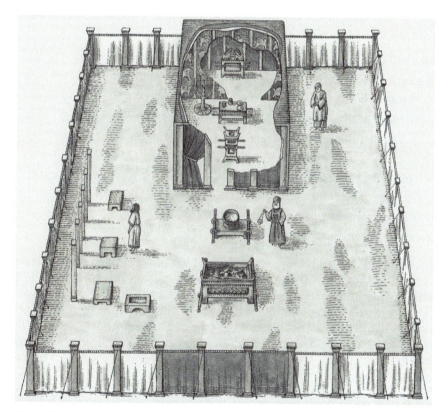

Illustration of the tabernacle.

---

*We must point out that the literal historicity of the story up to about this point—the years of the divided kingdom—is subject to much debate. There are those, of course, who say it must all be accepted as factual, usually on religious grounds. Others point out that there is no archaeological or other hard evidence for all or even much of the narrative before the tense times of Israel and Judea leading up to the Exile. Then, or during the Exile and afterward, most of the actual writing was done. What went before, they say, including the tales of David and Solomon and everything earlier than those rulers, must be taken as tradition rather than strict history—though the narratives are no less significant for that. But scholarly matters such as these are largely beyond the scope of this book.

prosperity is necessarily a sign of God's favor, as they do on several issues. One of the Psalmists is compelled to ask, understandably, why in God's world, the ungodly, despite their arrogance and venality, so often seem to prosper (Ps. 73: 1–14). The Book of Job, among the profoundest books in the Hebrew Scriptures, tells the story of Job, a righteous and honest man who was caused to suffer terribly, but who refused to follow the advice of his friends and confess he was suffering because of his sins, when he honestly did not believe they were proportionate to his ordeal. Finally, God revealed to him the splendor of Heaven and Earth, the magnificence of the first day "when the morning stars sang together, and all the songs of God shouted for joy" (Job 38:7). Then Job recognized a mystery deeper, brighter, and more joyous than he could comprehend, and he worshiped it.

The low point in this period came in 586 B.C.E., when the Babylonians took Jerusalem, destroyed the temple, and carried off leading citizens to Babylon for a life of exile and servitude. Prophets like Jeremiah blamed this on the failings of the king and the nation. When, some decades later (the year 538 B.C.E. is often given), Cyrus of Persia took Babylonia and allowed the exiles to return and the temple to be rebuilt (an event celebrated in Isaiah 40 to 66 and described in Nehemiah and Ezra), it seemed a marvel beyond hope or belief, a victory of God when all was darkest, and the "marvel" is so sung in Isaiah 58:8 and many passages of similar power:

> *Then shall your light break forth like the dawn,*
> *and your healing shall spring up speedily;*
> *your righteousness shall go before you,*
> *and the glory of the Lord shall be your rear guard.*

Or in a Psalm like 126:

> *When the Lord restored the fortunes of Zion,*
> *we were like those who dream.*
> *Then our mouth was filled with laughter,*
> *and our tongue with shouts of joy.*

Yet for all that, the religious experience of Israel was not fully satisfied with the "return" from Babylon, for it was also a return, like all such returns, to the ambiguities of ordinary life in history. There were new problems and new challenges. These were faced by the new temple and, even more significantly, by a new affirmation of Judaism as a religion of the Torah, or of the Law of Moses, and by new developments in literature and belief. The last centered on a literature of wisdom and the growth of a belief in a Last Day and a Messiah. But first let us look at the story of those times.

FROM THE SECOND TEMPLE TO THE TALMUD

Some twenty years after the first Jews were permitted to return to Jerusalem by Cyrus the Great in about 538 B.C.E., the foundations of a smaller but nonetheless adequate second version of the temple were laid in the Holy City by Zerubbabel and Haggai. It was completed in 515 B.C.E. But the work of rebuilding Jewish society in the land of Israel—of which the reconstruction of the temple was an important aspect—is epitomized in two men who subsequently were leaders in the religious and political spheres, respectively—Ezra and Nehemiah. Each has his book in the Hebrew Scriptures. The promulgation of the Torah, or Law, by Ezra in 444 B.C.E., together with the people's assent to it (Nehemiah 8 to 10), is of immense religious importance, for it vividly displays the changes that exile and distance from the site of the temple had wrought in Judaism.* Though the temple was rebuilt, the religion became more and more what it would ultimately become, a religion of **synagogues** ("gathering places"), where worship consisted of prayer and the study of the Scriptures without sacrifices.

Menorah, yarmulke, prayer book, and tallith (prayer shawl); items used in Jewish practice.

Although details are unclear, tradition has it that the text of the Torah and eventually all the Hebrew Scriptures were edited and finalized over these years by an assembly of learned scholars called the Great Synagogue, founded by Ezra. These developments must have been accelerated by exile, when Jews had to make do religiously without temple rites and were far from their homeland. Instead it was necessary to gather, to pray, and to sing what they could recall or had written down, to hear the words of the wise and of the books proclaiming the Law and the words of men of God, to eat and drink and hold festival in accordance with the Law, and to remember. This is the essence of synagogue life to this day. Though the temple was rebuilt, more and more Jewish communities near and far worshipped mainly in the synagogue style, and within a few centuries this form of worship prevailed.

Here is that history. After the "return," the land of Israel remained a province of the Persian empire, locally ruled under the emerging law by the chief priests of the restored temple and by lay leaders such as Nehemiah, a Jew who had risen high in the civil service and arranged to have himself appointed governor of Judea. In 331 B.C.E., Alexander the Great conquered the Persian empire and, with it, the homeland of the Jews. Alexander's empire, after his early death, was divided among his leading generals, Egypt going to the house of Ptolemy, and Syria to that of Seleucus. Palestine went at first to Egypt but was later transferred to the Seleucids. In 168 B.C.E., the Syrian ruler Antiochus IV, seeking to impose Greek civilization on all his people, desecrated the temple and prohibited the practice of Judaism.

This led to a rebellion much celebrated in Jewish lore. The Maccabee brothers mounted a campaign to drive out the oppressor. Then, in 164 B.C.E., they relit the lamps of the holy temple, a joyous event commemorated in the festival of **Hanukkah** (to be

---

*Most scholars believe that the Law read by Ezra at this time was essentially what is known as the Priestly Code, the legal, ritual, and moral prescriptions contained in the Book of Leviticus and large parts of Exodus and Numbers, or a portion of that code. Much earlier, before the exile, the righteous King Josiah (r. 640–609 B.C.E.) had promulgated a book of the Law, which was probably essentially the biblical Deuteronomy. Certainly the Law has a long history, much of it now lost, prior to Ezra. But Ezra's recitation and the people's response to it is of immense importance, for it represents the triumph of the Torah—and so of the Torah's God—as the supreme, unquestioned authority in normative Jewish religion. Before, especially before the purgation of exile, we read much of the admixture of Yahwist religion with various forms of paganism and idolatry. On another level, the charisma of the prophets, profoundly inspiring and disturbing, had reached its height in figures such as Isaiah, Jeremiah, and Ezekiel before and during the exilic era. It had then shared pride of place with the emerging Torah tradition, but it now quickly fades also, subordinated to a scriptural text that contained (though in legal rather than poetic form) the Yahwist and Mosaic values for which the prophets had stood and, in time, their own "books." (The poetic tradition was perpetuated in the "wisdom" books of the Bible, such as the Psalms, large parts of which are certainly postexilic.) After Ezra, we hear nothing of idolatry within Judaism and very little of fresh prophecy. Judaism from this point on was basically the religion of the Torah and its elucidation, and Jewish identity was intimately bound up with the life of the Torah.

"248 Chapter 7 • Keeping Covenant with God in History

discussed more later). For over a century (166–63 B.C.E.), Judea existed as a tiny and precariously independent state under first the Maccabees and then their descendants, kings of the Hasmonean house, who increasingly combined high priestly and royal functions in Jerusalem. Rome brought the Holy Land into its empire in 63 B.C.E., ruling sometimes directly, sometimes through client kings such as Herod the Great and his lineage.

During these difficult years, the Jewish religious tradition, based on the now-established Torah, was being consolidated by a succession of distinguished **rabbis**, men such as Hillel, Gamaliel, and those of the school known as the Pharisees. They composed commentaries and case applications of the Law, in part validated by the contention of the Pharisees that there was an oral law given to Moses as well as the written, the former living as Judaism's succession of teachers and giving guidance to their exposition of the latter. These labors were compiled in the **Mishnah** (c. 200 B.C.E. to 200 C.E.), a compilation of stories that fill in the gaps in the oral Torah, and the **Gemara** (c. 200 to 500 C.E.), rabbinical commentaries on the Mishna to connect it to the written Torah; together they make up the great multivolumed text known as the **Talmud**. Jewish scholars prepared out of close argumentation these vast commentaries on the Law, which made it both precise and flexible enough to be applicable to the new times in which Jews were more likely to be an urban minority than rural farmers and herders.

Next to the Scriptures, no book is of more importance to Judaism than the multivolumed Talmud. It is a vast and ever-fascinating collection of religion, folklore (**aggadah**), ethics and jurisprudence (the Law, **halakhah**), and it is the text to which all learned Jews instinctively turn first for illumination of the tradition's thought on virtually any issue, though its role is understood differently by liberal and orthodox authorities.*

The new age brought forth other responses, too. Jewish tradition divides the Hebrew Scriptures into three parts: the Torah; the Prophets, which also includes historical books; and the Writings, containing other books of history, such as Ruth and Esther, as well as the "wisdom" literature (Psalms, Proverbs, Job, Ecclesiastes, and the Song of Solomon). Although the Wisdom Books incorporate much preexilic material, they were compiled in their final scriptural form in the days of the Second Temple or even later. These works are often called Wisdom Books because they are primarily concerned with presenting timeless words of devotion, reflection, moral advice, and philosophy. They are remarkably diverse. To one whose view of the Bible is chiefly shaped by those parts concerned with God's Law, judgment on sin, or calls to faith, passages in the Wisdom Books may seem amazingly skeptical or speculative.

Belief in the eventual coming of the **Messiah** also has preexilic roots, but it flourished most in the atmosphere of extreme alternating hope and disillusionment and of the precarious national existence that characterized Israel after the Return. Prophetic proclamation of God's judgment led to growing expectation of a final,

---

*It is important to point out that Jewish Orthodoxy does not mean the kind of direct, unmediated adherence to the scriptural text characteristic of Christian fundamentalism. Rather (as in the case of also so-called Muslim fundamentalism, with its insistence on strict adherence to the *shari'ah*, the Islamic law developed case by case over centuries by its recognized interpreters), Orthodoxy does not mean individual recourse to the original biblical Law but acknowledgment both of its divine inspiration and its legitimate interpretation and application by a recognized succession of rabbis, down to the rabbinical courts operative in Orthodox Judaism today. The findings of this succession are recorded in the Talmud and the later "responsa" of eminent jurisprudents. Rabbinical decisions, like those of any court, are bound to honor and take into account precedent, though variations along accepted lines may be mooted. The "fundamentalism" of Orthodox Judaism, then, lies in the literalistic acceptance of Talmudic and subsequent rabbinical teaching, not directly in scriptural literalism. Though the Hebrew Torah is believed to be literally inspired by God, word by word and even letter by letter, its explication is beyond the power of the unaided individual human intellect and requires the authoritative guidance of the tradition.

culminating judgment of the entire world and the making of a new, purified heaven and earth. Related to this idea was the believing hope that, before that great event, a Messiah (the word means "anointed one," because anointing with oil was the way of designating a king in ancient Israel) or sublime hero and king would be sent by God. He would defeat Israel's enemies and rule in perfect justice and peace. Many expected even nature to be bountiful beyond imagining in the messianic age.

MEDIEVAL AND MODERN JUDAISM

Just as one sees changes in Judaism from the desert wanderers' religion of Abraham or Moses to the temple of Solomon, the spiritual center of a kingdom, and a religion of a largely farming society, one also sees Judaism has continually adjusted to new situations through its long subsequent history. As we have seen, there was the destruction of the first temple and the exile to Babylon, but the temple was rebuilt. It was destroyed again by the Romans in 70 C.E., and from then on Judaism survived in **diaspora**—that is, in many widely dispersed communities. During this time, Judaism made its transition to a way based on the home-centered ethical and ceremonial precepts of the Law, without the temple with its bleating animals, its heavy smells of blood and incense, and its richly vested priests. The transition was not as difficult as it might seem, for synagogue practice and study had already taken hold everywhere except in Jerusalem. Pilgrimage to the temple had once been the main bond of worldwide Jewry. Now cohesion lay in the "Fence of the Torah," following the Law as interpreted by the Talmud, which gave inwardly, and in the eyes of others, a separate identity in a world of change and confusion. There were other kinds of flexibility, too; Philo Alexandria (first century C.E.), for example, interpreted the Scriptures allegorically in terms of Platonic philosophy.

The "Fence of the Torah" style of Judaism persisted through the Middle Ages and into modern times, as Jews dwindled to very small numbers in their homeland (first ruled by Christians and then by Muslims). But Jews became important minorities in

A lone Hassidic Jew prays next to two schoolboys at the Western or "Wailing" Wall.

European and Near Eastern cities and spread as far as India and China. When they did not suffer persecution, they generally flourished, and many Jews rose to prominence in Christian or Muslim societies. Their education and diligence, fruits of the careful study that the Law required, were frequently superior to that of their neighbors.

Several new developments colored medieval Judaism. The form of Jewish mysticism called the **kabala** had its supreme expression in the Zohar, or Book of Splendor, probably composed within a developing tradition by Moses de Leon in Spain about 1275.[2] On the basis of finding deeper, allegorical meanings in the words and letters of the Hebrew Torah that point to metaphysical realities, it held that God in himself is infinite and incomprehensible but that his attributes provide windows of insight into God as he relates to humanity. As topics of meditation, certain basic attributes of God drawn from the Scriptures are arranged into a pattern of male–female polarities and on different levels in the hierarchy of spiritual things called the "kabalistic tree." Meditation on their dynamic interaction provides a subtle and often profound spiritual path.

Herbert Weiner, a Reform rabbi who some years ago investigated Kabbalistic mysticism and wrote a book about his search entitled *9 1/2 Mystics* (he himself was the half-mystic), started his book by citing a favorite image of Kabbalists. "The primal light, they say, is simply too bright for finite eyes to behold. Paradoxically, it becomes more communicable—if somewhat dulled and altered—as it is 'veiled' and transmitted through darkening vessels." (See endnote 3 below.) He tried to peek a little behind those veils.

In Jerusalem, Weiner discovered a synagogue of Kabbalist practitioners, but he found that, like adepts of esoteric pathways in many religions, at first they discouraged outside inquirers until it could be ascertained how serious they were. But in time Weiner spoke with a rabbi, David ha-Cohen, considered an authority in the field.

Approaching this reverend individual's home, Weiner thought of how the Kabbalists say that everything in the world above has its analogue below. The city of Jerusalem in which he was walking was only a pale reflection of the heavenly Jerusalem on high, the rabbi's garden but a poor imitation of the eternal Garden of Eden.

Rabbi ha-Cohen, who turned out to be more cherubic than intimidating, warned Weiner of the dangers of excessive or premature Kabbalistic study, telling him tales of persons who had come to madness or worse through its pursuit. Nonetheless, the two got into a discussion of a few basics. The difference between Kabbala and Eastern mysticism, with its view that the apparent world is maya, "illusion," is that for the Jewish esotericist, the phenomenal world is indeed real. But its mountains, seas, and people are only like the visible part of an iceberg, and the substance above, beneath, and behind them is far bigger than the fragments of reality we see with our everyday eyes, perhaps bigger than we can imagine and far more powerful than we likely anticipate if we begin to try to manipulate the universe's mighty but invisible levers.

The distinguished rabbi left Weiner with a blessing, then added: "Not a finger is moved here...but it is noticed above." (See endnote 3 below.)

Since the 1960s when Weiner's book was published—and partly because of its impact—Kabbala has become popular among both Jews and non-Jews in Europe and in America as well as in Israel, with a number of groups and institutions devoted to its study on various levels. Though many persons and organizations have come and gone in this mysterious world, and possibly some have found the Kabbala more than they could handle, it has become a permanent part of the face of Judaism today as it had in the Middle Ages.

Kabbalism had many areas of influence—from magic to messianic movements. The most important is the more popular form of Jewish mysticism called **Hasidism**.

This is a pietistic movement that started in Eastern Europe in the eighteenth century through the teaching of Ba'al Shem Tov (1700–1760). Hasidism is a feeling-oriented reaction against rabbinic emphasis on learning and legalism and against stifling social conditions. It teaches Jews to follow the Law but to make it an expression of fervent love for God. (The colorful stories and doctrines with which its venerated teachers explain the meaning of love for God and the symbolism of ritual law are deeply dyed with kabalistic lore. They emphasize pious love and the wisdom of the person of simple devotion.) Music, dancing, and even uncontrolled ecstatic behavior are frequently part of Hasidic worship. Small but vigorous groups of Hasidic background, such as the Lubavitcher movement, which has done much to encourage a return to Orthodox practice, are still active in Israel and America.[3]

Menorah with the Star of David, a symbol of Judaism.

One of the many sayings attributed to great Hasidic rabbis is this: "When the poor, ignorant village peddler returns to town shortly before dark, and, ignoring his fatigue and hunger, hastens to the House of Prayer to recite the afternoon and evening services, then the Seraphim and Ophanim [Wheels of Fire or Thrones, a class of angelic beings] tremble before his worship, for it splits the very Heavens."[4]

Here we see that it is not great learning, whether legal or Kabbalistic, that is important but inner dedication and fervor. Yet the worship and the way of life is Orthodox; the peddler does not change that but only the dedication with which he performs it despite weariness. In the process, he creates an example that is on the lips of those revered teachers, sometimes almost worshiped in themselves, who became the driving spirits of Hasidic movements.

Another strand of modern Judaism, the liberal and rationalistic, has roots in both certain ancient schools and the thought of the medieval philosopher Moses Maimonides (1135–1204), whose commentaries on the Talmud and law codification made use of Greek philosophy and presented a smooth, logical face to the faith. It was not until the eighteenth-century Enlightenment, however, that this lineage exercised its full influence on Jewish life. Particularly in Germany, Jewish leaders and thinkers, such as Moses Mendelssohn (1729–1786) emphasized acculturation to non-Jewish European life and the critique and defense of Judaism through philosophy. In the end—although this was not Mendelssohn's intention—many Jews in Western Europe became more or less secularized, like countless Christians of the same period, more interested in the mainstream of European culture than in the Law and the synagogue.

Modern Jewish life is a conflux of several forces. It has been touched by traditional Orthodoxy, Hasidism, and Enlightenment secularization and liberalism, as well as the many cultural milieus in which Jews in the diaspora can be found. For example, customs and styles of worship of the **Ashkenazi** (Jews from Northern and Eastern Europe) differ from those of **Sephardim** (Jews from the Iberian Peninsula) and Eastern Jews. It is also influenced by the bitter effects of persecution in Russia in the late nineteenth and early twentieth centuries and by a milder but ugly anti-Semitism widespread in Europe and America, restricting Jewish participation in many areas of life.

Most horrible of all Jewish experiences was the Holocaust under Nazism, in which some six million Jews perished before and during World War II, and traditional

Jewish life in Europe was devastated. All Jewish life since then has been interwoven with sorrowful remembrance of this terrible event and with the attempt to cope with it. It has deeply affected Jewish–Christian dialogue.

JUDAISM IN AMERICA

Immigration has made America a reservoir of Jewish strength. Today, that land is home to some six million Jews—more than contemporary Israel (4.5 million).

American Judaism is not homogeneous but is divided into four main traditions. **Orthodox Judaism** teaches the full following of the Law, or Torah, and is quite traditional in Talmudic scholarship, theology, and forms of festival and worship. **Reform Judaism**, which calls its places of worship "temples" rather than "synagogues," has roots in the German Enlightenment experience. It is liberal in attitude, oriented more to the prophets than the Law, and believes the essence of Judaism does not involve following the Law legalistically. Many Reform Jews follow it hardly at all, save for major festivals, though they refer to its underlying principles in thinking about ethical and moral questions. Between Reform and Orthodox is **Conservative Judaism**, which takes Jewish Law and history seriously as a guide to life but believes that the Law's provisions can and should be adjusted to suit the conditions of modern living. **Reconstructionist Judaism**, which has roots in humanism and is the most radical in terms of reform, holds that Judaism should be ever-evolving to meet the challenges of the contemporary age, and it rejects "chosenness" (discussed further later) in favor of an all-inclusive Judaism.

The discussion below of the beliefs, practices, and sociological elements of Judaism reflects American Judaism in all its diversity, as well as Judaism around the world.

JEWISH BELIEFS

Judaism is often presented as a religion in which the importance of formal, theological doctrine is minimized. In a real sense this is true. No dogma is as significant to most Jews as adherence to the Jewish community, a relationship many feel better expressed through practice—participation in the **Sabbath** worship, festivals, customs, and observances traditional to the community—and through a living sense of being part of the Jews' long history, than in creedal affirmations. Jewish theoretical and ideological expression, on the part of both theologians and ordinary believers, has accordingly been remarkably free and varied. Practitioners of Judaism as a religion, or as a communal tradition, have ranged from literal believers in God as presented in the Scriptures to agnostics and atheists.

Nonetheless, it is fair to say that over the centuries a broad theological consensus has survived among the majority of serious Jews. A conventional touchstone for its delineation has been thirteen principles of faith put down by the great medieval thinker Moses Maimonides:

1. God is Creator and Guide.
2. God is One in a unique way.
3. God does not have a physical form.
4. God is eternal.
5. God and God alone is to be worshipped.
6. God has revealed his will through the prophets.
7. Moses is the greatest of the prophets.

8. The Torah was revealed to Moses.

9. The Torah is eternal and unchanging.

10. God is all-knowing.

11. God gives rewards and punishments.

12. The Messiah will come.

13. The dead will be resurrected.

Whether interpreted strictly or liberally, these principles appear to have four main emphases. First, they affirm the existence of a God who is creator and sustainer of the world and who is absolutely one without a second. This expresses the uncompromising monotheism that is Judaism's central religious theme and most distinctive gift to humanity. Second, the principles affirm that this God is an active God, in some way continually involved in human history. He has revealed his will through prophets and Scripture in the context of history and is preparing a messianic culmination of history. Third, they affirm the complete religious adequacy of Judaism, its greatest prophet—Moses—and its Torah. Fourth, they powerfully elucidate depth, meaning, and righteous judgment in individual human life, as they affirm that God knows each life thoroughly, bestowing rewards and punishments to each in a manner not fully specified. By speaking of personal resurrection, Maimonides avows the eternal significance of each individual life.

Like all other creeds, this statement cannot be wholly detached from its historical context. In this case, Judaism lived amid Christianity and Islam. The opening stress on God's oneness, incorporeality, and eternity as metaphysical categories reflects the profound influence of Greek thought on the philosophical expression of all three faiths and so establishes common ground. On the other hand, the principles indirectly distinguish Judaism from Christianity by making no allowance for the Trinity or the Incarnation of God in Christ, insofar as these tenets compromise God's oneness and bodilessness. They also clearly deny both Christian and Muslim assertions that Moses and the Torah were succeeded by greater prophets and more perfect scriptural revelations; and of course they disallow that the Messiah has already come. (Asked about the last point, most Jews will respond that while they much admire the Jew called Jesus as a heroic figure and great rabbi, he was not the kind of Messiah they expected and still anticipate, for after two thousand years the world is still painfully far from the reign of peace, justice, and abundance that prophecy declared the Messiah's age would bring.)

At the same time, some dimensions of Judaism are not mentioned in the principles. Most conspicuous in its absence is the concept of Jews as a "chosen people" having a special covenant relationship with God. As we have seen in connection with the traditional establishment of that covenant with Abraham, the momentous pact was not made with that patriarch alone but with all his descendants, and it was not made for their sake alone but for the blessing of all the human race. For Jews this "specialness" has certainly brought as much or more suffering as blessing by any ordinary worldly measure, though its inner, spiritual worth is immeasurable in such terms. In any case, most Jews are well aware of their peculiar role as the blessers and, often to extreme extents, sufferers of the world, and most religious Jews give this experience special meaning as the product of their divine chosenness.

The problem of combining existence in historical time, so inseparably intertwined with "chosenness," with Judaism's transcendent monotheism has been a crucial issue in modern Jewish thought. This has been all the more true since recent history has dealt Jews both opportunity and horror to unprecedented degrees—the emancipation of the Jews in early nineteenth-century Europe, the Enlightenment, the movement into the mainstream of Western culture, the immigration to the New World, the massacres and the unspeakable Nazi Holocaust, and the rebirth of Israel as a state. In all this, the God of Israel has been left behind by some, as though irrelevant to such new ways of life or such raw terror. Yet, some would say, never has the heart of Jewish faith been more needed. Here are three examples.

Franz Rosenzweig (1886–1929) insisted that divine revelation within historical time must be central to any religion that truly revolves around God and is not merely philosophical idealism or moral consciousness. This revelation is a relation between the eternal God and finite, time-bound individuals, a discourse between the divine subject as (to us) Thou and the dependent and autonomous I.

This "I–Thou" relationship became the key concept of Rosenzweig's friend Martin Buber (1878–1965), who was also heavily influenced by Hasidism. Without diminishing the importance of the divine–human I–Thou, Buber made the I–Thou concept a keystone of all authentic interpersonal relationships, in which the other is not simply an "it" to be used like an impersonal object, but a "Thou," full of inwardness and subjectivity like that of the "I."

Abraham Joshua Heschel (1907–1972), a Jewish thinker whose ideas often took mystical wing under kabalistic and Hasidic inspiration, celebrated the holiness hidden in all things and the possibility of an intense, passionate relationship between God and humans. Jewish practices sanctifying the whole of nature and life facilitate both realizations. Yet, as we shall see, Heschel also wrote of Judaism's particular emphasis on the manifestation of the sacred through time, whether in the stream of history or the annual round of festivals and holy days.

We must now turn to such sacred observances in Judaism. Before we leave the company of wise men, however, we might make one final observation: Both Buber and Heschel shared to the full the vicissitudes of modern Jewry. Both were raised in the richly traditional, scholarly Jewish culture of Eastern Europe; both were compelled to leave the Europe of Hitler's storm troopers to end their days in two relatively safe havens for Jews—Buber in Israel and Heschel in the United States.

JEWISH LIFE

Let us examine some of the specifics of Jewish life. It should be remembered always that there are various degrees of observance and various attitudes toward the importance of, for example, the dietary laws and strictness of Sabbath keeping. The differences are not only between the serious and the lax. Jews of equal inner commitment, insofar as this can be gauged, may place the emphasis on different strands of the tradition. (Differences of these kinds are, of course, found among the various traditions of all major religions.)

But throughout all of Jewish life a special chord reverberates. It is made up of a tradition of respect for education, an awareness of history, and a sense of being an often-persecuted minority group, as well as the specific festivals, customs, and religious rites of Judaism. The close family and community life of Judaism reflects this tone, through whichever of several possible styles of Jewish life it is expressed. There is always some sense of Jewish identity, too. It has often been commented that every Jew, however nonpracticing and secularized, knows that he or she is a Jew.

The sociological bedrock of Jewish life is the family. With only very few possible exceptions, such as the prophet Jeremiah and perhaps the Essene communities of Hellenistic times, religious celibacy has had no place in Judaism. One of the most consistent themes of all Jewish history, after the theme of being a special called-out covenant people, is that of the holiness of marriage and the procreation of children: a fundamental religious duty for the wisest and holiest rabbi as well as for any other

A Jewish wedding with the bride and groom under the chuppa (wedding canopy), while holding the ketubah (wedding contract).

Jew. It is not a concession to the weakness of the flesh but a sacred, as well as a joyful, way of life and a part of the covenant:

> The whole world depends on the holiness of the union between man and woman, for the world was created for the sake of God's glory and the essential revelation of His glory comes through the increase of mankind. Man must therefore sanctify himself in order to bring to the world holy people through whom God's glory will be increased....[5]

It is in the family, then, that religious observances begin. The Sabbath, festivals, and the dietary rules all involve, especially in Orthodox tradition, much more that is done at home than in the synagogue with the community as a whole: the Sabbath meal and prayers; holiday blessings and customs, such as Hanukkah lights and the Passover meal in which the head of the family is the religious leader; the hours spent preparing food according to religious regulation. Beside this, the synagogue is not where religion "happens" so much as where one receives instruction and inspiration to make it happen in its true locus, the home. But under the changed conditions of modern life, the tendency, especially in the more liberal traditions, is to express Jewish identity more through synagogue, temple, or community participation and less through the complicated and time-consuming home actions in their traditional forms. Even so, it must be emphasized that the home can still be a place where Jewish identity in its moral and cultural meaning is learned and deeply felt.

The cornerstone of Jewish practice is the observance of the Sabbath. This period of twenty-four hours from sunset Friday to sunset Saturday commemorates the Lord's day of rest after the work of creation, and it is intended for the rest and refreshment of both body and soul. On the Sabbath, no work is done, and there are feast and celebration and nourishment for the body and mind and soul at the table and in the synagogue. Far from being an onerous burden or a time of negative prohibition, the classical Jewish literature sees the Sabbath as a bountiful gift to God's people, as a lovely bride to be welcomed with eager love.[6] This act of love is encouraged for married couples on the Sabbath night as a culmination of the celebration and welcoming of the Sabbath bride.

Traditional Sabbath observance begins with concluding one's ordinary business, bathing, and putting on fresh garments reserved for that festive day on Friday afternoon. After sundown, the previously prepared Sabbath meal is eaten, with traditional Sabbath dishes and prayers and blessings over the food and the full cup of wine.

On the next day, there is public worship in the morning and late afternoon. Synagogue or temple worship consists basically of reading from the Torah and the other Scriptures, prayers, and chants, but the atmosphere of the worship varies considerably from one tradition to another. In Orthodox synagogues, men and women remain on separate sides; the liturgy is in Hebrew; and the preservation of many ritual customs, as well as in some cases a certain Hasidic exuberance expressed, perhaps, in swaying or dancing to the music, tells us that this is the Judaism most in continuity with that of Old World Europe. In Reform temples, the service will be plain and dignified, with more emphasis on the sermon. Conservative synagogues will follow a middle course. However, Reform and Conservative worship, like that of some once-staid Christian churches, is today in a new way discovering the Jewish heritage of lively music, dance, and chant, especially in services for young people. Reconstructionist services employ many traditional practices while being liberal in content.

The most important object in any Jewish place of worship is the Torah, the scroll of the Law, in its large ornamented box, called the Ark, at the front of the hall. A lamp continually burns before it. Opening the door and curtains in front of the Torah and finally removing it from the case for reverent reading are major actions in the drama of the service.

Items used or eaten during the Passover seder.

FESTIVALS AND PRACTICES

Besides the regular Sabbath worship, the Jewish year is marked by several festivals. Although not really as important as the weekly celebration of the Sabbath (only the Sabbath is mentioned in the Ten Commandments), many Jews today observe the **High Holy Days** (Rosh Hashana and Yom Kippur) and the Passover. The holidays can be divided into three groups. Because they follow the partially lunar Jewish calendar, the dates (like that of the Christian Easter) vary from year to year.

First are the High Holy Days, or "Days of Awe," which come in the autumn. **Rosh Hashana**, literally "Head of the Year," is kept as the anniversary of the creation and is the Jewish New Year's Day. Then, after a sacred season of ten days for repentance, comes **Yom Kippur**, the Day of Atonement. It is said to be the day when God reckons up the sins of every person for the previous year and, accordingly, sets their fate for the coming year. For some Jews, God's reckoning is only a metaphor, but it nevertheless sets the tone of Yom Kippur, a day when Jews assess themselves

A Bar Mitzvah in Jerusalem.

Jews celebrating Succoth at the Lion's Gate in Jerusalem.

in their hearts and determine how to amend their lives. The customs of the day create a backdrop for this inward strife and turning: fasting for twenty-four hours and a day-long synagogue service full of haunting, dirgelike music, and corporate confession.

Three happier festivals are basically grounded in the agricultural society of ancient Israel and fit the seasonal cycle of all archaic agricultural religion yet also have meaning as commemorating the mighty acts of God on behalf of Israel as recorded in the Bible. They orient the believer to God's work both in nature and in history. These are Passover in the spring, **Shavuot** in late spring or early summer, and **Sukkot** in autumn.

The Passover, or *Pesah*, recalls God's sparing, or "passing over," the firstborn of the Israelites and the hurried meal that the Israelites ate before leaving their enslavement in Egypt for the great events of the Exodus, the parting of the Red Sea, the receiving of the Law at Mount Sinai, and the entry into the Promised Land. An impressive family rite, the Passover meal, or **seder**, with its traditional foods (the paschal lamb, which is not actually eaten but is like a sacrifice; unleavened bread; roasted egg; vegetable; bitter herbs; wine; and so forth) and the questions and answers between the youngest son and the father concerning the meaning of the symbols, is deeply loved in Jewish homes and is the Jewish holiday best known to Christians because of its association with the death of Jesus.

Shavuot or Pentecost, seven weeks after Passover, was an ancient harvest festival for grain and is also commemorated as the anniversary of the giving of the Law on Mount Sinai. Traditional Jews mark it by all-night study of the Torah, and it is a customary time for religious confirmation and graduation exercises.

Bright and colorful Sukkot is the autumn harvest festival for fruit and vegetables. When possible, booths are set up on lawns and in temples, gaily decorated with apples, pomegranates, gourds, corn, and the like. The booths are covered with straw, boughs, or palm fronds but with spaces so that one can see the stars. People eat, study, and sometimes sleep in them. Like so much of Judaism, it is the sort of religious rite that children find exciting and unforgettable.

Finally, there are several minor holy days. Two of them are **Purim** and Hanukkah. Purim, in February or March, commemorates the story recounted in the Book of Esther: how the Jews were saved from the wicked designs of Haman, chief minister of the Persian king, by Esther the queen and her cousin Mordecai. Like Mardi Gras or carnival in Latin countries, which comes at approximately the same time, Purim is the time when religion gives sanction to the role of comedy, buffoonery, and "letting go" in human life. Tradition says one may drink until one cannot tell the difference between "Blessed be Mordecai" and "Cursed be Haman." During the reading of the story in the synagogue, children gleefully make a tremendous racket with noisemakers whenever the name Haman is spoken. Strolling players and schoolchildren perform farces in which solemn rabbis and elders might be spoofed most of all.[7]

Hanukkah comes at about the time of the Christian Christmas and has become popular in America partly as a result of this association. It commemorates the rededication of the temple in Jerusalem in 165 B.C.E., as we have seen. The event is too late even to have been included in the Hebrew Scriptures, although the Books of Maccabees do appear in the Roman Catholic Bible and in the Apocrypha of some Protestant versions. The celebration is simple and is carried out in the home. An eight-branch Hanukkah **menorah**, or candelabra, is lit, and a Hanukkah song is sung, over an eight-day period. On the successive nights, cakes and gifts are presented to the children.

Jewish boys undergo certain rites of passage: circumcision, performed as a religious act when the boys are eight days old; Bar Mitzvah, when the boy reads from the Hebrew Scriptures and begins the entry into manhood. In America, the **Bar Mitzvah** has often become the occasion of gala celebrations. In some Jewish traditions, a parallel festival for girls, the **Bat** (or **Bas**) **Mitzvah**, has been introduced.

The Jewish dietary laws have had an immense role over the centuries in keeping the faith alive and its people together, for the rules of food preparation are so exacting they make it almost a practical necessity—if they are to be kept—for one to eat with, and therefore live in and marry within, his or her own community. Today, however, their observance varies. Some follow them minutely; some give them only token honor such as the refusal to eat pork; some feel they are entirely irrelevant to the modern world and observe them not at all.

No restrictions govern food from plants; the law deals only with killing and eating conscious life. The basic rules are that animals eaten must have a split hoof and chew the cud; this includes cattle and sheep but excludes a large number: swine, reptiles, elephants, monkeys, horses, and all carnivorous beasts, among others. Of sea creatures, only those with fins and scales may be taken; birds of prey and insects are forbidden. Furthermore, meat must be slaughtered and prepared in special ways to be **kosher**, or edible by those keeping the dietary rules. The rules also forbid the eating of meat and dairy products together and expect that separate pots and plates will be used for each. The keeping of two sets of dishes (and a third for Passover) is a sure sign of a quite traditional Jewish home.

The tradition also requires men to pray morning and evening and to give time to Torah study.

In all these observances we see again that Judaism is not primarily oriented toward doctrine as its basis; one finds that ideas about God and such matters as the afterlife vary immensely. Yet the Jewish faith continues to be intensely felt as a way of life here and now. The reason may be that it is oriented toward time and history, rather than eternal ideas, as the source of human meaning and obligation. The Law is important because it comes out of past history and now controls present time, making time holy through demands on how it is spent and how biological events in time are sanctified. In turn, the Jewish hope of salvation is chiefly oriented toward future time. The tradition affirms that God will, in his time, send the Messiah, a hero heir to the greatest kings and prophets of old but greater than they, and that in his day and through his work, all evils on the Earth will be rectified and an era of joy initiated. Some interpret this hope literally; others figuratively, in terms of a "Messianic Age."

Judaism is a religion whose centers of value are in time: tradition out of the past and hope for the future. We are beings in time and history, and we are to look to the tradition and our hopes rather than to new revelation or mysticism alone to find what we need most to know and believe to live this human life as it is meant to be lived.

JUDAISM, GOVERNANCE, AND POLITICAL LIFE

What traditional Judaism says about political life from its beginning to the present day is difficult to identify precisely. As we have seen, Judaism traverses a vast and diverse landscape over four millennia—from its origins to prophets and kings, enslavement in Egypt, exile in Babylonia, and the long diaspora—to the advent of the State of Israel and its implications for Jews not only there but all over the world. To complicate the matter further, most of Judaism's traditional literature was written by Jews who lived under the sovereignty of others. Yet the Jewish people have survived through the millennia where other polities have not, despite exile, subjugation, and sometimes severe persecution in the foreign lands in which they have resided. Why have they survived? Exploring the Jewish polity's classical self-conception and the accommodations Jews have made to their shifting circumstances over the millennia provide many clues.

Foundational Concepts

The Jewish polity's self-conception begins with Eden and its loss. God created humankind to live in bliss in Eden. However, Adam and Eve lost Eden, and the animating desire of ensuing generations, then, was to regain Eden by doing what was necessary to build God's kingdom on Earth. As the Hebrew scriptural narratives recount, the Jews responded to God's call, however imperfectly, to reconcile themselves and thus redeem the Jewish people with and for God.

Perhaps no more defining moment for the Jews as a polity exists than the Exodus from Egypt. The Exodus narrative, the stories that follow, and their perceived meaning and outcome bring to the fore two central motifs: "freedom" from bondage and the "covenant," which, although they are evident earlier with Abraham, come even more profoundly to the fore at Sinai. There God, through Moses, makes covenants with the Jewish people. God's covenant at Sinai was at once with the whole of the Israel community and the individual people, who consented to and therefore participated in the covenant. God promised not to exercise unfettered power and to preserve the Jewish people, and the people promised to direct their God-given freedom toward obedience to God's Law.[8]

The Laws given by God to Moses—the Torah—have provided the basis for the Jewish polity for more than three millennia and are central to Judaism's political self-conception as well as its religious conception.[9] In this broad sense, as Saadia Gaon (882–942 C.E.) wrote in *The Book of Doctrines and Beliefs* in tenth-century Babylon, the Torah is a "constitution" for the Jews that lays down the basic normative principles that are to govern Jewish life—individual, social, and political.[10] That is, the original idea of the rule of the prophetic charismatic leader in the person of Moses eventually gave way to an emphasis on Torah Law and the rational analyses of rules and their application to create a political order and society conducive to living a good life worthy of God.

Of course, if human beings were capable of perfect obedience to God's commands, there would be no need of a governing authority. Because this is not the case, however, over time it was understood that political order is needed to keep the Jews pointed toward reconciliation with God, to avoid and resolve disputes, and for the security, social stability, and survival of the Jewish people.[11]

In sum, the bases for Jewish political and religious life are freedom, the covenant of the people to and with God, participation, the inherent worth of human beings, the Torah, and the survival of the Jewish people through a governing system that preserves Jewish identity and authority over the Jewish people wherever they may be found.

Structure of the Jewish Polity

As we have already seen, Judaism began with the individual, Abraham, and familial or tribal identification, especially with Jacob (also known as Israel). But latter Judaism held sovereignty over a whole community with the establishment of a kingdom (Saul, David, Solomon) and the authority of the priesthood in the Temple at Jerusalem. However, once kingdom, temple, and priesthood were no more and the Jews existed only in the diaspora, ideas for governance nevertheless drew from earlier sources for the formation and maintenance of communities. "Israel" (not the modern state but the Jews as a people) would persevere and survive.

Although implied in earlier times, in the Rabbinic era around 100 B.C.E., the idea of three spheres of authority, known as *ketarim* or "crowns" emerged: the king (*keter malkhut*), the high priest (*keter kehunah*), and the sage (*keter torah*). These three "crowns" served as God's representatives to and for the Jewish polity, and they are the classic understanding of the structure of Jewish rule. Eventually, the three crowns had a more general appeal as three distinct, but interdependent, spheres of power represented in the civil authority (kingship/*malkhut*), the religious authority (priest/*kehunah*), and the Torah authority (the sage/*torah*).[12] When the diaspora separated the people from any territory, and therefore any sovereign claims, and resulted in the abolition of the priesthood, the remaining "crown"—the Torah—became primary. The "Fence of the Torah" (referenced earlier) defined the Jewish people.

On the basis of covenant and consent, an understanding of an assembly of the whole people, known as the *edah*, developed. Inherent in the concept of the *edah* is the imperative that any governing bodies must be participatory. To ensure participation, there were three levels of governance: the whole people; the intermediate, which consisted at first of tribes and later involved territorial jurisdictions, known as *aratzot*; and the local. Each level was, then, organized and operated through covenants, agreements, and compacts derived from the original idea of the covenant of God and the Jews and was always governed by reference to the Torah.

Eventually, as the Jewish polity grew and circumstances changed, there were further organizational developments. In the fifth century B.C.E., a body called the *Anshei Knesset HaGedolah* ("Men of the Great Assembly") was established by Ezra and Nehemiah to govern the Jewish people. This *Knesset* (another word for *edah*) consisted of 120 representative sages, ten for each of the twelve tribes of Israel—a symbolic *minyan* (quorum) for each tribe.

During the seventh and eighth centuries, approximately 95 percent of the Jews worldwide lived within the territory ruled by the Islamic caliphate, with its capital in Baghdad. Under Arab Islamic rule, the Jews enjoyed much autonomy and consequently were able to maintain the *edah* and build on previous institutions, such as the *yeshivot* (a center for study and interpretation of Torah) of Babylonia. They were able to establish communication networks and institutions, which approximated the *edah*, which spanned the whole of the Muslim territories. The *yeshivot* in Babylonia provided responses (*responsa*), referenced earlier, to queries that it received from Jewish communities dispersed throughout the caliphate and beyond, which served as guides for governance as well as interpretation of Torah for individual, family, and community life even well after the Muslim empire had begun to break down.

Later, during the diaspora of the high Middle Ages in Europe (eleventh and twelfth centuries) local rule predominated. However, governance was still conducted according to the commentaries, codes, and the *responsa* literature, which provided a form of centralized identity and method for decision making and adjudicating cases. Consequently, despite the separation of, and distance between, communities, the Jews were able to maintain their identity as a whole people wherever they were found.

In the nineteenth century, when technological advances such as the railroad and telegraph made communication and travel more feasible, Jewish diaspora organizations were formed that filled the role of the *edah*. For example in 1897, the World Zionist Congress convened in an effort to reconstitute a representative modern-world Jewry. Other such organizations developed as well, providing a kind of *edah* governance for the uprooted diaspora Jewish people all over the world.

Theology of the Land and Current Tensions

Judaism's theological identity also has roots in the Land of Canaan, which, according to the Hebrew Scriptures, God promised to Abraham and his progeny. Consequently, returning to and dwelling in that land is a central motif in Jewish historical and scriptural narratives from Judaism's origins to the present. The Jews returned to this land after the Exodus from Egypt and again after Babylonian exile ended. They built their first and second temples there. After the Jewish rebellion that ended with the destruction of the Temple in Jerusalem by the Romans in 70 C.E., the Romans named the land "Palestine" and, as discussed earlier, the Jews were expelled and scattered in diaspora around the globe for nearly two millennia. Nevertheless, Jewish religious rituals included supplications to God for the Jews' return to Mount Zion (the Hebrew designation for Jerusalem) from then to modern times. For some Jews, full reconciliation with God is linked with their return to the land of God's promise; through their labor on the land, they would redeem not only the land itself but the Jewish people as well.[13]

The growing nineteenth-century nationalism in Europe led also to a rise of Jewish nationalism. Many Jews were inspired to dream of a national homeland in the area that had been known as Palestine in Roman times but was then part of Syria in the Turks' Ottoman Empire. That land, though never without a Jewish community, had been mainly Muslim for centuries, but Jews began settling there in the 1890s, often forging out new lifestyles, like that of the agricultural communes called **kibbutzim**. Recognizing and supporting this growing aspiration, Theodor Herzl published *Der Judenstaat* (The Jewish State) in 1896 and became the father of the movement known as **Zionism**—although it should be noted that when Zionism first appeared as an ideology, many religious Jews rejected it as a false messianism.

In 1917, the famed "Balfour Declaration" was issued, which stated that the British government supported the Zionists in their effort to establish their national home, presumably upon partition of the Ottoman Empire at war's end. After World War I, the League of Nations gave the British a mandate for the area they renamed Palestine, to which Jews would be permitted to emigrate. However, the British did not entirely make good on the Balfour Declaration, and a dispute arose about its meaning and intention. Then, after the horrific events of the Holocaust during the aftermath of World War II, American and European sympathies were with the Jews. The determination that such horrific persecution would never happen again immensely strengthened support for an independent Jewish homeland. Then, against all probability, the global vicissitudes of the twentieth century led to the birth of the state of Israel. The newly formed United Nations adopted a resolution on November 29, 1947, in support of the establishment of an independent Jewish state (and a corresponding Arab state) in Palestine, still under British mandate. On May 14, 1948, the Jews declared their independence, and the State of Israel was established on a part of the land that had been the ancient home of the Jews.

Not all Jews agreed with this development, however. On one hand, some held that taking action to reclaim the land was a usurpation of God's will. Those holding this view believed that the return of the homeland to the Jews should wait for God's intervention. On the other hand, some believed that the territorial claim had not gone far enough. These joined a movement to reclaim all of the land of the ancient covenant, believing that full redemption of the land should be the goal.

Consequently, when Israel won the Six Day War with the Arab nations in 1967 and began its occupation of additional lands gained in that conflict (among them the Gaza strip and the West Bank), some Orthodox understood this triumph as a sign of God's intervention to fulfill God's covenant with the Jews. Hence the "settler movement" was born, involving, for the most part, various religious Zionists who sought to reclaim the land in these newly conquered territories for their own by religious right.[14] Yet others, secular and religious Jews, including some Orthodox, believed that Israel should exchange land for peace, thus justifying the exchange on pragmatic terms. Such Orthodox find further support for this approach in the *halacha* value that saving Jewish lives overrides other concerns.[15] It follows from this reasoning that if the exchange renders Israel secure, then the additional territories should be released.

Tensions continue in what has become known as the "Israeli-Palestinian conflict" and remain a threat to stability in the Middle East.*

Israel and Governance

Estimates vary as to the percentage of the population that consisted of Jews in 1948 in the territory that became Israel that year. However, only six years after its founding, Israel was 90 percent Jewish because of increased immigration from Europe following the Holocaust; immigration from the Soviet Union because of continued oppression of the Jews there after the war; the settlement of the Jewish population from Arab states, such as Morocco, Egypt, Yemen, and Iraq; and the expulsion or fleeing of Arabs.[16] Consequently, if there were any question of the Jewish character of the people of the nation at the time of its founding, it was certainly dispelled by then.

Many of the characteristics and foundational concepts of the Jewish polity of the past can be seen in the political structure of the State of Israel today. Basic human rights of all residents are recognized and protected in recognition of human beings' inherent worth and liberty. The Israel parliament, known as the Knesset (which is the *edah* or assembly, referenced earlier), was named after the *Anshei Knesset HaGedolah* of the fifth century (discussed earlier). This governing institution recalls the covenant tradition of the Jewish people, which began with Abraham and Moses, in that it involves agreements among the members, as well as the imperative of participation—here through representatives. Just as its predecessor, the Knesset consists of 120 members, symbolically representing a *minyan* for each of the original twelve tribes. Furthermore, the three *ketarim* or "crowns" of authority in Jewish life are represented in Israel by the civil authority (*keter malkhut*) of the governmental institutions, local religious councils (*keter kehunah*), and the chief rabbi (*keter torah*), the latter two involving state-sponsored and quasi-state institutions.[17] Furthermore, participation from the bottom up is also exhibited by the Jewish polity in the State of Israel in that much authority is held by local governing bodies and in that government representatives at all levels are elected through democratic processes.

Significantly, the State of Israel was formed in large part to preserve and serve the Jewish people in a secure homeland, where they could maintain their Jewish identity without fear of persecution. Israel is important today as a cultural and religious focal point for world Jewry and is a center of Jewish learning. It is also important to many Jews to know there is one small place in the world that allows them to live free and that is definitely Jewish.

Although the State of Israel provides to non-Jews basic human rights, including freedom of religion and civil rights, such as citizenship and voting rights, it has policies and practices that otherwise privilege Jews. Examples include immigration policy and national symbols and rituals from Jewish traditions. Yet approximately 20 percent of Israel's citizens today are Arabs who call themselves Palestinian Israelis. They hold political rights and serve in government, some even in the military. Thus, Israel is not a theocracy; however, it also does not follow strict separation of religion and the state. Its "ethnic democracy" stands somewhere between.[18]

---

*See the sections in Chapter 9 entitled "Islam, Governance, and Political Life" for another perspective.

Diaspora Today

Although at its advent many Jews thought the State of Israel would become the center of the *edah*, that was not to be. Divergent views of the propriety of the establishment of the state at all as well as the divergent views of the relationship of the state to the Jewish people as a whole, among other things, has led to a continuance of diaspora organizations such as the World Jewish Congress, which was established in 1936 and is still active today. Consequently, although the establishment of the State of Israel was, of course, a significant development in the history of the Jewish people, it does not speak for Jews worldwide, nor does any other Jewish institution, although some aspire to that role.

Looking Back to Look Forward

Through its long history, the Jewish polity has persevered. Despite many trials and though quite diverse in their theological and political views, the people of Abraham, Moses, and Jacob (Israel) have survived, maintaining their distinct identity, while challenging their own communities and the world to keep the dialogue alive by continuing to ask difficult questions and saying—"Yes, but…".

WOMEN IN JUDAISM

Women in Traditional Judaism

Throughout its long history, Judaism has exhibited a certain ambivalence toward women. On the one hand, Jewish women, as wives and mothers, have been celebrated, some say even glorified, in Jewish tradition. Judaism's texts and traditions extol outstanding women as charismatic luminaries, heroines, intellectuals, devoted wives and daughters-in-law, and leaders. Two books of the Hebrew Scriptures are named after the exemplary women whose lives they recount. On the other hand, texts and traditions at times also reveal a profound suspicion of women and their sexuality, resulting in restrictive rules and disparaging pronouncements ("The uterus is a place of rot"[19]). And perhaps worse, education was the purview of men, and men have traditionally been the rulemakers and the keepers of the records. This has led to an androcentric perspective, which has resulted in the failure to account for many aspects of women's lives at all; thus, the rules reflect a concern only with the places in which women's lives intersect with men—marriage, divorce, sexuality, and the birth of offspring. Other than this, women, in effect, are invisible in the texts. Accordingly, the rules do not deal with such things as relationships among women.[20]

Perhaps unique to the Jewish tradition, however, is its apparent refusal to pin down one idealized conception of womanhood. While Proverbs 31 sets out the characteristics of an ideal wife, the

Woman lighting candles before a Passover seder.

Hebrew Scriptures provide accounts of women who have been significant participants in the unfolding of Jewish history in other ways.[21] For example, the Book of Judges tells us of Deborah, who, in addition to being a wife, was the "judge" of Israel at the time of the account (i.e., she was one of a succession of prophets and charismatics who guided the people of Israel). She was instrumental in Israel's success in a significant battle, having advised a military leader before and during the battle. In later lore (*aggadah*) there are stories of clever, saintly, and wise women.

Nevertheless, it is the role as wife and mother that takes center stage for women in traditional Judaism, and most of the traditions regarding women revolve around her role in the home. In particular, Jewish women's fertility was fundamental to her worth. Indeed, the greatest blessing and duty for the husband and wife was the bringing forth of children, particularly sons, to continue the patrilineal line. But this could be a two-edged sword for women because, while the birth of children was a blessing, it was believed that barrenness meant that God had judged a woman harshly,[22] and the failure to bear children was grounds for divorce.

Still, Judaism, at most times in its history, has offered women a greater role than many other traditions. Although their main province has been the home, Jewish women have rarely been restricted to the house, as in some other religious traditions. On the contrary, the traditional ideal Jewish wife is industrious in obtaining provisions for the home, strong and capable, and involved in buying and selling in the marketplace in addition to more generally recognized vocations for a wife, such as weaving, sewing, and providing food for the family. Moreover, a good wife is every bit the blessing for her husband that Eve was for Adam in Genesis. Indeed, according to Proverbs 31,

> *What a rare find is a capable wife!*
> *Her worth is far beyond that of rubies.*
> *Her husband puts his confidence in her,*
> *And lacks no good thing.*
> *She is good to him, never bad,*
> *All the days of her life.*[23]

And the Talmud, which generally advocates moderation, admonishes the husband to spend beyond his means when it comes to his wife and children.[24]

Yet from ancient times to the present, maleness has been praised while femaleness has been discounted. Again and again, the importance of the birth of a male child is emphasized, while the birth of a daughter is not even mentioned in the Hebrew Scriptures and is lamented in the Talmud, which includes in a traditional blessing: "[B]less thee with sons, and keep thee from daughters because they need careful guarding."[25] Perhaps most telling of this attitude is the daily prayer recited by traditional Jewish men:

> *Blessed art thou, O Lord, our God! King of the Universe who hath not made me a heathen.*
> *...who hath not made me a slave.*
> *...who hath not made me a woman.*[26]

These attitudes have been reflected in other aspects of Jewish tradition as well, resulting in the secondary status of women. The Laws given by Yahweh to Moses at Sinai (Genesis 20 and 21) and the story of the Levite's concubine (Judges 19) indicate that in ancient Judaism, women were considered men's property and not persons in their own right*—a disposition that has had an impact on later attitudes toward women.[27] For example, in Jewish tradition the marriage of a woman to her husband is the transfer of the father's rights in the woman to the husband.[28] Furthermore, the Talmud, the most influential book regarding the status of women in Judaism, is replete with suspicions and superstitions regarding women. One example is the belief that women are prone to sorcery. This reflects the view that women are dangerous if permitted to function outside the accepted institutions as independent persons. Therefore, women are deemed "holy" or "sanctified" when married and potentially "unholy" or "impure" when not.[29]

The emphasis on purity is also reflected in **niddah**—the rules regarding menstruation. These address the taboos that we have seen in other religious traditions regarding the avoidance by men of the blood of menstruation and childbirth. Some of the rituals and regulations concerned with these taboos (which involve avoidance of sexual contact and prohibiting women from entering the temple during proscribed times, as well as ritual cleansings) are still observed today in Orthodox Judaism.[30]

Significantly, the Talmud provides 613 obligations for men, including the obligation to appear at temple and to study the Torah. These obligations relate to the covenant with the God of Israel and reveal the many places in which a man's life touches the sacred. Yet only three obligations apply to women: lighting the candles for the Sabbath celebration, breaking the Sabbath bread, and observing *niddah*. Accordingly, women are neither required to attend temple services nor to study the Torah, because these requirements are thought to interfere with a woman's first obligation to fulfill her duties as wife, and, significantly, her involvement in them is not necessary for the fulfillment of the covenant with God. The result of this has been a general tendency to exclude women from study and to limit their participation and attendance at temple—those institutions that are the sacred centers of Judaism. As the Talmud says: "A woman may not read from the Torah because of the honor of the congregation."[31] And even when women were included in temple worship, they could not be counted in the *minyan* (the quorum of ten required for public worship). Of course, with such limitations, women were not considered for leadership roles in the synagogue and were not ordained as rabbis.

In traditional Judaism, marriage is a pivotal event for the immediate family as well as for the entire community, because the family is the basic component of the Jewish social structure.[32] The marriage is a contractual arrangement between the man and the woman set down in the **ketubah** (the marriage contract). But this not only has legal significance; it is also a profound religious commitment analogous to the covenant of Yahweh with Israel. Moreover, unlike in some other religious traditions we have seen, in Judaism sexuality is embraced as a gift from God and is to be enjoyed fully in the marital union as God's purpose. This sentiment is nowhere more beautifully expressed than in the Song of Songs of the Hebrew Scriptures, where mutual passion is glorified as analogous to the relationship of Yahweh to

---

*The story of the Levite's concubine (second wife) is one of the most disturbing stories in the Hebrew Scriptures. It is often cited by Jewish and Christian feminists as one of several passages exhibiting a disregard for the humanity of the women portrayed in the Bible and evidence of women's extremely low position in society at the time. The Levite (of the Levi tribe) was traveling with his concubine and was staying in the home of a man who had provided them shelter. While resting there, some men came and threatened the Levite, whereupon he threw his concubine out to them as an appeasement to be abused sexually by them through the night. In the morning, the Levite found his concubine dead on the doorstep. This incident was the catalyst for a fierce battle against those who had committed the outrage, but it is clear that the outrage was the offense against the Levite rather than the concubine in her own right. Thus, there was no condemnation of the husband for having thrown her out to the malefactors to a horrific death.

Israel, which, as Denise Lardner Carmody has said, "places sexual passion near the heart of the covenant."[33] For example, the Song of Solomon 1:2–4 declaims:

> *O that you would kiss me with the kisses of your mouth!*
>
> *For your love is better than wine,*
>
> *your anointing oils are fragrant,*
>
> *your name is oil poured out;*
>
> *therefore the maidens love you.*
>
> *Draw me after you, let us make haste.*
>
> *The king has brought me into his chambers.*
>
> *We will exult and rejoice in you;*
>
> *we will extol your love more than wine;*
>
> *rightly do they love you.*

Nevertheless, traditionally, while the woman's consent was required for marriage, divorce has been allowed only upon the husband's action (although at certain times and under certain circumstances, the wife's consent has been required). Grounds for divorce included such things as the woman's adultery (although tradition had it that the wife could not accuse the husband of adultery), childlessness, vociferousness, indiscretion, or immodesty. Only the husband could prepare and deliver the *get* (bill of divorce). The wife's only recourse, should she want a divorce, was to persuade her husband to divorce her. When a wife had good grounds for wanting a divorce (e.g., the husband's impotence, his refusing sex, his staying away from home too much, or severe illness such as leprosy), the rabbi would be prevailed upon to persuade the husband to divorce his wife, and sometimes the full weight of the Jewish courts would be brought to bear to this end. Unless the wife was involved in a scandal (which usually involved some breach of law or custom, such as not covering her head in public), she would be paid the amount set forth in the *ketubah* as the marital settlement. Once divorced, the man and woman were permitted to remarry others.[34] These traditions are still the practice in Conservative communities today and are enforced by Orthodox religious courts in Israel.

A very difficult situation for a woman is to become an *agunah*—a woman who is not free to remarry either because her husband refuses to provide the *get* or he disappears. This has been a considerable problem for Orthodox women whose husbands have not been accounted for after wars and, more recently, after the Holocaust. Unless a wife can find two witnesses (who must both be men, because women are not permitted to appear as witnesses in court), she is never free to remarry.

Jewish Women Today—Modernity and Feminism

While, as in all other religious traditions, women no doubt participated in ways unrecognized and unrecorded by the authorities, the Jewish tradition we have outlined prevailed as normative into the nineteenth century when modernity began to have an impact on Jewish culture. When the Jews were emancipated in Europe in the early nineteenth century, there was a move in some quarters to harmonize Jewish faith with reason and ethics. The encounter with Enlightenment ideas, such as democracy and pluralism, and the concomitant development of the notion of civil rights, caused Jews to reconsider the role of women in Judaism.[35]

Out of this ebullition of ideas arose Reform Judaism, which championed women's rights. In 1846, at its Breslau Conference, Reform Judaism spoke out for women's equality—an idea that began a slow unfolding into practice. Gradually attitudes toward women shifted, and the door to greater participation of women began to be opened. Finally, after much debate and resistance by more conservative forces within the ranks, Sally Priesand became the first publicly ordained woman rabbi in 1972.[36] Today there are women ordained as rabbis and cantors in Reform, Conservative, and Reconstructionist Judaism. Although Orthodox Judaism still does not ordain women, it now permits and encourages their study of the Torah, and women participate in some Jewish rituals.

Since the 1970s, Jewish feminism has had a considerable impact on the reform of Jewish traditions that affect women, and Jewish feminism is now found in every branch of Judaism. Jewish feminists have been challenging *halakhah* (Jewish law), uncovering androcentric biases, reinterpreting texts, including women's experience in them, challenging traditional attitudes toward women, and revalorizing the feminine to counter negative stereotypes and unfounded suspicions regarding women found in traditional texts. These efforts have resulted in a shift in attitudes, resulting in changes in theology and practice.[37]

Feminists have found that there is much in Judaism on which to base the equal dignity of womankind with mankind. One example is the Genesis account of creation in which God creates both man and woman in His image and does not blame the Fall on Eve alone, as later interpretations would have it. Another is the tradition that one cannot be "born" Jewish unless one's mother is Jewish, regardless of the father's religious heritage. Feminists have challenged the use of male-gendered language to describe God, concluding that, if God is male, and human beings are in God's image, then maleness is the norm of Jewish humanity and that therefore, that norm cannot stand.[38] To counter this, feminists have proffered traditional doctrine that holds that God is gender-neutral, concluding that there is no basis in tradition to refer to God as "He."[39] In addition, feminists have emphasized feminine images of the divine, readily accessible in the mystical tradition, which can be found in Jewish texts and traditions: **Shekhinah** (the spirit of God at the Sabbath, which is feminine) and Wisdom (imaged as female and present with God at the beginning of creation).

Feminists have unearthed evidence from early Judaism that reveals that some of the practices thought to be age-old Jewish traditions, for example, the separation of women and men in the temple, do not derive from Judaism. Rather, they are practices assimilated from surrounding cultural contexts. Women and men now generally sit together and women participate fully in Jewish rituals in all but Orthodox Judaism. In addition, women have revised old rituals and have created new ones. Now, as we have seen, girls in many synagogues, just as boys, have a rite-of-passage ritual—the *Bat* (or *Bas*) *Mitzvah*. The wedding ceremony has been revised. Whereas in the traditional ceremony only the males spoke, the revised ceremony includes statements by the bride. Progressive women have created new rituals for other passages in women's lives: childbirth, naming baby girls, marking menarche and menopause, and so forth.[40] Women, and progressive men as well, have worked to reform the language of the liturgy so that it is gender-inclusive.[41] Moreover, feminists have sought equality not only in being able to participate in ways that traditionally have been the exclusive domain of men but also by raising to consciousness the particular ways in which women approach the religious life, perhaps transforming Judaism in the process.[42]

But reform has not been an easy task because, as we have seen, the Jewish tradition itself is grounded in a patriarchal pattern of social relations and values. Many in Orthodox and Conservative Judaism contend that Reform and Reconstructionist Judaism have gone too far, resulting in an obscuring of the tradition, and there is concern among some traditionalists that Jewish feminist critique is ultimately a secularizing force that detracts from the Jewish tradition's religious significance. Jewish feminists must then face the question: How do we transform tradition and still maintain Jewish identity and community? This question has been answered by various feminists in several ways in the distinct branches of Judaism, and inroads have been made as they challenge the patriarchal structure itself. They point out that Judaism has traditionally envisioned its people as "Jews" (i.e., men) and "Other" (i.e., "other than" the norm—that is, women).[43] This tradition, Jewish feminists say, must change.

As Judith Plaskow has said;

> Once we begin to see women as a class, and gender as a central category for the analysis of any culture or tradition, we are bound to break out of a system which renders women's status invisible. At this stage, in any case, a feminist Judaism must insist on the importance of women's experience and, thus, on shaking up the categories and processes of Jewish life and thought.[44]

Such feminism seeks not only to reform tradition but to re-form it, making it accessible to relational models of leadership rather than hierarchy and to unity rather than separation and distinctions. Yet the conservative question is not without merit: When is the re-formation so counter to tradition that it results in something that is no longer Judaism at all? This question and the feminist challenge continue to be salient for Judaism in the twenty-first century.

Fundamental Features of Judaism

Theoretical

Basic Worldview	Universe is made by God but is an arena for humans to live in and enjoy, exercising free will, in cooperation with God's guidance.
God or Ultimate Reality	In traditional Judaism, a sovereign, personal, all-good creator God.
Origin of the World	Created by God.
Destiny of the World	Will be led by God through historical vicissitudes, until finally a messianic age brings it to a paradisal state.
Origin of Humans	Created individually by God.
Destiny of Humans	Chiefly in this world; with divine help and human cooperation, the human condition can become better and better until a paradisal age is reached.
Revelation or Mediation between the Ultimate and the Human	The Scriptures, especially the Torah, or Law, and its traditional interpretation in the Talmud.

Practical

What Is Expected of Humans: Worship, Practices, Behavior	To honor and serve God by following the Law of Moses in letter or spirit, to maintain the identity of the people, and to promote the ethical vision of the great prophets and humanitarians. Jewish customs are followed in the home as well as in the place of worship.

Sociological

Major Social Institutions	After the Jewish people as such, the basic unit is the congregation of Jews, forming a synagogue or temple. Jewish family life is also very important.

Summary

The pioneers of the tradition of the great monotheistic faiths were the ancient Israelites, the people of the Hebrew Scriptures. Their self-understanding as a people with a covenant relation to God, who was leading them for his ultimate purposes through suffering and success in historical time, gave them a special attitude toward God and history and a Scripture to interpret it. The Hebrew Scriptures contain the Torah, or Law of Moses—its first five books—giving the commandments God had given the people to set them apart and to reveal the covenant relationship: histories, showing the course of the relationship with God; prophetic books, giving the proclamations of divine spokesmen of what God says in particular situations; and wisdom books, with timeless poetry and philosophy from out of this historical experience.

The center of worship was the temple in Jerusalem, but around the beginning of the Christian era, because of the dispersal of the Jews and the destruction of the temple, worship and learning came to be centered on the synagogue, a gathering of the community for prayer and study. In the Middle Ages, Jews experienced widespread dispersion (diaspora) throughout Europe, where they were sometimes prosperous and sometimes persecuted. The mystical philosophy called kabalism arose. Since the beginning of modern times in the seventeenth century, Judaism has seen the rise of the popular mysticism called Hasidism in Eastern Europe, trends toward rationalism and secularism in response to the Enlightenment, persecutions culminating in the Holocaust during World War II, further dispersal through immigration, and Zionism—the successful movement to create a Jewish state in the Holy Land.

Judaism has the highest regard for marriage and the family; ideally, Jewish religious life revolves around the home even more than the synagogue. Its chief expression is the Sabbath with its special observances. The High Holy Days and festivals are yearly landmarks of faith. Jewish distinctiveness and faith are also shown through the rites by which persons are brought into the adult community and among some by following dietary laws.

American Jews are divided among Orthodox, Conservative, Reform, and Reconstructionist schools of interpretation. All have in common a sense of a unique Jewish experience and mission in the world and an emphasis on the sacred importance of time and history.

In Judaism, religion, law, and political life are intertwined. However, the Jewish people have lived most of their history under the sovereignty of others. The bases for Jewish political and religious life are freedom, the covenant of the people to and with God, participation, the inherent worth of human beings, the Torah, and the survival of the Jewish people through a governing system that preserves Jewish identity and authority over the Jewish people wherever they may be found. The structure of the Jewish polity developed around the idea of "three crowns" or *ketarim*, that is, the three spheres of authority—the king (*keter malkhut*), the high priest (*keter kehunah*), and the sage (*keter torah*)—and a conception of the Jewish people as a whole: the *edah*. The participation of the people directly or by representatives was also an early development. The "theology of the land" is important for some Jews, making the land of Israel sacred to them. Today the government of the State of Israel is an "ethnic democracy" based on some of Judaism's ancient ideals for a polity.

Traditional Judaism has reflected an ambivalent attitude toward women. On the one hand, it glorifies women as wives and mothers, and it recounts the lives of exemplary women and their contribution to Jewish history. On the other hand, it reveals an underlying distrust of female sexuality and independence, which has led to the traditional subordination of women to secondary status in the Jewish community. Enlightenment ideals of modernity and the feminist movement since the 1970s have had a profound impact on Judaism as a whole, particularly with respect to a change of attitudes toward women's equality with men. The question of whether and to what extent Jewish tradition can be transformed and still maintain Jewish identity and community is one of the most significant questions facing Judaism in the twenty-first century.

Questions for Review

1. Show how Judaism has produced both traditionalist and innovative expressions and has shown in various movements both feeling-oriented and rationalistic approaches.
2. Interpret the meaning to Judaism of the Jews as "chosen" or covenant people.
3. Discuss the Jewish Scriptures (Old Testament) as a drama of the relationship of God with humanity.
4. Summarize the history of Judaism from the second temple to the Middle Ages and the emergence of the Talmud, the synagogue, and the rabbinical tradition.
5. Cite the main features of medieval Judaism, such as its dispersion and kabalistic thought.
6. Cite the main features of modern Jewish history: Hasidism, the Enlightenment and Jewish responses to it, immigration to the New World, persecution and the Holocaust, and Zionism.
7. Discuss basic Jewish beliefs and the perspectives of important modern Jewish thinkers.
8. Talk about the meaning and role in Judaism of the family, the Sabbath, the High Holy Days and festivals, and the dietary laws.
9. Discuss initiation into Judaism through circumcision and the Bar Mitzvah.
10. Interpret the meaning of Judaism as a religion oriented toward time.
11. Explain the "three crowns" concept underlying Judaism's ideal polity, the idea of the *edah* and the role of the people in it, and how the state of Israel reflects these concepts.
12. Think about how the traditional views of women in Judaism resulted in their secondary status, while still glorifying women as wives and mothers.
13. Consider the ways in which traditional views toward women in Judaism must be altered in the Judaisms that wish to incorporate Enlightenment and feminist ideas.

Suggested Readings on the Hebrew Scriptures and Judaism

Hebrew Scriptures/Old Testament

Buber, Martin, *The Prophetic Faith*. New York: Macmillan, 1949.

Cross, Frank Moore, *From Epic to Canon: History and Literature in Ancient Israel*. Baltimore, MD: John Hopkins University Press, 1998.

Flanders, Henry Jackson, Robert W. Capps, and David A. Smith, *People of the Covenant: An Introduction to the Old Testament*, 3rd ed. New York: Oxford University Press, 1988.

Fretheim, Terence E., *Abraham: Trials of Family and Faith*. Columbia, SC: University of South Carolina Press, 2006.

Harrison, Roland Kenneth, *Introduction to the Old Testament*. Grand Rapids, MI: Eerdmans, 1969.

Heschel, Abraham, *The Prophets*. New York: Harper & Row, 1962, 1969.

McCabe, Elizabeth A., ed., *Women in the Biblical World*. Lanham, MD: University Press of America, 2009. Includes New Testament.

McNutt, Paula M., *Reconstructing the Society of Ancient Israel*. Louisville, KY: Westminster John Knox Press, 1999.

Rogerson, J. W., and Judith M. Lieu, eds., *The Oxford Handbook of Biblical Studies*. Oxford and New York: Oxford University Press, 2006.

Thompson, Thomas L., *The Mythic Past: Biblical Archaeology and the Myth of Israel*. New York: Basic Books, 1999.

Judaism

Borowitz, Eugene B., *Liberal Judaism*. New York: UAHC, 1984.

Brill, Alan, *Judaism and Other Religions*. New York: Palgrave Macmillan, 2010.

Bulka, Reuven P., *Dimensions of Orthodox Judaism*. New York: KTAV, 1983.

Cohn-Sherbok, Dan, *Judaism Today*. London and New York: Continuum, 2010.

de Lange, Nicholas, *An Introduction to Judaism*, 2nd ed. Cambridge, UK: Cambridge University Press, 2010.

Eisen, Arnold M., *Rethinking Modern Judaism: Ritual, Commandment, Community*. Chicago: University of Chicago Press, 1998.

Heschel, Abraham, *Between God and Man: An Interpretation of Judaism*. New York: The Free Press, 1965.

Katz, Steven T., *Interpreters of Judaism in the Late Twentieth Century*. Washington, DC: B'nai B'rith International, 1993.

Leaman, Oliver, *Jewish Thought: An Introduction*. New York & London: Routledge, 2006.

Lieberman, Joseph, The Gift of Rest: Rediscovering the Beauty of the Sabbath. New York: Howard Books, 2011.

Marcus, Ivan G., *The Jewish Life Cycle*. Seattle: University of Washington Press, 2004.

Neusner, Jacob, and Alan J. Avery-Peck, *The Blackwell Companion to Judaism*. Oxford & Malen, MA: Blackwell Publishing, 2000.

———, *The Life of Torah: Readings*. Encino, CA: Dickenson, 1974.

Rosenthal, Gilbert S., *Contemporary Judaism: Patterns of Survival*. New York: Human Sciences, 1986.

Roth, Cecil, ed., *Encyclopedia Judaica*, 18 vols. Philadelphia: Coronet Books, 1994.

Skolnik, Fred, ed. in chief, *Encyclopedia Judaica*, 10 vols., 2nd ed. Detroit: Macmillan Reference, 2007.

Wouk, Herman, *This Is My God*. Garden City, NY: Doubleday, 1959.

Judaism in America

Antler, Joyce, ed., *Talking Back: Images of Jewish Women in American Popular Culture*. Hanover, NH: Brandeis University Press/University Press of New England, 1998.

Blair, Sara, ed., *Jewish in America*. Ann Arbor: University of Michigan Press, 2004.

Elazar, Daniel Judah, *The Conservative Movement in Judaism: Dilemmas and Opportunities*. Albany: State University of New York Press, 2000.

Fishman, Sylvia Barauk, *Jewish Life and American Culture*. Albany: State University of New York Press, 2000.

Gurock, Jeffrey S. *Orthodox Jews in America*. Bloomington: Indiana University Press, 2009.

Kaplan, Dana Evan, ed., *The Cambridge Companion to American Judaism*. New York: Cambridge University Press, 2005.

Kugelmass, Jack, ed., *Key Texts in American Jewish Culture*. New Brunswick, NJ: Rutgers University Press, 2003.

Moore, Deborah Dash, *GI Jew*. Cambridge, MA: Harvard University Press, 2004.

Raphael, Marc Lee, ed., *The Columbia History of Jews and Judaism in America*. New York: Columbia University Press, 2008.

———, *Judaism in America*. New York: Columbia University Press, 2003.

Jewish Mysticism

Cohn-Sherbok, Dan, *Jewish Mysticism: An Anthology*. Oxford: Oneworld, 1995.

Dan, Joseph, ed., *The Heart and the Fountain: An Anthology of Jewish Mysticism Experiences*. New York: Oxford University Press, 2002.

Laenen, J. H., *Jewish Mysticism: An Introduction*. Louisville, KY: Westminster John Knox, 2001.

Matt, Daniel C. *The Essential Kabbalah*. New York: HarperCollins, 1996.

Scholem, Gershom G., *Major Trends in Jewish Mysticism*. New York: Schocken Books, 1961.

Weiner, Herbert, *9 1/2 Mystics: The Kabbala Today*. New York: Holt, Rinehart & Winston, 1969.

Judaism, Governance, and Political Life

Neusner, Jacob, "Judaism," in *God's Rule: The Politics of the World's* Religions, Jacob Neusner, ed. Washington, DC: Georgetown University Press, 2003.

Novak, David, *Covenantal Rights: A Study in Jewish Political Theory*. Princeton, NJ: Princeton University Press, 2000.

Sandler, Shmuel, "Judaism and Politics," in *The Politics of Religion: A Survey*, Jeffrey Haynes, ed. London; New York: Routledge, 2006.

Wald, Kenneth D., "The Religious Dimension of Israeli Political Life," in *Religion and Politics in Comparative Perspective: The One, the Few, and the Many*, Ted Gerard Jelen and Clyde Wilcox, eds. New York: Cambridge University Press, 2002.

Women in Judaism

Bach, Alice, ed., *Women in the Hebrew Bible*. London and New York: Routledge, 1999.

Bale, Rachel, *Women and Jewish Law: An Exploration of Women's Issues in Halakhic Sources*. New York: Schocken Books, 1984.

Baskin, Judith R., ed., *Jewish Women in Historical Perspective*. Detroit, MI: Wayne State University Press, 1991.

Blyth, Caroline, *The Narrative of Rape in Genesis 34: Interpreting Dinah's Silence*. New York: Oxford University Press, 2010.

Carmody, Denise Lardner, "Judaism," in *Women in World Religions*, Arvind Sharma, ed. Albany: State University of New York Press, 1987, pp. 183–206.

Goldman, Karla, *Beyond the Synagogue Gallery: Finding a Place for Women in American Judaism*. Cambridge, MA: Harvard University Press, 2000.

Greenspahn, Frederick E., ed., *Women and Judaism: New Insights and Scholarship*. New York: New York University Press, 2004.

Hartman, Tova, *Feminism Encounters Traditional Judaism: Resistance and Accommodation*. Waltham, MA: Brandeis University Press; Hanover, NH: University Press of New England, 2007.

Heschel, Susannah, ed., "Judaism," in *Her Voice, Her Faith*, Arvind Sharma and Katherine K. Young, eds. Boulder, CO and Oxford, UK: Westview Press, 2003.

———, *On Being a Jewish Feminist*. New York: Schocken Books, 1995.

Kates, Judith A., and Gail Twersky Reimer, eds., *Reading Ruth: Contemporary Women Reclaim a Sacred Story*. New York: Ballantine, 1994.

Levitt, Laura, *Jews and Feminism: The Ambivalent Search for Home*. New York: Routledge, 1997.

Nadell, Pamela Susan, *Women Who Would Be Rabbis: A History of Women's Ordination, 1889–1985*. Boston: Beacon Press, 1998.

Peskowitz, Miriam, and Laura Levitt, eds., *Judaism Since Gender*. New York: Routledge, 1997.

Plaskow, Judith, *Standing Again at Sinai: Judaism from a Feminist Perspective*. San Francisco: HarperSanFrancisco, 1990.

Ross, Tamar, *Expanding the Palace of Torah: Orthodoxy and Feminism*. Waltham, MA: Brandeis University Press, 2004

Umansky, Ellen M., "Feminism in Judaism," in *Feminism and World Religions*, Arvind Sharma and Katherine K. Young, eds. Albany: State University of New York Press, 1999.

Spreading the Word of God in the World

The Growth of Christianity

CHAPTER OBJECTIVES

After studying this chapter, you should be able to

- Place the life and teaching of Jesus in a historical context.
- Explain the historical development of the Christian religion.
- Summarize the teaching, practice, and institutional life of the major forms or denominations of Christianity.
- Discuss the position of Christianity in the world today.
- Understand Christianity's conception of the relationship of church and state as it has evolved throughout Christianity's history and its views of political institutions, as well as those views as they are expressed in denominations today.
- Discuss the theological views that have shaped attitudes toward women in Christianity and the impact of these views on women's struggle for equality and the twentieth- and twenty-first-century American debate on the "woman question."

ENCOUNTERING CHRISTIANITY

Years ago on a trip to Europe, I* visited many of the ubiquitous churches, shrines, and cathedrals that adorn the cities and villages all across that land. These monuments to faith are innumerable and represent various denominations. Yet I experienced a congruent sense of the piety of the adherents of this largest of the world's religions, which made the centuries of conflicts among those holding different Christian theological views unfathomable. As I encountered each sanctuary, humble or magnificent, with its own unique beauty and reverent appeal, a rush of compassion washed over me.

Nowhere did I experience that feeling more than when I entered the Sacred Heart Basilica in Paris (Basilique du Sacré Coeur). There my breath caught and eyes welled as I encountered, not a representation of the sacrificial Jesus on the cross, but the ascendant, resurrected Jesus in all

---

*Barbara McGraw

273

his majesty in an awe-inspiring ceiling mosaic—his arms open to all who seek God's love, acceptance, and forgiveness. No wonder, I thought, that Christians all across the globe believe that Jesus, born of the humblest of beginnings on Earth, now transcendent, cherishes the lowly and the high as equally worthy of his grace.

THE SCOPE OF CHRISTIANITY

Today Christians, or at least persons of Christian religious background, number over two billion, about a third of the world's overall population. This figure is up from a half-billion at the beginning of the twentieth century. At that time, the religion also represented about a third of the world's people—up from a fourth around 1800— but with a significant difference. In 1900, it was overwhelmingly European and Euro-American in its constituency and centers of power. Now its membership is predominantly persons of color in Africa, Asia, and Latin America, and its centers of real strength are rapidly moving to that part of the world. This is due to both population growth and growth by conversion, including (as we will see) the appearance of dynamic innovative forms of Christianity in lands new to it.[1]

Yet Christianity is also an ancient faith with a long history, and its areas of strength and "centers of gravity" have shifted dramatically before. At one time its major centers were around the eastern end of the Mediterranean, areas now largely Muslim. The "center" then moved to Western Europe and finally to "Anglo" North America; it now seems to be going south. But it is important to realize that the greater part of Christian history transpired before the Americas were settled by Europeans and was set in cultural environments immensely remote from those of the West. Most of the other major faiths, except Islam, are about five hundred years older than Christianity. Yet Christianity is scarcely behind any of them in the sense of antiquity imparted by its oldest shrines in the Old World. The comparatively new brick, glass, or wood churches that dot Christian America by the tens of thousands may give this religion an almost modern façade, far different from the impression it gives in other places. In Europe the church or cathedral is often the oldest structure in an old city, giving to Christianity a feel of the remote past.

The hymns and worship style Americans call the "old-time religion" largely date only from the nineteenth-century American frontier. Before that are eighteen other centuries of Christianity. Some of the forms it took in the past would be as unfamiliar to Americans as Tibet would seem to many Americans today, and much of this history is relatively little understood or known even by most American Christians.

In the waning days of the Roman Empire, Christians not only worshiped in underground burial tunnels called **catacombs** and met lions in the Coliseum, but they also wrote, argued, and took the faith to what they believed were "barbarian" tribes. These Christians built churches on wagons to follow the barbarians on their wanderings. After the fall of Rome, Western Europe lay in what some refer to as the "Dark Ages." During that time, worship in Constantinople—with its opulently robed priests, clouds of incense, and sonorous music—reached a splendor that visiting Russians reportedly said was closer to Heaven than to Earth. In the tenth century, the Nestorian Church of the East, following the caravan routes, was planted from Mesopotamia to the imperial city of the Tang Dynasty in China. A Christian church of Eastern Orthodox type has existed in South India since at least the fourth century. At the other end of the world, Irish monks let God guide their flimsy boats to remote islands and promontories, inhabited only by sea gulls, on which to build rough monasteries.

Then there are somewhat more familiar but no less colorful Christian images: medieval popes in monarchical splendor, crusaders, manuscript-copying monks,

Canterbury pilgrims, Protestant reformers, visionaries of the Blessed Virgin Mary at Lourdes or at Fatima, and missionaries on tropical islands. Christianity embraces worshippers at high Masses and at silent Quaker meetings, people for whom the faith is a liberal charter and those for whom faith demands the most rigorous conservatism on both social and theological issues.

JESUS

Like all other major religions, Christianity has integrated into itself meanings and practices from many places where it has dwelt. The process begins with the Greek vocabulary of the New Testament itself. But there is only one focal point which brings together all this diversity: the last two or three years of the earthly life of Jesus of Nazareth, called the "Messiah" or "Christ."

Jesus appeared publicly in Roman-occupied Palestine around the year 30 C.E. He was first visible as an associate of a man called John the Baptizer, a Jewish ascetic who had lived in the desert before coming into the Jordan Valley to preach fiery outdoor sermons calling on people to repent and change their ways, for God was about to judge the world and punish the wicked. Such **apocalyptic** expectation was rife at this time, all the more because the heavy hand of Roman tyranny seemed to block all nonsupernatural hope for the Jewish nation or for individuals, except those who curried favor with Rome.[2] The repentance John called for was marked by a ritual washing, or baptism, which he administered to his converts in the Jordan River.

Among those who received this baptism was a young man from Nazareth called Jesus (Joshua). Not much is definitely known about his background. The stories later told about his descent from David, his miraculous conception, his birth in Bethlehem, and his childhood are difficult to corroborate historically and are generally accepted or not on the basis of one's religious outlook; for Christians, they embody important religious truths about Jesus.

Shortly after Jesus' baptism by John, John was arrested and then executed. This arrest did not give Jesus the leadership of John's movement directly, but it did partly inspire him to gather disciples and start a ministry of his own, which was in some ways parallel to John's but came to develop distinctive characteristics.

Like John, Jesus began by proclaiming in his preaching that the **Kingdom of God** was at hand. The "Kingdom" meant the paradisal rule of God that would follow an apocalyptic distress and judgment. The Kingdom as a concept was intimately tied with the work of the Messiah, who would inaugurate it.[3] Jesus also taught that people should repent of their former ways and, in preparation for the Kingdom, live now as though in the Kingdom. The principles for this way of life are assembled in the Sermon on the Mount in Chapters 5, 6, and 7 of Matthew's Gospel in the Bible. The essence is to practice forbearing love and nonresistance of evil, because God will shortly be dealing with it in judgment, and to be perfect

Engraving of Jesus healing the sick by Gustave Doré.

even as the God who is to rule is perfect. By comparison, John's moral message was merely of repentance and following justice.

Unlike John, Jesus did not baptize, although his followers did. His work of healing was the major sign in his ministry of the power of the coming Kingdom, just as baptism had been John's major sign. His miracles of healing the sick, the insane, the blind, and the paralyzed, and his other miracles, such as feeding five thousand people with five loaves and two small fish, are presented as signs of the Kingdom's arrival. Healing was often understood as the exorcism of evil spirits from the disturbed. Jesus said, "If it is by the finger of God that I cast out demons, then the kingdom of God has come upon you" (Luke 11:20). He also performed nature miracles, like walking on water.

The nature miracles and healings bring to light other special features of Jesus' ministry—his aura of authority and his mingling with both sexes and with all classes of society. Jesus taught everywhere, not only in synagogues but also by the lakeshore and in open fields. Instead of using close argument or extensive scriptural analysis, he used stories, **parables**, and simple but acute aphorisms to make his points or, better, to catch up the listener in his vision of the Kingdom's nearness—so near its power is already breaking through and is within reach of those who see its rising light.

Just as the Kingdom was for everyone, but in a special sense for the poor who had so little, so did Jesus bring its message to everyone. He numbered among his associates fishermen, prostitutes, revolutionary zealots, despised tax collectors, and (though he also harshly upbraided them) members of the strict religious party, the Pharisees. He did not inculcate extreme asceticism but rather was known as the teacher who came eating and drinking, and his illustrations show a sympathetic awareness of the ways and problems of ordinary life with its sorrows, joys, and innocent festivities.

After only a short year or two of this life, however, the young wandering preacher and charismatic wonder worker of the Kingdom left Galilee, his homeland, and went down to Jerusalem shortly before the Passover, when Jews traditionally made a pilgrimage to the holy city. He clearly intended this journey, which God had laid upon him, to be a climactic appeal to Israel to accept the incoming Kingdom and to reject perversions of religion. To this end he made certain dramatic gestures: he entered the pilgrim-thronged holy city in a sort of procession (which has come to be commemorated as Palm Sunday), and he caused a disturbance overturning the tables of the currency exchangers and the chairs of the sellers of birds and animals for sacrifice in the temple courtyard. He and his disciples then withdrew for a few days to live in suburban Bethany and to teach in the temple precincts.

Yet in the edgy political situation, these gestures, combined with news of Jesus' popular appeal in Galilee, understandably came to the concerned attention of Roman and Jewish authorities alike. They perceived revolutionary political over-tones in the young prophet's activities and appeal. How far this perception was justified is much disputed by historians, but there is no doubt there were those among both supporters and opponents of Jesus who expected him to be at least the figurehead in an uprising against Rome and perhaps against the collaborating Jewish elite as well.[4] This was an upshot neither the Romans nor the Jewish elite wished. Before the end of the week in which Jesus arrived in the city, the decision had been taken and carried out to dispose of him.

Jesus was arrested with the help of Judas, a disgruntled radical among his disciples, and he was hastily, but decisively, tried by the various authori-ties concerned, ultimately before Pontius Pilate, the harsh Roman governor who throughout his tenure had shown no pity to protesters against Roman rule. (Indeed,

Rome finally recalled him for excessive cruelty.) On Friday in Passover week, Jesus was executed by **crucifixion**—being nailed to a structure made of two crossed beams set upright—the slow and agonizing death that Rome awarded to rebels. But the story did not end there.

THE EARLY JESUS MOVEMENT

The drama of this tragic death of one so young, beloved, and appealing to many inevitably worked deeply into the minds of those who had been committed to his movement and caught up in his vision of the Kingdom. They tried to find ways to understand the man and the event in categories familiar to them. Some thought of the Jewish tradition of a coming Messiah, "Anointed One" or King, and wondered if, as some of Jesus' words and deeds suggested, he were this figure. (The title "Christ" is the literal Greek translation of "Messiah.") In particular, they now joined the Messiah image with poignant passages in Isaiah about the "suffering servant"—the hero who saves his people not by military victory but by undergoing excruciating pain, baring his back to the smiters, his cheek to those who plucked out the hairs.

Some thought of the words "Son of Man," which he had often used—words that his hearers would have recognized as referring to the mysterious judge who would descend on clouds on the last day in the current apocalyptic expectations. It was frequently ambiguous whether Jesus meant the title to refer to himself or another coming one or if he meant both at the same time. Others, closer to the Greek religious tradition, thought of the titles "Lord" and "Son of God," used of Hellenistic kings and deities alike. Still others thought of philosophical concepts like **Logos** ("**Word**" or "Principle") or Sophia ("Wisdom") used to describe the creative power of God at work in the world in connection with the enigmatic and unforgettable man from Nazareth. As to exactly how he thought of himself and his mission, in his own subjectivity, who can say? Almost all we know of him, including the words he is reported to have spoken, comes to us through the hands of those who saw him in light of categories and concepts such as those just mentioned. Beyond all the words, however, there is mystery—the mystery of one whose charm and sternness, magic and endurance of torture, empathy and remoteness, combined to make him both unknown and unforgettable. He had the combination of mystery and clarification of all great religious images and symbols.

Soon enough he was a supreme symbol of the ineffable mysteries of life, death, and God, all of which he somehow seemed to bring into focus for many. His form and the instrument of his suffering were reproduced in gold and silver and gems around the world.

Michelangelo's La Pietà: Mary mourning over her son Jesus.

This kind of thinking took hold in the community of Jesus' disciples and followers. Christianity, which has never been a purely individual religion, was communal even before the crucifixion. The disciples, leaving job and family, formed a new social group around Jesus, and it was in the context of this group especially formed in expectation of the Kingdom that the teaching about the Kingdom and the wonders that foreshadowed it were imparted. The disciples were always at hand for Jesus' preaching and miracles, and it was they who were told the inner meaning of parables and signs.

On the Friday Jesus died on the cross, this community was dispirited and scattered; the **apostle** Peter went back to his fishing. But on the first day of the next week, word of a new event brought the community together again. It was reported by Mary Magdalene, a woman close to Jesus and the disciples, and then by Peter himself, that the tomb was empty and that Jesus was walking in the garden where he had been interred. More such accounts were quickly bruited about: he had joined two disciples walking to Emmaus, and when they broke bread together, he was known to them; the disciples were in a room with the doors shut, and he appeared in their midst; they were in a boat, and he appeared on the shore and cooked breakfast for them. He seemed the same and yet different in these postdeath appearances, as though partly in a different dimension. He ate. "Doubting Thomas" was able to touch Jesus' wounds to assure himself that Jesus was really the crucified one and not a ghost or imposter. Yet this Jesus was able to pass through shut doors and appear or disappear unexpectedly and by no pattern discernible to mortals. Finally, forty days after the first appearance in the garden, the resurrected Jesus appeared to them, we are told, in familiar Bethany. There, as they talked, he took them out to a nearby hill, blessed them, and was taken up into heaven.

By now, the nascent Christian community—the disciples, certain women such as Mary Magdalene and Mary the mother of Jesus, and peripheral followers—was vitalized and enthusiastic. The series of mysterious resurrection appearances, which came only to members of the community, greatly reinforced its thinking about who Jesus was along the lines of the categories and concepts discussed above. The supreme event came when, on the Jewish feast of **Pentecost** fifty days after Passover, shortly after his ascension into heaven, those who were gathered in an upstairs room suddenly felt tremendously shaken by a spiritual force they were certain was the Holy Spirit of God mentioned in the Old Testament and whose coming was remembered to have been promised by Jesus.

After receiving the Holy Spirit, the **apostles**, as the inner core of the group was now called, began preaching in the streets to the many peoples who crowded into the holy city. They preached basically that Jesus who had died was risen from the dead, that this event confirmed that he was and is both Lord and Messiah—the Christ—and so all the scriptural prophecies about both the Jewish and universal roles of the Messiah and the Last Days were fulfilled or will be in him.

Many heard and believed. Most were Jews, but some of the earliest converts to the truth and significance of this new happening in Judaism were Greeks, probably of a class called "proselytes," who, without undertaking the whole of the Jewish law, admired Judaism, worshipped its God, and accepted as much of its teaching and practice as possible. The incipient universalism of the Christian sect, with its proclamation of a new age when the reign of the Jewish God would be evident everywhere, and was now already present in Christ, must have greatly eased the spiritual plight of such people.

PAUL

The council of the apostles described in Acts 15, where only a minimal adherence to the Jewish law was required of non-Jews, gave preliminary definition to the presentation of Jesus as a manifestation of God who welcomed Jew and Greek alike. But it was in the work of Paul, the most notable convert and missionary in the days of the early fellowship, that this universalism in Christ fully came through.[5]

Paul, a Hebrew who was a Roman citizen, was originally called Saul. He was a strict follower of the Law of Moses and a persecutor of the new Christian sect. But while traveling from Jerusalem to Damascus in his anti-Christian efforts, at one place in the road he unexpectedly fell to the ground in a violent rapture. He experienced a vision of Jesus the Christ appearing to him and saying "Saul, Saul, why do you persecute me?"

Although he did not immediately begin his public missionary work, Paul was a great, if controversial, advocate of the new faith between about 45 and 62 C.E. and Christianity's first theologian. His labors on its behalf took him through Asia Minor, Greece, and finally to Rome. More and more he saw himself as the apostle to the **Gentiles** (non-Jews), and his calling was to show that in these days after Jesus, the Gentiles had been "grafted" into Israel as an alien branch onto an old tree. Consequently, when they prayed in the name of Jesus, they had all the privileges and responsibilities of being God's people, which had formerly been Israel's alone. But this did not mean, for Paul, that they had to follow the Jewish Law. They had only to believe the Gospel, or "Good News," about Jesus and have trust in him, and they would be brought into his oneness with God—not on their own merits but as a free gift of God transmitted even as they were grafted into old Israel through Jesus Christ. Jesus' death on the cross, Paul said, broke the sway of sin and death in the world, and his rising again brought new life. By joining oneself to Christ by faith (not only by belief but by a commitment of one's whole self) and by the acceptance of baptism (the ritual immersion in water representing initiatory rebirth), one received new life in Christ and was no longer of this world, which is passing away, but was entered into the everlasting reign of God.

VARIETIES OF EARLY CHRISTIANITY

By now a number of interpretations of the Christian message and community had become articulated. Some still thought of Jesus primarily as the Jewish Messiah who would soon return to vindicate Israel. Some thought of all of this as a continuation— one might say an "export version"—of Judaism, making its promises freely available to all apart from the Jewish social and dietary law. (One can compare the relation of Buddhism to Hinduism.) Others doubtless experienced it as something closer to the well-known Greek mystery religions, the purveyors of belief and experience that would give a blissful state after death to those who received it. The death and **resurrection** of Christ provided for them the pattern of such a deliverance, which one needed only to appropriate for oneself. All of these, and other philosophical and religious themes as well, found their way into the newly emerging and varied groups that together made up the early Jesus movement.

These various ideas were stirring in groups that Paul and the other apostles, as well as others, established throughout the Mediterranean world in such varied places as Judea, Syria, and Egypt, together with Rome itself. They were usually fringe groups to the Jewish community, but they embraced many others as well—rich and poor, slave and free, but more of the dislocated than of the well established in the polyglot, spiritually mobile Mediterranean world. The destruction of the Temple in Jerusalem by the Romans in 70 C.E., mentioned in connection with our discussion of Judaism in Chapter 7, and the dispersion of Jerusalem Jews, had a profound effect on the Jesus movement as well. By severely weakening the Jerusalem church, with its links to Judaism, the demise of the Temple and subsequent **diaspora** exacerbated a schism between Judaism and the followers of Jesus that has had a profound effect on Middle Eastern and Western history ever since— Christianity eventually becoming more Gentile in its makeup and universal in its teachings than Judaism had been.

One significant group of Christians in the earliest decades resided in Jerusalem under the leadership of the Apostle James, called "James the Just" and "the Brother of the Lord." He and his church were clearly highly respected by nearly all believers. James and the Jerusalem assembly were largely Jewish and were understandably concerned to include some aspects of the Jewish Law, especially in regard to food, in the Christian practice. They were, on the other hand, less concerned than Paul and others with philosophical doctrines about the nature of Christ and salvation. In the New Testament, we see Paul and James at opposite poles on many issues, with Peter endeavoring to mediate. But James himself was martyred in 62 C.E., and the Jerusalem church was dispersed by the Roman destruction of Jerusalem in 70 C.E., clearing the way for the "Gentile" church of Paul and Greek-speaking Christianity to prevail. A later group of Christians called Ebionites, who were vegetarian and identified themselves with the poor, claimed to be descended from the Jamesian church.

If the group around James represented a conservative perspective on Christianity (in the sense of staying close to its Jewish roots), other views, though also popular with some Jewish Christians, fully embraced language from Hellenistic and Eastern thought. An important early Christian movement was **Gnosticism**. Its oldest accounts of Jesus go back virtually as far as the "canonical" gospels and so represent an alternative interpretation of him and of Christianity. This alternative account has been particularly evident since the discovery in Egypt in 1945 of the Nag Hammadi library of Gnostic texts; the most famous of these is the Gospel of Thomas, portraying Jesus as a master of pithy and enigmatic sayings.

The various schools of Gnosticism differed considerably, but basic themes included ideas such as the following: this world is imperfect because it was created by a lower, bumbling emanation of the true God rather than the Father of Lights above; the inner essence of humans is light from the highest realm which is entrapped in material bodies in this imperfect world (thus we are only strangers here and heaven is our home); Jesus has come from the Halls of Light above to recall those scattered and snared sparks of light from the eternal Flame; by true *gnosis*, or wisdom imparted by Jesus, we can make the ascent out of this world, past the evil *archons*, or guardians who patrol this prisonhouse planet, and back to our true home above. Although little is known about Gnostic organization and church life, they seem mainly to have been like "schools" around particular teachers of the Wisdom but also to have had sacraments, charms, and mysteriously beautiful rituals and dances that enacted their teachings.[6]

Scholarship on Gnosticism has brought out the important role of women among Jesus' disciples, especially Mary Magdalene. The Gospel of Mary (probably 100–200 C.E.) presents Mary Magdalene as especially close to Jesus, frequently better able than the other apostles to interpret his meaning, and to ask the right questions. She was even called the "Apostle of the Apostles." The Gospel of Mary has Peter saying to her: "Sister, we know that the savior loved you more than other women. Tell us the words of the savior that you remember, which you know and we do not. We have not heard them."[7]

Even more challenging to conventional Christianity is the Gospel of Judas (from around 150 C.E.), a sensation when published in 2006, which offers the radical view that Jesus (who in this text, unlike in the New Testament, laughs a great deal) especially liked and trusted Judas, teaching him inner mysteries of the universe unrevealed to the other disciples, and then persuading him to do the necessary act of betrayal.[8]

Tales of this sort may appear outlandish to those whose view of Christianity is shaped by the books and doctrines that came to be accepted as standard. Nonetheless, it must be recognized that they are nearly as old as the recognized texts and that Christianity up to around 300 C.E., at least, was a religion of numerous varieties. Indeed, many scholars now believe that simply labeling, and perhaps dismissing, a wide spectrum of them as "Gnosticism" may be misleading. In any case, "Gnosticism" and much else could well have seemed as plausible as any other version of Christianity back then, and echoes of the Gnosis have resounded down the centuries in various "heresies."[9]

THE EMERGENCE OF NORMATIVE CHRISTIANITY

Eventually, the new faith coalesced around a standard narrative. As the first century advanced, the many communities of Jesus' followers began to write down and circulate what had previously been orally transmitted accounts of the sayings of Jesus and stories of the life of Jesus. These writings in many ways reflected the views of the various traditions of the communities from which the writings came—some emphasizing the death and resurrection of Jesus and others emphasizing the teachings of Jesus. Eventually, four of these writings became accepted as the four Gospels; there were others that were not. The first three of the Gospels, or lives of Jesus, are called the **Synoptic Gospels**. They obviously go together because long passages are virtually identical. The shortest, Mark, was evidently written first, probably between 65 and 70 C.E. Matthew (c. 70–80 C.E.) and Luke (c. 80 C.E.) borrowed much from Mark and added much of their own, emphasizing different aspects of the life of Jesus and his teachings. The fourth Gospel, John (its date is uncertain, but it is probably late first century), was evidently written from a completely different point of view. Concerned to present Jesus as the light and life of the world, the eternal Logos or principle of God's activity revealed to the eye of faith, it contains much that is religiously beautiful and profound, yet it is perhaps less close to the literal words of Jesus than the other three—though matters like this are the subject of continuing scholarly discussion beyond the scope of this book.[10]

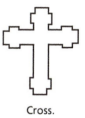

Cross.

Added to this growing corpus of Christian literature were the **Epistles** (letters) of Paul, written earlier than the Synoptic Gospels, only twenty to thirty years after the crucifixion and much treasured in the churches he had founded; the Acts of the Apostles by Luke (probably written 85–90 C.E.); and other writings of varying types, some of which finally became part of the Christian Bible and some of which did not.

At this time we also see the emergence of normative Christian beliefs, rites, and church organization in some localities, while others remained loosely organized groups. This stage, sometimes called "early Catholicism" because it obviously represents the beginning of the course of Christian development that led to the structure of the medieval church, can be found as far back as the New Testament "Pastoral Epistles" (I and II Timothy, Titus) and the Epistles of Peter. There were formulas of belief slowly becoming standardized into creeds (e.g., II Timothy 2:11–13), attacks on heretics (e.g., those found in I Titus 1:10–16), and a quieter, more sober and conventionally moralistic way of life. With the hope of many in the Christian community for an early appearance of the Lord in glory disappointed, the virtues of soundness and self-control were urged, being needed for a long-term sojourn as the children of light in the midst of a dark world (but one not yet passing away). The brilliant apocalyptic colors of the Gospels and the tumultuous early days of Acts fade; concern turns to sorting out true from false doctrine and the proper qualifications and prerogatives of church officers and various classes of members, such as young men and widows.

Yet the churches of those days had an appeal of their own. Each local church came to be headed by an *episcopos* ("overseer"—the term "bishop" is derived from this Greek word), assisted by a council of *presbyteroi* ("elders"—"priests" or "presbyters" in English), and by *diakonoi* ("servers"—"deacons" in English, whose special duty was caring for the needy). The churches apparently had many other categories or roles as well, from readers and healers to widows, each with special duties in worship and otherwise and with perhaps a special place to stand during services. Everyone was to have a definite and important part. The church did extensive welfare work among its membership. Like most other such organizations in the Roman world, it was a mutual aid society as well as a religious fellowship.

The church met for worship early in the morning on Sunday (of course, just another ordinary workday then), the day commemorating the Resurrection, and perhaps on other days as well. To avoid legal problems, Christians often gathered quietly and, until late in the third century when churches began to be built, in private homes or catacombs. Worship combined Scripture, prayer, and instruction with the **Eucharist** ("giving thanks"), the sacred communal meal representing the Last Supper which as the Mass, **Holy Communion**, or Lord's Supper, remains the principal act of worship of Roman Catholic, Eastern Orthodox, and some Protestant churches.

Imagine that you were at one of these services in those days when the church was a semiunderground body in the Roman Empire. At the back of the room, you would see the bishop seated and facing you from behind a table, with his presbyters seated on either side. In front of the table would stand the deacons, probably two in number. The service would begin with readings from the Scriptures of the Old Testament, with emphasis on the passages believed to prophesy the coming of Christ, and from the Psalms, used as hymns of praise. Many people might take part in these readings. The bishop, and possibly others, would discourse on their meaning. Perhaps letters of the apostles and accounts from the life of Christ would also be read; gradually these came to be more and more a formal part of Christian worship, until they evolved into the normative collection known as the New Testament. The bishop would then pray at some length, and the Kiss of Peace would be exchanged among those attending the service. After this, everyone would bring a gift of bread or wine up to the table. The bishop, standing behind the table with the elders, would raise his eyes to heaven and offer thanks for this food. Then the people would come forward to receive a piece of bread from the bishop and a bit of wine offered in a chalice held by a deacon, believing this to be a sacred meal in which Jesus Christ is mystically known and his grace imparted.[11] Not to be confused with the Holy Communion was the *agape*, or love feast, held afterward as a social communal meal.

The other great service was baptism. This initiation into the Christian life was generally held on Easter Eve. Only those who had received baptism would take part in the communion just described; *catechumens*, or those receiving instruction, and penitents going through a process of readmission after confessing a major sin would remain at the service only through the first part. Instruction would be very long and thorough, lasting perhaps for two full years, and it would be followed by careful intellectual and moral examination. Then during the week before Easter, the candidates would be given a final exam by the bishop on Wednesday, would bathe on Thursday, fast on Friday, be blessed and exorcised by the bishop on Saturday, keep an all-night vigil, and finally, early on Easter morning, would be baptized in a font or by having water poured over them and would immediately afterward receive Holy Communion.[12]

During this period, Christian intellectual life continued to increase the philosophical sophistication with which the faith was presented. Celebrated Christian thinkers such as Clement of Rome, Clement of Alexandria, Origen, Justin Martyr, Irenaeus, Tertullian, and others moved the emphasis from showing the continuity of Christianity with Judaism to showing its compatibility with Greek and Roman philosophy and its points of difference from it. This is natural, since the non-Jewish Greco-Roman world increasingly became the milieu of Christianity.

The tone of Christian thinkers ranged from the fiery Tertullian (c. 160–225 C.E.), a former lawyer who thought that everything **pagan** was alien to Christianity and who deemed faith alone and a very strict moral life the only proper Christian way, to the mild Clement of Alexandria who, with Origen, his fellow Alexandrian, emphasized that all truth leads to Christ, who is the Word or creative principle known to philosophy.

Everyone has heard of the persecutions of Christians under the Roman Empire: of **martyrs** hung upside down on crosses or burned at the stake or thrown to the lions in the Coliseum. Indeed, there were ghastly persecutions, although they were sporadic and local until the third century. Often Christians in the empire lived undisturbed lives, and while they were not an officially recognized religion, the general policy was to tolerate all groups, however bizarre, that did not present a clear threat to the government. Tradition has it that the Emperor Nero (r. 54–68 C.E.) instigated a persecution (in which the apostles Peter and Paul were killed) to deflect blame from himself for the disastrous fire at Rome; if so, such persecution was limited to the capital.

In the third century, however, persecutions were ordered for the entire empire under Decius (r. 249–251 C.E.), Valerian (r. 253–260 C.E.), and Diocletian (r. 284–305 C.E.). By this time, the numbers of Christians had grown quite visible, and troubles were increasing in the Roman state requiring both solidarity and scapegoats. In the face of external invasion and internal dissension, these emperors desperately wanted unity and did not yet realize that the empire and Christianity could converge and be mutually supportive, as they were to do within a century. Ironically, it was generally the most conscientious emperors who persecuted Christianity, for they took most seriously their responsibilities for unifying and strengthening the realm.

Usually the persecution was done in the context of a drive for all subjects of the empire to express loyalty to the sovereign, who was nominally regarded as divine. Few subjects took this seriously, but it was expected that they would express patriotism by burning a bit of incense before a portrait or image of the emperor, an act regarded as offering divine honor. At the times of persecution, Christians might be summoned by the authorities and required to make this and comparable gestures or suffer imprisonment and possibly death. Christians, regarding the token gesture as idolatry, frequently refused it. Such refusal was taken as proof that they were subversive—and they suffered the consequences.

Greatest havoc was wrought by Diocletian, a dedicated and capable man who strove desperately to save a rapidly disintegrating situation but who suffered many problems and bad advice. By his time Christianity had numerous churches, costly possessions, and large numbers. The emperor shrank at first from shedding blood but ordered all Christian buildings, artifacts, and books destroyed, seeking thereby to weaken the obstreperous movement. These actions did not work, however, and before long his agents were working torture and death as well among faithful Christians.

It must be noted that a certain cult of martyrdom flourished among Christians. Those who died violently under the various persecutions were afforded heroic status, and the bones and graves of many became relics and shrines. Here began the veneration of **saints**. There were those who looked to the example of Jesus Christ and the earlier martyrs and were fully prepared for, and even sought out, the martyr's death. Thus Ignatius, bishop of Antioch, was taken to Rome in the days of Trajan (r. 98–117 C.E.), where he met his death at the jaws of wild beasts in the amphitheater. Thinking no doubt of the Holy Communion, he wrote to the church at Rome while on his journey to death:

> I am God's wheat; I am ground by the teeth of the wild beasts that I may end as the pure bread of Christ. If anything, coax the beasts on to become my sepulcher and to leave nothing of my body undevoured so that, when I am dead, I may be no bother to anyone. I shall be really a disciple of Jesus Christ if and when the world can no longer see so much as my body. Make petition, then, to the Lord for me, so that by these means I may be made a sacrifice to God.

In this vein, he also wrote:

> The pangs of new birth are upon me. Forgive me, brethren, do nothing to prevent this new life.[13]

THE CHRISTIAN TRIUMPH

Not long in terms of world history was Christianity to dwell amidst the smell of beasts and blood, save in memory. In the early decades of the fourth century, Christianity emerged from its place as merely one of the competitors in the lavish spiritual marketplace of the Roman world to become first the dominant and then the sole official religion of the empire and, in time, of all Europe. This reversal happened with surprising speed. True, the church had done well during the long years of comparative peace since the end of the Decian persecution in 251 C.E. In some places, especially in Asia Minor, Christianity was the majority faith, and nearby Armenia had become the first officially Christian nation around 300 C.E. In many cities, including Nicomedia in Asia Minor (modern Turkey), to which Diocletian had moved his capital, stood impressive churches, and members of the emperor's family as well as the lowly supported them until his persecution of the church.

Nonetheless, the reasons for the triumph of Christianity around 312 C.E. are not all immediately apparent. The faith of Christ had no greater prestige than the Neoplatonic mysticism favored by philosophers or the Mithraism popular in the army or the ancient polytheisms nostalgically upheld by patrician traditionalists. Indeed, it had been only a few years earlier (303 C.E.) that, at the instigation of his son-in-law Galerius, the aging Diocletian imposed persecution.

But one of Diocletian's commanders, Constantine, who emerged in Western Europe after the former's abdication in 305 C.E. as an Augustus or "coemperor," favored the Christian cause. Another coemperor, Maximinus Daia, who continued sporadic persecution in the East, was defeated by another contender, Licinius. The latter met with Constantine in 313 C.E. to decree toleration of all religions in the Empire, via the **Edict of Milan**. Thereafter, Constantine and Licinius ruled together.

Deep psychological currents favorable to Christianity apparently ran through the complex mind of Constantine. His mother, Helena, had become a Christian, and at the famous battle of the Milvian Bridge, where he was victorious over a rival in 312 C.E., it is said he saw a cross in the sky and the letters IHS—the Greek beginning of the name Jesus or the Latin initials for *In Hoc Signo*, "By this sign."[14]

After 323 C.E., Constantine was the sole emperor. He established his capital in Byzantium, later named Constantinople (modern Istanbul), and pursued policies favorable to Christianity, although he was not himself baptized until he was on his deathbed. In 325 C.E., he sponsored a council of bishops at Nicaea, which made most of what is now the **Nicene Creed** the standard of doctrine. But Christianity did not become the official religion, the only one whose open practice was permitted, until the reign of Theodosius I (379–395).

During the same period, and largely in reaction to doctrinal disputes, the **canon** of authoritative New Testament scriptures was established. It was not finalized until a council of bishops at Carthage in 419. The final codification of scripture was thus fairly late and came after much of the development of Christian teaching, worship, and social organization. On the other hand, the selection was influenced by the previous acceptance of most of those books as canonical and therefore as authoritative by the most prominent churches. Still, many scholars think that the inclusion of the four Gospels, each reflecting a different perspective on the life of Jesus and his message (rather than choosing one as authoritative), represented a compromise among the various groups who wanted their account included in the canon. The last disputes over the canon were chiefly about the Pastoral Epistles, Jude, the Book of Revelation, and whether the Epistle to the Hebrews was actually written by Paul. Many then, as now, were dubious about its Pauline authorship but accepted it anyway as part of the New Testament.[15]

While the great **pagan** temples were turned into churches or public buildings and the centers of pagan learning were dispersed, **paganism** lingered a long time in the countryside. In the course of becoming the dominant religion of society and subsuming all the roles that had animated the former faiths—from folk religion to the mysteries to Neoplatonist philosophy—Christianity continued to develop. In church organization, the bishops remained in the cities where the faith had long held sway, becoming more and more the spiritual parallels of governors and magistrates. Successors of the *presbyteroi* of old, parish priests, ordinarily one to a church, strove to Christianize the archaic agricultural religion of the countryside. Festivals such as Christmas and Easter, which borrowed symbols from the indigenous pagan religions of conquered lands, became colorful public holidays, while pagan shrines and temples changed names. Moreover, the new faith spread rapidly among the restless Germanic tribes who were replacing Roman provinces with their rude kingdoms and dukedoms.

THE FOUNDATIONS OF MEDIEVAL CHRISTIANITY

Let us look more explicitly at the changes Christianity underwent during the medieval period in terms of the forms of religious expression.

Theoretical expression became more and more solidified, particularly in regard to an understanding of the **incarnation**—how God became human in Christ. This articulation took place by means of **General Councils**, meetings to which all bishops were invited. They sought to condemn **heresy**, or false teaching, and define correct, or **orthodox**, teaching.

There were four important General Councils, all dealing basically with issues involving the incarnation. The **Council of Nicaea** in 325 C.E., affirmed, in the Nicene Creed, that Christ is of one substance or essence with God the Father. This definition opposed that of others who held that Christ was only "like" God, a lower being sent as God's envoy. The **Council of Constantinople** reaffirmed the Nicaean position in 381 C.E. The **Council of Ephesus** in 431 C.E., affirmed Christ was always God from his mother's womb (so it called Mary, his mother, *Theotokos*—"God-bearer"), not a man who had been made Son of God. The **Council of Chalcedon** in 451 C.E., affirmed that Christ is both True God and True Man, two natures conjoined in one person.

A similar matter that underwent theological refinement at about the same time, although never the subject of a General Council, was the doctrine of the **Trinity**.

A rendering of the west facade of the Cathedral of Notre-Dame, Reims, France.

Christians had experienced God in three basic ways: as God the Heavenly Father, as the Son of God in Jesus Christ, and as the Holy Spirit who was promised by Christ and who filled the community in the upper room on Pentecost. Now it was written that these are three "persons" bound together in infinite love, who nonetheless are but one God.

In the West, Christians were less involved in the General Councils than in the East, but theological work continued there, too. The greatest figure for the West was **Augustine** (c. 354–430 C.E.), a North African bishop who taught about the Trinity and about **grace**, God's free gift or help, among other topics. Concerning grace, Augustine emphasized that God takes the initiative in relations between himself and us. All begins with grace, for we cannot seek God or do things pleasing to him unless he first enables us, because we are naturally self-centered and do not truly seek God or do selfless acts on our own. In such terms as these, Augustine explained **original sin**, the doctrine that holds that human beings inherit a sinful nature and without God's help we humans can do nothing that goes beyond our self-centeredness.

It is too easy, however, to stress the history of ideas in the church and forget that changes of similarly immense consequence were going on in worship and social organization. Indeed, as always, for the uneducated majority, what was experienced in worship and the socio-political role of religious institutions was much more influential than the discussions of theologians.

As the church moved out of the spiritual underground of the great cities and into spacious buildings, typically modeled on the basilica or the Roman court of law, or into the rural world of peasant and lord, the liturgy, or pattern of worship, also changed, becoming expressive and ornate. The clergy wore symbolically colored garments and moved with slow ritual, accompanied by music and incense, to present and bless the bread and wine of the Eucharist. In the West, the language of the service was Latin; in the East, it was Greek. These tongues, especially Latin, quickly became "sacred" languages, like Sanskrit in India, as the vernacular changed and numerous new peoples came into the orbit of the faith, for the Christian population was rapidly growing and changing.

During the fourth century, virtually all the peoples of the old Roman Empire were at least superficially Christianized—even those of areas no longer Christian today, such as North Africa, Egypt, Syria, Palestine, and Asia Minor. In the East, missionaries won converts in Ethiopia, Mesopotamia, Persia, and even India. In the West, Visigoths, Saxons, Vikings, Franks, and other North European tribes now ruled the lands only barely brought under the cross in the waning days of imperial order; the situation was often chaotic. By the year 1000, however, all but a few corners of Europe had been converted, and the rambunctious tribes had begun slow progress toward becoming nations.

Let us look briefly at two examples: England and Ireland. Christianity came to Roman Britain in the third century. Apparently it was brought by unknown soldiers and merchants, although stories were told in the Middle Ages that Paul himself had visited Britain or that Joseph of Arimathea (he who claimed the body of Jesus) had come there and planted the sacred tree known as the Glastonbury Thorn, a favorite object of pilgrimage. These legends are significant because they typify the believing world of medieval Christianity. The Celtic and Roman settler population had become widely Christian by the time Britain was cut off from Rome early in the fifth century.

Shortly afterward, massive invasions of Danes, Angles, and Saxons, still adherents of the old Germanic religion of Wotan and Thor, had pushed the Christianized Britons back to the far West, to what is now Wales and Cornwall and their vicinity. There they held out; the tales of King Arthur reflect in part the days of these beleaguered people, who still remembered something of Rome and Christ, as well as old Celtic religious motifs. But in 597 C.E. a missionary named Augustine (not the North African bishop) was sent out from Rome to Kent, the Saxon kingdom in the extreme southeast corner of England. Its king and people, through the agency of the king's Christian wife, were converted, and not long afterward all the Anglo-Saxon kingdoms—Wessex, Sussex, Mercia, and the rest—had submitted to the faith of Christ.

Ireland's conversion was accomplished by the famous Patrick, who died in 461 C.E. The population was still tribal, and the church followed tribal lines. It was full of zeal and its monks full of wanderlust. Missionaries from Ireland traveled to many parts of Europe. Ireland was Christian while England and much of the continent was not; in those confused times, Ireland was a preeminent center of Christian learning and effort in the West.

The classical pattern of bishops, who governed the church in geographical areas called *dioceses*, and of parish priests in each community was perpetuated wherever the church acquired a foothold. The bishops of major cities became known as "archbishops." The Council of Chalcedon made the bishops of five of the most important cities in the ancient empire—Constantinople, Antioch, Alexandria, and Jerusalem in the East, and Rome in the West—**patriarchs**, and the patriarch of Constantinople, the capital of the Byzantine Empire, was called the ecumenical or universal patriarch. With this title, he is still the chief dignitary of the Eastern Orthodox Church, though only as "first among equals." On the other hand, the patriarch of Rome came to be called the **pope**. He had long been looked upon as the chief arbitrator of disputes and heir of the church which, having been associated with the apostles Peter and Paul themselves, had an apostolic tradition of unquestionable soundness. Indeed, especially in the West, many said that the pope, successor to Peter as bishop of Rome, was heir to those promises that Matthew's Gospel records Jesus as having given to Peter:

You are Peter, and on this rock I will build my church, and the powers of death shall not prevail against it. I will give you the keys of the kingdom of heaven, and whatever you bind on earth shall be bound in heaven, and whatever you loose on earth shall be loosed in heaven. (Matthew 16:18–20)

Furthermore, in the confusion that attended the collapse of the Roman Empire, the popes, particularly strong popes such as Leo (r. 440–461 C.E.) and Gregory (r. 590–604 C.E.), emerged as dominant figures in both church and secular affairs, beacons of stability and hope in a dark and terrifying world. It is not surprising that by the Middle Ages, their sovereignty over the church in the West was firmly established.

One extremely important social development in Christianity was **monasticism**. In order to serve God better and in search of security and purity in a corrupt and

Statue of Saint Gudule, a seventh-century saint, and Saint Michael in the Cathedral of Saint Michael and Saint Gudule in Brussels, Belgium.

chaotic society, young men—and, not long afterward, young women—left society to remain unmarried and form communities focused on the worship of God. The monastic movement started in Egypt in the late third century when men such as Anthony and Pachomius went into the desert to pursue lives of prayer as hermits. Soon they were followed by disciples, and communities grew up. Before long the idea had spread throughout the Christian world. Benedict (c. 529 C.E.) established the Benedictine monastic pattern, which became normative for the church in the West. Monasteries quickly became centers of both missionary work and the preservation of learning, as well as orphanages, hospitals, and way stations.[16]

Parallel to monasticism was the general idea of celibacy, or the unmarried state, for the clergy. There was a widespread feeling, based both on the examples of the apparently unmarried Jesus and Paul the apostle and on lingering aversion to the "passions" derived from Greek philosophy, that the celibate life was holier and closer to perfection than the married. The actual situation in the early church was mixed, however. In the East, it was held that bishops should be celibate but that the ordinary clergy could be married. This pattern was established at least by the time of the General Councils and prevails in the Eastern Orthodox Church today. In the West, partly in response to the social disruptions, regional churches and finally the papacy enjoined celibacy for all clergy, and this was observed (at least officially) everywhere in the West by the Middle Ages.

Patterns of popular Christian worship also evolved strikingly. One feature was devotion to the Blessed Virgin Mary, mother of Jesus Christ, and to other saints. It had roots in the early church's veneration of martyrs and in Christian belief that all who are in Christ, whether in this life or the next, are one family and so able to communicate with and help one another. Now this area of the faith grew and expanded. Shrines and altars to saints and festivals for them appeared in both East and West. Statues in the West and icons (sacred paintings) in the East, as well as saints' relics—bones, clothing—came to focus this devotion. The cultus, especially for the vast illiterate masses now Christianized, provided a deeply felt color and warmth. With it also came pilgrimages, journeys for the sake of devotion to Jerusalem and other holy places.

Christian life now had two basic emphases: the winning of eternal life in heaven and the avoiding of hell after death and following Christian moral teachings while on Earth. Although the Last Judgment, typically portrayed on the rear wall of medieval churches, was much regarded, like death it was chiefly seen as a narrow portal to heaven. Heaven was gained through the **sacraments** (baptism, Holy Communion, and the "last rites" especially) and by prayer, penitence for sins, and a moral life. Morality included doing those things that would make earthly society just and stable, a worthy prologue to heaven. Thus Christian moral teaching helped to make the medieval world, which idealized itself as an unchanging human social order lying between the time of Christ and the Last Judgment.

MEDIEVAL CHRISTENDOM

Let us look at the religious life of a medieval peasant, typical of the vast majority of people in Europe between 800 and 1500 and in many places until much later. A peasant's life would center on the village where other peasants lived, on the manor or castle of the lord, and on the church. In some cases, the lord would actually be a bishop or an abbot; usually he would be a hereditary feudal lord, who would spend much of his time leading his knights in combat with other lords and their knights and who would probably name the priest of the church.

The center of this community was the parish church. This stone building was an island of relative grace and color in a drab world. It might have vivid paintings and windows showing supernal things: a radiant saint, the wondrous Mother of God with her warm open arms and compassionate look, Christ judging high and low alike on the dreaded Last Day.

On Sunday morning, bells from this church would ring out, and the lord and his family and knights would gather together with the peasants in the church for Mass, generally at nine o'clock. The priest in his vestments would stand before the altar, and with many bows and elaborate gestures, wavings of incense and strikings of bells, he would celebrate the Mass. It was the same offering and blessing of bread that the early Christians had performed in their catacombs and upper rooms, but the priest would now be muttering in an old and sacred tongue the words that made the wafers of bread and cup of wine the Body and Blood of Christ for the saving of souls in his parish. He might also give a sermon. Priest and church were supported by glebe lands, fields of the manor set aside whose revenues went to this cause.

Besides Sundays, numerous festivals of saints broke the tedium and hard work of village life. Then would come special services, dancing, fairs, and traditional practices; some of them, like the Procession of the White Lady of Banbury (cited in Chapter 2), which brought great delight to the peasants, had clear pre-Christian background.[17]

There were other breaks in the rhythm, too. Merchants and tradesmen were able to make pilgrimages to shrines where miracles were said to take place, as Chaucer's pilgrims did, both men and independent women like the Abbess and the wife of Bath, to Canterbury. Some even went as far as Jerusalem. In other ways, too, the pattern of medieval life was often broken, for the Middle Ages were by no means the static "Age of Faith" sometimes imagined. Changes and dissidents were always present. The vicissitudes of war and weather and often disease swept continually through medieval town and countryside.

Rumors of the Crusades—those remarkable combinations of bloodthirstiness, greed, and piety—must have reached almost everywhere. The Crusades expressed the very spirit of medievalism, but they helped to bring that age to an end by opening up contact with new ideas from the East and from the Greek culture better preserved there, as well as leading to deep-seated enmity between Christian Europe and Islam and between Eastern and Western Christianity.

In 1054, before the Crusades started (in 1095), came the formal rupture between the **Eastern Orthodox** and Western (Roman) Catholic churches, known as the "Great Schism." The official reason was the *filioque* question—whether the Holy Spirit proceeds from both God the Father and God the Son (as the Western version of the Nicene Creed stated) or from the Father alone (as the Eastern version had it)—and a few other similar theological and ecclesiastical issues of similar quality. But the real issue was the growing authority of the papacy in the West (the word *filioque*, "and the Son," had been added to the Western Nicene Creed by authority of the pope, not of a General Council) and even more perhaps by wide cultural differences emerging between Western Europe and the Byzantine East. The split was effectively made irrevocable by the Crusades; the sack of Constantinople by soldiers of the cross in 1204 left a bitter legacy that made lasting reconciliation impossible.

The greatest Western religious thinker in the Middle Ages was **Thomas Aquinas** (c. 1225–1274), the major figure of the style of philosophy known as scholasticism. Influenced by the Aristotelianism of the Muslim thinker of Cordova, Averroës (whose works had been discovered by the West during the Crusades), Aquinas was concerned to distinguish between the realm of nature where reason holds sway and the realm of faith where revelation adds its gifts. The existence of God, shown by nature, is (he stated) knowable through reason alone, but the way to salvation can only be known by revealed Christian faith. The result of this philosophical and theological labor was a vast synthesis of Aristotelian science and philosophy, Christianity, and medieval experience, which summed up the vision of that age and has been the most important intellectual force in Roman Catholicism to the present. In it, all beings under God—angels, humanity, matter, sound reason, and sure revelation—have their logical places and reasonable duties in reflecting God's glory, a vision expressed poetically in the *Divine Comedy* of Dante Alighieri.

The Middle Ages teemed with new religious movements centering on holy, charismatic personalities, increasingly so as time advanced. The important thing to note is that these were challenges to the medieval order by a new, sometimes cantankerous but always deeply felt individualism and a rejection of the old corporate village faith of the parish church and the succession of festivals.[18] It is important also to realize that there were skeptics and religiously indifferent persons in the Middle Ages just as there are today and that many areas were barely reached by the church.

Most of the new religious movements were reactions to the church in favor of "Gospel simplicity" and "inwardness." They favored asceticism, fervent religious feelings, and freedom of movement for religious persons in contrast to the comparative wealth, objective worship of shrine and sacrament, and rootedness in feudal village and agricultural patterns of the conventional church. The dissident movements were, significantly, strongest among the crafts- and tradespeople of the burgeoning towns, although they sometimes swept through countryside districts on a wave of social protest. They were a combination of the age-old "holy man" ideal (which was sometimes exemplified by women as well) and the modern severing of religion from its rural roots. Both motifs contrast with the medieval alliance of religious and feudal concepts and of Christianity and agricultural religion.

Some of these movements, like the one of Francis of Assisi and his friars, remained within the orbit of orthodoxy. Francis, the "Little Poor Man," lived and inspired many others to live a life of Christian perfection marked by poverty, universal love, and a new personal devotion to the

Sculpture of Saint Francis of Assisi by Alfiero Nena near Lago d'Orta in the Piemonte region, Italy.

human Christ in the manger and on the cross. In a remarkable episode in 1219 during the Fifth Crusade, Francis traveled to Egypt where he courageously went behind enemy lines to call unarmed on the Sultan, seeking to explain Christianity and achieve peaceful coexistence between the warring faiths. The Muslim ruler was impressed, thinking that if all Christians were like Francis, there would be no need for war.[19] Francis's order of friars, or "brothers," wandering, begging, and relatively free from control by bishop or parish priest, transmitted his message throughout Europe and soon enough to Latin America and the Orient.

Other such preachers, however, were considered heretical. Some, like the Albigensians or Cathari, who were the object of brutal persecution in the thirteenth century, were inspired by the ancient Gnostic-type religion called Manichaeism (which held that matter is the source of evil), as well as by simplicity and inwardness. The Albigensians so honored spirit above flesh that they held self-starvation to be a noble thing. Others, like the Waldensians, the Lollards, and the Hussites, were more concerned with conforming Christian life to their reading of the Bible.

THE REFORMATION AND MARTIN LUTHER

The next development was the Reformation, which carried all these trends to their natural conclusion—a new style of Christianity. Perhaps the onset of change was abetted by the Black Death, or bubonic plague, which swept across Europe, wiping out nearly a third of the population from 1348 to 1350, disrupting traditional patterns of society, leaving many parishes without clergy, and on a deeper level going far toward discrediting the traditional faith and church. (People asked themselves: "Why did good and bad alike succumb to the plague? Why did the prayers of the traditional church not protect us?")

At the same time, the prestige of the papacy as the unifying force in Europe and Christendom was greatly weakened by the abduction of the pope by agents of the French king in 1309 and the relocation of the papal residence to Avignon, under French domination, from 1309 to 1377. Above all, the papacy's image was tarnished by the resultant Great Schism of the West of 1378–1417, when two "popes" reigned, one in Rome and one in Avignon, each claiming to be the true ruler of the church and each holding the allegiance of several nations.

Against this background, groups such as the English Lollards, followers of John Wycliffe, began around 1380 to demand such reforms as abolition of clerical celibacy, of the use of images, of prayers for the dead, of pilgrimages, and of elaborate vestments. They demanded that the clergy should chiefly preach and that the scriptures should be freely available to all in the vernacular language. In Bohemia and Moravia, the Hussites, followers of John Hus, made similar demands, particularly asking that the church manifest poverty and that church lands be expropriated. Some, like John Hus in 1415, were executed as heretics by being burned at the stake.

It was not until the sixteenth century, however, that new ideas came into their own at a time of the slow decline of feudalism, the rise to prominence of towns, and the corresponding shift of Christian emphasis (even in Catholic mysticism) from churchly and sacramental religion to a preoccupation with inner motivation and experience. However, it would be an oversimplification to say that these changes caused the Reformation.

The Reformation was overtly focused on spiritual and theological issues, however. The man who by far most influenced its course, Martin Luther (1483–1546), was little concerned consciously with these matters of social history. He had been a scholarly friar of the Augustinian order since the age of twenty-one, though his father—a strict, pious, enterprising civic leader engaged in the mining business in

Statue of Martin Luther in Magdeburg, Germany.

the small German town of Eisleben—was typical of the kind of man the Reformation would help supersede knights, lords, and peasants. Nonetheless, it was Luther's deeply inward spiritual struggles that defined the issues, language, and direction of the Reformation.

In his monastery, Luther experienced grueling anxiety. His problem was that he felt himself a sinner, however blameless a life he had lived as a monk. As long as he thought of his life in terms of how much he had to do, what standards he had to meet, what religious acts he had to perform, and what devout feelings he had to feel, he could only live, it seemed, in a cruel uncertainty, which would virtually lead to madness if one were really serious about it—and Luther was nothing if not serious. He felt trapped; he was commanded to love God, but how could one love a God whose demands left one in such anguish? Could he ever know if he had done enough?

Then, in studying the scriptures, Luther struggled with the lines, "He who is righteous by faith shall live" (Habakkuk 2:4; Romans 1:17), until this saying provided a sunrise of new awareness that led to his doctrine of *sola fides*, "faith alone." He realized to the depths of his being that what set a person in right relationship with God was not the things he had been trying before but simple faith—sincere belief, trust, and intention—and this, as a matter of inner attitude, was available to anyone at any time. In fact, it is not really a matter of what we do at all, for faith is first of all a gift— a grace (from *gratia*, meaning "free") from God—

always free, always poured out in love, to which we only can respond with sincerity. When Luther realized this, all else appeared superfluous and likely to confuse. For this reason, he insisted also on the principle of *sola scriptura*, the Bible alone as guide to Christian faith and practice, for he felt that salvation by grace through faith was the clear and central message of the scriptures and that its obscuring had come about through overlays of human philosophy and ecclesiastical tradition.

Luther's new understanding of Christianity first brought him into conflict with its medieval version over the issue of the sale of **indulgences**. Indulgences were related to the doctrine of **purgatory**—a universally held medieval belief that there is an intermediate state between heaven and hell for those who die as neither saints nor hopeless sinners. Their souls suffer purging fires for a long or short time, until they have been cleansed of evil and justice is satisfied, and they can then await entry into the presence of God. The pope, it was believed, held the spiritual key to a "treasury of merit"—the superabundance of merit attained by Christ and the saints. Indulgences were certificates issued by the pope, the effect of which was to transfer to the penitent some of this merit. This affirmed that because the recipient had done an adequate number of acts of penitence and devotion, so many "days"—or possibly all—of his or her prospective suffering in purgatory had been remitted. Indulgences could be obtained for oneself or even by one person on behalf of another, living or dead.

This profoundly medieval doctrine was not without its attractive side. It was a concrete way of stating the benefits accrued from such extra and innocent religious acts as pilgrimage, and it suggested, in the exchange of merit idea, that Christians deeply share in one another's lives and can bear one another's burdens. It was an implementation of the communion of saints. Indulgences are still made available in the Roman Catholic Church, but in Luther's day, indulgences were being widely distributed in Germany with little consideration but for the donation of money customarily given by the recipient. In effect, they were being used as a means of church fund-raising, and a special drive had been implemented to raise funds for the building of St. Peter's Basilica in Rome. Moreover, the theology behind indulgences went very much counter to Luther's new inner discovery of salvation by grace through faith only. The use of indulgences by the Roman Catholic Church at that time also raised the hackles of nascent German nationalism, for many Germans felt that they were being exploited for the sake of interests in Rome.

On October 31, 1517, Luther reportedly posted ninety-five theses, or points for debate, on the door of All Saints Church in Wittenberg, which served as the bulletin board of the university where Luther taught theology and Bible. It was the eve of All Saints' Day, when many relics of the saints (a comparably questionable matter with Luther) would be exposed for veneration in that church. In the famous Ninety-five Theses, Luther spoke against abuses of indulgences, relics, and the like, but the tone was not extreme, nor did he question papal authority or the doctrine of purgatory as such. He stressed the supreme value of inwardness and of sharing the sufferings of Christ more than prematurely trying to take advantage of heaven: a theology of the cross rather than a theology of glory.

This challenge started as a theological dispute, but it quickly escalated beyond what one would normally expect of such arguments among monks. Luther was engaged in a course that finally led to his rejection of papal authority as its logical outcome, and this in turn produced his excommunication by Rome in 1521.

Public opinion in Germany tended to take Luther's side. Spurred on by his pamphlet "Address to the Christian Nobility of the German Nation," a sense of German national pride and identity, long smoldering under cultural and spiritual domination from southern Europe, was inflamed. When Luther was summoned before the Imperial Diet at Worms to defend himself, he may not actually have used the famous words, "Here I stand; God help me, I can do no other," but that was what he meant, and his defiance of resented authority deeply stirred many a German patriot. But this did not please the young Holy Roman Emperor Charles V, who desired to continue the alliance between his throne and that of the pope.[20]

The test of inward faith, rather than rites, sacraments, or pious deeds, was congruous with a longstanding German mystical bent. The precise theological points at issue may have mattered less to the knights and people at large than to scholars, but the common folk grasped the implication that the new teachings meant all persons were fully equal before God. When Luther's German Bible and simplified services in the vernacular soon appeared, people well understood both the new orientation toward inward faith and the implicit Germanic self-affirmation.

Luther had hoped to see the church purified and Christians everywhere find new inner freedom and peace. It was a cause of grief and bitterness to him that one of the most conspicuous results of reform was conflict—theological, political, and military. In the following century, conflict escalated into the devastating Thirty Years' War, finally settled at the peace of Westphalia in 1648. Scandinavia, most of northern Germany, and small minorities elsewhere were thereafter **Lutheran**.

Engraving of John Calvin.

CALVIN

The most important reformer after Luther was John Calvin (1509–1564). He was French but is associated mainly with Geneva in Switzerland. As a young man, he was a Renaissance **humanist**, but in 1533 he was converted to the Protestant movement that Luther had spearheaded. He immediately wrote his theological masterpiece, *Institutes of the Christian Religion*. The brief first edition was published in 1536, but Calvin kept revising and expanding it until the definitive edition of 1559.

After 1541, Calvin lived in Geneva, which had recently thrown out its ruling bishop and become Protestant. Calvin was invited to take over leadership. Reluctantly (he much preferred a quiet scholarly life), he accepted. During his stay, Geneva became a kind of holy community of the Reformed faith, dominated by Calvin and other clergy, who enforced strict moral rectitude and correct belief in church and city government alike.

Calvin's theology is based on a strong contrast between the infinite greatness and power of God and the sinfulness of humanity. God's glory fills the universe; the division between the sacred and the secular is done away with, for all is sacred. Furthermore, Calvin held to a doctrine of **predestination**—all that happens is due solely to God's will—from life and death to the smallest seemingly accidental events. Nonetheless, humankind is in rebellion against God; God permits this in order that his mercy may be shown in the salvation of those whom he chooses, while divine justice is affirmed by the punishment of the rest. Those whom God chooses for eternal life do not have any merit of their own; they are recipients of his grace which, as Luther (following Augustine) had emphasized, must come before anything right that humans can do. The "elect," those chosen through grace, will be marked by a righteous life and a seemingly spontaneous and persevering predilection for true religion. Calvin's theology also emphasized the mystical union of the Christian with Christ.

Calvin stressed, like Luther, the importance of the Bible alone as the normative guide for Christians. In church organization, he made greater changes than Luther had made. Doing away with bishops, he gave considerable place to local control and boards of elders, or **presbyters**. But like Luther he dealt harshly with dissenters. The sacraments of baptism and the Lord's Supper were greatly simplified in administration, and the preaching of the **Word of God**, the chief means by which people are called to faith and grace, was given new emphasis.

Calvinists insisted, as did other Protestants, that everyone should be able to read the Bible, and this gave much impetus to education. It should also be noted that **Calvinism** appealed especially to the rising business class in Western Europe. Its stress on the elect's sense of inner call, commitment, and righteousness in the midst of work in the world, rather than sacerdotalism or monasticism, and its stern ethics focusing on self-denial, hard work, and individual responsibility contributed to the psychology that made this class prosperous and, in fact, for several centuries second to none in worldwide influence. Sometimes prosperity was seen as in itself a sign of divine election and favor.

Today, churches known as Reformed, Presbyterian, or Congregational come from the Calvinist tradition, although Calvin's original message has been varyingly modified by them over the years. Calvinism became dominant in Holland,

Scotland, and parts of Germany and Switzerland. The Puritan movement in England and America was Calvinist as well and has had tremendous impact on life in those countries and in their spheres of influence. Minority Protestant churches in France, Hungary, and some other parts of Europe are also Calvinist in background.

THE ENGLISH REFORMATION

In England the Reformation took yet another form. It is natural that this country of Wycliffe and the Lollards, and of emerging nationalism as well, should have harbored many people who responded enthusiastically to news of the events in Germany. Yet the English character has always exhibited a sense of pragmatism, moderation, and appreciation of tradition as well as a thirst for reform. All of this is evident in the English Reformation. Significantly, it did not receive its impetus from a wholly engaged reformer such as Luther or Calvin but from a rather sordid political matter. The king, Henry VIII, had been an enthusiastic defender of the old faith against the reformers, but in the early 1530s he desired to divorce his queen, Catherine of Aragon, because she had been unable to give him a living male heir. This step required a dispensation from the pope, which the latter, Clement VII, was unwilling to authorize. Therefore, Henry called upon Parliament to sever relations with Rome and make the king supreme head of the church in England. The resultant Act of Supremacy was passed in 1534. Henry was divorced and married again—and not for the last time.

Although strained relations between Rome and England were not new, undoubtedly the continental Reformation created an atmosphere conducive for Henry to take this final step. But those who desired a more thoroughgoing reformation were initially disappointed. Monasteries, convents, and pilgrimage shrines were promptly dissolved and their wealth divided among Henry's henchmen, but otherwise little changed. Most of the same bishops remained in their sees, and the same celibate priests in their parishes, saying the same Latin Mass. The king rigorously enforced Catholic doctrinal orthodoxy, but after Henry VIII died in 1546, the dike could no longer hold. Calvinist influence now pouring in from Geneva overbalanced the conservative side. A new form of worship in the English language, the *Book of Common Prayer*, was produced in 1549. Essentially, it perpetuated the basic structure of the old Latin forms but with substantial concessions to Protestantism on sensitive issues, such as its formal elimination of devotion to saints.

It should be added that the Reformation was far from universally appreciated among the ordinary people, many of whom saw only the arbitrary destruction of a religion that had given beauty and meaning to their lives and that had taught what they had been heretofore believed was true.[21] It was over a century before the religious situation in England was fully stabilized, but the essential outline of its official form, the Church of England, was already apparent in the Prayer Book of 1549. It was characterized by continuity of church structure from the Middle Ages and by English-language worship, which was Catholic in outline but designed to be nonoffensive to moderate Protestants. A pragmatic mentality emerged more slowly, allowing for some divergence of theological opinion among individual clergy and members, especially between the Catholic and Protestant traditions that met in the **Anglicanism** of the Church of England and subsequently in its daughter churches around the world.

A minority in England maintained allegiance to the Church of Rome. Over the next two centuries, others separated themselves from Anglicanism into more fully Protestant groups: Puritan (Calvinist), Baptist, Quaker, and Methodist. We shall now examine the story of groups such as these.

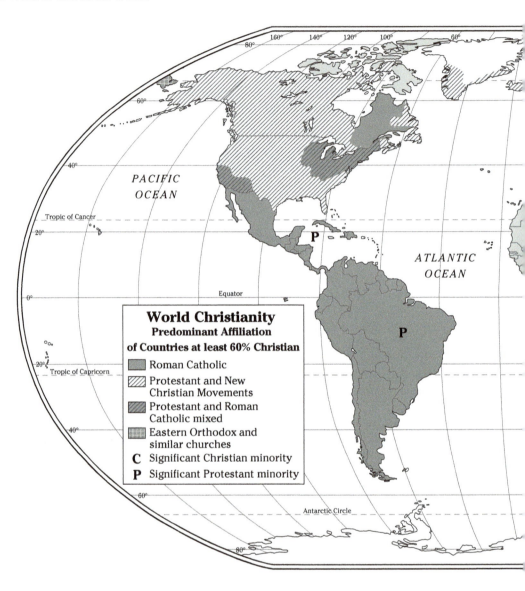

World Christianity
Predominant Affiliation
of Countries at least 60% Christian

Roman Catholic

Protestant and New
Christian Movements

Protestant and Roman
Catholic mixed

Eastern Orthodox and
similar churches

C Significant Christian minority

P Significant Protestant minority

RADICAL REFORM

Outside the great movements of Luther and Calvin and generally without the support
of rulers, the Reformation stirred up the zeal of many who wanted more far-reaching
changes in the church and often also in society. These movements typically stressed
the need for personal conversion experiences, moral perfection, and a close following of the New Testament both in faith and in social life. They varied from Anabaptists
(indirectly the forebears of modern Baptists in England and America), who rejected
the baptism of infants, insisting that Christians should have a personal conversion
experience and be baptized only after it; and Mennonites, who were perfectionists,
pacifists, and often communalists; to Unitarians, such as Michael Servetus, who
denied the doctrine of the Trinity and was burned at the stake in Calvin's Geneva.[22]

The non-Anglican Protestant groups in England have been particularly influential in world Christianity, because they have flourished wherever the far-flung
British people have settled overseas—especially in a nation as large and powerful

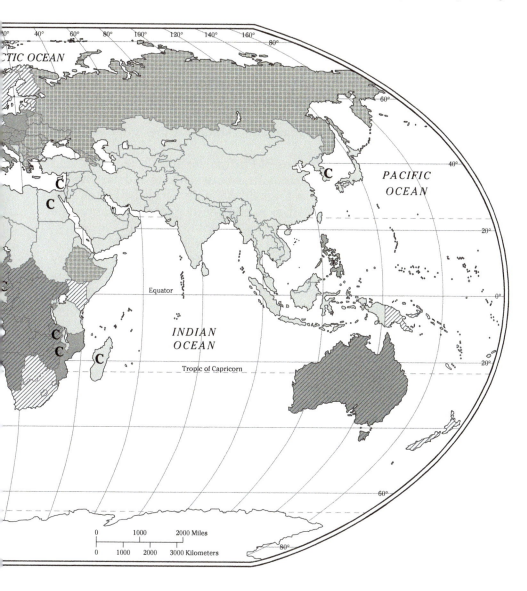

as the United States—and because they have generally been active in missionary work. Many of these Dissenters or Nonconformists, as they were called in England, emigrated overseas because of discrimination or persecution against them in the homeland. They have included the ancestors of today's Baptists, Methodists, Congregationalists (now the United Church of Christ), some Presbyterians (the background of others is in the established Church of Scotland), and **Quakers**, as well as newer American denominations founded by members of those churches in turn.

British nonconformity has its post-Reformation roots in the Puritan movement that began in the Church of England in the latter part of the sixteenth century. It was composed of highly Protestant-oriented Anglicans who wished to "purify" the church of what they saw as persisting elements of Catholicism. Puritans wanted simple (though long) services emphasizing preaching, biblical doctrine (with a Calvinist tone), moral earnestness, and an emphasis on the religious life and role of the laity.

Some of them preferred the Presbyterian or Congregational forms of church government to the bishops of the established church.

By the 1580s, some Puritans realized that the Church of England was not going to change its basic character (which was based on the Catholic–Protestant compromise known as the "Elizabethan settlement") in the direction they wished. Some of them felt compelled by conscience to worship apart from it with like-minded believers as the "gathered church." They were called "Independents" or "Separatists." These persons were severely repressed; some emigrated, like the "Pilgrims" who established Plymouth Colony in 1620.

In the seventeenth century, the fortunes of Puritanism and dissent rose and fell dramatically, becoming entangled in fierce battles between king and parliament, old aristocracy and rising middle class, as England painfully wrenched itself into the modern world. In general, the Stuart kings of the century strongly supported episcopacy and the Church of England (when they were not Roman Catholic sympathizers), while Parliament and the rising middle class favored Puritanism. Religion was not the only issue, but it was an age when religious positions were taken very seriously and became flags of allegiance of classes and interests as well as passionately held convictions. These struggles climaxed with the civil war between royal and parliamentary forces in the 1640s, the parliamentary Puritan victory and the beheading of King Charles I in 1649, as well as the subsequent rule of England by the faction controlled by Oliver Cromwell.

The 1650s, the decade of Cromwell's Commonwealth, were rife with radical social as well as religious movements. The Levellers wanted to abolish all hierarchical distinctions in society. The Diggers were agrarian communalists who, though harassed by both the law and violent mobs, endeavored to cultivate common land they said should be made available to the poor. The Ranters showed the interaction of radical political and spiritual protest by bringing to such causes their rejection of all authority of scripture or creed, holding instead only to an inner experience of Christ that makes all equal and free. The pacifist Society of Friends, known as the Quakers, the only of these groups from the Commonwealth period to survive institutionally down to the present, rejects such "outer" sacraments as water baptism and holy communion, and holds meetings for worship in which anyone is free to rise and speak. But hope that this radical decade signaled a new age in which the world would truly be "turned upside down" was dashed by the end of the Commonwealth in 1660.

In 1660, after Cromwell's death, the monarchy was restored, and Anglicanism was the established church. At first, despite the wishes of the new king, Charles II, for religious liberty, punishment was once again visited upon Dissenters. But gradually, as the bloody events since the Reformation made it clear that national uniformity in religion was a hopeless ideal, a trend toward accepting religious pluralism and liberty set in, culminating in the Toleration Act of 1689. It granted freedom of worship to all Christians except Roman Catholics and Unitarians. Their emancipation was not to come until much later.

These dramatic events had momentous consequences for the emerging denominationalism of the English-speaking world, including America—then a thin ribbon of seaboard colonies on the east coast of the New World. On both sides of the Atlantic, Congregationalism became the successor of

Engraving of Oliver Cromwell.

the independent Separatist congregations. English and American Baptists came from the same background; they were originally independent congregations who differed little from the others save in their rejection of infant baptism and their insistence that baptism can be given only to believers who have made a mature confession of faith. But as time went on, the general mood of Baptists shifted from Puritan Calvinism toward **Arminianism**—that is, emphasis on the individual's freedom to decide rather than on predestination. This is evident today in the tendency of Baptist preaching to stress the individual's responsibility to make a decision for faith in Christ.

The last great English dissenting movement was Methodism. It did not arise until the eighteenth century under the leadership of the Anglican clergyman John Wesley (1703–1791). After a youthful conversion experience, Wesley became an eloquent preacher who took all England as his parish, teaching the necessity of genuine conversion and the possibility of Christian perfection. This ministry made a powerful impact amid the social evils of the early Industrial Revolution (of which Wesley was well aware) in a time when the older churches were at a low ebb after the passions of the previous century. Societies and classes were formed in numerous communities to study and practice the Wesleyan approach. Although Wesley himself never intended that his movement should leave the Church of England, shortly after his death many of these groups, finding they could no longer keep their new wine in old bottles, became independent churches, both in England and in America. At least as many followers of Wesley remained within the Church of England to become the seedbed of an influential Anglican **evangelical** movement.

THE CATHOLIC REFORMATION

During the period of the Protestant Reformation, far-reaching developments were also taking place in the papal church against which the Protestants had rebelled, the church known—in distinction from Protestantism—as Roman Catholic. These developments are sometimes known collectively as the Counter-Reformation. But there was more to them than mere reaction to Protestant criticism, even though that formidable challenge certainly pressed Catholics to rethink and strengthen their tradition.

Some moves for Catholic reformation had been underway even before the Protestant reformers. The Fifth Lateran Council (1512–1517), on the eve of their Reformation, accomplished little but kept the idea of internal reform alive. Church leaders such as Cardinal Ximenez de Cisneros (1436–1517) in Spain had worked diligently for the improvement of clerical education and standards, but after Luther and Calvin, such efforts cried out for considerably augmented energy and scope. The need was answered by widespread renewed emphasis on Catholic education and discipline, especially among priests, and above all by new religious orders such as the Capuchins (1528) and the Jesuits (1540), who were dedicated to missionary work abroad and to holding the line against Protestantism in Europe.

The new situation also called for even greater Catholic unity and clearer definitions of the Catholic position, especially in regard to issues raised by the Protestant reformers. In that task the **Council of Trent** (1545–1563) is the centerpiece. At first attempting unsuccessfully to achieve reconciliation with the Protestants, the Council, during a second phase beginning in 1551, sought above all to purify and then defend the traditional Catholicism of the Middle Ages and before. The result of the Council's decrees was a church clearly governed by the pope and his "cabinet," or **Curia**, possessing a high degree of uniformity in doctrine and worship (centered on the Latin Mass); firmly maintaining such controversial teachings as purgatory and the invocation of saints; sure of its own authority based on both scripture and tradition rightly interpreted by its **magisterium,** or teaching jurisdiction; determined to uphold high levels of training and commitment; and prepared to win back what it could from the Protestants and to spread itself over the Earth. This was essentially the style of Catholicism that was to prevail for four centuries.

CHRISTIAN MYSTICISM AND DEVOTION

Before presenting the characteristics of the major branches of Christianity today, let us pause to look at the mystical and devotional side of the religion and its literary expression. By "mysticism," we mean experience interpreted as immediate contact with the divine, very frequently expressed in the language of unity: "I felt the oneness of all things"; "I was united with God." Such statements are the reasons why mystical experience is often said to be "beyond words," and mystics may shock the conventionally pious when they say that even prayer and meditation are practices to be surpassed.

Perhaps more than other religions, Christianity makes a clear-cut distinction between theological writing and mystical-devotional literature. In this respect, Christianity shows its difference from a religion like Buddhism, in which the equivalent of salvation would have to be the ultimate transformation of consciousness represented by Nirvana. But mainstream Christian theology and preaching are generally more concerned with salvation than with mystical experiences to which not every Christian is called.

The first Christian **mysticism** after the New Testament was deeply indebted to **Neoplatonic** philosophy for its terminology and philosophical concepts. But instead of developing language for laying out the Christian view of God, Christ, Holy Spirit, salvation, and so forth, mysticism was concerned to show how the soul inwardly rises to more perfect union with the One.

The most influential Christian mystical writings of this sort are those of the writer who called himself Dionysius the Areopagite—the Greek philosopher of the Book of Acts who heard Paul on Mars Hill (Areopagos) in Athens and who spoke of the God who is a "darkness which is beyond light." But the writings, which include *The Mystical Theology* and *The Divine Names*, are now believed to have been written by a Syrian monk of the sixth century.

This Dionysiac, Neoplatonist approach was most influential in the Christian mysticism of the Middle Ages and the Reformation.

But during the same Middle Ages, something else began stirring as well. A Christian mysticism of the affirmation of images was coming to flower. If the mysticism of the Neoplatonist, Dionysiac type asks its adherents to take away all that is not God and so is often called the "negative way," its counterpart is the affirming way of using images in the mind and before the eyes as stepping stones to God.[23] One example of an affirmative mystic was Francis of Assisi (1181–1226).

Francis of Assisi fervently promoted devotion to Jesus in the manger and on the cross, both affirmative pictures to which devotion could be affixed in mind and heart. Tradition credits the "Little Poor Man" of Assisi with making the first Christmas crèche and with receiving the **stigmata,** or marks of the nails and crown of thorns and wounded side of Christ on the cross, in his own flesh.

Protestant mysticism began in the age of Luther himself. Lutheran and Calvinist Christianity centered on inward faith and the inner workings of grace rather than the attainment of spiritual stages or mystical "states." Jacob Boehme (1575–1624), a German shoemaker, is widely considered the greatest Protestant mystical thinker. Boehme spoke of the divine infinity beyond words and concepts as the Original

Ground; its expression is accomplished through the interplay of opposites. All of this interplay is incarnate in humans, he held.

Movements like seventeenth-century Pietism on the European continent and Wesleyan Methodism in eighteenth-century England so stressed the importance of inwardly felt conversion in the believer that they easily led to positive devotional focus on the catalyst of the change—Jesus Christ. The result was a highly Christocentric Protestantism, still immensely powerful, which mentally pictures, prays to, and inwardly relates to Jesus himself. This Christian style is well expressed in such hymns as "O Sacred Head Now Wounded," or "I Come to the Garden Alone" ("And he walks with me and he talks with me").

Roman Catholic mysticism during and after the Reformation era reflected comparable lines of development. The Roman church's greatest mystics and spiritual writers in this period also tended to be great founders or reformers of religious orders who labored on the spiritual, intellectual, and practical levels to enable their church to meet its new challenges. In particular this was true of the great sixteenth-century Spanish mystics: Ignatius of Loyola (1491–1556), founder of the Society of Jesus (Jesuits) and author of the celebrated *Spiritual Exercises*; John of the Cross (1542–1591), monastic reformer and writer of the profound *Dark Night of the Soul*, which explores the stripping away of self and sense one must pass through to reach, through love alone, the unitive state; and Teresa of Avila (1515–1582), also a reformer and spiritual writer of great perception on the stages of gain and loss leading to union, where even God is momentarily forgotten as he is gained.

The spirituality of the Eastern Orthodox Church has remained very conservative, long adhering in its essence to the Christian Neoplatonism of the early Christian centuries, yet also long remaining more deeply entwined with the lives of ordinary believers than has often been the case in the West.

EASTERN ORTHODOXY

The branch of Christianity called Orthodox is the dominant religious tradition of Greece, the Balkans, and Russia. There is a scattering in other parts of the Near East, and of course it is found wherever immigrants from its homelands have come, including the United States. (A Russian Orthodox cathedral was established at Sitka, Alaska, as early as 1794.) The Orthodox churches, about 160 million strong, are often called "Eastern" because their center of gravity is in Eastern Europe, although this faith is of worldwide importance. They are sometimes called Greek Orthodox, since the cultural and historical background is Greek. The tradition took its definitive form in the culturally Greek Byzantine Empire, but the majority of Orthodox Christians are now Slavic rather than Greek. The Orthodox churches of various nationalities commonly go by national names, such as Russian Orthodox, Serbian Orthodox, or Rumanian Orthodox.

Orthodoxy likes to speak of itself as the oldest Christian church, and indeed geography makes its churches continuous with those that Paul and other apostles founded or visited in places like Thessalonika, Corinth, and Cyprus. But the ritual and ethos of the present-day Orthodox churches is essentially the form in which it crystallized in the Byzantine period before the fall of Constantinople to the Turks in 1453.

The word "orthodox" has varying uses and connotations in English. For the people of the Eastern churches it is an attractive and strong word, not primarily suggesting rigid and narrow attitudes. They believe, of course, that their churches alone preserve the correct, or orthodox, tradition of Christian teaching and life from earliest times. But they also like to point out that in Greek the word "orthodox" can mean

Orthodox Christian service inside the Kazan Cathedral in Saint Petersburg, Russia.

both "right teaching" and "right glory." The combination of these two gives insight into the world of Orthodox life.

A highly conservative mood informs the standard doctrinal teaching of the Orthodox churches. It is held that only a General Council can officially define doctrine, and only the seven councils held in Nicaea, Constantinople, Ephesus, and Chalcedon up to 787 C.E. are recognized. Moreover, Orthodox thought has been deeply influenced by **Platonism**, with its assumption that what is most real and true is unchanging. Thus, central to Orthodoxy is the reality of the Trinity, God as three in one—an eternal mystery that undergirds the world. Next is the eternal reality of the incarnation of God in Christ, not only a historical episode but also an eternal involvement of God in the material world, through struggle and suffering, through making the children of Earth divine, and through manifesting true glory.

On the one hand, this attitude has led to an exaltation of timeless contemplation, exemplified by devout Orthodox monks, such as those living virtually out of history on Mount Athos in Greece, whom all serious Orthodox regard as ideals and as unseen givers of life to the church. The goal, the Orthodox say, is to be deified in the sense of becoming "partakers of the divine nature," actual sharers in God's own life; contemplation raises us to this level.

Yet on the other hand, Orthodoxy greatly celebrates Christ's Resurrection and the anticipated Last Day when God will make the new heaven and earth and will be all in all. These events represent the triumph of God's suffering work in the world as he makes visible what the contemplative knows inwardly: the world is infused with divinity.

The worship side of Orthodoxy richly expresses these ideas. For one used to the plainness of much of Western Christianity, a first visit to an Orthodox church can be an overwhelming experience. The service is long and may be spoken in an unfamiliar tongue, but few will be untouched by the glowing color and the soaring, exotic music. The Divine Liturgy, as the main Sunday service is called, is also at heart the early church's offering and blessing of bread and wine. The ornate vestments shimmer richly; incense is swung into the music-laden air over and over; and the book of the Gospel and the elements of bread and wine are brought out in procession.

Across a partition (the *iconostasis*) before the altar and at the church entry and elsewhere will be seen *icons*—vividly colored stylized paintings of Christ and the saints. These, which the faithful reverently kiss and before which they burn candles, have a very special meaning in Orthodoxy. Made according to holy traditions, they are seen as radiating the Divine Glory of the subjects and so are like peepholes into eternity and the means of raising oneself to it. In fact, the whole Divine Liturgy is seen as an experience of moving up into another plane or conversely a breakthrough of heaven to Earth. The entire intricately wrought interior of the building may have a background in gold, representing eternity.

These experiences of the divine that the church is believed to make available here on Earth help one understand the activity of people in Orthodox worship. People will often be seen coming and going throughout the long service or getting up on their own to pray and light candles, perhaps with prostrations, at various icons. The sense of individual freedom suggests the church is more like a home than an institution. At the same time, Orthodoxy inculcates a deep sense of community within which this freedom is possible. A sense of simply belonging to the Orthodox community is an interior identity that goes beyond any particular forms of outward expression. There is much that is important and traditional in matters of worship, fasting, and so forth, yet they hardly stifle the homey and spontaneous tone with legalism.

Something of the same feeling permeates the other forms of Orthodox social expression; this was particularly the case in old Russia. No country except India has had as many wandering holy men as Russia before the Communist Revolution. In some ways, the Orthodox Christianity of "Holy Russia" was more Asian than Western in religious style. The *startsi*, holy monks or hermits, more often laymen than priests and familiar to readers of Dostoevsky, were venerated counselors and givers of blessing. Some remained in one place; some were perpetual pilgrims who wandered about the vast land—even as far as Jerusalem—with nothing but the clothes on their backs and perhaps a sacred book or two, begging or remaining silent unless pressed to teach. There were also the "Holy Fools," perhaps idiots, madmen by conventional standards, or cripples, who would babble nonsense, meow like a cat in church, or castigate a czar for his sins, yet before whom even nobility might bow with humility, for they were seen as embodiments of the suffering Christ and of the irrational side of God here on Earth.[24]

Thus, Eastern Orthodoxy has quite distinctive forms in the three areas of religious expression: theological emphasis on God in Trinity and incarnation as eternally unchanging yet present all through the world, even in the lowliest, and always breaking through in mystery and glory; a worship that expresses that glory; and social forms making room for tradition, homeliness, and spontaneity in individuals within a mystical community.

ROMAN CATHOLICISM

The Roman Catholic Church—the communion of Christians who recognize the supreme spiritual authority on Earth of the bishop of Rome, called the pope, and who share much else as well—is the largest Christian body. A billion people are within its spiritual, or at least cultural, orbit. It is the dominant religious tradition in most of Southern and Central Europe, Ireland, and Latin America, is an important minority

Statue of Pope John Paul II in the courtyard of the Basilica of Our Lady of Guadalupe, Mexico City.

in English-speaking North America and Australia, and has been growing dynamically in parts of Africa and Asia.

Needless to say, there is, and has long been, much diversity, based on various cultures and individual emphases, within a religious institution that large, as well as based on a common core of teaching and practice. Even the sign that outwardly links this realm together—acceptance of the pope as symbol and guarantor of Christian unity—has varied in appearance through the centuries. Popes have been weak and relatively little noted in some centuries, and in others, popes have been great potentates who played major roles in international politics, who lavishly patronized the arts, or who exercised near-absolute control over the church. Now understanding of the papal role, like much else, is changing. But its profoundest meaning, as a symbol of the catholicity, or universality, of the church, is likely to abide. With the papacy goes another characteristic that is also changing in nature yet that is deeply ingrained in the church's Roman past and Catholic present—an acceptance that some uniformity and centralized authority are good in the church, not only for practical reasons but also because of the opportunity they provide members for spiritual growth through obedience and self-discipline.

The papacy is far from being the only distinguishing mark of the Roman Catholic Church, however, and some would argue it is not one to be overemphasized, even though in some ways it symbolizes much that is distinctive about the Roman Catholic experience. Here are some other general characteristics[25]:

1. *Affirmation of sacramentality and visible forms.*This attitude, shared by Eastern Orthodoxy and many Anglicans and Lutherans, affirms the central importance of the sacraments, or acts by which divine grace is bestowed through material forms: water in baptism, bread and wine in Holy Communion. The Seven Sacraments recognized by the Roman Catholic Church are Baptism, Confirmation, Penance (confession of sins and absolution or forgiveness mediated by a priest), Holy Eucharist (the Mass or Holy Communion), Matrimony, Holy Orders, and Extreme Unction (anointing of the sick and dying, part of the "last rites"). The same sacramental and visible forms also affirm the appropriateness of colorful ceremonies, vestments, and images. They affirm through them the presence of the sacred in the church and the necessity of the church appearing to the world as a visible, organized community. The fundamental assumption behind sacramentalism is that God's work is not wholly invisible and unpredictable. Sacraments say that God does work through specific matter, people, and institutions. The incarnation of God in the matter of human flesh in Christ, Catholics say, authenticates the materiality of the sacraments, and God's promises confirm them. For Roman Catholics, the affirmation of appearances and the sacramental principle are ways of emphasizing that the world was created to be good

and that the church is a visible and specific work of God on Earth by which he comes to the world through the things of the world.

2. *The church as an instrument of mediation and communion between humans, including those departed—whether saints or sinners or mixed—and between humanity and God.* This characteristic interprets the role given the invocation of the saints as heavenly helpers, prayers for the spiritual growth of those who have left this life, and the importance of the church as God's "extended family" to Catholics. The principle of mediation also interprets the importance of ordained priests, who have a definite role as teachers and as mediators of grace through the sacraments. The institution of the priesthood has an objective side. The Roman Catholic Church maintains a clear pattern of doctrine, and priests and bishops are expected to uphold normative standards regarding devotional practices, celibacy of clergy, and moral issues such as abortion and birth control. The legal model is an inheritance of Roman law, to which is added the belief that Christ gave to his church a distinctive teaching authority.

3. *The church as an organic and growing institution.* Besides affirming the church's organization and authority, Catholics increasingly harbor another feeling about it, too: awareness that the Christian fellowship, the church, is an organic, growing, and thus changing institution. The papacy, the general councils, and the other organs of the church's teaching authority have power to direct this growth, yet it is believed to move under the guidance of the Holy Spirit, who is always helping Christians better understand the truth given to them. Changes in rite and custom and clearer definitions of what previously had been latent or unclear in doctrine (although doctrine itself does not change) accompany the church's pilgrimage through the ages. For example, the First Vatican Council in 1870 defined "papal infallibility" as the pope being preserved from error when he exercises this defining function in a formal way. The **Second Vatican Council** (1962–1965), an event of major significance, liberalized the theological, practical, and sociological forms of Catholic expression by such things as authorizing the use of everyday language (rather than Latin) in the liturgy of the church, authorizing and encouraging greater participation by laity in the church, acknowledging religious freedom and the relationship of each individual to God, and encouraging the openness of the church to the contemporary world.

The Roman Catholic Church, then, is an institution highly visible, sacramental, legal, and yet changing. While it certainly claims continuity with the church of the early centuries and the Middle Ages, it is not equally the same in all respects now as it was then. Let us look at some specific characteristics of present-day Roman Catholicism.

First, some essential doctrines. God is said to be accessible through reason. Faith means intellectual assent. In other words, one can know by reason that there is a God apart from the Christian revelation and that faith is recognizing in the mind that this is so. This is significant, for it indicates the partnership of religion and philosophy and the belief, important to many Catholic attitudes, that there are basic truths upon which the Christian faith builds. The added revelation that comes through Christ is mediated through both scripture and tradition, the Bible and the church's lore interacting to cast light upon each other. Its basic points are the Trinity and the incarnation of God in Christ.

The Roman Catholic Church makes much of the Mother of Jesus, the Blessed Virgin Mary. This emphasis is made fundamentally not only because her role guarantees the incarnation but also because she is seen—in her acceptance of God's request that she bear his incarnating son—as a representative of the human race as it was before sin arrived. She is humanity responding perfectly to God's will and receiving the fullness of God's grace and reward. This role of Mary is the meaning of the papally defined doctrines of the Immaculate Conception (1854): that Mary was herself conceived without original sin (the Immaculate Conception is not to be confused, as it often is, with the Virgin Birth of Christ) and that she was bodily assumed into heaven, as defined by the pope in 1950, which makes her an exemplar of the Resurrection and heavenly reward of all the redeemed.

St. Alfonso Liguori (1696–1787) said, "What Jesus has by nature, Mary has by grace." The prerogatives of Mary, distinctively Christian even if corresponding to the paradigm of the pre-Christian Mediterranean goddesses like Isis and Cybele and answering to the natural desire of many for feminine as well as masculine principles in religion, have made devotion to Mary notably popular. Her power in heaven is held to be immensely great, and her benevolence virtually unconditional. Marian piety has reached a high pitch in the last hundred years or so with the two previously mentioned definitions. They were paralleled by the widespread belief in appearances of Mary to heal and prophesy at such places as Lourdes in France in 1858 and Fatima in Portugal in 1917. These sites are now extremely popular pilgrimage centers, with their holy grottos or wells, their appealing statues of Mary appearing to artless peasant children, their dramatic torchlight processions, and their ongoing miracles. After the Second Vatican Council, there was a somewhat reduced interest in the Marian complex for a time, but it has revived in traditional form at shrines like Medugorje in Bosnia-Herzegovina and with new perspectives given by liberationist and feminist Catholics who have seen Mary as an ideal. Pope John Paul II was very devoted to the Holy Mother.

Other significant doctrines include purgatory and the **canonization** of saints, a process by which the pope (anciently, any bishop) declares that a given person of "heroic sanctity" is in heaven and so able to intercede on behalf of those who call upon him or her before the throne of God.

Worship is centered on the Seven Sacraments, although by no means is it limited to them. These include the initiatory rites of Baptism and Confirmation and the Mass. This last, the ancient offering of bread and wine, was always spoken in Latin until the Second Vatican Council, except in certain churches using rites similar to those of the Eastern Orthodox. The priest stood at the altar in stately vestments, his back to the congregation, and at the supreme moments when the bread and wine became the body and blood of Christ, he knelt and then elevated them to the accompaniment of bells. At a "high Mass" there would be a sermon, incense, and chanted music during the rite. Members of the congregation could follow the Latin service in a book with translations. Even if they did not, the rich atmosphere, so expressive of **numinous** "otherness" and of the contrast between the sacred and the ordinary, was conducive to prayer and meditation. Since the Second Vatican Council, the use of ordinary language and

A Catholic priest celebrating Mass.

a rather more informal mood, with the priest standing behind the altar facing the people as the host at a banquet, suggests something different: the church as a family of love, where the talents of all have a place.

Another sacrament is Penance, the forgiveness of sins. Traditionally, one was expected to make a private confession of his or her sins to a priest periodically, generally in the small boxlike structure in churches called the confessional. The priest has authority to impart a penance—commonly a set of prayers to say—and to give absolution, or impart God's forgiveness for the confessed wrongs. Today, group confessional prayers recited in church are often used instead.

Matrimony is another sacrament, for it is a gift of God and a means of grace. The Roman Catholic Church therefore has rules governing its members' marriages. Because the marriage bond is sacramentally permanent, remarriage after divorce is a matter that requires legal procedures within the church, and there is disapproval of abortion and "nonnatural" means of birth control.

Roman Catholicism is abundant in spiritual life apart from the sacraments. Devotion to the Blessed Virgin may take the form of the **rosary** that one uses to count repeated Hail Marys or of *novenas*, special sets of prayers on successive days, or it may take the form of pilgrimages to shrines. Today, creative diversity continues to emerge. The charismatic movement, for example, enriches Roman Catholicism with spontaneity and "speaking in tongues."

Roman Catholic social expression is complex and highly organized. At the head of the church is the pope, whose seat is located in Vatican City, a tiny independent state of which he is sovereign in the heart of Rome. He is elected by the College of Cardinals, an assembly of some seventy prominent archbishops, bishops, and a few others who have been named by a previous pope to this dignity. The pope is assisted by the *Curia,* a cabinet and bureaucracy whose department heads are generally cardinals. Beneath the papacy, the church is divided into provinces, headed by archbishops, dioceses headed by bishops, and local parishes under their parish priests. Today bishops are generally appointed by the pope, and parish priests by the bishops, although other arrangements (often with the state having a role) have obtained in the past and still do today in some places.

Parallel to this hierarchy are the orders of monks and nuns—persons who have undertaken not only the celibate state but also vows of poverty and obedience. They usually live communally in monasteries and convents; devote much time to worship together and private meditation; and engage in educational, missionary, or charitable work, or, if they reside in an "enclosed" order, they live in a combination of labor, study, corporate prayer, and contemplation. Orders, such as the active Franciscans, Dominicans, Jesuits, the Brothers of the Christian Schools (or "Christian Brothers"), as well as the more contemplative Benedictines and Cistercians (including the Trappists), and their distinctive traditional garb, are well known. Today the "religious life," as this way is called, is also undergoing considerable modification, but it remains a bulwark of Roman Catholicism. Indeed, persons of all spiritual traditions or none have increasingly found making retreats at monasteries or convents of great personal value.

Under Popes John Paul II (served 1978–2005) and Benedict XVI (served 2005–), the Vatican has tended to move in a conservative direction. While the changes of Vatican II have certainly not been undone, doctrinal orthodoxy has been firmly upheld, opposition to abortion and the ordination of women rigorously maintained, and such traditional landmarks as Marian devotion and the optional Latin Mass encouraged. Recently, Pope Benedict XVI has conducted Mass in the pre-Vatican II form, suggesting the option for priests to return to the older tradition style of worship. In a body as large and diverse as the Roman Catholic Church, Vatican policies are always going to be controversial, even as Rome's authority must ultimately be acknowledged. For some, the steadfastness of papal policy in a confusing and changing world is reassuring.

PROTESTANTISM

The term **Protestantism** is generally taken to include all non–Roman Catholic and non–Eastern Orthodox churches that directly or indirectly derive from the sixteenth-century Reformation in Northern and Western Europe. We have already looked at this event and some of its principles. Although the vast collection of Protestant **denominations** may suggest almost chaotic variety, they do have in common certain basic attitudes traceable to the Reformation. Even points upon which they differ tend to fall into certain predictable categories. Churches of Reformation background range from certain very formal and "ritualistic" Anglican and Lutheran churches to silent Quaker meetings and **Pentecostalist** groups that stress spontaneous shouts and "speaking in tongues." But apart from a few exceptions, Protestant worship cannot be mistaken for any other.

Let us look at some common themes of Protestantism, recognizing that they have different meanings and applications in different Protestant traditions.

As far as theoretical expression is concerned, the central emphasis for most informed Protestants remains justification by God's grace through faith in Christ and all that implies. The important thing is that one's consciousness and feelings be centered on God and open to his will and grace. What is of value, then, is what evokes and expresses this centering. Thus, Protestantism, in doctrine and story alike, is inclined to apply the principle of parsimony—to cut away everything not essential to hearing and receiving the word of God in the scriptures, to cut away all that might distract from one's personal relationship to God.

The other major, but related, Protestant theme—the sufficiency of scripture alone—finds expression in diverse ways. They range from those who stress that the Bible must judge church life to those, particularly some Anglicans, who—like Roman Catholics and Eastern Orthodox—emphasize the importance of interpreting scripture within the context of church tradition.

There is also a difference between fundamentalist interpretations, which insist on a "literal" rendering of such points as the virgin birth and the miracles of Jesus, and "liberal" interpretations, which hold that scripture must be interpreted in a way consistent with present-day historical and scientific knowledge. This distinction means, in effect, that fundamentalism often functions as a vehicle of resistance to modern culture, while liberalism tries to relate Christianity to the current scientific and scholarly worldview. But on some issues, especially political, the roles may be reversed when fundamentalism speaks for a majority culture.

A continuum is also seen in styles of worship. They range from the solemn and formal services of Anglicans, Lutherans, and Reformed to the folksy worship of many Methodists and Baptists and the often ecstatic meetings of Pentecostals. In mainstream Protestantism, preaching and reading the scriptures are the primary means to inspiring faith.

The response to grace also finds other diverse expressions, ranging from an emphasis on the ethical life and good works (and here some stress personal morality and others stress Christian responsibility for society as a whole) to an emphasis on spiritual states and their expression through conversion, inward joy, and ecstatic phenomena. The most formal expression has generally been that of the **state church** Protestants of Europe and their American counterparts. But the recent growth of informal services and charismatic or Pentecostal phenomena all through Protestantism has changed this pattern.

In general, however, a simplification motif is clearly evident in worship, even though Protestant worship has often become stylized. The typical service contains an opening hymn, scripture reading, a prayer, a sermon, the offering, the benediction, and a closing hymn. A simple service of Holy Communion is also offered, though not every Sunday in the majority of Protestant churches. The congregation mainly participates in singing, although in some churches the people offer prayers as well. Otherwise the minister, as a trained religious specialist, is the principal communicator of the mainly verbal experience.

In social expression, the ideal generally is recovery of the New Testament church, since seldom (except in Anglicanism) is post–New Testament tradition given much authority. However, the New Testament scriptural paradigm means different things to different wings of Protestantism, and there is a considerable variety in modes of government. Some are ruled by bishops, some by boards of presbyters, some by the local congregation. In practice, the historical situation has also influenced structural form.

After the Reformation, Protestantism had state church status in a number of countries—for example, the Church of England or state Lutheran and Reformed churches in Germany, Scandinavia, Scotland, or Holland, or their colonial American branches. As a consequence, its organization had to fit in with the laws of the realm. As might be expected, then, the types of organization have varied widely between churches that come out of the state church tradition.

On the other hand, as we have seen, there were independent movements—the Radical Reformation—that sprang up as alternatives to the state churches and that usually had, at least originally, **sectarian** characteristics: charismatic leaders, local control, strict moral codes, and greater stress on subjective feelings. Such groups, small and fairly powerless, focused on the local church as an important entity. In America after the Revolution, particularly on the frontier, Protestantism was independent of the state and highly fluid. This led to a wealth of new forms of expression that were usually rooted in the authority of the local group or in the charisma of the traveling evangelist.

With all the differences that can be seen among the many Protestant denominations, however, Protestant social organization has in common the tacit or explicit assumption that the whole of the Christian church cannot be visible and entire in the world today. It is at best only the sum total of many Christian bodies, and its true membership cuts cross all sorts of lines—and it is known only to God.

INDEPENDENT CHRISTIANITIES

Varieties of Independent Christianities around the World

Besides the major branches of Christianity we have looked at, Eastern Orthodox, Roman Catholic, and Protestant (and sometimes Anglican listed as a separate fourth), another is increasingly cited as a distinctive group: Independent Christianity. These are Christians who are unaffiliated with any of the foregoing, and even if Protestant in religious style, as the majority are, they do not see themselves as stemming directly from any of the Reformation churches.

The fluid nature of these movements and the differences over just how distinct a group has to be from the historic churches to be considered independent make it difficult to give exact numbers. The authoritative *Status of Global Missions* report for 2011 numbers 378 million Independents, only slightly less than the number of historic Protestants.[26] The *World Christian Encyclopedia* puts the number at 386 million, making Independents more numerous than Protestants and second only to Roman Catholics among world Christians.[27] In any case, the number is substantial, perhaps 20 percent of all Christians, and the number is growing, especially in the Southern Hemisphere where Christianity is expanding most rapidly.

Who are these Independent Christians? First, we might look at North America. Here are several Christian groups like Calvary Chapel and the Vineyard, with roots in the "Jesus Movement" that arose among young people in the aftermath of the 1960s counterculture. They are often described as "postdenominational." Though evangelical and moderately Pentecostal in style, they are not the offshoot of any particular church but see themselves as based directly on the Bible and the experience of Jesus and the Holy Spirit. These churches, cumulatively numerous, are often counted in Independent Christianity.

However, these postdenominational churches are far from the first in the United States to attempt to go behind the Reformation and recover New Testament Christianity. In the early nineteenth century, the "Restoration movement," centered on what was then the frontier, also attempted to do so. Out of it arose three substantial denominations, the Churches of Christ, the Christian Church, and the Disciples of Christ, which are now really part of the American Protestant mainstream. Apart from a few distinctive practices, such as having Holy Communion every Sunday, they are not too different from many other Protestant denominations. Should they be numbered as Protestant or Independent? It's hard to say, and perhaps the quandary is an indication of why religious statistics should not be taken too seriously.

It is when we move to relatively newly missionized lands that the distinction between traditional denominations and Independents goes into high relief. There, traditional churches were established by missionaries that largely transplanted styles of worship and values of the mission-sending homelands to alien settings. The Independents, on the other hand, were founded by native leaders who, though they may have originally contacted the faith through missionaries, were quick to adapt it extensively and often dramatically to the traditional culture. These vary from quiet, unobtrusive movements in such Asian countries as Japan and China to colorful new groups in Africa and Latin America.

For the former, let us take, for example, Mukyokai, or "No Church" Christianity, in Japan. Founded by Uchimura Kanzo (1861–1930), it is a form of Christianity that claims no formal doctrines, services, liturgies, sacraments, or clergy. (It does, however, embrace pacifism, and the movement was a center of resistance to Japanese militarism in the 1930s and 1940s.) Followers simply meet for Bible study and quiet prayer, and its ranks include a number of intellectuals. "No Church" Christianity spread to Taiwan and Korea; Ban Ki-Moon, the Korean diplomat made Secretary General of the United Nations in 2006, is a "No Church" Christian.

In China today, it is reported that somewhere between 30 and 70 million Christians worship in informal, independent "house churches," far more than the 13.3 million members of officially registered Christian bodies. Worship is informal, including prayer and Bible study, and may include a shared meal. Some house churches are Roman Catholic in commitment, bringing together believers loyal to the pope rather than the official government-controlled Catholic Church, which is estranged from the Vatican. Many more are Protestant in style but prefer casual home-based assemblies to the government-endorsed denominations. Hence both may be perceived, at least by officials, as potential centers of dissent. House churches have sometimes been persecuted in the People's Republic of China and their adherents disadvantaged in opportunities for good education and jobs. It can be hoped their situation will improve if liberalization advances. In any case, the Chinese house church people, insisting on their right to worship in their own way and with whom they will worship while free of government regulation, are a prime contemporary example of Independent Christianity.

Moving to places where Independent Christianity has had fewer political problems, at least in recent decades, but clearly represents drives for freedom for an indigenous form of spiritual and cultural expression, we may turn to Africa. A good example is the Mai Chaza Church. It originated in what is now Zimbabwe but has spread through several countries in Southern Africa. It is named after the founder, a woman called Mai (Mother) Chaza, originally a Methodist who, in 1953–1954, became seemingly deranged and moreover had a near-death experience. But she recovered and reported that she had met God while in a coma. After a subsequent retreat in the mountains, she was given healing power. As she became well known in this work, she also established *Guta ra Jehova,* Cities of Jehovah, centers of healing said to be modeled on heavenly cities whose architecture was revealed to Chaza. These are now impressive places of pilgrimage, where followers of the religion, wearing uniforms, live and worship.

After her death in 1960, Mai Chaza has been religiously exalted to the role of Messiah and mediator of God to her people. Indeed, she has been made into an African female expression of Jesus. A book of her deeds and sayings is used in services alongside the teachings of Jesus.* Worship is colorful, with drums, processions, confessions, and exorcisms. At the time of confession, a white sheep with a black head, called John the Baptist, goes around and points out those in the congregation who must confess. Festivals are dramatic and important in the Mai Chaza church.[28]

Another Independent African Christian movement is The Church on Earth by the Prophet Simon Kimbagu (to be discussed in Chapter 10). In both it and Mai Chaza, we see an example of a prophet or messianic figure originally inspired by Christian teaching who mediated a new movement in which the Holy Spirit reportedly spoke in ways particularly congenial to African needs and customs.

Many Independent Christian churches are Pentecostal, emphasizing the gifts of the Spirit and, of course, the independent ministry to which many open to the Spirit can feel called. In Africa, an example is the Zion and Apostolic churches of South Africa, which practices divine healing and speaking in tongues, supported by such practices as baptism by triune immersion, use of symbolic objects such as blessed water and staffs, and the wearing of white robes with colored belts and sashes. These churches also sometimes allow polygamy, which is traditional in Africa.

Independent Pentecostal churches have also become very important in Latin America. One is the Universal Church of the Kingdom of God (Igreja Universal do Reino de Deus) in Brazil, founded in 1977 by Edir Macedo; it has grown dynamically with the help of a popular radio ministry, having now some six million members in 46 countries. The Universal Church's media empire, noisy worship style, emphases on exorcizing demons, anti-Catholicism, and frequent calls for money offerings have made it both powerful and controversial. A church like this is characteristic of many movements in rapidly changing societies through its use of modern communications technology and response to the needs of persons moving out of a traditional

---

*Some scholars distinguish between Independent Christianity and Marginal Christianity, the latter being groups who are not only independent of the historic Christian churches but also regard another book and/ or founder as equal to the Bible and Jesus, though they may revere the latter. The Mai Chaza Church is clearly an example.

Mormon Temple, Idaho Falls, Idaho, U.S.A.

peasant life (with which traditional religion, whether African or Catholic, is associated) into an exciting but baffling modern, urbanized, industrialized world with all its opportunities and perils. In this setting, the more colorful and Pentecostal styles of Independent Christianity have clearly found a place.

The Church of Jesus Christ of Latter Day Saints (the Mormons)

The Church of Jesus Christ of Latter-Day Saints, whose adherents are commonly called Mormons, has a special place in the Christian story. The LDS church was founded in 1830 by Joseph Smith (1805–1844) in western New York. Following a vision of Jesus Christ, he reportedly found and translated a set of Golden Plates containing a text published as the Book of Mormon.[29] It told the story of ancient Hebrews who came to the New World, the eventual appearance of Jesus Christ to them after his ministry in Palestine, and the further teaching he then gave. On the basis of this teaching and in the spirit of the contemporary Restoration Movement mentioned above, Smith sought to reestablish the Christian church in a purified form. Distinctive doctrines included belief in the progression of souls from human to divine status, baptism on behalf of the dead, and polygamy (which was discontinued in 1890).

The church faced fierce opposition, including the killing of Joseph by a mob in 1844. Shortly afterward, the second major leader, Brigham Young, led a large number of Mormons to settle Utah. There Mormonism, with its great temple and tabernacle in Salt Lake City, retains its geographic and spiritual center. Temples are especially important as sites for special rites of initiation and marriage restricted to members of the church in good standing. In the twentieth and twenty-first centuries Mormonism has spread to many parts of the world and has even been called by some sociologists a future world religion. In recent decades, it has tended to downplay highly distinctive doctrines and presents itself as a force for conservative family and community values.[30]

CHRISTIANITY, GOVERNANCE, AND POLITICAL LIFE

Apolitical Christianity Becomes Political: Christianity and Politics in Historical Context

Unlike Judaism or Islam, Christianity was apolitical in its origins. Jesus' "kingdom of God" stood against the "kingdom" of the world, especially Rome, and was understood to be attainable in the future—at the end, at the *eschaton*, not fully in the here and now. Consequently, New Testament accounts of Jesus' teaching and early Christianity provide no guidance for what political arrangements would be appropriate for Christians. Rather, according to the Gospels, Jesus famously proclaimed, "My kingdom is not of this world" (John 18:36), and he admonished his followers, "Render unto Caesar the things which are Caesar's, and unto God the things that are God's" (Mathew 22:21). Whether this reflected the idea of the separation of religion and the state is in dispute; however, it can at least be said that here Jesus was counseling his hearers to value the promise and vision of the future heavenly kingdom and not earthly realms.[31]

As a rabbi of a marginalized sect of Jews under Roman authority, Jesus held no political power. Instead, he aligned himself with the lowly and the oppressed and challenged existing authorities, both priestly and civil. For his efforts, he was crucified as a criminal. Yet Jesus' promise of the coming kingdom of God sustained his followers, and they knew they must be ready for it.

As we have seen, although Christianity began within Judaism, it was not a religion of an ethnic group or particular place but was universal in its message. People are called from the world to become a new community of believers—to set aside the things of this temporal world and to aim for the glory of eternity. Christians did not need to give attention to this world, when the next world was at hand. Paul counseled the new Christians, however, that in the meantime, they should be obedient to the existing civil authorities, stating, "Let every person be subordinate to the higher authorities, for there is no authority except from God, and those that exist have been established by God" (Romans 13:1). God is the sole sovereign over all, even earthly kings; hence their rule must be God's will. Yet although generally Paul's new Christians remained obedient to the civil laws of the Roman Empire and did not resist authority, they were persecuted for refusing to recognize the divinity of the emperor and to participate in the civil ceremonies of allegiance.

When in 313 C.E., Emperor Constantine authorized Christianity in his realm, however, political Christianity was born in a new empire that eventually joined Christianity to the state. Yet the two realms did not become one. They remained divided in separate institutions, which had developed over the preceding three centuries. Hence, a tension between the two remained, although the status of Christianity, its bishops in particular, was elevated as Christians, at least the leaders, joined the elites of society.

The General Councils (referenced earlier) of the period that followed had political overtones, for the theological issues were often identified with parties or nationalities of political significance within the empire, and in some cases they were called together by political authorities (e.g., Constantine, the First Council of Nicaea) to resolve potential socially disruptive disputes. In particular, issues were frequently polarized between Egypt and the northern part of the empire. The Bishop of Rome, being an outsider to Eastern squabbles, could often mediate these problems. This increased his authority and helped develop his office into the medieval and modern papacy.

From the outset, however, Christianity recognized two distinct realms—the realm of this world and the realm of heaven—in a dualistic tension. How the relationship of those two realms was understood in the doctrines of the many variants of Christianity throughout its history signaled their views of politics.

By the beginning of Christendom,* the Church had become highly institutionalized, its organizational structure having been influenced significantly by Roman civil institutions and structures, which led some to dream of a reunified Christian empire. However, that was not to be. Earlier, after Rome was sacked by the Goths in 410, Augustine of Hippo (referenced earlier) claimed for the Christians

---

*Although Christendom can refer to Christianity as a whole, the word often is used, as it is here, to refer to European Christianity in the historical period that begins with the collapse of Rome (c. 476 C.E.) and ends with the advent of Protestant Reformation (c. 1517).

a Christianity not tied to any earthly realm, but as a godly "city"—a society of those whose aim is heaven, perfect and unachievable by man alone but through the grace of God, and which stands in contrast to the City of Man, the realm of those who have strayed. Christianity is eternal and would not die with the Roman Empire, to which its fortunes had been tied, because Christianity was not a religion of a time or place, not merely a kingdom that was passing away. Christianity's universal message and the people who follow it would prevail, not needing the political to sustain them.

As the Roman Empire collapsed, any immediate hope of a unified Christian empire was dashed, but the dream did not die. Still holding the two realms in tension, the Roman Pontificate claimed sovereignty as God's vicar on Earth and sought to assert the authority of the Church as ultimate. Pope Gelasius I crystallized this view, which became known as the doctrine of the "two swords," in a 494 c.e. letter to the Byzantine Emperor Anastatsius.

> There are two powers, august Emperor, by which this world is chiefly ruled, namely, the sacred authority of the priests and the royal power. Of these, that of the priests is the more weighty, since they have to render an account for even the kings of men in the divine judgment.[32]

Gelasius was asserting that the two powers, that is the "two swords"—one temporal and one spiritual—derive from God and therefore ultimately fall under the purview of the Church. It follows from this view that the Church, by divine right, not only had the authority to run its own affairs without interference from civil authorities but also the authority to criticize civil authorities when the Church thought their rule had strayed from what is right and just. By the thirteenth century, the two swords doctrine was interpreted by the pope not only as requiring Church autonomy from encroachments by civil authority and as providing the right of the Church to serve as bulwark against autocratic tendencies of civil authority, but also as claiming the Church's authority to sanction or nullify the actions or even the entire authority of civil rulers, making the latter's legitimacy dependent on the Church.

As a consequence, from the fall of Rome to the Protestant Reformation, the Roman Church held sway over much of the territory that had once been the sovereign lands of the Empire. During this time, power and authority became centralized in the pope, and the Church became the focal point of increasingly rigid doctrine. The civil rule of kings and "Holy Roman Emperors" was legitimized by coronations conducted by Church representatives, sometimes by the pope himself.

By the fourteenth century, however, in response to the pope's claim of sovereignty, civil rulers began to assert the "Divine Right of Emperors," and the controversy was joined.[33] Corruption in the Church and struggles for power between popes and kings joined with a theological tradition in Christianity that legitimized resistance to unjust authority, while other developments (including the rise of the merchant class) led to the development of towns and eventually nation-states as the prevailing political structure in Europe. These were the emerging conditions that existed when Luther's protest led to the Protestant Reformation, which was both a religious movement and political movement. The German nobility aligned their fortunes with Luther when he defied the Roman Church. German pride joined with religious protest as a national identity began to emerge—with profound ramifications for state and church, which were replicated throughout Europe.

Some new nation-states married their religions with national identity, and their monarchs claimed absolute power and authority as the "Divine Right of Kings," as was the case in England (Anglican) and Sweden (Lutheran), for example.[34]

(It is interesting to note that the regalia—the symbols of royalty—of England's monarch, who reigns as both head of state and head of the Church of England, include two swords of justice, one spiritual and one temporal.)

The Thirty Years' War, a religious war between Protestants and Catholics, began in the Holy Roman Empire's German states, but spread throughout most of Europe. It ended in 1648 with a treaty known as the Peace of Westphalia. The treaty, adopted the doctrine of *cuius regio, eius religio* ("whose the region, his the religion"), which derived from an earlier treaty among the German states and which settled the religious dispute by recognizing the ruling magistrate's religion (Roman Catholic, Lutheran, or Calvinist) as the official religion of that ruler's state.

Further developments involved the role of radical dissenters, which were significant, especially for North America.

As we have seen, John Calvin had joined church and state in working toward an ideal in his Geneva city-state. Calvinist influences led to the Puritan movement in England, including its separatist off-shoot known as the Pilgrims. Both were persecuted, which led to the beginning of their migration to the New World in the early seventeenth century. The Puritan takeover in 1649 of the government in England resulted in the austere commonwealth of autocratic rule under Oliver Cromwell, who stripped away (i.e., "purified") the pomp and ritual of the Anglican Church and British society in general. However, the commonwealth lasted only until 1660 when the monarchy was restored. Thereafter, England's Puritans were marginalized and oppressed, as was the case with their Calvinist-influenced counterparts in greater Europe—for example, the Presbyterians (Scotland), the Morovians (Germany), and the Mennonites (Holland).

These representatives of what came to be known as the "free church" movement (i.e., free from state control) necessarily dissented against the state religious establishments, and as a consequence, they suffered ridicule and even persecution. Many left their original homelands for the hope of establishing a new religious community, based on their own free church doctrines and practices, in North America, a land too far away for governing authorities and others to be able to harass them. But established-church Lutherans and Anglicans, as well as Catholics, eventually came, too (as did Jews and Muslims, albeit in much smaller numbers).

The free church tradition of dissent can be traced from the Christian doctrine permitting resistance to the state for injustice and the understanding of the "two swords" of authority—one civil and one spiritual. The question of who is the appropriate wielder of those two swords, however, came to fore significantly in the Christians' New World home in the years leading to the founding of the United States. Should the wielder be the church or the state? Not trusting ecclesiastical authorities, Catholic or Protestant, who had been known to abuse their authority, nor trusting the state, which in many countries had claimed absolute or near absolute authority under monarchies and parliaments resulting in abuses as well, it was understood that something different was required. The answer eventually came: the authority would be vested in the people, who, it was believed, would be better guardians of their own well-being than popes, bishops, kings, or parliaments unelected by them. This was so, even in states that had nominally "established" churches.

There had been precursors to the concept of popular sovereignty in the governing structures of dissenting churches, as well as in the ancient realms of Greece's and Rome's republican period, and these were profound influences for the founders of the United States. The new nation and its states would be structured as a republic, with popular democratic elections, authority balanced and checked, and the church would not be bound by the state nor would it bind the state. The people would be free to be and to do good in their new society, in accordance with their various beliefs about what God requires of them, as long as certain "inalienable" rights to life, liberty, equal dignity, and, therefore, the pursuit of happiness were respected.[35]

Since its advent, Christianity has provided support for many different political institutional structures, including autocracy and democracy, and later socialism, and has been used to justify both persecution and toleration, both isolationism and imperialism, and both church/state separation and national churches. Let's take a look at Christianity's main expressions today for a brief discussion of their current approaches to the role of religion in political life.

Roman Catholicism

Because Roman Catholicism has always recognized the importance of human activity in the world (e.g., the doctrine of works) as central to its conception of faith, its doctrine of eternal salvation has been linked inextricably to conduct in the temporal world. Since the late nineteenth century, however, Catholicism's this-world focus has taken a new turn. Once the church of empires, the Roman Catholic Church wields the two swords differently today.

Previously, the Catholic Church had taken a strong stance against modernity and liberal movements within Catholicism. However, it gradually began to engage the world on issues of social justice. Going beyond evangelizing solely for the salvation of souls, although not abandoning that aim, the Catholic Church turned its attention more profoundly to the plight of the poor and oppressed. Pope Leo XIII's encyclical letter *Rerum Novarum* (1891) on labor marked the beginning of a series of encyclicals in which the Church set out a moral basis for just social policies—marrying its previous emphasis on charitable works with direct challenges to political, economic, and culturally entrenched systems and structures that result in suffering. Such letters formed the basis for Catholicism's "social teachings," which now have a prominent place in the Church.

By the Second Vatican Council, the Catholic Church had eschewed a theology that mainly emphasized transcendence and had embraced the realm of human activity as a location of God's redemptive endeavors. This led in turn to the Council's embrace of liberty of conscience (and therefore religious pluralism and formal separation of church and state) and a new regard for human beings' many cultural manifestations around the world. Understanding the work of the Holy Spirit to be catholic (i.e., universal), albeit most completely expressed through the redemptive work of the Catholic Church, Catholicism no longer claimed the exclusive authority of the spiritual sword and instead harnessed its deep commitment to the inherent worth and dignity of every human person, giving rise to its own dedication to human rights around the world.

Having also relinquished its claim to temporal authority over the state, the Catholic Church now wields its temporal sword through the institutions of "civil society"—those institutions that operate between the individual and the state. Its understanding of human beings as social and political by nature leads the Catholic Church to promote a conception of the common good, which exceeds and at the same time serves the individual by not subverting the individual good to the purposes of a potentially authoritative collective.[36] Consequently, whereas the Catholic Church once defended autocratic rule, today it embraces democratic reforms framed by the principles of liberty and equal dignity and a profound appreciation of diversity. In this effort, Catholicism serves as a moral voice, guided by the principles of *subsidiarity* (leaving authority at the lowest level of any hierarchy as is practically possible); *socialization* (everyone is interconnected and interdependent); and *solidarity* (serving the poor as the "preferential option").

In service of these goals, the Roman Catholic Church calls to the whole world to abandon activities, policies, and culturally entrenched practices that undermine human flourishing. Using the "sword" of persuasion, the Church engages in politics, participating in public policy debates and inspiring its adherents and others to take up its causes for health, education, workers' rights, liberty, economic justice, and enhanced participation of the people in democratic processes.

Eastern Orthodoxy

Originating from the Byzantine Empire where religion and the state worked together presumptively for the benefit of the people, Eastern Orthodoxy spent long centuries under Muslim or Mongol rule after the fall of the empire. Under both the Byzantine Empire and sympathetic later modern nation-states, and in a different way under the Ottoman Empire, the Orthodox Church has been very closely linked to the state, and in many places, it has consisted of state churches, such as the Greek Orthodox, Russian Orthodox, and Serbian Orthodox churches. However, under Communist regimes, which were cold toward church and religion, it was suppressed.

Orthodoxy's self-understanding is that Orthodoxy has inherited the legacy of the early Christian church, which called its followers to become a new community whose citizenship is not of this world but of the coming Kingdom of God. Here, individual conscience is not the focus of religion, as it is to varying degrees in those variants of Christianity that have self-consciously confronted modernity. Rather, religion is the interrelational community of the people of God who are the lifeblood of the polis. While they live under the authority of the state, the people of God's transforming role is what shapes the culture out of which politics emerges.

That transforming role derives from Orthodoxy's Eucharistic service—its Liturgy—through which the people of God participate in the otherworldly Kingdom of God. Through the mystery of the Liturgy, the participants experience "a foretaste" of the otherworldly ideal to which they aspire, not as a goal, but through their transformative becoming.[37] In this way the Kingdom of God becomes present in the here and now, as the people of God go out into the world and transform the world by their participation in it, working together with other people of goodwill, while also preparing the world for the coming ideal at the *eschaton*.

Thus, for Orthodoxy, the concept of a separation between church and state that emphasizes individuals and their voluntary associations in a private sphere divorced from the life of the polis has little meaning. Rather, Orthodoxy emphasizes experience through the aesthetic, the mysterious, and the sacred rather than the rational and the doctrinal, which often has been the emphasis of church-state relations in the West. Still, through the people of God, Orthodoxy's otherworldly Kingdom is for the world—transforming culture, moving ever closer, if not fully achieving, the ideal, which can be attained only at the end of time.

Protestant Churches

Today Protestantism is the state religion of several nations of Europe. Although a few began as absolute monarchies by "divine right," religious toleration gradually became the norm, as well as democratic reforms. Thus today, with some exceptions, religious liberty prevails.

But, as noted earlier, it was in what is now the United States that the "free church" movement of Calvinist influence staked its claim. Although the free churches began with their own theocratic aspirations, requiring sanctification not just of individuals but of the whole society and its government as well, they came to view government, even good government, with suspicion, especially if aligned with religion. As a consequence, they came to support the idea of the separation of church and state. In addition, the theology and style of church life left by John Calvin contributed immensely to the development of democracy: indirectly through its new emphasis on the equality of all before God, for the elect might be found in any social station, and directly through the model of its Presbyterian or Congregational forms of church organization, which gave many sorts of people experience in decision-making responsibilities and did not fit as well with feudalism or absolute monarchy as did bishops.

These influences aligned with other developments in political philosophy (most notably that of the Enlightenment) and led to the revolutionary spirit that demanded democratic representation in government. By the time of the founding of the United States, the idea of limited government and disestablishment of religion was beginning to take hold, influenced in part by the descendents of the dissenting "free churches." Both ideas were memorialized in the United States Constitution. The states soon followed, disestablishing what remained of the states' religions, including elimination of government support of religion. America's first generation had looked back in history and found both authoritative religion and the state lacking as sources of moral authority; the new governments placed the authority for interpreting the word of God in the people, who would then vote their consciences.

At the same time, the tradition of resistance and dissent, the "Protestant protest," endured—and still endures as America's religious continue to call politicians and public policy makers to the protestors' understandings, whether "conservative" or "liberal," of the moral good, which many Christians and others believe arises out of the West's "Judeo-Christian" tradition. Therefore, many dissenters hold, politics should not be uprooted from that tradition. Yet the meaning, scope, and import for society of that tradition is variously understood by those in different denominations, and so the debates continue. Nevertheless, liberty, equal justice, and the people's right to participate in government, all of which are memorialized in the constitutions of the United States and its constituent states, can credibly be attributed, in part, to the theological strain in Christianity that adheres to the doctrines of free will and the inherent equal dignity of every human being.

CHRISTIANITY IN AMERICA: A WELLSPRING OF DENOMINATIONALISM

Because of the special nature of religious history in America, denominationalism is a key to understanding it. In practice, even Judaism, Roman Catholicism, and Eastern Orthodoxy—all very important to American religious life—have had to fall in with styles of social expression that the American context creates.

The basic facts in American religious life are (1) immigration by peoples of numerous religious cultures and the adoption of foreign imports by those already in America; (2) numerous homegrown religious movements; (3) the United States is perhaps the only major society in the world substantially settled by religious dissidents, persons persecuted for religious reasons elsewhere, or their descendents; this background has profoundly shaped the unique American religious mentality; (4) the emergence of a new society with a need for cohesion and for a sense of creating a new political and spiritual way of being in the world; and (5) the political **separation of church and state**. These facts have resulted in **pluralism** rather than a single official or heavily dominant religious institution, as obtains in most other societies. Yet they have also meant that most groups have found themselves affirming common American ethical and social ideals—democracy, patriotism, social concern—together with their distinctive doctrines and worship.

The general history of religion in America reflects these centrifugal and centripetal drives. In the colonial period, immigrants of diverse religious backgrounds settled in different areas, often in order to find a religious haven: Puritans in Massachusetts, Baptists in Rhode Island, **Quakers** in Eastern Pennsylvania, Lutherans in Western Pennsylvania, Roman Catholics in Maryland, and Anglicans in Virginia and along the southern seaboard. From 1720 to 1740, the movement for a deeper, more intellectually serious and also more feeling-oriented Christianity, called the **Great Awakening**, swept across parish, denominational, and colonial lines. The first vital expression of the American centripetal force, it paved the way for the Revolution in that it gave the populations of the thirteen colonies a new sense of being a distinctive American people with their own spiritual concerns, rather than merely transplanted Europeans.

The Revolution, of course, brought the sense of national unity to a high pitch and culminated religiously in the First Amendment to the Constitution, which made the United States of America the first society in the history of the world to mandate full religious freedom and the separation of church and state. It guaranteed freedom and equality for all faiths and the absence at the national level of any official religious endorsement or support. In this situation, there were many who felt that, forced to stand on its own in a new society and shorn of feudal trappings, religion would wither away, or (as the concurrent Unitarian movement in New England suggested) become very "rational." But such was not to be.

Instead, during the period of westward expansion, nation building, and belief in a special American "Manifest Destiny," both geographical and spiritual, religion flourished in a cornucopia of forms. Evangelical revivals swept the frontier. They brought tremendous growth to the Methodist and Baptist churches, and they produced new denominations such as the Disciples of Christ. New movements, such as **Spiritualism**

Easter Sunday services at a Baptist church in New York.

and the Latter-Day Saints ("Mormons"), originated in upstate New York (discussed earlier). Utopian communes and numerous colleges were planted in the name of religion. In an expansive era, the centrifugal and centripetal drives reinforced each other and showed, despite some tension, that religious pluralism, in the absence of state interference or support, need not weaken religion but can liberate it to flourish.

But this primal "era of good feeling" was not to last. Just as Eden ended with the discovery of sin, so the optimism of the first decades after independence was darkened by the confrontation with the shadow side of American life—slavery. The middle decades of the nineteenth century were rent by controversy over slavery, and denominations were divided by it on North–South lines, so that we came to have Northern and Southern Baptists, Presbyterians, and Methodists (the Methodists were reunited in 1939, the Presbyterians in 1984). After the Civil War, most of the freed slaves entered exclusively black churches. For many decades, black churches were the only important institutions controlled by blacks, and their ministry the most esteemed profession generally available to them. Out of the black churches came a distinctive style of religious life characterized by close community feeling, a free spiritual expression in which the important worldwide movement of **Pentecostalism** is rooted, as well as leaders in the civil rights movement, such as Martin Luther King Jr.

During the same years, and up until 1920, new immigration vastly increased American population with a mixed multitude. During the 1840s, American Roman Catholicism grew by immigration from a small minority to the largest single church in the nation—a position it has held ever since. Jews, Eastern Orthodox, and German and Scandinavian Lutherans also immigrated in the millions during the latter half of the nineteenth century. All this was in the context of great social change: the growth of cities, of industry, of widespread education, and of life based on modern technology. The older Protestantism tended to react in two ways: conservatism, which came to be known as fundamentalism and which sought to preserve the religious values of frontier revivalism and religious surety in a changing world, and the more liberal **social gospel** movement, which strove to correlate religion to new ideas in science and society and to recover the old dream of making America into a new "people of God" through social reform.

The strands of this history are expressed in the panorama of American denominations (some of which are discussed earlier as "Independent Christianities"). However, they are far from the whole story of American religion. There was also the centrifugal drive toward a **civil religion**—a common American ethic and vision that cuts across denominations. On the other hand, important issues such as fundamentalism versus the social gospel have polarized denominations from within and have found expression in distinctive denominations. Yet "one issue" denominations without concomitant ethnic or sociological roots have generally not been very successful.

American denominational **pluralism** is an important phenomenon. Derived from the unique history of colonial settlement, the frontier flux, the slavery controversy, and immigration, it is as distinctive in its way as Tibetan Buddhism. No other society, except to a lesser extent such British Commonwealth nations as Canada and Australia, which have had superficially comparable religious histories, approaches the particular form of sociological expression of religion found in America.[38]

MISSIONARIES AND THE MODERN EXPANSION OF CHRISTIANITY

Christianity calls forth more than the image of established cloisters and churches. It also evokes scenes from its geographical front lines: the Spanish friar building his sun-washed missions surrounded by native people of the Americas; the

Interior of the Sacred Heart Basilica in Montmartre, Paris, with its famous ceiling mosaic of the risen Christ.

Image of the Virgin Mary in a Greek Orthodox church.

nineteenth-century Protestant missionary marching into the jungles of "Darkest Africa" or onto the shores of a "Cannibal Isle," Bible in hand.

These are pictures that evoke in us a profound diversity of responses; the missionary's front-line soldiering on behalf of the Cross has usually been controversial, both in the sending and in the receiving countries. He or she has been admired for incredible heroism, and millions have been deeply grateful for the medical, educational, and spiritual benefits they have received. Yet the missionary's calling has also given rise to gnawing doubts about the right of one religion to impose itself upon people of another, about the relation of modern missions to Euro-American expansionism, and about the long-term impact of the missionary upon cultures around the world whose ancient ways have been challenged and sometimes shattered peremptorily.

The story of Christian missions since the days of Columbus is as complex as these responses imply. But one thing is certain: the Christian missionary endeavor, together with European immigration in these five centuries, has radically changed the religious map of the world. From being mostly the faith of a relatively small corner of the Earth—Europe—Christianity has overwhelmed whole continents and islands across vast seas, and it is represented in nearly every nation of the Earth. A third of the world's population is, at least nominally, under its spiritual sway.

At the time of Columbus's first voyage to the Americas in 1492, Christianity was gradually recovering from a low ebb. In the previous century, the faith had been sorely weakened in numbers or morale by the Black Death, the Great Schism, and Muslim advances in the East. The last culminated in the Turkish capture of Constantinople in 1453 and the final demise of Christendom's bulwark to the East, the Byzantine Empire.

But in the fifteenth century, new life was stirring. In those years, Spain and Portugal, having just expelled the last of the Muslims, stood proud, robust, and full of enthusiastic Catholic faith, facing the broad Atlantic and ready to conquer new worlds for king and Christ. Commerce may have been its real dynamic, but kings and seafarers alike sincerely believed that they were acting at the will of God and that conversion of the "pagans" was the greatest objective of their voyages. Christian explorers laid claim to the lands and peoples that they "discovered" for their Christian monarchs as sanctioned by fifteenth century Papal Bulls, by virtue of which natives peoples were enslaved or killed, although they were sometimes spared if they converted to Christianity.[39]

Within a remarkable half-century after 1492, brutal but effective Spanish conquests had subdued the great centers of Native American civilization, Mexico and Peru, and had established colonial outposts from Argentina to the northern Caribbean. In the wake of armies, missionaries baptized thousands daily, bringing the native masses nominally under the cross. The Spanish priests built churches in imposing baroque style, often on the location of major pre-Christian temples. They devised ways to inculcate the rudiments of Christian faith to their illiterate charges. Elaborate sacred dramas, simple hymns and chants, and colorful processions, as well as fiery preaching in both Spanish and native tongues, supplemented the mystery of the Mass.

Missionaries were also sent to the East. An example is Matteo Ricci (1552–1610), an Italian Jesuit, and his companions in China. Coming to the East with the Portuguese, Ricci entered China through Macao in 1583 and finally reached Peking (now Beijing) in 1601, where he remained the rest of his life. Ricci and his Jesuits pioneered a new approach to missions. Rather than imposing European cultural forms on the people, before beginning their work, they mastered the Chinese language and studied Chinese culture in depth. Ricci became thoroughly Chinese in all nonessentials, wearing a mandarin robe and ingratiating himself with the intellectual class through his teaching of Western science and geography. While his number of converts was not large, he established the Christian church in China and won intellectual prestige for it through his own example. But his willingness to employ Chinese language and Confucian practices, such as ancestral rites, in Christian worship created a long-standing controversy within the Catholic Church. The "Rites Controversy," as it was called, was essentially over the significant issue of to what extent Christianity can adapt itself and its worship to the ways of the various lands to which it travels. The matter was decided against the Jesuits in the eighteenth century, but in 1939 the Vatican adopted a more liberal policy, and the Second Vatican Council expressed considerable new openness toward local adaptations of Catholicism, in effect vindicating Ricci's position—although such adaptations have been viewed by some as manipulations of the poor and illiterate.

The modern expansion of Christianity has come in great waves. The first, essentially Roman Catholic, followed the Spanish and Portuguese movement East and West. By the seventeenth century, this wave had crested. In that century and the next, Christianity continued vigorous expansion but far more through immigration than direct missionary activity. Christian Europeans, both Protestant and Catholic (especially from the British Isles, France, Holland, and Germany), settled in North America and South Africa, where their colonies formed the seeds of nations of predominantly Christian faith.

The beginning of the nineteenth century saw the onset of a new wave of European imperial and commercial as well as emigration expansion. Even as the old colonies of the New World won independence, this new outpouring centered on Asia, the South Pacific, Australia, and later Africa. Protestant nations such as Britain and the Netherlands, and later Germany as well as the United States, were most involved, as was Catholic France.

With the loss of the American colonies, British interest turned substantially eastward to India, Australia, Asia, and the archipelagos of the South Pacific, which had been lately visited by Captain James Cook. This interest coincided with the late eighteenth-century rise of the evangelical movement, which fired missionary zeal, as well as with the expansion of Euro-American commerce, emigration, and colonial empires.

Christian missionary expansion in the modern era has been far-reaching, finding itself in all corners of the globe: the London Missionary Society work in the South Seas, beginning in 1796; the work of William Carey in India, beginning in 1794; Anglican and Methodist missionaries in early nineteenth-century New Zealand; the continued work of missionaries in China and Japan; the exploration and missionary work of David Livingstone (1813–1873) in sub-Saharan Africa; and more. Christian missionary expansion is still a powerful force today.

Santuario de Guadalupe, a Spanish Catholic mission in the southwest of the United States.

The work of Mother Teresa, which continued in India after her death in 1997, is but one notable example.

The missionary movement spawned numerous new forms of Christian life as Christianity was adopted by native peoples in various ways, whether or not intended by the missionaries themselves. Interestingly, however, it has also contributed immeasurably to Christian unity. It is primarily out of the missionary endeavor that the modern **ecumenical movement**, dedicated to interchurch cooperation, understanding, and ultimately reunion, has arisen. In the nineteenth century various missionary conferences, regional or among allied denominations, were held. These culminated in the World Missionary Conference in Edinburgh, Scotland, in 1910, bringing together representatives of the missionary work of all major Protestant churches. It led directly to the World Council of Churches, the main ecumenical agency, which the Eastern Orthodox churches later joined. In more recent years Roman Catholics have also cooperated with the World Council as nonmember "observers" and have in other ways striven to promote ecumenical understanding.

The missionary enterprise has had a reverse impact on Europe and America, too, one doubtless unexpected at first. Just as missionaries shattered the isolation of countless tribes and nations around the globe, so have their reports shattered the complacency and spiritual isolation of the older Christian nations. They opened up a wide world that many found to be far more complex, spiritually and culturally, than anticipated.

First, questions about the moral underpinnings of Christendom slowly began to arise in the minds of thoughtful Christians as a result of experiences such as those of the first Portuguese missionaries in Africa, who found that the natives they had brought under the Gospel of love quickly fell away when brutal slavers arrived flying the same flag as they.

Second, questions about the absolute superiority of Christianity were raised by missionary reports of non-Christian cultures, which the unbiased mind could only see as equal or even in some ways superior to those in the West. In Asian countries such as India, China, and Japan, missionaries encountered civilizations and religions of great sophistication, and they found themselves regarded as barbarians. Missionary scholars were, in fact, among the first to translate and bring to the West the great spiritual classics of the East, which some in the West discovered to be as appealing as the Bible. The reports of Jesuits such as Ricci from Confucian China, with its respect for education, its civil service examination merit system, and its apparently tolerant and primarily ethical religion, made that ancient empire seem something of a utopia to intellectuals in an early eighteenth-century Europe struggling toward democracy and just emerging from the bloody religious wars of the seventeenth century. The Chinese image had a significant impact on the emergence of the eighteenth-century Enlightenment ideals of reason, deistic religion, tolerance, the civil service, and democracy—much more of an impact than Europe, despite those missionaries, had had on China in the same century.

We see then that the missionary expansion of Christianity, together with exploration and economic exchange, resulted in a nascent move toward globalization, the impact of which was as profound then as it is today in its continued evangelizing endeavors throughout the world, especially in Third World countries. It also made Christianity by far the largest and most widespread religion in the world, embracing no less than a third of the world's population by 2010. That is largely because, for all the questions missionizing raises, its successes have been unquestionable. All this has created the new Christianity of the twenty-first century: mainly nonwhite, centered south of Europe and of "Anglo" North America.[40]

WOMEN IN CHRISTIANITY

We have seen in the many other cultures that we have studied thus far that the dominant religion in large part shapes social conventions, including those regarding women. This is no less the case in the West where Christianity has dominated Western thought from the fourth century to at least the nineteenth century, and some would say even today.

The West has seen an expansion of women's rights and roles in society that is unprecedented in many other countries around the world. Christianity, together with its attitudes toward women, traveled a long road, however, before it reached its current configuration. It is important to explore that road in order to appreciate better the historical context in which the debate on the "woman question" in the West—particularly in the United States—now finds itself. As we shall see, "woman's place" in society and its religious institutions has been a much-debated topic in Christianity from the very beginning and is no less so today.[41]

Women in the Early Jesus Movement

There is considerable evidence that the Jesus movement, at its outset, provided a place for greater participation by women than had been the case in much of Greek and Roman society at that time.[42] Significantly, there are many New Testament references to women—this, at a time when most customs and traditions held that women were to remain in the background. Not only do Mary Magdalene and Mary, the mother of Jesus, figure prominently in the stories of Jesus, but several other women are referenced as well. The Gospel of Luke 8:1 indicates that highly stationed women—for example, Herod's steward's wife, Joanna—traveled with Jesus. Some women are mentioned as benefactresses of the newly emerging movement. In the parable of the lost coin in Luke 15:8, Jesus used a woman to represent God. Even more significantly, all four gospels present women as the first witnesses to Jesus' resurrection.

In addition, in Luke 10:38, we find the story of Martha and Mary. The travels of Jesus and his followers took them to the home of Martha. Mary, who was Martha's sister, was not helping Martha in the household tasks (which probably included serving the guests). Instead, Mary was sitting with the men, listening to the teachings of Jesus. When Martha complained, Jesus replied: "Martha, Martha, you are worried and distracted by many things; there is need of only one thing. Mary has chosen the better part, which will not be taken away from her." This is remarkable at a time when the custom was to exclude women from study. Here, Jesus was saying that his teachings were the "better part" even for a woman such as Mary.

New Testament books written later reference women in roles of leadership in the newly emerging movement. In Romans 16:1, Paul acknowledges Phoebe as a deacon (i.e., a minister) and a benefactor (i.e., a provider, implying some status) of the church. Later in the same chapter, Paul refers to Andronicus and Junia (or Julia) as apostles. Junia is a feminine name (although often translated as the masculine Junius), which indicates that there were women apostles who were respected members of the early community.[43]

On the other hand, there are the often-cited passages of the New Testament indicating that women should be subordinated to men. First Corinthians 14:34 is a case in point. There the author admonishes women to be silent in church and remain subordinate to their husbands. And Titus 2:3–6 expressly directs women to be submissive to their husbands. Other passages state clearly that women are not to hold positions of authority in the church but are to remain committed only to their husbands and the duties of the home.

Yet Christianity was wholly open to everyone, including women. The baptismal formula cited in Galatians 3:28 makes this expressly clear: "There is no longer Jew or Greek, there is no longer slave or free, there is no longer male and female; for all of you are one in Christ Jesus." And while I Corinthians sets up a hierarchy—God as head of Christ, Christ as head of men, husbands as head of wives (11:3), it also acknowledges that women "pray and prophesy" in the church (11:5), which is contrary to the I Corinthians passage referred to above that appears to demand their silence.

Biblical scholars have noted these various passages and others, and many explanations have been offered for the seeming inconsistencies. One theory has it that some of these letters, such as the letters to Timothy, Titus, the Ephesians, and probably the Colossians, were written pseudonymously (i.e., writing in the name of another, e.g., in the name of Paul the Apostle), a common practice at the time, or that certain passages were interpolated by men of a later period. Removing these from Pauline authorship greatly reduces negative passages about women in the New Testament.[44] Those who hold this theory surmise that perhaps the later writers were concerned that the newly emerging movement, with its greater role for women, would not be accepted in the Hellenistic culture of the time and that, therefore, it would be suppressed. Accordingly, they brought women into line with the customs of the greater society and of its patriarchal social patterns.

Whatever the case, by the second century, the Jesus movement retreated from what was probably a liberating trend for women. Significantly, the early church fathers developed a disparaging attitude toward sexuality. Because men associated women with sexuality, women were disparaged as well, and by the second century the most influential sects of the early Jesus movement became extremely misogynistic. Tertullian (c. 155–220), considered by many to be the first theologian of the West, is reported to have called women "the devil's gateway," blaming them for the sin of humanity that necessitated the death of the savior.[45] Not surprisingly, with such prevailing views, celibacy became the ideal, marriage being a second, less holy, choice, and women came to be viewed as extraneous at best and dangerous at worst to the spiritual life of men.

By the fourth century, when the church was officially recognized by the Roman Empire and the church patriarchy was well established, women's role was limited in many of the same ways we have seen in the other religions we have studied. A woman's place was in the home; she was to be subservient to her husband; she was to remain chaste; her main function was to produce children, particularly sons, to continue her husband's family line; and she was to keep silent.[46] But in addition to all of this, a misogynistic strain in Christian theology remained that framed the debate about women in Christianity.

Christian Dualism, the Medieval Vision, and their Impact on Attitudes toward Women

The two most influential Christian theologians who provided the foundations of much of Christian theology and, therefore, attitudes about women, were Augustine (354–430) and Thomas Aquinas (1224–1274). While both wrote works that had an impact on Christianity as a whole, after the Protestant Reformation Thomas Aquinas continued as the greater influence on Catholicism, Augustine as the greater influence on the major Protestant denominations; Martin Luther was an Augustinian monk. However, both developed views that promoted a dualism that greatly influenced both Catholic and Protestant church attitudes toward women.

As we have seen, Augustine's famous treatise, the *City of God*, espoused the view that there are two realms of existence—the City of God and the City of Man.

The City of God is the realm in which the faithful are in tune with God's will and are not sinful. The City of Man is the realm of human beings' defective will, which resulted from the original sin of Adam and Eve, who had failed to obey God when they ate the forbidden fruit of the tree of the knowledge of good and evil. As Augustine's works were interpreted and incorporated into later church doctrine, the dual realms of the City of God and the City of Man were equated with the realm of the eternal, that is, heaven, and the realm of finite world, that is, the natural world (the world of the "flesh"), respectively. The natural world was considered the locus of temptations to sin and, therefore, everything "natural" became suspect—including the inclinations of the body. Not surprisingly, the natural desire for the pleasure of sex was equated with sin; and women, being associated by men with sex, were, from their point of view, a primary temptation to sin. Moreover, Augustine linked the transfer of original sin to sexual intercourse and birth.

Still, Augustine's views of women were more favorable than those of many others of his time who stressed the evils of women as a justification for the adoption of a celibate life. Many of these men disparaged the body, sex, and procreation altogether and thought that marriage was an evil to be avoided. At the time, some Christians promoted a heterodox theology that bringing more children into the world depleted the spiritual realm; therefore, women were unnecessary to, or even counter to, the good. Augustine maintained a different view. Although Augustine, too, favored the celibate life, he was a defender of marriage, and he attempted to legitimate sexual relations as part of God's intention for men and women. He held that children are the first "good" of marriage and that women's legitimate purpose is to procreate.

Even though Augustine's views might have been more favorable toward women than those of many of his contemporaries, the debate that he had joined reveals the generally negative perspective toward women. At this point in Christianity's history, women were not even valued for their place in the home as central to the family, as was the case in Judaism, Confucianism, Hinduism, and Islam. Because celibacy was promoted as the highest ideal, women were seen as temptresses who were the cause of conflicts in men between the life of the spirit and the world of "flesh." Augustine was attempting to modify this view, but the spirit–flesh dualism that he inherited from Greek thinkers placed women on the side of sin.[47]

Thomas Aquinas, adopting for the most part the views of women that had been held by the famous Greek philosopher **Aristotle**, believed that women are inherently inferior to men and that men represent the full expression of humanity, while women are lesser beings—"misbegotten males"—who should be subordinate to men. Accordingly, women's roles in the church were severely limited; as secondary creatures, they could not appropriately hold any position of authority. The only reason for a woman's existence, it was thought, was procreation, where her contribution to the child was the lesser part—matter—whereas the man's contribution was to "prepare" the matter to receive the "form" or soul—what made one human—which was provided by God. He further taught that the operation of the soul in a woman was weakened by her inferior body. As a result, she exhibited a defective mind and will.

As in the case of Augustine, however, Aquinas's views represented a softening of especially negative attitudes toward women at the time. Aquinas argued that although women were lesser beings, they nevertheless contributed to the completeness of the world and, like men, were created directly by God and not by angels, as others had contended. Still, Aquinas fostered dualistic views that had considerable impact on women's lives in the West to modern times. The sinfulness of the pleasure of sexuality continued as a dominant theme, and celibacy remained the ideal for those who kept to the tradition of Aquinas. Consequently, women, associated by men only with sex and childbirth, were identified with sin, and they and their roles as wives and mothers were marginalized as inferior.

Rosemary Radford Ruether, a well-respected Christian feminist scholar, has argued that dualistic conceptions of reality in Christianity led to theological justifications for the subordination of women to men. Men associated themselves with what they deemed to be the higher pursuits of the mind and spirit, the realm of the sacred, and linked women with the body and the passions—that which they deemed to be the realm of the profane. It followed then that if reason should rule the passions, men should rule women. Otherwise, spirit could not prevail over the profane world.[48]

Christian Women in Europe during the Middle Ages: Wives, Nuns, Charismatics, and Heretics

The Middle Ages were difficult times for most Europeans. This was a time of insecurity, as many wars between the various lords were fought and the people suffered from disease, including the infamous bubonic plague. The feudal system lent a degree of safety to the masses but brought with it serfdom and the commensurately oppressive existence that went along with it. Women worked alongside their husbands in the fields. Their many pregnancies greatly shortened their lives.

Yet the local church, even more than the lord's manor, was a center of community life. Because the people were illiterate (the parish priest himself often only semiliterate), the practical expression of religion was a more dominant force than specific applications of high church theology. As a result, many pre-Christian folk practices were assimilated into the many ceremonies and festivals of church life—for example, the egg hunt at Easter, the maypole dance as Spring bloomed, the lighting of the Yule fire at Christmas. Accordingly, the actual lives of women were a confluence of many factors, and religion was more a "little tradition," where women's participation was certainly more prominent than the official tradition would suggest. Nevertheless, official church doctrine still tended toward oppressive ideologies and practices regarding women, and although the practical effect of these depended in large part on the inclinations of the local parish priest, they certainly influenced the attitudes exhibited in the culture.

As a result of the developing dualistic views of early Christianity, as we have seen, women's roles as wife and mother did not receive the high regard in the Christendom of the Middle Ages that it did elsewhere. Women were a suspect group. Their main functions in life did not exemplify their participation in the ideal of the religion. Instead, the socio-religious ideal was a rejection of such mundane matters and an embracing of the spiritual life—not as an adjunct to mainstream society as we saw with Buddhism but as the primary social vision. As the Middle Ages progressed, however, in no small part because of the influence of the writings of Augustine and Thomas Aquinas, the extremely misogynistic views toward women softened to some degree. Marriage became a sanctified institution. By 1439 the Council of Florence included marriage in its definitive list of the Seven Sacraments of the Church—a means by which divine grace is transmitted through matter.

In addition, there were exceptions to the prevailing views of the time. The rise of notions of chivalry (which some scholars have argued were instigated by aristocratic women) and the platonic romanticism of the troubadours for married women certainly influenced views such as those of Dante Alighieri (1265–1321), who wrote of his Beatrice: "Her least salutation bestows salvation on this favored one, and humbles him until he forgives all wrong," suggesting that divine beauty in the female face can be a sacrament of salvation. But scholarship has shown that such views

A sculpture of the Madonna and Child by Barbara Hepworth.

did not translate into enhanced status for women in the Middle Ages as had once been suggested.[49]

Increasingly, Mary, the mother of Jesus, imaged as infinitely compassionate, sexless, and ever-virgin (even after childbirth), became the venerated image of woman. Mary became the divine mediator, and popularly held beliefs about such things as her immaculate conception and assumption into heaven upon her death (which later became official Catholic dogma in 1854 and 1950, respectively) abounded, as well as ceremonies in her honor. On the other hand, Eve, now blamed entirely for the Fall of humankind in the Garden of Eden, became the symbol of the inherent sinfulness of women. Weak of will and mind, she was easily tempted by the serpent. In addition, during this time the serpent became increasingly associated with Satan, a figure who now began to take on a more prominent role in Christian theology.[50]

Women, too, wished to overcome the sin of sexuality to which they had been linked, and therefore many gave up marriage, sexuality, and childbirth in an attempt to exemplify the religious virginal ideal. St. Clare (1194–1253), founder of the Poor Clares, a companion religious order to the Franciscans, reminds us that life in the convent was long a spiritual path available to women. As early as the second century, women's religious communities seem to have existed, and in the Middle Ages, they became significant institutions.

The early convents were well endowed because women's dowries were given to the religious houses they entered. Accordingly, convents enjoyed considerable independence and power. As a consequence, convents were able to offer an alternative life for women where they experienced a degree of autonomy. There they were well educated, held positions of leadership within the convent, taught, and went on pilgrimages. The story of convents in the Middle Ages is mixed, however. Sometimes they were placed under the authority of the male bishops, their funds distributed to other institutions, and their independence and authority limited. Later in the period, the authorities demanded a more stringent cloistering of nuns, which greatly limited their activities.[51]

Still, exemplary women, whether or not nuns, were able to transcend negative attitudes of the day toward women. In some ways comparable to the shamaness tradition we saw in China and Japan, charismatic women and women mystic ascetics gained credibility by virtue of their experiences of the Divine, which often included claims to special revelations from Jesus or Mary. If such women were deemed by the officials of the church or popular opinion to be authentic visionaries, they were respected members of the Christian community, and some became leaders and teachers. Thus women notable for asceticism, ecstatic visions, or deep spiritual wisdom were highly honored and, like Clare, sometimes recognized in their lifetime or later as saints.

Hildegaard von Bingen (1098–1179), a German nun, was a visionary as well as a woman remarkably accomplished in several spheres. She has today become perhaps the most famous of all medieval women, remembered for the richness of her visions, described in books which she illustrated herself, for her splendid correspondence, and for her musical compositions. She saw men and women as equal before God in the "creative greenness" of Spirit. She was recognized by the church and was extremely well respected in her time, becoming a very popular abbess of an influential convent.

Another visionary was Margery Kempe (c. 1373–1439), an Englishwoman who, unlike Hildegaard, was married and had no fewer than fourteen children. After the fourteenth, she convinced her husband to permit her to live a celibate life. Alone and often on foot, she went on pilgrimages that took her as far as Jerusalem. From time to time, she underwent intensely emotional experiences in which she participated in the agonies of Christ on the cross and equally in the joy of her own close relationship to Christ, whom she saw as her heavenly spouse.

Her emotional outbursts brought her to the attention of church authorities, however, who in turn brought her before the archbishop under charges of heresy. However, the archbishop judged Margery Kempe authentic, and the charges were dropped. Now officially sanctioned by the church, Kempe became a charismatic preacher, developed a very large following, and gained considerable respect and status. She is remembered today primarily because she recounted the events of her life in what was the first autobiography in English literature—*The Book of Margery Kempe* (1426).

Dame Julian of Norwich (c. 1342–1415), an anchoress (an enclosed solitary contemplative nun) who had been visited by Margery Kempe, is known for the splendid visions she described in her *Revelations of Divine Love* (sometimes translated as *Showings*). There she put great stress on love and the feminine as well as the masculine nature of God and, thus, spoke of Christ as "mother" and of the "motherhood" of God.

There were many other exemplary women, but most women's lives were extremely limited. The contemporary views of the time reflected the dualism we discussed previously. Consequently, women were blamed for the sins of the world, deemed especially vulnerable to the wiles of Satan, had no legal or religious rights, were denied education, and had no options other than the convent or a married life restricted by prevailing views about keeping silent and submitting to their husband's will, which were modified only in part by local practices and folk beliefs.

As we have seen, Christian women in the Middle Ages were involved in the "little traditions" that were practiced alongside the officially sanctioned tradition. But as the Middle Ages came to an end, the consequences of this proved to be disastrous.

Many remnants of the pre-Christian shamanistically based religions continued into the Middle Ages. Observances involved such things as folk medicine, the care of women in childbirth, and magic for such things as finding a husband or wife. These were largely practiced by women—frequently by such village figures as the "wise woman" or the midwife. Furthermore, as we mentioned, peasants continued to practice many of the pagan folk festival celebrations, and women played significant roles there—in contrast to their limited role in church celebrations. In the late Middle Ages, the tolerance of earlier times for these practices collapsed as church leaders felt more and more compelled to clamp down on folk religious practices, which were increasingly stigmatized as dangerous and diabolical.

The general suspicions toward women were conflated with the perceived need to root out these "evils." Because women were the main practitioners of these old ways and they were thought to be more subject to the temptation of sin, the male clergy sought to bring women under a more stringently imposed authority of the church. Now these poor females were labeled "witches," and many among the clergy sought to purge Christendom of them. A tract of 1486, the **Malleus Maleficarum** (*Hammer against Witches*) by two Dominican monks, did much to spark more than two centuries of vicious persecution by secular and ecclesiastical authorities of alleged witches, mostly women, whose sins generally lay only in the twisted imaginations of the witch finders. Often a woman labeled as a witch had merely stepped out of line of the authoritative ideal for womanhood. She was too beautiful and therefore probably not pure; she was too vocal about things she did not like and therefore not obedient; she was too popular as a "wise woman" of the village and therefore not subject to male authority.

After unspeakably horrible tortures, many of which were deliberately directed toward the woman's sexuality, such women might confess to pacts with Satan and name others as "witches." They were then burned at the stake to free their immortal souls from the grips of evil. Undoubtedly, there lay much significance in the fact that the persecutors were men (often male clergy) and the victims mostly women, thought to be especially susceptible to the wiles of Satan. The antiwitch campaign was particularly harsh in Spain and Germany, where some towns had very few women left after a visit from the witch finders (two towns in Germany in 1585 had only one left), but the antiwitch campaign also reached Britain and Salem, Massachusetts.

There have been many speculations as to the actual number of women accused of witchcraft who were burned at the stake, hanged, or died in prison during the period from the thirteenth to the eighteenth century when the witches were purged from first the Catholic and later the Protestant churches. Estimates range from forty thousand to 9 million.[52] Regardless of the actual numbers of women physically persecuted, the threat of being called in to the witch finder or inquisitor must have provided a strong incentive for women to fall into line with the orthodox position of the relevant church regarding women's place, and the threat certainly closed doors to alternative avenues of spiritual expression and leadership.

Women and Reform

The most significant change for women under the Protestant Reformation was that Martin Luther proclaimed that marriage, home, and family are the calling of human beings. He rejected celibacy outright, declaring it to be a sin against God who has commanded people to "be fruitful and multiply," and thus Luther called monks and nuns to leave their monastic orders in order to marry. Protestant Christianity embraced family life as the realm of the sacred where virtue is learned, while rejecting the Catholic dogma that marriage is a sacrament. Women were obviously a necessary part of this sacred center, and they gained respect and status for their holy role as bearers and nurturers of children. Sex within the bonds of marriage was, then, something good in the eyes of God and was praised and celebrated by Luther.

These doctrines were well reflected in other Protestant churches as well. The marriage service of the Church of England, adopted in 1549, combined something of the older sacramental idea with the new Reformation valuing of family life. It speaks of marriage as an "honourable estate," and when the groom gives the ring to his bride, he says: "With this ring I thee wed; with my body I thee worship; with all my worldly goods I thee endow; in the Name of the Father, and of the Son, and of the Holy Ghost. Amen." This rite clearly sees the woman and man as, in their physical bodies, the sacramental means of love and grace one to another and even implies that sex is a kind of holy communion.

On the other hand, the major Protestant denominations, having adopted, for the most part, the theological underpinnings of Augustine, melded some of the previously held ideas of the Roman Catholic Church with the newly configured Protestant Church and, therefore, the dualistic thinking that had pervaded Christianity persisted. The natural world was still the world of sin, and while sex was a gift from God, it was considered suspect unless controlled. Women, still equated with nature and the body and believed to have whatever reason they possessed clouded over by emotion, were thought to be more tempted to sin and lust. Accordingly, although the authoritative doctrine offered a degree of mutuality between husband and wife, women functioned mainly as an adjunct to men for procreation, and men were the rulers of their wives. Unmarried women were suspect, having no recognized place in society. Significantly, an alternative way of life for women—the convent—was eliminated in Protestantism, undoubtedly leaving fewer means of fulfillment available than before to women whose bent went more toward education and art than vocations associated with home life. Women's sphere became the home, and they had no place of authority in church life.

Christianity and Women in America before the Twentieth Century

Early American Christianity was primarily Protestant. In the very beginning, much of it lay in the tradition that we have called "radical reform," involving such groups as the Puritans. For the most part, early American Christianity continued attitudes toward women that had prevailed in the European Protestantism we explored previously. Here, as there, men were expected to guard themselves against the wiles of women. The only accepted role for women was that of the good wife. And women who attempted to step outside the prescribed bounds of society to gain any kind of status or independence were quickly reined in or rejected outright. Some were even accused of witchcraft. Anne Hutchinson's story is a case in point.

Anne Hutchinson (1591–1643), born in England, joined the Massachusetts Bay Colony in 1634 and commenced work as a teacher, holding Bible classes in her home. When she began to promote her own teachings regarding the importance of freedom of conscience and individual inspiration on the basis of what she claimed were revelations from God, she was seen by the authorities as a threat to the religious orthodoxy. She was tried as a witch and, though exonerated of witchcraft, was expelled from the Colony in 1637.

Yet there are many stories of distinguished women throughout American history, who had an impact on the landscape of American Christianity. There are the stories of Mother Anne Lee (1736–1784), who founded the Shaker movement, and of Mary Baker Eddy (1821–1910), who founded the Church of Christ, Scientist, both having emphasized the motherly and fatherly features of God, an inward and sensitive feeling-oriented approach to religion and the nurturing, healing aspects of spiritual leadership. There is also the story of Mother Elizabeth Ann Seton (1774–1821), founder of the Sisters of Charity, the first American Roman Catholic religious order. She is often called the mother of the Catholic parochial school system and was beatified by the Roman Catholic Church in 1963. Space does not permit the mention of but a few such names.[53]

There is, however, a story of women in American Christianity that exemplifies the American religious spirit of the nineteenth century and that is particularly informative for us as we face the contemporary debate about the "woman question" in America. The debate on this issue, as we see it in our contemporary popular press, has been framed in terms of the goals of liberal feminists, deemed primarily secular, and the goals of the conservative traditionalists, deemed religious. As we shall see, however, religion played a pivotal role in the advancement of feminist causes. Let us now turn to that story.

The eighteenth century was witness to a development in American Christianity that was to have a far-reaching effect on the lives of women—The Great Awakening of the mid-1700s. This, as we have seen, brought a feeling-centered element to American religion. Emphasis on feeling made the central values of religion more accessible than before to women, with their generally limited education—and women felt called to the spirit in a new way. Now, the great authority of religion was not the doctrinal interpretations of church leaders; instead, it was one's subjective experience of being infused with the spirit of God that was the single most important power dictating how one should live.

The Great Awakening only opened the door slightly to a new way of participating in religion and, therefore, had only a small impact on everyday life for women in general. But it was the precursor to a new wave of awakenings—the **Second Great Awakening**, which began in the early decades of the nineteenth century and was led at first by Charles Grandison Finney (1792–1875), a Presbyterian minister. The impact of this movement was felt in the depths of the American imagination, which held dear the importance of freedom of individual conscience. And those imbued with the Holy Spirit—especially women—took this to heart as they were called in great numbers to a progressivist-liberal message for society.

Women's participation in this "holiness" movement had vast implications for America. Spirit-led women embraced the new experience-centered theology and felt called by God to participate in public prayer and give testimonies of their conversion experiences. Women began to preach to large congregations of seekers. As Nancy Hardesty and the Daytons have written: "It encouraged, indeed compelled women to burst the cocoon of 'women's sphere,'"[54] and, thus, it broke through the traditional duality that had kept women in the home.

This development was not welcomed by the church leaders of the day, however, who sought to conserve tradition. "The Bible commands women's silence in the church!" such leaders countered. And many women were not inclined to go against the grain of the biblical tradition in which they had been raised. But the transformative energy of evangelical conversion and the experience of total **sanctification** (i.e., experiencing the power of the Holy Spirit to preserve one from sin and realize Christian perfection, often called the "second blessing") was felt by many women and held sway. Infused with that confidence, they began to challenge notions held by church leaders that the Bible justified such things as slavery, the subordination of women, the limitations of women's education, and the refusal to ordain women.

Together with like-minded men, these women became leaders of progressivist causes that disputed church orthodoxy. Strong in the belief that full reception of the Holy Spirit made women and men spiritually equal, they participated in all manner of social justice activities. Phoebe Palmer, an early leader who experienced sanctification on July 26, 1837, and thereafter published several books expounding her newfound faith, such as *The Way of Holiness and Faith and Its Effects*, preached to and inspired other women, proclaiming that "Holiness is Power." One of her converts was Catherine Booth who, with her husband William Booth, went on to found the Salvation Army.

Charles Finney (referenced earlier) was instrumental in these developments. Although roundly criticized by mainstream clergymen for his work, he nevertheless encouraged women to play a greater role in American religious life and to work toward the realization of a vision for equality in American social and political life as well. Frances Willard, founder of the reformist Women's Christian Temperance Union, is a notable example.

Significantly, educational opportunities for women had been severely limited, and therefore women's ability to gain recognition in religious hierarchies as ordained ministers or as leaders in secular institutions was extremely difficult. Under Finney's leadership, Oberlin College became the first coeducational college in the United States and thus the first to admit women to its degree-granting programs. The first women in the United States to receive a Bachelor of Arts degree did so at Oberlin in 1841. Oberlin produced several graduates who became leaders on behalf of reform movements, including Lucy Stone, the abolitionist and suffragist, and Antoinette Brown, the first woman to be ordained (1853).

Sojourner Truth (1797–1883), a former slave, although not directly involved in the holiness movement, was nevertheless inspired by her experience of the spirit to speak out against slavery and was a powerful women's rights advocate. She is remembered for her tremendous oratory skills, although she had no formal education. Her now legendary speech at the 1851 Woman's Rights Convention in Akron, Ohio, stands as but one example of her work. Countering the arguments of the ministers there (who justified the subordination of women by claiming that men have superior intellect and that God meant for women to be inferior because Christ was a man and Eve took the apple from the serpent), Sojourner Truth, who was a strong presence standing six feet tall, responded:

"That man over there." Her long finger shot toward the minister in question. "He says women need to be helped into carriages and lifted over ditches and to have the best everywhere." She smiled, shaking her head gently. "Nobody helps me into any carriages, over mud puddles, or gets me any best place...And ain't I a woman?" Sojourner cried out. "Look at me!" She bared her powerful right arm and raised it high in the air. "Look at my arm. I have plowed. And I have planted. And I have gathered in barns. And no man could head me. And ain't I a woman?"

"I could work as much and eat as much as a man—when I could get it—and bear the lash as well! And ain't I a woman? I have borne children and seen most of them sold into slavery, and when I cried out with a mother's grief, none but Jesus heard me. And ain't I a woman?" ...

"That little man in black there! He says women can't have as much rights as men, 'Cause Christ wasn't a woman.'" Her arms stretched wide as if to evoke the cross, and her eyes burned. "Where did your Christ come from? Where did your Christ come from?" Her question rolled over the packed, silent pews. "From God and a woman!" She looked witheringly at the minister in question. "Man had nothing to do with him!"[55]

While African Americans had gained their political freedom during the Civil War, they had not gained an accepted place in society. Amanda Smith, another former slave, who had received sanctification in 1868, challenged religious and social norms by preaching and singing in holiness meetings in America and later in the British Isles and Africa. Her very presence and the felt authenticity of her message inspired many who had held on to racial prejudice to abandon such notions as contrary to the Holy Spirit.

But these movements were cutting against the grain of mainstream conservative Christian religious tradition, which, as we have seen, projected a certain ideal for Christian womanhood. The church fathers (and many women) of several denominations were often the most vocal opponents of women's advancement, as well as opponents of some of the causes that the women of the holiness movement (and like-minded men) promoted, such as the abolition of slavery. These church fathers

Elizabeth Cady Stanton, feminist and Suffragette.

cited scriptural passages and appealed to the now well-worn dualistic thinking of tradition (i.e., the inherent inferiority of women and their tendencies toward sin) to justify such things as limited roles for women in institutional structures, placing men over women as their rulers, limited education for women, and providing no legal standing for women (such as requiring a woman to be represented by her husband, just as if she were a minor). Permitting women a greater voice on their own behalf and in society at large would undermine the social order ordained by God, such clergymen argued.

Pivotal in the controversy was the Bible. How were those inspired by the Holy Spirit to reconcile their real felt experience with the injunctions against women in the Bible? While there were women who acquiesced in their silencing by church leaders because of biblical pronouncements, others found that the Bible itself provided the support they needed for their participation. For example, Phoebe Palmer cited Acts 2:17–18, which restates the promise of Joel 2:28: "In the last days it will be, God declares, that I will pour out my Spirit upon all flesh [or people], and your sons and your daughters shall prophesy.... Even upon my slaves [or servants], both men and women, in those days I will pour out my Spirit; and they shall prophesy." Others sought to reinterpret the Bible, arguing that its main message is one of liberation for all peoples. The Quaker Grimke sisters were of this bent. They, too, had been inspired by Finney's revivalism and were major participants in the abolition movement and the women's rights movement, although they later set aside their work for women's rights, having been convinced that linking slavery to women's oppression *might undermine their ability to convince a majority of those in power to abolish slavery!* Others rejected the Bible outright as authoritative, seeing it as a product of writers from a patriarchal time and not binding for their time. This was the approach of Elizabeth Cady Stanton.

Elizabeth Cady Stanton (1815–1902) is well known for being, among other people, the first person to organize women in an effort to obtain the right to vote and to be ordained as ministers in the churches. Because she herself had been converted by Charles Finney's revivalism, the inspiration for her religious views arose out of a personal religious conviction. But hers was not one that demanded adherence to a text that she found counter to her experience. Instead, she placed much of the blame for the subordinate position of women in society and women's acceptance of subordination squarely on the Bible itself and on clergymen's interpretation of it. Her alternative was the *Woman's Bible*, which she edited and published in 1895. In her introduction to the first edition, she wrote:

From the Inauguration of the movement for woman's emancipation the Bible has been used to hold [women] in the 'divinely ordained sphere,' prescribed in the Old and New Testaments.... While [women's] clergymen told them on the one hand, that they owed all the blessings and freedom they enjoyed to the

Bible, on the other, they said it clearly marked out their circumscribed sphere of action: that the demands for political and civil rights were irreligious, dangerous to the stability of the home, the state and the church.... No wonder the majority of women still, and with bowed heads, accept the situation.[56]

Legal, political, and religious rights that women in America now take for granted can be traced to the work of such luminaries as Phoebe Palmer, Lucy Stone, Francis Willard, Sojourner Truth, Elizabeth Cady Stanton, and the religious movements that stood against the tide of those who wished to maintain the status quo of women's subordination and the slavery of African Americans.[57]

The "Woman Question" in American Christianity in the Twentieth Century and Beyond

After the Civil War, the intensely felt reformist and abolitionist spirit that was present in the years leading up to that war between the states seemed temporarily exhausted. The holiness movement turned more conservative and inward-looking, and the movement for women's rights became more political than explicitly religion-based, perhaps because religious leaders were instrumental in blocking women's advancement. Women's right to vote was not granted until 1920, and the efforts for ordination of women until then had been of only limited success. However, by the 1950s, ordination of women again became a major topic of discussion in many Protestant denominations. Methodists and Presbyterians began ordaining women in 1956. As the new feminist movement of the 1960s took hold, women began to enter theological seminaries in large numbers both in those denominations as well as in others that did not yet permit ordination.

From the 1970s on, many more Protestant denominations granted women's ordination, and a few women have been raised to the office of bishop in them: Marjorie Matthews in the United Methodist Church in 1984 and Barbara Harris in the Episcopal Church in 1989. The Church of England began ordaining women in 1992.

The Roman Catholic and Eastern Orthodox churches have felt themselves unable to take this step, although the participation of women in many levels of leadership—educational, leading services in the absence of a priest, pastoral work in parishes and college chaplaincies—has increased dramatically in the Roman Catholic Church since the liberalizing of Catholicism under the Second Vatican Council. Still, as Rosemary Ruether has noted, "Women's presence in world Christianity in all continents can be seen as a broad-based pyramid in which women are present in large numbers at the base and increasingly small numbers as one moves up the hierarchical ladder."[58]

Most interestingly, there is a confluence of trends the outcome of which is not yet determinable. The 1980s witnessed a new Christian spirit moving

Emergent leadership of women in religion: Barbara Harris became the first female bishop in the history of the Anglican Church in 1989.

through America that became a powerful political, as well as religious, force in the 1990s—the so-called Christian right. Their voices are still prominent in debates about social issues and their views have tempered previous liberal trends. Concerned that American values are at stake, these conservative Christians advocate a return to a literal interpretation of the Bible, including the biblical injunctions regarding women. Contemporary society appears to them to have lost its original moral ground. As a consequence, they are advocating a return to traditional social conventions reflecting the old duality in order to bolster what is, for them, a religiously legitimate social order. The late twentieth century saw the rise of the Promise Keepers, a movement of men who hold to this view, as well as the 1998 Southern Baptist Convention amendment of its official statement of belief, the "Baptist Faith and Message." It now states that husbands and wives are of "equal worth before God," but that "[a] wife is to submit graciously to the servant leadership of her husband even as the church willingly submits to the headship of Christ" and that a husband "is to love his wife as Christ loved the church. He has the God-given responsibility to provide for, to protect, and to lead his family." This is a very significant statement of faith in that the Southern Baptists constitute the largest American Protestant denomination at sixteen million members.[59]

On the other hand, while the 1960s "second wave" of feminism appeared to many to turn away from religion as an oppressive institution in society, since then the experience of the spirit in another direction has taken hold. Spirit-led women of a feminist bent have been instrumental in revitalizing worship in the liberal churches, many of which now profess their faith to God as Mother and Father.

While conservative Christians are holding to the inerrancy of the Bible, archeological finds and considerable scholarship have been providing insight into the social and political context in which Christianity was born, and new information as to how the New Testament came into being is, at the same time, challenging tradition. Modified biblical interpretations have arisen out of that scholarship, and Christian feminist scholars have had a part in it. Elisabeth Schussler Fiorenza, in her pivotal work *In Memory of Her*, and Karen Torjesen, in her work *When Women Were Priests*, are just two who have contributed to a feminist reinterpretation of the scriptures that runs counter to the interpretations adhered to by traditionalists.

Significantly, womanist and *mujerista* writers (African American and Hispanic American, respectively) have pointed out that feminism has been a movement of white women seeking to overcome the oppressions associated with gender and, therefore, the focus has been too narrow. The work of womanist and *mujerista* women has revealed that oppression is multidimensional, involving not only gender but race and class as well. Their insights have opened up the theological discourse to include, as Linda A. Moody has written, a "theology across the boundaries of difference."[60] United States *mujerista* scholars and Latin American women theologians have been influential in **Liberation Theology** movements, which have had a long-range impact globally.

Most important, Western Christian woman's scholarship has generated a global discourse about women and religion. Today we find this scholarship having an impact on some aspect of every religion in the world. In Christianity today, no less than in all the other major religions of the world, however, the battle for women's rights is made against the backdrop of tradition. What can be retained of tradition while widening the arena of opportunities for women? How can religion provide a place for women's voices in the shaping of theology—the traditionally exclusive sphere of men? What is women's proper role in family and society? How far should women's rights extend when women are the bearers of the future generation? What is the proper relationship of women and men? The outcome of the many discourses these questions have generated are shaping the lives of women in every corner of the globe.

CHRISTIANITY IN THE WORLD TODAY

Today, Christianity remains the largest religion in an anxious world, full of strains, paradoxes, and ominous portents almost beyond imagining. In some places, a new age of high technology, symbolized by space probes and sophisticated computers, is being ushered in. Yet it is not a transformed world, and the bodies and minds of countless children shrivel for lack of bread. Even as prospects of amazing progress in science, medicine, and all branches of learning gleam, not for centuries has the future been so feared. For beside that glittering computerized future (and what it might do to human values, nobody knows) loom the grim shadows of the new four horsemen of the Apocalypse: tyranny, war, economic disaster, and famine.

Just because of its phenomenal worldwide spread, the Christian third of humanity finds itself today at all corners of the world's dilemmas. It is the church of wealthy consuming nations and the church of the starving, of countries old and new, of lands and classes with little in common and much reason to see themselves at cross-purposes. Moreover, it particularly finds itself in confrontation with rising Muslim and Hindu self-affirmations.

In 1900 the world's most powerful countries were Christian, ruled by professedly Christian emperors, kings, and presidents. Moreover, it was widely boasted that Europe and America's Christianity had something to do with their manifest superiority over the rest of humanity. Not a few Christians prophesied that since the day of

Fundamental Features of Christianity

Theoretical

Basic Worldview	A world made by God, but fallen far from harmony with God's will; Jesus Christ bridges the gap between God and humanity. In this situation faith and love are required.
God or Ultimate Reality	A sovereign, personal, all-good creator God.
Origin of the World	Creation by God.
Destiny of the World	At the end of time, to be judged and then remade as a paradise of God.
Origin of Humans	Created individually by God.
Destiny of Humans	Judgment and resurrection on the last day; eternal life.
Revelation or Mediation between the Ultimate and the Human	Supreme self-manifestation by God in Jesus Christ the mediator; revelation in scripture and, especially in the Roman Catholic, Eastern Orthodox, and Anglican traditions, the tradition and authority of the Christian church.

Practical

What Is Expected of Humans: Worship, Practices, Behavior	To seek to know God, to worship God, to practice the ethics of love and service.

Sociological

Major Social Institutions	The Christian church, divided into many traditional denominations; also monastic orders, missionary works, numerous associations.

the other religions and their outmoded cultures was clearly past, the whole planet might be converted within a generation.

By the end of the twentieth century, even though Christian numbers had greatly increased over that tumultuous century, the confidence of those expansive times was long gone. Wars and revolutions toppled ancient Christian as well as Confucian thrones; movements of national independence brought resurgent affirmations of Hinduism, Buddhism, and Islam; in Europe, America, and elsewhere, immense social and intellectual changes weakened the grip of the traditional religion, Christianity, on the minds of many.

Yet Christianity survives and thrives. It retains its complex denominationalism, its amazing diversities of forms of worship and theological opinion, and its chronic inability to find a common voice with which to address a problem-ridden world. Still, there is no doubt that Christianity remains a major presence to be reckoned with as it continually adapts to new places and circumstances, and takes on new challenges.

Summary

Throughout its two thousand years of history, Christianity has achieved a wide diversity of forms, but they all derive ultimately from the person, life, and teaching of Jesus. The teaching centers on the Kingdom of God, Jesus' proclamation of God's reign or rule, which is both present in the world and coming into it. Jesus was executed on a cross by the Roman authorities; reports spread among his followers that he had risen three days later from the dead. For the religious movement that formed around him, whose teachings were supremely articulated by the apostle Paul, Jesus was a divine savior; through faith in him one could share his life eternally.

For the sometimes-persecuted early Christian church of the Roman Empire, Christian life was arduous. It centered on baptism, the major rite of entry into its fellowship, and the Holy Communion, the sacred meal that repeated Jesus' Last Supper before his crucifixion.

After the triumph of Christianity under the Emperor Constantine, the religion faced new problems and opportunities. Doctrinal differences were resolved by General Councils, which emphasized that Jesus Christ is of one substance with God the Father, truly God and truly human. Christian worship became more elaborate; the church became the official religion of the empire and over the next few centuries converted most of Europe. The medieval style of Christianity that followed seemed outwardly to express the stable social order with a steady round of festivals and Sunday masses that were the medieval ideal, but beneath the surface were tensions that gave rise to radical movements and that set the stage for future developments.

The sixteenth-century Protestant Reformation was sparked by the monk Martin Luther's conviction that salvation was not won by the amount of one's piety or good works but was freely given by God as grace and received by faith. In opposition to medieval church life, he proposed an alternative style centered on scripture, preaching, and the ideal of inward faith. The second great reformer, John Calvin, emphasized the sovereignty of God and his calling of people by grace to his service and salvation. The Reformation in England was more conservative than that on the continent, resulting in a church with both Catholic and Protestant features. On the other hand, England was also a main center of radical reform—movements of more extreme Protestants who favored a simple church of believers, social change, and separation of church and state. From out of the radical wing of the Reformation came such denominations as those of the Congregationalists, Baptists, Quakers, and, later, Methodists.

Christian mysticism and devotion have run deep over the centuries, in two great, though sometimes converging, channels: the way of the negation of images, which seeks to know God by taking away all words and concepts less than God; and the way of the affirmation of images, using ideas and mental images to lift one to God. Both have expression in each of the three main divisions of Christianity: Eastern Orthodoxy, Roman Catholicism, and Protestantism. But in these and other respects, the three show differences as well.

Highly traditional, the Orthodox Church centered in Eastern Europe presents firm doctrine, ornate worship, and a deep affiliation with the cultures of the countries in which it is predominant. Its spiritual life combines freedom with a feeling for the meaning of corporate church life and the resurrection of Jesus.

The Roman Catholic Church is distinguished by the papacy, a sense for the importance of combining freedom with order, and an emphasis on the sacraments in Christian life. In it, traditionalism combines with a capacity for change.

Protestantism displays wide diversity but is generally characterized by relative simplicity of worship, emphasis on scripture and preaching, and often a desire for local and democratic control of church government.

Christianity began as a movement separate from the Roman state. Thus, from the beginning Christianity recognized two distinct realms—the realm of this world and the realm of heaven—in a dualistic tension, which eventually were reflected in the doctrine of the "two swords." That doctrine claimed for the pope the ultimate authority over kings and empires, calling authoritarian rule to adhere to Christian precepts. Eventually, however, emperors and kings, especially after the Protestant Reformation, asserted their own "divine right," claiming absolute authority.

War between Catholics and Protestants ended with the Peace of Westphalia, which adopted the doctrine of *cuius regio, eius religio*. Radical Christians of the "free church" movement dissented from state religious establishments and the state's resulting religious intolerance. Many dissenters migrated to the New World, where their influence played a significant role in the development of the democratic institutions of the United States and the tradition of protest and dissent that remains prevalent today.

The Roman Catholic Church, having relinquished its claim on direct authority over governments, now works indirectly through the institutions of "civil society." Although, this church once defended autocratic rule, today Catholicism embraces democratic reforms framed by the principles of liberty and equal dignity and a profound appreciation of diversity. In this effort, the Catholic Church serves as a moral voice, guided by the principles of *subsidiarity* (leaving authority at the lowest level of any hierarchy as is practically possible); *socialization* (everyone is interconnected and interdependent); and *solidarity* (serving the poor as a "preferential option").

For the Eastern Orthodox, religion is the interrelational community of the people of God who are the lifeblood of the polis. While they live under the authority of the state, the people of God's transforming role is what shapes the culture out of which politics emerges.

Protestantism sometimes aligned with other developments in political philosophy (most notably that of the Enlightenment), which inspired the revolutionary spirit that demanded democratic representation in government, limited government, disestablishment of religion, and freedom of religion, among other inspirations and demands.

During the last five hundred years, Christianity has expanded to become the largest and the most worldwide religion. Beginning with the work of Catholic missionaries in the wake of Vasco da Gama and Christopher Columbus, Christianity has expanded remarkably through a combination of missionary work and European emigration. The nineteenth century, when Protestant as well as Catholic missionaries were active, was particularly a period of growth. As the twenty-first century opens, much of the future of Christianity lies in Asia, Africa, and Latin America where, as the result of missionary expansion there, many forms of Christianity have thrived, from the traditional, such as Roman Catholicism, to those with ecstatic practices, such as Pentecostalism, to new religious movements, such as the Mai Chaza Church.

The writings of the early Jesus movement reflected more inclusion of women than was the norm at the time; however, this was countered with biblical admonitions that have provided justification for placing women under the authority of their husbands and silencing them in church affairs. The early institutionalized church made celibacy, rather than home and marriage, the ideal, and limited women's participation. However, women found an alternative in the life of the convent where they could be educated. The Protestant Reformation included women's place in the home as wives and mothers in its sacred center, the nuclear family. But European Christendom from the fourteenth century through the seventeenth century sought to purge many of the folk customs that remained a part of the religious practices of the people, resulting in the removal of women's spheres of influence in the "little traditions" of local church life. This also resulted in the outright persecution of women as "witches." Although conservatism and religion are often thought to go together, religious movements of the nineteenth century, such as the "holiness movement," proved to be fertile ground for the development of women's rights. Today, just as in other religions in the world, Christianity is involved in a debate about women, tradition, and reform, the outcome of which will have a great impact on women in the twenty-first century.

In the late twentieth century, Christianity faced many problems and many prospects. Now, in the twenty-first century, it remains a worldwide faith, with much variation in its appearance from one part of the world to another.

Questions for Review

1. Summarize the life and central teaching of Jesus.
2. Summarize the basic teaching of Paul the apostle.
3. Give a description of life in the early church: its forms of worship, way of life, organization, and fundamental beliefs.
4. Explain the reasons for persecution of Christians under the Roman Empire and the Christian attitude toward martyrs.
5. Interpret what the triumph of Christianity under Constantine meant to the religion. What new problems appeared? What new opportunities? What new forms of Christian life arose?
6. Summarize the meaning and teaching of the first four General Councils.
7. Trace the development of medieval Christianity and outline its major features.
8. Interpret the nature of Martin Luther's basic religious experience, and cite the main points of his teaching.
9. Explain some fundamental features of Calvinism.
10. Outline the course of the Reformation in England, and tell how and why it was different from that on the continent of Europe.
11. Discuss the nature of radical reform, explaining who the Puritans were and the background of such denominations in the English-speaking world as Congregationalists, Baptists, Quakers, and Methodists.
12. Trace the course of mysticism within Christianity.
13. Summarize the main features of Christian teaching, practice, church organization, and life within Eastern Orthodoxy, Roman Catholicism, and Protestantism. Be sure to include variations within each of these major branches of Christianity.
14. Explain the doctrines of the "two swords" and *cuius regio, eius religio* ("whose the region, his the religion") and their legacy for the development of ideas about the relationship of church and state.
15. Discuss Roman Catholic, Eastern Orthodox, and Protestant views toward religion, governance, and political life today.
16. Trace the history of the expansion of Christianity in the last five hundred years, referring to the worldwide role given Christianity and the questions it has raised.
17. Explain how Christian dualism has had an impact on Christian attitudes toward women and remains influential in Western culture as a whole.
18. Trace the history of women in Christianity from its earliest times to the present.

Suggested Readings on Christianity

General

Atwood, Craig D., *Handbook of Denominations in the United States*, 13th ed. Nashville: Abingdon, 2010.

Balling, Jakob, *The Story of Christianity: From Birth to Global Presence*. Grand Rapids, MI: Eerdmans, 2003.

Brown, Candy Gunther, ed. *Global Pentecostal and Charismatic Healing*. Oxford and New York: Oxford University Press, 2011.

Cambridge History of Christianity, Series. New York and Cambridge: Cambridge University Press.

Gerrish, Brian A., *The Faith of Christendom: A Source Book of Creeds and Confessions*. New York: World, 1963.

Gonzalez, Justo L., *The Story of Christianity*, 2 vols. San Francisco: Harper & Row, 1984.

Gonzalez, Ondina E., *Christianity in Latin America: A History*. Cambridge and New York: Cambridge University Press, 2008.

Herring, George, *An Introduction to the History of Christianity: From the Early Church to the Enlightenment*. London: Continuum, 2006.

Jenkins, Philip, *The Next Christendom*. Oxford and New York: Oxford University Press, rev. ed. 2007.

Lindberg, Carter, *A Brief History of Christianity*. Malden, MA and Oxford: Blackwell, 2006.

Livingston, James C., et al., *Modern Christian Thought*. Minneapolis: Fortress, 2006.

Martin, David, *The Future of Christianity*. Farnham, UK and Burlington, VT: Ashgate, 2011.

Moffett, Samuel Hugh, *A History of Christianity in Asia,* 2 vols. Maryknoll, NY: Orbis, 1998, 2005.

Niebuhr, H. Richard, *Christ and Culture*. New York: Harper Torchbooks, 1956.

Pelikan, Jaroslav, *Jesus through the Centuries*. New Haven, CT: Yale University Press, 1985.

Underhill, Evelyn, *Mystics of the Church*. London: J. Clarke & Co., 1925.

Woodhead, Linda, *An Introduction to Christianity*. New York and Cambridge: Cambridge University Press, 2004.

The New Testament

Carter, Warren, *The Roman Empire and the New Testament: An Essential Guide*. Nashville, TN: Abingdon Press, 2006.

Clark-Soles, Jaime, *Death and the Afterlife in the New Testament*. New York: T & T Clark, 2006.

Donaldson, Terence L., *Jews and Anti-Judaism in the New Testament*. Waco, TX: Baylor University Press, 2010.

Herzog, William R., II, *Prophet and Teacher: An Introduction to the Historical Jesus*. Louisville, KY: Westminster John Knox, 2005.

Holliday, Carl R., *A Critical Introduction to the New Testament*. Nashville: Abington, 2005.

Koester, Helmut, *From Jesus to the Gospels: Interpreting the New Testament in Its Context*. Minneapolis: Fortress Press, 2007.

Meeks, Wayne A., *The First Urban Christians: The Social World of the Apostle Paul*. New Haven, CT: Yale University Press, 1983.

The Early Christian Church

Bingham, D. Jeffrey, *The Routledge Companion to Early Christian Thought*. London and New York: Routledge, 2010.

Denzey, Nicola Frances, *The Bone Gatherers: The Lost Worlds of Early Christian Women*. Boston: Beacon Press, 2007.

Harding, Mark, *Early Christian Life and Thought in Social Context: A Reader*. Nondon and New York: T & T Clark, 2003.

Harvey, Susan Ashbrook, and David G. Hunter, T*he Oxford Handbook of Early Christian Studies*. Oxford and New York: Oxford University Press, 2008.

Pagels, Elaine, *The Gnostic Gospels*. New York: Random House, 1979.

Rhee, Helen, *Early Christian Literature: Christ and Culture in the Second and Third Centuries*. London and New York: Routledge, 2005.

Waddell, Helen, *The Desert Fathers*. Ann Arbor: University of Michigan Press, 1957.

Eastern Orthodoxy

Angold, Michael, *Eastern Christianity*. Vol. 5 of the *Cambridge History of Christianity*. Cambridge, UK: Cambridge University Press, 2006.

Binns, John, *An Introduction to the Christian Orthodox Churches*. Cambridge University Press, 2002.

Fedotov, G. P., *A Treasury of Russian Spirituality*. London: Sheed & Ward, 1952.

McGuckin, John Anthony, ed., *The Encyclopedia of Eastern Orthodox Christianity*, 2 vols. Chichester, UK and Malden, MA: Wiley-Blackwell, 2011.

O'Mahony, Anthony, and Emma Loosley, *Eastern Christianity in the Modern Middle East*. London: Routledge, 2010.

Ware, Timothy, *The Orthodox Church*. Baltimore, MD: Penguin Books, 1963.

Roman Catholicism

Cunningham, Lawrence S., *An Introduction to Catholicism*. Cambridge, UK: Cambridge University Press, 2009.

Linden, Ian, *Global Catholicism: Diversity and Change since Vatican II*. New York: Columbia University Press, 2009.

McNamara, Jo Ann Kay. *Sisters in Arms: Catholic Nuns Through the Millennia*. Cambridge, MA: Harvard University Press, 1996.

Norman, Edward R. *The Roman Catholic Church: An Illustrated History*. Berkeley: University of California Press, 2007.

Schwaller, John Frederick, *The History of the Catholic Church in Latin America*. New York: New York University Press, 2011.

Protestantism

Dorrien, Gary, *The Making of American Liberal Theology*. Louisville: Westminster John Knox, 2003.

Harris, Harriet A., *Fundamentalism and Evangelicals*. Oxford: Clarendon, 1998.

Haverstick, John, *The Progress of the Protestant*. New York: Holt, Rinehart and Winston, 1968.

Hillerbrand, Hans J., ed., *Encyclopedia of Protestantism*, 4 vols. New York: Routledge, 2004.

MacCulloch, Diarmaid, *The Reformation*. New York: Viking, 2004.

Marsden, George M., *Fundamentalism and American Culture*, 2nd ed. New York: Oxford University Press, 2006.

Martin, David, *Pentecostalism: The World Their Parish*. Oxford: Blackwell, 2002.

McGrath, Alister E., and Darren C. Marks, *The Blackwell Companion to Protestantism*. Oxford, UK and Malden, MA: Blackwell, 2004.

Miller, Donald E., and Tetsunao Yamamori, *Global Pentecostalism: The New Face of Christian Social Engagement*. Berkeley: University of California Press, 2007.

Noll, Mark A., *American Evangelical Christianity: An Introduction*. Oxford: Blackwell, 2001.

Williams, George, *The Radical Reformation*. Philadelphia: Westminster, 1962.

Christianity, Governance, and Political Life

Berman, Harold J. *Law and Revolution: The Formation of the Western Tradition*. Cambridge, MA & London: Harvard University Press, 1983.

Coppa, Frank J., *Politics and the Papacy in the Modern World*. Westport, CT: Praeger, 2008.

Haynes, Jeffrey, "Christianity and Politics," in *The Politics of Religion: A Survey*, Jeffrey Haynes, ed. London; New York: Routledge, 2006.

Jacob Neusner, ed., *God's Rule: The Politics of the World's Religions*. Washington, DC: Georgetown University Press, 2003. See chapters on Primitive and Early Christianity, Roman Catholic Christianity, Reformation Christianity, and Orthodox Christianity.

Kidd, Thomas A. *God of Liberty: A Religious History of the American Revolution*. New York: Basic Books, 2010.

Lahr, Angela M., *Millennial Dreams and Apocalyptic Nightmares: The Cold War Origins of Political Evangelicalism*. Oxford and New York: Oxford University Press, 2007.

McGraw, Barbara A., *Rediscovering America's Sacred Ground: Public Religion and Pursuit of the Good in a Pluralistic America*. Albany, NY: State University of New York Press, 2003.

Plant, Raymond, *Politics, Theology, and History*. Cambridge, UK: Cambridge University Press, 2011.

Wilson, John F., and Donald L. Drakeman, eds., *Church and State in American History: Key Documents, Decisions and Commentaries from the Past Three Centuries*. Boulder, CO: Westview, 2003.

Witham, Larry, *A City Upon a Hill: How Sermons Changed the Course of American History*. San Francisco: HarperOne, 2007.

Witte, John, Jr., and Frank L. Alexander, eds., *The Teachings of Modern Protestantism on Law, Politics, and Human Nature*. New York: Columbia University Press, 2007.

Christianity in America

Ahlstrom, Sydney E., *A Religious History of the American People*. New Haven, CT, and London: Yale University Press, 1972.

Balmer, Randall, and Lauren F. Winner, *Protestantism in America*. New York: Columbia University Press, 2002.

Bednarowski, Mary Farell, *The Religious Imagination of American Women*. Bloomington: Indiana University Press, 1999.

Bridges, Lynn, *The American Religious Experience: A Concise History*. Lanham, MD: Rowman and Littlefield, 2006.

Carey, Patrick, *Catholics in America: A History*. Westport, CT: Praeger, 2004.

Davidson, James D., and Ralph E. Pyle, *Ranking Faiths: Religious Stratification in America*. Lanham, MD: Rowman and Littlefield, 2011.

Frykholm, Amy Johnson, *Rapture Culture: Left Behind in Evangelical America*. New York and Oxford: Oxford University Press, 2004.

Gillis, Chester, *Roman Catholicism in America*. New York: Columbia University Press, 1999.

Lippy, Charles H., and Peter W. Williams, eds., *Encyclopedia of the American Religious Experience*, 2 vols. New York: Scribners, 1988.

Maffly-Kipp, Laurie F., Leigh E. Schmidt, and Mark Valeri, eds., *Practicing Protestants: Histories of Christian Life in America, 1630–1965*. Baltimore, MD: Johns Hopkins University Press, 2006.

Morone, James A., *Hellfire Nation: The Politics of Sin in American History*. New Haven, CT and London: Yale University Press, 2003.

Numbers, Ronald L., *The Creationists*, expanded ed. Cambridge, MA: Harvard University Press, 2006.

Ostling, Richard N., and Joan K., *Mormon America*. San Francisco: HarperSanFrancisco, 1999.

Raboteau, Albert, *Slave Religion*. New York: Oxford University Press, 1978.

Robins, R. G., *Pentecostalism in America*. Santa Barbara, CA: Praeger, 2010.

Theis, Jeffrey, *Mexican Catholicism in Southern California: The Importance of Popular Religiosity and Sacramental Practice in Faith Experience*. New York: P. Lang, 1993.

Varacalli, Joseph A., *The Catholic Experience in America*. Westport, CT: Greenwood Press, 2006.

See also "Protestantism" and "Christianity, Governance, and Political Life" above and "Women in Christianity" below.

Women in Christianity

Barstow, Anne Llewellyn, *Witchcraze: A New History of the European Witch Hunts*. San Francisco: HarperSanFrancisco/Pandora, 1994.

Clark, Elizabeth A., and Herbert Richardson, *Women and Religion: The Original Sourcebook of Women in Christian Thought*, rev. ed. San Francisco: HarperSanFrancisco, 1996.

Fiorenza, Elisabeth Schussler, *In Memory of Her: A Feminist Theological Reconstruction of Christian Origins*, 10th anniv. ed. New York: Crossroad, 1994.

Gerhart, Mary, "Christianity," in *Her Voice, Her Faith*, Arvind Sharma and Katherine K. Young, eds. Boulder, CO and Oxford, UK: Westview Press, 2003.

Hunt, Mary E., and Diann L. Neu, *New Feminist Christianity: Many Voices, Many Views.* Woodstock, VT: Skylight Paths, 2010.

Isasi-Diaz, Ada Maria, *Mujerista Theology: A Theology for the Twenty-first Century.* Maryknoll, NY: Orbis Books, 1996.

Keller, Rosemary Skinner, and Rosemary Radford Reuther, eds., *Encyclopedia of Women and Religion in North America.* Bloomington: Indiana University Press, 2006.

Lutz, Jessie G., *Pioneer Chinese Christian Women: Gender, Christianity, and Social Mobility.* Bethlehem, PA: Lehigh University Press, 2010

Mabee, Carleton, *Sojourner Truth: Slave, Prophet, Legend.* New York: New York University Press, 1993.

Malone, Mary T., *Women and Christianity.* Maryknoll, NY: Orbis Books, 2001.

Raughter, Rosemary, *Religious Women and Their History: Breaking the Silence.* Dublin: Irish Academic Press, 2005.

Ruether, Rosemary R., "Feminism in World Christianity," in *Feminism and World Religions*, Arvind Sharma and Katherine K. Young, eds. Albany: State University of New York Press, 1999.

Torjeson, Karen, *When Women Were Priests: Women's Leadership in the Early Church and the Scandal of Their Subordination in the Rise of Christianity.* San Francisco: HarperSanFrancisco, 1993, 1995.

Townes, Emilie M., ed., *A Troubling in My Soul: Womanist Perspectives on Evil and Suffering.* Maryknoll, NY: Orbis Books, 1993.

Warner, Laceye C. *Saving Women: Retrieving Evangelistic Theology and Practice.* Waco, TX: Baylor University Press, 2007.

Westerkamp, Marilyn J., *Women and Religion in Early America, 1600–1850: The Puritan and Evangelical Traditions.* New York: Routledge, 1999.

9

Submitting to the Will of God

Building the House of Islam

CHAPTER OBJECTIVES

After studying this chapter, you should be able to

- Discuss the basic teachings and practices of Islam.
- Explain the historical role of the Islamic faith.
- Summarize the major schools of Islam.
- Begin to understand the role of Islam in governance and political life.
- Interpret the place of Islam in the world of today.
- Talk about the role of women in Islam past and present.

THE MEANING OF ISLAM

Over 1.6 billion people, over one-fifth of the world's population, adhere to the faith of Islam, the youngest of the world's great religions. Despite important variations within Islam, it is also the most homogeneous and self-consciously an international community of the three great cross-cultural faiths: Buddhism, Christianity, and Islam.

Islam is a community that does indeed cut across many cultures. Non-Muslims often envision Islam as the faith of Arabs in desertlike lands, but only a minority of Muslims are Arab, and only a tiny minority are desert dwellers. The largest single Muslim nation is tropical Indonesia, where the faith of Muhammad is superimposed on a South Asian culture. Other Muslims in great numbers are farmers and craftspeople in India, Pakistan, and sub-Saharan Africa, where Islam is growing, or businesspeople in the cities of Turkey, Iran, or Malaysia. Even in the Arab countries, where Islam originated, the population is largely urban or engaged in intensive, sedentary agriculture in fertile strips like those along the Nile and the Two Rivers. In fact, historically, normative Islam has been preeminently a faith of citified, mobile, internationally minded people, sometimes conquerors, but more often urban businesspeople, and through them it has spread from culture to culture.

Partly because of this base, Islamic culture has a quite visible unity as well as a great diversity. From Morocco to Java, the Muslim **mosque** presents a distinctive atmosphere. Few would mistake a mosque for a church, synagogue, or Hindu temple. The mosque, a place of prayer to the infinite Lord, has no picture, image, altar, flowers, or candles—only a vast, clean, cool, austerely beautiful empty space. The floor may be spread with rich carpeting and the walls and ceiling or dome with the delicate, fantastic tracery of arabesque. But nowhere will realistic representational art be found. Only a bare niche in the wall serves to orient prayer in the direction of Mecca, the holiest of cities; only a modest affair like a seat atop a staircase serves as pulpit.

On the streets of a Muslim country, the pervasive influence of the religion is also felt. Five times a day—sunrise, noon, afternoon, just after sunset, at dark—a crier, called the **muezzin** (nowadays often replaced by a recording and a loudspeaker system), summons the faithful to prayer from the **minaret**, the tower attached to every mosque. His plaintive cry replaces the bells of Christendom. Then, believers prostrate themselves in prayer in shops and homes, wherever they are, as well as in mosques.

In the markets, veiled women are not seen as much as formerly, but they are still common in some parts of the Muslim world. Although the Muslim admonition against alcoholic drink is not always strictly observed, it is in coffee shops and teahouses rather than pubs or bars that one sees the men gathered of an evening to discuss the affairs of the day. Finally, if one is at all familiar with the local language, one will be struck by the frequency of expressions such as "If Allah wills" in daily conversation.

Minaret, Hassan II Mosque, Casablanca, Morocco.

The very heart of Islam is submission to the total will of **Allah**, or God. (Allah is not the name of a god, but simply means "The God"—the one and only God.) God's will for humanity, Muslims believe, was most fully given in the **Qur'an**, the book revealed through the prophet Muhammad. The word **Islam** means "submission," and the name tells us that the central idea of this faith is simply full and complete submission to the will of God. An adherent of the faith is called a **Muslim**, one who has made the submission.[1] So it is that the muezzin in his five-times-daily cry says:

God [Allah] is great! God is great!

There is no god but God,

And Muhammad is his prophet!

Come to prayer! come to prayer!

Come to abundance! come to abundance!

(At dawn, he here adds:

Prayer is better than sleep!

Prayer is better than sleep!)

God is great! God is great!

There is no god but God!

That is the central motif of Islam—the greatness of God alone. Because Allah is great and sovereign, all the world and all the affairs of humankind belong only to him. For this reason, Islam does not lavishly embellish the religious sphere with rites and symbols and priesthood; if Allah is truly great, Islam says, he can be worshipped anywhere by anyone in the simple forms prescribed by the Qur'an

Muslims praying in Afghanistan.

and by tradition. If God is truly sovereign, what he has commanded for all of society—law, ethics, government—is just as important as the religious commandments and inseparable from them. For this reason, Islam is experienced as a total and indivisible way of life. It is deeply consistent with the basic premise of the faith—the absolute sovereignty of God over all situations and over every atom of the universe—that whenever feasible, Muslims not only establish Muslim worship but also create Muslim societies under Muslim rulers based on Qur'anic law. Modern conditions have often mandated reinterpretations of this ideal. But the Qur'an remains the fountainhead of the true law and the true culture and a summons to submission in every area of life: political, economic, and family life, as well as such conventionally religious matters as how one says prayers.

MUHAMMAD

At the core of Islam lies the experience and faith of Muhammad (570–632 C.E.) himself. He lived in Arabia, having been born and raised in the city of Mecca, a commercial center already sacred to the Arabs. Its holy sanctuary, which drew numerous pilgrims, was the home of many polytheistic gods—chiefly those of the moon, the stars, and the days of the year—and the resting place of a sacred stone, probably meteoritic, considered to have come down from heaven. The area around this place of worship was a neutral zone where representatives and merchants of many tribes, often at war with each other, could meet in peace.

Muhammad came from a respected merchant family of modest means, which was part of the prestigious Quraysh tribe who were custodians of the sacred places of Mecca. According to tradition, he became a camel driver as a young man. When he was twenty-five, he entered the service of Khadija, a wealthy widow much older than he. Before long he married her, and she bore his daughter Fatima.

Muhammad was always a serious, thoughtful, and rather withdrawn man. But until he was about forty, his life was not outwardly much different from that of the other merchants of the sacred city. At that age, however, he found himself going into the mountains more and more to devote himself to meditation.

About the year 610, Muhammad began to have a remarkable series of experiences in these solitary meditations in mountain caves. A mysterious darkness would come over him, and then the luminous figure of the archangel Gabriel would appear and recite words to him from Allah, God, which he could remember clearly. These words were first of all about the unity of God—that there is but one single god, "Lord of the worlds," who abominates idolatry and will judge the Earth on a day of fire and anxiety; and God calls upon all humanity to accept his sovereignty.

For ten years (611–621) Muhammad implored his fellow Meccans to obey this call to acceptance of the oneness of God, but with little success. Indeed, it seemed to many that his fervent message threatened the lucrative polytheistic cultus, and

Muhammad found his position in Mecca untenable. In 622 he accepted an invitation from the city of Yathrib (now Medina) to teach, and he and his followers migrated there. His journey to Yathrib is called the **Hijra** (flight or emigration). The date of the *Hijra* now marks the first year of the Muslim calendar.

But Medina was not a place of peace. The fledgling Muslim community was soon required to fend off attacks from the Meccans. Battles ensued, which continued intermittently until 630 C.E. when Muhammad led an army, ten thousand strong, against the Meccans. The prophet's former fellow-citizens surrendered in the face of such a force. Contrary to custom at the time, however, Muhammad showed mercy to the vanquished, and soon a majority of Meccans converted to Islam.

It may be helpful to consider for a moment the context of Muhammad's work. The Near East in Muhammad's day was dominated by the political, economic, and ideological rivalry of three great powers: the Byzantine and Ethiopian Empires, which were Christian, and the Persian Empire, which was Zoroastrian but harbored influential minorities of Jews and non-Orthodox Christians. The Byzantine and Persian empires, arch foes, fought interminable and debilitating wars, which usually ended in standoffs.

In this situation, Arabia was by no means the barbaric backwater sometimes imagined, but it was nonaligned, a no-man's-land between superpowers. There were Christians and Jews in Arabia who were thought to lean, respectively, to Byzantium and to Persia. But the merchants of Mecca and Yathrib, well aware of world affairs through trading contacts in the great imperial cities, realized that their well-being required them to avoid overdependence on either side.

Yet many were also well aware that the religions of the great powers were more "modern" than their own polytheism. Belief in a sovereign deity—whether the Christian God or Ahura Mazda or the God of the Jews—was clearly the new progressive thing upon which great civilizations were being built. Moreover, "new occasions teach new duties," and the prosperous, individual-enterprise Meccan merchants found the old sense of identity in the tribe breaking down deep within them. A new doctrine and ethic was called for, emphasizing mercantile values, individual responsibility, and the sacredness of the individual betokened by personal judgment and immortal life. The new teaching might draw from Zoroastrianism, Judaism, and Christianity, or at least parallel them, in its idea of one God and moral choice, but it had to be politically independent of other ideologies. Some, called **Hanifs**, had already moved in this direction; they are not fully understood, but apparently they were a pious, though not highly organized, people who shunned the worship of idols and affirmed a generalized monotheism. Other Arabs to the north were Christian. But in this situation, an Arab prophet was lacking, one who as an Arab would bespeak the common national and spiritual concerns of the Arabs.

That is what Muhammad did visibly during his ten years in Medina, and he did it so well that the message he espoused carried conviction far beyond the Arab world. Using Medina as a base, in addition to Mecca, he brought nearly all of Arabia under his control. He became at once the religious leader, the political ruler, and the military commander of the Arabs and remained so right up to the end of his life. He died just two years after his triumph in Mecca—his divine revelations continuing through it all, to the end. Together those revelations make up the text of the Qur'an, the Holy Scripture of Islam.

THE QUR'AN

Unlike the Judeo-Christian Bible, the Qur'an is not a collection of diverse material from over hundreds of years. It was all delivered in a period of no more than twenty-two years to one man in the form of communications from God through his angel in 6,000 verses (*ayat*), later organized into 114 chapters (*surahs*). It is not a book of history or a life of Muhammad or a philosophical treatise. It is a book of proclamation: proclamation of the oneness and sovereignty of God, of his coming judgment, of the need to submit to him for the sake of righteousness and to build a just society. In passing, it also presents a Muslim view of previous religious history, especially of the earlier prophets such as Abraham, Moses, and Jesus. From time to time, it gives instructions to the faithful as a moral guide.

To Muslims, the Qur'an is a miracle—the most convincing miracle of all as validation of their faith. In the original Arabic, the Qur'an, exquisite in its incomparable beauty of rhythm and expression, is said to be untranslatable. That one man, and he illiterate according to tradition, could be the merely human author of "the Glorious Qur'an, that inimitable symphony, the very sounds of which move men to tears and ecstasy,"[2] seems to Muslims incredible. The Holy Qur'an, they deeply believe, is the full and complete message of the infinite Divine Mind to humanity. Thus, it is not only studied but also chanted, memorized, and recited on all sorts of occasions, venerated both as words and as a book. Even its way of speaking is divine; it represents the personal style of Allah and so transmits something of God's essence. Its very choice of rhythm, metaphor, and rhetorical method, in other words, reveals something of how God thinks and feels, just as do its contents.

It is necessary to bear in mind always the Qur'an's purpose—to proclaim the oneness and sovereignty of God. It does not develop a philosophy or tell a story because those are not its purposes. The Qur'an is intended only to state one basic truth; it repeats itself to reinforce that one simple truth. As A.J. Arberry has put it, the repetition of the Qur'an's truth is like being surrounded by a gallery of paintings all on the same subject.[3] The Qur'an's accounts of some matters common to other faiths, such as the lives of Abraham or Jesus, may seem twisted to those of such other faiths. However, it must be remembered that Muslims are not, after all, Jews or Christians. They are under no obligation to regard those other religions' versions as authoritative. In fact, Muslims consider the older Hebrew and Christian scriptures to be incomplete and corrupted by human intervention, while the Qur'an is believed to be the complete and full expression of Allah because it is his direct word, Muhammad being only, in effect, a scribe. However, because of Muslims' common heritage with Jews and Christians beginning with Abraham and a recognition of the validity of the prophets of the Bible including Jesus, Muslims consider Jews and Christians of higher status and of closer kinship to Muslims than those in "idolatrous" religions that do not share such heritage. Jews, Christians, and Muslims are all "People of the Book."

The Qur'an begins with the following prayer, which sums up its basic spirit and message well:

> *In the Name of Allah, the Compassionate, the Merciful*
>
> *Praise be to Allah, Lord of the Creation,*
>
> *The Compassionate, the Merciful, King of Judgment-day!*
>
> *You alone we worship, and to You alone we pray for help.*
>
> *Guide us to the straight path,*
>
> *The path of those whom You have favoured,*
>
> *Not of those who have incurred Your wrath,*
>
> *Nor of those who have gone astray.*[4]

The book continues to describe the wonders of creation: how God made humankind from the union of the sexes, out of clots of blood, and through the mysterious development of the embryo. God, it says, created man of ideal form. It exhorts humans not to deny but to show gratitude for this panorama of mercy and marvel, for when the judgment comes, wrongdoers will not be asked about their sins but will be known by the expressions on their faces. The deniers of the Lord's blessings will then suffer in hell, but those who have regard for the divine majesty will find themselves in surroundings fit for heroes: gardens full of flowing springs, lush fruits, and dark-eyed damsels. Like the paradises of most religions, this one has the brightly colored, gemlike, opposite-of-the-ordinary quality of dream, poetry, and sensuous youthful joy. But the deeper meaning of the Qur'an's message is less reward and punishment than the inescapable fact of Allah himself:

> *Roam the earth and see how Allah conceived Creation. Then Allah will create the Second Creation. Allah has power over all things;*
>
> *He punishes whom He will and shows mercy to whom He pleases. To Him you shall be recalled.*
>
> *Neither on earth nor in heaven shall you escape His reach; nor have you any beside Allah to protect or to help you.*[5]

> *And again:*

> *To Allah belongs the east and the west. Whichever way you turn there is the face of Allah. He is omnipresent and all-knowing.*[6]

The fundamental faith of the Qur'an, then, is consistent monotheism. It is expressed in the coming judgment, the absolute sovereignty of Allah over all things, over both the making and the fortunes of the present world, and the issue of who will be brought into joy in the Second Creation. Muhammad is the envoy of God and the last, or seal, of the prophets. This fact is not, for Muslims, an addition to consistent monotheism but the way God guarantees that this truth shall be known.

Muslims believe that Islam is the ultimate religion, the complete religion. It is the religion of Abraham, the primal monotheism of the beginning come back in finalized form. It is the ultimate form of religion because it is in fact the simplest and clearest. It is just the essence of religion—plain and perfect submission to the absolute God in all areas of life.

The Qur'an indicates that before Muhammad, a series of prophets, all to be greatly honored, labored to call humankind back to this perfect *islam*, or submission. They included Abraham, Moses, Isma'il, Idris (Enoch), and Jesus. But it was through Muhammad that the final, complete message came, superseding all that went before: it was the culminating message of God for humankind.

The role of Jesus in the Qur'an and in this series of prophets usually puzzles Christians. The Qur'an makes Jesus the greatest before Muhammad. He was called to preserve the Torah

Muslim boys studying the Qu'ran during Ramadan.

of the Jews and was a wise teacher of deep inward holiness. (This last quality has made him especially beloved of the esoteric mystics of Islam.) Jesus has, to say the least, been far more highly regarded by Muslims than Muhammad has been by Christians.

The Qur'an accepts the virgin birth of Jesus and calls Mary one of the greatest among women, but it says Jesus was born under a palm tree rather than in a stable. It mentions the Last Supper, but it denies that Jesus was actually crucified. It says that people only thought he died on the cross; instead, he was taken directly to heaven. It is believed that Jesus will return just before the Last Judgment to defeat Al-Masih ad-Dajjal, or the False Messiah, who will also appear in those end-times. But Islam does not make Jesus the "Son of God," for in Muslim eyes such a concept would be polytheistic and idolatrous.

However different the life and meaning of Jesus may here appear, in looking at Islam and the Qur'an, Christians may, in the words of Seyyed Hossein Nasr, "come to understand how the sun of their own spiritual world is also a shining star in the firmament of another world." [7]

One of the loveliest passages of the Qur'an reads:

God is the light of the heavens and the earth.

The likeness of His light is as a niche,

Wherein is a lamp, the lamp in a glass, the glass like a glistening star, kindled from a blessed tree,

An olive neither of the east nor of the west,

Whose oil would almost shine had no fire touched it.

Light upon light: God guides to His light whom he will:

God brings similitudes for men and God has knowledge of all things.[8]

In all ways then the light of God is added to light; the final revelation is not inconsistent with what was presented by earlier prophets, even though the other People of the Book may have distorted their heritages. But Islam gives the final luster of a perfect glass to the light of God agelessly hidden in the lamp of the world.

All the way through, then, the central message of Islam is oneness; the unity of the line of true prophets, the oneness of the final prophet and the book, the oneness of the People of God, the one submission to be made, and, finally, the supreme oneness of God.

Islamic submission to oneness is expressed in part through avoidance of **shirk**, idolatry, or putting other gods beside the One. It is typified by the avoidance of images and often of any representational art in Muslim religion and culture. This is not a condemnation of the world of created things, for Islam has little asceticism of that sort. It extols the joys of marriage and the table, and paradise itself is described in sensual terms. But these are gifts of God, to be accepted and enjoyed for themselves with gratitude. They are not to be worshipped or even artistically recreated as symbols for God, who needs no such help.

The submission of Islam is not just a private, personal matter. It is not meant to be the sort of following of inner "leadings" that often merely indulges whims and sanctifies self-inflation. To be sure, Islam has not lacked colorful but dubious figures who have claimed special divine calls. But the tradition has tried hard to combat the human proclivity to mix piety and egotism through the **Shari'ah**, or law. *Shari'ah* is the Qur'an as it is explicated and expanded by recognized jurists who depend in this process upon the *Sunnah* (extra-Qur'anic sayings and examples in the life of Muhammad), which are recorded primarily in the **Hadith**.

The lineage of prophets, and living the Islamic way of life now, is part of the great historical process leading up to the culmination of history, the Last Day for, as we have seen, Islam, like Judaism and Christianity, is a religion of God acting in history, and that history has a definite beginning and ending. As the opening of the Qur'an says:

> *In the Name of God, the Merciful, the Compassionate*
> *Praise belongs to God, the Lord of all Being,*
> *the All-merciful, the All-compassionate,*
> *the Master of the Day of Doom.*[9]

And, giving a vivid picture of that Day, the sacred book in Sura 82 adds:

> *When the sky is torn*
> *When the stars are scattered*
> *When the seas are poured forth*
> *When the tombs are burst open*
> *Then a soul will know what it has given and what it has held back.*[10]

Islamic scripture and tradition add further details, some clearly in line with earlier Jewish and Christian apocalyptic belief. We are told that as the Day approaches the world will more and more abandon divine law and degenerate into chaos. The heroic figure called the *Mahdi*, or "rightly guided one," will appear to restore the world for a short time. But he will be followed by the previously mentioned al-Masih ad Dajjal, impostor messiah or anti-Christ, a deceiver who promises true revelation but delivers only its opposite: more confusion and tribulation.

But his time is short, for then trumpets sound. The world is shaken as all that is familiar collapses, but tombs open and the souls of the dead are reunited with their bodies, to stand before the mighty judgment. The righteous enter paradise, the unrighteous the flames of hell.

The Muslim paradise is literally *al-Jannah*, "the Garden." One might have expected a desert people, like the first Muslims, to imagine paradise as like the lush, well-watered oases for which they yearned as they crossed their hard dry land, and so it was. Paradise is enclosed, cool, filled with sparkling streams, abundant with luscious fruit and with male and female companions, taken by some commentators to represent mystical states of consciousness, for the greatest boon of paradise is the nearness of God.

As for hell, its destroying flames are said to manifest the anguish and self-destruction of a life in denial of God. As to whether hell is eternal, or more like a purgatory one can leave if the evil in one has been truly burned away, is an open question. For one *hadith*, or saying of the Prophet, says, "He shall make men come out of hell after they have been burned and reduced to cinders," and another has God say of the damned in hell, "Let those leave hell whose hearts contain even the weight of a mustard seed of faith."

And to show even this much faith, Islam offers clear guidelines for practice, beginning with the Five Pillars.

THE FIVE PILLARS OF ISLAM

Let us examine some aspects of traditional and normative Islamic life based on *Shari'ah* as derived from the Qur'an and *hadith*. These center on the **Five Pillars of Islam**: the confession of faith, prayer five times a day, giving of alms to the poor, fasting in the month of **Ramadan**:, and the **hajj**, or the pilgrimage to Mecca.

Thousands of Muslims circumambulate the Ka'bah in the Grand Mosque in Mecca, Saudi Arabia, during the hajj.

The first of the Five Pillars is to say, "There is no god but God (Allah), and Muhammad is the *rasul* (Prophet or messenger) of God." This statement sums up in a few words the simple Muslim faith. The basic concept of the oneness of God has been discussed. When Muhammad is called the **rasul** or messenger of God, it means that he is God's appointed spokesman, the mouthpiece through which God chose to deliver his call for submission and his final commandments to the world. True, Muhammad is also considered a paragon of virtue and fountain of wisdom, so that his sayings and acts, as transmitted by tradition, are basic precedents in Muslim law. But he is not a saint, seer, wonder worker, divine incarnation, or even a profound mystic like the Buddha or a peerless philosopher like Confucius. It is emphasized that Muhammad's birth was biologically normal and that he performed no miracles except the delivery of the Qur'an itself. The Qur'an attributes virgin birth to Jesus and miracles to earlier prophets: Moses changed a staff into a serpent; Jesus is said by the Qur'an not only to have been taken up into heaven but also to have caused some clay birds to come to life and fly away. These are appropriate to the son of Mary, for he is the prophet of mystic and marvelous holiness; similar powers are recognized, as we shall see, in numerous Muslim *wali*, or saints. But Muhammad's own calling was not to this sort of thing but simply to be the spokesman of God. His miracle is the Qur'an itself; its production by a man like him in enigmatic circumstances and the wonderful emergence of the Islamic community around him are considered sufficient evidence of his authority. Muhammad needed to dispense no other, more trivial, miracles as calling cards.

The second of the pillars is prayer, done five times a day. In the next part, we shall examine how these formal prayers are performed.

Muslims praying at the Juma Masjid (mosque) in Delhi, India.

Muslim father and son reading the Qur'an during Ramadan.

The third pillar is almsgiving. The fundamental obligation is to give a relatively small but variable percentage of one's wealth to the needy within the Muslim community; expanded, the obligation covers good works and comradely attitudes in general, a helping hand and friendly smile for one's neighbor. This pillar reaffirms the social and ethical dimensions of Islam. The Muslim faith strives to remember it is a community of submission and service, working for a more just world, not just a personal path to salvation. Strictly speaking, almsgiving should be done out of religious commitment rather than compulsion (although it has been collected, from Muslims only, as a tax in traditional Islamic states). But many modern reformers have seen in the almsgiving principle a rationale for social welfare programs or socialism as an application of the Islamic community ideal under contemporary conditions.

The fourth pillar of Islam is the fast of Ramadan. Ramadan is a lunar month of about twenty-eight days in the Muslim calendar; during this period the faithful are neither to eat nor drink between daybreak and dark but to give attention to prayer and religion. Commonly, family and friends will gather at night to dine as soon as it is permitted, and there are traditional Ramadan dishes. Often the meal will be combined with reading aloud from the Qur'an and with prayer and will continue far into the night. The daylight hours will be for rest and further prayer. At the end of Ramadan comes *Eid al-Fitr,* a festive celebration that commences when the first sliver of a new moon indicates the end of the month of fasting and the beginning of the next month.[11]

Because the Muslim calendar is lunar, the occurrence of Ramadan moves progressively through the seasons. When it falls in the short, cool days of midwinter, it is relatively easy to endure, but amid the long summer days of a hot, dry climate, going without food or even a sip of water provides a stern test of Muslim loyalty. Understandably, some partially successful attempts have been made in recent times to reinterpret Ramadan in view of the exigencies of modern urban life. For innumerable devout Muslims, however, Ramadan remains a strenuous test of faith, softened by support from culture and tradition and the "we're all in it together" mood of a Muslim society's observance. For many, too, the opportunity for a deepening of one's life of prayer and Qur'anic study is genuinely welcome.

The fifth pillar is one known to almost everyone who has heard anything about Islam: the pilgrimage to Mecca called the *hajj.* Mecca, the immemorially holy city and birthplace of Muhammad, is the focal point of Islam. As though aligned along rays to a sun, Muslims at prayer face toward this vale in the Arabian Desert, and once in a lifetime their feet are to take them down that ray to the holy place. Every year a million or more Muslims gather at Mecca in the month of pilgrimage; this assembly affords, like nothing else, that sense of unity and identity for which Islam is justly famous.

Not all Muslims, of course, make the pilgrimage even once. Minors, the elderly, the infirm, and those without financial means are among those exempted from the obligation. For those who do go on the *hajj*, the rewards are substantial, not only in spiritual fulfillment but also in prestige within the Islamic family. Back in the home community, wherever it lies, the returned pilgrim may add the title *hajji* to his or her name and will be afforded special honor.

The pilgrimage is properly made in Dhu-al-Hijjah, the last month of the Muslim calendar. The pilgrimage is thus a meeting of sacred ultimates—a return just before the beginning of a new year to the place where Islamic history began.

Muslim belief about Mecca and the *hajj* combines the city's pre-Islamic role as a sacred center, a sanctuary for combative tribes, and a place of polytheistic worship, with beliefs about Abraham and the revelation through Muhammad. According to traditional Muslim belief, Mecca is the navel of the world, the spot where creation began. Abraham (Ibrahim in Arabic), the primal prophet of the original pure mono-theistic religion, was then called by God to proceed to the valley where Mecca is now located.

This he did, together with Hagar his wife and Isma'il (Ishmael) his son, forefa-ther of the Arabs. On one occasion, Hagar was lost in the desert with Isma'il, and she ran desperately about, up and down the hills there, looking for water for the infant until she found that a well had sprung up where she had lain Isma'il, right under his heel as it lay on the sand. Later, Abraham under God's instructions built the cubical shrine at Mecca—the *Ka'bah*—with the help of Isma'il. In the corner of the *Ka'bah* was placed the Black Stone brought from heaven by the angel Gabriel. On another occasion, in a variant of the account of the sacrifice of Isaac in the Judeo-Christian Bible, Abraham was commanded by God to sacrifice his son Isma'il. As they went to the place of sacrifice, Satan appeared three times to Isma'il and tempted him to reject his father's demand, but Isma'il kept faith and refused. At the last moment, a ram was substituted for the boy.

The *Ka'bah* is now the center of the great open-air mosque of Mecca and is the real focal point of all Muslim worship. Other mosques have a niche in a wall fac-ing in the direction of Mecca; this mosque, because it is the focal point, surrounds the *Ka'bah*, or Holy House, which stands at its center. The *Ka'bah* itself is covered with black-and-gold cloth and has a gold-encrusted door, seldom opened. The sacred black stone is visibly inserted in a corner of the Holy House. Around it is a broad marble pavement, where pilgrims circumambulate the shrine, and beyond this, plat-forms for prayer.

In Muhammad's day the *Ka'bah* contained 360 images of heathen gods (so far had the faith of Abraham declined), but the prophet had these destroyed. Now the *Ka'bah* holds nothing but a few lamps. Yet for Muslims, whose faith is in the infinite God alone, in its emptiness the shrine is all the more holy. The *Ka'bah* is said to be an exact replica of the house of God in paradise above, around which angels circle as the faithful on Earth circle the earthly *Ka'bah*. Heaven, tradition says, is closer to Earth at Mecca than anywhere else, so prayers are heard best from there. Nothing comes between the *Ka'bah* and the abode of Allah; airplanes are not allowed to pass over it, and it is said that even birds will not fly above the Holy House. Nearby is *Zamzam*, the well of Hagar and Isma'il, reputed to have curative powers.

Interestingly, Muhammad developed his teaching about Meccan pilgrimage dur-ing the time he was at Medina, when it was by no means clear that he would ever be reconciled with his home city. The teaching may, of course, have had political motives aimed at appeasing his kinsmen. Yet it also suggests that for the exile, Mecca had the quality of many pilgrimage centers of being "the center out there"—a place remote from the center of present action on the worldly plane yet a place of access to ultimate origins and ultimate goals. So has Mecca ever been.[12] Indeed, after the time of Muhammad, Mecca's role as a commercial center declined, and the holy city has since depended economically almost entirely on its sacred role.

The carrying out of the *hajj* is marked by many careful rituals. As he (or she, because women also undertake the *hajj*) approaches the city, probably from the sea-port and airport city of Jiddah on the coast, the pilgrim stops to separate himself or herself from the ordinary world by ablutions, as before prayer. The pilgrim then dons special white garments; thereafter, until the rites are completed, he or she must abstain from killing human beings, beasts, and plants; from sexual activity; and from cutting hair or nails.

Upon arriving at the sacred site, the pilgrim kisses (or if that is not possible because of the crowd, touches) the sacred Black Stone and then circumambulates the *Ka'bah* seven times.

Next the pilgrim runs seven times up and down a colonnade between two hills about 450 yards apart, reenacting Hagar's search for water for Isma'il.

Then the pilgrim proceeds outside Mecca to Mina, where he or she probably finds quarters in a vast tent city with a temporary population of a million or so; this gathering in itself gives pilgrims an experience of the power and unity of Islam. The next day the pilgrims all proceed to **Mount Arafat**, upon which they must stand between noon and sundown. There, seated on a camel, Muhammad gave his farewell sermon on his own last pilgrimage to Mecca.

This "standing at Arafat" is the culminating act of the *hajj* and the one act that cannot be omitted. It is the archetypal assembly of the faithful as a united army drawn out of all kindreds and tongues in submission to God. Like Muhammad's followers, they will listen to a sermon by an eminent Muslim scholar as they stand at Arafat. The assembly is said to bring to mind the gathering of all peoples for judgment on the Last Day, and it repeats the first assembly that Muhammad himself commanded so heroically.

After this, the final rites represent a process of desacralization. Returning to Mina, the pilgrim throws rocks at three stone pillars said to represent devils, recalling the three temptations of Satan that Isma'il rejected.

On the last day of the formal, sacred pilgrimage, the pilgrim will sacrifice a ram or goat in a certain field; part of the meat is supposed to be given to the poor. On the same day throughout the Muslim world, an animal is similarly sacrificed. Its head is pointed toward Mecca, and the Muslim cuts its throat, saying, "In the name of Allah." This recalls the ram substituted for Isma'il in Abraham's rite.

Next, in Mecca, the pilgrim has his or her hair cut. The hair, a token of oneself, is left behind as a sign of dedication. The pilgrim circumambulates the *Ka'bah* a final time.

Most pilgrims will then proceed to Medina, although this journey is optional. There, in this second most sacred city of Islam, they visit Muhammad's mosque and tomb. Some Muslims desire to come to Medina to die and be buried there with the prophet and his family.

The *hajj* is a collection of diverse traditional acts. Some may seem very Islamic and meaningful; some, like the running and stoning of the "devils," rather primitive and bizarre. Yet Muslims find them all spiritually significant, though none more so than the pilgrimage itself. Many Muslims, including the most mystical, have found deep inward meanings in all the traditions; stoning the pillars, for example, is made to represent striking down sinful desires within one's self.

Perhaps the best explanation is that of the great medieval theologian al-Ghazali.[13] He pointed out that the *hajj* is meant to be a supreme act of Islam, of submission and self-abnegation. That which is less than rationally appealing or satisfying to refined feeling can do much to purify and eliminate the egotism that easily lingers in a heart that considers itself refined. The *hajj* is an act of sheer devotion and of sheer identification with the inscrutable mind of God and with the Islamic tradition. It affirms that at the center of true religion is the finite human facing the infinite mystery of God, not the satisfaction of human inclinations.

PRAYERS AND MOSQUES

Hundreds upon hundreds of the faithful line up rank on rank, bowing and prostrating in unison in the mosque at noon Friday and spilling over into the plaza in front of it. This is a common sight in Islamic lands that never fails to impress visitors. It expresses eloquently the unity and devotion of Islam.

Equally impressive, and even more frequent, are the five-times-a-day prayers said regularly by believers wherever they are. The manner of saying these prayers and preparing for them is carefully prescribed by Islamic law; their combination of legalistic form and tenacious, fervent faith is close to the spiritual heart of Islam. Five times a day, the faithful Muslim's mind and heart, perhaps prompted by the *muezzin,* turns away from the things of the world to prayer:

1. Early in the morning, when dawn has become bright but before the sun has well risen.
2. Noon or early afternoon.
3. Late afternoon.
4. Directly after sunset.
5. Night, between darkness and dawn; usually about two hours after the sunset prayers.

If worshippers cannot perform the prayers at the time they are called, the prayers may be performed at any time until the next prayer is proclaimed.

Before prayers, one must be in a state of purification. This is attained by formal washing: the hands and arms are washed up to the elbows, the mouth and nostrils are rinsed, and the feet are bathed to the ankles, all thrice. Mosques and most homes will have water available in tanks, urns, or fountains for this purpose; one may also wash in an oasis. If sufficient water is not present, sand may be used.

Several further conditions should be met, if possible, out of respect for this sacred action. One should pray in a clean place free of defilement. For this reason, many Muslims use special small carpets, prayer rugs, which they spread over the place of prayer. One must be modestly dressed; for women, this means the body must be entirely covered except face, hands, and feet. Before beginning the prayers, one must articulate in one's mind the intention to say the right prayers. Finally, one must pray facing in the direction of Mecca.

The prayers begin and end with the petitioner standing upright, but they include bowing and prostration. They are spoken in Arabic, the language of Muhammad and the Qur'an, rather than in the vernacular language of the one who prays.

Muslim sisters in prayer at home on their prayer rug.

The Muslim first stands to say *Allahu-akbar*, "God is greater [than all]." Then still standing, he or she recites the *al-Fatiha* or opening verse of the Qur'an, given on page 371, and another short chapter of the scripture. The Muslim then bows and says thrice or more, "Glory to the Lord, the Exalted." He or she stands, saying: "God hears him who praises him. Our Lord, to thee belong praise." And then he or she kneels, touching the forehead to the ground, to say, "Glory to my Lord, the most High," thrice or more often. Finally, the petitioner stands, saying again *Allahu-akbar*. This whole procedure is called a *rak'ah*, and it is the basic unit of prayer. It is repeated a varying number of times, depending on the time of day. The whole is concluded by a prayer, not from the Qur'an, asking God to exalt and bless Muhammad and his followers.

We have dwelt in some detail with the prayers and their performance because they provide an intimate perception of Islam as it is lived and practiced day by day and as an incomparable view of its spirit. The rules surrounding the prayers may suggest that Muslims are burdened with an onerous task in fulfilling this basic obligation of their religion. Certainly, the prayers are not meant to be a trivial, lightly regarded part of one's life but a constant punctuation of every day recalling one to his or her first identity and responsibility. But for the devout, they are a welcome expression of faith and an added dimension to daily life. They remind the believer that he or she is a Muslim, one who worships and serves God before anything else.

Furthermore, they remind the person who prays that to be a Muslim means to be a part of the worldwide community, which, like any real community, has its traditions, its rules, and its center. One expresses this identity by performing one's prayers not haphazardly but at the same time, in the same way, and facing toward the same center, like one's comrades in the community. The prayers, then, rank with the *hajj* in creating a deep sense of Muslim identity. It may be noted that, although one may say the prayers with a special intention for some personal need and may pray at any other time on behalf of one's personal petitions, there is no prayer here for individual needs, such as for daily bread or for personal favors. The Muslim knows that one's relation to Allah should be first of all one of faith, praise, gratitude, obedience, and identity with the Islamic community and that God knows one's special needs before one can ask.

The prayers may be said individually wherever one is, but Muslims have always preferred to say them congregationally whenever possible. The mosque is the ideal place for corporate prayers, and the noon prayers on Friday are generally recited there. Friday marks the major weekly Muslim service; in it certain additional prayers are offered, and two sermons, separated by a short break, are delivered by the **Imam**, or learned teacher, retained by the mosque.

Women are expected to pray but are exempted from congregational prayers. They may pray in the mosque, in a separate section behind the men, but it is more traditional for them to pray at home.

The typical architecture of the mosque was originally inspired by the Arab house with its large courtyard and by the basilica-type Christian churches of conquered lands, some of which were converted into mosques. But the mosque has developed into a unique religious structure that sublimely represents the spirit of Islam. Far simpler in ornamentation than most churches and temples of other faiths, yet imposing and monumental, the mosque reflects well the austerity and majesty of Islam and its God.

The feature of a mosque that will first attract the attention of most visitors to the Islamic world are the *minarets*. These are the high towers beside the mosque proper. They are usually capped with the star and crescent moon, which is the symbol of Islam, said to be derived from the moon and single star that lighted the Prophet's way on his *Hijra* from Mecca to Medina. Great centers of worship may have as many as six minarets standing by the shorter and squatter building of the mosque. As we have seen, it is from the minaret that the *muezzin* cries out the call to prayer five times daily.

Approaching the mosque, the visitor enters a wide courtyard. It will probably contain water to be used for ablutions before prayer, and it is a favorite meeting place of the community. Indeed, mosques with their attached structures have traditionally functioned at once as virtually every sort of public building. Schools and libraries were and are connected with them, and their spacious facilities have served in the past as a place for gathering armies and as courts of justice. While modern states have felt that separate sites are more appropriate for such activities, their traditional affiliation with the mosque reminds us of the close alliance of Islam with all aspects of the life of the community.

The interior of the mosque characteristically possesses a clean, cool, open ambiance, yet the nonrepresentational ornamentation is sufficient to add a note of transcendent richness. The floor is covered with mats or carpets, often highly decorative. The walls and ceilings may be adorned with stunning arabesque designs or calligraphed Qur'anic verses. But one sees no furniture to speak of except the **minbar**, or seat, at the top of steps, which serves as a pulpit. Occasionally, a screened box provides protection for a worshipping ruler. A niche, called the **mihrab**, points prayer in the direction of Mecca. By its architecture and appearance, the mosque well expresses the two orientations of Islam—to God and to the community of believers, symbolized by Mecca, which is its earthly center.

The mosque also expresses well an already mentioned feature of Muslim life: its focus in the city or town. The rhythm of Muslim religious obligations; the daily prayers called by the *muezzin*; the ablutions and fasting; the *hajj*, which usually followed trade routes; and the law courts all seem to fit the outlook and pattern of life of the urban trader or craftsperson. Even Muslim farmers have generally wanted to live in villages with mosques. In particular, the Friday noon prayers are supposed to be said in a **Friday Mosque**, a great mosque theoretically large enough to hold the entire community, in contrast to smaller edifices that may be used for daily prayers. The Friday Mosque again affirms that Islam is meant to be lived in community, and it perceives the city as the ideal earthly expression of community.[14]

JIHAD

Out of the community ideal of Islam comes the often misunderstood concept of **jihad**. Sometimes referred to unofficially as the "sixth pillar of Islam," *jihad* means to "struggle" or "strive" in the realization of God's will on earth.[15] *Jihad* requires one to strive to live a life of righteousness and to struggle for social justice achieved through a just social and political order. Thus *jihad* is a multidimensional concept that includes one's own personal struggle (*jihad akbar*); striving for a just society (*unmaic jihad*); and the "lesser" *jihad* (*jihad ashgar*), which permits Muslims to defend themselves with violence if necessary. This lesser *jihad* also has been interpreted to permit under certain circumstances a "holy war" against injustice or to spread Islam,[16] although not to force individual conversions, which is forbidden in doctrine, even though there are reports that it has happened in some places. While many claim that *jihad* as holy war is highly restricted by the Qur'an and is legitimate only to address the plight of the oppressed or under conditions similar to those that would permit war under a Christian Just War Theory, others have interpreted *jihad* to permit any war aimed at eradicating what is forbidden, especially that which is promoted by the enemies of God—"the infidels."[17]

Still, since Islam in principle is a community as well as a religion, presumably only an absolute pacifist would be able to reject the theory of *jihad* as holy war out of hand, since other communities also fight to defend or expand their ways of life. However, on the deepest level, *jihad* is as much a spiritual struggle against enemies of faith within oneself as against outer foes.

HISTORIC ISLAM

In 632, the year of the Prophet's death, all these themes were coalescing to form the new faith of the newly unified Arab people. Returning from his triumphal pilgrimage to Mecca, Muhammad preached a farewell sermon, and shortly afterward, he died with his head in the lap of Aisha, his favorite wife. He was mourned, yet his death came at a propitious moment.

Star and Crescent.

Through a brilliant combination of diplomacy and militancy, Muhammad had united nearly all of Arabia under his command. He was the charismatic hero of the hour; he died before his hour of supreme glory had had a chance to pall.

His religious mission was apparently fulfilled; the revelations that he delivered were gathered to form the Qur'an within twenty years of his death.

Unlike other religious founders, Muhammad died a popular hero among his people, a ruler, a successful diplomat, a politician, and a general. Even though he was also a mystic visionary, there was nothing ethereal about him. Instead, he seemed to his people a man larger than life in many senses: warmhearted, full of cheerful humor, a planner of stratagems, a marshal who rode into battle with his troops and held his following together by the force of his personality when all seemed darkest— yet also a seer deep in prayer and vision alone in the desert, a rock of convinced faith and principle, and a man of a trustworthy and sympathetic nature. From this complex and extraordinary man came the Islamic faith, a faith that seems at once made for humans as they are, with their needs for politics, laws, wars, and sexual expression—and made for God as he is at his most magnificent: personal, creative, sovereign, and glorious, calling humans to total submission.

Inspired by fresh memories of Muhammad striding through Arabia, the Arabs were ready, at the moment of his death, to carry Islam out of his native land. They did this under new leadership with a rapidity that ever since has amazed the world. Within a century, the **caliphs** ("deputies" of the Prophet as temporal ruler), who were successors of Muhammad, ruled from Spain and Morocco to the Indus in the East. They came near to conquering Europe, but they were stopped by Charles Martel at the battle of Tours in 732 in what is now France. The weary Byzantine Empire reeled before their sway and lost vast provinces—once-Christian Egypt, Palestine, Syria, and part of Asia Minor. The Persian Empire collapsed entirely and passed to Muslim faith and sovereignty. After 750, Baghdad was the seat of the caliph who ruled all of this realm except Spain. That imperial city typifies that early expansive Islam was fundamentally a faith of urban merchants and men of affairs.

The years of the Baghdad caliphate (750–1258) and of the Cordova caliphate in Spain (755–1236) were the glorious years of early Islamic civilization. In the caliphates, art, science, and philosophy matured—thanks in part to Muslim revival of ancient Greek wisdom and the transmission of lore from India to the West. Modern mathematics has roots in the Arabic system of numbers and the zero, which the Muslims borrowed from India but whose use they explored. The Greek classics, including the philosophy and science of **Plato** and Aristotle, came back to Europe in the late Middle Ages and in the Renaissance by way of the Muslim world.

After the wars that Christian Europe called the Crusades, which engendered bitter feelings and much misunderstanding between the two faiths (not yet healed) and after the fall of the caliphates, Islam broke down into smaller units. The Turks finally took Constantinople (modern Istanbul) and caused the death of the Christian Byzantium in 1453. Most of the Arab lands ended up as parts of the Turkish-ruled Ottoman Empire (though the Turks are not Arab). Farther East, Persia and the Mughal Empire in India became splendid Islamic civilizations.

But gradually, it seemed, the Muslim world grew stagnant. By the nineteenth century, most of it was under European influence or direct colonial rule. The reasons for this decline from its brilliant and dynamic early life are complex. In part, it was due to external factors: incursions of conquerors such as Genghis Khan and European advances in technology and world exploration. Internally, the *Shari'ah* became more and more fixed in case after case. Believed to have divine sanction, the law inevitably made society static, putting a premium on conformity rather than innovation and new ideas.

In the twentieth century, however, Islam exhibited a new burst of life. It served as a vehicle for identity from North Africa to Indonesia and recovered something of its old dynamic sense of the unity of the diverse peoples who are followers of the Meccan prophet. We shall examine modern Islam in more detail later.

FEATURES OF CLASSIC ISLAMIC CIVILIZATION

Urban Settings and Family Life

As we have seen, Islamic religious culture comes most fully to flower in urban settings. Never was this more true than in the classical Golden Age of Islamic civilization, when fabled cities like Baghdad and Granada were centers of brilliant culture as well as flourishing political and commercial hubs. Let us examine some characteristics of life in these communities.

A traveler to a great classical Muslim city might first be struck and perhaps a little disappointed by the lack of monumental grandeur and imposing vistas. True, the Islamic city would be dominated by the impressive domes and minarets of its principal mosques and perhaps by a castle or fortress, like the Alhambra of Granada, Spain. But streets, especially in residential areas, would tend to be narrow and twisting and often would lead to dead ends. Houses, rather than presenting an ostentatious facade, would be likely to display only a rough whitewashed wall with a gate and balconies on the upper stories. The main business and shopping sections would be in the *suq* in many Muslim areas, a covered street lined with shops, displaying a fascinating interior that is not apparent from any outside vantage point.

The significant reality about the classical Islamic city, which interprets its distinctive features, is that the mazelike exterior is, so to speak, full of secrets. Just as Islam tells us that the created world veils and reveals the great secret of the universe—the power and sovereignty of Allah—so the city conceals, while expressing to the discerning eye, its more mundane social structures. Each of the little urban nooks and crannies created by the seemingly chaotic web of streets may house a subcommunity of practitioners of a particular craft or trade. Even more important, behind each wall and gate would be the intimate world of a family. Beyond the gate would be a courtyard and around it the house, with its quarters for women, children, and servants. For in a society in which women have traditionally been veiled and

Alhambra, 14th century palace of Muslim rulers in Granada, Spain.

enclosed and in which the education of young children frequently took place in the home, the house was a private realm with profound meaning for the personal lives of those who resided in it. Much business was conducted in its court; here, at prosperous houses, would arrive merchants, storytellers, wandering holy men, officials, and teachers, bringing the world to the home.

The Development of Islamic Culture

Among the other important motifs that governed classical Islamic civilization was the close relation in Islam between religion and law and the historical role of Muslims as conquerors and then rulers of their portion of the world. This reality had two important, but rather different, effects. First, it meant that Islamic law, with its often benign but ultimately conservative effects, firmly shaped the contours and limits of this civilization. For even the most powerful ruler, whether caliph or Ottoman sultan, was in theory supposed to be only an upholder of the existing law and to innovate nothing.

Second, it meant that the courts of kings and caliphs were immensely influential centers of cultural creativity. The average person thought of them as Arabian Nights realms of splendor and wonder. The reality may have been a little less fabulous, but the wealth, power, and entertainments of Baghdad and Granada at their height were the marvel of the world. Courts patronized poets, artists, musicians, philosophers, and theologians, and they drew talent and sophisticated appreciators of culture to their circles. In turn, because lines of trade and communication ran from the capitals like Baghdad, and later Cairo, Delhi, Isfahan, and Istanbul, to the far-flung reaches of the Islamic world, those cities served as centers of cultural dissemination. That Islam was a religious culture of a relatively few great capitals and had relatively great political cohesion during much of its most creative period has as much to do with the considerable uniformity of Islamic culture as it does with a faith of well-traveled soldiers and traders.

The Role of Nonrepresentational Art, Calligraphy, and Literature in Islamic Culture

The Muslim antipathy to representational art has also played a potent role in creating a highly distinctive Islamic culture. Although not directly Qur'anic, the idea that representation leads to idolatry early became almost universal in the Muslim world. Though observed with varying degrees of literalness in various times and places, it has meant that Islamic art has been essentially decorative and that pen and brushwork have largely been limited to calligraphy and book illustration—the latter being the medium wherein representational art has been accepted by all but the strictest Muslims. Islam has also accepted representation in such relatively minor forms as household tiles, figurines, and china, but never in monumental sculpture or painting. However, gifted Muslim artists have explored the acceptable media to the limits and have created a remarkable artistic heritage.

Islamic calligraphy and painting derive their power—and their Islamic validity—from their capacity to reveal the secret that the power and sovereignty of God is everywhere, so truth and paradisal beauty lurk beneath contrary appearances. Calligraphed lines from the Qur'an join with arabesques to adorn the clean walls and domes of mosques. The latter display the transcendent beauty of the One God; the former add, also through the medium of beauty, that the same God can be known and is known above all through the revealed words of the scripture. For example, Sura 68 of the Qur'an tells us it is "by the pen, and what it writes" that we are blessed and not cursed. But Islam universally holds that it is no sin and much virtue to make those words as appealing to the eye as possible through art and so to impress even more strongly their power.

So also the paintings that illumine the pages of books and sometimes the walls of schools and tombs give more a sense of conveying mystical rather than ordinary reality. They are flat and two-dimensional, with perhaps a gold background suggesting eternity rather than depth perspective. The saints and kings are mythic figures; the birds and gazelles are creatures from paradise. In the same way as the arabesque, these ostensibly representational works do not actually show the world as it is but as it appears to one whose eyes are opened to the presence of the God within and above all that is, so they present a sacred, not a worldly or idolatrous, vision. The famous Persian carpets also often have a comparable sacred message: the spot in the center upon which the elaborate design focuses is an opening from time into eternity.

In Islamic literature, poetry has been of far more importance than prose, for the two most influential literary languages of Islam—Arabic and Persian—lend themselves well to poetry and have highly exalted poetic feeling. Besides religious verse, they both have an exceedingly rich

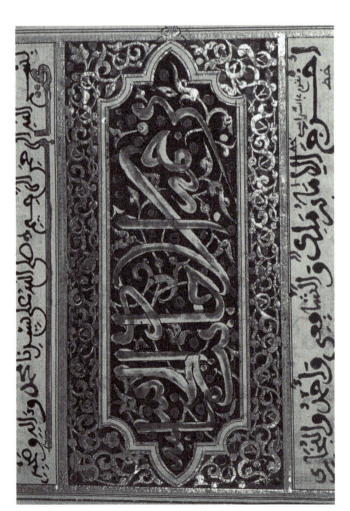

Eighth-century manuscript showing Arabic calligraphy in the Maghrebi style.

storehouse of secular verse: humorous, amorous, bacchic, and historical, together with odes celebrating the deeds of princes and warriors.

Perhaps because of these associations, poetry has not been well regarded by the most orthodox Muslims. The great exception, of course, is the Qur'an itself, which, though not always strictly poetry, is composed with unique and powerful patterns of rhythm and rhyme. But the position of the Qur'an in Islamic letters is paradoxical. As the text from which traditional Muslims learned to read, of which they had memorized long passages, and which they constantly heard recited, its majestic cadences must have been deeply embedded in their conscious and unconscious minds. Yet the Qur'an has been held to be beyond either imitation or criticism; to attempt either is presumptuous sacrilege. Thus, save in commentaries and pious treatises where it is directly quoted, one does not see an immediate influence of the Qur'an on literary theme or style.

For these reasons, one finds little good religious poetry associated with mainstream Islam. Rather, it is in the mystical tradition, above all in Persia, that the spiritual verse of Islam flowers. As much influenced by the secular poetry of wine and love as by the Qur'an, these songs of the spirit boldly use the language of intoxication and carnal passion to speak of the relation of the soul to God, the supreme Friend and Lover. They celebrate the "inebriate of God" beside himself with divine love, yet still able to express that love in soaring verse.

Islamic mysticism also came to express itself in elegant books. The most famous example is *The Conference of the Birds* by Farid ad-Din Attar (1119–1230), an allegory relating the quest of thirty birds for the Simurgh, a mythical bird who represents God. When they finally found that splendid being, the questing avians asked him to explain the mystery of the unity and multiplicity of reality. The Simurgh answered (in a mystical image that would be questioned by orthodox Islam) that his form was a sunlike mirror. He who looks at God sees himself reflected there in all his many parts, yet the mirror is one.

Philosophy, Science, and the Intellectual Life of Islam

Another very important motif, intrinsic to Islam and related to court and mosque alike, is the prestige given to scholarship because of the importance of the law and therefore its right interpretation. Members of the **ulama**, or body of learned men, adorned courts and presided in mosques; they also founded universities and searched out the philosophical underpinnings of faith. Because the language of scripture and its legal commentaries was Arabic, in whatever part of the world they dwelt, they had to work in that language. The immense authority of Arabic scholarship also worked powerfully on behalf of Islamic cultural homogeneity. For although popular religion and culture might vary considerably, this factor meant that the "great tradition" of learning and of "correct" interpretation would diverge far less, even when the Islamic world was not politically united.

The scientific work of the Golden Age of Islamic civilization has rightly been much acclaimed. Learned Arab men of the Baghdad caliphate and the Spanish caliphate preserved classical Greek and Roman scholarship and transmitted to Europe much of importance from farther East, such as the already mentioned concept of the zero in mathematics (which had been developed in India). They also made substantial advances in such varied fields as astronomy, optics, medicine, geography, and chemistry. All this, as we have said, occurred during the Middle Ages of Europe. Had it not been for the world of Islam, ancient learning would undoubtedly have been lost to a much greater extent than it was, and important advances that set the stage for modern science would not have been possible.

Although the highest intellectual life for the Muslim remained the divine sciences (understanding the mystery and majesty of God and the application of his revealed law), the openness of the conquering Arabs toward what remained of Greek natural science in the Middle Eastern countries they ruled was remarkable. As one might have expected, conservatives were highly dubious of such foreign and unrevealed lore. Yet more than enough people were of the opinion that all learning about Allah's creation was good and to his glory and that science and logic could assist in the understanding of God. For them natural and theological queries were complementary rather than at odds. A story tells us that the ninth century Caliph al-Ma'mun had a dream in which Aristotle appeared to him and that after some philosophical discourse, told him to treat scientists as gold and to hold to the Oneness of God—the fundamental Muslim doctrine. The great philosopher al-Ghazali, although he also emphasized mystical intuition, strongly affirmed that the study of Greek logic was a necessary preliminary to the study of doctrine and religious law.

Islamic philosophy had to deal with the impact of Greek thought to find what it could use of Plato, Aristotle, and the Neoplatonists and what no longer seemed applicable in the light of new revelation. Interestingly, the Islamic appropriation of Greek ways of thinking followed the sequence of Greek thought's own development—from rationalism to Neoplatonic mysticism.

Rationalism and Mysticism in the Development of Islamic Thought

A very significant early school of Islamic thought was the **Mu'tazila**, founded by Wasil ibn Ata (699–749). It exhibited a strong rationalist tendency. What God does is always what is best according to reason, and reason is equal to revelation and superior to tradition as a source of truth, according to the Mu'tazila thinkers. They explained anthropomorphic language about God in the Qur'an and contended that scripture was created in time, in opposition to the view of those who considered themselves more orthodox that scripture is the eternal Word of God. The Mu'tazila were supported by the same Caliph al-Ma'mun (r. 813–833) who entertained Aristotle in his dream, but their supremacy was short-lived.

A reaction that was to condition all subsequent mainstream Islamic theology came through the writings of Abul-Hasan al-Ash'ari (873–935), from which **Ash'arism** developed. He taught that divine actions cannot be explained in terms of human reason. God is simply absolute power and grace, mysterious rather than reasonable on the human level, to be adored and obeyed. This view won the allegiance of both political and spiritual leaders, and it set the stage for more and more emphasis on the basic Islamic concepts of God's oneness and sovereignty. It led toward determinism or predestination in theology and **pantheist** tendencies in mysticism: in either case, the sole controlling reality in the creation is God, whether viewed in terms of his ever-present will or of his ever-present being.

In the eleventh and twelfth centuries, two scientist–philosophers at opposite ends of the Muslim world labored vigorously to revive the rational approach and in the process profoundly affected European thought. Both ibn-Sina (980–1037) in Persia, known to the West as Avicenna, and ibn-Rushd (1126–1198) in Spain, known as Averroës, were deeply influenced by the Greek tradition. Both wrote important scientific and medical works, as well as pure philosophy, and both strove to assert the primacy of reason and science over revelation, although toward the end of his life Avicenna moved more and more in a mystical direction. But that thinker provocatively held to such assertions as the eternality of the universe and that only the soul survives death. Believing the Greeks had proved conclusively these matters by reason, he required that the Islamic doctrines of creation and resurrection be interpreted in a nonliteral way.

Al-Ghazali, following in the Ash'arism tradition that the ways of God are beyond searching out, attacked these positions in such works as *The Incoherence of the Philosophers*, in which he tried to show that the notion of matter as eternal and uncreated does not even stand up to reason and furthermore that reason itself is a poor guide to ultimate things. Averroës responded with, among his many books, *The Incoherence of the Incoherence*, strongly reasserting reason, though he was able to find a position somewhat more closely approximating orthodoxy than Avicenna's on the resurrection at the end of the world: while reason and science make it incredible that one's literal physical body could be resurrected, God could supply a new likeness of it on the Last Day.

Averroës's mind, though, was wide-ranging and free. He asserted the superiority of Islam over Plato's ideal state because the former seeks the happiness of all, not just a philosophical elite, but he also showed himself unorthodox when he regretted that Islam did not afford women the same equality he thought that Plato had afforded in his *Republic*.

However, such a liberal outlook was not to be characteristic of subsequent Islamic thought. Instead, the devout antirationalism of Ash'arism and al-Ghazali, more and more colored by Sufi mysticism (which will be discussed later in this chapter), was predominant in the last great classical school—that of Shihab al-Din al-Suhrawardi (1155–1191), of ibn al-Arabi (1165–1240), and of Sadr al-Din al-Shirazi (d. 1640), which pursued a high Neoplatonism, influenced also by Zoroastrian concepts of light and darkness, portraying a multilevel reality within the sole being of God.

Classical Islamic civilization, then, created a world of rich diversity and brilliance but all constrained by the sometimes flexible parameters of a worldview whose touchstone was the Qur'anic revelation.[18]

SUNNI ISLAM

We shall now examine some of the variations of belief and practice within Islam. The most important division today is between the Sunni and Shi'a traditions. **Sunni Islam** is the normative Islam of most places except Iran. Shi'a Islam is the official Islam of Iran, is dominant in southern Iraq, and is represented by minorities in Lebanon, Pakistan, India, Yemen, and elsewhere.

Sunna means "well-trodden path," and it refers to the consensus of traditional legal and social practices, as well as to the majority Islamic community that claims to be founded on the authentic and correct consensus tradition. It is a tradition given to accommodation of differences and tolerance within the overall Islamic perspective, often citing as its precedent the Prophet's saying, "Differences of opinion within my community are a blessing." The 85 percent or so of the world's one billion Muslims who are Sunni nonetheless maintain considerable overall homogeneity of belief and practice without a centralized organization or authority, for while some nostalgia for the caliphate remains, Sunni Islam today is self-governing in each Muslim country.

In Sunni Islam the fundamental authority, after the guidance of the Qur'an, is Muslim law. It is interpreted not by a single individual but by a consensus of learned men who base their decisions on tradition, *hadith*, and analogy. Although al-Azhar University in Cairo has long been considered the most venerable repository of such learning, Sunni interpretation is decentralized. Its emphasis is on the basic Five Pillars of Islam and on a rather formal—though deeply felt—style of devotion. Its legal bent stresses putting all of life under God and the Qur'an. Different schools of law interpretation exist within Sunni Islam, though they are not competitive but recognized alternatives. Sunni Islam also embraces some submovements; one is the Wahhabi movement, dominant in Saudi Arabia, which is a conservative, puritanical reform dating from the eighteenth century.

SHI'A ISLAM

Shi'a Islam, the Islam of Iran, southern Iraq, and minorities elsewhere, is different in tone and more complex. Shi'ites believe that after Muhammad there was intended to be a succession of divinely appointed and authoritative teachers of Islam—Imams—to guide the faithful. The first was Ali, Muhammad's cousin, and after him Ali's eldest son, Hasan, and then Ali's second son, Husayn. There were then nine others in family succession, down to the twelfth, who was born in 869.

All of these, except the last, died mysteriously and are said by the Shi'ites to have been killed at the instigation of various caliphs. From the Shi'a point of view, the caliphates represent dark usurping powers seeking to destroy the true spokesman in each generation of the house of the prophet of God. The twelfth Imam is said to be still living but invisible. In the fullness of time, he will reappear to bring justice to the Earth, sometimes under the title of **Mahdi**, or "Guided One." Subsects of the Shi'a recognize only part of the lineage or variations on it. Understandably, colorful claimants to the title of Mahdi have appeared from time to time in Muslim history.

Shi'a devotion puts most emphasis on Husayn (also spelled Hussein), the third Imam and the most worthy and tragic of all. In the sixty-first year after the *Hijra*, he and his companions were killed by the forces of the Caliph Yazid in a great battle at Karbala, in southern Iraq. The death of this splendid young hero has been made by Shi'a into an event that demands eternal recompense by fervent mourning and reenactment. Husayn's shrine at Karbala is a mighty place of pilgrimage.

The death of Husayn is commemorated by Shi'ites in the festival of **Muharram**, the first month of the Muslim calendar. During the first ten days of the year, Shi'a communities exhibit great religious fervor. At the end of the old year, black tents are set up in the streets with memorial arms and candles to remind passersby of the martyr. On the first day of Muharram, the devout cease from bathing or shaving. The story of Husayn is vividly recited from pulpits in the tents; the listeners respond with wailing and tears. Occasionally, groups of men roam the streets venting their anguish by inflicting sword wounds on themselves, dragging chains, dancing wildly, and pulling out their hair.

The climax of this remarkable commemoration of a hero's death occurs on the tenth day of Muharram. The battle of Karbala and the death of Husayn are enacted in a colorful passion play, with horsemen in bright costumes charging and recharging each other, battering their comrades in sport with wooden staves. The crowd becomes more and more excited; finally, Husayn is taken and is seen to suffer excruciatingly from thirst while the cruel foemen make sport of him. At last he is beheaded.[19]

The atmosphere of Shi'a Islam, as reflected in the Muharram and the beliefs about the mysterious martyred or hidden Imam, is clearly different in tone from that of Sunni Islam. The Shi'a world, far from being one in which submission to the revelation of Allah steadily and progressively triumphs, is a darker sphere where treachery and cruelty are all too likely to prevail on the outer plane. Heroes and true prophets of God suffer and die in anguish, while ruthless imposters sit upon thrones; the number of true faithful is small compared to that of frauds; and the faithful are known chiefly by the fervor of their righteous wailing for the evils of this hard world and the keenness of their hope in God's inward, invisible plans.

The Shi'a mentality is conditioned by centuries of experience of almost always being a religious minority within Islam, save under the Fatimid Dynasty, which ruled medieval Egypt and surrounding areas in the tenth and eleventh centuries, and in Iran since the Safavid Dynasty made it the official faith early in the sixteenth century. But history as old as Islam itself lies behind the Shi'a experience.

When the Shi'a movement began, it appeared on the surface as more of a political than a religious caucus. It was the party (Shi'a means "party" or "faction") supporting Ali and his descendants for the caliphate against the line recognized by the Sunni majority. According to the Sunni tradition, Muhammad left no designated successor. Upon his death, the community selected Abu Bakr, the Prophet's closest companion and the father of his wife Aisha, to be its leader. He died after only two years, but he appointed as his successor Umar (r. 634–644), the real organizer of the Arab empire. From then on, the control of the empire by Meccans, of the Umayyad and later (after 750) of the Abbasid house, was clear, despite a brief and challenged caliphate by Ali himself from 656 until his assassination in 661.

According to the Shi'a account, Muhammad appointed Ali as his successor before his death, but while the latter was still mourning the Prophet's passing and before he could assume active leadership, a clique within the companions of the Prophet had advanced the elderly Abu Bakr to the fore, and Ali's party felt compelled to accept him temporarily in order to prevent division at this critical juncture for Islam, despite knowing it was contrary to Muhammad's wishes. The bitterness of the Ali party was only increased during Ali's caliphate by the attack mounted against him by Mu'awiyah, governor of Syria, an exceptionally able ruler to whose banner the majority of Muslims turned as Ali's rule appeared weak and precarious. But the Ali party won sympathy from the discontented, especially the Bedouin tribesmen, with its demands for social justice and its opposition to the increasingly luxurious aristocracy of the empire. Furthermore, the movement's emotional tone was, as we have seen, deepened when Ali's son Husayn was cut down trying to raise a revolt against the Umayyads with a small but heroic army in 680. The Shi'a faction also had roots in ancient antagonism on the part of South Arabians and their powerful allies in Iraq and Iran where Ali found support—regions where Shi'a is still strong—against the North Arabian Mecca-Medina power base of the ruling **Sunni** Islamic establishment in the caliphate era.

As Shi'a Islam persisted despite failure in the military and political arenas, its theoretical concept of the divinely ordained Imam grew more and more exalted. The Sunni caliph was viewed as "successor" to Muhammad only in the latter's role as administrative leader of the Islamic community. No caliph presumed to share the Prophet's unique religious vocation as mediator of divine revelation. But Shi'a concepts of the Imam made his a unique and sacred spiritual office, though they varied from conservative doctrines in which he was little more than a divinely blessed caliph to extremist theologies that saw him as specially chosen by Allah to be divine and the sole interpreter of the Qur'an, who is to be obeyed absolutely. What might be called the Shi'a mainstream was satisfied to hold that, by divine grace, the Imam is without sin, that he has various sorts of superhuman wisdom and power and that he is able to interpret the Qur'an infallibly. However, since the "hiding" of the Imam, these extraordinary functions have been exercised by him through visible spiritual leaders who participate in some way in the Imam's prerogatives.

It is not surprising to find, then, that most sectarian movements within Islam have been Shi'a. The considerable majority of Shi'ite accept the standard list of twelve Imams before the hiding of the twelfth, and they are therefore called **Twelvers**, or **Ashariyah**. Like the Shi'a of Iran, they hold to the moderate position concerning the Imam outlined above. But a smaller faction, generally called

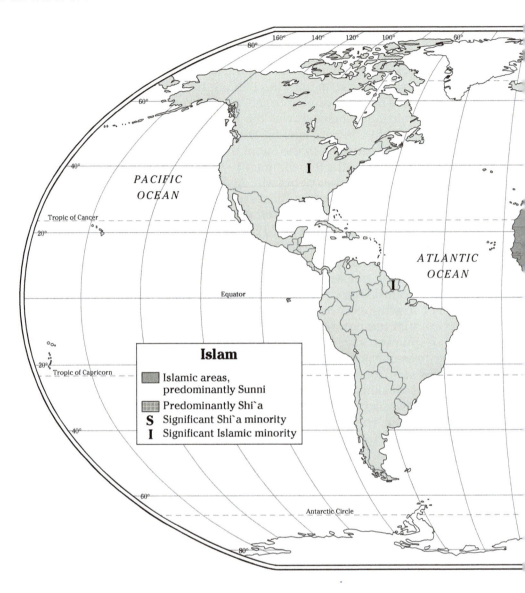

Islam

Islamic areas, predominantly Sunni

Predominantly Shi`a

S Significant Shi`a minority

I Significant Islamic minority

Ismailis, though sometimes also **"Seveners,"** accept only the first seven Imams and differ on the identity of the last. The Twelvers contend that the younger son of the sixth Imam inherited his dignity because the elder son, Ismail, was guilty of the sin of drinking wine. But Ismailis assert that the succession did pass to Ismail; moreover they claim that he was the last visible Imam and that his son Muhammad at-Tamm will return as the Mahdi, the divine figure who many believe will appear just before the Last Judgment to establish righteousness.

The Ismaili system of belief has been deeply influenced by esotericism of Gnostic and Zoroastrian background. It holds that the Qur'an contains veiled concepts of the **Neoplatonic** sort—doctrines of divine emanations, of levels of reality, and of the mystic significance of the number seven, for example. Ismailism takes a cyclical view of history and views all actual, public religions relativistically.

Ismaili history is fascinating. In the ninth century, an Ismaili order called the Qarmatians arose in southern Iraq and Bahrain. The Qarmatians practiced communal living, holding all things in common and serving one another's needs. But they

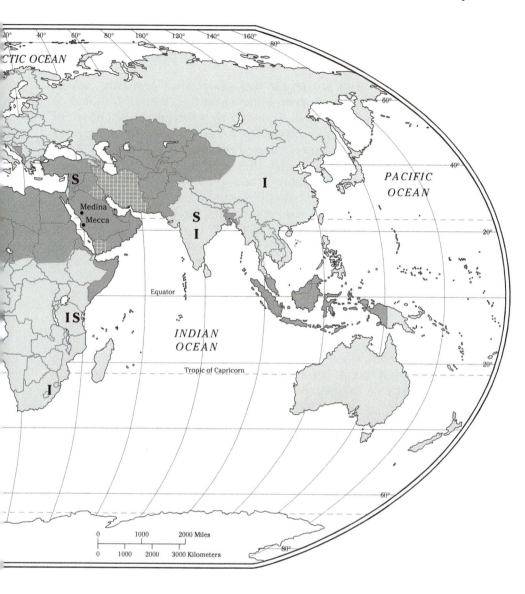

also defied the caliphate, engaging in terrorism against those they regarded as their foes. They achieved such exploits as sacking Mecca and temporarily carrying off the Black Stone of the *Ka'bah* in 930 C.E.

The Qarmatians prepared the way for something even greater: the rise of the Ismaili Fatimid Dynasty. At once imperial and revolutionary, this house perceived its mission in highly ideological terms. Its ruler was himself the quasi-divine Mahdi, and his tasks were to destroy the hated usurping caliphate in Baghdad, to convert Sunni Muslims to the true faith, and to establish a world empire under the world's true sovereign. Originating in North Africa (though claiming descent from Muhammad's daughter Fatima), the Fatimid house conquered Egypt in 969, making Cairo their capital and building a great university and mosque there. Besides armies, which tried to press ever closer to Baghdad, the Fatimids sent out missionaries to spread subversion and terror as well as to make converts in the lands of the enemy. But after reaching a high point in 1059, when they actually held Baghdad for a year, the Fatimids went into decline, harried not only by the caliphate, itself in decline, but also by the rising power of Turks and of Christian crusaders. Their regime was also made ultimately untenable because the majority of Muslims simply could not accept Ismailism or the legitimacy of Fatimid claims. Ismaili believers themselves came to lose faith in them, and the dynasty ended in 1171.

The Fatimid dynasty left a grim progeny in the order called Assassins, which flourished in the mountains and, through secret agents, in the cities of Iraq and of Iran and in adjacent areas from 1099 to 1266. Founded by a fervent Ismaili missionary and a deposed claimant to the Fatimid throne, the Assassins lived by raiding and terror, believing that the murder of those considered enemies was a religious duty. The name "Assassins" derived from the hashish they allegedly took to steel themselves for their bloody deeds. They were finally put down by invading Mongols, who also took Baghdad in 1258, ending the caliphate there and indirectly allowing Islamic culture to flourish all the more elsewhere—in Persia, India, Egypt, and later Turkey. A strictly religious, nonpolitical caliphate was set up in Cairo, where it remained until 1517. Thereafter, the title was taken by the sultans of the Ottoman Empire who held it until 1926, when the ancient dignity of the Commander of the Faithful and Successor of the Prophet vanished from the Earth.

The Ismailis today survive in several groups. The Druzes, a people of highly esoteric and initiatory faith centered in southern Syria, believe their creed was founded by al-Hakim, the sixth Fatimid ruler, who in 1017 proclaimed himself the latest incarnation of God. In 1021 he disappeared. Though others opine that he was deranged and murdered, the Druzes have taken him at his word ever since and regard him as the hidden Imam. Other Ismaili sects are centered in India and Yemen. The best known, with a following in the millions, is the Nizari movement, whose spiritual leader is now known as the Aga Khan. Aga Khan III (1877–1957) was much celebrated in the twentieth century as a philanthropist, sportsman, and Indian statesman. Since 1957, that philanthropic legacy has been carried forward by Aga Khan IV, who founded and chairs the Aga Khan Development Network.

But despite its wide dispersal and political origin, it is undoubtedly no accident that Shi'a Islam has its oldest roots in the Valley of the Two Rivers, where in ancient times New Year's (which Muharram really is) included rites of battle with chaos by the hero Marduk and wailing for the dead Tammuz. (One is reminded of the enacted battle and wailing for Husayn.) Shi'a is also strong in formerly Zoroastrian Iran, with its belief in a cosmic battle of good and evil, a hidden coming prophet, and an apocalyptic reversal to which the faithful looked forward. Christian and Manichaean influences on Shi'a cannot be excluded either, for Husayn emotionally becomes virtually a suffering savior. Shi'a attitudes undoubtedly had some part in setting the stage for the Iranian revolution of 1979, discussed later, under the leadership of **ayatollahs**, whose authority is believed to be conferred by the hidden Imam.

ISLAMIC MYSTICISM

A discussion of Islam would be superficial if it dealt only with its outward, official history and practices and left out the mystical wing, which has frequently given the faith of Muhammad another face. This tradition is known to the West as **Sufism** and its practitioners as Sufis. Their God is the same God as that of the Qur'an and the tradition, but they seek not only to follow his external commandments but also to know him intimately and even to lose themselves in love into the depths of his being. Around the Sufis' mystic quest have clustered a number of auxiliary features, many of great beauty: spiritual masters, parables and wisdom tales, spiritual fraternities, schools of meditation, and techniques of attaining ecstasy through music, chanting, and dance.

"Whirling Dervishes" in Syria.

Sufis believe their approach is grounded in the inner experience of the Prophet himself. Muhammad clearly prayed deeply and knew God intimately, even experiencing trance and rapture. Certain verses of the Qur'an, such as this one cited earlier, support the quest for mystical awareness of God everywhere: "To Allah belongs the East and the West. Whichever way you turn there is the face of Allah."[20]

Another Sufi approach suggests the esoteric side of things: we are told that Allah took his servant from a holy mosque to a farther mosque to reveal certain divine signs.[21] According to some traditions, this last passage refers to God's mysteriously transporting Muhammad in a single night from Mecca to Jerusalem and then taking him up into heaven to show him sights not seen by other mortals. Secondhand accounts of this journey probably helped inspire Dante's *Divine Comedy*.[22]

Thus many Sufis believe not only that their way is that of Muhammad himself but also that Sufism is really a timeless path known to the wise in all generations, just as Muhammad's declaration was in a sense but a restoration of the true primordial faith of Abraham and of Eden. Doubtless there is truth to this, represented historically by the parallels and possible influence between Sufism and Asiatic shamanism, Greek Neoplatonism, Christian monasticism, and the lore of Hinduism and Buddhism. But within Islamic history, Sufism became visible as a movement about a century after Muhammad. Like Shi'a but in a different way, Sufism was a reaction against the luxury and corruption, the loss of original desert simplicity and pure faith, which many serious Muslims saw overtaking the newly triumphant Islamic world of the caliphates.

The origin of the word *Sufi* is disputed, but the majority of scholars attribute it to the Arabic word for wool, *suf*, alluding to the coarse wool garments worn by ascetics seeking a more inward way and as a mark distinguishing them from those content with outward conformity to Islam.

Sufi inwardness made of greatest importance one's personal relationship of faith and love to God, a love which was its own reward. Never has this attitude been more eloquently expressed than by the mystic Rabiʻa al-Adawiya of Basra (713–801), a former slave who had been trained as a flute player. At night she would pray thus:

> Oh my Lord, the stars are shining and the eyes of men are closed, and kings have shut their doors, and every lover is alone with his beloved, and here am I alone with Thee.

She also said:

> I saw the Prophet in a dream, and he said to me, "O Rabiʻa, dost thou love me?" I said, "O Prophet of God, who is there who does not love thee? But my love to God so possessed me that no place remains for loving or hating any save Him."

And again:

> It is a bad servant who serves God from fear and terror or from the desire of a reward....Even if Heaven and Hell were not, does it not behoove us to obey Him?[23]

This is a pure Sufi spirit echoing down through the ages. As time went on, this sheer love of God came to be more and more organized, with particular practices and doctrines and societies shaping the lives of those who followed its path.

Thus, Abu Yazid al-Bistami (d. 874) described the stages of the spiritual life leading up to **fana**, a complete passing away of the separate individual self into God. The fana state was often manifested in ecstatic spiritual intoxication. In that state, al-Bistami, hardly knowing whether it was he or God in him whose words they were, did not shrink from such expressions as "I am your Lord," "Praise be to me, how great is my majesty," or "My banner is greater than that of Muhammad." The conventional were duly shocked.

Finally, in 922, one of these God-possessed persons of uninhibited rapture, al-Hallaj, was executed at Baghdad for saying "I am the Truth"—"Truth" being an attribute of Allah. The tragic al-Hallaj had taken Jesus, in Islam the exemplar of the inward mystic, as his model of the God-incarnate man, and he was sentenced to the same fate as Jesus: crucifixion.

At the same time, a reaction in favor of a more orthodox Sufism set in. Junayd of Baghdad (d. 911) emphasized that the claims of mystical experience cannot be given priority over normative moral and customary demands of religion and that the nature of love itself demands that, even in the mystic's "identity" with God, there be also a difference between him and God.[24]

The great al-Ghazali (1058–1111), who had been a conventional Muslim scholar until he experienced and then sought to interpret the mystic path, made Sufism a respectable part of Islam. He interpreted Sufi inwardness as an attitude to accompany the outward acts and bring them to life, as we have seen in his treatment of the *hajj*.

The philosopher and Sufi master ibn al-Arabi (1165–1240), a spiritual follower of al-Ghazali, moved in the direction of a pantheist philosophy as the intellectual expression of what the Sufi "knows" and enacts. For him, God was not only the source of all but also the sole reality. Within the divine, however, are gradations; between the human and the divine is a realm of images that reflect in the human imagination—angels, the Day of Judgment, and so forth—and on these images religious visions and events are grounded.

The Sufi way has made much of **shaykhs**, spiritual teachers and masters, and *wali*, saints. Drawing initially from Shi'a sources, Sufis have also talked of hidden holy ones and of the coming Mahdi. According to Sufism, the saints are different from the prophet Muhammad but are in their own way nearly as great. For a Sufi to attain sainthood, becoming a "friend of God," was as good a goal as outward Islam's submission.

Indeed, by the tenth and eleventh centuries, the twin goals of sainthood and submission came together, as the notion gained force in Sufi circles that one should submit to one's *shaykh*, or spiritual guide. The *shaykh*, called farther East around India a *pir* or a *murshid*, was more or less an Islamic parallel to the Hindu *guru*. The very self-abnegation of one's submitting to his *shaykh*'s commands "as a dead body in the hands of its washers" was an experience of egolessness and bore its own spiritual reward, whether the guide was wise or not.

Many were wise, and their wisdom was often expressed in peculiar tales and gnomic wisdom. We are told, for example, that a certain man fell down in a seizure on a street of perfume sellers. People tried to revive him with various sweet odors of the tradesmen, but to no avail. Finally, someone thrust sharp, pungent, ammonious ordure before his nose, and he arose. The implication is that only by the different, even the disconcerting, can the walking dead be brought to life.[25] *Shaykhs* have employed the methods of differentness with their paradoxes and their chanting, dancing, and trances.

Since the labors of al-Ghazali, Sufi masters have generally emphasized doing the normative devotions of Islam but with a special mind to the inward as well as the outward aspects. But beyond that, there are particular ecstatic techniques for knowing God that the *shaykhs* taught: practices such as *dhikr* (or *wird*), reciting the beautiful names of God on beads; or even whirling dances like those of the **dervishes**, or feats of shamanistic fervor like rending garments, eating glass, or cutting oneself without pain to show one's divine absorption.

Practices such as these were developed by the great Sufi orders that spread across Islam after the tenth century. They still exist, although since around 1900 their power has diminished. For the most part they were not celibate monastic orders, although in some instances an inner core of devotees or leaders might—whether officially married or not—exemplify a level of commitment comparable to that of monks or abbots in other faiths. But for the bulk of lay adherents, the orders were more like lodges: one would receive a formal initiation by a *shaykh* or a *pir* of the order and would then practice its devotion corporately at periodic meetings and otherwise privately. Some Sufi orders, especially in the Turkish Empire, had political and revolutionary overtones. Some have been suppressed by modern Islamic governments because the whole Sufi attitude was considered by modernizers to inculcate a medieval, superstitious, nonproductive mentality; ironically, at the same time, Sufism has been discovered and much appreciated by many outside of Islam.

Sufi orders with their saintly masters were and are a great proselytizing force for Islam. It was primarily in their gentler, more mystical form that Islam entered India and Indonesia. It is easy to speculate that, apart from its empathetic presentation by such mystic Sufi saints, Islam might have had little success in these cultures. Today, Sufi orders are having success in spreading Islam in Africa.

The prestige of the *shaykh* made much of Islam into a cult of personalities. *Shaykhs* became saints who had cosmic as well as temporal meanings. It was said that the saints kept the world together generation after generation. In an invisible hierarchy were varying degrees of saints: "successors," "pegs," "pillars," and finally the *qutb*, the "pole" or "axis" of the universe. There is only one *qutb*, according to a popular tradition, in every generation, and when one dies, he is replaced by another.

The members of this hierarchy are the true pivots upon which the world in its inner life turns. They may not be known to the general public—indeed, a saint in his humility may not even know himself that he is a saint, much less an axis of the world—but should he fail in the mysterious work his inward sanctity enables him to accomplish, the social order and the Earth itself would fall apart. Finally, *Sufis* spoke of the enigmatic leader of the saints themselves, al-Khidr, "the Green One," a generally invisible but immortal and ever-youthful guide who appears at time of need in the dreams or waking sight of the sincere questor on the mystic path. [26]

The Muslim public knew well the reputations of the more visible saints. It flocked to their presences and, after their deaths, to their tombs. In the heyday of popular Sufism—the twelfth through the nineteenth centuries—legends of saints were rife, and pilgrimages to their holy places rivaled Mecca in popularity. Many of them are still much frequented. In Shi'a areas, the shrines of *Imams*, like that of Husayn himself at Karbala in Iraq, are thronged. Countless village mosques contain tombs of local saints, unmarked by image or picture but well known and visible because of their coffin shape, inscription, and the many colored flags on buildings.

In the valley of Bamian in Afghanistan, famous for its ancient Buddhist monastic caves and towering Buddhist images (later destroyed by the Taliban), but whose population is now strongly Muslim, I* came across a shrine of an "ice-burning saint." According to the local legend, this mystic had once come with his disciples into the valley and begged for fuel with which to cook food for himself and his band. But the villagers, not recognizing him for what he was, hardened their hearts against his request. The saint then sent a disciple into the nearby mountains to get some ice, and by a miracle he caused the ice to burn and used it for firewood. Thereupon the awestruck villagers believed in him and besought the holy man to stay, which he did. When he died, the shrine was built over his tomb, a modest domed edifice of mud with a wall around it, all festooned with red banners. I saw bearded men of the village circumambulate the tomb inside the walls muttering *dhikr* as they went; in setting out, each stooped to pass under a table holding the Qur'an.

I sensed here both the devotional power of popular Islam and the basic similarities of the central Asiatic myths and *culti* of men of power, whether in shamanistic, Hindu, Buddhist, Muslim, or Christian forms—for the "wizard saint" has been a constant in all the many faiths that have swept across the wild mountains, deserts, and forests of that vast area of the Earth.

Islam generally believes that the saints have power to perform miracles. Muhammad did none, except the miracle of the Qur'an itself. But the saints have a different calling from that of the public envoy of God, one at once more arcane and more popularly appealing. They must work wonders to show the transcendence of spiritual attainment over the material and do works of mercy that help hold the universe together. They are masters of the realm of archetype and dream that lies above this world and below God, as written in the philosophy of al-Ghazali and of ibn al-Arabi. The *baraka*, or the numinous power of the saints, rests eternally over their tombs and relics, and for this reason, pilgrims to these sites are often healed and blessed.

ISLAM, GOVERNANCE, AND POLITICAL LIFE

Islam was political in its formation. Like Jesus, Muhammad was a revolutionary figure; unlike Jesus, however, Muhammad gained political power. He governed first a city and then most of Arabia, and he died a hero in the eyes of its people. The defining

---

*Robert Ellwood

moment for Islam was the establishment of the first Islamic community; thus, the Islamic calendar begins not with Muhammad's birth but with that central event—the *Hijra*—when Muhammad and his followers went to Yathrib, which became al-Medina, "the City."

Islam's Community Ideal and Authority

The religion Muhammad established was never only about how one thought of God and said one's prayers but also about how it is lived with others in a just society, guided by divine law. Based on the supreme and absolute sovereignty of God, Islam wants to make sure that sovereignty extends to every area of life: family, law, community, and government. Consequently, Islam makes the Qur'an not only a book of God's self-revelation but also, through *Shari'ah*, a source of practical and moral regulations covering such matters as marriage, almsgiving, relations with non-Muslims, as well as public policy, governance, and punishment of criminals. Through the use of analogy and by determining consensus, legal scholars decide how Qur'anic law is to be applied to concrete cases before them. Many argue, therefore, that authentic Islam does not permit the relegation of Islam to a "private sphere" divorced from public life. Rather, the ideal of submission to God joins the Muslim to the others who make the same submission to bring about the ideal Islamic community ordained by God.

How that ideal Islamic community is to be actualized, as well as how *Shari'ah* is to be applied, is not an easy question. Although traditional Islamic societies, like traditional societies almost everywhere, have tended to be absolute monarchies, this is not required in Islam, and in fact, Muslim states have been, and are today, monarchies, autocracies, theocracies, and democratic republics—and sometimes a combination of two or more of these. Nevertheless, the traditional Islamic community has three main foci—the community itself (the *ummah*), the concept of justice expressed in the *Shari'ah* (*adalah*), and leadership (*imamah*)—and three groups who are supposed to work cooperatively and in balance with each other: the religious scholars (the *ulama*), who interpret Islamic law; the judges (the *qadis*), who resolve disputes; and the *caliph*, the head of state, who serves as "guardian" leader of the community.[27]

In addition, there has been considerable debate among Islamic scholars through time about what a just society entails. In that regard, a central idea in Islam, even when not practiced, is economic justice. This derives from the almsgiving principle, which eschews policies that are believed to exploit the underprivileged, such as usury and unfair exchange values. Furthermore, stark disparities in wealth and social status are regarded as inherently immoral, leading in turn to overall moral decay. Consequently, the Islamic ideal supports the just distribution of income and wealth. But whether this should accomplished through markets, socialist programs, through wealthy benefactors, or otherwise has been a much-debated subject. In any case, however, Islam holds that it is immoral for the politically and economically powerful to exploit the poor and disadvantaged for unjust gain.

All of this raises the question of authority. Ultimately, in Islam the sole authority is God, but what God wants of human beings necessarily requires the interpretation and the application of the *Shari'ah* in every age and place. Who legitimately serves in this function is an ongoing question in Islam around the world today.

In 2010–2011, the world was astounded to see a series of popular uprisings throughout the Arab Islamic world, first in Tunisia and then extending to Egypt and beyond. The crowds surging into the streets, often braving tanks and bullets, were expressing another voice of Islam—that of the people on the streets. For while the concept of divine sovereignty has sometimes been expressed through absolute human rulers claiming to be the "shadow of God," traditionally governance also requires *ijma*, consent of the faithful. This is a principle of *Shari'ah*, based on the *hadith*: "My community shall never be in agreement in error." Customarily, the *hadith* meant agreement of the *ulama*, but it has always been recognized that ultimately, it means the spoken or tacit consensus of all believers. What happens when those in power confront *ijma* with a different idea?

Tension with the West

In the first decades of the twentieth century, most Muslims were either subject to Western colonial rule—in the British and French Middle East, in British India, in the Dutch East Indies (Indonesia), in Russian central Asia, and in British and French Africa—or they were subjects of the backward Ottoman or Persian empires. Throughout the twentieth century, these lands generally acquired nominal independence, but they remained far from equal in most other ways. Muslim societies were conspicuously weak on the international stage, beset by poverty (except for some very unequally distributed oil wealth) and often finding themselves in considerable economic dependence on the West. It is not surprising, then, that many Muslims were alarmed by the disparity in economic and political power between the Islamic world and the largely Christian "West"—Europe and North America.

Muslims began to ask the following questions: Must Islamic societies, and by implication Islam, be modernized? Or must they experience continued decline? Or were Islamic societies weak and undeveloped only because Islam had not been truly lived?

Reactions have varied. In some places, Westernization has been embraced as welcome reform compatible with Islamic values and structures—for example, economic liberalism as a means to lift up the poor and increase their life prospects and the recognition of the rights of women, as we shall see later in this chapter. In other places, such trends were viewed as undermining the social and political order because of those trends' corrupting proclivities. Traditional moralists declared that letting the West inside the gates of Islam would lead to materialism, consumerism, hedonism—all of which undercut traditional values, including the family and the Islamic commitment to justice and equality. Many Muslims were aware that even if there is a long-term uplifting effect, Western market capitalism often seems, at first, to widen the gap between rich and poor into a canyon and to glorify a life based only on the fulfillment of material desires, thereby making a mockery of the Islamic ideal of a holy community in submission to God. Moreover, alarmed observers perceived that not only was the West coming in through the gates but also that a certain number of nominal Muslims already inside—including some in very high places—were enablers, putting profitable alliances with Western governments and corporations ahead of the well-being of their own people or of Islamic values. All this embodies the background of Islamicism, the movement sometimes called, somewhat misleadingly, "Islamic fundamentalism."

Islamicism

Islamicism is a movement within Islam that seeks to establish what its participants believe was the original Islamic political and social order of Muhammad's era. Islamicists generally view themselves as fulfilling a goal today similar to that of Muhammad in his day. Muhammad fought against the forces of the "pagan ignorance" (*jahiliyyah*) of competitive polytheistic tribes; Islamicists fight against the *jahiliyyah* of the West, which is understood to be even worse than the *jahiliyyah* of Muhammad's era.[28] Consequently, Islamicists resist Western political and economic domination, and some Islamicists resort to violence, with *jihad* as holy war understood as a just rebellion against those responsible for moral and social decay (including Muslims aligned with modernizing foreign powers or Muslims who illegitimately usurp power and wealth at the expense of ordinary people).

Some Islamicist movements seek not only to reestablish what they understand to be just wealth distribution and social cohesiveness but also social organizational rules that restrict education, communication with the world outside their utopian community, and family life, rules reflected particularly in the restricted lives of women. The goal of extreme Islamicists is an eventual worldwide Islamic caliphate, ordering personal, family, social, economic, and political institutions according to strictly interpreted Islamic doctrines. Rejecting entirely the idea that religion can be separated from the state in any way, Islamicists embrace instead a conception of society that requires salvation of the whole society, not merely individuals or groups within it.

Take for example, Sayyid Qutb (1906–1966). He was a leading ideologist of the Egyptian-based Muslim Brotherhood and was a significant Islamicist leader. As a young man, Qutb had been enamored with the West. He loved English literature and took a position with the Egyptian Ministry of Education. But he reacted against the British because of what he perceived as their domination of Egypt during World War II and afterward and because of the creation of the State of Israel in Britain's Palestinian mandate. Qutb then came to the United States to study, but he felt humiliated by what he experienced as a denigrating American attitude toward Arabs. He finally concluded that young, Westernizing Muslims like himself tried too hard to fit alien models and win acceptance by Europeans or Americans. They should instead proudly affirm their Muslim and Arab culture, realizing that rightly applied, Islam could provide a superior alternative to both capitalism and Communism.

Qutb and his Muslim Brotherhood were not well received by the leaders of his own Egyptian nation, exactly the sort of people radicals like himself saw as far too compromising. He was arrested in 1954 for alleged participation in a Muslim Brotherhood plot to kill Egyptian President Gama Abdul Nasser. Then, in 1966, he was again arrested and secretly executed for his last book, *Maalim Fi al-Tariq* (*Signposts on the Road*). This "dangerous" book emphasized the absolute Lordship of God, the equality of all people, and undeviating following of the Qur'an and Islamic tradition as the only foundations for a good society; the book also argued that the present corrupt leadership had instead returned a supposedly Muslim society to *jahiliyya*.[29]

The way to undo decay, Qutb and other advocates like him stressed, is to make the *Shari'ah*, interpreted by qualified teachers and scholars, the fundamental law of the state; to distribute wealth in accordance with Islamic ideals of justice and brotherhood; and to restrict severely outside (non-Muslim) influences in society. Reportedly, Qutb is a major intellectual influence on the *Al-Qaeda* movement, whose leader, Osama bin Laden, allegedly was responsible for the September 11, 2001, attacks on the United States. Bin Laden has been lauded as a hero by many Islamicists around the world for his terrorism against the West's encroachments into the Middle East.

It must be recognized, however, that Islamicist groups represent only one voice within Islam. There are also Muslim pacifists and advocates of nonviolence, as well as those who believe that war is sometimes justified, just as there are within virtually all religions.

Turkish man wearing a fez.

Governments in the Islamic World

Islam has led to various approaches to government throughout the Muslim world. Let us consider just a few examples.

TURKEY: A SECULAR DEMOCRATIC REPUBLIC   Turkey is the homeland of the Turks, the non-Arab race whose sultan long ruled most of the Arabic-speaking peoples in the days of the Ottoman Empire and who fostered Islam wherever he ruled. By the nineteenth century, this sprawling imperial state was slipping from the sultan's grasp, and after World War I, Turkey lost its empire and set off in a radically new direction under the iron rule of Kemal Ataturk (1881–1938). Ataturk sought to establish a Westernized and strictly secular state. Ataturk's **secularization** program ended religious courts and schools, put secular law in the place of the Shari'ah, abolished the caliphate and Sufi orders, substituted the Roman alphabet for the Arabic in the writing of Turkish, forbade religious garb outside places of worship, and made Sunday the weekly holiday instead of Friday. Wearing the fez, a hat traditionally associated with old Turkey and with Islam, was outlawed.

Today Turkey remains a secular state. Its constitution provides for a political structure similar to those found in the West with secular law and balance of powers between three branches of government: executive, legislative, and judicial. However, Islamicist traditionalist political parties continue to challenge strict secularism there.

IRAN: ISLAMIC THEOCRATIC REPUBLIC   To the east of the Arab world lies Iran, a mainly non-Arab, Persian Shi'a Muslim nation. Under the leadership of the **Ayatollah** Khomeini, the Shah (monarch) Muhammad Pahlavi was toppled in 1979 and an Islamic republic was established in which *Shari'ah* was proclaimed to be normative and clergy like Khomeini took a decisive role. Enforcement of traditional values was effected with much religious fervor.

Today Iran's government nominally involves a system of checks and balances. However, ultimate political and religious authority rests with the "Supreme Leader," a cleric in the tradition of the Ayatollah Khomeini, who is elected and supervised by the Assembly of Experts, who are Islamic scholars. The Iranian president, who is elected by the people, is subject to the authority of the Supreme Leader but often acts independently as governor of day-to-day matters of state. However, the Council of Guardians, which answers ultimately to the Supreme Leader, determines the eligibility of presidential candidates.

Moderate reformers and Islamicist-oriented clerics struggle to assert their differing visions of a just social and political order in Iran today, and the tensions between them are ongoing.

SAUDI ARABIA: ISLAMIC AUTOCRATIC THEOCRACY   Saudi Arabia is in effect an Islamic **theocracy** with autocratic rule vested solely in a king who is chosen by and from amongst the members of the royal Saudi family. The king, as ultimate arbitrator of practical and religious matters, is the final authority over the social and political order of the nation's Islamic society—all ostensibly in accord with *Shari'ah* and the Qur'an, the "constitution" of the state.

Saudi Arabia, convulsed by oil wealth and inevitable social change, is striving to become both a modern and a conservative Muslim state at the same time, while an impoverished and alienated underclass is becoming increasingly agitated. The strict

Islamicist Sunni Wahhabi (Salafis) sect, which rejects mysticism of the Sufi sort and demands a state based on a strict traditional and literal interpretation of the Qur'an and *Shari'ah,* dominates.

PAKISTAN: ISLAMIC FEDERAL REPUBLIC   In the Indian subcontinent, Pakistan, founded as an Islamic state at the time of the independence and partition of the former British Indian empire in 1947, retained a legal system based on English law. However, in 1979, *Shari'ah* became law under pressure of an Islamicist resurgence there.

Today Pakistan is a federal representative democratic republic. Pakistan's constitutional governing structure consists of several states and a central government, president, prime minister, and two legislative bodies—a Senate and a National Assembly. Adherence to *Shari'ah* is embedded in structure of the judiciary, which among its courts includes the Federal Shariat Court and a Shariat Appellate component of the Supreme Court, which arguably are not independent of political pressures. Muslim religious political parties, such as the Pakistan Muslim League, wield considerable influence in the government.

Alternatively under military and democratic rule, and with an increasingly vocal and violent Islamicist resurgence, Pakistan, a nuclear power, remains one of the most unstable nations in the world.

INDONESIA: REPRESENTATIVE DEMOCRATIC REPUBLIC   Today, Indonesia, the world's fourth most populous nation, is a representative democracy with a Muslim majority. Islamic moderates there have promoted liberalizing reforms, which tout the compatibility of Islam with democratic ideals. However, a large majority of Muslims, which make up about 87 percent of the population, believe that Islamic values should dominate society, and the Council of Ulama has been giving them support by issuing edicts that prohibit the reinterpretation of traditional Islam as being consistent with secular and liberal values. At the same time, others who hold to democratic rule eschew the idea of an "Islamic state" and embrace the possibilities of economic globalization and religious pluralism, in acknowledgement of Indonesia's strong Hindu, Buddhist, and indigenous spiritual and cultural influences, which predate Islam's majority in that island nation.

PALESTINE: REFUGEES AND NATIONALISM   The Holy Land of Jews and then Christians, which was known as Palestine in Roman times, came under Muslim rule soon after Muhammad's death. Jerusalem was conquered by Muslims in 635 C.E., and except for a brief period of Christian Crusader rule (1099–1187), it remained Muslim until British conquest during World War I. Under Ottoman Empire rule for more than four hundred years, it was then part of Syria. The territory was then given its former Roman name "Palestine," and the British governed it until after World War II.

Many Muslims claimed the territory was God's religious gift to them and therefore their Holy Land. Jerusalem was revered in the Qur'an; Muhammad had directed Muslim prayers to Jerusalem before redirecting them to Mecca. Important Islamic sacred sites reside there, in particular al-Aqua Mosque and the Dome of the Rock, completed in 692 C.E., which holds the rock from which Muslims believe Muhammad was taken to heaven to receive the Islamic prayers he then brought back to his followers.

In 1948, following World War II, the United Nations sanctioned the territory's partition into a Jewish state and an Arab state. While this development was met with jubilation on the part of many Jews, Arabs resisted. Israel was founded on part of the territory, but the remaining lands came under the control of the surrounding Arab states. The 1948 Arab-Israeli War and other conflicts followed, the territory not finding a settled peace.

Displaced by the conflicts, many Arabs remained in the parts of the territory bordering Israel that were controlled by Arabic states. Not assimilated into those Arab nations and hoping for return to what had now become Israel, the displaced became refugees in the Arab-controlled lands that had been part of British Palestine. Then Israel gained control of those areas in the 1967 War. Out of this turmoil emerged a nationalist identity, as the refugees and resisters understood themselves to be a people—the Palestinian people.[30] The secular nationalist Palestine Liberation Organization (PLO) and the Islamicist Hamas (*Harakat al-Muqawama al-Islamiyya*, meaning "Islamic Resistance Movement") arose as nationalist competitors for the hearts and minds of the Palestinian people, who claimed Palestine as their homeland.

Tensions continue in what has become known as the "Israeli-Palestinian conflict" and remain a threat to stability in the Middle East. International efforts to find a "two-state solution" have yet to be successful.*

ISLAM IN EUROPE

One of the most significant developments in Islam in recent decades has been the marked increase in the Muslim population of northern and western Europe and the social and political tensions that have followed as a result. While southeastern Europe has had a large Muslim population for centuries, the Islamic influx into nations of northern and western Europe, heretofore mostly homogeneous in religion and ethnicity, has produced tensions. At first embracing "multiculturalism" (many cultures within a nation), some traditional European peoples there have been alarmed by what they view as a threat to their way of life by the significant influx of Muslims with their very different culture and views of society.

Here are some figures giving Muslim percentages of total population, according to a Pew Report of October 2009: Austria, 4.2; Belgium, 3; France, 6; Germany, 4; Netherlands, 5.7; Switzerland, 4.3; United Kingdom, 2.7. (For comparison, the same report gives the U.S. Muslim numbers as 0.8 percent of the total population.) Moreover, these percentages are growing owing to both immigration and natural increase. A subsequent Pew Report estimated that by 2030 the percentages for certain countries will be as follows: Austria, 9.3; Belgium, 10.2; France, 10.3; Sweden 9.9.

When a distinctive percentage of any population reaches double digits, it is bound to have political and cultural consequences, and such has been the case in Europe. While many have welcomed Muslims as new friends and neighbors, as well as willing workers, others have found the Muslim presence disturbing, not only because of fear of terrorism but also because the Muslim way of life often seems alien to European values, above all with regard to the role of women. The distinctive dress of some Muslim women has often been a flashpoint. Much publicity has been given to political backlash in France, which in 2004 outlawed the wearing of distinctively religious dress in schools, clearly aimed primarily at Muslim schoolgirls with the *hijab* or distinctive headscarf, and in 2011 banned the *burqa*, or full-body cover everywhere in public. On another front, in a 2009 referendum, Swiss voters banned the building of minarets, the distinctive tower beside mosques from which the call to prayer is uttered. In 2011, legislation was introduced into the Dutch parliament outlawing the

---

*See the sections in Chapter 7 entitled "Judaism, Governance, and Political Life" for another perspective.

methods of animal slaughter required to make meat *hallal*, or acceptable to Muslims, although it wasn't adopted. (The legislation would also have outlawed slaughter for Jewish kosher.)

All these moves have generated vociferous debate over religious freedom versus enforcing values thought to be egalitarian or humane and fundamental to the European way of life. Muslims, and their supporters in these battles, have claimed that such legislation singles them out ultimately because of simple bigotry toward people who are different or because of a visceral European dislike of Islam perhaps going back to the Crusades. The other side has claimed that if Muslims want to live in Europe, they must accept the values upon which European civilization is based. What seems certain is that Islam will continue to be a presence and no doubt the spark and tinder of arguments in Europe for years to come.

ISLAM IN AMERICA

Islam is a minority religion but a growing presence in the United States. Immigration, important diplomatic and commercial relationships between the United States and the Islamic world, and conversion have all contributed to the remarkable growth in numbers and visibility of this faith in the United States since the middle of the twentieth century. Impressive mosques and Islamic centers have been built in many major American cities, their minarets now joining the spires and domes of Christian churches and Jewish temples. These edifices have enabled American Muslims and visitors from Islamic lands to worship in familiar ways and have enabled non-Muslim Americans to observe the practice of Islam and engage in dialogue with Muslims without leaving their homeland.

For immigrant Muslims, the experience of being Muslim in America has been challenging and often rewarding. Sometimes they have suffered suspicion, prejudice, and abuse because of negative stereotypes of Muslims held by many other Americans—caricatures no more true of all Muslims than are similar stereotypes of other racial and religious groups true of all their members. Sometimes American Muslims, especially women, have felt conspicuous because of the traditional dress they hold is required by their faith. Practices such as regular prayer five times a day and the fast of Ramadan have not always been easy in the context of work and life in the United States. Since the events of September 11, 2001, tensions between Muslim and non-Muslim Americans have been greatly exacerbated, despite the efforts of many religious and political leaders to calm them and to insist rightly that the many adherents of a religion cannot be implicated in the crimes of a few.

At the same time, learning how to be a Muslim in America has helped many Muslims to understand their religion in new and exhilarating ways. They have come to discriminate between what they now hold to be the essentials and what is merely cultural. Most Islamic centers serve Muslims from many parts of the Islamic world—Arabs, Africans, Iranians, Pakistanis, Indonesians, and others—contributing to a fresh and vital sense of Islam as a world community. Like religionists of other faiths in the United States, they have learned to hold to their faith and community without any sort of state support in a pluralistic and open society.

American Muslims have been of different strands. The majority of immigrants, though from many different countries, have been Sunni Muslims, and most immigrant-based mosques have been of this style. Shi'a Muslims from Iran and elsewhere have often worshipped at the same centers, there being no discrimination, though occasionally Shi'ites have established separate mosques. There have also been a smaller number of immigrants (or converts) of sectarian Islamic groups: Ismaili, Druze, Ahmadiyya, and others, who have organized their own denominations.

A number of movements that have appealed to Westerners not of Islamic background have their roots in Sufism. Sufism, with its sacred dance, its wonderful poetry, and its rich sense of the immediate presence of God, has a universal appeal that has inspired many. Groups range from the Western followers of various Sufi *shaykhs* or spiritual leaders to those that have become quite independent of normative Islam. The cultural influence of Sufi poetry, like the famous *Rubaiyat of Omar Khayyam*, must also be mentioned.

Many converts to Islam in the United States have been African American. The most influential force in this activity has been the work of Elijah Muhammad (1897–1975), founder of the Black Muslims or Nation of Islam, as they were called. The movement originally possessed unorthodox doctrines and staunchly advocated the separation of African and white Americans, but since Elijah Muhammad's death, it has moved closer to normative Islam. Its best known adherent, Malcolm X, supported this move toward the end of his life. Today the mainstream of African American Islam no longer has a distinctive organization and strives to be simply Muslim. Some splinter "Black Muslim" groups, of which the most prominent is the Nation of Islam of the controversial Louis Farrakhan, have maintained the separatist mentality.

The multiracial **Bahá'í** faith, though it does not identify itself as Islamic, has roots in the Muslim culture of Persia and also has a presence in the United States.

American Islam, like the faith, generally has a varied and colorful history. It is bound to have a gradually increasing influence on American life.

WOMEN IN ISLAM

In the West, it is common for the uninformed to think of Islam as one monolithic religio-cultural phenomenon. Instead, as we have seen, just like Christianity, Islam has taken many forms. While all have the Prophet Muhammad and the Qur'an at their core, Islam's many sociological expressions, theoretical interpretations, and practices have been greatly influenced by the cultural contexts in which Islam is found. Accordingly, the Islam of Egypt differs from that of Saudi Arabia, just as both differ from Islam found in the United States.

In no area are these differences more profoundly revealed than in the attitudes, customs, practices, and laws that involve the role of women. Hence, it is extremely difficult to say anything much that would serve as a generalization for all of the half billion Muslim women all around the world and for all times.[31] Still, in an effort to provide a context for the contemporary discourses on women and Islam, we will provide some background information regarding classical Islam as it developed in the Middle East. Then we will turn to developments there today.

Islam and the Question of Women's Role

It is often said that the founding of Islam improved the status of women in its time. I* remember a lively conversation with an American Muslim man some years ago in which he stated that Islam proclaimed the equal status of women at a time "when some Christians were still contemplating whether women were fully human beings

---

*Barbara McGraw

with souls!" Yet there is considerable contemporary debate about this issue. On the one hand, the Qur'an provides much support for the equality of women and men. It is of no small account that the Qur'an addresses women explicitly, making clear that women as well as men are equally significant in God's eyes. For example, the Qur'an states:

> Those who believe, men and women, befriend one another, and enjoin what is right and prohibit what is wrong. They observe their devotional obligations, pay the zakat [alms], and obey God and His Apostle. God will be merciful to them, for God is all-mighty and all-wise.[32]

In addition, there are sayings of the Prophet included in the *hadith* that make clear that equality is a central message of Islam: "All people are equal, as equal as the teeth of a comb. There is no claim of merit of an Arab over a non-Arab or of a white over a black person or of a male over a female. Only God-fearing people merit a preference with God."[33] On the other hand, however, certain passages in the Qur'an and *hadith* appear to modify this message, indicating that men are superior to women (e.g., one male witness is equal to two female witnesses in court) and that men are to be women's protectors.

More important, the interpretation of passages in the Qur'an can lead to very different conceptualizations of Islamic law respecting women. Take, for example, the following two translations (i.e., interpretations) of Qur'an 4:34—a passage that is often invoked when the subject of women's position in Muslim society is discussed.

One translation makes clear that women are to be subordinated to men:

> Men are in charge of women, because Allah hath made the one of them to excel the other, and because they spend of their property (for the support of women). So good women are the obedient, guarding in secret that which Allah hath guarded. As for those from whom ye fear rebellion, admonish them and banish them to beds apart, and scourge [i.e., beat] them. Then if they obey you, seek not a way against them. Lo! Allah is ever High Exalted, Great.[34]

Another translation of the very same passage reflects a completely different interpretation. Here, men are admonished to treat women well—even women they find "averse":

> Men are the support of women as God gives some more means than others, and because they spend of their wealth (to provide for them). So women who are virtuous are obedient to God and guard the hidden as God has guarded it. As for women you feel are averse, talk to them suasively; then leave them alone in bed (without molesting them) and go to bed with them (when they are willing). If they open out to you, do not seek an excuse for blaming them. Surely God is sublime and great.[35]

Throughout the centuries and in different localities, the ambiguities arising from seemingly conflicting passages and different interpretations have resulted in various views of Islam's injunctions with respect to women. One thing is clear, however. Like Buddhism, Islam took the "woman question" to heart in its primary texts. Unlike Buddhism, however, Islam addressed the role of women in society at large, providing an adjusted vision of women's rights and role in society from what had preceded it.

Early Islam after Muhammad: The Continuation of Patriarchal Patterns

Whatever may have been intended regarding the status of women, soon after its founding, Islam adopted most of the patriarchal patterns of the monotheistic religions—Judaism, Christianity, and Zoroastrianism—that prevailed in the Middle East and along the Mediterranean at the time of Islam's founding.[36] Islam also supplanted the polytheistic religions that had remained, along with their goddesses and the priestesses who served them.

There are accounts of women of considerable independence, education, and wealth who lived before the founding and popularization of Islam, some of whom, like Muhammad's sponsor and wife Khadija, were involved in commerce. Islam itself, however, moved toward a more restricted role for women in the home in the years following Islam's founding when Islam became feudalistic. The patriarchal family structure with the male as head of the family, the woman leaving her natal home to join her husband's family, and the female family members being placed in subordinate positions replaced the variety of family structures that were found outside the monotheistic norms of the time. For example, previously there had been matrilineal families where the woman remained in her natal family tribe and the husband visited her there.[37]

Still, in many ways, Muslim women were provided with rights unavailable to other women of the same time and place. For example, marriage was not to occur without the bride's consent, and women were given the right to negotiate the terms of their marriage contracts, including the amount of the bride price to be paid by the groom (marriage being a contractual matter and not a sacrament in Islam). The bride price was paid to the bride herself, as a token of love and sincerity on the part of the groom, rather than to her father. Women were permitted to keep the bride price after marriage and, in most cases, even after divorce. Women were also permitted to maintain and manage their own finances, and the husband was to support his wife in accordance with his means regardless of his wife's own wealth. If special provisions were negotiated into the marriage contract regarding divorce or if there were other sufficient grounds (e.g., desertion, abuse), a woman had access to divorce (although for men divorces were much easier to obtain). Divorced and widowed women were permitted to remarry, and women were given rights to their children. Under the Qur'an, women could own and inherit property, although a woman could only inherit one-half that of a man because, unlike him, she was not expected to provide for a family.[38] In addition, women's religious obligations were the same as men's, reflecting the Qur'anic teaching that men and women are equally worthy in the eyes of God.

Attitudes and taboos regarding menstruation and childbirth, which we have seen in other religions, were greatly curtailed in Islam.[39] Sex within marriage was not stigmatized, since a good marriage relationship was considered ideal, as opposed to celibacy, which is more highly regarded in most of Hinduism and some forms of Christianity, as well as in other religions. Furthermore, the Qur'an and the Prophet Muhammad spoke against certain common practices regarding females that had prevailed among pre-Islamic Arabs, such as the inheritance of women as "property" and the practice of burying female infants alive.

In addition, polygyny (marrying many wives), which was a common practice in pre-Islamic society, was severely limited. In some pre-Islamic tribes, each man had numerous wives—over seventy-five in some cases. However, the Qur'an permitted men to marry only up to four wives, and then only if the wives could be treated equally by the husband. The Qur'an also states that it is unlikely that wives can be treated equally and so urges the husband to choose only one.[40] Moreover, many Islamic scholars have argued persuasively that the main reason Islam permitted

Several veiled Muslim women ride in a donkey cart with a solitary man walking along on a street in Cairo, Egypt.

polygyny was to provide for women who would not otherwise have husbands in a world that offered women no acceptable alternative to marriage and childbearing. In other words, marrying additional wives was a charitable thing to do. This act of charity was exemplified by Muhammad, who after his first wife Khadija died, married, in addition to Aisha, unmarriageable women—for example, an older widow and a woman who had come from a family of non-Muslims and who was later abandoned by her husband through divorce.[41]

However, many of these developments were, in practice, greatly diminished as Islam developed. By the third century of Islam, despite the rights granted in the Qur'an, practices and customs of the localities prevailed. The father or other male head of household arranged the marriages of the daughters and, while nominally hers, the wife's property generally was administered by her husband. Despite Qur'anic passages to the contrary, sons were preferred over daughters because of economic considerations—the son being perceived as being more able to add to the wealth of the family.[42] Divorce, which had always been easier for a husband to obtain than a wife, became even more readily obtainable for men. A practice evolved that required only that the husband proclaim three times that his wife was divorced. Thereafter the divorce was irrevocable. Equality in religious obligations was also undermined. Women were admonished to pray in the home rather than in the mosque, and it was the general practice that when women did attend services at a mosque, they were to remain in the rear.[43]

In addition, the apparent sanctioning of polygyny in the Qur'an provided religious justification for those men who wished to continue the practice. Regardless of what may have been intended by the Qur'an, its express acknowledgment that men can marry several wives led not to reform (as many have argued was the original intention) but to abuses, including the development of a restrictive harem system.

Many restrictive Islamic practices with respect to women were originally customs of neighboring peoples and conquered peoples that were assimilated into Islamic society. In *Women and Gender in Islam*, Leila Ahmed contends that the Islamic practice of segregating the sexes was not endemic to Islam but came from the practices of the Christians and Jews of the Middle East. Similarly, she contends that the practice of veiling women (which, in some countries even today, involves covering the woman from head to toe with a veil called the **chador** in Iran or in its more severe version, the *burqa* in Afghanistan) came from the people of Sassania (Persia) who were conquered by the Muslims.[44]

Most significantly, until very recently, the Qur'an was interpreted by men who were in authority. Because women's education was limited, women generally were ignorant of Qur'anic teachings that might have mitigated against the restrictions placed on them.[45]

Whatever the source of the restrictive practices for women, religious sanctions for them were soon found by those interpreting the scriptures, and such practices have prevailed to such a degree that they have become identified inextricably with Middle Eastern Islam. By medieval times, the *Shari'ah* was codified, and many customs and traditions of the times regarding women were included, despite dubious authority for them in the Qur'an.[46]

Significantly, interpretations favoring restrictive practices regarding women reflected a Muslim ideal of womanhood that we will recognize, at times in their various histories, as mirroring the ideal we have found in many other religions, including Christianity—as well as the same suspicions and negative stereotypes. Here, as there, motherhood, chastity, purity, fidelity, obedience to the father and husband, beauty, and modesty became the watchwords of the lives of women. A woman was to be self-sacrificing, being concerned only with the well-being of her husband and children, and she was to be agreeable and sexually available to her husband.[47]

Motherhood has always held a highly respected place in Islamic society, however, providing mothers with considerable status in the home—one that could be a source of great pride and self-esteem. Still, women were valued primarily for their ability to produce sons for their husbands' families—the birth of a girl bringing discredit to the mother. Because polygyny was expressly permitted in Islam, a woman's failure in this regard was a threat to her status in the home. If she did not produce sons, another wife could be brought into the home to serve that purpose, or a wife might be divorced.

Furthermore, women were considered to be ignorant—unfit for high learning—and in many ways inferior to men, and they were generally disparaged as untrustworthy. Accordingly, control of women was considered justified. Many *hadiths* reflect these attitudes.[48]

As we have seen in other religions, virginity was highly valued in Islam. A woman who was found not to be a virgin on her marriage night was considered a grave dishonor to her family. Sometimes she was killed in order to remove the disgrace. To guard against such shame and dire consequences, women were kept secluded from the outside world in the home (a practice known as **purdah**); thus, her association with others was highly guarded and her education was restricted to her domestic vocation.

Islam continued the common practice of circumcising male children. In addition, the practice of female circumcision was adopted in many places and continues today, despite there being no authority for it in the Qur'an. The circumcision of females is much more involved than for males because it involves a clitoredectomy, usually without anesthesia, when the girl is between seven and eight, and in some locales, the operation is even more involved. It was apparently a widespread cultural practice in the Arabian peninsula, as well as other areas in the world at the time of the rise of Islam. According to Nawal al-Saadawi, it was even practiced in Europe and could be found there as late as the nineteenth century.[49]

Nawal al-Saadawi (b. 1931) is an Egyptian woman who overcame her religious and cultural circumstances to become a doctor and a leading Islamic feminist, activist, and prolific writer. In her book *The Hidden Face of Eve: Women in the Arab World*, Saadawi provides a graphic account of her own circumcision. She recounts that she was taught that it was necessary in order to purify her of an offending and shameful organ on her body and to make her a more suitable and chaste wife.[50] Today the practice seems to be limited, for the most part, to countries in Africa such as Egypt and the Sudan. It has been outlawed officially in Egypt with the highest court there upholding the ban in December 1997 after a three-year battle between reformists who opposed the practice and traditionalists who wished to continue it. However, despite the ban, it is extensively practiced in Egyptian villages. It has been banned in other countries as well, but though perhaps declining, it continues to be practiced by some. Female circumcision has been raised as a social and a legal issue in the United States and elsewhere when families from Africa who continue the practice settle in those countries.

Veiling, segregation, seclusion, and female circumcision (where it has been practiced) can all be seen as the strategies adopted by Islam to achieve the same goals we have seen in nearly all of the preceding religions we have studied: the control of women's sexuality for the preservation of chastity and the reproduction of sons for the husband's family. In medieval times, when the *Shari'ah* was codified, such restrictive practices were rigorously followed. Significantly, such practices became symbols of a family's social status and have continued into modern times in many Islamic lands, particularly in the urban environments of the upper and middle classes, despite the call for reform by those who argue that these traditions have no place in an authentic Islam.

Interestingly, throughout Islam's history, rural women have generally not been segregated, secluded, or veiled. Consequently, rural women may have had more opportunity to participate in the social situations in which they found themselves; however, such expanded opportunities should not be overstated because rural peoples, who tend to be poor, are limited in other ways related to their economic conditions. Moreover, because such practices have been symbols of status, a family that becomes upwardly mobile is likely to adopt them as a reflection of the ideal.

Muslim Women: Leaders, Saints, and Practitioners

These extremely restrictive practices and the severe limitations they placed on women's lives do not tell the whole story, however. From the beginning, there have been women who have figured proudly in Islamic heritage and have served as models. One especially notable example is the Prophet Muhammad's first wife, Khadija, who was considerably older than he. She was a wealthy and independent trader who hired merchants, such as Muhammad, to trade for her abroad. She married Muhammad and provided him with financial support, making his religious vocation possible. It was she who assuaged his doubts about his first revelations and convinced him to make them known. Some argue that Khadija's independence and wealth reflect more the attitudes toward women of pre-Islamic culture, which permitted more expanded roles for women than Islam. Nevertheless, Khadija figures prominently in the development of Islam and is honored for the part that she played.

After Khadija's death, as noted earlier Muhammad married several women including Aisha, who became his favorite wife after Khadija. Unlike Khadija, Aisha lived a more secluded and protected life in the home. It is reported that she was required to speak to others from behind a partition. (Some Islamic interpreters have used this as a justification for the veiling of women.)[51] Nevertheless, Muhammad prized Aisha for her wisdom and insight, and it is reported that he received some of his revelations in her presence and that he died in her arms.[52] She lived for over forty years after Muhammad's death, and her accounts of the household have provided Islam with a wealth of information about the Prophet. Those accounts, in turn, have been some of the most important contributions to the *hadith* and have had a significant influence on the interpretation of the Qur'an.[53] It is said that the Prophet told his followers to take half of the knowledge of his revelations from Aisha and the other half from all the rest of his companions.[54] More important, Aisha apparently had considerable authority in the early fledgling Muslim community.[55] (Some reformers have argued that her authority provides evidence that women held high status in the early Medina community, and, therefore, that it should be so today.) [56]

Another important female figure in the early history of Islam is Fatima, Muhammad's daughter with Khadija. Fatima was the only child through whom Muhammad had descendents, including Hasan and Husayn. Today she is a highly revered saint of Islam who has been referred to by one scholar as "the fountainhead of female spirituality in Islam."[57]

It is interesting to note, as well, the pivotal role Aisha and Fatima played in the Shi'a/Sunni separation. Shi'a's successor lineage descends from Muhammad's son-in-law, Ali, and Fatima. However, Aisha's father, Abu Bakr, was the first caliph in what later became the Sunni tradition. Because of acrimony between the two factions, when Ali was named the fourth caliph, Aisha raised an army against him, which resulted in the first Muslim civil war.

We have already encountered one of the most revered women in the history of Islam, Rabi'a al-Adawiya (713–801), a mystic poet who lived a life as an ascetic in total submission to Allah. The great Muslim reformer Al-Ghazali cites Rabi'a, who was a considerable influence on him, as an important Islamic saint. Rabi'a, who never married, is especially known for having expressed her pure devotion to God as love. Her poems are prominent in Sufi literature, and many legends regarding her abound in Islamic lore. As Charis Waddy has pointed out, Rabi'a's acceptance as a saint, as well as the reverence for other women as saints, makes it clear that women could be as saintly as men, although this fact often seems to have required additional explanation because of the generally disparaging attitudes toward women.[58]

In general, Islamic women have proven to be as resourceful as other women around the world and throughout history who have been forced by custom and religion into living narrow lives. Here, as we have seen elsewhere, a "little tradition" has evolved. Many Islamic women seek out and provide access for others to the world of spiritual powers involving warding off evil, healing, good omens, and the like. Viewed as heretical by the authorities, such practices nevertheless inhere in Islam whether or not they are officially sanctioned.

As for the official practice, again, women are restricted, being admonished to pray in the home. Nevertheless, women are significant participants in certain ways. One primary obligation of Muslims is to give alms. Generally, it is the women who actually perform this duty for the household. Moreover, Muslim women are frequent visitors to the shrines of saints such as Fatima. There, women have the opportunity to meet with other women outside the seclusion of the family home; there women pray to saints for the good of the family, asking for help in matters pertaining to health, marriage, economic benefits, and the like.[59] Women also participate in the *hajj*. The custom is that the pilgrims dress in a manner that does not distinguish them from others on the basis of wealth, class, and, to some degree, sex.[60] This custom is to reflect the basic equality of all peoples before God.

Muslim Women and the Winds of Change

Modern feminism in Islam formally began with the publishing of *The Liberation of the Women* by Oasin Amin, a male Egyptian lawyer, in 1899. Badran and Cooke contend, however, that an "invisible" feminism existed from the mid-1800s, when middle- and upper-class women's publications were read by women in the harems. From the 1920s, however, feminism became very visible as women began to organize public movements—first in Egypt and later in Lebanon, Syria, Iraq, and the Sudan. Women organized the Egyptian Feminist Union in the 1920s, the Arab Feminist Union (a pan-Arab organization) in 1944, and the Arab Women's Solidarity Association (also a pan-Arab organization) in the mid-1980s, among others.[61]

Today reformists argue that the Qur'an must be read in the context of its time. This means that the egalitarian spirit held by such reformists to be at the core of the Qur'an is what should hold sway, particularly with respect to women, rather than applying the law in contemporary situations as it was applied in the past. Traditional interpretations and applications of the law, they argue, have more to do with acknowledging the social circumstances at an earlier time rather than establishing set rules for all time.[62] For example, they argue that when the Qur'an states that men are to be women's "protectors," it is acknowledging the precarious position that women experienced in the Prophet's time; the Qur'an did not establish a permanent paternalism that should apply in all times and places.

Further, economic considerations are influencing changes in many Islamic countries. Women have moved out of the home and into the workplace. While this may be viewed by some as an advance because it opens doors to greater choices for women, others point out that often the opportunities provided are not nearly those provided

Queen Noor of Jordan prays at the grave of her husband King Hussein I with their two daughters Princesses Iman and Raya, as well as with Princess Rania who later became Queen.

to men. In those countries where segregation of the sexes is still the norm, segregation is the norm in the workplace as well. As a result, women are generally limited to what becomes "women's work." Not surprisingly, these are the lower-level tasks. Many women work in the domestic, food, and textile fields.[63] Still, in some countries, such as Egypt, Pakistan, Turkey, Bangladesh, and Jordan, Muslim women hold important positions in leadership. Women are governmental officials, doctors, and professors, and they hold positions in other professions as well. As these women shatter the mold of the stereotypes of women, there is an increasingly loud call to shatter the religious justifications for restrictive practices as well. On the other hand, the Islamicist resurgence we spoke of earlier has led in some places to a return to strict tradition.

Women and men who favor women's rights are reinterpreting the Qur'an and the *Shari'ah* and pushing for reforms that they contend are consistent with the original egalitarian spirit of Islam. There has been a revival of the principle of **ijtihad** (creative original interpretation) that was used by the early interpreters of the Qur'an but was abandoned when the *Shari'ah* became codified in the twelfth century.[64] Texts reinterpreted through *ijtihad* have provided fodder for a feminist critique and reconsideration in modern times of Islamic practices regarding women.

Interestingly, today, the veil has become a significant symbol for both the reformers and the traditionalists. On the one hand, those who seek reform view the veil as a symbol of oppression and the act of casting it off as the claiming of women's autonomy and the rejection of subjugation. On the other hand, the traditionalists view the veil as a symbol of a strong and clear Islamic tradition. For them, taking up the veil is a moral act and a rejection of Western mores and practices, which are held by them to be corrupting influences.

It is important to recall that the reformist/traditionalist conflicts with respect to women are inextricably intertwined with nationalist sentiments in parts of Islam. Much of Islam was colonized by the British, Dutch, French, or Italians over the course of the nineteenth century. British and Dutch rule left the Islamic culture largely intact. However, the French and Italians required assimilation into European cultural and religious norms, placing additional stress on those cultures. Those countries where the Islamic culture was most threatened have, for the most part, a less favorable attitude toward reform. Understandably, they want to return to their own ways, including practices pertaining to women. In countries such as Iran after the Ayatollah Khomeini came to power, many women have willingly taken up the veil as a symbol of the return to tradition after it had been denied, while others who oppose it are nevertheless subjected to the laws enforcing a return to tradition. In countries such as Egypt, where the Islamic culture was not as threatened, the social environment is more conducive to change, and because of this Egypt has been a primary generator of ideas regarding reform for women. There nationalism has supported reforms for women as the people sought to move away from practices that they view as "backward" and that were used as justifications for colonial paternalism by the British.[65]

As we have noted in respect to Europe, the wearing of distinctively Muslim dress by women has often been a cause of friction, both with non-Muslims and even within the Muslim community or family, as a symbol of traditionalism versus modernization and assimilation into a non-Muslim culture. Many non-Muslims, both men and women, assume that such a tradition is oppressive, because they are unable to understand how a culture in which a woman could not wear a T-shirt or a bikini if she so chose could be anything other than oppressive. But some Muslim women have argued the opposite: that the Western enslavement of women to fashion and sex appeal (as they understand it) is what is really degrading, reducing a woman to a sex object judged by her looks rather than her inner quality. Young Muslim women, in places where wearing the headscarf has been under attack, have demonstrated,

Fundamental Features of Islam

Theoretical

Basic Worldview	The world is for humans but under the absolute rule of God.
God or Ultimate Reality	God, sovereign, personal, revealing himself and giving specific guidance to humanity.
Origin of the World	Created by God.
Destiny of the World	To be destroyed on the Last Day, the day of judgment.
Origin of Humans	Created by God.
Destiny of Humans	To be judged on the Last Day and to receive reward or punishment in the Second Creation.
Revelation or Mediation between the Ultimate and the Human	The revelation in the Qur'an given through Muhammad, the last and greatest of the prophets.

Practical

What Is Expected of Humans: Worship, Practices, Behavior	To worship and serve God in accordance with his commandments: to observe the Five Pillars and the rest of *Shari'a*.

Sociological

Major Social Institutions	The whole Islamic community; the local Friday Mosque community; the *ulama*, or body of teachers and preachers; Sufi orders; the ideal of the Islamic society.

holding up signs saying, "Hijab is my choice," or, "The hijab is women's liberation." There is no doubt that this will be an ongoing controversy for some time, but it is important to understand the reasoning of both sides.

The stories of woman converts to Islam may shed further light on the situation. Margot Badran, in "Feminism and Conversion," presents the example of Batool Al Toma (formerly Mary Geraghty), a British woman of Irish background.[66] Feeling unable to find rational answers to her religious questions in her natal religion, she believed that she saw signs of those answers in Islam. After seven or eight years of investigation, she converted. At first in her reading, she "was very comfortable about how Islam presented women and saw women." Further reading, however, brought before her eyes appalling information on the actual experience of some Muslim women in Muslim cultures. Far from being turned away from Islam by this material, however, Al Toma was convinced that all that those women experienced was a perversion of Islam. The rational and egalitarian Islam of her first enthusiasm was still the real Islam for her.

Al Toma threw herself, together with other Muslim women, into the cause of Islamic feminism (though she does not use that term). Not hesitant to study and think for herself, she drew her own intellectual conclusions like any other theologian reinterpreting her or his own religion for contemporary times. In 1993 she founded the New Muslim Project in England, editing this association's newsletter *Meeting*

Point. The Website is for both men and women, particularly new converts, but its orientation toward Islam's affirmation of the full equality of all human beings, already mentioned, is clear. As editor of *Meeting Point* and as education officer in the Islamic Foundation, Al Toma continues to play a sensitive and significant role in dialogue between old and new Islam, between Muslims and non-Muslims, and between the genders in her chosen faith.

Contemporary Islam is replete with contradictions that reflect the competing winds of reform and tradition. These competing forces are playing themselves out in various ways in different contexts in the vast and varied forms of Islam found not only in the Middle East but also all around the world. Where women stand within these various contexts depends on many things: the traditional customs of each area in which Islam is found; the degree to which such customs have been assimilated into Islam; the resolution of the reformist/traditionalist debate in each society; the degree of acceptance or rejection of Western ideas of modernity; and the contributions of Islamic feminism. Consequently, Islam is likely to remain ever varied as it continues to spread throughout the world in the twenty-first century, and its attitudes and practices with respect to women will be just as widely varied as well.

Summary

Islam is a religion with a highly distinctive cultural and spiritual atmosphere. The word *islam* means "submission"; the faith centers on the submission of individuals and communities to the absolute sovereignty of Allah, God, in all areas of life.

Muhammad, the Prophet of Islam, was a trader from Mecca who began at the age of forty to receive lines of powerful and beautiful Arabic while meditating in a cave. These lines included words of warning to repent, moral admonishments, and above all, revelations of God's greatness. They were recorded by scribes, and after the Prophet's death, they were compiled into the Qur'an, the book believed by Muslims to be the last and greatest divine revelation to humanity, just as Muhammad is seen as the last and greatest in a line of prophets sent to restore the simple, primal religion of justice and pure monotheism. Muhammad's spiritual purification movement also became a political movement. This development is understandable because the Qur'an emphasizes that while conversion to Islam should never be performed by force, its faith and moral strictures should be practiced in a society that abides by them and seeks to implement them in all human spheres of activity, including the political and economic. By the time of Muhammad's death, most of Arabia had been united under his banner; within a century Islamic forces had spread across much of Africa and Asia to create an empire ruled by a caliph or by a successor to Muhammad in the political realm. The caliphs reigned over a brilliant Islamic civilization for several centuries, but finally their realm was replaced by several regional Muslim empires, such as the Mughul, the Persian, and the Ottoman. Still later, after the experience of European colonial rule in some places, these Muslim empires were succeeded by the numerous Islamic nation–states of today.

The practice of Islam centers on what are commonly called its Five Pillars: reciting the creed that states that there is no God but Allah and that Muhammad is his Prophet; praying five times daily; giving alms; keeping a fast during the month of Ramadan; and once in one's life, if possible, making the pilgrimage to Mecca. The daily prayers are said according to certain set procedures, facing in the direction of Mecca; thus, like the pilgrimage, they reinforce the communal sense of Islam. On Friday at noon, prayers are customarily said congregationally in a mosque, accompanied by sermons. The mosque, with its austere ornamentation and its niche pointing in the direction of Mecca, together with its traditional role as community, educational, and judicial center, is a beautiful expression of the spirit of Islam.

Sometimes referred to informally as the "sixth pillar," *jihad* is a multidimensional concept meaning to "struggle" or "strive" in the realization of God's will on Earth. Jihad as holy war is the "lesser" *jihad*. On the deepest level, *jihad* is as much a spiritual struggle against enemies of faith within oneself.

Islamic culture has been shaped by several factors: the predominance of the city, of the court, and of trade in its social and economic world and of the discouragement of representational art and of religious poetics imitative of the Qur'an. Islam's art has therefore emphasized ornamentation and calligraphy; within these limits, it has developed splendid forms that well suggest the universal presence of God. Its poetic and prose literature has been chiefly developed within the mystical traditions; it often borrows boldly from verses of love and intoxication to describe the relation of the soul to God. During the golden age of the Caliphate, science, philosophy, and theology were extensively cultivated. Learned men not only preserved the best of classical thought but also made important advances, which were finally transmitted to Europe.

Islam is divided into two main groups. Sunni Islam emphasizes the traditional path of Islamic life as interpreted by the consensus of scholars and the community. Shi'a Islam, while following the traditional path, also puts its faith in the authority of Imams who are Muhammad's hereditary successors. Now, the true Imam is said to be in hiding but is expected to emerge at the apocalyptic moment. Shi'a Islam has been productive of most sectarian movements within Islam; it predominates in Iran and in southern Iraq.

Islamic mysticism, called Sufism in the West, focuses on the presence of the divine oneness everywhere and offers paths to the attainment of union with God. Several great orders of Sufis are spread across the Muslim world. Their practices include chanting, dancing, whirling, and meditation. The role of the *shaykh*, or spiritual mentor, is very important. Great mystics have often been venerated, in life and after death in their tombs, as great saints capable of working miracles. The literature of Sufism is often of remarkable beauty and has won much admiration both in the Islamic world and outside it.

Islam was political in its formation; the sovereignty of God extends to the whole society and encompasses law, social ethics, and government, as well as personal devotion and submission. The ideal Islamic community strives for social and economic justice by following the *Shari'ah*; however, the Qur'an does not dictate a particular political form. Consequently, Islam is expressed in various political forms throughout the world. Early in the twentieth century, Muslim countries such as Turkey sought to meet the demands of the modern world by secularization, but later, as in the Iranian revolution of 1979, a strictly conservative Islam has emerged. Political and economic tensions with the West and the marginalization and alienation of many in the Islamic world have led to Islamicist movements that sometimes resort to violence to achieve their goals—a more just political and social order than that offered by the West or by authoritarian regimes at home, often supported by the West. This resurgent Islam is a major force in the world today.

In the world today, Islam is experiencing much vitality, particularly in comparison to its situation in the nineteenth century. Muslim nations are becoming wealthy and important in world politics; there are many signs of spiritual revitalization. Islam is a growing phenomenon in Europe and the United States, as well as elsewhere around the world. Its strong Qur'anic traditions and egalitarian values, variously interpreted, find much appeal all around the world.

It is very difficult to make generalizations about women in Islam because its practices differ in the many places it can be found around the world. Moreover, there is considerable debate about the "woman question" in Islam, and the answers to that question differ on the basis of various interpretations of the Qur'an and *hadiths*. In general, it can be said that when founded, Islam provided women with greater rights than had been experienced by women before. Yet, just as we have seen with many other religions, attitudes and customs from the social context in which Islam has found itself have been assimilated into Islamic culture, and religious justifications have been found for them. Although motherhood has always held a place of high esteem for women in Islam, practices such as seclusion (*purdah*), veiling, segregation, and, in some places, female circumcision have limited women's lives greatly. Nevertheless, there have been prominent women in Islam's history who have provided alternative models for women. Today there is much tension between reformists and traditionalists. The reformists take a progressivist stance toward the role of women in Islam and seek to reinterpret the Qur'an in order to return, in their view, to Islam's original intention. After suffering the travails of European colonialism, the traditionalists wish to return to the core of Islamic tradition, including the return of women to their traditional place in the home. Casting off or embracing the practice of veiling women has become a major symbol in this struggle.

Questions for Review

1. Describe the "feel" and characteristics of Islamic society.
2. Discuss ways in which Islam relates to the individual and to the community, and ways in which its legalistic and mystical (or sainthood) aspects are expressed.
3. Summarize the life of the prophet Muhammad, placing his life in the context of his times and assessing the nature of his immense impact on both religion and history.
4. Talk about the Qur'an as a book of revelation, referring to its style, content, message, and meaning.
5. Outline the faith and practice of the Five Pillars of Islam: the statement of faith, the prayers, the giving of alms, the fast of Ramadan, and pilgrimage to Mecca.
6. Describe how the Muslim's five daily prayers are performed and what they mean.
7. Describe the characteristic architecture, the interior arrangements, and use of the mosque.
8. Describe the history and main features of such principal areas of Islamic culture as art, poetry, prose literature, science, philosophy, and theology.
9. Explain the difference between Sunni and Shi'a Islam, and summarize the history of the Shi'a movement.
10. Discuss Islamic mysticism or Sufism, explaining where it has been in tension with mainstream Islam and in what ways it has deepened and widened Islam's life.
11. Explain the relationship between Islam and politics throughout Islam's history, as well as in Muslim nations today, including the concept of *jihad*.
12. Survey the position of Islam in the modern world, giving special attention to its varied responses to the changes wrought by modernization, including the Islamicist resurgence.
13. Discuss the prospects of dialogue among the three great monotheistic faiths: Judaism, Christianity, and Islam.
14. Discuss the impact on differing interpretations of the Qur'an on Islamic women.
15. Describe how customary practices of people of the surrounding regions were assimilated into Islamic law.
16. Talk about the role of women and the ways in which it is discussed as a central topic in contemporary Islam.

Suggested Readings on Islam

General

Armstrong, Karen, *Islam: A Short History*. New York: Modern Library, 2000.

Ayoud, Mahmoud, *Islam: Faith and History*. Oxford: Oneworld, 2004.

Brown, Daniel W., *A New Introduction to Islam*. Malden, MA and Oxford, UK: Wiley-Blackwell, 2009.

Denny, Frederick M., *An Introduction to Islam*, 3rd ed. Upper Saddle River, NJ: Pearson Prentice Hall, 2006.

Esposito, John L., *Who Speaks for Islam? What a Billion Muslims Really Think*. New York: Gallup Press, 2007.

———, ed., *The Oxford History of Islam*. New York: Oxford University Press, 1999.

Geaves, Ron, *Aspects of Islam*. Washington, DC: Georgetown University Press, 2005.

Glassé, Cyril, *The New Encyclopedia of Islam*. Walnut Creek, CA: Altamira Press, 2001.

Gordon, Matthew S., *Islam*. New York: Oxford University Press, 2002.

Grieve, Paul, *A Brief Guide to Islam*. New York: Carroll and Graf, 2006.

Hewer, C. T. R., *Understanding Islam: An Introduction*. Minneapolis: Fortress, 2006.

Leirvik, Oddbjørn, *Images of Jesus Christ in Islam*, 2nd ed. London: Continuum, 2010.

Lings, Martin, *Muhammad: His Life Based on the Earliest Sources*. London: George Allen and Unwim, 1983; Rochester, VT: Inner Traditions, 2006.

The Qur'an (Koran)

Arberry, Arthur J., *The Koran Interpreted*, 2 vols. New York: Macmillan, 1955.

Esack, Farid, *The Qur'an: A User's Guide*. Oxford: Oneword, 2005.

Mattson, Ingrid, *The Story of the Qur'an*. Malden, MA and Oxford, UK: Blackwell, 2008.

McAuliffe, Jane Dammen, *The Cambridge Companions to the Qur'an*. Cambridge University Press, 2006.

Islamic Mysticism

Arberry, Arthur J., *Sufism*. New York: Harper Torchbooks, 1970.

Knysh, Alexander D., *Islamic Mysticism: A Short History*. Boston: Brill, 2000.

Kugle, Scott Allen, *Sufis and Saints' Bodies: Mysticism, Corporeality, and Sacred Power in Islam*. Chapel Hill: University of North Carolina Press, 2007.

Rozehnal, Robert, *Islamic Sufism Unbound: Politics and Piety in Twenty-first Century Pakistan*. New York: Palgrave Macmillan, 2007

Schimmel, Annemarie, *Mystical Dimensions of Islam*. Chapel Hill: University of North Carolina Press, 1975.

Smith, Margaret, *Readings from the Mystics of Islam*. London: Luzac, 1950.

Islam, Governance, and Political Life

Akhtar, Shabbir, *Islam as Political Religion*. Abingdon, UK and New York: Routledge, 2011.

Ayoob, Mohammed, *The Many Faces of Political Islam: Religion and Politics in the Muslim World*. Ann Arbor: University of Michigan Press, 2008.

Baran, Zeyno, ed., *The Other Muslims: Moderate and Secular*. New York: Palgrave Macmillan, 2010.

Bowen, John Richard, *Why the French Don't Like Headscarves: Islam, the State, and Public Space*. Princeton, NJ: Princeton University Press, 2007.

Esposito, John L., with Natana J. De Long-Bas, "Classical Islam" and "Modern Islam," in *God's Rule: The Politics of the World's Religions*, Jacob Neusner, ed. Washington, DC: Georgetown University Press, 2003.

Feldman, Noah, *The Fall and Rise of the Islamic State*. Princeton, NJ: Princeton University Press, 2008.

Heristchi, Claire, and Andrea Teti, "Rethinking the Myths of Islamic Politics," in *The Politics of Religion: A Survey*, Jeffrey Haynes, ed. London; New York: Routledge, 2006.

Peters, Rudolf, *Jihad in Classical and Modern Islam*. Princeton, NJ: Markus Wiener Publishers, 1996.

Rennie, Bryan, and Philip L. Tite, *Religion, Terror, and Violence*. New York and London: Routledge, 2008.

Islam in America

Ahmed, Akbar, *Journey into America: The Challenge of Islam*. Washington, DC: Brookings Institute Press, 2010.

Ba-Yunus, Ilyas, *Muslims in the United States*. Westport, CT: Greenwood Press, 2006.

Barrett, Paul, *American Islam: The Struggle for the Soul of a Religion*. New York: Farrar, Straus, and Giroux, 2007.

Curtis, Edward E., IV, *Islam in Black America*. Albany: State University of New York Press, 2002.

Haddad, Yvonne, *The Muslims of America*. New York: Oxford University Press, 1991.

Kahn, M. A. Muqtedar, *American Muslims: Bridging Faith and Freedom*. Beltsville, MD: Amana Publications, 2002.

Marable, Manning, ed., *Black Routes to Islam*. New York: Palgrave Macmillan, 2009.

Smith, Jane I., *Islam in America*, 2nd ed. New York: Columbia University Press, 2010.

White, Vibert L., *Inside the Nation of Islam*. Gainesville: University of Florida Press, 2001.

Contemporary Islam

Davidson, Laurence, *Islamic Fundamentalism: An Introduction*, rev. ed. Westport, CT: Greenwood Press, 2003.

Esposito, John L., *The Future of Islam*. New York: Oxford University Press, 2010.

Fish, M. Steven, *Are Muslims Distinctive? A Look at the Evidence*. New York: Oxford University Press, 2011.

Geaves, Ron, *Islam Today*. London: Continuum, 2010.

Gemie, Sharif, *French Muslims: New Voices in Contemporary France*. Cardiff: University of Wales Press, 2010.

Herrara, Linda, and Asef Bayat. *Being Young and Muslim*. New York: Oxford University Press, 2010.

Sniderman, Paul M., and Louk Hagendoorn, *When Ways of Life Collide: Multiculturalism and Its Discontents in the Netherlands*. Princeton, NJ: Princeton University Press, 2007.

Women in Islam

Abdul-Ghafur, Saleemah, *Living Islam Out Loud: American Muslim Women Speak*. Boston: Beacon Press, 2005.

Abu-Lughod, Lila, ed., *Remaking Women: Feminism and Modernity in the Middle East*. Princeton, NJ: Princeton University Press, 1998.

Ahmed, Leila, *Women and Gender in Islam: Historical Roots of a Modern Debate*. New Haven, CT, and London: Yale University Press, 1992.

Badran, Margot, *Feminism Beyond East and West: New Gender Talk and Practice in Global Islam*. New Delhi: Global Media Publications, 2007.

———, and Miriam Cooke, eds., *Opening the Gates: A Century of Arab Feminist Writing*. Bloomington and Indianapolis: Indiana University Press, 1990.

Bowen, John Richard, *Why the French Don't Like Headscarves: Islam, the State, and Public Space*. Princeton, NJ: Princeton University Press, 2007.

Bullock, Katherine, ed., *Muslim Women Activists in North America*. Austin: University of Texas Press, 2005.

Fernea, Elizabeth Warnock, *In Search of Islamic Feminism: One Woman's Global Journey*. New York/London/Toronto/Sydney/Auckland: Doubleday, 1998.

Haddad, Yvonne Yazbeck, *Muslim Women in America: The Challenge of Islamic Identity Today*. New York: Oxford University Press, 2006.

———, Jane I. Smith, and Kathleen M. Moor, *Muslim Women in America*. New York: Oxford University Press, 2006.

Hassan, Riffat, "Feminism in Islam," in *Feminism and World Religions*, Arvind Sharma and Katherine K. Young, eds. Albany: State University of New York Press, 1999.

———, "Islam," in *Her Voice, Her Faith*, Arvind Sharma and Katherine K. Young, eds. Boulder, CO and Oxford, UK: Westview Press, 2003.

Hekmat, Anwar, *Women and the Koran: The Status of Women in Islam*. Amherst, NY: Prometheus Books, 1997.

Kassam, Zayn R., ed., *Women and Islam*. Santa Barbara, CA: Praeger, 2010.

McGinty, Anna Mansson, *Becoming Muslim: Western Women's Conversions to Islam*. New York: Palgrave Macmillan, 2006.

Pemberton, Kelly, *Women Mystics and Sufi Shrines in India*. Columbia: University of South Carolina Press, 2010.

Roded, Ruth, ed., *Women in Islam and the Middle East: A Reader*. New York: I. B. Tauris; St. Martin's Press, 1999.

al-Saadawi, Nawal [El Saadawi], *The Hidden Face of Eve: Women in the Arab World*, Sherif Hetata, trans. and ed. Boston: Beacon Press, 1982.

Shirazi, Faegheh, *Velvet Jihad: Muslim Women's Quiet Resistance to Islamic Fundamentalism*. Gainesville: University of Florida Press, 2009.

Smith, Margaret, *Rabi'a: The Life and Work of Rabi'a and Other Women Mystics in Islam*. Oxford: Oneworld, 1994.

Stowasser, Barbara Freyer, *Women in the Qur'an, Traditions, and Interpretation*. New York: Oxford University Press, 1994.

van Nieukerk, Karin, *Women Embracing Islam: Gender and Conversion in the West*. Austin: University of Texas Press, 2006.

10

Spirits Rising
New Religious Movements

CHAPTER OBJECTIVES

After studying this chapter, you should be able to

- Discuss circumstances in which new religious movements are particularly likely to arise.
- Cite and explain the seven types of new religious movements discussed in this chapter.
- Explain the features of new religious movements.
- Give a few good examples of new religious movements.

THE WORLD OF NEW RELIGIONS

Since the eighteenth century, certain intellectuals have predicted the withering away of religion—the "Death of God." But God or Gods and Goddesses have died many times, and new Gods and Goddesses have arisen to fill the vacuum. Their names may hardly yet have the glow of the old and the holy, and they may come from segments of society little involved in the religious commerce of the previous age. The Buddha was of *kshatriya* rather than **brahmin** caste; Muhammad came from Arabia rather than one of the main religious powers of his time; Jesus came from the peasantry in Galilee, not from Jerusalem. But sometimes such religious leaders and their movements bear the future, like the obscure, tiny, furry mammals in the age of dinosaurs.

It is nothing new for prophets to appear who proclaim that the extant religion is ready to be superseded. So spoke the Buddha, in effect, of the old Brahminism and its rites, and Muhammad of the old gods of stars and moon, and so do some of those whose charismatic messages spawn new movements today. In all the countless religious changes Earth has seen, the religious quest has been renewed, but it has often changed course and set out in unexpected directions. Sometimes, at first, its new forms have hardly seemed like "religion" at all, compared with the older elaborate structure. At first, the Buddha's methods may have seemed more like an ancient version of psychotherapy and the cause of Muhammad more like a radical political movement than an institution that would, in time, show equivalents to other, older faiths. These movements may seem more like breaths of fresh wind, which sweep away all the old gods and clean the skies. Indeed, the worldwide religious scene *is* like the weather; change is always in the wind. As much as purists throughout the centuries may have wished to maintain tradition, religious thought, practice, and institutions are always changing shape—sometimes in almost unperceivable increments and sometimes by leaps and bounds.

It is essential, obviously, to know the main features of the major religions, and that is what we have studied so far in this book. But we must also realize that every one of them was once a new religion and would always be challenged by other new religions. Some "new religions," such as Buddhism, Christianity, and Islam, have gone on to become major world religions themselves. Many other new religions have not become large or have not survived at all. But often they have left traces in their cultures and have played a part in world history. Most important of all, they have frequently met the religious needs of the people of their times and places, needs that the major, established religions on the scene could not meet or perhaps did not even recognize.

New religions may arise under many circumstances. They may be a way of dealing with extreme disruption of a traditional society, when the former religion seems powerless or discredited and only a new revelation can offer hope. They may be the result of rapid social change, even if sometimes equated to "progress," which seems to require a new religious worldview. They may even appear in a society that from the outside appears full of hope and doing well but is experiencing internal, maybe intergenerational, dislocations—like the United States in the 1840s (Spiritualism), in the 1960s (Nichiren Shoshu and many other new religions from East and West), or in the 1980s (the New Age Movement). Some may say that the Divine reaches out to the world with a new call for a new time and circumstance. Whatever the case, the result is that some people within the society find that the old religion has lost authority and doesn't seem to be in touch with "what's happening now" and that therefore they require a new religion as a flag of their new, distinctive identities. Or it may be that people feel called to a new way of worship and a new way of being in the world—just as others have felt called to the major world religions.

Nothing is automatic about the emergence of new religions in particular times and places. They do not always seem to be the result of stresses greater than the usual, and some moments of crisis in human history have produced a conservative return to a strict and recognized tradition rather than new religious responses. The appeal of a new religious movement is a complex combination of a setting that has produced some deep-level dissonance between religion and people's present experience, together with just the right message or, in some cases, with a charismatic prophet, neither too conventional nor too radical, who has the right vocabulary to inspire followers.

TYPES OF NEW RELIGIONS

New religions are of varying types. Of course, we cannot presume to categorize all new religious movements in the world, and even if we could, few would present characteristics that fall neatly into only one category. Nevertheless, it is useful to speak in terms of "ideal types," while recognizing many variations in practice.

Reactive Movements

"Reactive Movements" are those movements that involve a response to stress, usually social or political. Take, for example, the Mansren-Koreri movement in Irian Jaya (then Western New Guinea, part of the Dutch East Indies). This religion is commonly regarded as the first of the modern "cargo cults" that have swept particularly through such areas of Melanesian culture as this one. Like most other new religions, it is based on older traditions. In western Irian Jaya, natives had long believed in a paradisiacal future state called *Koreri* and in prophets called *konor*, who were its heralds. The golden age of the Mansren-Koreri religion was, like many in world mythology, really a return to an ideal state at the beginning. Irian Jaya had been ruled by a beautiful young king called Mansren. Then, when his people rebelled against him, Mansren left them and went far away. But, it was believed, he would return someday to reestablish the realm of happiness, peace, and abundance.

In 1867, while Irian Jaya was under Dutch colonial rule, a *konor* had a vision that led him to call on the people to gather every night to sing new songs and enact dramatizations of the Mansren story; regular work was disrupted. By the 1880s, the imminent arrival of the golden age was being prophesied, and in 1886 another *konor* declared that a ship loaded with cargo for Mansren's people was on the way. The enthusiasm took many forms, not a few of which obviously reflected tensions between the natives and their Dutch overlords. It was said that since Mansren would soon establish a new and better society, it was no longer necessary for the natives to pay taxes or grow crops. These provocations caused some *konor* to be arrested and imprisoned for their trouble. Tension also arose between natives and white missionaries. Many of the former were nominal Christians, and their Mansren rhetoric came to include themes obviously inspired by the Bible, but some believers claimed that Mansren was greater than Christ and abandoned the mission churches.[1]

Many movements like this one swept through the South Pacific during the colonial era. Often the claim would be made that the whites had taken from the natives what was rightfully theirs but that a native hero or god, like Mansren, would come to restore them to their heritage. With him would arrive a great ship, or later an airplane, a vehicle like the one the Europeans used in their trade but this time loaded with goods for the natives. In many places, cargo cultists ritually built docks or airstrips expressly for these vehicles. At the same time, as a sign of the coming of a new age, they would stop work on things of the old and perhaps abandon or give away all their goods.

Similar movements have occurred in North America. The words quoted on page [40/was 42] are attributed to a leader of the Ghost Dance ceremony, part of a Native American movement of the 1890s at the very end of independent indigenous culture, when, prophets said, that if certain dances calling back the ancestors were performed, the whites would be driven away and the vast buffalo herds that had once ranged the plains would return. Native Americans would then be able to hunt freely across the immense prairies instead of being cooped up on reservations, where they had to break the soil and farm to survive.

Accommodationist Movements

"Accommodationist Movements" are movements that arise out of well-established religions that have been introduced into a new cultural context. The Church on Earth, the Kimbanguist Church in the Democratic Republic of the Congo, formerly Zaire and, before that, the Belgian Congo, is a Christian movement of this type. It was founded by Simon Kimbangu (1889–1951), who was converted to Christianity in 1915 by Baptist missionaries and was at first a lay evangelist. But after recalling a childhood vision of a man "neither black nor white" appearing with a Bible, he became more and more of an independent prophet, performing, it was widely rumored, many miraculous healings like Jesus himself. When he was imprisoned by the Belgian colonial authorities, the Christlike drama of his life, as it was seen by his growing number of followers, advanced further, and he was viewed as a living martyr and a special prophet called to bring Christ to the Africans. His church is now a flourishing institution with widespread religious, educational, and social service works. While avoiding any direct political involvement, it played a part in the development of the modern African consciousness that led to independence and nationhood in the Congo and elsewhere.

Spirit Movements

"Spirit Movements" are movements in which the participants claim a special connection with beings from the spiritual realm: angels, ghosts, ancestors, nature spirits, and the like. These groups tend to emphasize a feeling-centered approach to religion and have sometimes been associated with reformist social causes, especially in their early years. The United States has been host to many movements of this type. One example is Spiritualism, a religion based on belief in communication with the spirits of the dead, primarily through mediumship. Its birth as a movement can be pinpointed quite precisely to the evening of March 31, 1848, in the home of John Fox, a farmer in Hydesville, New York, near Rochester. The family had two daughters at home, Margaretta, eleven, and Kate, eight. They had been hearing strange noises in the house, rappings that sounded like the recently invented Morse code. That evening Kate was said to have snapped her fingers at the rappings and said, "Here Mr. Splitfoot [the devil], do as I do," and commenced to work out a code with them. The mysterious sounds then identified themselves, not as those of the devil but coming from the spirit of a peddler who had been murdered in the house several years before the Foxes had moved in.

Reports of these goings-on created an immediate sensation in upstate New York and soon across the country. Committees investigated them; newspapers presented long accounts of them; and, most important, countless other people tried communicating with spirits. Soon "voice mediumship"—the spirit speaking through the lips of a "medium" in trance—proved to be much more efficient than communicating by raps or other means.

By the 1850s, Spiritualism was a vogue in the United States, and it quickly spread around the world. Popular mediums and Spiritualist lecturers drew large crowds, and "home circles," wherein people gathered during an evening to experiment with the new phenomena, became popular. In some places, like the Western Reserve section of Ohio (around Cleveland), regular churches were reported to be nearly empty as crowds thronged to meetings of the new faith. Persons as prominent as Horace Greeley, Abraham Lincoln, and Queen Victoria were said to have been interested in it.

Spiritualism also made connections with contemporary developments. It claimed to be the most "scientific" of religions, since its claims, unlike those of older religions depending on faith or authority, could be tested empirically. It also declared that its spirits were coming through particularly now because they were at the forefront of the progress, both scientific and social, that was now clearly sweeping the world. Spiritualistic messages thus tended to support the abolition of slavery, the welfare of prisoners, humane education, and the rights of women: indeed, Spiritualist mediumship and ministry were forms of religious leadership open to women when virtually no "mainstream" church offered them similar opportunities. Spiritualism thus met the needs of many in a new American generation born since the birth of the republic, a generation hopeful of a new world through science, democracy, and social reform and open to new ideas and testing them directly. But popular enthusiasm for the new faith faded as some mediums were found to be fraudulent or unreliable and as national attention was swallowed up by the Civil War. Nonetheless, Spiritualist churches can be found in America and Britain to this day.[2]

Some of the groups that are loosely referred to under the rubric "New Age" fall within the "Spirit Movement" category. Contact with divine beings of one sort or another—angels, spirits, UFOs, biblical figures (although not in any sense recognized by mainstream denominations)—is a popular topic in New Age literature and practice. We might therefore follow nineteenth-century Spiritualism with a glimpse at twentieth-century UFO "contactees" and the religious movements that followed some of them. The UFO contacts and the messages received from outer space visitors,

Pagan elder, Andras Corban-Arthen, gives a blessing during a ritual at the Rites of Spring gathering in Massachusetts.

Santería altar and attendant.

like the entities received through New Age "channeling," have much in common with the spirits of the older Spiritualism faith. They come from a mysterious level higher than the human but lower than God; they speak through enigmatic signs or mediumistic deliverances, often including ecstatic states reminiscent of primordial shamanism; yet they also claim that they are in line with the latest science. Also, as in Spiritualism, the recipients of the extraterrestrial messages tend to be very ordinary people otherwise, residing in rural or proletarian settings.

The well-known analytic psychologist Carl Jung, in an essay on "flying saucers," speaks of them as "technological angels": essentially religious envoys from above the human plane, like the descending angels, bodhisattvas, gods, or spirits of old but now, in the space age, arriving in futuristic spacecraft as wise visitors from another planet. Often they come with words of alarm about Earth's disastrous direction, such as our development of atomic energies for which we are not morally ready. Their earthly "contacts" are thus put in the position of prophets. Jung commented on the UFO contactee experience in words that have religious overtones and that may help us to understand many new religious movements:

> We have here a golden opportunity of seeing how a legend is formed, and how in a difficult and dark time for humanity a miraculous tales grows up of a attempted intervention by extra-terrestrial "heavenly" powers—and this at the very time when human fantasy is seriously considering the possibility of space travel and of visiting or even invading other planets.[3]

Some years ago, I* had the opportunity to attend the then-annual Space Convention at Giant Rock, on the Mojave Desert in California, a site where not a few flying saucer sightings and contacts had been reported. The two-day meetings consisted mainly of a series of lectures by noted contactees. There was something of the atmosphere of the old-fashioned evangelical camp meeting, though the message and the testimonials were different, at least on the surface. But old and new had in common the proclamation of salvation through a savior come down from heaven, one as incarnate deity, the other in the space vehicle of a civilization far greater and nobler than ours.

Among the speakers was Orfeo Angelucci (1912–1993), to whose story Jung devotes some ten pages in *Flying Saucers*. Angelucci, a mild-mannered factory worker of Italian-American background, told how in 1952 he had met a wonderful man and woman from another world. They subsequently took him in their splendid vehicle to their paradisal planet, promised to help misguided humanity, and designated him to publicize this experience. The religious—no less the shamanistic and mystical—character of the encounter was evident in the language he used. In his book, he said that with the marvelous friends he had felt an exaltation "as though momentarily I had transcended mortality and was somehow related to these superior beings" and that on first encounter, "a blinding white beam flashed from the dome of the craft." "Momentarily," he went on, "I seemed partially to lose consciousness. Everything expanded into a great shimmering white light...IN THAT SUBLIME MOMENT I KNEW THE MYSTERY OF LIFE!"[4] That religious quality was equally manifest in the simple, utterly sincere tone of his presentation, attitudes just as present when later I had the opportunity of talking with him in his modest home. It must be noted that Angelucci had suffered serious physical and neurological disabilities earlier in life, including what was then called a "nervous breakdown," and nervous tension just before the

---

*Robert Ellwood

apparitions. Was his behavior like the shaman's initiatory ordeal? Angelucci says that when he asked his celestial friends if they could grant him strong physical health, they replied they could not: "It is only because your physical body is weakened and your spiritual perceptions thereby keener that we have been able to contact you."[5] Overall Angelucci was a man who would not have stood out in a crowd but who had very remarkable experiences, and the same can be said of many another contacted by spirits in guises old or new.

Some of the other groups described later also speak of contact with the spirit world, and religions always have a component that is in many ways like the "Spirit Movements." Sometimes the "Spirit" spoken of by a group is not a particular entity like an angel or an ancestor. Instead, it is Spirit in a general sense.

A comparison can also be made to similar groups arising out of mainstream religions. The holiness revival discussed in the section "Women in Christianity" in Chapter 8, like Spiritualism, was an experience-based, feeling-oriented religious movement in which people were moved by the Holy Spirit to work for liberal social goals such as abolition of slavery and the rights of women.

New Revelation Sects

Another type includes a great number of new religious groups; we call this type "New Revelation Sects." A new religious movement of this type is like a sect—a group that represents very strict, demanding adherence to the normative religion of the society—but that differs in that it offers new revelatory teachings as well. At its outset, Christianity was a movement of this type. As we discussed in Chapter 8, Christianity arose out of Judaism, Jesus having provided the new revelations. But many other religious movements have arisen as well—some that have survived and become mainstream religions in their own right, or at least large denominations within a religion, and some that have remained small or have died out.

Mother Anne Lee (1735–1784) was the first leader of the United Society of Believers in Christ's Second Appearance, an American group commonly called the Shakers, which falls within the "New Revelation Sect" category. The Shakers' theology is based on Christianity, but Anne Lee's revelatory visions led her to teach that people should live in harmonious equality and that God is both male and female. The Shakers held to a life of simplicity and celibacy. After her death, her followers claimed that Anne Lee's presence on Earth was Jesus' Second Coming in female form. The Shaker movement declined after the Civil War, and today only one traditional Shaker community remains active, in Sabbathday Lake, Maine.

The Family International, formerly known as the Children of God and Family of Love, also falls within this type. Family International arose out of the Jesus Movement in the United States in the early 1970s and is still active today. Its founder, David Berg, was considered by the adherents as a "prophet" of the end times. He had received revelations about the need to abandon worldly institutionalized structures, including traditional religious ones, and to establish pure Christian communities.

Another example is the Church of Jesus Christ of Latter-Day Saints, also known as the Mormon Church, discussed in Chapter 8, which has become a major worldwide Christian denomination, today boasting more than 13 million members worldwide.

An all-encompassing version of this type is the Bahá'í faith. Bahá'í adherents claim that Bahá'u'lláh (1817–1892), upon whose ideas the faith is based, brought forth a new revelation—the oneness of all the major religions of the world and of humanity. Although the Bahá'í faith arose out of Islam, its founder an Iranian Shi'ite, it claims to fulfill Islamic, Zoroastrian, Jewish, and Christian prophesies and to be the ultimate expression of divine faith. Bahá'í now has five million members worldwide and approximately 170,000 in the United States.

A relatively new movement of this type is Mai Chaza Church in Africa (discussed in Chapter 8), whose founder Mai Chaza established healing centers in the *Guta ra Jehova*, the "Cities of Jehovah."

In 1999 and 2000, much worldwide attention was attached to a new Chinese movement of this type, the Falun Gong, because of its persecution as a dissident group by the Chinese government. This movement, in the Chinese Buddhist-Daoist tradition, is based on the authority of the founder, Li Hon Zhi. Li's charismatic power is said to enable people to use certain meditation and movement practices to arouse spiritual energy, to maintain radiant health, and to become enlightened. The authoritarian government of the People's Republic of China, in banning the fervent and rapidly growing group, has alleged that its unconventional healing has actually caused death. The government is no doubt also threatened by the Falun Gong's movement for independence from its control.

Import Religions

Another type is what we call "Import Religions." Import religions are those that demonstrate the transcultural nature of many new religious movements as they are new to one country but are established religions in other countries. The International Society for Krishna Consciousness (the Hare Krishna Movement) belongs to the

Hari Krishna women and girl.

bhakti tradition of India but was an entirely new religious movement for the United States when it was founded there by A. C. Bhaktivedanta Swami Prabhupada in 1966. Similarly, Christian groups are "Import Religions" when they are introduced in counties dominated by another world religion, for example Christianity in Buddhist and Shinto Japan. Christian Pentecostalism in Africa (discussed in Chapter 8) is also an import religion.

Several years ago I* attended a chapter meeting of Nichiren Shoshu of America (NSA), as it was then called, another import religion, in a modest one-story frame house in a suburban California city. This group was essentially an American branch of Soka Gakkai, the Nichiren lay Buddhist movement discussed in Chapter 5. Often counted as one of the "New Religions" of Japan, it has been a dynamic force in that nation since 1945. Far from a stereotypical Buddhist group with an air of monks and unworldly meditation, modern Japanese Nichiren Buddhism is an up-to-date religion with youth rallies, marching bands, and an emphasis on chanting to receive worldly as well as spiritual benefits.

The living room of the bungalow where this chapter of NSA met had been converted into a shrine room. At the end of it, opposite the door, a cabinetlike box had been set up, with its doors open to display a rectangular sheet of heavy paper crowded with characters. When I arrived at seven in the evening, four or five young people were already seated on the floor, chanting. Others kept coming in, until thirty-five or forty

---

*Robert Ellwood

were present. The rapid chant went on, and more and more people joined it, humming and bouncing along with the energy of an express train, using the words of the *Daimoku, Nam Myoho Renge Kyo* ("Hail the Marvelous Teaching of the Lotus Sutra").

Then came time for testimonials. I heard people talk about how chanting had helped someone to sell a house and another to reconcile a daughter with her parents and how it had enabled someone to land a good job and another to get into a closed college class in ceramics. One person even said that chanting would find one a parking place when the search seems hopeless. But everyone also emphasized that the benefits of chanting are not just materialistic—that the spiritual change within that comes from chanting is really more important and profound. It's just that, as Nichiren Buddhism says, *esho funi*, "inner and outer not separate." If you change the inner through chanting, your outer circumstances will also change for the better; if you put good things into your outer life, your inner state of mind will improve, too.[6] Nichiren Shoshu is no different from most new religions in claiming that, unlike conventional faiths, it can produce visible benefits here and now in the real world.

Golden Age Movements

"Golden Age Movements" involve what is believed by the adherents to be a return to the faith of a prior "golden age," when people were closer to the Divine. Such movements often draw from existing religious traditions in the development of their practices but do not identify themselves as a part of or as derived from such existing religions. Two subgroups of this type that are expanding especially in Europe, the United States, Canada, and Australia are the Feminist Spirituality Groups and the Pagan Groups. Often the two are intertwined and therefore not readily distinguishable, although we will attempt to discuss them separately here for clarity.

Feminist Spirituality Groups are loosely aligned as a conglomerate often referred to as the "Goddess Movement." A foundational belief of most of the groups within the Goddess Movement is that before the Patriarchal Revolution, men and women lived harmoniously with each other and with nature in egalitarian agrarian communities and worshipped a Goddess as "Mother of All" in her many aspects. In such communities, art proliferated, and all was beauty. The adherents seek to return to the practices and social situation of that time. Some groups consist of men and women working together toward this goal. Other groups are "separatist," consisting of only men or only women who believe that a return to equality is not possible until each gender separately works through biases that have been assimilated from the patriarchal culture in which both genders now live. Such groups may draw syncretistically from other contemporary or older sources to develop their practices—sometimes from ancient or contemporary Pagan sources. Some groups' ceremonies evolve out of an artistic creative process involving many of its members and are not ritually repeated but recreated for each ceremony.

The Temple of Isis in California is a Goddess Movement group that involves both men and women. It is part of the Fellowship of Isis, an international group with headquarters in Clonegal, Ireland, and founded by Olivia Lawrence and Pamela Durdin-Robertson in 1976. It has about fifteen thousand members in the United States, Great Britain, Ireland, and Nigeria. While the adherents call their group the Temple of Isis, for them Isis incorporates all manifestations of the Goddess around the world. In the words of one adherent: "We support the resurgence of the Goddess and the realization of a sustainable and peaceful future."

Several years ago I* attended a Temple of Isis celebration on a beach outside Los Angeles at dawn. There gathered men and women, dressed in colorful robes

---

*Barbara McGraw

and bedecked with flowers, to celebrate the "Sisters of the Sea." The ceremony began with the blowing of a conch shell horn to call the participants to the ceremony. All formed a circle, sand at their feet and the sea breeze blowing in their hair as the sun rose, casting streams of brightly colored light across the peaceful ocean. Then the priestesses called to the four directions of the world and asked that the Goddesses corresponding to the directions join the circle for the ceremony.

A slow, deep drumming commenced, and one of the priestesses led the circle into a procession, dancing rhythmically to the music of chimes and bells that had joined the beating drum. The group gathered in turn at each of four altars for the four "sisters of the sea"—Isis (Egypt), Aphrodite (Greece), Mari (or Mary in her many aspects around the world), and Yemaya (Yoruba)—and received blessings from the priestesses there. In succession, the participants tasted the sweetness of chocolate at the altar for Aphrodite; received a blessing of scented oil placed on the forehead at the altar for Mari; and at the altar of Yemaya, received a blessing of cool waters sprinkled over their heads and copper pennies, which they then cast into the ocean as an offering to the Goddess. The ritual culminated at the altar of Isis, where the participants gathered around a small boat that had been made by the priestesses out of willow branches and leaves. Each person placed flower petals, shells, herbs, or feathers into the boat as he or she made a prayer wish. The boat was then launched into the sea to send the wishes to the Goddess.

The other subgroup, the Pagans or Neo-Pagans, also wishes to return to a prior "golden age." For them, however, it involves a return to the pre-Judeo-Christian roots of a prior faith. The prior faith is usually the shamanistically based indigenous religion of a particular place, such as one of the Native American or First Peoples religions of America or one of the folk religions of old Europe, mostly known as Wicca, or "Witchcraft" (not to be confused with the negative images of "witches" as portrayed in fairy tales), as Odinism-Asatru, or as Druid. Usually such groups' thought and practices involve the reverence of nature as sacred and full of "spirit" (as we saw in the discussion of indigenous religions in Chapter 2); the celebration of seasonal festivals; the use of magical means to experience the Divine and to effect positive changes in one's own life or in the world; and the celebration of the Divine as both God and Goddess. Because of their belief in the sacredness of nature, such groups are often involved in the ecology movement, which itself often has religious overtones.

Hybrid Religions

The last type involves groups that have assimilated ideas and practices from the monotheistic world religions into an indigenous, shamanistically or spirit based religious tradition. We refer to these as the "Hybrid Religions." For example, many new religions, like Voodoo in Haiti and New Orleans; Santería in Cuba, Puerto Rico, and Florida; Umbanda and Candomblé in Brazil (discussed in "The New Face of World Christianity" section in Chapter 8) are syntheses of African religions and Roman Catholicism. Several years ago, we[*] went to a Voudon temple in New Orleans. Brightly colored altars were filled with figures sacred to the priestess there, including figures of Jesus, Catholic saints such as Mary, and Africa deities such as Ezili and Papa Legba.

A good example of this type is Santería. Santería, "the way of the saints," is a religious movement combining African and Roman Catholic features. It arose among the African population in Cuba but spread to other parts of the Caribbean and, especially after the Cuban exile of 1959, to the United States. Now Santería can be found in most large North American cities, but it is strongest in Florida. It has many similarities

---

*Robert Ellwood and Barbara McGraw

Santería religious ceremony, part of Carifest in Santiago de Cuba.

to other non-Protestant Afro-American religions, such as Voodoo in French Creole-speaking Haiti and Umbanda and Candomblé in Brazil.

Santería is fundamentally the traditional religion of the Yoruba people of West Africa. But in the New World setting, their gods, called Orishas, are also identified with Roman Catholic saints so that Chango, a great king and warrior, who also represents fire, thunder, and lightning, becomes Saint Barbara, who is associated with thunder and lightning and who is a patron saint of soldiers; and so that Yemaya, a lovely black mother goddess, whose power derives from the sea, is also the Blessed Virgin Mary, Mother of Jesus, and Star of the Sea. In worship, sacrifices (most commonly chickens) are offered, and devotees often go into ecstasy and are possessed by their patronal *orisha*. Divination, done by priests called *babalawos*, is frequently practiced. The rituals, costumes, and altars of Santería are very colorful and filled with fascinating symbolism.[7]

Other Ways to Categorize New Religions

There are other ways to categorize new religions as well. Examples include Millennialist (or Millenarian), emphasizing the coming of a paradisiacal age; Thaumaturgical, emphasizing magical powers; Healing; Prophetic; Communalist, in which members live together, perhaps without personal property; Legalistic, emphasizing strict adherence to rules; Mystical, emphasizing methods of meditation and inner realization; Initiatory, like the Greek "mysteries," emphasizing programmed transformative experiences; Devotional; and Philosophical. And it is important to remember that many new religious movements exhibit characteristics of more than one category.

In addition, as we have mentioned, there are groups that represent a very strict, demanding adherence to the normative religion of the society, like the Amish or Jehovah's Witnesses in America, which are called "sects." Those centered on a new or imported teaching are often called **cults**. But these terms should be used with great caution because they have become highly pejorative and are based on stereotypes, although not intended as such by the sociologists of religion who originally coined the terms.

NEW RELIGIONS AROUND THE WORLD

The few examples given here have barely begun to suggest the wealth of religious experience and diversity found in new religious movements around the world. It should be remembered that new religions are increasingly mobile, no longer likely to be confined to just one cultural area. In preceding chapters and previously in this chapter, we have already looked, to some degree, at new religions in Japan, Korea, Vietnam, Brazil, Africa, and China.

In the United States and Canada, several hundred new religions, many of them adapting or related to indigenous, occult, or Eastern religions, can be found, some of which have been named in the previous section. They reflect the pluralistic nature of religion in these societies and the tendency of some people to be seekers and spiritual experimenters. Asian and Latin American immigration has also brought many new religions to the United States and Canada.

In Europe, new religions comparable to those in the United States and Canada—in fact, often the same ones—are plentiful. They can be ascribed not only to some of the same factors influencing U.S. and Canadian religions but also to the spiritual vacuum left by relatively low attendance at the services of conventional churches. In Russia and in the former Soviet bloc nations, the collapse of Communism has left a situation of social confusion and seeking that has spurred the growth of new religions, too.

The Islamic world has produced a number of new religious movements, some of them arising out of Sufi mysticism. Sufism in many forms has been brought to North America as well. Perhaps the best-known new religion to appear out of the Islamic world is the Bahá'í faith, already mentioned.

India also has a host of movements, often based on particular spiritual masters like Ramakrishna, whom we mentioned in Chapter 3, and typically presenting not only his or her charisma and spiritual authority but also a certain method of yoga, meditation, or devotion. One from the twentieth century, the Brahma Kumari movement, allows only female leadership, although both men and women may join as ordinary members. Other movements in India include the Sai Baba movement, which has a presence in Europe and in North America, and the Ammachi, or "hugging saint," movement. The yoga movement, originally an important spiritual practice within Hinduism, was adopted in the West in a reduced form as mere exercise. Now it is reengaging the whole person in holistic self-realization through breathing meditations and body postures and is growing around the world, especially in the United States.

Africa has been estimated to host no fewer than eight thousand new religious movements. New movements are abundant in Latin America as well.

An interesting phenomenon is the wealth of new religious movements of many types in Japan, which exemplify the vividly diverse panorama of doctrines and practices that new religions throughout the world may exhibit. Tenrikyo ("Religion of Heavenly Wisdom"), mentioned in Chapter 5, has practices that include the performance of sacred dances with gestures of sweeping movement to symbolize clearing away spiritual dust. Members of Perfect Liberty, believing that "life is art" and that all aspects of life need to be integrated into a total work of art, emphasize sports and, when possible, build their churches near golf courses. The Church of World Messianity offers *johrei*, in which the "Divine Light of God" is channeled through the cupped hand of one who administers it to a recipient. Most new Japanese religions were founded by strong shamanists such as Miki Nakayama (1798–1887), foundress of Tenrikyo, one of the oldest and most prototypical of the new religions, and Bunjiro Kawate, founder of Konkokyo, who had a shamanistic vision in which a folk religion deity revealed himself to be actually a monotheistic High God.

In all the new Japanese religions, we see evidence of syncretism, which is often the case with new religious movements around the world that are not "sects,", although even new "sects" may exhibit syncretistic elements as well. Ideas from East and West are combined into new mixes in the new Japanese religions; for example, Jesus is quoted in their literature along with the Buddha. Seicho-no-Ie, a group teaching that "all is perfect," draws both from the Western "New Thought" positive-thinking tradition, which places full responsibility for one's condition in the individual—a ramification of the modern isolation of the individual in contrast to archaic village or tribal society and religion—and from the Mahayana Buddhist belief in the universal and unstained One Mind.

Communal life in the new Japanese religious movements is especially represented in their sacred centers. Like Tenri City of Tenrikyo and the headquarters of Perfect Liberty with its immense golf course near Osaka, the new Japanese religions tend to have architecturally striking headquarters surrounded by large communities. They are places of pilgrimage that profess to show what the world will be like when the "new age" arrives. In the new Japanese religions, every member may be taken seriously and given a part to play. This makes them appealing to the dislocated millions who have been moved by modernization far from ancestral shrines to impersonal industrial cities.

Of course, it is not possible here to discuss all of the individual new religions in detail; only a taste of the multitude of flavors can be given. However, some perspective may be provided by noting that, although there is great diversity represented in the new religious movements, they all have some characteristics in common. Let us then look at some general features of new religious movements.

FEATURES OF NEW RELIGIOUS MOVEMENTS

We shall look at features of new religious movements in terms of the three forms of religious expression presented in Chapter 1. What is likely to be in each of them?

First, in the theoretical or "What do they say?" form of expression, a new religion will probably show enough continuity with the religion already accepted in its society that ordinary people can recognize it as religion. But it will then put a new face on the old religion, one that appeals to vague uneasy feelings that people may have that the old religion is outmoded or irrelevant to the crucial problems of the present. Thus, in the Mansren movement, an old story was renewed in contemporary terms when the folk hero was said to be returning to supersede colonial rule and bring a modern ship full of goods, like those of the Europeans. Current new American religions of Eastern background speak of God, like Judaism and Christianity, but by "God," they tend to mean something more impersonal, inward, and universal, like Brahman or the Dao, than the personal God of the traditional religions.

At the same time, another common feature of the beliefs of new religions, suggested by Spiritualism, is a tendency to fill up the "intermediate" range of the sacred cosmos between human earthly experience and ultimate transcendence with a range of finite but supernatural beings: spirits, angels, gods, goddesses, ascended masters, and the like. These beings are, of course, no more than the gods and spirits of **animism** and polytheism, or the equivalents of Hindu Gods and Goddesses

An Amish girl, making handicrafts. Groups such as the Amish represent "sects" that involve strict adherence to the dominant religion of a society, rather than a new or imported teaching.

or Buddhist Buddhas and *bodhisattvas* in modern dress. But while much modern religion has downplayed or eliminated such gods and spirits, human beings nevertheless claim to encounter them.

In addition, a new religion usually offers something the adherents feel is new in the way of its thinking about the social structure of society. This generally takes two forms: a progressivist-reform message or a purist-reform message. Both are messages of change. Often the rights and roles of women or other gender issues become central in either form.

In terms of practices, worship, or "What do they do?" new religions tend either to center on one repeatedly taught and emphasized practice that is like a *single*, *simple*, *sure key* to a personal encounter with the sacred, like some of the new Japanese religions, or to develop a community worship practice in which the creative process of developing unique ceremonies, as in the Feminist Spirituality Groups, is part of the particular movement's religious mystique. Recall again that a new religion must have a draw strong enough to counter the natural appeal of conventional faiths, which have the support of family, ethnicity, and community. Because they have been around for a long time, established religions may have a variety of services, practices, and emphases, from celebrating popular holidays to ways of private prayer and meditation, but they involve activities that strike the sort of person drawn to a new religion as lukewarm and too compromised with the culture. Yet it is difficult for a person to make the break from the conventional established religion unless the alternative presents a definite experience of greater intensity and more immediate reward, spiritually and sometimes also materially, than the conventional.

The sociology of new religious movements, on the one hand, may be like the practical form of expression in that it must offer a person enough to compensate for breaking one's "natural" ties—familial, ethnic, and communal—to a birthright religion. The appeal of a highly charismatic spiritual leader, a "guru" or a prophet, may have this effect on some people; they want to be near him or her and receive far more from that person and the new practice than they do anywhere else. The same may be said about the group that forms: it is intense, fervent, committed, and ideally also loving and sharing. It is not a "natural" group in the sense above but one made up of people who have made a self-conscious, intentional choice to enter it. This makes it a group with a highly different "feel" from the conventional, a "feel" which, for some, provides a chosen "family" that overcomes the perceived failures of the birth family. Such a group is also more likely to be more demanding of its adherent's time and energy.

New religious movements can also operate sociologically in another way: as very diffuse influences that do not compete directly with conventional religion or make the same kinds of demands. While there is often an "inner circle" of adherents who are dedicated practitioners of their faith, other adherents do not attend formal services as often as they attend lectures and classes, read books and pamphlets, or, nowadays, listen to CDs and DVDs sold through the mail or listen, read, or watch Internet offerings. In America today, many conventional churchgoers may also take a yoga or meditation class during the week or read and reflect on a Spiritualist-type or New Age book once in a while. These are examples of what one means by the diffuse type of influence new and unconventional religious movements can have.

Summary

New religious movements have been found worldwide and throughout history and are very numerous today. They appear under many conditions but especially in times of social stress and rapid social change or in answer to new ideas and visions in the air. New religions are of various types, although in practice none fit neatly into only one type. The types we have discussed in this chapter are Reactive Movements, Accommodationist Movements, Spirit Movements, New Revelation Sects, Import Religions, Golden Age Movements, and Hybrid Religions. Basic features of new religious movements are likely to be a different but recognizable doctrine; a practice centered on a single, simple, sure technique or a creative group process and practice; a charismatic founding and leadership or an intense, highly demanding group. On the other hand, they may involve a diffuse type of influence that is not directly competitive with mainstream religion. In every case, though, a new religious movement must offer inner rewards sufficiently effective and convincing to compensate for a break with the conventional faith.

Questions for Review

1. What are some circumstances in which new religious movements might be particularly likely to appear?
2. What are the different types of new religions we have discussed in this chapter, and what are the characteristics that define them?
3. What are some common features of new religious movements?
4. Discuss the common features of new religious movements in terms of the three forms of religious expression.
5. Give some examples of new religions from different parts of the world.

Suggested Readings on New Religious Movements

General

Clarke, Peter B., ed., *Encyclopedia of New Religious Movements*. London and New York: Routledge, 2006.

Daschke, Dereck, and W. Michael Ashcraft, *New Religious Movements: A Documentary Reader*. New York: New York University Press, 2005.

Hume, Lynne, and Kathleen McPhillips, *Popular Spiritualities*. Aldershot, UK and Burlington, VT: Ashgate, 2006.

Lewis, James R., *Violence and New Religious Movements*. Oxford and New York: Oxford University Press, 2011.

————, ed., *The Oxford Handbook of New Religious Movements*. Oxford and New York: Oxford University Press, 2004.

————, and Jesper Aagaard, eds., *Controversial New Religions*. New York: Oxford University Press, 2005.

————, and Sarah M. Lewis, eds., *Sacred Schisms: How Religions Divide*. Cambridge: Cambridge University Press, 2009.

Mooney, Annabelle, *The Rhetoric of Religious "Cults."* New York: Palgrave Macmillan, 2005.

Siegler, Elijah, *New Religious Movements*. Upper Saddle River, NJ: Prentice Hall, 2007.

Strmiska, Michael F., ed., *Modern Paganism in World Cultures: Comparative Perspectives*. Santa Barbara, CA: ABC/CLIO, 2005.

Zeller, Benjamin E., *Prophets and Protons: New Religious Movements and Science in Late Twentieth-Century America*. New York: New York University Press, 2010.

Native American, African, and Oceanic Movements

Barrett, Leonard E., *The Rastafarians*. Boston: Beacon Press, 1988.

Cave, Alfred A. *Prophets of the Great Spirit*. Lincoln: University of Nebraska Press, 2006.

Lawrence, Peter, *Road Belong Cargo: A Study of the Cargo Movement in the Southern Madang District of New Guinea*. New York: Humanities Press, 1964.

Maroukis, Thomas Constantine, *The Peyote Road: Religious Freedom and the Native American Church*. Norman: University of Oklahoma Press, 2010.

Metraux, Alfred, *Voodoo in Haiti*. New York: Schocken, 1989.

Ojo, Matthews A., *The End-Time Army: Charismatic Movements in Modern Nigeria*. Trenton, NJ: Africa World Press, 2006.

Truner, Harold W., ed., *Bibliography of New Religious Movements in Primal Societies*, 5 vols. New York: Macmillan, 1977–1992.

New Religions in Asia

(See also the Bibliography and Notes for Chapter 5 for Japan, Korea, and Vietnam.)

Ashby, Philip H., *Modern Trends in Hinduism*. New York: Columbia University Press, 1974.

Brooks, Charles R., *The Hare Krishnas in India*. Princeton, NJ: Princeton University Press, 1989.

Chan, Wing-Tsit, *Religious Trends in Modern China*. New York: Columbia University Press, 1953. (Though now somewhat dated, a classic study of modern movements up to the revolution and their relation to Western influence.)

Elliott, Allen J. A., *Chinese Spirit Medium Cults in Singapore*. London: Royal Anthropological Institute, 1955.

MacKenzie, Rory, *New Buddhist Movements in Thailand*. London and New York: Routledge, 2007.

Porter, Noah, *Falun Gong in the United States*. Parkland, FL: Dissertation.com, 2003

Reader, Ian, *Religious Violence in Contemporary Japan: The Case of Aum Shinrikyo*. Honolulu: University of Hawai'i Press, 2000.

Stalker, Nancy K., *Prophet Motive: Deguchi Onisaburo, Oomoto, and the Rise of New Religions in Imperial Japan*. Honolulu: University of Hawai'i Press, 2008.

York, Michael, *Pagan Theology: Paganism as a World Religion*. New York: New York University Press, 2003.

Religious Movements in North America

Adler, Margot, *Drawing Down the Moon: Witches, Druids, Goddess-Worshippers, and Other Pagans in America*. New York: Penguin Books, 1979, 2006.

Bednarowski, Mary F., *New Religions and the Theological Imagination in America*. Bloomington: Indiana University Press, 1989.

Chryssides, George D., and Margaret Z. Wilkins, eds., *A Reader in New Religious Movements*. New York and London: Continuum, 2006.

Clifton, Chas, and Graham Harvey, *The Paganism Reader*. New York and London: Routledge, 2004.

Coleman, James William, *The New Buddhism: The Western Transformation of an Ancient Tradition*. New York: Oxford University Press, 2001.

Cowan, Douglas E., and David G. Bromley, *Cults and New Religions: A Brief History*. Malden, MA and Oxford: Blackwell, 2008.

————, *Cyberhenge: Modern Pagans on the Internet*. New York and London: Routledge, 2005.

Curtis, Edward E., IV, and Danielle Brune Sigler, *The New Black Gods*. Bloomington: Indiana University Press,

2009. Important update of the 1944 classic, Arthur Fauset, *Black Gods of the Metropolis.*

Dawson, Lorne L., ed., *Cults and New Religious Movements: A Reader.* Malden, MA and Oxford: Blackwell, 2003.

Ellwood, Robert S., *Alternative Altars: Unconventional and Eastern Spirituality in America.* Chicago: University of Chicago Press, 1979.

———, and Harry B. Partin, *Religious and Spiritual Groups in Modern America*, 2nd ed. Englewood Cliffs, NJ: Prentice Hall, 1988.

Gallagher, Eugene V., *The New Religious Movements Experience in America.* Westport, CT: Greenwood Press, 2004. Excellent bibliography.

———, and W. Michael Ashcraft, eds., *Introduction to New and Alternative Religions in America,* 5 vols. Westport, CN: Greenwood Press, 2006.

Miller, Timothy, ed., *America's Alternative Religions.* Albany: State University of New York Press, 1995.

Palmer, Susan J., *Aliens Adored: Rael's UFO Religion.* New Brunswick, NJ: Rutgers University Press, 2004.

Pike, Sarah M., *New Age and Neopagan Religions in America.* New York and Chichester, West Sussex: Columbia University Press, 2004.

Rocheford, E. Burke, *Hare Krishna Transformed.* New York: New York University Press, 2007.

Shupe, Anson, and Susan E. Darnell, *Agents of Discord: Deprogramming, Pseudo-Science, and the American Anticult Movement.* New Brunswick, NJ and London: Transaction Publishers, 2006.

Ward, Martha, *Voodoo Queen: The Spirited Lives of Marie Laveau.* Jackson: University Press of Mississippi, 2004.

Women in New Religions

Eller, Cynthia, *Living in the Lap of the Goddess: The Feminist Spirituality Movement in America.* Boston: Beacon Press, 1995.

Griffin, Wendy, "Goddess Spirituality and Wicca," in *Her Voice, Her Faith,* Arvind Sharma and Katherine K. Young, eds. Boulder, CO and Oxford, UK: Westview Press, 2003.

———, ed., *Daughters of the Goddess: Studies of Identity, Healing, and Empowerment.* Walnut Creek, CA: Altamira Press, 1999.

Palmer, Susan J., *Moon Sisters, Krishna Mothers: Women's Roles in New Religions.* Syracuse, NY: Syracuse University Press, 1994.

Puttick, Elizabeth, *Women in New Religions: In Search of Community, Sexuality, and Spiritual Power.* New York: St. Martin's Press, 1997.

Wessinger, Catherine, ed., *Women's Leadership in Marginal Religions: Explorations Outside the Mainstream.* Urbana: University of Illinois Press, 1993.

A FINAL WORD

WE HAVE SURVEYED THE RELIGIONS OF THE WORLD. WHAT HAVE WE LEARNED?

We have learned from the study of the history of the world's religions their theoretical, practical, and sociological forms of religious expression. We have learned about founders, dates, doctrines, rites, reforms, the diverse roles of women and men in many faiths, as well as how each religion views the world and how we should live in it.

But something else too may be in the mix: the dynamics of religion. Some might like it otherwise, but it should be apparent from our examination that the religions on planet Earth are in a continual process of change and evolution and that therefore, sometimes, one religion is replaced by another. Christianity becomes strong in the Southern Hemisphere even as it fades in some parts of the Northern Hemisphere; Islam is increasingly a presence in Europe and North America, as are Hinduism and Buddhism; Confucianism was once in decline, but now it seems to be regaining its role as a moral influence in East Asia. New religious movements mushroom on every side; some survive long, others do not.

Sometimes the process of change is so fast as to be dizzying; sometimes it is much slower than generational change so that a religion may seem impermeable. Sometimes people look to the past for authentic religion, sometimes to the here and now, and sometimes to the future. Even then, often something of the ages is brought forward to the present. Sometimes a new revelation builds upon or clarifies ancient ones, suggesting perhaps that the Divine is still speaking to us as it always has through the ages. Still, even within the most traditional or conservative of religions, we find that most people today do not worship exactly as their grandparents did; new music, the influence of television and the Internet, and subtle changes in culture and values make certain a new form of worship.

WHAT THEN OF THE FUTURE?

Some say religion is declining, that it is not compatible with the science, technology, and lifestyles of the present and that it is weakened by too many scandals and mistakes. Others contend that something like religion is necessary for a comprehensive worldview and that religion is the ultimate foundation for valid values that shape self, family, community, and good governance. The past and the present, our concerns in this book, suggest in any case that the impulse behind religion is deeply embedded in human nature, or at least in the nature of most humans. It is capable of expressing itself in radically new ways when the time is right, in some ways perhaps that would barely seem religious to those of another generation, in some ways that pass on to a new generation an inspiration from ancient wisdom. We can only wait and see, unless we ourselves are among those responsible for shaping the religious faith of years to come.

In any case, we can only end with the thought with which we began this adventure: now is an exciting time to study the religions of the world.

APPENDIX

Studying the World's Religions

I. WRITING A TERM PAPER

One assignment you may have in a class on world religions is to write a paper on a selected topic in this area. Here are some ideas on how to go about it.

Topic

Unless the topic is assigned, be sure that you select one that is neither too broad nor too specialized for a student at your level. Attempting to write about all of Buddhism or Hinduism in one paper could result in only extremely superficial coverage. On the other hand, a specialized subject more suitable for a Ph.D. dissertation would usually not be recommended. For the typical six- to twelve-page research paper something in the middle range would be best, such as the life and teaching of a major religious figure—Shinran, Confucius, Luther, Muhammad. Another approach would be the story of a religious group or denomination within a major religion—Nichiren Buddhism, Southern Baptists. One could also select a particular text, like the Diamond Sutra or the Gospel of Mark; or a particular rite or practice, like Zen meditation or the Roman Catholic Mass. A few special religious sites, the Ise shrine or Mecca and the pilgrimage to it, would also be suitable. You could write about one of the Hindu gods or Buddhist *bodhisattvas* or something comparable. Those who are philosophically minded might wish to take a basic concept like *nirvana, karma,* or redemption and study it. On the other hand, don't overlook the importance and fascination of popular religion, like the celebration of festivals such as Durgapuja, Christmas, or Passover; or pilgrimages; or how weddings and funerals are done; or beliefs and practices concerning the dead.

These are only a few ideas; the possibilities are almost endless.

Sources

When you select your topic, be sure that adequate resources on it are available to you. We suggest you first read about the topic in a good encyclopedia, such as the *Britannica*, the *Encyclopedia of Religion*, or the *Abingdon Dictionary of Living Religions*, to get an overview and to look at its bibliography. Encyclopedia resources can be found on the Internet as well, of course. For more bibliography entries, look in this textbook, in bibliographies in textbooks on the religion, and in sources like Vol. 4 of *The Reader's Adviser*. In addition, you may choose to use Internet databases. If so, refer to "III. Internet Research Guide" below.

Then, use at least four good scholarly books or articles. They should be as specialized as possible; if you are writing about Krishna, use books about him or at least about Hindu deities generally or about Hinduism, not just encyclopedias or general world religion textbooks. There is always material in good scholarly journal articles, too. Ask your librarian to help you find them. In many cases, you will not need to read all of a book. Learn how to skim and how to use the contents and the index to locate what you need. Be careful with the spelling of non-English names and terms.

Notes and Bibliography

In your paper, be sure to use a proper format for notes. Footnote or endnote all quotations and sources of particular, specialized information. If you use computerized sources, either CDs, information networks, or websites, they must be fully cited the same as any other source. Remember that in most schools plagiarism, or the unacknowledged use of material other than your own in a paper, is grounds for expulsion. Include a bibliography of all the sources you used, in proper form, at the end of the paper.

Organization

Your paper should first have a one-paragraph introduction; second, a body of several paragraphs organized around the history and the three forms of religious expression to which we have referred several times in this book; and finally, a one-paragraph conclusion. Here is a proposed outline. (If you decide to write about ethics, art, or religious experience more specifically than what is set out in the outline below, be sure to add additional sections to the outline to accommodate that material clearly.)

1. *Introduction.* This is a short introductory paragraph to the whole paper.
2. *History.* Here, give the history and background of the subject: for example, if the subject is a person such as Shinran, the story of his life; if the subject is a teaching or school, how it came into being and developed over time. Be sure not to confuse myth and history here.
3. *Teaching.* Here, present the subject's most important teachings about the Divine or Ultimate Reality and the nature of human life, ethical duties, and the meaning and destiny of life as given by the person, text, or school associated with the deity or practice. Some will be obvious. Some, like the teachings behind a rite or festival, will require a little digging, but they are there. Important myths, such as those about a deity or a festival, come in here; analyze what those myths are saying about God, nature, and human life.
4. *Practices.* What forms of worship, meditation, and activity are associated with the subject? How is the deity worshipped? What practices did the leader himself follow and teach his or her followers? How is the rite actually done? How is the text used in real worship, or what worship does it imply? Is the purpose of the practice to elicit a mystical or other special experience? Does art play a part in the practice of the religion? Be as specific as possible. Don't just write, for example, "meditation," but describe just what method of meditation is used in this context.
5. *Sociology.* Here describe such things as the social role of the teacher, the role of disciples, and the organization of a school or denomination. And answer questions, such as the following: Who performs a particular rite or worships a particular deity? What does that mean socially? Who makes the pilgrimage and why? What is the "leadership" or "authority"? The discussion should include relevant material on the nature of leadership, social and institutional structures, the interaction of leaders and members of a group, the place of women and other particular classes, and the relationship of a religious group or practice to the larger society.
6. *Conclusion.* Here, set out what you have drawn from exploring the material discussed in the paper. You may also, but need not, give your own critical reaction to the topic.

Proofreading and Grammar.

Be sure to proofread very carefully, double-checking the spelling of technical and non-English names and terms. (Although there are different methods of transliteration from some languages, try to use one method consistently.) Take care of all typos, misspellings, bad grammar, and messiness.

II. WRITING A RELIGIOUS VISIT PAPER

Another assignment you may have in a class like this is to visit a place of worship, presumably one that is new to you, and to write a report on it. In most cases, this will be a visit to a service.

Here are some ideas on how to organize this paper based on the three forms of religious expression. It is assumed that this paper is intended to be a descriptive or "phenomenological" account of the religious activity, neither laudatory nor critical. On this particular occasion, the purpose is just to observe carefully and empathetically, in the way discussed in Chapter One, what is actually done. It is also assumed that this report is to be based on firsthand observation, deliberately avoiding the use of secondary sources, so notes and bibliography are not needed. However, in some cases you may need to get a little background through prior reading or through material available at the religious site to understand better what you see; if used, be sure to cite those. Interviews may also be helpful, as well as perusing the website for the group, if it has one; if used, also be sure to cite those.

Most religious places welcome sincere students as visitors. Remember to be quiet, respectful, appreciative, and appropriately dressed.

Here is the outline for a descriptive or "phenomenological" paper:

1. *Field Information.* Give the full name, exact address, and religious affiliation of the group. (For example, don't just say "a Buddhist temple"; be sure to specify the school, or denomination, and the national background.) Give the exact date and time of the visit; give the name and type of service (if any) attended.

2. *Preliminary Placing Information.* Describe the outside and inside appearance of the building, the way visitors are greeted, and the sort of people in this group (that is, their apparent social class, lifestyle, ethnic background, gender, average age, the number present, and so forth).

3. *Description of Activity or Symbolism.* If you attend a service or formal presentation on the religion, describe what happened from beginning to end. Try to give some sense of the emotional tone and subjective spiritual meaning of the scenario. (For example: Was the opening dramatic or casual? Is congregational participation emotional or reserved? Is much of the service spontaneous or ritualized?)

   If you did not attend a regular service, discuss in detail the significance of the art, architecture, and symbolism in and around the site.

4. *Analysis.* Analyze the topic in terms of the three forms of religious expression: theoretical (teaching), practical (worship), and sociological (leadership and group type), and include art, ethics, and experience as appropriate. At least one-third of the paper should cover these topics.

   a. *Theoretical.* What, essentially, does this religion teach? As far as you can tell from this one experience, what is the main message this religion gives through its sermons, practices, symbols, and so on?

   b. *Practical.* What is the basic nature of the worship? Formal or informal? Ancient or modern? Structured or spontaneous? What message about how this group conceives of the role of religion does the nature of the worship communicate?

   c. *Sociological.* What kind of group is it? Close-knit or diffused? Does it consist mostly of people drawn to the religion by family or ethnic ties? Or does it consist mostly of committed converts of different backgrounds? What role does the priest or leader play? What message about religious experience and meaning is communicated by the nature of the leadership and the group?

A discussion of the art, ethics, and mystical or other special religious experiences of the group may also be discussed under the above three categories as they apply. For example, the art may have implications for the theoretical, practical, or sociological aspects of the group; the practical aspect may be used to evoke a special experience.

Writing a religious visit paper should be an interesting adventure. Best wishes!

III. INTERNET RESEARCH GUIDE

One method for doing research is to use resources on the Internet. Although the Internet should not be a substitute for a trip to the library, it can be a valuable additional tool for locating sources for your term paper. Here are a few suggestions for doing research online.

Search Engines

One way to begin working in a new field you haven't worked in before is to use a search engine. Many people prefer Google (www.google.com), but there are several other search engines that may be helpful, particularly those that search the databases of several search engines. These are the so-called metasearch engines, and they include Ixquick (www.ixquick.com) and Mamma (www.mamma.com). Using search engines effectively requires the development of some skill in choosing search terms. However, once you develop the knack for it, search engines can be very helpful, although evaluating the sources you find this way can be tricky. (See below on the process of evaluating sources.) Subject directories such as Yahoo! (www.yahoo.com) categorize various   resources on the Internet by subject. These can also be helpful tools in your research.

Evaluating Sources

The Internet can be a wonderful source of information, but you will need to be careful about the Internet sources you choose to use for your term paper. Some Internet sources are "authoritative" and are therefore appropriate. Others are sites that primarily involve opinions that may be uninformed or very biased or are sites whose main focus is commercial. Being careful to discern the difference will be very important. In general, you should rely on material written by experts in the field—for example, those associated with universities or with institutes or centers associated with universities.

Still, keep in mind that sometimes nonauthoritative websites can provide good links to other websites that do provide authoritative materials; however, use of specialized directories and databases are more likely to be helpful in screening for authoritative sources (see below for these).

Finding appropriate sources in hard copy can also be challenging at times. Scholarly journals and books published by university presses or professional associations are generally authoritative sources and good places to locate material written by other authoritative sources, although these are not the only places.

Specialized Directories and Databases

Specialized directories and databases provide sources that are not readily available, or in some cases not available, through search engines. So you have to know how to find them. A good place to start is to ask your library's research librarian for current Internet database lists for which your library has special access. Another place to find databases is going to a website that lists them. You can also try using a search engine by combining "database" with a search term that best represents the subject of your search.

A few websites that we have found helpful are the following:

Religion in America—The Pluralism Project http://www.pluralism.org
Religion-Online http://www.religion-online.org
Religious Worlds http://www.religiousworlds.com
Virtual Religion Index http://virtualreligion.net/vri/
Wabash Center Internet Guide http://www.wabashcenter.wabash.edu/resources/guide_headings.aspx

Your Research Librarian

At the beginning of this section, we suggested that the Internet was not a substitute for a trip to the library. One good reason for that suggestion is that the research librarian in your library is probably your most valuable resource for information on how to search the Internet for sources, as well as for locating other research tools in the library. Don't be too shy to ask questions!

GLOSSARY

Aborigine/Aboriginal People Usually refers to the original peoples of Australia, but can also refer more generically to what are believed to be original peoples of any land, sometimes also referred to as "first peoples."

Abrahamic religions Collective term for the three religions that honor the founding role of Abraham: Judaism, Christianity, and Islam.

Adept Highly skilled practitioner of religious techniques.

Advaita Vedanta Philosophy emphasizing nondualism; teaches that all is really Brahman; what appears as other than Brahman is *maya* or Brahman's appearance in forms not absolute in themselves.

Aggadah The part of the Talmud devoted to folklore.

Ahimsa Literally, harmlessness. Ancient yoga, Buddhist, and Jain term. A main principle standing behind the nonviolent resistance movement of Mohandas Gandhi, who led the movement for Indian independence, and, following Gandhi's example, Dr. Martin Luther King Jr., who led the civil rights movement in the United States during the tumultuous 1960s.

Ahriman (Angra Mainya) In Zoroastrianism, the evil spirit, also called "the Lie," who opposes Ahura Mazda, the High God, who is righteous.

Ahura Mazda In Zoroastrianism, the High God, who is righteous and who combats Ahriman, the evil spirit, in a universal battle—a battle between Truth and the Lie.

Allah "The God." The Muslim title for the one sovereign God.

Altar of Heaven A huge tiered mountain in Beijing (Peking) where the emperor of China would worship Heaven at the Winter Solstice.

Amida Buddha *See* **Amitabha Buddha**.

Amitabha Buddha The Buddha of Pure Land Buddhism; the Buddha of the Western Paradise. It is said that countless ages ago, he was an aspirant who vowed (the "Original Vow") that when he attained full and perfect enlightenment, out of compassion he would bring all who called upon his name into his Buddha paradise. Emiduo in Chinese and Amida in Japanese.

Anatman No self or no ego. The Buddhist teaching that there is no separate individual human self; humans are instead an impermanent collection of parts, the five skandhas (form, sense, perception, karmic impulses, consciousness).

Ancestral spirits The souls of ancestors, believed by many peoples to continue to take an active interest in their communities and capable of great harm if displeased.

Ancestrism The veneration of ancestors as semideified figures to whom offerings and worship are presented.

Androcentric/Androcentrism Man-centered/man-centeredness, as opposed to human-centered/human-centeredness, which includes women.

Anglicanism The post-Reformation term for the Church of England and its daughter churches throughout the world, such as the Episcopal Church in the United States; it retains both Catholic and Protestant features.

Animism Belief that everything in nature has a soul or spirit and that therefore all of existence involves the widespread presence of spirit beings, both of the departed and of animated natural objects.

Apostle From the Greek for "a person sent forth," one of the original disciples of Jesus, and, in addition, Paul, who began missionary work subsequent to the life of Jesus on Earth.

Aquinas, Thomas (c. 1225–1274) Dominican monk and greatest Western religious philosopher of the Middle Ages in the scholastic tradition of the Catholic Church; influenced by Aristotelian philosophy.

Arhant One who has obtained complete enlightenment without having become a savior of others as a *bodhisattva* or a Buddha; the term is especially characteristic of Theravada Buddhism.

Aristotle (384–322 B.C.E.) Greek philosopher and scientist who emphasized the use of logic in understanding God, the universe, and human ethics. Greatly influenced Christian theology through Thomas Aquinas, as well as Islamic thought through the Mu'tazila movement.

Arminianism belief that one has free will to decide for or against faith in Christ, in contrast to a strict Calvinist view of divine election and predestination.

Ascetic/Asceticism One who denies oneself the pleasures of the world; in religion, in order to prepare oneself for receiving enlightenment, God's will, God's love. Asceticism is the institutionalization of ascetic practice.

Ash'arism The immensely influential school of Muslim theology that emphasizes that the ways of God are beyond human understanding; human knowledge of God, it says, can only be based on revelation.

Ashkenazi Jews from northern and eastern Europe. Originally, "Ashkenazi" referred to Jews of Germany and France. However, in 1182 the Jews were expelled from France. Many moved to Spain and Poland, as well as Germany. Their special language, Yiddish, developed primarily in Germany and Poland, and their religious practices were also influenced by the cultures of those countries. While Ashkenazi Jewry is generally considered of German descent, the real center became Poland, but it eventually spread throughout Europe. Most Jews in the United States are Ashkenazi.

Ashrama   In Hinduism, a stage of life, or a retreat, under the guidance of a guru.

Atman   The soul or essence of one's self said to be actually nothing other than Brahman.

Augustine, Saint   (354–430). Early Christian convert, bishop, and theologian noted for his autobiographical *Confessions*, his book *The City of God* on the ideal society, and many theological writings, especially those on the Trinity, grace, and predestination. His concept of the church influenced Catholic thought and the Protestant reformers Luther and Calvin on grace and predestination.

Avatars   Animal or human forms taken by a God on Earth; an incarnation of a God, like Rama or Krishna.

Axial Age   Term originally coined by historian Karl Jaspers but used differently by others following him, which denotes a period of many parallels among the civilizations of the world, especially in religion, during the period centering on the fifth century B.C.E, but which could be expanded to extend from 900 B.C.E. until approximately 600 C.E.

Ayatollah   In Shi'ite Islam, a legal and religious teacher regarded as possessing very great learning and righteousness who can make independent religious judgments. A twentieth-century term meaning "Sign of God."

Bahá'í   A religion that centers on the unity of all peoples and the oneness of God and all religions. It was founded by Bahá'u'lláh, who is considered by followers to be the latest among messengers (e.g., Moses, Buddha, Jesus, and Muhammad) to bring a message from the Divine Source for his time.

Bardo   The dharmakaya and the heavenly or transcendent-but-with-wondrous-forms expression of the Buddha-nature in Tibetan Buddhism.

Bar Mitzvah   In Judaism, the rite of passage for a young man when he is able to read the Hebrew scriptures in the synagogue or the temple, thereby undertaking the obligation of the Law.

Bat (or **Bas**) **Mitzvah**   In Reform and Conservative Judaism, the rite of passage for a young woman equivalent to the Bar Mitzvah for young boys.

Bhagavad-Gita   Classic Hindu quasi-scriptural text emphasizing karma-yoga and bhakti.

Bhakti   Hindu spiritual path based on love for one's chosen deity.

Bhakti-yoga   "Devotion yoga"; the Hindu practice of seeking liberation and union with the divine through loving, often ecstatic devotion to one of the personified deities. Presented in the Bhagavad-Gita and other texts.

Bodhidharma   The half-legendary sage from India who brought Zen or Chan Buddhism from India to China.

Bodhisattva   "Enlightenment being." In Mahayana, where there may be numerous *bodhisattvas*, a being on the path to enlightenment who has taken a vow to help all other beings and who works through wisdom and compassion for them in the world. In Theravada, the one entity preparing to become the next Buddha.

Boxer Rebellion   The "Boxers" was the name given by foreigners to members of a secret society in China known as the Fists of Righteous Harmony, practitioners of martial arts. They were recruited by the Empress Dowager Tsu Hsi to rid China of foreigners and foreign influences, which had forced the Chinese government to make humiliating concessions in furtherance of foreign trade. In 1900, this resulted in a rebellion during which foreign diplomats and their families were placed under siege by the Boxers and repeatedly attacked for two months. The foreign diplomats and their families were rescued by an international army. It subdued the Boxers and the Chinese imperial forces, weakening the power of the Ching Dynasty.

Brahman   the universal being; God, understood to be not so much personal as the source and essence of all existence.

Brahmin   The priestly caste in Hinduism.

Buddha   An enlightened or awakened one.

Caliph   Leader of Islam regarded as successor of Muhammad in his capacity as temporal (political, this-worldly) ruler of the faithful.

Calvinism   The Reformation teaching and practice of John Calvin, who emphasized God's sovereignty in calling whom he will to salvation—a concept often called divine predestination.

Canon   (of Scripture) The proper selection and order of books to make up a scriptural authority; in the case of Christianity, the books of the Old and New Testaments.

Canonization   In the Roman Catholic Church, the procedure by which the pope officially recognizes a person as a saint.

Cao Dai   A spiritualistic and syncretistic new religious movement in Vietnam.

Caste   social group traditionally believed to be an expression of dharma and based on relative purity; caste may determine with whom one may eat, and one's residence, marriage, and occupation.

Catacombs   Underground cemeteries, such as the early Christian catacombs of Rome.

Chador   A covering from head to toe worn by some Muslim women. The practice of wearing the chador is called "veiling." The *burqa* is a more severe version.

Chakras   In some yogic teaching, centers of spiritual power along the spinal column, which can be opened by raising the kundalini.

Chan School of Chinese Buddhism, influenced by Taoism, emphasizing meditation, interaction of master and disciple, and nature; Zen in Japan.

Chi or **Qi** Chinese word for the inner biological/spiritual energy of nature, including that found in human beings, which is invoked in martial arts and is manipulated in acupuncture. Ki in Japanese.

Ch'ondogyo An important new religious movement in Korea that has advocated worship of the God of Heaven, a combination of features of all major Korean spiritual traditions, and of social reform.

Civil religion A term used to encompass the symbols, ideas and myths, and ritual-like practices of a society that legitimize social and political institutions. In a society in the United States, this may include religious and secular elements.

Conditioned reality Reality as we ordinarily experience it, limited and constrained by space, time, and the patterns of thought and feeling that shape our response to it.

Confucius (Kong Fuzi in Chinese) One of the most influential men in Chinese history and philosophy. He emphasized a good social order based on hierarchy, mutuality, and ritual.

Conservative Judaism School of Judaism teaching that the principles of the law are important but that their practice may be modified to meet contemporary conditions.

Cosmic religion Religion centered on nature—the turn of the seasons and sacred places such as holy trees and mountains, all of which are understood as being in the natural order of all things.

Council of Chalcedon In 451 C.E., the fourth ecumenical council of the Roman Catholic and Eastern Orthodox churches, which taught that Jesus had two natures, divine and human, coexisting in one person and one substance in Christ.

Council of Ephesus In 431 C.E., the third ecumenical council of the Roman Catholic and Eastern Orthodox churches, which affirmed that Jesus was both divine and human from conception and birth. Hence, Mary, his mother, could be called *Theotokos*, "Bearer of God" or "Mother of God."

Council of Nicaea In 325 C.E., the first ecumenical council of the Roman Catholic and Eastern Orthodox churches, called by Emperor Constantine, to settle the exact nature of Jesus' relation to God; the result was the line in the Nicene Creed, which sets out the standard doctrine that Jesus Christ is of one substance with the Father.

Council of Trent 1545–1563, a Roman Catholic council held to address issues raised by Protestantism and to institute reform in the church.

Crucifixion The common method for executing lower-class rebels and criminals in Rome; involved nailing the condemned's hands and feet to a structure made of two crossed beams set upright in the ground, thereby leaving the condemned to die a slow, agonizing death.

Cult A term used by sociologists to denote a nontraditional minority religion characteristically centered on a charismatic leader. The term has been used negatively by the news media and others to designate a group perceived as making high demands on its members and controlling their lives in ways potentially dangerous to themselves and to society.

Cultus A particular form of worship or devotion.

Curia The "Roman Curia" consists of the officials who assist the pope in governing the Roman Catholic Church; they come from a consortium of departments and institutes, including the Secretariat of State, congregations, tribunals, pontifical councils, and other offices.

Daijosai In Japan, the harvest festival as celebrated by the emperor after his accession to the throne.

Dao (Tao) Way, Existence, Nature, or God; the Chinese term for infinite Reality.

Dao De Jing (Tao Te Ching) The book, purportedly written by Laozi, the legendary founder of Daoism. "Dao De Jing" means something like "The Book of the Dao and How to Apply Its Strength."

Daoist Popes Hereditary leaders of religious Daoism noted for their blessing of widely distributed amulets. Formerly located on Dragon and Tiger Mountain in central China, they are now headquartered in Taiwan.

Dengyo Daishi Originally Saicho (762–822), he brought the teachings of the Tiantai school of Buddhism in China to Japan, which became Tendai Buddhism there, holding that the Lotus Sutra is the culminating expression of the Buddha's teachings.

Denomination In Protestant Christianity, a church organization composed of a number of local churches, having a distinctive and autonomous structure and probably some distinctive doctrines and forms of worship, while recognizing itself as only a part of the larger church of Christ on Earth, for example, the Methodist, Baptist, or Presbyterian churches.

Dervish Literally, "doorway." The "whirling dervishes" (the Mevlevi Order) were founded by Jelaluddin Mevlana Rumi, who was a mystic and a poet. Wearing long white robes with wide skirts, the dervishes do a whirling dance, which is believed to bridge the material and spiritual worlds.

Deus otiosus "Resting god"; term used for a creator god who, after making the world, withdraws from it, leaving day-to-day affairs in the hands of secondary Gods and spirits.

Devotionalism Emphasis on deeply felt prayer and meditation, that is, devoting oneself to the divine, usually pictured in some concrete form such as a deity or savior.

Dharma In Hinduism, the social order, which works for righteousness in accordance with *rita*, the cosmic order, and to which the righteous adhere; also one's own duty. In Buddhism, the Buddha's teachings, which are related to the cosmic order.

Dharmakaya The expression of the Buddha-nature as the essence of the universe. Called "the Clear Light of the Void" in The Tibetan Book of the Dead.

Diaspora Literally, "dispersion." Refers to many widely dispersed communities of a people. In Judaism, specifically, it refers to the Jewish people who have been dispersed throughout the world because of persecution; however, the term is also applied to others with similar fates, for example, the Tibetan Buddhists, whose leader, the Dalai Lama, has met with Jewish leaders to discuss ways to continue religious and cultural identity in "diaspora."

Doctrine A statement expressing basic beliefs of a religion in propositional form.

Dong Zhongshu A very influential Chinese thinker (c. 179–104 B.C.E.) instrumental in creating what may be called the Han Synthesis, which combined aspects of Daoism and Confucianism.

Dynasty A family of rulers in succession.

Eastern Orthodoxy A family of ancient Christian churches centered in Eastern Europe and the Middle East, divided into autonomous national bodies, that is, Greek Orthodox, Russian Orthodox, and so on. Descended from the church of the Byzantine Empire, they are characterized by ornate ritual, rich spirituality, and doctrinal conservatism.

Ecstasy In religion, a state of powerful rapture, trance, or alteration of consciousness believed to open one to spiritual experience, inspiration, or possession.

Ecumenical Movement The modern movement for mutual understanding among the branches of Christianity, striving for increasing cooperation among them, with the hope of eventual Christian reunification.

Edict of Milan The edict of Constantine in 313 C.E., which declared that it was no longer legal to persecute Christians.

Eightfold Path Right understanding, thought, speech, action, livelihood, effort, mindfulness, and concentration or *samadhi*—the fundamental ideals of Buddhist life and practice as taught by the Buddha.

Epistles Formal letters; a term generally used for letters by apostles included in the New Testament of the Bible.

Eschatology/Eschatological Doctrines concerning the "last things": death, heaven, hell, judgment, resurrection of the dead, the end of the present world.

Eucharist The sacred communal meal representing the Last Supper, which remains the principal act of worship of Roman Catholic, Eastern Orthodox, and some Protestant churches. *See* **Holy Communion**.

Evangelical Term widely used to refer to those forms of Protestantism that emphasize the supreme authority of Scripture and salvation by faith—sometimes expressed by a powerful conversion experience—in the atonement of Jesus; also, sometimes connotes "evangelizing," that is, spreading the "good news" of the Gospels to others.

Exodus The journey of the Israelites under Moses out of Egypt to the Promised Land.

Fana Sufi term for mystical absorption in the divine.

Feng liu In Daoism, "wind and stream"; a metaphor for spontaneity, acting according to the movement of what is happening day by day.

Feng-shui An elaborate art that involves determining the Yin–Yang "bearings" of locations for houses, businesses, tombs, and temples, as well as the arrangements of rooms and the objects within them.

Filial piety Important aspect of Confucian society. It refers to the obligation of children to negate their own feelings and individuality in deference to the wishes and pleasure of their parents.

Five Pillars of Islam The confession of faith, prayer five times a day, giving of alms to the poor, fasting in the month of Ramadan, and participating in the *hajj* (the pilgrimage to Mecca).

Five relationships (The) In Confucianism, society is believed to be based on these five relationships: (1) ruler and subject, (2) father and son, (3) husband and wife, (4) elder and younger brother, and (5) friend and friend.

Four Noble Truths The truth of suffering; the truth of attachment as the cause of suffering; the truth of the end of attachment; and the Eightfold Path as the way to end it—the basic Buddhist teaching as presented by the Buddha in his first sermon.

Friday Mosque A mosque large enough to hold the entire population of a community, designated as the place for its Friday noon service.

Gemara The part of the Talmud that is a collection of rabbinical commentaries (c. 200–500 C.E.) on the Mishna in order to connect it to the written Torah.

General Council A meeting of bishops recognized as authoritative by the Eastern Orthodox and Roman Catholic churches; the former accepts only the first seven General Councils, the latter a longer list, including the Second Vatican Council. *See*, for example, **Councils of Chalcedon**, **Trent**, **Ephesus**, and **Nicaea**, and the **Second Vatican Council**.

Gentiles The name given by Jews to people who are not Jews. Saint Paul saw himself as the apostle to the Gentiles.

Gnostic, Gnosticism Ancient spiritual movement that took many forms, largely Christian, emphasizing that the human soul is divine but that it is entrapped in the material world, which was created by a lower God; the soul can be liberated through mystical knowledge (*gnosis*) imparted through Christ.

Gohei   In Shinto, zigzag paper streamers (sometimes made of hemp) that are waved over a person's head for purification.

Grace   Strengthening and saving power, above all the power to believe or have faith, freely given by God or a transcendent source, a concept especially important in Christianity, Islam, Bhakti Hinduism, and Pure Land Buddhism. Special emphasis is put on the way grace comes as a free and loving gift quite apart from the recipient's doing anything to deserve it and so is to be received with faith and thanksgiving.

Great Awakening   Christian movement in America occurring from approximately 1720 to 1750 and based on revivals emphasizing conversion and Christian seriousness.

Great Cultural Revolution   Chinese Communist movement from 1966 to 1969, perhaps contrived by the aging Mao Zedong himself, to renew revolutionary fervor at the expense of social stability. His cohorts disrupted education, harried enemies, defaced monuments of the past, and left nearly all religious places ransacked and closed. Such religious life as survived went deep underground.

Guru   In Hinduism, a spiritual teacher or guide; the disciple's relation to the guru is generally considered sacred.

Hadith   Traditions of what the Prophet Muhammad did or said which, in Islamic law and traditional scholarship, are believed divinely inspired and have great authority, together with the Qur'an, in establishing orthodox teaching and practice.

Haiden   The hall of worship in Shinto where the laity pray and sacred dance is offered.

Hajj   The Muslim pilgrimage to Mecca.

Halakhah   The Jewish law, especially as expressed in the Talmud.

Han Dynasty   A period (206 B.C.E.–220 C.E.) in Chinese history, which paralleled the contemporary Roman Empire in cultural sophistication, and during which China became a Confucian state.

Han Synthesis   A way of thinking about Chinese religion and culture that developed during the Han Dynasty that combined aspects of Daoism and Confucianism. The Dao, Yin–Yang, and cosmic cycles and correspondences were central ideas.

Hanifs   Believers in one God who predated Muhammad.

Hanukkah   Minor Jewish holiday. A joyous event commemorating the relighting of the lamps of the holy temple in the year 165 B.C.E, during the campaign of the Maccabee brothers to drive out the oppressor.

Hasidism   Popular Jewish mystical and devotional movement, which began in eighteenth-century Eastern Europe.

Hatha-yoga   The yoga of physical postures.

Heresy   From Greek, meaning "choice"; doctrines or opinions at odds with orthodoxy.

High God   A sovereign deity who created the world or humankind, who may sustain the moral law but who may not be involved in everyday affairs.

High Holy Days   In Judiasm, Rosh Hashana and Yom Kippur.

Hijra   Muhammad's flight from Mecca to Medina in 622 C.E.; the date from which the Muslim calendar begins.

Hoa Hao   A new religious movement in Vietnam with roots in Theravada Buddhism.

Holy Communion   The rite of consecrating and consuming bread and wine in remembrance of Jesus' Last Supper with his disciples before the crucifixion; the principle service of worship in Roman Catholic, Eastern Orthodox, and some Protestant churches; also called the Eucharist (an ancient and sometimes Anglican term, now often used in ecumenical contexts), Divine Liturgy (Eastern Orthodox), Mass (Roman Catholic), and Lord's Supper (Protestant).

Honen   The founder of Amidism in Japan, known as the Jodo-shu or Pure Land sect.

Humanist   In the Renaissance, one who engaged in the recovery of classical learning and values. Today, one who believes in the importance of human values and meeting human needs in this world, as opposed to supernatural, otherworldly values and needs.

Ijtihad   In Islam, the creative original interpretation of the Qur'an, as opposed to strict adherence to traditional interpretations.

Imam   A trained Muslim teacher and preacher; in Shi'a Islam, a supernaturally endowed supreme teacher and leader of Islam who is a hereditary successor of the Prophet.

Incarnation   Becoming flesh. In Christianity, the doctrine that in Jesus Christ, God (i.e., God the Son, the second person of the Trinity) took on flesh and became a human being. In Hinduism, broadly speaking, the avataras or descents of Vishnu or other Hindu gods.

Indigenous Peoples   The peoples who are identified as being, or who identify themselves as being, the original peoples of a particular land, sometimes also referred to as "first peoples" or aborigines.

Indulgences   Certificates issued by the pope, the effect of which is to transfer to the penitent some of the grace or merit attained by Christ and the saints and "stored" by the Catholic Church. The perceived abuse of the issuances of indulgences by the pope was one of the main causes of the Protestant Reformation.

Initiation   A process, often arduous, through which a person passes, usually in a traditional programmatic way, to acquire spiritual power and social status within a community, whether as adult member or as shaman.

Islam "Submission" in Arabic; name of the religion.

Ismailis or **"Seveners"** A minority within Shi'a who differ from the "Twelvers" on the identity of the seventh imam, who, they believe, is the last and hidden one. Ismailism has incorporated many esoteric elements into its beliefs.

Izanagi The male primal parent of the national myth of Japan, which is set out in the Kojiki and Nihonshoki.

Izanami The female primal parent of the national myth of Japan.

Jainism Ancient Indian religion emphasizing the attainment of freedom from karma and material existence, as taught by sage–ascetics.

Jihad In Islam, holy war; also allegorical of the spiritual struggle.

Jñāna-yoga "Knowledge yoga"; the Hindu discipline of seeking spiritual knowledge and liberation through meditation. Presented in the Bhagavad-Gita and other texts.

Jodo Shinshu "True Pure Land" Buddhism, a denomination founded by Shinran (1173–1262), the "Martin Luther of Japan."

Jodo-shu "Pure Land" Buddhism, a denomination founded in Japan by Honen (1133–1212).

Junzi The superior man, who, as the Confucian ideal suggests, is a man at once a scholar, a selfless servant of society, and a gentleman steeped in courtesy and tradition; as an official and family head, he continually puts philosophy into practice.

Ka'bah The cubical temple of Mecca that is the focus of pilgrimage.

Kabala Medieval system of Jewish mystical philosophy.

Kamakura Period and Reformation The Kamakura was a period in Japanese history (1185–1333), during which several new forms of Buddhism emerged (e.g., Pure Land, Nichiren, and Zen), all of which represented a radical Buddhist simplification presenting a single, sure key to salvation. Parallels can be drawn to the Protestant Reformation in Europe.

Kama-sutra A Hindu text, which describes the ways to achieve sensuous and sexual pleasure.

Kami Shinto deities.

Karma Activity; cosmic and personal cause and effect by which one's thoughts and deeds determine what happens to one, whether good or bad, including one's future rebirths. In *moksha*, one transcends *karma*.

Karma-yoga Attaining liberation through selfless work in the world and following one's own *dharma*.

Karuna In Buddhism, the great virtue of compassion.

Ketubah In Judaism, the marriage contract. It is often an elaborately decorated work of art as well.

Kibbutzim Agricultural communes in Israel.

Kingdom of God or **Kingdom of Heaven** The reign or rule of God, where God's will is done and his power is evident. Jesus said this reign or rule is both present and coming through his ministry.

Koan In Chan or Zen, an enigmatic riddle or saying intended to challenge ordinary rational thought and to help one realize one's true nature.

Kobo Daishi Originally Kukai (773–835), he was the founder of Shingon Buddhism and wrote a book in which he attempted to synthesize Daoism, Confucianism, and Buddhism.

Kojiki One of two texts that sets out the national myth of Japan. *See* Nihonshoki.

Kosher In Judaism, keeping "kosher" is adherence to the Hebraic dietary laws.

Krishna One of the principal devotional deities of bhaki in India, regarded either as a form of the supreme God or as an avatar of Vishnu; above all, a God of love worshipped through love, though also the great teacher of the Bhagavad-Gita.

Kuan-yin The "Goddess of Mercy" or "Goddess of Compassion" in Chinese Buddhism. Also known as Guanyin in China, as Kannon in Japan, and as Kwanseum in Korea. Originally, this *bodhisattva* was the male Avalokiteshvara in India.

Kundalini In some yogic teaching, coiled power at the base of the spine that can be raised for spiritual growth.

Laozi (Lao-tzu) The legendary founder of Daoism.

Li Confucian term for rites, propriety, courtesy; it suggests that doing things with correct form has religious and cosmic meaning.

Liberation Theology A theological movement that began in the Latin American Catholic Church; it emphasizes the need of the church to identify with the poor and help them overcome all forms of oppression.

"Little tradition" The name given to beliefs, practices, and social institutions that are outside the major institutional expression of a religion, as in folk religion or popular religion. Although historically women have played only minor roles in the authoritative institutions of the various world religions, they have often played a great role in the "little traditions" that often emerged alongside the official tradition.

Logos Literally, "Word." Divine expression or action; a title for Christ in his universal, divine nature.

Lotus Sutra A sutra of Indian origin extremely influential in Chinese and Japanese Buddhism, especially Tian Tai, Tendai, and Nichiren. It emphasizes simple devotion and the universal grace of the Buddha.

Lutheranism   The Reformation teaching and practice of Martin Luther, who emphasized the sole authority of scripture and "justification by faith," the receiving of God's saving grace through inward faith, as cornerstones of Christianity; the term is used more in America than in Europe.

Magisterium   The teaching jurisdiction of the Roman Catholic Church; it bestows the authority to teach doctrine.

Mahdi   In Islam, a teacher who will come just before the Day of Judgment to restore true religion and righteousness. Not a required belief but widely held.

Magi   Order of priests or seers in ancient Persia and the Hellenistic world.

Mahaprajapati   The Buddha's aunt and foster mother. She asked the Buddha to permit herself and five hundred women to join the Buddha as his followers. When he finally agreed, the order of Buddhist nuns was created.

Mahayana   The "Great Vehicle," Buddhism of the northern tier of Buddhist countries, including China, Tibet, and Japan; it emphasizes the *bodhisattva*, the Buddha-nature in all things, and the use of many methods and paths to enlightenment.

Maitreya   The Buddha of the future who will bring a new paradisal era. *See also* **Miluo**.

Malleus Maleficarum   A book published by two Dominican monks in 1486; it sets out the methods for discovering witches and obtaining confessions from them, usually through horrific tortures.

Mandala   In Buddhism or Hinduism, a meditation diagram showing arrangements of Buddhas and *bodhisattvas* or deities.

Mandarins   The quasi-priesthood of Confucianism; a class of scholar-bureaucrats who administered and educated society. (Also known as the *Ru*.)

Mandate of Heaven   In China, the right of a sovereign to rule as a representative of Heaven.

Manichaeism   An ancient religion founded by the Iranian prophet Mani (216–?274 C.E.), using an elaborate mythology to present an extreme dualism of spirit and matter, respectively good and evil, and the salvation of human souls from out of the prisonhouse of matter. The religion survived under various names well into the Middle Ages in both Europe and Asia.

Mantra   A set of sacred words or syllables chanted or meditated in order to bring spiritual power or to unite one with the deity they represent.

Mao Zedong   (1893–1976) The founder and the first chairman of the People's Republic of China. Because he was early deified by many, historians have likened his leadership and his followers to a religious cult. His charismatic leadership and ideas led to the Cultural Revolution. Also spelled Mao Tse-Tung.

Mappo   In Japanese Buddhism, the last age, when doctrine and morality will deteriorate so much that one can be saved only by faith, if at all; concept of considerable importance during the Kamakura Reformation.

Martyr   From Greek for "witness," one who dies for a faith or cause.

Matsuri   Shinto festival.

Maya   Brahman manifest in the world of forms; illusion when these forms are seen as other than Brahman.

Megalithism   The practice in many late Neolithic cultures around the world of erecting monuments of large upright stones, sometimes oriented toward the seasonal rising of astronomical bodies. They often mark burial and ritual sites, but in some cases their purpose is not fully understood. One of the best-known examples is Stonehenge in England.

Mencius   (372–289 B.C.E.) Next to Confucius himself, the greatest philosopher of Confucianism, who held that human nature is basically good and is impeded only by an evil social environment.

Menorah   In Judaism, the eight-branch candelabra which holds candles that are lit successively during the eight-day Hanuka celebration.

Messiah   The "Anointed One." In Judaism, an expected deliverer and Sublime King who will establish a divine reign of righteousness. In Christianity, Jesus the Christ. The word "Christ" is a direct Greek translation of *Messiah* (which also means "Anointed One").

Middle Way   The Buddha's path, understood as avoiding attachment to all extremes or conditioned, partial realities, conceived of as coming in pairs of opposites.

Mihrab   The niche indicating the direction of Mecca in a mosque.

Miluo   The Buddha of the future, depicted in China as the fat, laughing Buddha surrounded by playing children. *See also* **Maitreya**.

Minaret   The tower beside many mosques from which the muezzin calls out the times of prayer.

Minbar   The seat atop a short flight of steps in a mosque from which the imam delivers sermons.

Ming Dynasty   (368–1644) Chinese dynasty characterized by the perfection of the Confucian civil service examination system and the idealist Neo-Confucian philosophy of Wang Yang-ming (1472–1529).

Mishnah   A compilation of Hebrew stories (c. 200 B.C.E. to 200 C.E.) that fill in the gaps in the oral Torah.

Moksha   Spiritual liberation in Hinduism.

Monasticism   The way of life of the monk or nun, a person who characteristically is celibate (unmarried for religious reasons), has no or few personal possessions, and lives a regulated life of prayer, work, study, and service in a community of such persons. The residence may be called a monastery or convent and is placed under a superior (abbot, prior, father superior, mother superior) to whom the others owe obedience. Distinctive garb is usually worn by monastics.

Monism The philosophy that the universe is one unitary whole.

Monotheism The doctrine that there is only one God.

Mosque Place of Muslim public worship.

Mount Arafat The hill outside Mecca where Muhammad gave his farewell sermon and where the faithful on pilgrimage stand throughout the afternoon.

Muezzin One who calls the faithful to prayer at the proper times from the minaret of the mosque.

Muharram The first month of the Muslim calendar, occasion of the Shi'ite festival which commemorates the death of Husayn, the third Shi'a Imam and the most worthy and tragic of all.

Muslim One who adheres to Islam; of or relating to Islam, as in "Muslim art."

Mu'tazila An early rationalist school of Islamic thought.

Mysticism Experience or teaching about direct inward experience of divine reality.

Myth A story that expresses in narrative form something of the fundamental worldview of a society.

Neo-Confucianism Refers to the Confucian movement and philosophy of the twelfth century and after which stressed its metaphysical aspects.

Neolithic "New Stone Age"; the period of the development of archaic agriculture.

Neo-Platonism/Neo-Platonic doctrine Ancient philosophical movement stemming from the thought of Plotinus (205–270 C.E.), stressing that all reality emanates from the One, which can be known through mystical experience. It profoundly influenced Jewish, Christian, and Islamic mysticism.

Nicene Creed The standard doctrine of Christianity, attributed to the Council of Nicaea and the Council of Constantinople (381), though it did not reach its present form until later.

Nichiren The founder (1222–1282) of Nichiren Buddhism, which focuses on the Lotus Sutra.

Niddah In Judaism, the rules regarding menstruation.

Nihonshoki One of two texts that sets out the national myth of Japan. *See* **Kojiki**.

Nirmanakaya The expression of the Buddha-nature as ordinary, "waking" reality.

Nirvana Unconditioned reality, experienced without form or limit when all attachments have been negated and the fires of craving blown out; the ultimate Buddhist goal.

Numinous Spiritual or supernatural.

On-giri In Japan, the relationship between a benefactor and client, resulting in an obligation.

Ontological From ontology; the philosophical study of being or reality. Also, the reality of a thing or a person, or the universal whole.

Original Sin The Christian doctrine that human beings are inherently sinners because they are descendants of Adam, who failed to obey God. The doctrine was fully developed in the writings of St. Augustine.

Orthodox Correct in doctrine; the name of the ancient Christian churches of the East, which recognize the first seven General Councils

Orthodox Judaism School of Judaism that emphasizes a strict following of the Law as traditionally interpreted.

Pagan Religion/Paganism Originally "pagan" was a Latin term used by Romans to mean country folk. Later the term was used by adherents of the Abrahamic Religions, especially Christians, to refer primarily to all non-Abrahamic religions, including the pre-Christian official religion of the Roman Empire. The term is sometimes used pejoratively to refer to nonmainstream religions, including indigenous religions. In recent decades, the term has been adopted by those in a growing religious movement in the United States and Europe who adhere to a collection of religions based on, derived from, or reconstructed from pre-Christian folk religion roots of Old Europe.

Pagodas Temples in South and East Asia; the term is most commonly used for the several-storied towerlike Buddhist temples characteristic of China, Korea, and Japan.

Paleolithic "Old Stone Age"; the cultural stage of hunting and gathering before the development of agriculture.

Pantheist One who holds that the universe itself is the divine being.

Parables Allegorical stories, which are used to convey an idea. Jesus used parables to make his points.

Passover The spring holiday of Judaism that commemorates the freeing of the Hebrew slaves from Egyptian oppression and the Exodus from Egypt of the Hebrews to the promised land. God "passed over" the dwellings of the Hebrews when he smote the first born of the Egyptians.

Patriarch A title given the bishop of certain ancient and important cities; in particular, the Patriarch of Constantinople (Istanbul); the senior official of the Eastern Orthodox Church.

Patriarchy Literally, the "rule of the fathers." Term used by feminists and others to denote a society in which authority is held by men.

Pentecost In Judaism, the "Feast of Weeks," which celebrates the receipt of the Law by Moses on the fifteenth day after the Exodus from Egypt. In Christianity, the celebration on the seventh Sunday after Easter, commemorating the descent of the Holy Spirit on the apostles; also known as Whitsunday.

Pentecostalism Form of Christianity that emphasizes practices such as "speaking in tongues" as evidence of the presence of the Holy Spirit.

Plato (428–348 B.C.E.) Greek philosopher who taught the ultimate oneness of reality, the existence of a realm of absolute and unchanging ideals and values of which our world is only a reflection, the immortality of the soul, and (in the *Republic*) the outlines of an ideal society. He greatly influenced Jewish, Christian, and Islamic thought.

Pluralism The condition, especially apparent in the modern world, in which many different options for belief and lifestyle exist together in the same society.

Pope The Bishop of Rome who, as successor of St. Peter, is believed by Roman Catholics to be head of the Roman Catholic Church on Earth and the representative of Christ.

Popular Religion "Religion of the people" as opposed to "official" or authoritative religion. *See also* "**little tradition**."

Practical form of religious expression A religion's form of worship, prayer, meditation, pilgrimage, and the like. To find a religion's practical expression, start by asking yourself, "What do its adherents do?"

Prajna Intuitive wisdom in Hinduism and Buddhism.

Prajnaparamita "Wisdom that has gone beyond"; the highest intuitive–enlightenment wisdom in Mahayana; also, the name of a goddess who personifies it.

Predestination The Christian doctrine that all that happens to human beings is due solely to God's will, particularly whether one is predestined to go to heaven or hell.

Presbyters "Elders"; in the Presbyterian Church, ordained ministers or lay leaders.

Prophet In the biblical tradition, one who speaks on behalf of God in the context of a particular historical situation.

Protestantism Christian sects that developed in "protest" to the practices of the medieval Roman Catholic Church during the sixteenth century.

Puranas Books deriving from the early Middle Ages, which set out accounts of the popular deities of the indigenous traditions of India. Many of these gods became the devotional gods of bhakti—for example, Sarasvati, Durga, Kali, Shiva, Vishnu, and Krishna.

Purdah The practice of secluding women by confining them to the home, thus isolating them from society and limiting their education to domestic vocations.

Pure Land Form of Buddhism strong in China and Japan, which emphasizes the believer's entry into paradise (the Pure Land) through faith in the vow of the Buddha Amitabha (Emiduo or Amida) to save all who call upon his name. Called Jodo in Japanese.

Purgatory In Roman Catholic teaching, an after-death state in which sins insufficient to warrant eternal punishment in hell are purged away so that the soul can eventually enter heaven.

Purim The Jewish holiday in February or March that commemorates the story recounted in the Book of Esther: how the Jews were saved from the wicked designs of Haman, chief minister of the Persian king, by Esther the queen and her cousin Mordecai.

Quakers Religious sect, known formally as the "Society of Friends," founded in the 1650s in England by George Fox and others. They were called "Quakers" because they would "quake" when they communed with God inwardly.

Qur'an (sometimes **Koran**) The sacred scriptures of Islam.

Rabbi A Jewish scholar or teacher, particularly the spiritual leader of a congregation.

Ramadan The month of the Islamic calendar during which Muslims fast from sunrise to sundown.

Rasul Muhammad's calling in relation to God; the term means prophet, envoy, messenger, apostle, ambassador, or spokesman.

Reconstructionist Judaism School of Judaism that has its roots in humanism and is most radical in terms of doctrinal reform.

Rectification of names In Confucianism, "becoming what one is." In other words, fulfilling one's proper role (e.g., father, son, wife, mandarin) in society to the fullest, motivated by *ren* (virtue) so that one contributes to the harmonious "dance" of society.

Reform Judaism liberal interpretation of Judaism that emphasizes ethics over following the Jewish Law legalistically.

Reincarnation The religious doctrine of several religions, including Hinduism and Buddhism, that after death human beings are born again in this world or in other worlds as humans or as animals.

Ren Confucian term for virtue; it suggests humanity, love, high principle, and living together in harmony.

Resurrection A rising from the dead.

Rinzai School of Zen Buddhism that developed in Japan during the Kamakura period (1185–1333), which taught that the way to enlightenment occurs through spontaneous insight.

Rita The Vedic term for the cosmic law or order.

Rosary In Roman Catholicism, a string of beads with a crucifix hanging on it, which one uses to count repeated "Hail Marys," or novenas, which are special sets of prayers on successive days. It also refers to the sets of prayers themselves. There are also rosarylike devices in Buddhism, Hinduism, and Islam.

Rosh Hashana In Judaism, the New Year holiday, commemorated by fasting and solemnity.

Ru *See* **Mandarin**.

Sabbath   The seventh day of the week (Saturday) and a Jewish weekly holy day, it is marked by observant Jews with many special practices and by strict abstention from work.

Sacraments   Certain rites believed to convey God's grace directly and to be generally necessary to Christian salvation. Many Protestant churches celebrate baptism and Holy Communion, whether using the term "sacrament" or not, while Roman Catholic, Eastern Orthodox, and Anglican churches acknowledge five additional sacraments: confirmation, marriage, holy orders, penance, and extreme unction ("last rites").

Sadhu   A "holy man" or renunciant who has set aside worldly goals for the sake of the spiritual life.

Saint   In Christianity, a person recognized by a church as possessing exceptional holiness.

Samadhi   The highest state of concentration or meditation, when the mind is one with the divine.

Sambhogakaya   The expression of the Buddha-nature as paradisal heavens ruled by radiant Buddhas and *bodhisattvas*.

Samgha   (sometimes **Sanga**) The Buddhist monastic order.

Samsara   The wheel of rebirth; the world.

Samskaras   Hindu "sacraments" or "rites of passage" performed at definite stages of life, from birth through entry into adulthood.

Sanctification   The "making holy" of a person or an object; in Pentacostalism, the reception of the Holy Spirit.

Sannyasin   A wandering monk who renounces all ties of ordinary life.

Sati (or **Suttee**)   In traditional Hinduism, a practice wherein the wife immolates herself on the funeral pyre of her dead husband.

Second Great Awakening   A movement in Christianity that occurred during the early nineteenth century in America; it was characterized by a feeling-centered approach to religion, powerful conversion experiences, an emphasis on individual conscience, and frontier revivals; it also motivated some individuals toward social action on such issues as women's rights and the abolition of slavery.

Second Vatican Council   An ecumenical council of the Roman Catholic Church, convened by Pope John XXIII and, after his death, presided over by Pope Paul VI. The purpose of the council was to renew the Catholic Church for the modern era by implementing significant developments in liturgy (e.g., authorization of conducting the liturgy in the vernacular rather than only in Latin), in theology (e.g., including an openness to religious freedom), in the role of the bishops, and in the relationship of the Catholic Church to the modern world, to other Christian churches, and to non-Christian religions.

Sect   A term used by sociologists to denote a religious group related to a mainstream religion (e.g., Christianity) but whose adherents believe represent a more intense commitment than the average adherent to the religion to which they are related (e.g., the Amish or the Jehovah's Witnesses in relation to mainstream Christianity).

Sectarian   Characterized by sects; the term may also imply partisanship between sects.

Secular   Worldly, temporal things not generally considered to be sacred or religious.

Secularization   Denotes a shift from the religious orientation of a society, an institution, a person, a symbol, and so on, to a worldly one; the term also often denotes the shift of social institutions from religious authority to civil authority.

Seder   The name for the Passover meal, which includes a ritual conducted each year in the spring by Jewish families, celebrating the Exodus of the Jews from Egypt under Moses' leadership and, therefore, freedom itself.

Separation of church and state   A central concept in the development of U.S. government, which seeks to maintain a separation of civil and religious authority in society. *See also* **State church** for an alternative approach.

Sephardim   Jews from the Iberian peninsula. The word "Sephardim" derives from the word for "Spain" in Hebrew. All Jews who did not convert to Christianity were expelled from Spain in 1492. Sephardic Jewish practices were influenced by their association with Spain, and their special language, Ladino, is a combination of Hebrew and Spanish.

Shakti   Spiritual power, often identified with the various female Hindu deities that correspond to male deities.

Shaman   A person who in many indigenous peoples' societies, through special initiation, has powers of spirit-control, divination, healing, and contacting Gods and spirits, usually exercised through elaborate performances and in a trance.

Shamanism   The experiences and practices of the shaman.

Shari'ah   The body of Muslim Law.

Shavuot   Jewish "first fruits" or harvest festival in late spring or early summer.

Shaykh   A Sufi, or a mystical, Islamic spiritual teacher and guide.

Shekhinah   The spirit of God at the Sabbath, which is feminine.

Shi'a Islam   The "party" of Ali; the minority, some 10 to 15 percent of all Muslims, who traditionally believe that Islam should be headed by a divinely guided Imam who is a hereditary successor of the Prophet through Ali, Muhammad's cousin.

Shingon Buddhism   Esoteric form of Buddhism founded in Japan by Kobo Daishi (773–835), based on Tantric Buddhism and the Great Sun Sutra. Shingon emphasizes realizing one's Buddha nature through the use of mantras, mudras, and meditation.

Shinko shukyo Japanese term for the new Japanese religions; literally, "newly arisen religions."

Shinran Founder (1173–1262) of Jodo Shinshu, True Pure Land Buddhism, in Japan.

Shin-shin-shukyo Japanese term for new Japanese religions founded since the 1950s.

Shinto "Way of the Gods"; the indigenous polytheistic religion of Japan.

Shirk Idolatry, putting anything else in the place of God; the ultimate and unforgivable sin in Islam.

Shiva Hindu God considered a personification of the Absolute.

Shogun In Japan, a hereditary military ruler, ostensibly under the authority of the emperor, but who held nearly complete control over the nation until 1867, when the rule of the Shoguns ended.

Sikhism Indian religion emphasizing monotheism and equality; its worship centers on its sacred scripture, the Holy Granth.

Sinicize To make something Chinese.

Skandhas Basic constituents of reality in Buddhist thought; five of them—form, sense, perception, reactions, and consciousness—make up a human being.

Social gospel A movement that strove to correlate religion to new ideas in science and society and to recover the old dream of making America into a new "people of God" through social reform.

Sociological form of religious expression A religion's forms of group life, leadership, relation to outside society, governance, and interpersonal relations. To find a religion's sociological expression, start by asking yourself, "How do the people involved in the religion relate to each other?" and "How are they organized?"

Soka Gakkai A new Japanese religion in the Nichiren tradition, which was very prominent in the mid-twentieth century and remains an international religious movement.

Song Dynasty (Sung Dynasty) (960–1279) Chinese dynasty characterized spiritually by the resurgence of Confucianism, especially in the work of the great Neo-Confucian philosopher Zhu Xi (1130–1200) and his school. In Buddhism, Chan (Zen) continued to flourish and reached a high point in its artistic expression.

Soto School of Zen Buddhism that developed in Japan during the Kamakura period (1185–1333), which taught that the way to enlightenment occurs through quiet meditation sessions.

Soul The principle of life and consciousness, commonly believed to have a destiny separate from the physical body.

Spiritualism A religious movement that that believes in the continuity of life after death; its practices include contact with the spirits of the departed through mediumship.

State church The officially recognized church of the governing authority of a nation. *See also* **Separation of church and state** for an alternative approach.

Stigmata Marks of the nails on the hands and feet, of the crown of thorns, and of the stab-wounded side of Christ on the cross, which have been experienced by some ardent Christians.

Sufism The mystical tradition in Islam.

Sukkot Jewish autumn festival, originally agricultural, notable for the building of festive outdoor "booths."

Sunna The body of established Islamic faith, morals, and practice, established by the consensus of jurists and the faithful.

Sunni Islam The majority body of Muslims, who stress sunna and consensus.

Sutra A Sanskrit text, especially scriptural texts in Mahayana Buddhism.

Svadharma In Hinduism, one's personal *dharma*; one's place in the "great dance" of the social order.

Synagogue A Jewish congregation and its meeting place, where worship consists of prayer and instruction rather than the sacrificial offerings of the temple.

Synoptic Gospels The first three Gospels of the New Testament. Believed by most scholars to have been written between 65 and 80 C.E. They are called "synoptic" (derived from *synopsis*, which in Greek means "view together") because they are parallel to each other in ways that the Gospel of John, the fourth Gospel, is not.

Tabernacle A moveable shrine in which Yahweh was worshipped by the Hebrews until Solomon built a great temple; it contained the written Torah. Its design and method of construction were given by God to Moses at Mount Sinai.

Taboo A prohibition, as against eating a certain food or going to a certain place or touching certain things (e.g., blood); it is enforced through fear of anger of Gods or spirits if the forbidden act is done.

Talmud A vast, authoritative commentary on the Hebraic Law, including aggadah and halakhah, composed by rabbis and completed about the sixth century C.E. Next to the Torah, it is the most important book in Judaism.

Tang Dynasty (618–907) Chinese dynasty that represented the "golden age" of Buddhist activity in China until the persecution of Buddhist temples and monasteries by the Tang court in 845. Daoism also flourished in this era, and Confucianism was enhanced by the development of the civil service system, which was based on examinations in the Confucian classics.

Tantrism Spiritual path emphasizing initiation, esoteric rituals, and sexual symbolism.

Tathagata "One who has gone thus" or "come thus"—a title of the Buddha emphasizing his passing from worldly existence into Nirvana.

Tendai Buddhism The form of Buddhism founded by Dengyo Daishi (762–822), who held that the Lotus Sutra is the final and culminating expression of the Buddha's teaching. Dengyo Daishi studied Tiantai Buddhism in China and then returned to Japan to establish a great monastery on Mount Hiei, which became a most significant influence on the spiritual history of Japan.

Tenrikyo (Religion of Heavenly Wisdom) One of the modern new religions of Japan; monotheistic.

Theocracy A government established and maintained in accordance with religious authority.

Theoretical form of religious expression A religion's stories, concepts, ideas, doctrines. To find a religion's theoretical expression, start by asking yourself, "What do its adherents say?"

Theragatha "Psalms of the Male Elders"; early Buddhist text.

Theravada The "Way of the Elders." The school of Buddhism emphasizing the historical Buddha and a conservative adherence to his teachings as Theravadins understand them; the school is predominant in the Buddhist countries of South Asia and Southeast Asia.

Therigatha "Psalms of the Female Elders" or "Psalms of the Sisters": early Buddhist text. This is a collection of beautiful accounts of the enlightenment of over seventy women elders who are believed to have been among the first nuns of Buddhism.

Three Refuges or **Three Jewels** The Buddha as the ideal teacher; the *Dharma* as his teaching or "gospel," and the *Samgha*, or order of monks, as the ideal community—three ideals that a person affirms on formally becoming a Buddhist or a Buddhist monk or nun.

Tian Chinese word usually translated as "heaven" but also means the supreme ruler or moderator of the universe who gives rain, victory, fortune or misfortune and who regulates the moral order.

Tibetan Book of the Dead The book that is Tibet's most famous contribution to the world's religious thought. It sets out an account of the experiences of a deceased person after death. Properly known as the Bardo Thodol or "Book of the In-Between."

Torah In traditional Judaism, the most important part of the Hebrew Scriptures, consisting of the first five books and containing the Hebraic Law.

Torii The gently curved archway that leads into the precincts of a Shinto shrine.

Totem An animal or plant believed to have a special spiritual relation to a particular tribe or subgroup.

Trikaya The three "bodies" or forms of expression of the Buddha-nature.

Tripitaka The oldest Buddhist scriptures; written in the Pali language, they are the only ones considered authoritative by Theravada Buddhism.

Trinity The Christian doctrine that there are three "persons"—the Father, the Son (Christ), and the Holy Spirit—in the one God.

Twelvers (Ashariyah) The majority of Shi'ites, who accept the first twelve of the Imams in the line of Ali, believing that the twelfth has gone into hiding to return as the Mahdi, or messianic savior, who will establish a paradisal reign on Earth just before the end of the world and the judgment.

Ulama Collective term for Muslim religious scholars and teachers who, by consensus, establish correct teaching.

Unconditioned reality The opposite of conditioned reality; reality in its absolute nature equally present in all times and places and not limited in any way.

Unification Church A group founded by the Rev. Sun Myung Moon (1920–2012), which combines Christian, shamanistic, and messianic features. Its adherents are often referred to pejoratively as "Moonies."

Upanishads The last and most philosophical of the Vedas, centering on the message that Atman is Brahman and that one's true self is the universal Divine Reality.

Vajrayana "Diamond" or "Thunderbolt" vehicle. The esoteric, or Tantric, school of Buddhism emphasizing initiation, mantras, visualizing, and a special elaborate set of symbols and pictures.

Varnas Major groupings of castes in Hinduism; literally, "colors." The four main varnas are (1) *Brahmins*, or priests; (2) *kshatriyas*, or rulers and warriors; (3) *vaishyas*, or craftsmen and merchants; and (4) *shudras*, or farmers and peasants. *Harijans*, or untouchables, are not one of the varnas, because they are outcasts.

Vedanta A tradition of Hindu philosophy that has generally been the most prestigious in India and is best known outside of that country by this name.

Vedas The ancient Hindu scriptures in Sanskrit composed of the Rig Veda, the Brahmanas, the Aranyakas, and the Upanishads. The first three parts are concerned mainly with the words, the rituals, and the meaning of the sacrificial rites of the Brahmin priests. *See* **Upanishads**.

Vihara A center of Buddhist practice and teaching.

Vipassana Theravada method of meditation that aims at analyzing one's experience until one realizes that conditioned reality is impermanent, is unsatisfactory, and has no "self."

Vishnu One of the major devotional gods of bhakti. Vishnu is God as the force on behalf of order and righteousness. He descends from the highest heaven in incarnate form whenever righteousness declines, working to restore good in the world. Krishna is an incarnate form of Vishnu.

Wang Yangming A leading Neo-Confucianist (1472–1529) who taught that the principle of the myriad separate things is actually within the mind itself and that therefore the supreme requisite is sincerity of mind. Also known as Wang Shouren.

Word, or **Word of God** (1) Jesus Christ as manifestation of God; (2) the Scripture understood as directly revealed by God. (An emphasis on the "Word" aspect of Christianity usually entails an emphasis on Scripture, preaching, and a relation of inward faith to Jesus Christ.)

Wu-wei In Daoism, nonbeing or not doing; the spontaneous flow of the endless stream of flux and change. A person who practiced "not doing" in the sense of letting the Dao act through him or her would be a sage in harmony with the Dao.

Xunzi A great Confucian philosopher (fl. 298–238 B.C.E.), who said that man is basically evil in the sense of being self-centered and that therefore man needs education and social control to become good.

Yang and Yin *See* **Yin**.

Yantra In Tantric Hinduism and Buddhism, a diagram consisting of lines, with no depictions of deities, Buddhas, or *bodisattvas*. It is used in meditation.

Yin and Yang From China, the interacting cosmic principles, respectively feminine and masculine, and ultimately included in the Dao.

Yoga A spiritual path designed to unite one with God or one's true self; in a more restrictive sense, spiritual exercises involving postures, breathing, and meditation.

Yom Kippur In Judaism, the Day of Atonement, which occurs ten days after Rosh Hashana and which is commemorated by fasting and prayer.

Zen *See* **Chan**.

Zend Avesta The scriptures of Zoroastrianism. Although it contains the Gathas (hymns ascribed to Zoroaster himself), it also contains much material of a later and more priestly character.

Zhu Xi A Neo-Confucianist leader (1130–1200) who taught that the one great ultimate is manifested in the principles of the myriad separate things. Also known as Chu Hsi.

Zhuangzi The first great Daoist writer (died c. 300 B.C.E.) after Laozi's vision. Also known as Chuang-tzu.

Zionism The movement to establish a Jewish homeland in the area of the Middle East called Palestine in ancient times and by the British.

ENDNOTES

Chapter 1

1. Joachim Wach, *Sociology of Religion* (Chicago: University of Chicago Press, 1944).
2. Baldwin Spencer and F.J. Gillen, *The Native Tribes of Central Australia* (London: Macmillan, 1938), 388–391. See also Bruce Chatwin, *The Songlines* (New York: Viking, 1987).
3. Susan Sered, *Women of the Sacred Groves: Divine Priestesses of Okinawa* (New York: Oxford University Press, 1999), 145.
4. Robert Ellwood, *Mysticism and Religion* (New York and London: Oxford University Press, 1958).
5. Rudolf Otto, *The Idea of the Holy* (New York and London: Oxford University Press, 1958).
6. Roger Bannister, *First Four Minutes* (London: Lyons & Burford, 1955), 11–12.
7. A book on ethics in the world religions, which combines description and critique, is Denise Lardner Carmody and John Tully Carmody, *How to Live Well: Ethics in the World Religions* (Belmont, CA: Wadsworth Publishing, 1988).
8. See David Lewis-Williams, *The Mind in the Cave* (London: Thames and Hudson, 2002).
9. For further reflections on the Axial Age and the development of the major religions, see Robert Ellwood, *Cycles of Faith* (Walnut Creek, CA: AltaMira Press, 2003).
10. See Karen Armstrong, *The Great Transformation: The Beginning of Our Religious Traditions* (New York: Knopf, 2006).
11. Wilfred Cantwell Smith, *The Meaning and End of Religion* (Minneapolis: Augsburg Fortress Press, 1991, org. 1963).

Chapter 2

1. International Work Group for Indigenous Affairs, http://www.iwgia.org/regions, retrieved January 19, 2013.
2. Ruth Murray Underhill, *Red Man's Religion* (Chicago: University of Chicago Press, 1965), 79.
3. See *Cosmos and History* (New York: Harper & Row, 1959); and *The Sacred and the Profane* (New York: Harper & Row, 1961).
4. "Internal Conversion in Contemporary Bali," mimeographed, 1961, 3. Cited in Robert N. Bellah, *Religion and Progress in Modern Asia* (New York: The Free Press, 1965), 176.
5. James G. Frazer, *The Belief in Immortality* (London: Macmillan, 1913), 1: 72–73, quoting A. J. Kruijt.
6. Leo Frobenius and Douglas C. Fox, *African Genesis* (New York: Stackpole, 1937), 215–220. Presented also in Joseph Campbell, *The Hero with a Thousand Faces* (Princeton: Princeton University Press, Bollengen Series, 2nd ed. 1968), 303–307.
7. James L. Brain, "Ancestors as Elders in Africa-Further Thoughts," *Africa,* 43, no. 2 (April 1973): 130.
8. This narrative follows a personal account of the Vision Quest in Peter Nabakov, *Two Leggings: The Making of a Crow Warrior* (New York: Thomas Y. Crowell, 1967), 55–58. (Nabakov's account was based on a field manuscript prepared by William Wildschut.) See also Robert H. Lowie, *The Crow Indians* (New York: Rinehart, 1956).
9. Frazer, *Immortality*, 250–254.
10. Rita M. Gross, "Tribal Religions: Aboriginal Australia," in Arvind Sharma, ed. *Women in World Religions* (Albany, NY: SUNY Press, 1987), 43, citing Catherine H. Berndt, "Women and the 'Secret Life,'" in R. B. and C. H. Berndt, eds. *Aboriginal Man in Australia* (Sydney: Agnus and Robertson, 1964), 154. The other information on Aboriginal women for this segment was obtained from Rita Gross's article as well.
11. Mircea Eliade, *Shamanism: Archaic Techniques of Ecstasy*, trans. Willard R. Trask, Bollingen Series 64 (New York: Bollingen Foundation, 1964), 190–197. © 1964 by Princeton University Press. Reprinted by permission of Princeton University Press.
12. Peter Freuchen, *Book of the Eskimos* (New York: Fawcett World Library, 1965), 168–171.
13. See, for example, Peter T. Furst, ed., *Flesh of the Gods: The Ritual Use of Hallucinogens* (New York: Praeger, 1972); Michael J. Harner, ed., *Hallucinogens and Shamanism* (London and New York: Oxford University Press, 1973); and Barbara G. Myerhoff, *Peyote Hunt: The Sacred Journey of the Huichol Indians* (Ithaca, NY: Cornell University Press, 1974).
14. Mircea Eliade, *Shamanism: Archaic Techniques of Ecstasy*, 60–61.
15. See Eliade, *Shamanism*; and Andreas Lommel, *Shamanism: The Beginning of Art* (New York: McGraw-Hill, 1967), 11–12.
16. Franz Boas, *The Religion of the Kwakiutl*, Columbia University Contributions to Anthropology, 10, part 2 (New York: 1930), 1–11. Summarized in Claude Lévi-Strauss, *Structural Anthropology* (Garden City, NY: Doubleday, 1967), 169–173.
17. Ichiro Hori, *Folk Religion in Japan* (Chicago: University of Chicago Press, 1968), 203–206.
18. For further anthropological discussion of the American Halloween, see Victor W. Turner, *The Ritual Process* (Chicago: Aldine, 1969), 172–174.
19. Frank G. Speck, *Naskapi* (Norman: University of Oklahoma Press, 1935), 83–94.
20. See John Batchelor, *The Ainu and Their Folk-Lore* (London: Religious Tract Society, 1901), 483–495; and

Joseph M. Kitagawa, "Aimu Bear Festival (Iyomante)," *History of Religions*, 1, no. 1 (Summer 1961): 95–151.

21. For a critical assessment of hunting ritual and its relation to hunting reality, see Jonathon Z. Smith, *Imagining Religion* (Chicago: University of Chicago Press, 1982), 57–65.

22. Margaret Ehrenberg, *Women in Prehistory* (London: British Museum Publications, 1989), 50–62.

23. Ibid.

24. James Mooney, "The Ghost-Dance Religion and the Sioux Outbreak of 1890," *Annual Report of the Bureau of American Ethnology*, 14, no. 2 (1896): 721, 724. Cited in Eliade, *The Sacred and the Profane*, 138.

25. Mircea Eliade, *Myth and Reality* (New York: Harper & Row, 1963), 104–105.

26. Michael J. Harner, *The Jivaro: People of the Sacred Waterfall* (Garden City, NY: Doubleday, 1972), 147.

Chapter 3

1. Betty Heimann, *Facets of Indian Thought* (London: George Allen & Unwin, 1964).

2. See Gregory Possehl, *The Indus Civilization: A Contemporary Perspective* (Walnut Creek, CA: Altamira Press, 2002), 247; Dilip Chakrabarti, ed. *Indus Civilization Sites in India, New Discoveries* (New Delhi: Marg Publications, 2004); Jane R. McIntosh, *A Peaceful Realm—The Rise and Fall of the Indus Civilization* (Boulder, CO: Westview Press, 2002), 24; Jonathan Mark Kenoyer, *Ancient Cities of the Indus Civilization* (Karachi: Oxford University Press, 1998), 105–127, 174; Vishal Agarwal, "What is the Aryan Migration Theory," *Journal of Interdisciplinary Studies in History and Archaeology* 2, no. 1 (Summer 2005): 1–46.

3. Most of the European languages, including English, are also from the Indo-European language family, which is why many words in Sanskrit seem to be cognate to English words.

4. See Edwin Bryant, *The Quest for the Origin of the Vedic Culture* (New York: Oxford University Press, 2001).

5. Rigveda 1.164.46.

6. There is a collection of similar words, confusing at first, that are built on this root. Brahma is the creator god in some Indian mythology. Brahman (the neuter form) is used in philosophical writing from the Upanishads on to refer to the impersonal Absolute. The Brahmanas are sacred ritual texts that are a part of the Vedas. Brahmans are the priestly caste, presumably so-called because they possessed mysterious and magical power like that by which the world is sustained. For the sake of clarity, in this book the common spelling Brahmin will be used for the priests.

7. Mircea Eliade, *Yoga: Immortality and Freedom* (New York: Bollingen Foundation, 1958), chapter 3.

8. Swami Prabhavananda and Frederick Manchester, trans., *The Upanishads: Breath of the Eternal* (New York: Mentor Books, 1957), 123–124. Copyright © 1957 by The Vedanta Society of Southern California. Reprinted with permission.

9. Ibid., 18–19.

10. On this period and the following, see Basham, *The Wonder That Was India*.

11. Swami Prabhavananda and Christopher Isherwood, *The Song of God: Bhagavad-Gita* (New York: Mentor Books, 1951), 37. Copyright © 1944, 1951 by The Vedanta Society of Southern California. Reprinted with permission.

12. Ibid., 40–41.

13. Ibid., 79.

14. Ibid., 67.

15. Ibid., 69.

16. Ibid., 91–93.

17. On Shankara and Advaita Vedanta, see Eliot Deutsch, *Advaita Vedanta: A Philosophical Reconstruction* (Honolulu: East-West Center Press, 1969); Eliot Deutsch and J. A. B. van Buitenen, *A Source Book of Advaita Vedanta* (Honolulu: University of Hawaii, 1971); Y. Keshava Menon and Richard F. Allen, *The Pure Principle: An Introduction to the Philosophy of Shankara* (East Lansing: Michigan State University Press, 1960); and Swami Prabhavananda and Christopher Isherwood, *Shankara's Crest-Jewel of Discrimination* (New York: Mentor Books, 1970).

18. See Rai Bahadur, *Siva Samhita*, trans. S. C. Vidyarnava (Allahabad, India: Lalit Mohan Basu, 1942); Eliade, *Yoga*; and A. Bharati, *The Tantric Tradition* (Garden City, NY: Doubleday, 1970).

19. Swami Prabhavananda, *Srimad Bhagavatam: The Wisdom of God* (New York: Capricorn Books, 1968), 199–200. Copyright © The Vedanta Society of Southern California. Reprinted with permission.

20. See Milton Singer, "The Great Tradition of Hinduism in the City of Madras," in Charles Leslie, ed. *Anthropology of Folk Religion* (New York: Vintage Books, 1960). The spirit of Krishna devotion is evident in the "Hare Krishna" movement in America with its fervent bhaktic singing and dancing. This movement derives from a Krishna devotional tradition started by Sri Chaitanya (c. 1486–1533) in Bengal. He and the movement regard Krishna as the supreme, personal God, and not as just an avatar of Vishnu or an expression of an ultimately impersonal Absolute like Advaita Vedanta.

21. See Wendy O'Flaherty, *Asceticism and Eroticism in the Mythology of Siva* (London: Oxford University Press, 1973).

22. See Ernest A. Payne, *The Saktas* (Calcutta: YMCA Press, 1933); and John G. Woodroffe, *Shakti and Shakta* (Madras: Ganesh, 1951). See also David R. Kinsley, *The Sword and the Flute: Kali and Krsna, Dark Visions of the Terrible and the Sublime in Hindu Mythology* (Berkeley: University of California Press, 1975).

23. Rabindranath Tagore, trans., *Songs of Kabir* (New York: Macmillan, 1917), 45–46. Hari is a name for Vishnu. Karim means a Muslim wonder-working saint. Ram is, of course, Rama. A pir is a Muslim Sufi teacher comparable to a Hindu guru.

24. Edward Luce, *In Spite of the Gods: The Rise of Modern India.* (New York: Anchor Books, 2008), 2750–2788 (kindle).

25. Anand Giridharadas, *India Calling: An Intimate Portrait of a Nation's Remaking* (New York: Times Books/Henry Holt & Co., 2001).

26. On ancient Hindu women, see Katherine K. Young, "Hinduism," in Arvind Sharma, ed., *Women in World Religions* (Albany: SUNY Press, 1987), 60–72; Paul Thomas, *Indian Women through the Ages* (Bombay: Asia Publishing House, 1964); A. S. Altekar, *The Position of Women in Hindu Civilization* (Delhi: Motilal Banarsidass, 1962).

27. Katyayana Shrautasutra 1.1.7 *et seq.*

28. Ibid. See also, e.g., Aitareya Brahmana 2.9, in which a young girl, Kumari Gandharva-Grhita, is cited as an authority on the *agnihotra* ritual.

29. Sharada Sugirtharajah, "Hinduism," in Jean Holm, ed., *Women in Religion* (New York: Pinter Publishers, 1994), 61.

30. Young, "Hinduism," 70.

31. Vasudha Narayanan, "Brimming with *Bhakti*, Embodiments of *Shakti*: Devotees, Deities, Performers, Reformers, and Other Women of Power in the Hindu Tradition," in Arvind Sharma and Katherine K. Young, eds., *Feminism and World Religions* (Albany, NY: State University of New York Press, 1999), 37.

32. Basham, *The Wonder That Was India*, 182; Prabhati Mukherjee, *Hindu Women: Normative Models*, rev. ed. (Calcutta: Orient Longman, 1994), 10–11; see generally, also, Pundita Ramabai Sarasvati, *The High Caste Hindu Woman* (New Delhi: M. C. Mittal Inter-India Publications, 1888, reprinted 1984), especially chapter 4.

33. Young, "Hinduism," 69.

34. G. Buhker, trans., *The Laws of Manu, Sacred Books of the East* (Delhi: Motilal Banarsidass, 1964), 195–197; Manu, 5, 147–165.

35. Ibid., 327–330; Manu, 9, 2–16.

36. Young, "Hinduism," 64; Ramabai Sarasvati, *The High Caste Hindu Woman*, chapters 3 and 4. See also Mukherjee, *Hindu Women: Normative Models*, rev. ed. (Calcutta: Orient Longman, 1994).

37. Carmody, *Women and World Religions*, 47.

38. Mary Daly, *Gyn/Ecology: The Metaethics of Radical Feminism* (Boston: Beacon Press, 1978), 120–121.

39. See, e.g., Veena Talwar Oldenburg, *Dowry Murder: The Imperial Origins of a Cultural Crime* (New York: Oxford University Press, 2002).

40. Ramabai Sarasvati, *The High Caste Hindu Woman*, 109.

41. On permitting Hindu widow remarriage, see e.g., Atharavaveda 9.5.27; Rigveda 10.40.2. But see Manusmriti 5.158; 5.162; Apastamba Dharmasutra 2.6.13–14 on prohibiting remarriage. On evidence of widows remarrying in ancient times, see Manusmriti 9.175. See also N. K. Dutt, "Widow in Ancient India," in *The Indian Historical Quarterly* 14, no. 4 (December 1938): 661–679.

42. Ram Kumar Chaube, *India as Told by the Muslims* (Varanasi, India: Prithivi Prakashan, 1969), 233–234; Arvind Sharma, et al., *Sati: Historical and Phenomenological Essays* (New Delhi, India: Motilal Banarsidass, 1988).

43. Benjamin Walker, *The Hindu World: The Encyclopedic Survey of Hinduism* (New York: Praeger, 1968), 2: 464, quoted in Daly, *Gyn/Ecology*, 117.

44. Young, "Hinduism," 85–86.

45. Michael Allen, "The Hindu View of Women," in Michael Allen and S. N. Mukherjee, eds., *Women in India and Nepal* (Canberra: Australian National University, 1982), 16–17.

46. See Doranne Jacobson, "Golden Handprints and Red-Painted Feet: Hindu Childbirth Rituals in Central Indian," and Susan Wadley, "Hindu Women's Family and Household Rites in a North Indian Village," both in Nancy Aver Falk and Rita M. Gross, eds., *Unspoken Worlds: Women's Religious Lives* (Belmont, CA: Wadsworth Publishing, 1989), 59–71; 72–81, respectively; reprinted in Doranne Jacobson and Susan S. Wadley, *Women in India: Two Perspectives* (Columbia, MO: South Asia Publications, 3rd ed., 1995), 137–155, 157–170, respectively.

47. Vasudha Narayanan, "Brimming with *Bhakti*, Embodiments of *Shakti*: Devotees, Deities, Performers, Reformers, and Other Women of Power in the Hindu Tradition" in Arvind Sharma and Katherine K. Young, eds., *Feminism and World Religions* (Albany, NY: SUNY Press, 1999), 34.

48. Lindsey Harlan, "Abandoning Shame: Mira and the Margins of Marriage," in Lindsey Harlan and Paul B. Courtright, eds., *From the Margins of Hindu Marriage: Essays on Gender, Religion and Culture* (New York: Oxford University Press, 1995), 205–206.

49. Narayanan, "Brimming...Women of Power in the Hindu Tradition," 40.

50. Sugirtharajah, "Hinduism," 67–68.

51. Young, "Hinduism," 91.

52. Carmody, *Women and World Religions*, 49.

53. Narayanan, "Brimming...Women of Power in the Hindu Tradition," 25–77.

54. Saul David, *The Indian Mutiny: 1857* (London: Penguin, 2004), 367.

55. See June McDaniel, *The Madness of the Saints* (Chicago: University of Chicago Press, 1989).

56. William Dalrymple, *Nine Lives: In Search of the Sacred in Modern India* (New York: Knopf, 2010), 204.

57. For an excellent discussion of the reform movement and its impact on the independence movement in India, as well as the status of women in contemporary India, see Katherine K. Young, "Women in Hinduism," in Arvind Sharma, ed., *Today's Woman in World Religions* (Albany, NY: SUNY Press, 1994), 77–135. This subsection and the next are based in part on this essay.

58. Ramabai Sarasvati, *The High Caste Hindu Woman*, 78; Kiran Devendra, *Status and Position of Women in India: With Special Reference to Women in Contemporary India* (Delhi: Shakti Books, 1986), 9.

59. Narayanan, "Brimming…Women of Power in the Hindu Tradition," 35.

60. Joanna Liddle and Rama Joshi, "Gender and Imperialism in British India," *Economic and Political Weekly*, 20, no. 43 (1985): WS–77, quoted in Young, "Women in Hinduism," 83.

61. Kiran Devendra, *Status and Position of Women in India: With Special Reference to Women in Contemporary India*, ix.

62. Young, "Women in Hinduism," 86.

63. Suhag Sukla, "Hindu Women: Hear Them Roar," *Huffington Post Religion Blog*, http://www.huffingtonpost.com/suhag-a-shukla-esq/hindu-women-hear-them-roar_b_850005.html (April 18, 2011).

64. See, e.g., Vanamala Bhawalkar, *Women in the Mahabharata* (New Delhi, India: Sharada Publishing House, 1999); Chaturvedi Badrinath, *The Women of the Mahabharata—The Question of Truth* (Hyderabad, India: Orient Longman, 2008); Narayanan, "Brimming…Women of Power in the Hindu Tradition," 25–77; T. P. Saxena, *Women in Indian History: A Biographical Dictionary* (Ludhiana, India: Kalyani Publishers, 1979); and R. C. Majumdar and Swami Madhavananda, *Great Women of India* (Calcutta, India: Advaita Ashrama, 1993).

65. Young, "Women in Hinduism," 46.

66. See Falk, "*Shakti* Ascending: Hindu Women, Politics, and Religious Leadership during the Nineteenth and Twentieth Centuries," 298–334.

67. Narayanan, "Brimming…Women of Power in the Hindu Tradition," 44.

68. Dalrymple, *Nine Lives*, 4–8.

69. See Mrs. Sinclair Stevenson, *The Heart of Jainism* (New Delhi: Munshivam Manoharlal, 1970; Oxford University Press, 1st ed., 1915); William de Bary, *Sources of Indian Tradition* (New York: Columbia University Press, 1958, 1966), chapters 4 and 5; and P. S. Jaini, *The Jaina Path of Purification* (Berkeley: University of California Press, 1979).

70. Trilochan Singh et al., *Adi-Granth: Selections from the Sacred Writings of the Sikhs* (New York: Macmillan, 1960; London: George Allen and Unwin, 1960; reprinted New York: Samuel Weiser, Inc., 1974), 24. Reprinted by permission of George Allen and Unwin, Ltd., and Samuel Weiser, Inc.

71. See E. Allen Richardson, *East Comes West* (Cleveland: The Pilgrim Press, 1985), 17–50.

72. See, e.g., The Hindu-American Foundation, *www.hafsite.org*.

73. On American Hindu religious movements, see Robert S. Ellwood and Harry B. Partin, *Religious and Spiritual Groups in Modern America* (Englewood Cliffs, NJ: Prentice Hall, 2nd ed., 1988), chapter 7, and Timothy Miller, ed., *America's Alternative Religions* (Albany, NY: SUNY Press, 1995), chapters 17, 18, and 19.

74. The authors express thanks to Hindu scholars who reviewed this chapter and made insightful comments: Acharya Arumuganathaswami, Vishal Agarwal, and Ramdas Lamb.

Chapter 4

1. On the life of the Buddha, see E. J. Thomas, *The Life of the Buddha as Legend and History* (London: Routledge and Kegan Paul, 1927) and the shorter summary in Richard H. Robinson, *The Buddhist Religion: A Historical Introduction* (Belmont, CA: Dickenson, 1970).

2. Edward Conze, *Buddhist Scriptures* (Harmondsworth, UK: Penguin Classics, 1959), 55–56. Reproduced by permission of Penguin Books Ltd.

3. Ibid., 186–187.

4. In some sources this tradition is called Hinayana ("Little Vessel"). That term, however, originated as a derogatory label used by Mahayanists for the other camp in debate and is not used by Theravadins themselves. It seems more courteous to keep to the word "Theravada."

5. In early centuries C.E., Mahayana was strong in the areas of central Asia that are now Kashmir, Afghanistan, and surrounding regions; from this part of the world, it spread to China. But it has been replaced there by Islam. It was also strong in medieval times in much of Southeast Asia, including the Khmer Empire in present-day Cambodia, with its great Buddhist temples of Angkor Wat (originally Hindu, then Mahayana, then modified to Theravada) and in present-day Indonesia (where it has been replaced by Islam). The story of the interaction of Hinduism, Theravada, and Mahayana in Southeast Asia up to early modern times is a very complex one.

6. On the role of the monk, see Jane Bunnag, *Buddhist Monk, Buddhist Layman* (London and New York: Cambridge University Press, 1973); Robert C. Lester, *Theravada Buddhism in Southeast Asia* (Ann Arbor: University of Michigan Press, 1973), Part 2; Richard F. Gombrich, *Precept and Practice: Traditional Buddhism in the Rural Highlands of Ceylon* (London: Oxford University Press, 1971); and Melford E. Spiro, *Buddhism and Society.* (New York: Harper & Row, 1970), Part 4.

7. The order of some of the *lokas* varies in different sources; this list follows Lester, *Theravada Buddhism*, 39–41.

8. The techniques of samadhic meditation are vividly described in B. A. Maitreya, "Buddhism in Theravada Countries," in Kenneth Morgan, ed. *Path of the Buddha* (New York: Ronald Press, 1956), 113–152. Original texts are found in Edward Conze, *Buddhist Meditation* (New York: Harper & Row, 1969).

9. For a personal account of the practice of *vipassana* meditation, see Eric Lerner, *Journey of Insight Meditation* (New York: Schocken Books, 1977).

10. On the concepts and practices of popular Buddhism in Theravada lands, see Bunnag, *Buddhist Monk, Buddhist Layman*; Lester, *Theravada Buddhism*; Gombrich, *Precept and Practice*; Spiro, *Buddhism and Society*; Maitreya, "Buddhism in Theravada Countries"; and Winston L. King, *A Thousand Lives Away* (Cambridge, MA: Harvard University Press, 1964).

11. A scholarly translation of the Lotus Sutra is Leon Hurvitz, *The Scripture of the Lotus Blossom of the Fine Dharma*. (New York: Columbia University Press, 1975). See also *The Lotus Sutra*, trans. by Burton Watson (New York: Columbia University Press, 1994).

12. On Nagarjuna and his philosophy, see T. R. V. Murti, *The Central Philosophy of Buddhism* (London: George Allen & Unwin, 1955); and Frederick J. Streng, *Emptiness: A Study in Religious Meaning* (Nashville, TN: Abingdon Press, 1967).

13. On *prajnaparamita* thought, see two books by Edward Conze: *Buddhist Thought in India* (Ann Arbor: University of Michigan Press, 1967), 198–204; and *The Prajnaparamita Literature* (The Hague, Netherlands: Mouton, 1960). These books contain references to the author's more technical scholarship in this area.

14. There is no general introductory book in English on the *bodhisattva*. For easily accessible summaries, see Robinson, *The Buddhist Religion*, 54–63; and Edward Conze, *Buddhism in Essence and Development* (New York: Harper Brothers, 1959), 125–130.

15. On Mind Only, see Conze, *Buddhist Thought in India*, 250–260; and D. T. Suzuki, *Studies in the Lankavatara Sutra* (London: Routledge, 1930). On a closely related school based on the Avatamsaka Sutra, see Francis D. Cook, *Hua-yen Buddhism: The Jewel Net of Indra* (University Park: Pennsylvania State University Press, 1977).

16. For an account of most of the Buddhas and *bodhisattvas* of practical importance in Mahayana art and devotion, see Alice Getty, *The Gods of Northern Buddhism* (Oxford: The Clarendon Press, 1928). See also Walter E. Clark, *Two Lamaist Pantheons* (Cambridge, MA: Harvard University Press, 1937).

17. Fascinating accounts of Tantric apprenticeships can be found in Herbert V. Guenther, *The Life and Teaching of Naropa* (London: Oxford University Press, 1963); and W. Y. Evans-Wentz, *Tibet's Great Yogin Milarepa* (London and New York: Oxford University Press, 1969).

18. Translations include Francesca Fremantle and Choguam Trungpa, *The Tibetan Book of the Dead.* (Berkeley and London: Shambhala, 1975); W. Y. Evans-Wentz, *The Tibetan Book of the Dead.* (New York: Oxford University Press, 1927, 1960); and Robert A. Thurman Jr., *The Tibetan Book of the Dead: The Great Book of Natural Liberation through Understanding in the Between* (New York: Bantam, 1993).

19. The standard treatment is S. J. Heinrich Dumoulin, *A History of Zen Buddhism* (New York: McGraw-Hill, 1965). For a readable history presented through the lives of the great Chan/Zen masters, see Thomas Hoover, *The Zen Experience* (New York: New American Library, 1980).

20. Peter G. Friedlander, "Buddhism and Politics," in Jeffrey Haynes, ed. *The Politics of Religion: A Survey* (London; New York: Routledge, 2006), 5, and see generally on Buddhism and politics.

21. Quoted in Todd Lewis, "Buddhism: The Politics of Compassionate Rule," in Jacob Neusner, ed. *God's Rule: The Politics of the World's Religions* (Washington, DC: Georgetown University Press, 2003), 240.

22. Quoted in Ibid.

23. Ibid., 241.

24. Ibid., 237–238.

25. Friedlander, "Buddhism and Politics," 6.

26. Lewis, "Buddhism: The Politics of Compassionate Rule," 251.

27. Friedlander, "Buddhism and Politics," 12 (noting also that the term "engaged Buddhism" was coined by Thich Nhat Hanh).

28. Sandy Boucher, *Opening the Lotus: A Women's Guide to Buddhism* (Boston: Beacon, 1997), 54.

29. Rita M. Gross, *Buddhism after Patriarchy: A Feminist History, Analysis, and Reconstruction of Buddhism* (Albany: State University of New York Press, 1993), 23.

30. Rita M. Gross, "Buddhism," in Jean Holm with John Bowker, ed., *Women in Religion* (London and New York: Pinter, 1994), 3–4; Nancy Schuster Barnes, "Buddhism," in Arvind Sharma, ed. *Women in World Religions* (Albany, NY: SUNY Press, 1987), 105–133, an excellent summary of the role of and attitudes toward women in the various forms of Buddhism.

31. Nancy Auer Falk, "The Case of the Vanishing Nuns: The Fruits of Ambivalence in Ancient Indian Buddhism," in Nancy Auer Falk and Rita M. Gross, eds, *Unspoken Worlds: Women's Religious Lives* (Stamford, CT: Cengage Learning, 3rd ed., 2000), 201–203; Gross, Buddhism after Patriarchy, 37; see also Gross, "Buddhism," 6.

32. Falk, "The Case of the Vanishing Nuns," 201–203.
33. For example, the Buddha is reported to have said that "[w]omen folks are uncontrollable...envious...greedy...weak in wisdom.... A woman's heart is haunted by stinginess...jealousy...sensuality." Aguttaranikaya, iv. 8.10, quoted by Cornelia Dimmitt Church, "Temptress, Wife, Nun: Woman's Role in Early Buddhism," *Anima: An Experiential Journal*, 1, no. 2 (Spring 1975): 55.
34. Rita M. Gross, "Buddhism," in Arvind Sharma and Katherine K. Young, eds., *Her Voice, Her Faith* (Boulder, CO: Westview Press, 2003), 64. See also K.A. Cissel [Kathryn A. Tsai], *The Pi-ch'iu-ni chuan: Biographies of Famous Chinese Nuns from 317–516* (Ann Arbor, MI: University Microfilms, 1972), 161; Barnes, "Buddhism," 107–109.
35. Falk, "The Case of the Vanishing Nuns," 201–203.
36. Barnes, "Buddhism," 109.
37. Ibid., 124. See also generally Cissel [Kathryn A. Tsai], *The Pi-ch'iu-ni chuan: Biographies of Famous Chinese Nuns from 317–516*.
38. *Book of the Gradual Sayings*, trans. by F. L. Woodward and E. M. Hare. 5 vols. (Pali Text Society, 1932–1936). Reprint (London: Luzac and Co., 1952–1965), vol. 3, 56–57, cited in Barnes, "Buddhism," 108, n. 1.
39. Diana Paul, *Women in Buddhism: Images of the Feminine in Mahayana Tradition*. (Berkeley, CA: Asian Humanities Press, 1979), 27–59.
40. Denise Lardner Carmody, *Women and World Religions* (Englewood Cliffs, NJ: Prentice Hall, 2nd ed., 1979, 1989), 71.
41. Falk, "The Case of the Vanishing Nuns," 204–209.
42. Barnes, "Buddhism," 109; Carmody, *Women and World Religions*, 73–74; Rita M. Gross, "The Householder and the World Renunciant: Two Modes of Sexual Expression in Buddhism," *Journal of Ecumenical Studies*, 22, no. 1 (Winter 1985): 81–96, cited in Carmody, *Women and World Religions*, 73–74.
43. Gross, "Buddhism," *Her Voice, Her Faith*, 89, quoting Chatsumarn Kabilsingh, *Thai Women in Buddhism* (Berkeley, CA: Parallax Press, 1991), 26.
44. Ibid., 89.
45. Gross, "Buddhism," *Women in Religion*, 8–9.
46. Gross, *Buddhism after Patriarchy*, 10.
47. Diana Paul, *Women in Buddhism*, 187–190.
48. Ibid., 230.
49. Ibid., 190–199.
50. Gross, "Buddhism," *Women in Religion*, 10–11.
51. Barnes, "Buddhism," 121.
52. Cited in Joanna Rogers Macy, "Perfection of Wisdom: Mother of All Buddhas," in Rita M. Gross, ed. *Beyond Androcentrism: New Essays on Women and Religions* (Missoula, MT: Scholars' Press, 1977), 318.
53. Cited in Gross, *Buddhism after Patriarchy*, 103.
54. Ibid., 102.
55. Gross, *Buddhism after Patriarchy*, 108.
56. Quoted in Miranda Shaw, *Passionate Enlightenment: Women in Tantric Buddhism*. (Princeton, NJ: Princeton University Press, 1994), 153.
57. Ibid., 80–81.
58. Ibid., 92; Gross, "Buddhism," *Women in Religion*, 16–17.
59. Barbara Aziz, "Moving Toward a Sociology of Tibet" in Janice D. Willis, ed. *Feminine Ground: Essays on Women and Tibet* (Ithaca, NY: Snow Lion, 1987), 79, cited in Gross, *Buddhism after Patriarchy*, 81.
60. Gross, *Buddhism after Patriarchy*, 87.
61. Gross, "Buddhism," *Her Voice, Her Faith*, 62.
62. Gross, *Buddhism after Patriarchy*, 39.
63. Ibid., 88.
64. Gross, "Buddhism," *Her Voice, Her Faith*, 90.
65. Rita M. Gross, "Strategies for a Feminist Revalorization of Buddhism," in Arvind Sharma and Katherine K. Young, eds., *Feminism and World Religions* (Albany, NY: SUNY Press, 1999), 98–99.
66. Ibid., 87–91.
67. Ibid., 97.
68. Ibid., 101.
69. Nancy J. Barnes, "Women in Buddhism," in Arvind Sharma, ed. *Today's Woman in World Religions* (Albany, NY: SUNY Press, 1994), 137–169. This is an excellent review of issues with respect to women in contemporary Buddhism and was used throughout this section as a resource.

Chapter 5

1. Marcel Granet, *Chinese Civilization* (New York: Meridian Books, 1958), 170–179.
2. See Judith M. Treistman, *The Prehistory of China* (New York: Natural History Press, 1972), 111–116.
3. In this chapter, the Pinyin System of transliteration of Chinese into the Roman alphabet is used. This system, adopted by the People's Republic of China, is quite phonetic for English if one remembers that q=ch and x=sh, approximately. In some cases, the older Wade-Giles form is given in parentheses. It will be the one found in many books.
4. The standard translation of the complete set of nine books is the nineteenth-century work of James Legge (Oxford, UK: The Clarendon Press, various dates), although, of course, its scholarship has now been superseded in various particulars.
5. See Harlee G. Creel, *Sinism* (Chicago: Open Court, 1929).
6. For translations of the Xiao Jing, the "Classic of Filial Piety," see James Legge, Hsiao King (Oxford: Oxford University Press, 1899); and Sister Mary Makra, *The Hsiao Ching* (Annapolis, MD: St. John's University Press, 1961).

7. Creel, *Sinism.*

8. Arthur Waley, *The Way and Its Power* (London: George Allen & Unwin, 1934), Introduction.

9. James Legge, trans., "Tao Te Ching, by Lao-Tzu," in *Sacred Books of the East*, vol. 39 (1891) resourced January 18, 2013, from Internet Sacred Text Archive at http://www.sacred-texts.com/tao/taote.htm, verse 1.

10. Excerpts from the Tao Te Ching on page 181 and the carryover quotation 181–182 are from ibid., verses 1, 10, 20, and 2, respectively.

11. Ibid., verse 18.

12. Ibid., verse 18.

13. See Burton Watson, *Chuang Tzu: Basic Writings* (New York: Columbia University Press, 1964); and A. C. Graham, *Chuang Tzu: The Inner Chapters* (London: George Allen & Unwin, 1981).

14. Fung Yu-Lan, *A Short History of Chinese Philosophy* (New York: Macmillan, 1960), chapters 19–20, contains a good brief summary of the Daoism of this period.

15. The best introduction to religious Daoism, as well as to other aspects of Daoism, is Holmes Welch, *Taoism: The Parting of the Way* (Boston: Beacon Press, 1965). See also Michael R. Saso, *Taoism and the Rite of Cosmic Renewal* (Pullman: Washington State University Press, 1972), which provides a striking description of modern religious Daoism, together with useful and informed comments on the history and meaning of religious Daoism. Peter Goulart, *The Monastery of Jade Mountain* (London: John Murray, 1961), offers a vivid if uncritical picture of Daoist life in mainland China in the decades before the Communist revolution. The same can be said of John Blofeld, *The Secret and Sublime: Taoist Mysteries and Magic* (London: George Allen & Unwin, 1973). Two older multivolumed works, J. J. M. de Groot, *The Religious Systems of China*, 6 vols. (Leiden: E. J. Brill, 1892–1910; reprinted Taipei: Literature House, 1964); and Henri M. Doré, *Researches into Chinese Superstitions*, 13 vols., in English (Shanghai: Tusewei Press, 1914–1938; reprinted Taipei: Chéngwen Publishing, 1968), provide an immense wealth of material on the Daoist pantheon and related rites and beliefs, as well as on other matters, although the scholarship and attitudes are dated.

16. See Mircea Eliade, *The Forge and the Crucible* (New York: Harper and Brothers, 1962), chapter 11.

17. The best general book on Chinese Buddhism is Kenneth Ch'en, *Buddhism in China* (Princeton, NJ: Princeton University Press, 1964). Also useful is Arthur F. Wright, *Buddhism in Chinese History* (Stanford, CA: Stanford University Press, 1959). For the actual life of Chinese Buddhist monasteries and popular devotion, see Holmes Welch, *The Practice of Chinese Buddhism, 1900–1950* (Cambridge, MA: Harvard University Press, 1967); and J. Prip-Møller, *Chinese Buddhist Monasteries* (New York: Oxford University Press, 1937, 1967).

18. See Wright, *Buddhism in Chinese History*, 36–37.

19. This area is well portrayed in Wolfram Eberhard, *Guilt and Sin in Traditional China* (Berkeley: University of California Press, 1967).

20. The most useful translations are John Blofeld, *I Ching* (New York: Dutton, 1968); and Richard Wilhelm, *I Ching, or Book of Changes* (New York: Pantheon Books, 1950).

21. Arthur Waley, trans., *Monkey: Folk Novel of China by Wu Ch'eng-En* (New York: Grove Press, 1958); Anthony Yu, trans., *The Journey to the West*, 4 vols. (Chicago: University of Chicago Press, 1977–1983).

22. Mark Csikszentmihalyi, "Confucianism," in Jacob Neusner, ed. *God's Rule: The Politics of the World's Religions* (Washington, DC: Georgetown University Press, 2003), 221 and generally.

23. *Classic of Documents (Shujing)*, quoted in Ibid., 227.

24. D. C. Lau, trans. *Mencius*. (Harmondsworthk, England: Penguin Books, 1970), 183.

25. Adam Yuet Chau, *Miraculous Response: Doing Popular Religion in Contemporary China*. Stanford, CA: Stanford University Press, 2006.

26. "Believers on the Rise in China," *Religion Watch*, 6, no. 2 (March 2007).

27. Philip Jenkins, "Who's Counting China?" *Christian Century*, August 10, 2010, 45.

28. Ian Johnson, "The Rise of the Tao," *New York Times Magazine*, November 5, 2010. *www.nytimes.com/2010/11/07/magazine/07rel.*

29. Peter Gwin, "Battle for the Soul of Kung Fu," *National Geographic*, 219/3 (March 2011), 94–113.

30. Louisa Lim, "China's Leaders Harness Folk Religion For Their Aims," National Public Radio, July 24, 2010. *www.npr.org/templates/story/story.php.*

31. Quoted in "China on the Rise," *University of Chicago Magazine* (August 2006), 25–26, at 25.

32. Nicholas D. Kristoff, "China's Winning Schools?" *New York Times*, January 17, 2011. *www.nytimes.com/2011/01/opinion/16krist*

33. Stewart McFarlane, "Chinese Religions," in Jean Holm with John Bowker, eds. *Women in Religion*, (London and New York: Pinter Publishers, 1994), 161, citing James Legge, *Li chi, Book of Rites*, 2 vols., C. C. Chai and W. Chai (New York: University Books, 1967), vol. 1, 441.

34. Cited in Denise Lardner Carmody, *Women and World Religions*, (Englewood Cliffs, NJ: Prentice Hall, 2nd ed., 1979, 1989), 71.

35. McFarlane, "Chinese Religions," 163.

36. Theresa Kelleher, "Confucianism," in Arvind Sharma, ed. *Women in World Religions* (Albany, NY: SUNY Press, 1987), 144, citing Nancy Lee Swann, *Pan Chao: Foremost Woman Scholar of China* (New York: Century Co., 1932), 83.

37. Ibid.

38. Theresa Kelleher, "Confucianism," 140. This article was particularly helpful to the author throughout this section.

39. Cited in Kelleher, "Confucianism," 148.

40. Ibid., 145.

41. Margery Wolf, "Women and Suicide in China," in Margery Wolf and Roxane Witke, eds. *Women in Chinese Society*, (Stanford, CA: Stanford University Press, 1975), generally, cited in Kelleher, "Confucianism," 146.

42. Margery Wolf, *Women and the Family in Rural Taiwan* (Stanford, CA: Stanford University Press, 1972), 32–37, and Margery Wolf, *Revolution Postponed: Women in Contemporary China* (Stanford, CA: Stanford University Press, 1985), 9–12, cited in McFarlane, "Chinese Religions," 162.

43. Carmody, *Women and World Religions*, 95–96.

44. James Legge, trans., "Tao Te Ching, by Lao-Tzu," in *Sacred Books of the East*, vol. 39 (1891) resourced January 18, 2013, from Internet Sacred Text Archive at http://www.sacred-texts.com/tao/taote.htm, verse 6.

45. Ellen Chen, "Nothingness and the Mother Principle in Early Chinese Taoism," *International Philosophical Quarterly* 9 (1969), 391–405, cited in McFarlane, "Chinese Religions," 165 and Kelleher, "Confucianism," 162–163.

46. McFarlane, "Chinese Religions," 166.

47. Carmody, *Women and World Religions*, 101.

48. Barbara Reed, "Taoism," in, Arvind Sharma, ed. *Women in World Religions* (Albany, NY: SUNY Press, 1987), 167–168.

49. Ibid., 175.

50. Ibid., 179–180.

51. Ibid., 176–177.

52. Ibid., 173.

53. Ibid., 168–169.

54. This section is based on the work of Beverley Jackson in *Splendid Slippers: A Thousand Years of an Erotic Tradition* (Berkeley, CA: Ten Speed Press, 1997). See also Fan Hong, *Footbinding, Feminism, and Freedom* (London and Portland, OR: Frank Cass, 1997).

55. Mary Daly, *Gyn/Ecology: The Metaethics of Radical Feminism* (Boston: Beacon, 1978), 136. This is one of Mary Daly's classic works in radical feminism and is an especially critical assessment of footbinding and other mutilations of the female body.

56. Appiah, Kwame Anthony, *The Honor Code: How Moral Revolutions Happen* (New York, NY: W.W. Norton & Company, 2010).

57. Louisa Lim, "Painful Memories for China's Footbinding Survivors," NPR, January 30, 2012. *http://www.npr.org/templates/story/story.php?storyId=8966942*.

58. Miriam Levering, "Women, the State, and Religion Today in the People's Republic of China," in Arvind Sharma, ed. *Today's Woman in World Religions* (Albany, NY: SUNY Press, 1994), 171–224.

59. The best translations are Donald M. Philippi, *Kojiki* (Tokyo: University of Tokyo Press, 1968); and W. G. Aston, *Nihongi* (London: George Allen & Unwin, 1896, 1956).

60. See Aston, *Nihongi*, Part 2, 65–67, for the traditional account.

61. Harper Havelock Coates and Ryugaku Ishizuka, *Honen the Buddhist Saint* (Kyoto: Choinin, 1925); Alfred Bloom, *Shinran's Gospel of Pure Grace* (Tucson: University of Arizona Press, 1965).

62. Masaharu Anesaki, *Nichiren the Buddhist Prophet* (Cambridge, MA: Harvard University Press, 1916).

63. See James W. White, *The Sokagakkai and Mass Society* (Stanford, CA: Stanford University Press, 1970).

64. See Robert N. Bellah, *Tokugawa Religion* (Glencoe, IL: The Free Press, 1957); Warren W. Smith, *Confucianism in Modern Japan* (Tokyo: Hokuseido, 1973).

65. Karen A. Smyers, "Women and Shinto: The Relation Between Purity and Pollution," in *Women and World Religions*, Lucinda Joy Peach (Upper Saddle River, NJ: Prentice Hall, 2002), 117–125, 120.

66. Ibid., 118.

67. Ibid., 119.

68. Denise Lardner Carmody, *Women and World Religions*, 116–117.

69. See, generally, William R. LaFleur, *Liquid Life: Abortion and Buddhism in Japan* (Princeton, NJ: Princeton University Press, 1992).

70. Vera Mackie, *Feminism in Modern Japan* (Cambridge, UK: Cambridge University Press, 2003), 3–6.

71. Ibid., 4–7. See also Dina Lowy, *The Japanese "New Woman"* (New Brunswick, NJ and London: Rutgers University Press, 2007.

72. See Sandra Buckley, ed., *Broken Silence: Voices of Japanese Feminism* (Berkeley: University of California Press, 1996); Vera Mackie, *Feminism in Modern Japan* (Cambridge, UK: Cambridge University Press, 2003); Dina Lowy, *The Japanese "New Woman."*

73. Material on Korean religion can be found in Charles Allen Clark, *Religions of Old Korea* (New York: Garland, 1981; 1st ed., 1932); James H. Grayson, *Korea: A Religious History* (London and New York: Routledge, 2002). On special topics see Roger Janelli, *Ancestor Worship in Korean Society* (Stanford, CA: Stanford University Press, 1982); Robert E. Buswell, Jr., and Timothy S. Lee, eds., *Christianity in Korea* (Honolulu: Univeristy of Hawaii Press, 2007); and two highly readable books by Laurel Kendall, *Shamans, Housewives, and Other Restless Spirits* (Honolulu: University of Hawaii Press, 1985) and *The Life and Hard Times of a Korean Shaman* (Honolulu: University of Hawaii Press, 1988).

74. On Vietnamese religion, see Philip Taylor, *Goddess on the Rise: Pilgrimage and Popular Religion in Vietnam*

(Honolulu: University of Hawaii Press, 2004); Philip Taylor, ed., *Modernity and Re-enchantment: Religion in Post-revolutionary Vietnam* (Singapore: Institute of Southeast Asian Studies, 2007); and Hum Dac Bui and Ngasha Beck, *Cao Dai: Faith of Unity* (Fayetteville, AR: Emerald Wave Publishing, 2000).

75. Rupert Isaacson, *The Horse Boy: A Father's Quest to Heal His Son* (New York: Little, Brown, 2009).

76. Nomi Morris, "Buddhism Flowers in Mongolia," *Los Angeles Times*, September 11, 2010, AA7.

Chapter 6

1. See R. C. Zaehner, *The Teachings of the Magi: A Compendium of Zoroastrian Beliefs* (London: George Allen & Unwin, 1956; New York: Macmillan, 1956), 53–55.

2. Jacques Duschesne-Guillaume, *The Hymns of Zarathustra* (Boston: Beacon Press, 1963), is a good translation of the Gathas. The bulk of the Zend Avesta is translated in *The Sacred Books of the East*.

3. Rustom Masani, *The Religion of the Good Life* (New York: Collier Books, 1962), gives an account by a Parsee of their beliefs and practices.

Chapter 7

1. Transliterated into Roman letters, the name of God, called the tetragrammaton, is *YHVH*. The pronunciation must have been something like Yahweh or Yehveh. The name Jehovah of the King James Bible is an older attempt at pronouncing the same name by supplying the vowels of the title *Adonai*, "The Lord." Devout Jews, of course, would not make the attempt to pronounce the name; as in the Bible, God is spoken of not by name but by terms like *Adonai*.

2. See Gershom G. Scholem, *Major Trends in Jewish Mysticism* (New York: Schocken Books, 1961), 156–204.

3. Colorful accounts of Hasidism can be found in the writings of Martin Buber and in Herbert Weiner, *9 1/2 Mystics* (New York: Holt, Rinehart & Winston, 1969).

4. Louis I. Newman, *The Hasidic Anthology* (New York: Schocken Books 1963), 501.

5. Rabbi Nahman of Bratslav (1772–1811), cited in Arthur Hertzberg, ed., *Judaism* (New York: George Braziller, Inc., 1961), 91–92. Reprinted with the permission of the publisher.

6. The meaning of the Sabbath is vividly described in Herman Wouk, *This Is My God* (Garden City, NY: Doubleday, 1959), 55–66. See also Abraham Joshua Heschel, *The Sabbath: Its Meaning for Modern Man* (New York: Farrar, Strauss, and Giroux, 1951).

7. Wouk, *This Is My God*, 96–99, contains a particularly colorful account of Purim.

8. Jacob Neusner, "Judaism," in Jacob Neusner, ed. *God's Rule: The Politics of the World's Religions* (Washington, DC: Georgetown University Press, 2003), 38.

9. Ibid., 20.

10. Quoted in Ibid., 14. See also, Martin Sicker, *What Judaism Says About Politics: The Political Theology of the Torah* (Northvale, NY; London: Jason Aronson, 1994), 124.

11. Martin Sicker, *What Judaism Says About Politics: The Political Theology of the Torah.* (Northvale, NY and London: Jason Aronson, 1994), 128–130. See also, Daniel J. Elazar, ed. *Authority, Power, and Leadership in the Jewish Polity: Cases and Issues* (Jerusalem; Lanthan: University Press of America, 1991), 3–4.

12. Elazar, *Authority, Power, and Leadership in the Jewish Polity*, 11, and generally for the discussion of the *edah* and the "three crowns."

13. Jacob Neusner, "Judaism," in Jacob Neusner, ed. *God's Rule: The Politics of the World's Religions* (Washington, DC: Georgetown University Press, 2003), 46.

14. Kenneth D. Wald, "The Religious Dimension of Israeli Political Life," in Ted Gerard Jelen and Clyde Wilcox, eds., *Religion and Politics in Comparative Perspective: The One, the Few, and the Many* (New York: Cambridge University Press, 2002), 114.

15. Ibid., 117.

16. Ibid., 102.

17. Daniel J. Elazar, ed. *Authority, Power, and Leadership in the Jewish Polity,* 11.

18. Kenneth D. Wald, "The Religious Dimension of Israeli Political Life," 103.

19. Cited in Denise Lardner Carmody, "Judaism" in Arvind Sharma, ed. *Women in World Religions* (Albany, NY: SUNY Press, 1987), 204.

20. Ibid., generally 183–206. This is an excellent summary of the subject and was helpful to the authors throughout this section.

21. Alexandra Wright, "Judaism," in Jean Holm with John Bowker, ed., *Women in Religion* (London and New York: Pinter Publishers, 1994), 114.

22. Carmody, "Judaism," 187.

23. *The Writings—Kethubim.* Copyright by The Jewish Publication Society of America, 1982.

24. Denise Lardner Carmody, *Women and World Religions* (Englewood Cliffs, NJ: Prentice Hall, 2nd ed., 1979, 1989), 146.

25. Ibid., 147.

26. *The Form of Daily Prayers: According to the Customs of the German and Polish Jews*, trans. by Joseph Guns (Budapest: Jos. Schlesinger Library, 1938).

27. See Phyllis Trible, *Texts of Terror: Literary-Feminist Readings of Biblical Narratives* (Philadelphia, 1984).

See also Susan Niditch, "Portrayals of Women in the Hebrew Bible," in Judith R. Baskin, ed., *Jewish Women in Historical Perspective* (Detroit, MI: Wayne State University Press, 1991).

28. Carmody, *Women and World Religions*, 139.

29. Ibid., 145.

30. See Rachel Biale, *Women and Jewish Law: An Exploration of Women's Issues in Halakhic Sources* (New York: Schocken Books, 1984), chapter 6. This is a good resource for Jewish law regarding women.

31. Cited in Susannah Heschel, "Preface," in Susannah Heschel, ed. *On Being a Jewish Feminist*, 16.

32. Originally, Judaism permitted polygyny. The practice is recounted in the Hebrew scriptures and was continued into the Talmudic period, although it appears that no rabbi referenced in the Talmud had more than one wife. See Wright, "Judaism," 125. Polygyny was abolished by Rabbenu Gershom (960–1028) who propounded a takkanah (new ruling). The practice was then discontinued in countries in the West. See Rachel Adler, "The Jew Who Wasn't There: Halakhah and the Jewish Woman," in Susannah Heschel, ed. *On Being a Jewish Feminist*, 16.

33. Carmody, "Judaism," 187.

34. Ibid., 198.

35. Carmody, *Women and World Religions*, 135.

36. A woman named Regina Jonas was ordained privately as a reform rabbi in 1935 in Germany. She was put to death at Auschwitz in 1944. See Katharina von Kellenbach, "'God Does Not Oppress Any Human Being': The Life and Thought of Rabbi Regina Jonas," *Yearbook of the Leo Baeck Institute*, vol. 39 (1994), 213–226, cited in Heschel, "Preface," in Susannah Heschel, ed. *On Being a Jewish Feminist*.

37. See Cynthia Ozick, "Notes toward Finding the Right Question," in *On Being a Jewish Feminist*, generally.

38. Judith Plaskow, "The Right Question Is Theological," in *On Being a Jewish Feminist*, 228.

39. See Rita M. Gross, "Female God Language in a Jewish Context," in Carol P. Christ and Judith Plaskow, eds. *Womanspirit Rising: A Feminist Reader in Religion* (San Francisco: HarperSanFrancisco, 1979, 1992), 170–171, and Plaskow, "The Right Question Is Theological," in 229.

40. Heschel, "Preface," in *On Being a Jewish Feminist*, xxiii.

41. Ibid., xxii.

42. See Judith Plaskow, "The Right Question Is Theological," in 230–231 and Heschel, "Preface," in *On Being a Jewish Feminist*, xii–xvi, generally.

43. Plaskow, "The Right Question Is Theological," 224.

44. Judith Plaskow, "The Wife/Sister Stories: Dilemmas of the Jewish Feminist," in Diana L. Eck and Devaki Jain, eds. *Speaking of Faith* (Philadelphia: New Society, 1987), 125–126, cited in Carmody, *Women and World Religions*, 156.

Chapter 8

1. See Philip Jenkins, *The Next Christendom: The Coming of Global Christianity* (New York: Oxford University Press, 2003).

2. See Robert M. Grant, *A Historical Introduction to the New Testament* (New York: Harper & Row, 1963).

3. See John Bright, *The Kingdom of God* (Nashville, TN: Abingdon Press, 1953).

4. For a presentation of the theory that Jesus was involved with political revolutionaries, see S. G. F. Brandon, *Jesus and the Zealots* (New York: Scribner, 1967).

5. See Gunther Bornkamm, *Paul*, trans. D. M. G. Stalker (New York: Harper & Row, 1971); John Knox, *Chapters in a Life of Paul* (London: Adam and Charles Black, 1954); and Richard Longenecker, *Paul: Apostle of Liberty* (New York: Harper & Row, 1964).

6. Two introductory books on Gnosticism that can be highly recommended are Stephan A. Hoeller, *Gnosticism: New Light on the Ancient Tradition of Inner Knowing* (Wheaton, IL: Quest Books, 2002); and Elaine Pagels, *The Gnostic Gospels* (New York: Random House, 1978). Like many contemporary presenters of Gnosticism, both discuss parallels, behind the often strange-sounding Gnostic myths, between the inner meaning of the ancient faith and modern existentialism, feminism, and psychology, especially Jungian.

7. Willis Barnstone and Marvin Meyer, eds., *The Gnostic Bible* (Boston and London: Shambhala, 2003), 479. See also Karen L. King, *The Gospel of Mary of Magdala: Jesus and the First Woman Apostle* (Santa Rosa, CA: Polebridge Press, 2003).

8. Rodolphe Kasser, Marvin Meyer, and Gregor Wurst, *The Gospel of Judas* (Washington, DC: National Geographic Society, 2006). See also Elaine Pagels and Karen L. King, *Reading Judas: The Gospel of Judas in the Shaping of Christianity* (New York: Viking, 2007).

9. Among the many books on Gnosticism, these may be particularly helpful to beginning students: Marvin Meyer, *The Gnostic Discoveries* (San Francisco: HarperSanFrancisco, 2005); and *The Secret Teachings of Jesus: Four Gnostic Gospels* (New York: Random House, 1984). See also note 6 above.

10. See John Marsh, *The Gospel of St. John*. (Harmondsworth, UK: Penguin Books, 1968); and Oscar Cullmann, *The Johannine Circle* (Philadelphia: Westminster Press, 1975).

11. See Dom Gregory Dix, *The Shape of the Liturgy* (London: Dacre Press, 1945), 36–45.

12. J. W. C. Wand, *A History of the Early Church* (London: Methuen & Co., 1937), 97.

13. From the *Epistle of St. Ignatius of Antioch to the Romans*, vols. 4 and 7; Francis X. Glimm and others, *The Apostolic Fathers* (New York: Christian Heritage, 1947), 109–110.

14. See Hermann Dorres, *Constantine the Great*, trans. Roland Bainton (New York: Harper & Row, 1972).

15. See Robert M. Grant, *The Formation of the New Testament* (New York: Harper & Row, 1965).

16. See Helen Waddell, *The Desert Fathers* (Ann Arbor: University of Michigan Press, 1957); Justin McCann, *Saint Benedict* (Garden City, NY: Doubleday, 1958); and David Knowles, *Christian Monasticism* (New York: McGraw-Hill, 1969).

17. See George C. Coulton, *Medieval Panorama*. (New York: Macmillan, 1938); and two works of readable history by H. Daniel-Rops, *The Church in the Dark Ages*, trans. Audrey Butler (New York: Dutton, 1959); and *Cathedral and Crusade: Studies of the Medieval Church, 1050–1350,* trans. John Worthington (New York: Dutton, 1957).

18. On spiritual dissidents in the Middle Ages, see Steven Runciman, *The Medieval Manichee*. (Cambridge: Cambridge University Press, 1960); and Norman Cohn, *The Pursuit of the Millenium: Revolutionary Millenarians and Mystical Anarchists of the Middle Ages* (New York: Oxford University Press, 1976).

19. Paul Moses, *The Saint and the Sultan: The Crusades, Islam, and Francis of Assisi's Mission of Peace* (New York: Doubleday, 2009).

20. A readable life of Luther is Roland H. Bainton, *Here I Stand* (New York: Abingdon-Cokesbury Press, 1950). For the entire period see Harold J. Grimm, *The Reformation Era 1500–1650* (New York: Macmillan, 1973).

21. See Eamon Duffy, *The Stripping of the Altars: Traditional Religion in England 1400–1580* (New Haven, CT: Yale University Press, 1992).

22. See George Harrison Williams, *The Radical Reformation* (Philadelphia: Westminster Press, 1962).

23. See Charles Williams, *The Figure of Beatrice* (London: Faber, 1943). Williams describes the longstanding distinction between two kinds of mysticism and devotion: that of "negation of images" and that of "affirmation of images."

24. Three books that provide real insight into the soul of Eastern Orthodox spirituality, especially in old Russia, are Jon Gregerson, *Transfigured Cosmos* (New York: Ungar, 1960); and *The Way of a Pilgrim*, and the *Pilgrim Continues His Way*, trans. R. M. French (New York: Seabury Press, 1974).

25. These characteristics are based in part on those in the article by Richard McBrien, "Roman Catholicism," in *The Encyclopedia of Religion*, vol. 12 (New York: Macmillan, 1987), 437–439.

26. *Status of Global Missions Report 2011*. (South Hamilton, MA: Gordon Conwell Theological Seminary, 2011). *www.gordonconwell.edu/.../StatusofGlobalMission.pdf*.

27. David B. Barrett, George T. Kurian, and Todd M. Johnson, eds., *World Christian Encyclopedia* (New York: Oxford University Press, 2nd ed., 2001).

28. David B. Barrett, *African Initiatives in Religion*. (Nairobi: East African Publishing House, 1971), 110–120.

29. Grant Hardy, ed., *The Book of Mormon: A Reader's Edition* (Champaign: University of Illinois Press, 2003).

30. There are many books on Mormonism, both by Mormons and by non-Mormons. One of the latter is Richard N. Ostling and Joan K. Ostling, *Mormon America: The Power and the Promise* (San Francisco: Harper, 1999). The edition of the Book of Mormon cited above is edited by a distinguished Mormon scholar.

31. Martin Marty, "Reformation Christianity," in Jacob Neusner, ed. *God's Rule: The Politics of the World's Religions* (Washington, DC: Georgetown University Press, 2003), 115.

32. "Letter of Pope Gelasius to Emperor Anastasius," in trans. J. H. Robinson, *Readings in European History* (Boston: Ginn, 1905), 72–73.

33. John Neville Figgis, *The Divine Right of Kings* (Cambridge, UK: Cambridge University Press, 1922), 45.

34. Ibid., generally.

35. McGraw, *Rediscovering America's Sacred Ground: Public Religion and Pursuit of the Good in a Pluralistic America* (Albany, NY: State University of New York Press, 2003), chapters 2 and 3.

36. Charles E. Curran, "Roman Catholic Christianity," in Jacob Neusner, ed. *God's Rule: The Politics of the World's Religions* (Washington, DC: Georgetown University Press, 2003), 70, and generally for the subject of this section of the text.

37. Petros Vassiliadis, "Orthodox Christianity," in Jacob Neusner, ed. *God's Rule: The Politics of the World's Religions* (Washington, DC: Georgetown University Press, 2003), 95, and generally for this the subject of this section of the text.

38. For more information on the numerous denominations and religious groups in the United States, see Atwood, Craig D., *Handbook of Denominations in the United States* (Nashville: Abingdon Press, 13th ed., 2010), and *National Council of Churches of Christ in the U.S.A., Yearbook of American and Canadian Churches* (Nashville: Abingdon Press), published annually.

39. See Stephen T. Newcomb, *Pagans in the Promised Land: Decoding the Doctrine of Christian Discovery* (Golden, CO: Fulcrum Publishing, 2008) and

"The Doctrine of Discovery," *www.doctrineofdiscovery .org*. See also the writings of Bartolomé de las Casas (c. 1484–1566), an historian and Dominican friar, especially "A Short Account of the Destruction of the Indies," wherein he recounts what the Native Peoples in the West Indies experienced at the hands of the colonizers.

40. Jenkins, *The Next Christendom: The Coming of Global Christianity* (New York: Oxford University Press, 2003).

41. For an excellent overview of issues regarding women in Christian thought from the New Testament accounts to the twentieth century, including excerpts from original sources, on which this segment is based in part, see Elizabeth A. Clark and Herbert Richardson, *Women and Religion: The Original Sourcebook of Women in Christian Thought*, new ed. (San Francisco: HarperSanFrancisco, 1996).

42. See note 30, chapter 7.

43. See generally, Elisabeth Schussler Fiorenza, *In Memory of Her: A Feminist Theological Reconstruction of Christian Origins*, tenth anniversary ed. (New York: Crossroad, 1994).

44. Clark and Richardson, *Women and Religion*, 11.

45. Denise Lardner Carmody, *Women and World Religions* (Englewood Cliffs, NJ: Prentice Hall, 2nd ed., 1979, 1989), 171, citing Tertullian, De Cult. Fem., 1:1.

46. For a discussion of how the original church turned from a more egalitarian view of women to subordination of women, see Karen Torjeson, *When Women Were Priests: Women's Leadership in the Early Church and the Scandal of Their Subordination in the Rise of Christianity* (San Francisco: HarperSanFrancisco, 1993, 1995).

47. These views probably were derived from Gnostic and Manichean theologies, which were eschewed by early church leaders but nevertheless found their way into the institutionalized views of the church. See Clark and Richardson, *Women and Religion*, chapter 2.

48. Rosemary Radford Ruether, "Motherearth and the Megamachine," in Carol Christ and Judith Plaskow, eds. *Womanspirit Rising: A Feminist Reader in Religion* (San Francisco: HarperSanFrancisco, 1992), 43–45.

49. Clark and Richardson, *Women and Religion*, 90–91, citing Barbara A. Hanawalt, "Golden Ages for the History of Medieval English Women," in Susan Mosher Stuard, ed. *Women in Medieval History and Historiography* (Philadelphia: University of Pennsylvania Press, 1987), 17.

50. Clark and Richardson, *Women and Religion*, 121.

51. Ibid., 92.

52. See Anne Llewellyn Barstow, *Witchcraze: A New History of the European Witch Hunts* (San Francisco: HarperSanFrancisco/Pandora, 1994); Joseph Klaits, *Servants of Satan: The Age of the Witch Hunts* (Bloomington: Indiana University Press, 1985); Hugh Trevor-Roper, *The European Witch-Craze of the Sixteenth and Seventeenth Centuries* (Harmondsworth, UK: Penguin Books, 1969).

53. For a wonderful collection of articles on women in Christianity and Judaism, see Rosemary Ruether and Eleanor McLaughlin, eds., *Women of Spirit: Female Leadership in the Jewish and Christian Traditions* (New York: Simon and Schuster, 1979).

54. Nancy Hardesty, Lucille Sider Dayton, and Donald W. Dayton, "Women in the Holiness Movement: Feminism in the Evangelical Tradition," in Rosemary Ruether and Eleanor McLaughlin, eds., *Women of Spirit*, 244. The authors found this article to be especially helpful in this segment.

55. The accounts of Sojourner Truth's Akron, Ohio, speech vary. This version is based primarily on the report of Frances Gage as given in Jacqueline Bernard, *Journey Toward Freedom: The Story of Sojourner Truth* (New York: The Feminist Press at the City of New York, 1967, 1990), 165–167, with some modifications based on other accounts. See also Carleton Mabee, *Sojourner Truth: Slave, Prophet, Legend* (New York: New York University Press, 1993), 67–78 and Nell Irvin Painter, *Sojourner Truth: A Life, a Symbol* (New York/London: W. W. Norton & Company, 1996), 167–168.

56. Quoted in Denise Lardner Carmody and John Tully Carmody, *Exploring American Religion* (Mountain View, CA: Mayfield Publishing Company, 1990), 121–122.

57. Nancy Hardesty, Lucille Sider Dayton, and Donald W. Dayton, "Women in the Holiness Movement: Feminism in the Evangelical Tradition," 225–254.

58. Rosemary R. Ruether, "Christianity and Women in the Modern World," in Arvind Sharma, ed. *Today's Woman in World Religions*, (Albany, NY: SUNY Press, 1994), 285.

59. Larry B. Stamer, "A Wife's Role Is 'to Submit,' Baptists Declare," *Los Angeles Times*, June 10, 1998.

60. Linda A. Moody, *Women Encounter God: Theology across the Boundaries of Difference* (Maryknoll, NY: Orbis Books, 1996).

Chapter 9

1. Formerly, Westerners often called the religion Muhammadanism and its followers Muhammadans in analogy to Buddhism or Christianity. But Muslims object to this label and never use it themselves, saying that they do not worship or idolize Muhammad but rather submit to God's will as revealed in his prophetic ministry. Today these feelings are rightly respected, and the proper terms Islam and Muslim are generally used.

2. Mohammed Marmaduke Pickthall, *The Meaning of the Glorious Koran* (New York: Mentor Books, n.d.), vii.

3. A. J. Arberry, *The Holy Koran* (London: George Allen & Unwin, 1953), 26–27.

4. N. J. Dawood, trans., *The Koran* (Penguin Classics 1956, 5th rev. ed., 1990), 15. Copyright © N. J. Dawood, 1956, 1959, 1966, 1968, 1974. Reproduced by permission of Penguin Books, Ltd.

5. Ibid., 194.

6. Ibid., 336.

7. Seyyed Hossein Nasr, "Jesus through the Eyes of Islam," *The Times*, July 28, 1973.

8. Kenneth Cragg, trans., *The House of Islam* (Belmont, CA: Dickenson, 1969), 39. Reprinted by permission of the publisher.

9. A. J. Arberry, *The Koran Interpreted* (New York: Macmillan, 1955), I, 29.

10. Michael Sells, trans., *Approaching the Qur'an: The Early Revelations* (Ashland, OR: White Cloud Press, 2nd ed., 1999), 52.

11. A vivid account of Ramadan, and of much else of Islam in an Iraqi Shiá setting, may be found in Elizabeth Warnock Fernea, *Guests of the Sheik* (Garden City, NY: Doubleday, 1969).

12. For an illuminating discussion of pilgrimage, which indirectly casts much light on the meaning of the *hajj*, see Victor Turner, "The Center Out There: Pilgrim's Goal," *History of Religions* 12, no. 3 (February 1973), 191–230.

13. G. E. von Grunebaum, *Muhammadan Festivals* (New York: Henry Schuman, 1951), 44–47. The entire discussion of the *hajj* in this book, 15–49, is very useful.

14. See Xavier de Planhol, *The World of Islam* (Ithaca, NY: Cornell University Press, 1959), 6–7.

15. John L. Esposito with Natana J. De Long-Bas, "Classical Islam," in Jacob Neusner, ed. *God's Rule: The Politics of the World's Religions* (Washington, DC: Georgetown University Press 2003), 135.

16. Claire Heristchi and Andrea Teti, "Rethinking the Myths of Islamic Politics," in Jeffrey Haynes, ed. *The Politics of Religion: A Survey* (London; New York: Routledge, 2006), 31.

17. John L. Esposito with Natana J. De Long-Bas, "Classical Islam," in Jacob Neusner, ed. *God's Rule: The Politics of the World's Religions* (Washington, DC: Georgetown University Press, 2003), 136.

18. For useful overviews of many aspects of Islamic culture, see Bernard Lewis, ed., *Islam and the Arab World.* (New York: Knopf, 1976).

19. See the account in von Grunebaum, *Muhammadan Festivals,* 81–94. Fernea, *Guests of the Sheik,* contains a colorful firsthand account of the first ten days of Muharram, 216–266.

20. Dawood, *The Koran,* 336.

21. Ibid., 228.

22. See J. R. Porter, "Muhammad's Journey to Heaven," *Numen* 21, fasc. 1 (April 1974), 64–80.

23. From Margaret Smith, *Rabi'a the Mystic* (New York: Cambridge University Press, 1928), 22, 99, 100. Reprinted by permission of the publisher.

24. See the discussion of Junayd in R. C. Zaehner, *Hindu and Muslim Mysticism* (New York: Schocken Books, 1969).

25. Idries Shah, *Tales of the Dervishes* (New York: Dutton, 1970), 143.

26. See the discussion of Muslim saints in Fazlur Rahman, *Islam* (Garden City, NY: Doubleday, 1968), 162–65; and in von Grunebaum, *Muhammaden Festivals,* 67–84.

27. John L. Esposito with Natana J. De Long-Bas, "Classical Islam," in Jacob Neusner, ed. *God's Rule: The Politics of the World's Religions* (Washington, DC: Georgetown University Press, 2003), 139.

28. Mehran Tamadonfar, "Islamicism in Contemporary Arab Politics: Lessons in Authoritarianism and Democratization," in Ted Gerard Jelen and Clyde Wilcox, eds., *Religion and Politics in Comparative Perspective: The One, the Few, and the Many* (New York: Cambridge University Press, 2002), 144.

29. Yvonne Y. Haddad, "Sayyid Qutb: Ideologue of Islamic Revival," in John L. Esposito, ed., *Voices of Resurgent Islam* (New York: Oxford University Press, 1983), 67–98.

30. Edward W. Said, *The Question of Palestine D.C.* (New York: Random House, 1980), x.

31. Jane I. Smith, "Islam," in Arvind Sharma, ed., *Women in World Religions* (Albany, NY: SUNY Press, 1987), 235; Margot I. Duley, "Women in the Islamic Middle East and North Africa," in Margot I. Duley and Mary I. Edwards, eds. *The Cross-Cultural Study of Women: A Comprehensive Guide,* (New York: The Feminist Press, 1986), 407.

32. *The Qur'an,* trans. Ahmed Ali (Princeton, NJ: Princeton University Press, 1988), 9: 71.

33. Quoted in Charis Waddy, *Women in Muslim History.* (London/New York: Longman, 1980), 28.

34. *The Qur'an* 4:34, cited in Denise Lardner Carmody, *Women and World Religions* (Englewood Cliffs, NJ: Prentice Hall, 2nd ed., 1979, 1989), 193.

35. *The Qur'an,* trans. Ali, 4:34. See also Asghar Ali Engineer, *The Rights of Women in Islam* (New York: Saint Martin's Press, 1992), 46, regarding different interpretations of this passage.

36. Carmody, *Women and World Religions,* 186.

37. Leila Ahmed, *Women and Gender in Islam: Historical Roots of a Modern Debate* (New Haven, CT, and London: Yale University Press, 1992), 4.

38. Jane I. Smith, "Islam," 239–240; Engineer, *The Rights of Women in Islam,* 30–37.

39. Engineer, *The Rights of Women in Islam,* 45.

40. Ibid., 21–22.

41. Carmody, *Women and World Religions*, 189.
42. Engineer, *The Rights of Women in Islam*, 36.
43. Leila Badawi, "Islam," in Jean Holm with John Bowker, ed., *Women in Religion* (London and New York: Pinter Publishers, 1994), 109.
44. Ahmed, *Women and Gender in Islam*, 5.
45. Smith, "Islam," 240.
46. Engineer, *The Rights of Women in Islam*, 36.
47. Ibid., 57.
48. Smith, "Islam," 242; Carmody, *Women and World Religions*, 195.
49. Nawal al-Saadawi (also El Saadawi), *The Hidden Face of Eve: Women in the Arab World*, trans. and ed. Sherif Hetata (Boston: Beacon Press, 1982), 40.
50. Ibid., 7–10, 33–43.
51. Smith, "Islam," 240.
52. Badawi, "Islam," 89.
53. Waddy, *Women in Muslim History*, 18–25.
54. Engineer, *The Rights of Women in Islam*, 43.
55. Ahmed, *Women and Gender in Islam*, 43, 73.
56. Smith, "Islam," 240.
57. Saadia Khawar Khan Chishi, "Female Spirituality in Islam," in S. H. Nasr, ed., *Islamic Spirituality: Foundations* (New York: Crossroad, 1987), 207, quoted in Carmody, *Women and World Religions*, 197.
58. Waddy, *Women in Muslim History*, 59–60.
59. Smith, "Islam," 244–245.
60. Carmody, *Women and World Religions*, 190.
61. Smith, "Islam," 248.
62. Engineer, *The Rights of Women in Islam*, 6.
63. Margot Badran and Miriam Cooke, "Introduction," in Margot Badran and Miriam Cooke, eds., *Opening the Gates: A Century of Arab Feminist Writing*, (Bloomington and Indianapolis: Indiana University Press, 1990), xxii–xxiii.
64. Engineer, *The Rights of Women in Islam*, 41–45.
65. Ibid.
66. Margot Badran, "Feminism and Conversion," in Karin van Nieukerk, ed., *Women Embracing Islam* (Austin: University of Texas Press, 2006).

Chapter 10

1. Friedrich Steinbauer, *Melanesian Cargo Cults*, trans. by Max Wohlwill (St. Lucia, Queensland, Australia: University of Queensland Press, 1979), 5–9; Peter Worsley, *The Trumpet Shall Sound* (New York: Schocken Books, 1968), 123–146.
2. See Ann Braude, *Radical Spirits: Spiritualism and Women's Rights in Nineteenth Century America* (Boston: Beacon Press, 1989).
3. Carl G. Jung, *Flying Saucers: A Modern Myth of Things Seen in the Sky* (New York: Signet Books, 1969), 27.
4. Orfeo Angelucci, *The Secret of the Saucers*. (Amherst, WI: Amherst Press, 1955), 34.
5. Ibid., 27.
6. Based on the account in Robert S. Ellwood, *The Eagle and the Rising Sun: Americans and the New Religions of Japan* (Philadelphia: Westminster Press, 1974), 69–74.
7. Joseph Murphy, *Santería: An African Religion in America* (Boston: Beacon Press, 2nd. ed., 1992); Migene Gonzalez-Wippler, *The Santería Experience* (Englewood Cliffs, NJ: Prentice Hall, 1982), a well-written first person account of the Santeria world; and Isamur Flores-Peña and Roberta J. Evanchuk, *Santería Garments and Altars* (Jackson: University Press of Mississippi, 1994), with beautiful color illustrations of the altars and vestments.

CREDITS

Text Credits:

Chapter 1: **p. 06–07**, Source: Based on content from Pearson; **p. 12**, Roger Bannister, FIrst Four Minutes. London: Lyons & Burford, 1955. pp. 11–12;

Chapter 2: **p. 33**, Eliade, Mircea; Shamanism. © 1964 Bolligen, 1992 renewed Princeton Univer- sity Press, 1972 paperback Ed., 2004 2nd. Paperback with new foreword Reprinted by permis- sion of University Press; **p. 38**, Source: Based on content from Pearson; **p. 48**, © Moment Open/Getty;

Chapter 3: **p. 57**, **p. 59**, Swami Prabhavananda and Frederick Manchester, trans., The Upanishads: Breath of the Eternal (New York: Mentor Books, 1957), pp. 123–24. Copyright © 1957 by The Vedanta Society of Southern California; **p. 64**, Source: Based on content from Pearson; **p. 66**, **p. 67**, **p. 68**, Swami Prabhavananda and Christopher Isherwood, The Song of God: Bhagavad-Gita (New York: Mentor Books, 1951), p. 40–41. Copyright © 1944, 1951 by The Vedanta Society of Southern California; **p. 74**, Swami Prabhavananda, Srimad Bhagavatam: The Wisdom of God (New York: Capricorn Books, 1968), pp. 199–200. Copyright © The Vedanta Society of Southern California. Reprinted with permission; **p. 78**, Rabindranath Tagore, trans., Songs of Kabir (New York: Macmillan, 1917), pp. 45–46; p.103, Singh, Trilochan. The Sacred Writings of The Sikhs. Copyright © 2009. United Nations Organization for Education, Science and Culture (UNESCO).

Chapter 4: **p. 134**, Source: Based on content from Pearson; **p. 118**, Buddhist Scriptures (Harmondsworth, UK: Penguin Classics, 1959), Edward Conze, pp. 55–56. Copyright © Edward Conze, 1959. Reproduced by permission of Penguin Books Ltd; **p. 150**, Based on Diana Paul, Women in Buddhism: Images of the Feminine in Mahayana Tradition (Berkeley, CA: Asian Humanities Press, 1979), 27–59; **p. 152**, Miranda Shaw, Passionate Enlightenment: Women in Tantric Buddhism (Princeton, NJ: Princeton University Press, 1994). Reprinted by permission of Princeton University Press.

Chapter 9: **p. 348**, **p. 349**, **p. 371**, The Koran (Penguin Classics 1956, 5th rev. ed, 1990), N. J. Dawood, trans., p. 15. Copyright © N. J. Dawood, 1956, 1959, 1966, 1968, 1974. Reproduced by permission of Penguin Books, Ltd.

Photo Credits:

Chapter 1: **p. 16**, Peter Dennis/Dorling Kindersley, Ltd; **p. 18**, Karen Trist/Rough Guides/ Dorling Kindersley, Ltd.

Chapter 2: **p. 30**, Dorling Kindersley, Ltd; **p. 32**, Brice Minnigh/Rough Guides/Dorling Kinder- sley, Ltd; **p. 33**, AP Photo; **p. 36**, Lutz Braun/Berlin/Art Resource, NY; **p. 41**, Dave stamboulis/ Alamy; **p. 43**, Tim Draper/Rough Guides /Dorling Kindersley, Ltd;

Chapter 3: **p. 48**, M.Freeman/Photolink/Getty Images; **p. 59**, Steve Gorton/Dorling Kinders- ley, Ltd; **p. 72**, Photo Researchers, Inc; **p. 74**, Barnabas Kindersley/Dorling Kindersley, Ltd; **p. 77**, Tony Souter/Dorling Kindersley, Ltd; **p. 82**, David pearson/Alamy; **p. 83**, Barbara McGraw; **p. 83**, Jagdish Agarwal/The Image Works; **p. 86**, Dorling Kindersley / Dorling Kindersley, Ltd; **p. 87**, Barbara McGraw; **p. 89**, Fox Photos/Stringer/Getty Images; **p. 91**, Tim Draper/Rough Guides/Dorling Kindersley, Ltd; **p. 96**, Barbara McGraw; **p. 101**, Mimi Forsyth; **p. 102**, Shawlin Mohd/Fotolia; **p. 103**, B.P.S. Walia/Dorling Kindersley, Ltd; **p. 104**, teracreonte/Fotolia.

Chapter 4: **p. 114**, Tim Draper/Dorling Kindersley, Ltd; **p. 117**, Martin Richardson/Rough Guides/ Dorling Kindersley, Ltd; **p. 123**, Martin Puddy/The Image Bank/Getty Images; **p. 125**, Burt Glin/ Magnum Photos; **p. 128**, Colin Sinclair/Dorling Kindersley, Ltd; **p. 130**, Linda Whitwam/Dorling

Kindersley, Ltd; **p. 133**, Ian Cumming/Dorling Kindersley, Ltd; **p. 137**, Photo Researchers, Inc; **p. 139**, Demetrio Carrasco/Dorling Kindersley, Ltd; **p. 140**, Martin Hladik/Dorling Kindersley, Ltd; **p. 147**, © Getty Images/Josef Polleross/Contributor; **p. 150**, Henri Carter Bresson/Magnum Photos.

Chapter 5: p. 166, Colin Sinclair/Dorling Kindersley, Ltd; **p. 168**, Colin Sinclair/Dorling Kindersley, Ltd; **p. 173**, © world of vector / Shutterstock; **p. 175**, Eugene Gordon/Pearson; **p. 177**, Topham Picture Source/The Image Works; **p. 179**, Julia Waterlow/Eye Ubiquitous/Corbis; **p. 180**, ©World History Archive / Alamy Stock Photo; **p. 188**, Nigel Hicks/Dorling Kindersley, Ltd; **p. 195**, Colin Sinclair/Dorling Kindersley, Ltd; **p. 201**, PhotoAlto / Alamy; **p. 204**, SSPL/Science Museum / Art Resource, NY; **p. 209**, Jmarshall - tribaleye images / Alamy; **p. 211**, Demetrio Carrasco/Dorling Kindersley, Ltd; **p. 212**, Demetrio Carrasco/Dorling Kindersley, Ltd; **p. 214**, Oote Boe Photography / Alamy; **p. 215**, Burt Glin/Magnum Photos; **p. 219**, imagebroker / Alamy; **p. 223**, Chris Stowers/Dorling Kindersley, Ltd.

Chapter 6: p. 230, Joel Fishman/Photo Researchers, Inc; **p. 236**, Andy Crawford/Dorling Kindersley, Ltd.

Chapter 7: p. 245, Dorling Kindersley, Ltd; **p. 247**, Stephen Oliver/Dorling Kindersley, Ltd; **p. 249**, Richard T. Nowitz/Corbis; **p. 251**, Sidney Bernstein / Photo Researchers, Inc; **p. 255**, Israel images / Alamy; **p. 256**, Dorling Kindersley, Ltd; **p. 263**, Kathy Sloane/Photo Researchers, Inc.

Chapter 8: p. 275, Philip Gendreau/Bettmann/Corbis; **p. 277**, Alinari/Art Resource, NY; **p. 286**, Dorling Kindersley, Ltd; **p. 288**, Demetrio Carrasco/Dorling Kindersley, Ltd; **p. 290**, © julie woodhouse / Alamy Stock Photo; **p. 292**, James Tye/Dorling Kindersley, Ltd; **p. 294**, Georgios Kollidas/Fotolia; **p. 298**, Georgios Kollidas/Fotolia; **p. 302**, Borderlands/Alamy; **p. 304**, Paul Franklin/Dorling Kindersley, Ltd; **p. 306**, Muskopf Photography, LLC/Alamy; **p. 312**, Andy Holligan/Dorling Kindersley, Ltd; **p. 319**, Kathy McLaughlin/The Image Works; **p. 322**, Mimi Forsyth; **p. 328**, Kim Sayer/Dorling Kindersley, Ltd; **p. 334**, Bettmann/Corbis; **p. 335**, © Getty Images / Steve Liss / Contributor.

Chapter 9: p. 345, Cecile Treal and Jean-Michel Ruiz/Dorling Kindersley, Ltd; **p. 346**, Steve McCurry/Magnum Photos; **p. 349**, paul thuysbaert/grapheast/Alamy; **p. 352**, Kazuyoshi Nomachi/HAGA/The Image Works; **p. 356**, Sally and Richard Greenhill / Alamy; **p. 361**, Demetrio Carrasco/Dorling Kindersley, Ltd; **p. 362**, Cecile Treal and Jean-Michel Ruiz/Dorling Kindersley, Ltd; **p. 371**, © Shutterstock / sinerji; **p. 378**, © imranahmedsg / Shutterstock; **p. 385**, Bert Gehr/Black Star; **p. 389**, © Salah Malkawi.

Chapter 10: p. 403, Janine Wiedel Photolibrary/Alamy; **p. 406**, Marc PoKemper/*MIRA.com*; **p. 409**, Jeff Greenberg/AGE Fotostock.

Color Inserts:

1A, Guillem Lopez/Alamy; **1B**, © P Lawrence / Alamy Stock Photo; **2A**, Kenneth M. Highfill/Photo Researchers, Inc.; **2B**, Art Wolfe / Science Photo Library, Inc; **3A**, Gary Ombler/Photo Researchers Inc.; **3B**, © Getty Images / Premium UIG; **4A**, Peter Wilson/Photo Researchers Inc.; **4B**, Susan McCartney/ Photo Researchers, Inc; **5A**, Linda Whitwam/Dorling Kindersley, Ltd; **5B**, Chuongy/Fotolia; **7A**, © Getty Images / Peter Ptschelinzew; **7B**, © Getty Images / Danita Delimont; **8A**, Paul Thuysbaert/Grapheast/ Alamy; **8B**, DPA /NSR/The Image Works; **9A**, © Getty Images / Scott Eells; **9B**, © Getty Images / ullstein bild / Contributor. **10A**, EyeEm Mobile GmbH / Alamy Stock Photo; **10B**, © Alberto Paredes / Alamy Stock Photo.

INDEX